Kraus'

Recreation and Leisure
in Modern Society ELEVENTH EDITION

Daniel D. McLean, PhD
University of Nevada, Las Vegas

Amy R. Hurd, PhD, CPRE
Illinois State University

Denise M. Anderson, PhD
Clemson University

JONES & BARTLETT
LEARNING

World Headquarters
Jones & Bartlett Learning
5 Wall Street
Burlington, MA 01803
978-443-5000
info@jblearning.com
www.jblearning.com

Jones & Bartlett Learning books and products are available through most bookstores and online booksellers.
To contact Jones & Bartlett Learning directly, call 800-832-0034, fax 978-443-8000, or visit our website,
www.jblearning.com.

Substantial discounts on bulk quantities of Jones & Bartlett Learning publications are available to corporations,
professional associations, and other qualified organizations. For details and specific discount information,
contact the special sales department at Jones & Bartlett Learning via the above contact information or send an
email to specialsales@jblearning.com.

10687-9

Production Credits
VP, Executive Publisher: David D. Cella
Publisher: Cathy L. Esperti
Acquisitions Editor: Sean Fabery
Editorial Assistant: Hannah Dziezanowski
Director of Production: Jenny L. Corriveau
Director of Vendor Management: Amy Rose
Vendor Manager: Juna Abrams
Director of Marketing: Andrea DeFronzo
VP, Manufacturing and Inventory Control:
  Therese Connell
Composition: codeMantra U.S. LLC
Project Management: codeMantra U.S. LLC
Cover Design: Kristin E. Parker
Director of Rights & Media: Joanna Gallant
Rights & Media Specialist: Robert Boder
Media Development Editor: Shannon Sheehan
Cover Image (Title Page, Part Opener,
  Chapter Opener): © Hero Images/Getty;
  © franckreporter/Getty
Printing and Binding: LSC Communications
Cover Printing: LSC Communications

Library of Congress Cataloging-in-Publication Data
Names: McLean, Daniel D. | Hurd, Amy R., author. | Anderson, Denise M., 1970, author.
Title: Kraus' recreation and leisure in modern society / Daniel D. McLean, PhD, University of Nevada,
Las Vegas Amy R. Hurd, PhD, CPRE, Illinois State University, Denise M. Anderson, PhD, Clemson University.
Description: Eleventh edition. | Burlington, Massachusetts : Jones & Bartlett Learning, [2018] |
Includes bibliographical references and index.
Identifiers: LCCN 2017020271 | ISBN 9781284106817 (pbk. : alk. paper)
Subjects: LCSH: Recreation–North America–History. | Leisure–Social aspects–North America. |
Play–North America–Psychological aspects. | Recreation–Vocational guidance–North America.
Classification: LCC GV51 .M34 2015 | DDC 790.097–dc23
LC record available at https://lccn.loc.gov/2017020271

6048

Printed in the United States of America
21 20 19 18 17   10 9 8 7 6 5 4 3 2 1

Brief Contents

Contents

Preface

Recreation and leisure touch the lives of almost everyone, whether through participating in sports and games, attending a theater production, visiting an art museum, traveling to another country, attending a street concert, or simply enjoying a local park. A world without recreation and leisure is unfathomable—no parks, no open space, no swimming, no lounging on beaches, and no traveling to other parts of the world just for fun. We often take these things for granted. The purpose of *Kraus' Recreation and Leisure in Modern Society, Eleventh Edition*, is to assist students in achieving an understanding and appreciation of the value of leisure and the leisure-service industry from multiple perspectives. This text provides a comprehensive survey of the leisure spectrum and profession, exploring its foundation, history, expansiveness, and continuing evolution. Leisure participation is viewed from the perspective of age, race, gender, and ethnicity and includes societal and personal benefits. It will demonstrate that recreation and leisure is a viable career option employing hundreds of thousands of people in North America. A career overview includes knowledge about public, commercial, nonprofit, and therapeutic recreation and the growing areas of tourism and sports.

This is the eleventh edition of a text that has been used by hundreds of departments of recreation, parks, and leisure studies at colleges and universities throughout the United States. It is designed for use in courses covering the history and philosophy of recreation and leisure and the role of organized leisure services today in American communities. This text is revised to reflect recent societal changes and the challenges that face leisure-service managers in the twenty-first century. It also provides an in-depth analysis of the basic concepts of recreation and leisure, the motivations and values of participants, and trends in the overall field of organized community services. Throughout the text, several important themes and emerging issues are emphasized, including the following:

◆ The dynamic dialogue surrounding the nature of the political, economic, and social environment that has forced parks and recreation agencies to reevaluate traditional approaches to delivering public park and recreation services by becoming simultaneously innovative, responsive, and entrepreneurial.

◆ Recreation and leisure are increasingly tied to the maturing fields of tourism and sport. Understanding these relationships is important for the success of leisure service managers.

◆ Wellness continues to be a major issue in the field, with obesity being the most immediate concern facing public parks and recreation agencies. Major efforts are being made to provide health and wellness opportunities, control obesity, and preserve cardiovascular health through parks and recreation. *Well-being* has become an inclusive term, looking beyond traditional wellness indicators.

◆ Tourism is the world's largest economy. Many communities are presenting themselves as a tourist destination in order to increase resources available to community members through jobs, attractions, and revenue generation.

◆ The baby boomers are retiring at a rate of more than 10,000 per day, and the millennial generation has become the largest generation. The impact and influence of these two generations on the parks and recreation profession requires organizations to rethink traditional service models. Boomers have more discretionary income than ever before and are willing to spend it on experiences—through travel and tourism, participating in programs, health and fitness activities, and adventure recreation. Millennials expect "now" activities and opportunities that simultaneously offer individual and group engagement, and they are impatient for change.

◆ Sport is increasing its influence and importance in the local, national, and international arena. Youth sport is taking on the forms and actions of professional sport, frequently to the detriment of the participants. Sport and tourism have become major community partners emphasizing economic community development. However, youth sport influence and participation has begun to wane as parents have become aware of life-changing injuries happening at young ages that may appear immediately or years later.

- There is a loss of an environmental ethic in the United States. Open space is shrinking due to community development of subdivisions, businesses, and more. Americans are using more than their share of natural resources: They comprise only 5% of the world's population but use 25% of all natural resources.
- The growth of the nearby nature and nature deficit disorder movements recognize the negative impacts of not having contact with nature.
- Globalization has impacted leisure through the ability to share models, lessons learned, adaptation to local settings, and the greater awareness that a global perspective brings to the profession.
- Socioeconomic status impacts leisure through available opportunities, activity choices, and the ways in which leisure is experienced. Urban communities often provide expanding services at increasing consumer costs, while inner-city urban areas continue to struggle to provide basic leisure services to residents.

Society is changing so rapidly that it is a challenge to capture the diversity and depth of change. The latest research, trends, and issues in the field are included in this edition. The parks and recreation profession is continually faced with providing services to a diverse population expanding far beyond race and gender. The latest edition of this text focuses on service provision for all people. A considerable amount of discussion is aimed at the role of parks and recreation departments on the health and wellness of our communities, as well as a means to combat the obesity epidemic that is plaguing North America. New case studies incorporated in the chapters allow students to apply knowledge of technology in leisure, the value and benefits of play, and changing family structures, to name a few.

Recreation's expanding roles in health, wellness, the obesity epidemic, quality of life, and environmental awareness and disengagement are examples of the breadth of the profession. Where once recreation professionals delivered programming and provided areas, facilities, and resources, they now face the need to partner, nurture, follow, and lead into new opportunities. Gone are the old socially contrived boundaries between disciplines and professions, replaced by a fluid composite of public, private, and nonprofit organizations and ever-growing numbers of unique stakeholders, all with a claim on recreation and leisure. Expectations of recreation professionals involve knowing about its history and foundations while embracing today's emerging social and physical challenges. It involves simultaneously honoring what was known yesterday and selectively engaging what will be known tomorrow. The fluidity of change in the leisure profession is captured in this text and challenges the reader to look to the past in looking to the future, ultimately learning from that past to strengthen the future. The text concludes with a strong assessment of the challenges and opportunities the future may promise.

WHY WE STUDY RECREATION AND LEISURE

This text is intended to provide comprehensive information that will help its readers develop sound personal philosophies, gain a broad awareness of the leisure service field, and answer questions, not with learned-by-rote solutions, but rather through intelligent analysis, critical thinking, and problem solving. Leisure-service professionals should have an in-depth understanding of the full range of recreational needs and motivations as well as agency programs and outcomes. This understanding should be based on a solid foundation with respect to the behavioral and social principles underlying recreation and leisure in contemporary society. To have a sound philosophy of the goals and values of recreation and leisure in modern life, it is essential to understand recreation's history and to be aware of its social, economic, and psychological characteristics in today's society. Should recreation be regarded chiefly as an amenity, or should it be supported as a form of social therapy? What are the recreation needs of populations such as girls and women, those who are aging, those who are disadvantaged, ethnic and racial minorities, persons with disabilities, or others who have not been fully served in the past?

Throughout this text, these contemporary issues are discussed in detail. This text promotes no single philosophical position; its purpose is to clarify the values promoted by recreation and leisure in modern society. What environmental priorities should recreation and park professionals fight to support, and how can outdoor forms of play be designed to avoid destructive ecological outcomes? How can leisure-service practitioners strike a balance between entrepreneurial management approaches, which emphasize fiscal self-sufficiency, and human service programming that responds to individual and community needs? Ultimately, these values are responsible for the field's ability to flourish as a significant form of governmental or voluntary agency service or as a commercial enterprise.

KEY FEATURES

◆ *Learning Objectives:* Guide the reader through the content and set the stage for focused reading. The learning objectives are provided as a guide to assist students in identifying key learning outcomes.
◆ *Case Studies:* Provide the reader a basis for in-depth exploration of current issues that are relevant to each chapter. The questions that follow the case studies allow the reader to apply the knowledge gained to real life scenarios, provoking further discussion and exploration.
◆ *Side Bars:* Highlight important information on current and related topics.
◆ *Questions for Class Discussion or Essay Examination:* Feature critical thinking questions to spark discussion and classroom engagement with the topics presented in the chapter.

ORGANIZATION

In the following chapters, this text focuses on multiple aspects of leisure and recreation. The content provides the reader with an in-depth discussion of present-day recreation, leisure, sports, tourism, and parks in American culture. The intended outcome is for the reader to gain an enhanced appreciation and understanding of how leisure affects individuals, groups, and society, and the roles that leisure plays in people's lives and in our society. This text looks at the roles of leisure in everyday life; the impacts of leisure on our culture; and how leisure influences individual choice, society mores, social engagements, the economy, and individual and community quality of life.

Chapter 1 introduces the concept of recreation and leisure. It discusses what recreation and leisure means to different people, along with who participates in recreation and why. It also introduces the reader to theories of play and leisure, focusing on their origins, influences, and importance to earlier and contemporary society. Six views of leisure provide students with insights into how theorists, practitioners, and participants view leisure today. The foundation provided in this chapter prepares the student to understand how leisure fits into our society, is influenced by societal change, and influences society and individuals. The terms *leisure, play,* and *recreation* and their various interpretations are also discussed in this chapter, providing the reader with insights into their use by researchers, practitioners, and participants.

Chapter 2 is an introduction to motivations for participating in leisure and recreation. It includes an in-depth discussion of physical, social, and psychological motivation as it relates to recreation participation. The chapter also examines motivation from the perspective of taboo recreation and serious leisure.

Chapter 3 recognizes the growing influence cultural and social factors have on leisure. Included in this chapter are discussions of gender, sexual orientation, race and ethnicity, and socioeconomic status. Understanding how these factors have traditionally affected leisure is as important as understanding how the factors are changing the perceptions of leisure and recreation in the twenty-first century.

Chapter 4 narrates the history of recreation and leisure from early civilizations to the present day. It is influenced by a European and North American perspective but recognizes the increasing influences from other cultures emerging in local and national society. The discussions of modern-day leisure are American, focusing on the influences of religion, colonization, and societal organization, and trace how different historical periods have acted on our perceptions of leisure and recreation. The chapter focuses on the dramatic changes that have occurred since World War II, recognizes the growing influence of globalization, and introduces the impact of technology on how people play and recreate.

Leisure and recreation traditionally have been represented from a community perspective and as a community resource. In Chapter 5, the 10 social functions of leisure are discussed. Social functions of leisure influence public policy, public commitment to organized leisure and recreation, and community development, all of which are critical in the twenty-first century.

Chapter 6 presents the different types of leisure-service organizations. The three organizational types include government, nonprofit, and commercial. This chapter identifies the three types of organizations, expands on them to address subtypes, compares and contrasts them, discusses their purpose, and generally identifies who is served, types of programming, types of services and areas, and intended outcomes.

Specialized leisure service organizations and areas are discussed in Chapter 7. Included are therapeutic recreation services for people with disabilities, armed forces recreation for military personnel and their dependents, employee services recreation for corporate employees, campus recreation for university students, and private-membership recreation for private club members. This chapter concludes with a comparison of the different types of organizations.

Chapters 8 and 9 address travel, tourism, and sport. Both of these industries have grown independent of leisure and recreation in recent years, yet their roots remain firmly within the leisure field. Chapter 8 provides an overview of the travel and tourism aspect of the hospitality and leisure industries. This approach allows the reader to better understand how travel, tourism, and leisure complement each other. Chapter 9 shows how sport has grown into a major commercial enterprise over the last 30 years and is increasingly seen as an economic engine versus a leisure experience. However, much of sport remains strongly fixed in the leisure sector. This chapter explores the growth of sport as a worldwide phenomenon, its place in the business sector, its roots in the leisure context, and the role of participation and spectating. Finally, it looks at sport from a business perspective.

Chapter 10 considers the leisure industry, what makes it a profession, and philosophies of leisure service delivery. Finally, Chapter 11 addresses the future of leisure and recreation and specifically looks at trends, influences, economic impacts, societal impacts, and predictions for the future. The chapter presents the influence of technology; how demographics and the growth of minorities are changing the way leisure is perceived and delivered; the impact of youth and a youth culture on society, especially as it contrasts with the baby boomer culture; global climate change issues, local environmental concerns, and how they relate; and finally, globalization and its influence on leisure and recreation.

NEW TO THE *ELEVENTH EDITION*

For the *Eleventh Edition* we have added a new coauthor to provide a fresh view of leisure. Among the most notable changes, we have condensed four of the chapters into two chapters, while other chapters have been rearranged to create a better flow of content. We feel the changes are advantageous to the text and the student and allow the instructor greater flexibility in the delivery of the material.

Many of the case studies have been replaced, with the previous ones now appearing in the instructor materials. Other case studies have been updated to reflect recent trends. In general, chapter content has been updated to reflect changes in the field since the last edition. Chapter 11 includes a limited discussion of how the 2016 presidential election might impact parks and recreation, but as this text goes to press, much is still being decided by the new administration.

- Chapter 1 combines what was previously Chapters 1 and 2. These have been integrated in order to strengthen the text's introduction. New first-person case studies have been added with a focus on individual perceptions of the leisure experience and planning a leisure experience from a senior's perspective.
- Chapter 2 provides updates on physical activity and health data, including obesity rates, and incorporates two new case studies.
- Chapter 3 features an expanded discussion of race and ethnicity, as well as their implications for leisure. New case studies have been developed.
- Chapter 4 combines the previous edition's two history chapters, providing one comprehensive look at the history of the field from early civilization through the present day. New case studies and a timeline have been added, along with new trend information related to health, diverse populations, and other areas of relevance to today's practitioners.
- Chapter 5 incorporates changes to two of the functions discussed. "Improving intergroup and intergenerational relations" has been expanded to "educating and uniting community members" to showcase the role parks and recreation plays in this important function within a community. The last function has been expanded from promoting health and safety to also include wellness, as parks and recreation is a key player in overall community wellness.
- Chapter 6 creates a foundation for the delivery of leisure by looking at 10 major elements of the delivery system. Added for the first time are small business enterprises, which have been a mainstay of

the commercial aspect of recreation and leisure. Updates have been incorporated into the sections on different agencies in government providing recreation services, as well as the private and nonprofit sector.

- Chapter 7 includes new statistics on the impact of travel and the ever-evolving trends in the industry as well as new case studies emphasizing these trends.
- Chapter 8 adds new information on ADA and the therapeutic recreation job analysis, as well as data on inclusion practices. New case studies have been added, and more current information related to MWR programming and employer-provided benefits related to wellness was added.
- Chapter 9 features updated sport participation levels, as well as the removal of the Sport Fan Index. The content has been refreshed with new and updated information.
- Chapter 10 showcases a new set of professionals and what their careers are like on a day-to-day basis. They are all young professionals that current students can aspire to be in the near future.
- Chapter 11 updates the future challenges presented and examines mandates. It reorganizes, updates, and presents twenty-first century agendas from a new perspective, demonstrating how they interact. This chapter reflects that the millennial generation has come of age and taken its rightful place as a key influencer of leisure. An aging society remains a key component of the leisure fabric, and coverage of this facet in this chapter has been updated and strengthened. Detailed information about each agenda has been updated with current data and expanded where necessary. Climate change remains an important focus. The "Technology and Time" section has also been significantly revised.

FOR THE INSTRUCTOR

Qualified instructors can receive access to the full suite of instructor resources, all of which have been revised to reflect the content of the *Eleventh Edition*. These resources include the following:

- Instructor's Manual, including chapter outlines, suggested assignments and projects, and additional case studies
- Slides in PowerPoint format, incorporating more than 400 slides
- Test Bank, featuring more than 300 questions
- Sample Syllabus

FOR THE STUDENT

Additional resources are available online for the student, including the following:

- Interactive eBook, featuring embedded weblinks and practice Knowledge Check questions tied to specific sections of the text
- Flashcards
- Slides in PowerPoint format
- Lecture Outlines

Recreation and Leisure in Modern Society is meant to make readers think about the field and how it impacts their lives on a daily basis. Its aim is to make the reader appreciate the recreational opportunities that are available in North America and to educate each reader on what it means to be a parks and recreation professional.

Acknowledgments

There is little more valuable to the completion of this text than the stories, examples, brochures, reports, photos, and information provided by the numerous public, private, nonprofit, commercial, and other organizations that have given material to us. Although it is difficult to thank everyone who has supported this edition, we truly appreciate the support of the University of Nevada (Las Vegas), Illinois State University, and Clemson University, as well as our families who understand the sacrifices needed to complete this project. In addition, we thank the National Recreation and Park Association and SHAPE America for providing examples of their services.

In addition to these sources, we also acknowledge the important contributions made by a number of leading recreation and leisure-studies educators whose writings—both in textbooks and scholarly articles—influenced our thinking. While it is not possible to name all of these individuals, they include the following: Lawrence Allen, Maria Allison, John Crompton, Dan Dustin, Geoffrey Godbey, Tom Goodall, Karla Henderson, Debra Jordan, John Kelly, Leo McAvoy, James Murphy, Ruth Russell, Wayne Stormann, and Charles Sylvester.

We welcome Denise Anderson of Clemson University as our new coauthor. She brings a rich knowledge of parks, recreation, and leisure that helps to keep this text current and relevant. Finally, Dan McLean, who is retiring with this edition, thanks all of the professionals, educators, students, volunteers, and others it has been his pleasure to work with and call colleagues since his first part-time playground leader summer job in Modesto, California, in 1965. That experience changed his life and focus forever.

We thank the reviewers of the *Eleventh Edition*, whose comments and suggestions have truly made this a better text:

- Paul Ankomah, PhD, of North Carolina A&T State University
- Glen Bishop, PhD, of Arkansas Tech University
- T. Jason Davis, PhD, of East Tennessee State University
- Gwendolyn S. Dawkins, EdD, CTRS, LRT, of Jackson State University
- Carla Jellum, PhD, of Central Washington University
- Larry McFaddin, MEd, of North Country Community College—SUNY
- Anna Park, MA, of Manchester Community College
- Paulette Shuster, MS, RTC, RC, of California State University, Northridge
- John Valentine, EdD, of Kean University
- Debbi Ware, EdD, of Gardner-Webb University

This text could not have been published without the efforts of the staff at Jones & Bartlett Learning: Sean Fabery, Acquisitions Editor; Hannah Dziezanowski, Editorial Assistant; Juna Abrams, Vendor Manager; Robert Boder, Rights & Media Specialist; Shannon Sheehan, Media Development Editor; Andrea DeFronzo, Director of Marketing; and Dhayanidhi Karunanidhi, Project Manager.

We are particularly indebted to the late Dr. Richard Kraus, who has left a tremendous gap in the parks and recreation field. To carry on his work is both important and critical. His efforts for more than 40 years as a writer, practitioner, and educator helped to shape this profession. This text has become a standard, and as future editions are prepared, we hope to stay close to the roots that Dr. Kraus nurtured while remaining current with the changes in the profession.

Foundations of Recreation and Leisure

My Passion: My Guitar

I am fairly certain that everyone in life has a passion, and if you don't have one, you haven't found it yet. If you haven't, I highly suggest exploring to find it to increase the quality of your life. From a very young age mine has been playing the guitar. I am definitely by no means a virtuoso and you won't hear me on next week's Top 40, but I absolutely love it.

Playing the guitar helps me in many ways. In my case it not only gave me a constructive activity to do, it kept me out of trouble as a youth. It helps me to relieve stress and escape from the daily struggles in life. The creativity and possibility for creativity are endless, the amount of things that you can learn are immense. No matter how good you get, or how good you think that you are, there is always a style of play or music that you can learn and improve on.

My father has played guitar for the majority of his life, and growing up in the house we were always around the guitar. At family get-togethers it was always something that we would do as a family and extended family. My father gave me a ukulele at the age of 7, but I didn't really become interested until the age of ten. He showed me three chords: G, D, and C, and told me that if I practiced these three chords, I could learn a great deal of songs. I practiced and practiced until my fingers were raw, and finally I learned the chords. After that, there was no stopping me, I couldn't get enough. I taught myself how to read and before long I was accompanying my Dad. This was the best part, I got to share something with him, spend time with him, and to this day we still play when we get together. As a teen it was how I communicated with my father, and I will forever have fond memories of these times spent with him, quality time.

Not only do I have this passion that I share with my father, I am passing the love for music and the guitar to my daughter. In the evening, when I pull out the guitar, my daughter is often found strumming along with me or dancing to the music that is played. She often strums along with her toy guitar and I can see how the passion for the guitar is being passed from one generation to another.

When I started practicing and practicing, my parents and I realized that I reached the ceiling of what I would be able to attain without formal lessons. We looked for a while and finally found one. This really helped because I learned not only about the guitar, but the theory behind it. How to read music and understand why certain notes sound good together. My understanding skyrocketed and soon I was learning more and more. My playing improved as well as my understanding of Music.

I took lessons for years and in high school stopped taking lessons when other activities such as sports took my time. I have never stopped playing and to this day I pick up the guitar whenever I have a chance.

My love for the guitar has extended past playing. I have been so intrigued by the guitar that I would like to learn how to build them. When I retire, I would love to use my Montgomery GI Bill that I will have received from serving my country in the U. S. Marine Corps to learn how to become a master craftsman. This way I can build the instrument that has greatly improved the quality of my life and the people around me from the joy to me. This way I can give that joy to others.

– "My Passion, My Guitar," Courtesy of D. Dunn

Learning Objectives

1.   Discuss the motivations for participation using the concepts of presence of diversity, and participation in leisure and recreation.

2.   Coherently express the development of the theories of play and how the theories contributed to contemporary views of play.

3.   Discuss how an understanding of the flow principle impacts and influences individual and group perception of participation.

4.   Explain individually and collectively how the six views of leisure meaning contribute to the definition of leisure.

5.   Articulate and defend the meaning (definition) of recreation.

6.   Acknowledge that play, leisure, and recreation have similarities and differences; explain the relationships between the three concepts and the importance and value of their study.

7.   Link the theories, views, and definitions of play, leisure, and recreation into a coherent and defensible "first" philosophy of recreation and leisure.

INTRODUCTION

Recreation and leisure have multiple meanings based on individual experiences and perceptions. Recreation is defined from an individual perspective. It could include watching television, attending an opera, base jumping, mowing the lawn, taking your children to the zoo, playing checkers, downloading music, writing a book, spending an evening on the town, or whatever one chooses to make it. Leisure theorists struggle to agree on what to call these types of experiences. Is it recreation, leisure, free time, available time, creativity, selfishness, or hedonism? One's own perceptions are so important in the defining of leisure and recreation that researchers continue to debate their meaning to society, individuals, and culture. However, as this text will show, recreation, parks, and leisure services have become an important part of government operations and a vital program element of nonprofit, commercial, private-membership, therapeutic, and other types of agencies. Today, recreation and leisure constitute major forces in our national and local economies and are responsible for millions of jobs in such varied fields as government, travel and tourism, popular entertainment and the arts, health and fitness programs, hobbies, participatory and spectator sports, and travel and tourism. Beyond its value as a form of sociability, recreation also provides major personal benefits in terms of meeting physical, emotional, philosophical, and other important health-related needs of participants. In a broad sense, the leisure life of a nation reflects its fundamental values and character. The very games and sports, entertainment media, and group affiliations that people enjoy in their leisure help to shape the character and well-being of families, communities, and society at large.

For these reasons, it is the purpose of this text to present a comprehensive picture of the role of recreation and leisure in modern society, including (1) the field's conceptual base, (2) the varied leisure pursuits people engage in, (3) their social and psychological implications, (4) both positive and negative outcomes of play, (5) the network of community organizations that provide recreational programs and related social services, (6) the development of recreation as a rich, diversified field of professional practice, and (7) trends influencing the future of recreation and leisure.

VARIED VIEWS OF RECREATION AND LEISURE

For some, recreation means the network of public agencies that provide facilities such as parks, playgrounds, aquatic centers, sports fields, and community centers in thousands of cities, towns, counties, and park districts today. They may view these facilities as an outlet for the young or a means of achieving family togetherness; pursuing interesting hobbies, sports, or social activities; or as a place for growth and development for all ages.

For others, recreation may be found in a senior center or golden age club, a sheltered workshop for people with cognitive disabilities, or a treatment center for physical rehabilitation. For some, traveling, whether it be by trailer, motorcoach, airplane, train, or cruise ship, is the preferred mode of recreation. The expansion of the travel and tourism industry has been staggering. Travel clubs have become increasingly popular, with several airlines built around short trips through extended travel. Disney has initiated a line of cruise ships that focuses on family, and has extended the idea of travel and tourism yet again. Resort destinations from Vail, Colorado, to Orlando, Florida, to Las Vegas, Nevada have developed travel and tourism with new levels of services and lodging, including a dramatic growth in timeshares.

Recreation occurs in many forms with group involvement highly desirable for some individuals.
© Germanskydiver/Shutterstock.

For a growing generation of young people, recreation and leisure have taken on new meanings of adventure, risk, excitement, and fulfillment as they seek to meld technology and recreation. The idea of recreation participation may not include any physical activity, but focus instead on Internet-based games, social networking, sharing music, instant messaging, and new ventures yet to emerge. The activity may be as dissimilar as sitting in front of a computer to being involved in extreme activities such as skateboarding on a Bob Burnquist–designed and –built 360-foot skateboard ramp with a 70-foot gap that must be negotiated to safely complete the experience. It may involve participation in ESPN's X-Games as a participant, spectator, or video game player. ESPN has used key sponsorships and promotion to give extreme sports a cultural definition. The X-Games include activities such as inline skating, BMX racing, snow sports including snowboards and free-style skiing, surfing, streetball, and motorcycles.

Environmentalists may be chiefly concerned about the impact of outdoor forms of traditional and emerging play on our natural surroundings—the forests, mountains, rivers, and lakes that are the national heritage of all Americans. More frequently, the environmental movement includes a growing awareness and global perspective.

Without question, recreation and leisure are all of these things. They represent a potentially rewarding and important form of human experience and constitute a major aspect of economic development and government responsibility today. It is important to recognize that this is not a new development. Recreation and leisure are concepts that have fascinated humankind since before the golden age of ancient Athens. Varied forms of play have been condemned and suppressed in some societies and highly valued and encouraged in others.

Today, for the first time, there is almost universal acceptance of the value of play, recreation, and leisure. As a consequence, government at every level in the United States has accepted responsibility for providing or assisting leisure opportunities through extensive recreation and park systems, tourism support systems, and sport facilities and complexes. Nonprofits and a wide variety of commercial enterprises provide recreation opportunities and experiences. Twenty years ago, the breadth of recreation and leisure opportunities was just beginning to explode.

Diversity in Participation

Often we tend to think of recreation primarily as participation in sports and games or in social activities, and ignore other forms of play. However, recreation includes an extremely broad range of leisure pursuits, including travel and tourism, cultural entertainment or participation in the arts, hobbies, membership in social clubs or interest groups, nature-related activities such as camping or hunting and fishing, attendance at parties or other special events, and fitness activities. What was considered nontraditional 10 years ago has become mainstream. Today's recreation opportunities and experiences are expanding in ways not conceivable as little as 10–30 years ago.

Recreation can occur anyplace and includes a variety of activities.
© Trevor Buttery/Shutterstock.

Recreation may be enjoyed along with thousands of other participants or spectators or may be an intensely solitary experience. It may be highly strenuous and physically demanding or may be primarily a cerebral activity. It may represent a lifetime of interest and involvement or may consist of a single, isolated experience.

As discussed elsewhere in this text, the diversity and depth of participation are similar to looking inside a three-dimensional box (Figure 1.1) and seeing on the horizontal plane the diversity represented by the different kinds of activities and experiences one might engage in as part of recreation and along the vertical plane the depth or intensity of participation. On the third plane, which gives the box dimension, the aspect becomes more complex because one has to take into account why people participate (psychological aspects) as well as with whom they participate (social aspects), the time (free time versus obligated time) spent in the activity, and the costs associated with involvement or away from other activities (economic). Figure 1.1 shows in a very simple way the challenges faced when exploring a leisure activity. Researchers have invested years and written thousands of articles attempting to explain the leisure experience. Figure 1.1 depicts that challenge but fails to take into account individual perceptions of the experience, which are all-important. This text explores each of these aspects in detail. By the conclusion, readers will have gained an understanding of the diversity and complexity of the leisure environment, services, involvement, and participation.

Motivations for Recreational Participation

Many participants take part in recreation as a form of relaxation and release from work pressures or other tensions. They may be passive spectators of entertainment provided by television, movies, or other forms of electronic amusement. Other significant leisure motivations are based on the need to express creativity, develop hidden talents, enhance physical skills, or pursue excellence in varied forms of personal expression.

For some participants, active, competitive recreation may offer a channel for releasing frustration and aggression, or for struggling against others or the environment in adventurous, high-risk pursuits. Others enjoy recreation that is highly social and provides opportunities for making new friends or cooperating with others in group settings.

Other individuals take part in leisure activities that involve community service or that permit them to provide leadership in fraternal or religious organizations. Still others take part in activities that promote health and physical fitness as a primary goal. A steadily growing number of participants enjoy participation in the expanding world of computer-based entertainment and communication, including CD-ROMs, Internet games, video

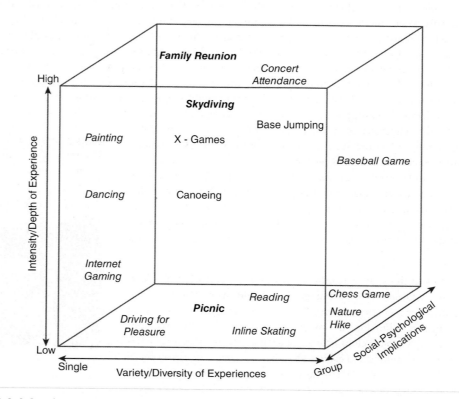

FIGURE 1.1 Simplistic Representation of the Complexity of Recreation and Leisure Experiences

AN ANALYSIS OF MY PASSION, MY GUITAR

The introduction to this chapter provides an excellent opportunity to analyze a leisure experience.

The experience is a lifetime engagement with a leisure activity, beginning as a young child. The exposure of the narrator's father playing the guitar was a motivation to "try it" for himself.

The author draws on the ukulele experience of learning how to play the instrument, sharing the discovery of learning the three chords and the motivation to learn more coming from that experience.

Watching a pit crew is part of the experience for NASCAR fans.
© Walter G Arce/Shutterstock.

- Can you relate to a leisure experience in your life where you have been motivated to learn more after mastering the basics? Did you experience a greater intensity or depth as a result of your motivation? How did you feel as you became more competent and comfortable with your skill set? It doesn't matter if it was playing a guitar, skiing down a bunny slope, drawing a picture, playing a sport, or any myriad of leisure activities.
- In regard to Figure 1.1, there is an intensity related to this experience. There is also longevity to the experience. The depth can relate to the intensity of feeling toward the music being played. It can also relate to the technical challenge of a piece of music and, as it is practiced and perfected, a sense of mastery. The author related the social psychological implications when sharing feelings of stress relief and escape from daily struggles. Yet, the need to learn "there was no stopping me" addresses self-development and mastery.
- Finally, the author talks of sharing the music and playing with his father. He already anticipates sharing his love with his daughter and mastering the construction of guitars. As will be discussed later in this text, the author has moved to "serious leisure," a form of leisure that takes the participant to deeper and constructive levels of experience.

games, smart phones with applications, iPods, the Internet, and much more. Others are deeply involved in forms of culture such as music, drama, dance, literature, and other forms of fine arts. Exploring new environments through travel and tourism or seeking self-discovery or personality enrichment through continuing education or various educational activities represents other important leisure drives.

AN ANALYSIS OF PLAY, RECREATION AND LEISURE

Any consideration of the broad field of recreation and leisure should include a clarification of terms and concepts. The words *play, leisure,* and *recreation* are frequently used interchangeably, as if they mean the same thing. However, although related, they have distinctly different meanings and it is important for both students and practitioners in this field to understand their varied implications and the differences among them.

PLAY AND DEVELOPMENT

"Many children in public school are getting less and less time outside, despite the documented benefits of free play."[1] Play has long been determined essential for physical and emotional development of children. During the past two decades, play fell out of favor among some educators and parents, but not among park and recreation professionals. Today, there is a resurgence of research across many fields about the value and importance of play. By play, we mean unstructured or "free play," unbound from parental perceptions, video intrusions, planned activities, and the like. Researchers are suggesting that play is an organic way of learning, that unstructured play builds skills that will create happy and productive adults, and that under the right conditions, schools that integrate play will enhance the learning, self-awareness, and confidence of their students. Play, long a fabric of cultures across the world, is finding greater evidence to support its importance to children and adults.

Case Study

Photography as Leisure: Why I take Photos

It sometimes feels like I have been taking photos for an eternity. I purchased my first "good" camera while I was in college, but I had been exposed to photography for years. My grandfather took photos for as long as I can remember. They were almost always photos of friends and family, but on occasion they were photos of scenes. I have inherited many of his photos from the 1940's, all of them taken as 35mm slides. As opposed to today, all photos were taken using film and you could do 24 or 36 photos to a roll. The film was expensive as was the processing, but when you got the photos back in slide format (for viewing through a projector) it was all worth it. Because of the expense we didn't take a lot of photos of the same subject. We took time to compose and think about the photo - much like the best photographers still do. Somewhere in my younger years I became fascinated with photography, but could not afford a good camera. I read books, took a college course, and finally purchased my first 35 mm single-lens reflex (SLR) camera. Ansel Adams, a noted western landscape photographer, was one of my heroes, as was Alfred Eisenstaedt, a noted photojournalist.

Having my own camera opened a whole new world for me. Learning to see the world through a viewfinder changed the way I saw the world! I wanted to take lots of "great" photos, but learned early on that great was in the eyes of the beholder. As a young father I took lots of photos of family, photos that years later have great meaning to myself and my family. At the time I was just trying to capture experiences. Now, as I near retirement, my children and grandchildren have fond memories. I would never have thought how my old family photos would find their way onto Facebook and other sites and bring meaning to so many people.

I've never really asked myself why I take photos. It was just something I wanted to do. I enjoyed the experience. Sometimes, like on a cold winter morning before dawn, I hoped that the clouds would be just right for photos of a desert mountain. Other times I hoped I could capture a special moment in one of my children's lives, one that could be shared. I originally took photos for selfish reasons - because I wanted to. It was not long, however, before I realized that I was helping to build family history and contributing to knowing who we were. These reasons became important to me.

Photography really is a single person activity. There may be lots of people around, but the act of shooting a photo is a single person activity (for me). I choose the location, I choose the time of day, I choose the day of the week, I choose the camera lens, I choose the lighting, the color, and so much more. For landscape photography I am at the mercy of the environment. I may want a calm clear day with no clouds, but instead get a blustery and overcast day. I have to learn how to adapt, to change my expectations, and to focus my creativity in a different way to achieve the results I hope for. The same is true for portrait photography, except the person being photographed has a significant influence on the outcome.

At the end of the day I pull my SD card out of the SLR and drop it into my computer, download the photos (no longer waiting for a week or more to see my photos), look at them, use various software to alter the light, the saturation, the contrast, the size, style and on and on. What used to take hours of time and experimentation in the darkroom can now be accomplished in minutes on a computer. On one trip returning from Europe I was able to sort, catalog, select, adjust, and have photos ready for processing by the time the airplane landed.

Why do I shoot pictures. It really gets down to the experience. It makes me feel good. It is something I like to do. It provides me with a sense of accomplishment and creativity. It builds my awareness of the world around me. It allows me to feel creative. At the end of a session of working with photos, whether shooting or adjusting, I feel positive about who I am and what I have accomplished

Questions to Consider

1. When you participate in recreation how are your feelings and motivations similar or different to those described in this case study? Why do you think they might be similar? Different?
2. Select a recreation activity you enjoy and write about it. Answer the following questions:
   a. When did you begin to participate in the activity?
   b. How do you feel when you participate? Is it a different feeling than when you first started to participate?
   c. Why do you participate in the activity?
   d. How do you feel when you are done with the activity? Is there any carryover of feelings to a later time?
   e. Look at Figure 1.1 and place your activity on the graphic. Explain why you placed it where you did.

The rationale for stressing such conceptual understanding is clear. Just as a doctor must know chemistry, anatomy, kinesiology, and other underlying sciences to practice medicine effectively, so too the recreation and park professional must understand the meaning of leisure and its motivations and satisfactions if he or she is to provide effective recreation programs and services. Such conceptual understandings are critical to the development of a sound philosophy of recreation service and to interpreting leisure-service goals and outcomes to the public at large.

THE MEANING OF PLAY

The word *play* is derived from the Anglo-Saxon *plega,* meaning a game or sport, skirmish, fight, or battle. This is related to the Latin *plaga,* meaning a blow, stroke, or thrust. It is illustrated in the idea of striking or stroking an instrument or playing a game by striking a ball. Other languages have words derived from a common root (such as the German *spielen* and the Dutch *spelen*) whose meanings include the playing of games, sports, and musical instruments. Although play is traditionally considered a child's activity, it is often recognized that people of all ages take part in play.

It is difficult to arrive at a single definition of play because it takes so many forms and appears in so many contexts. However, a general definition would describe play as a form of human or animal activity or behavioral style that is self-motivated and carried on for intrinsic, rather than external, purposes. It is generally pleasurable and often is marked by elements of competition, humor, creative exploration and problem solving, and mimicry or role playing. It appears most frequently in leisure activities but may be part of work. It is typically marked by freedom and lack of structure but may involve rules and prescribed actions, as in sport and games.

Historical Perspectives

In ancient Greece, play was assigned a valuable role in the lives of children, based on the writings of Plato and Aristotle. The Athenians placed great value on developing qualities of honor, loyalty, and beauty and other elements of productive citizenship in children. For them, play was an integral element of education and was considered a means of positive character development and teaching the values of Greek society.

Later, as the Catholic Church gained dominance among the developing nations of western Europe, play came to be regarded as a social threat. The body was thought to detract from more spiritual or work-oriented values, and every effort was made to curb the pleasurable forms of play that had been popular in the Greek and Roman eras.

Gradually, however, educators and philosophers such as Froebel, Rousseau, and Schiller came to the defense of play as an important aspect of childhood education. For example, Froebel wrote of play as the highest expression of human development in childhood:

> Play is the purest, most spiritual activity of man at this stage. . . . A child that plays thoroughly with self-active determination, perseveringly until physical fatigue forbids, will surely be a thorough, determined man, capable of self-sacrifice for the promotion of the welfare of himself and others.[2]

EARLY THEORIES OF PLAY

In the nineteenth and early twentieth centuries, a number of influential scholars evolved comprehensive theories of play that explained its development and its role in human society and personal development.

Surplus-Energy Theory

The English philosopher Herbert Spencer, in his mid-nineteenth-century work *Principles of Psychology,* advanced the view that play was primarily motivated by the need to burn excess energy. This theory asserts that running, playing soccer, or jumping rope on the playground are done because people have excess energy to use. A criticism of this theory is that play also occurs in people with little energy and does not account for nonphysical play.

Relaxation Theory

An early explanation of play that was regarded as the converse of surplus energy was relaxation theory. Rather than to burn excess energy, play was done to restore it. Play was seen as a means to energize a person who was exhausted from work, school, or the stresses of daily life. It was believed that when a person is either mentally or physically tired, play can restore energy. So, exercising after a long day at work can serve to help an individual relax and restore. Spending time on Facebook during a study break or playing after school are both examples of relaxation theory.

Preparation Theory

Preparation theory suggests that play is a means for children to practice adult life. Children who play house, doctor, or school are preparing to experience these things as older children or adults. Preparation theory also suggests that people learn teamwork and role playing in their play. A weakness of this theory is that it does not account for adult play.

Catharsis Theory

The catharsis theory is based on the view that play—particularly competitive, active play—serves as a safety valve for the expression of bottled-up emotions. Among the ancient Greeks, Aristotle saw drama as a means of purging oneself of hostile or aggressive emotions; by vicarious sharing in the staged experience, onlookers purified themselves of harmful feelings. Biking a long distance after a hard day at work, playing a musical instrument after an argument with a friend, and hitting a bucket of golf balls to blow off steam after a nonproductive meeting are all examples of the catharsis theory of play.

Coupled with the surplus-energy theory, the catharsis theory suggests a vital necessity for active play to help children and adults burn excess energy and provide a socially acceptable channel for aggressive or hostile emotions and drives.

CONCEPTS OF PLAY IN MODERN SOCIETY

During the first three decades of the twentieth century, a number of psychologists and educators examined play, particularly as a developmental and learning experience for children.

Self-Expression Theory

Two leading physical educators, Elmer Mitchell and Bernard Mason, saw play primarily as a result of the need for self-expression. Humans were regarded as active, dynamic beings with the need to find outlets for their energies, use their abilities, and express their personalities. The specific types of activity that an individual engaged in were, according to Mitchell and Mason, influenced by such factors as physiological and anatomic structure, physical fitness level, environment, and family and social background.[3]

Play as a Social Necessity

During the late nineteenth century, leaders of the public recreation movement called for the provision of organized recreation for all children. Joseph Lee, who is widely regarded as the father of the play movement in America and who promoted the establishment of numerous playgrounds and recreation centers, was instrumental in the public acceptance of play as an important force in child development and community life. Jane Addams, founder of the Hull House Settlement in Chicago and a Nobel Peace Prize winner, advocated the need for organized play opportunities that served as an alternative to the difficult life children living in poverty faced on the streets. These values continue to be embraced by contemporary communities, as is evidenced by public and private support of parks and recreation departments, community recreation programs, after-school programs, and other play-based activities.

Typologies of Play Activity

In the twentieth century, more and more social and behavioral scientists began to examine play empirically. One such investigator, the French sociologist Roger Caillois, examined the play experience itself by classifying the games and play activities that were characteristic of various cultures and identifying their apparent functions and values. Caillois established four major types of play and game activity: agon, alea, mimicry, and ilinx.

Agon refers to activities that are competitive and in which the equality of the participants' chances of winning is artificially created. Winners are determined through such qualities as speed, endurance, strength, memory, skills, and ingenuity. Agonistic games may be played by individuals or teams; they presuppose sustained attention, training and discipline, perseverance, limits, and rules. Clearly, most modern games and sports, including many card and table games involving skill, are examples of agon.

Alea includes games of chance—those games or contests over whose outcome the contestant has no control; winning is the result of fate rather than the skill of the player. Games of dice, roulette, and baccarat, as well as lotteries, are examples of alea.

Mimicry is based on the acceptance of illusions or imaginary universes. Children engage in mimicry through pretend play. This category includes games in which players make believe, or make others believe, that they are other than themselves. For children, Caillois writes:

Case Study

. . . .

Senior Playgrounds

According to a National Public Radio report, "Within parks, people tend to be more physically active on trails, at playgrounds and at sports facilities." (Research) This is, in fact, true for people of all ages. Age doesn't matter: People are more physically active at playground type places. Think about to the last time you were at a playground. For me, it was when I took my children to play. I sat playing on my phone, but the laughing and fun going on around me was contagious. Pretty soon I was running around with my kids, running up the play structure, and sliding down the slide. My teenage kids were playing a game of 'horse' and I jumped in and played too. I really enjoyed myself that afternoon and I know that my kids enjoyed having me there with them. But I asked myself, "What if I didn't have children? What if I am a senior and I want to be active? Where could I go and what would the playground be like?"

Yesterday's adult playground equipment is static, uninviting, and mostly unused. Today's planners have greater options than ever before. While youth playgrounds have been reinvented numerous times since the 1970s, adult playgrounds, for the most part remained static. That is all changing! "Today's planners of fitness-zones have modernized alternative moving away from static to fitness devices with moving parts, as well as updated classics. Today's fitness zones have grouped stations in a single area, creating an outdoor fitness zone where people can work out together or individually.

As a bonus and because park and recreation agencies focus on all ages and abilities, many of the "stations are created to accommodate anyone from teens to seniors and out-of-shape newbies to highly fit, regular exercisers. In some parks, the equipment is so popular that lines often form as people wait their turn to use the stations. In addition, these new all-weather machines require little upkeep and maintenance, and are made to last." (Madren)

While talking to my uncle, he told me how their Florida retirement community has 20 different senior parks. He said they are wonderful and have gotten him and his wife out enjoying life again. They even have adult recumbent 'tricycles' that they ride.

There are significant benefits that are physical, social and emotional to the participants. KaBOOM! suggests the areas are "a great connector for adults and seniors and the children in their lives." Research suggests there are cognitive and physical benefits of play, that can include stress reduction. Community parks with adult playgrounds can serve as a gathering spot, combatting the isolation and loneliness some seniors have, nurturing social and mental health. Some new senior parks feature adult focused low-impact exercise equipment for seniors and those who have not exercised for some time. These parks were started abroad, but now the US is on board with having them. In 2012 England, Finland, Germany, Spain and throughout Asia senior parks were a reality.

The term bio-healthy parks have been applied to senior parks. The focus is on movement, socialization, and keeping the mind exercised. Research shows that participation in physical activity, even if it is not stressful of extended, positively influences physical and cognitive well-being in seniors. The challenge for seniors not living in planned communities is to get them out of their home and engaged in physical and mental activities.

In Spain, senior parks are all the rage. "On one recent morning, in the Spanish coastal town of Vilassar, a kiddy park with its slides and seesaws is empty. But right next to it, 20 retirees shout out during roll call. Then they take up positions by tiny balance beams, elevated walkways, pedals fixed to benches and twisting metal bars. The day's workout session begins. 63-year-old retiree Manuel Francisco Martin spins a suspended metal disk with two hand cranks, while walking in place. "The point is to be able to keep going, he said. "To never stop. Because once you stop moving, things go badly." Several grey heads nod in agreement. "If you exercise you feel better," he says. "When you go up a couple of steps you don't get out of breath. When you walk for 10 minutes you feel calm and relaxed." The body is like everything else, he said: any parts that aren't used eventually break down. This outdoor exercise park was designed somewhere with a decidedly short season for parks: Finland. The company behind the project was Lappset and they've sold tens of thousands of these parks worldwide. But Spain has been an especially good market. It has 600 already and orders in for hundreds more. Each time a new park opens here, Lappset physical therapist Paz Vidal shows up to explain how each station works. They're not overly complicated. But Paz said the seniors generally need a walk-through. And encouragement…These parks aren't just about getting winded. They're designed for the mind too. A few of the stations are in fact games, where you match colors, or shapes, or numbers…The point of these outdoor exercise spots isn't just to give elderly folks something to do. Officials say it makes good fiscal sense as well. Analysts estimate that 40 to 45 percent of the population in Spain will be retirees by 2050. Spending a few bucks on parks to keep that population alert and healthy, the thinking goes, could save a lot in expensive health care costs." (Hadden) I thought it was very interesting that Spain wasn't just thinking about the health benefits of senior parks, but also that it made good fiscal sense too.

Questions to Consider

1. How many people over 60 do you know who exercise on a regular basis?
2. Compare them to people who don't exercise on a regular basis. Is there a visible difference?
3. Do you think that a person can keep exercising after they turn 75 or 80? Why? Why not? What do you think the limitations would be?
4. How can recreation and park planners improve opportunities for seniors to be engaged in physical activity?

Sources

Brenoff, A. (n.d.). Playgrounds for seniors Improve Isolation. http://www.huffingtonpost.com/2015/06/04/playgrounds-for-seniors_n_7452270.html.

Hadden, G. (n.d.). Playgrounds are a big hit with Spain's elder set. http://www.pri.org/stories/2014-04-01/playgrounds-are-big-hit-spains-elder-set.

Liliana Bettencourt and Rui Neves. (n.d.). Senior playgrounds in the promotion of physical activity among the elderly - characteristics of use. https://www.researchgate.net/profile/Rui_Neves/publication/301351623_Senior_playgrounds_in_the_promotion_of_physical_activity_among_the_elderly_-_characteristics_of_use/links/5714cecf08aec4e14da7f2b9.pdf.

Madren, C. (2013). Hit the (Outdoor) Gym: A New Era of Fitness Trails and Outdoor Gyms Helps Communities Stay Healthy. https://www.questia.com/magazine/1G1-335188120/hit-the-outdoor-gym-a-new-era-of-fitness-trails.

Renzulli, L. A. (n.d.). Playgrounds for Seniors Popping up in U.S. http://www.governing.com/generations/government-management/gov-senior-playgrounds-popping-up.html.

Research, A. L. (n.d.). Parks, Playgrounds and Active Living. http://activelivingresearch.org/files/Synthesis_Mowen_Feb2010_0.pdf.

Willard, L. (n.d.). Playgrounds for senior citizens. http://www.upworthy.com/playgrounds-for-senior-citizens-genius-idea.

> The aim is to imitate adults. . . . This explains the success of the toy weapons and miniatures which copy the tools, engines, arms and machines used by adults. The little girl plays her mother's role as cook, laundress and ironer. The boy makes believe he is a soldier, musketeer, policeman, pirate, cowboy, Martian, etc.[5]

Ilinx consists of play activities based on the pursuit of vertigo or dizziness. Historically, ilinx was found in primitive religious dances or other rituals that induced the trancelike state necessary for worship. Today it may be seen in children's games that lead to dizziness by whirling rapidly and in the use of swings and spring riders. Among adults, ilinx may be achieved through amusement park rides such as roller coasters and a variety of adventure activities, including skydiving and bungee jumping.

Contrasting Styles of Play

Caillois also suggested two extremes of play behavior. The first of these, *paidia*, involves exuberance, freedom, and uncontrolled and spontaneous gaiety. The second, *ludus*, is characterized by rules and conventions and represents calculated and contrived activity. Each of the four forms of play may be conducted at either extreme of paidia or ludus or at some point on a continuum between the two.

The Play Element in Culture

Probably the most far-reaching and influential theory of play as a cultural phenomenon was advanced by the Dutch social historian Johan Huizinga in his provocative work *Homo Ludens* (*Man the Player*). Huizinga presented the thesis that play pervades all of life. He saw it as having certain characteristics: It is a voluntary activity, marked by freedom and never imposed by physical necessity or moral duty. It stands outside the realm of satisfying physiological needs and appetites. It is separate from ordinary life both in its location and its duration, being "played out" within special time periods and in such special places as the arena, the card table, the stage, and the tennis court. Play is controlled, said Huizinga, by special sets of rules, and it demands absolute order. It is also marked by uncertainty and tension. Finally, it is not concerned with good or evil, although it has its own ethical value in that its rules must be obeyed.

In Huizinga's view, play reveals itself chiefly in two kinds of activity: contests for something and representations of something. He regarded it as an important civilizing influence in human society and cited as an example

ESSENTIAL CHARACTERISTICS OF PLAY, C. 1948

In 1949, Elmer Mitchell and Bernard Mason identified the essential characteristics of play in their book *The Theory of Play*.[4] They acknowledged an absence of consensus on the meaning of play, but suggested that there was more agreement on the characteristics of play.

1. Play is activity; it is not idleness, but is in contrast with it. Loafing and dawdling are not play … a slumping of activity because of lack of interest, indicates a loss of the play spirit.
2. Play is not limited to any particular form of activity; it may be neuromuscular, sensory, mental, or a combination of all three.
3. The value of play in education is due to its power to interest the player, absorb his attention, and arouse him to enthusiastic and persistent activity.
4. Whether an activity is play or not depends on the attitude of the mind of the doer toward the thing he is doing. It follows there is no particular activity. What is play one day may be drudgery another day.
5. There is a general accord … that the play spirit is an attitude of mind, but there is not so full an agreement as to the nature of this attitude.

the society of ancient Greece, which was permeated with play forms. He traced historically the origins of many social institutions as ritualized forms of play activity. For example, the element of play was initially dominant in the evolution of judicial processes. Law consisted of a pure contest between competing individuals or groups. It was not a matter of being right or wrong; instead, trials were conducted through the use of oracles, contests of chance that determined one's fate, trials of strength or resistance to torture, and verbal contests. Huizinga suggested that the same principle applied to many other cultural institutions:

> In myth and ritual the great instinctive forces of civilized life have their origin: law and order, commerce and profit, craft and art, poetry, wisdom, and science. All are rooted in the primeval soil of play.[6]

PSYCHOLOGICAL ANALYSIS OF PLAY

Over the past several decades, numerous authorities in the fields of psychology and psychoanalysis have examined play and its role in personality development, psychoanalytical perspectives, play as creative exploration, and related areas.

Play in Personality Development

The theoretical foundations of play have a long history with little consensus on one overall theory of play. Over the past 40 years, much research has been done on the benefits of play. The psychological aspects have been prominent. Personality is shaped by play in many different ways. Play prompts enjoyment, freedom, and fun. It prompts self-expression, creativity, imagination, and self-confidence. Play allows children to learn to interact with others through cooperative, sharing, and conflict-resolution activities. All of these experiences affect an individual's personality and contribute to the type of person the individual will become.

Psychoanalytical Perspectives on Play

Sigmund Freud, the father of modern psychoanalysis, had a number of distinctive views regarding the meaning and purpose of play. Freud saw play as a medium through which children are able to gain control and competence and to resolve conflicts that occur in their lives. He believed that children are frequently overwhelmed by their life circumstances, which may be confusing, complex, and unpleasant. Through play, they are able to reexperience threatening events and thus to control and master them. In this sense, play and dreams serve a therapeutic function for children. In general, Freud thought that play represented the child's way of dealing with reality—in effect, by playing with it, making it more acceptable, and exerting mastery over it.

Play can be viewed from developmental, psychological, anthropological, creative, and cultural perspectives.
© Photos.com/Getty.

The American Academy of Pediatrics released a report about the importance of play and stated that "Play is essential to development because it contributes to the cognitive, physical, social, and emotional well-being of children and youth. Play also offers an ideal opportunity for parents to engage fully with their children. Despite the benefits derived from play for both children and parents, time for free play has been markedly reduced for some children."[7]

> Might we not say that every child at play behaves like a creative writer, in that he creates a world of his own, or, rather, rearranges the things of his world in a new way which pleases him? It would be wrong to think he does not take his play seriously; on the contrary he takes his play very seriously and he expends large amounts of emotion on it. The opposite of play is not what is serious but what is real.[8]

A number of Freud's other theories, such as the "pleasure principle" and the "death wish," have also been seen as having strong implications for the analysis of play. The Freudian view of play influenced many psychotherapists and educators in their approach to childhood education and treatment programs. Bruno Bettelheim, Erik Erikson, and Anna Freud, Freud's daughter, all experimented with the use of play in treating children with mental and emotional issues.

Play as Creative Exploration

Other contemporary theories of play emphasize its role in creative exploration and problem solving. Studies of arousal, excitement, and curiosity led to two related theories of play: the stimulus-arousal and competence-effectance theories.

Stimulus-Arousal Theory   This approach is based on the observation that both humans and animals constantly seek stimuli of various kinds, both to gain knowledge and to satisfy a need for excitement, risk, surprise, and pleasure. Often this is connected with the idea of fun, expressed as light amusement, joking, and laughter.

However, the expectation that play is always light, enjoyable, pleasant, or humorous can be misleading. Often, play activities can be frustrating, boring, unpleasant, or even physically painful—particularly when they lead to addiction (as in the case of drug, alcohol, or gambling abuse) and subsequent ill health or economic losses.

Competence-Effectance Theory   A closely related theory holds that much play is motivated by the need of the player to test the environment, solve problems, and gain a sense of mastery and accomplishment. Typically, it involves experimentation or information-seeking behavior, in which the player—whether human or animal— observes the environment, tests or manipulates it, and observes the outcome. Beyond this, the player seeks to develop competence, defined as the ability to interact effectively with the environment. Often this is achieved through repetition of the same action even when it has been mastered. The term *effectance* refers to the player's need to be able to master the environment and, even when uncertainty about it has been resolved, to produce desired effects in it.

Csikszentmihalyi "Flow" Principle   Related to the competence-effectance theory is Mihaly Csikszentmihalyi's view of play as a process in which ideally the player's skills balance the challenge level of the tasks. If the task is too simple, it may become boring and lacking in appeal. If it is too difficult, it may produce anxiety and frustration, and the player may discontinue the activity or change the approach to it so that it becomes more satisfying. This balance between skill and challenge results in what is called "flow." Csikszentmihalyi suggests that a sense of flow is a unique element in true play, which he identifies as a sense of flow. This is the sensation players feel when they are totally involved with the activity. It includes a feeling of harmony and full immersion in play; at a peak level, players might tend to lose their sense of time and their surroundings, and experience an altered state of being. Such flow, he argues, could be found in some work situations, but it is much more commonly experienced in play such as games or sport.[9]

With the obesity epidemic at record levels, a new focus has been put on the value of play. Organizations such as the U.S. Play Coalition, Voice of Play, and many others are providing resources and information on the value of play to parents, community leaders, and parks and recreation professionals. This overview of play theories and the role of play provides a foundation for the value of play that should be instilled in recreational professionals.

If the waves match the surfer's ability, surfing is an optimal activity in which an individual might experience flow.
© iStockphoto/Thinkstock/Getty.

Case Study

. . . .

Organizing My First Ukulele Summer Camp

THE IDEA

Camp Villages is a nine-week summer program for the grandchildren, ages 5 to 18, of the residents of The Villages, the largest 55+ community in Florida. 2016 was the 16th summer for the program. Resident clubs organize the programs. I volunteered in 2015 with the Air Gun Club program. I thought our Ukulele Players Club could sponsor a summer camp program in 2016. I took the idea to our club's Performance Group, our core ukulele players. They agreed to help and placed me in charge.

ORGANIZING

The recreation department limits the Camp Villages programs to 2 hour sessions. The sessions can be offered as often as a club wishes. Clubs submit proposals to the special activities director, outlining what's being offered, number of sessions, requested dates and times, resource requirements, and limits on number and ages for participation.

For the Ukulele program, we requested two sessions, one each in July and August. We limited participation to 20 grandchildren per session, ages 10 and up. The recreation department provided a list of dates and times from which we chose. We asked for copy support (student handbooks), room setup, water, ice, coffee, digital projector, and screen. A recreational department liaison was assigned to assist.

A first priority was ukuleles. Initially we anticipated borrowing ukuleles from club members. Upon reflection, we decided to raise money and purchase as many ukuleles as possible so the campers would be playing similar instruments. When I explained what we were doing to a local music store, they gave a significant discount. We raised money from donations from club members of our club, as well as members of two other ukulele clubs. Additionally, one member donated a ukulele which we raffled off. We were able to raise enough to purchase twenty-two ukuleles and buy support materials such as binders, ukulele straps, and tuners.

We also wanted gift bags for the campers. We contacted several ukulele vendors asking for promotional items. The response was excellent. They sent catalogs, lanyards, stickers, wooden nickels, pens, etc. One company did even more, sending ten free ukuleles in addition to their other materials. One of our members was able to get a local business to provide bags for the gifts. At each session, campers were presented with a bag containing catalogs, stickers, lanyards, pens, and a binder with songs and lesson materials.

Next was developing the ukulele lessons for the camp. With two hours for the session, we developed five lessons. We modified a lesson plan template we found on the internet and developed first an outline of the lessons, then full lesson plans. Finally, we took the lesson plans and wrote computer presentations including diagrams, chord charts, fill in sections, and songs. Picking appropriate songs that would catch the interest of young campers but still include all the musical information was a challenge.

The whole summer camp program is built on volunteers, and, the ukulele camp was no different. Our club has upwards of two hundred members. During the summer many are gone. Our Performance Group provided the bulk of our volunteers. With twenty campers each session we planned for fifteen volunteers. This gave us sufficient people for a minimum of one volunteer for each two campers, plus people to check in the campers, someone to run the computer during the lessons, a photographer, and a presenter. Eighteen different volunteers took part during the two sessions.

Volunteers brought snacks and drinks to each session.

After each session we had a brief discussion of the pros and cons of the session and discussed improvements. Several improvements were included in the second session.

RESULT

The first session went very well, the second even better. Both sessions were near to full. The grandparents, who by camp rules, had to be present, seemed to enjoy the camp as much as the campers. Because of the extra ukuleles, some grandparent had the opportunity to take part. With extra ukuleles we were able to have a drawing each session, and one lucky camper went home with their ukulele. The recreation department liaison was very happy with the results and asked us to increase the number of sessions next year. Importantly, the volunteers were extremely pleased and proud of what we'd done. Some of the campers came to our regular club meeting later in the week and played with us.

LESSON LEARNED

Planning is everything. Having more lessons than we could possibly get through meant we didn't have to worry about running out of material. Limiting each lesson to 25 minutes or less kept the campers attention. When working with campers as young as 10, having enough volunteers was critical. We usually place one volunteer with each of the youngest campers. Having a book with all the student material and songs for the campers was important. They took notes, filled in blanks on the diagrams, and used it as reference. Some of the songs just didn't work. Either they were in the wrong key for the presenter to sing or they weren't age appropriate. Next year we'll replace some of the songs. Tempo for strumming, chord practice, and singing songs had to be keep slower than normally. Changing chords is difficult when you're first learning. Have time during the practice when only the campers are playing (volunteers stop and watch).

HOW DID IT FEEL?

Campers, grandparents, recreation department personnel, and volunteers, all agreed that it was successful. All the hard work, time, and money were well invested. The club is already planning for next year's Villages Ukulele Camp.

(Courtesy, D. R. McLean)

Questions to Consider
1. What do you think were the recreation experiences for this senior group as they provided a recreation activity?
2. What were the potential recreation experiences for the participants and their grandparent(s)?
3. What was the value of this program to the participants? to the leaders?
4. Could this be considered a leisure activity for both groups? Why? Why not?

THE MEANING OF LEISURE: SIX VIEWS

What exactly is leisure? The concept of leisure as a unique, desirable component of the human experience was first articulated by ancient Greeks. In more recent centuries, scholars attempted to define leisure in terms of both its role in society and impact on the individual. For the Athenians particularly, leisure was the highest value of life and work the lowest. Because the upper classes were not required to work, they were free to engage in intellectual, cultural, and artistic activity. Leisure represented an ideal state of freedom and the opportunity for spiritual and intellectual enlightenment. Within modern philosophies of leisure that have descended from this classical Athenian view, leisure is still seen as occurring mostly in time that is not devoted to work. However, it is considered far more than just a temporary release from work used to restore one for more work. Etymologically, the English word *leisure* seems to be derived from the Latin *licere*, meaning "to be permitted" or "to be free." From *licere* came the French *loisir*, meaning "free time," and such English words as *license* (originally meaning immunity from public obligation) and *liberty*. These words are all related; they suggest free choice and the absence of compulsion.

The early Greek word *scole* or *skole* meant "leisure." It led to the Latin *scola* and the English *school* or *scholar*—thus implying a close connection between leisure and education. The word *scole* also referred to places where scholarly discussions were held. One such place was a grove next to the temple of Apollo Lykos, which became known as the *lyceum*. From this came the French *lycée*, meaning "school"—again implying a bond between leisure and education.

The Classical View of Leisure

Aristotle regarded leisure as "a state of being in which activity is performed for its own sake." It was sharply contrasted with work or purposeful action, involving instead such pursuits as art, political debate, philosophical discussion, and learning in general. The Athenians saw work as ignoble; to them it was boring and monotonous. A common Greek word for work is *ascholia*, meaning the absence of leisure—whereas we do the opposite, defining leisure as the absence of work.

Case Study

. . . .

Finding Flow

Csikszentmihalyi's flow principal requires that a person's skill matches the skill at hand. If there is not a balance between skill and challenge, the individual experiences boredom if they are too skilled, or anxiety and frustration if they are under skilled for the challenge. For an individual to experience flow in play there are several factors that must exist. The activity should provide:

1. **A clear set of goals:** The outcomes, or goals, of activities are known. For example, games and sport have clear goals because rules guide play; music is dictated by a score; a marathon runner has a goal to finish. These goals are attainable based on the skill of the individual.
2. **Immediate feedback:** It is clear how well the individual is performing in relation to the activity at hand. A runner knows how well they are progressing, an artist sees his or her work come together, and a team understands how well they are doing in a game.
3. **A loss of self-consciousness:** People do not worry about how they look or are performing; they simply feel good about the activity and their involvement in it.
4. **A sense of distorted time:** The individual loses all sense of time and what seems like minutes can actually be hours.
5. **An autotelic experience:** One participates for the activity itself (intrinsic motivation) and no other reward. Pure enjoyment of the activity is the only justification needed.
6. **Strong concentration and commitment:** The individual totally focuses on the activity and directs all concentration toward it.
7. **A sense of personal control:** The individual feels she or he is in control of the situation and her or his skills to achieve the desired outcome.

Questions to Consider

1. Describe an activity that you enjoy. Does it enable you to experience flow? What elements of flow do you most experience with this activity?
2. Could work allow you to experience flow? Why or why not?
3. Is flow a state that younger people could achieve more so than older people? Justify your answer.

Source

M. Csikszentmihalyi, *Finding Flow: The Psychology of Engagement with Everyday Life* (New York: Basic Books, 1997).

How meaningful is this classical view of leisure today? Although the Greek view of leisure as a necessary and integral piece of a holistic life has merit, this view has two flaws. First, it is linked to the idea of an aristocratic class structure based on the availability of a substantial underclass and slave labor. When Aristotle wrote in his *Treatise on Politics* that "it is of course generally understood that in a well-ordered state, the citizens should have leisure and not have to provide for their daily needs," he meant that leisure was given to a comparatively few patricians and made possible through the strenuous labor of the many.

In modern society, leisure cannot be a privilege reserved for the few; instead, it must be widely available to all. It must exist side by side with work that is respected in our society, and it should have a meaningful relationship to work. The implication is that leisure should be calm, quiet, contemplative, and unhurried, as implied by the word *leisurely*. Obviously, this concept would not apply to those uses of leisure today that are dynamic, active, and demanding or that may have a degree of extrinsic purpose about them.

Leisure as a Symbol of Social Class

The view of leisure as closely related to social class stemmed from the work of Thorstein Veblen, a leading American sociologist of the late nineteenth century. Veblen showed how, throughout history, ruling classes emerged that identified themselves sharply through the possession and use of leisure. In his major work, *The Theory of the Leisure Class,* he points out that in Europe during the feudal and Renaissance periods and finally during the industrial age, the possession and visible use of leisure became the hallmark of the upper class. Veblen attacks the "idle rich"; he sees leisure as a complete way of life for the privileged class, regarding them as exploiters who lived on the toil of others. He coined the phrase "conspicuous consumption" to describe their way of life throughout history. This theory is dated because of the rise of greater working-class leisure and because many members of extremely wealthy families work actively in business, politics, or other demanding professions.

To some degree, however, Veblen's analysis is still relevant. The wealthy or privileged class in modern society continues to engage in a wide variety of expensive, prestigious, and sometimes decadent leisure activities even though its members may not have an immense amount of free time. They tend to travel widely, entertain, patronize the arts, and engage in exclusive and high-status pastimes. Recent scholars have characterized contemporary leisure in Western cultures as consumerist and motivated by the pursuit of diversionary experiences that can be purchased. Ramsey expresses the following critique of consumerist leisure:

> So the nasty face of consumerist leisure expresses acquisitiveness, possessiveness, what the ancient Greeks called *plenoxia:* the desire for more than one's appropriate share. . . . The paradox around obligation-free leisure time is the drive quality, the compulsions and obsessions around purchase and use, to which many people are vulnerable due to the sheer vastness and success and ease of consumerism.[10]

Leisure as Unobligated Time

The most common approach to leisure is to regard it as unobligated or discretionary time. Discretionary time is time that is not used for work obligations and personal maintenance. This view of leisure sees it essentially as time that is free from work or from such work-related responsibilities as travel, study, or social involvements based on work. It also excludes time devoted to essential life-maintenance activities, such as sleep, eating, and personal care. Its most important characteristic is that it lacks a sense of obligation or compulsion. This approach to defining leisure is most popular among economists or sociologists, who are particularly concerned with trends in the economic and industrial life of the nation. Other scholars, including feminists, have found this definition useful in the study of time constraints faced by working adults in contemporary society.

Although this definition appears to be convenient and largely a matter of arithmetic (subtracting work and other obligated tasks from the 24 hours that are available each day and coming out with a block of time that can be called leisure), it has some built-in complexities. For example, is it possible to say that any time is totally free of obligation or compulsion or that any form of leisure activity is totally without some extrinsic purpose? Is it also possible to say that all unobligated time is intrinsically rewarding and possesses the positive qualities typically associated with leisure? For example, some uses of free time that are not clearly work or paid for as work may contribute to success at work. A person may read books or articles related to work, attend evening classes that contribute to work competence, invite guests to a party because of work associations, or join a country club because of its value in establishing business contacts or promoting sales. Within community life, those nonwork occupations that have a degree of obligation about them—such as serving on a school board or as an unpaid member of a town council—may also be viewed as part of a person's civic responsibility.

The strict view of leisure as time that lacks any obligation or compulsion is suspect. If one chooses to raise dogs as a hobby or to play an instrument in an orchestra, one begins to assume a system of routines, schedules, and commitments to others. When this happens one has to question if it is really leisure by this definition of unobligated time.

Leisure as Activity

A fourth common understanding of leisure is that it is activity in which people engage during their free time. Obviously, this concept of leisure is closely linked to the idea of recreation (as you will see in the section on recreation) because it involves the way in which free time is used for activity purposes. Early writers on recreation stressed the importance of activity; for example, Jay B. Nash urged that the procreative act be thought of as an active, "doing" experience. Recuperation through play, he wrote, isn't wholly relegated to inertia—doing nothing—but is gained through action.

For many individuals, Nash's view of leisure would be too confining. They would view relatively passive activities, such as reading a book, going to a museum, watching a film, or even dozing in a hammock or daydreaming, to be appropriate leisure pursuits, along with forms of active play.

Feminist scholars have criticized conceptualizations of leisure as activity as irrelevant for many women whose everyday life experiences cannot be easily categorized into a work/leisure dichotomy. Furthermore, definitions of leisure as activity do not accommodate individual perceptions about particular activities. Some individuals may view preparing a meal as a pleasurable activity of self-expression, whereas others view the activity as a monotonous, domestic obligation. In response to this criticism, contemporary scholars who study leisure as activity are primarily concerned with the outcomes of a particular activity rather than the activity itself.

Leisure as a State of Being Marked by Freedom

The fifth concept of leisure places the emphasis on the perceived freedom of the activity and on the role of leisure involvement in helping the individual achieve personal fulfillment and self-enrichment. Neulinger writes:

> To leisure means to be engaged in an activity performed for its own sake, to do something which gives one pleasure and satisfaction, which involves one to the very core of one's being. To leisure means to be oneself, to express one's talents, one's capacities, one's potentials.[11]

This concept of leisure implies a lifestyle that is holistic, in the sense that one's view of life is not sharply fragmented into a number of spheres such as family activities, religion, work, and free time. Instead, all such involvements are seen as part of a whole in which the individual explores his or her capabilities, develops enriching experiences with others, and seeks "self-actualization" in the sense of being creative, involved, expressive, and fully alive. The idea of leisure as a state of being places great emphasis on the need for perceived freedom. Recognizing the fact that some constraints always exist, Godbey defines leisure in the following way:

> Leisure is living in relative freedom from the external compulsive forces of one's culture and physical environment so as to be able to act from internal compulsion in ways which are personally pleasing and intuitively worthwhile.[12]

Such contemporary leisure theorists stress the need for the true leisure experience to yield a sense of total freedom and absence from compulsion of any kind. Realistically, however, there are many situations in which individuals are pressured to participate or in which the activity's structure diminishes his or her sense of freedom and intrinsic motivation.

Leisure as Spiritual Expression

A sixth way of conceptualizing leisure today sees it in terms of its contribution to spiritual expression or religious values. Newly founded faith-based social welfare organizations in the late nineteenth century were a driving force behind the growth of public and philanthropic leisure services during that time. During the early decades of the twentieth century, play and recreation were often referred to as uplifting or holy kinds of human experiences.

A more modern approach to spirituality moved beyond religion to an inner peace, understanding of the values that drive a person, and the meaning people assign to their lives. Leisure's connection to spirituality may not seem immediately obvious. However, leisure plays a major role in spirituality. The most common spiritual leisure pursuits are outdoor and nature activities. Walking through the woods, sitting on the bank of a creek, or paddling a canoe across a calm lake are means to spirituality for some. Others may prefer meditation, yoga, or other relaxation and contemplative exercises.

Leisure Defined

Recognizing that each of the six concepts of leisure just presented stems from a different perspective, a general definition that embraces several of the key points follows.

Leisure is that portion of an individual's time that is not directly devoted to work or work-connected responsibilities or to other obligated forms of maintenance or self-care. Leisure implies freedom and choice and is customarily used in a variety of ways, including to meet one's personal needs for reflection, self-enrichment, relaxation, pleasure, and affiliation. Although it usually involves some form of participation in a voluntarily chosen activity, it may also be regarded as a holistic state of being or even a spiritual experience.

THE MEANING OF RECREATION

In a sense, recreation represents a fusion between play and leisure and is therefore presented as the third of the important concepts that provide the framework for this overall field of study. The term itself stems from the Latin word *recreatio,* meaning that which refreshes or restores. Historically,

Volunteers form Adopt-a-Park programs to enhance local parks and build social capital within the community.
Courtesy of Deb Garrahy.

recreation was often regarded as a period of light and restful activity, voluntarily chosen, that permits one to regain energy after heavy work and to return to work renewed.

This point of view lacks acceptability today for two reasons. First, as most work in modern society becomes less physically demanding, many people are becoming more fully engaged, both physically and mentally, in their recreation than in their work. Thus, the notion that recreation should be light and relaxing is far too limiting. Second, the definition of recreation as primarily intended to restore one for work does not cover the case of persons who have no work, including the growing retiree population, but who certainly need recreation to make their lives meaningful.

In contrast to work, which is often thought of as tedious, unpleasant, and obligatory, recreation has traditionally been thought of as light, pleasant, and revitalizing. However, this contrast too should be reconsidered. A modern, holistic view of work and recreation would be that both have the potential for being pleasant, rewarding, and creative and that both may represent serious forms of personal involvement and deep commitment.

CONTEMPORARY DEFINITIONS OF RECREATION

Most modern definitions of recreation fit into one of three categories: (1) Recreation has been seen as an activity carried on under certain conditions or with certain motivations; (2) recreation has been viewed as a process or state of being—something that happens within the person while engaging in certain kinds of activity, with a given set of expectations; and (3) recreation has been perceived as a social institution, a body of knowledge, or a professional field.

Typically, definitions of recreation found in the professional literature have included the following elements:

1. Recreation is widely regarded as activity (including physical, mental, social, or emotional involvement), as contrasted with sheer idleness or complete rest. Recreation may include an extremely wide range of activities, such as sport, games, crafts, performing arts, fine arts, music, dramatics, travel, hobbies, and social activities. These activities may be engaged in by individuals or by groups and may involve single or episodic participation or sustained and frequent involvement throughout one's lifetime.
2. The choice of activity or involvement is voluntary, free of compulsion or obligation.
3. Recreation is prompted by internal motivation and the desire to achieve personal satisfaction, rather than by extrinsic goals or rewards.
4. Recreation is dependent on a state of mind or attitude; it is not so much what one does as the reason for doing it, and the way the individual feels about the activity, that makes it recreation.
5. Although the primary motivation for taking part in recreation is usually pleasure seeking, it may also be meeting intellectual, physical, or social needs. In some cases, rather than providing "fun" of a light or trivial nature, recreation may involve a serious degree of commitment and self-discipline and may yield frustration or even pain.

Within this framework, many kinds of leisure experiences may be viewed as recreation. They may range from the most physically challenging pursuits to those with much milder demands. Watching television, listening to a symphony orchestra, reading a book, or playing lacrosse are all forms of recreation.

Voluntary Participation
Although it is generally accepted that recreation participation should be voluntary and carried out without any degree of pressure or compulsion, often this is not the case. We tend to be influenced by others, as in the case of the child whose parents urge him to join a Little League team, or the gymnast or figure skater who is encouraged in the thought that he or she might become a professional performer. Although ideally recreation is thought of as being free of compulsion or obligation, once one has entered into an activity—such as joining a company bowling league or playing with a chamber music group—one accepts a set of obligations to the other members of the team or group. Thus, recreation cannot be entirely free and spontaneous and, in fact, assumes some of the characteristics of work in the sense of having schedules, commitments, and responsibilities.

Motives for Participation
Definitions of recreation generally have stressed that it should be conducted for personal enjoyment or pleasure—ideally of an immediate nature. However, many worthwhile activities take time to master before they yield the fullest degree of satisfaction. Some complex activities may cause frustration and even mental anguish—as in the case of the golf addict who is desperately unhappy because of poor putting or driving.

In such cases, it is not so much that the participant receives immediate pleasure as that he or she is absorbed and challenged by the activity; pleasure will probably grow as the individual's skill improves.

What about the view that recreation must be carried on for its own sake and without extrinsic goals or purposes? It is essential to recognize that human beings are usually goal-oriented, purposeful creatures.

James Murphy and his coauthors have identified different recreational behaviors that suggest the kinds of motives people may have when they engage in activity:

- *Socializing behaviors:* Activities such as dancing, dating, going to parties, or visiting friends, in which people relate to one another in informal and unstereotyped ways.
- *Associative behaviors:* Activities in which people group together because of common interests, such as street rod car clubs; stamp-, coin-, or gem-collecting groups; or hobbyists.
- *Competitive behaviors:* Activities including all of the popular sport and games, but also competition in the performing arts or in outdoor activities in which individuals compete against the environment or even against their own limitations.
- *Risk-taking behaviors:* An increasingly popular form of participation in which the stakes are often physical injury or possible death.
- *Exploratory behaviors:* In a sense, all recreation involves some degree of exploration; in this context, it refers to such activities as travel and sightseeing, hiking, scuba diving, spelunking, and other pursuits that open up new environments to the participant.[13]

To these may be added the following motives:

- *Vicarious experiences:* Activities such as watching movies or sports events.
- *Sensory stimulation:* Activities that might include drug use, sexual involvement, or listening to rock music.
- *Physical involvement:* Activities that are done for their own sake, as opposed to competitive games.
- *Creative arts:* Activities that stimulate creativity and imagination through such mediums as the visual or performing arts.
- *Intellectual pursuits:* Activities that require cognitive skill such as reading, puzzles, strategic games, playing a musical instrument, or crocheting.

Recreation as an Outcome

Recognizing that different people may have many different motives for taking part in recreation, Gray and Greben suggest that it should not be considered simply as a form of activity. Instead, they argue that recreation should be perceived as the outcome of participation—a "peak experience in self-satisfaction" that comes from successful participation in any sort of enterprise.

> Recreation is an emotional condition within an individual human being that flows from a feeling of well-being and self-satisfaction. It is characterized by feelings of mastery, achievement, exhilaration, acceptance, success, personal worth, and pleasure. It reinforces a positive self-image. Recreation is a response to aesthetic experience, achievement of personal goals, or positive feedback from others. It is independent of activity, leisure, or social acceptance.[14]

Historically, leisure researchers have focused on the social-psychological outcomes of recreation. More recently, significant attention has been given to physical outcomes. Researchers and practitioners are particularly interested in the relationship between recreation participation and physical health outcomes, including reduction of obesity and other chronic health conditions.

Recreation as a Social Institution

Recreation is identified as a significant institution in the modern community, involving a form of collective behavior carried on within specific social structures. It has numerous traditions, values, channels of communication, formal relationships, and other institutional aspects.

Once chiefly the responsibility of the family, the church, or other local social bodies, recreation in contemporary society is the responsibility of a number of major agencies in today's society. These may include public,

People are motivated to engage in high-adventure activities because of the risk involved.
Courtesy of Billy Heatter/U.S. Air Force.

EMOTIONAL COMMITMENT TO SPORT

The degree to which many individuals become deeply committed emotionally to their recreational interests may be illustrated within the realms of sports and popular entertainment. So fervently do many Americans root for popular sports teams and stars that sport has increasingly been referred to as a form of religion. The glorification of leading athletes as idols and the national preoccupation with such major events as the Stanley Cup, the World Series, or the Super Bowl demonstrate the degree to which sports—as a popular form of recreation—capture the emotional commitment of millions of Americans today.

Gardening is an example of a recreation activity that is freely chosen and has elements of intrinsic and extrinsic motivation.
© Photodisc/Getty.

nonprofit, or commercial organizations that operate parks, beaches, zoos, aquariums, stadiums, or sports facilities. Recreational activities may also be provided by organizations such as hospitals, schools, correctional institutions, and branches of the armed forces. Clearly, recreation emerged in the twentieth century as a significant social institution, complete with its own national and international organizations and an extensive network of programs of professional preparation in colleges and universities.

Beyond this development, over the past century, there has been general acceptance of the view that community recreation, in which citizens take responsibility for supporting organized leisure services to meet social needs, contributes significantly to democratic citizenship. Community recreation is offered through city or county park and recreation departments.

Recreation Defined

Acknowledging these contrasting views of the meaning of recreation, the following definition of the term is offered. Recreation consists of human activities or experiences that occur in leisure time. Usually, they are voluntarily chosen for intrinsic purposes and are pleasurable, although they may involve a degree of compulsion, extrinsic purpose, and discomfort, or even pain or danger. Recreation may also be regarded as the emotional state resulting from participation or as a social institution, a professional career field, or a business. When provided as part of organized community or voluntary-agency programs, recreation should be socially constructive and morally acceptable in terms of prevailing community standards and values.

RELATIONSHIPS AMONG PLAY, LEISURE, AND RECREATION

Obviously, the three terms discussed in this chapter are closely interrelated. Leisure, for example, provides an opportunity to carry on both play and recreation. Much of our free time in modern society is taken up by recreation, although leisure may also include such activities as continuing education, religious practice, or community service, which are not usually thought of as forms of recreation. In turn, it should be understood that although play and recreation tend to overlap, they are not identical. Play is not so much an activity as a form of behavior, marked stylistically by teasing, competition, exploration, or make-believe. Play can occur during work or leisure, whereas recreation takes place only during leisure.

Recreation obviously includes many forms of play, but it also may involve distinctly nonplay-like activities such as traveling, reading, going to museums, and pursuing other cultural or intellectual activities. As a social institution, recreation has broader applications than play or leisure in two ways: Recreation is often provided by institutions that do not have leisure as a primary concern, such as the armed forces or business concerns; and recreation agencies often provide other social or environmental services and may in fact become an important linkage between municipal governments and the people they serve.

Leisure is a subject of scholarly study for many economists and sociologists; it also has come increasingly under the scrutiny of psychologists and social psychologists. However, to the public at large, leisure tends to be a somewhat abstract or remote concept. Although many academic departments and some community agencies use the term *leisure* in their titles, it lacks a sense of urgency or strong appeal as a public issue or focus of government action.

Of the three terms, *recreation* is at once the most understandable and significant for many people. It is easily recognizable as an area of personal activity and social responsibility, and its values are readily apparent for all age groups and special populations as well. For these reasons, it is given primary emphasis in other chapters, particularly in terms of program sponsorship and professional identity.

The themes that have just been introduced are explored more fully throughout this text, as the historical development of recreation and play and the evolution of the present-day leisure-service system are described. Throughout, issues related to the social implications of recreation and leisure and to the role of recreation and park professionals are fully discussed, along with the challenges that face practitioners in this field in the twenty-first century.

Summary

Play, recreation, and leisure represent important basic concepts that are essential aspects of the overall field of organized leisure services. They have been explored by philosophers, psychologists, historians, educators, and sociologists from ancient Greek civilizations to the present.

Play may best be understood as a form of activity or behavior that is generally nonpurposeful in terms of having serious intended outcomes, but that is an important element in the healthy growth of children and in other societal functions. The chapter presents various theories of play, ranging from the classical views of Herbert Spencer to more contemporary concepts that link play to Freudian theory or to exploratory drives of human personality.

Six concepts of leisure are presented that depict it as the possession of the upper classes or aristocrats throughout history, as free time or activity, as a state of being, and as a form of spiritual expression. Recreation is also explored from different perspectives, with a key issue being whether it must be morally constructive or socially approved to be considered recreation. The role of recreation as an important contemporary social institution and force in economic life is also discussed.

Questions for Class Discussion or Essay Examination

1. Read the case study Photography as Leisure: Why I Take Photos. Conduct an analysis of the case study, answering: 1) Why this is recreation? 2) Identify what you believe to be the recreation components of the activity, explaining each of the components.

   _____

   _____

2. If motivation is important in the study of recreation and leisure, explore some of the motivations you identify in leisure participation. How does knowing your motivations for participation in recreation and leisure influence your desire to study recreation and leisure?

   _____

   _____

3. Compare and contrast the early theories and contemporary theories of play. First, identify the commonalities in the theoretical development of play, and secondly, the differences. How has play been influenced by leisure and play theorists?

   _____

   _____

   _____

4. Discuss the contrasting meanings of play, leisure, and recreation, and show how individually and collectively they overlap and differ from each other in their meanings. Which of the three do you feel is the more useful term as far as public understanding of leisure and recreation is concerned?

   _____

   _____

   _____

5. Play is considered by many to be the domain of youth, and yet we see the creation of senior playgrounds, adult sport activities, and participation by adults in more and more recreation activities that could be called "play." Explain why play is defined as a youth activity and adults use the term recreation. Are they really that different? Are the motivations similar? Expand on this discussion.

_____

_____

_____

_____

_____

6. Examine your free time as a student. Do you have more or less free time than you did before college? Explain how your free time has changed. Compare it with your parents' or older siblings' free time and explain the difference. What causes these differences?

_____

_____

_____

_____

_____

Endnotes

1. Westervelt, Eric, "Where the Wild Things Play," National Public Radio (2014). http://www.npr.org/sections/ed/2014/08/04/334896321/where-the-wild-things-play.
2. Friedrich Froebel, cited in George Torkildsen, *Leisure and Recreation Management* (London: E. and F. N. Spon, 1992): 48–49.
3. The original source of this theory was W. P. Bowen and Elmer D. Mitchell, *The Theory of Organized Play* (New York: A. S. Barnes, 1923).
4. Mitchell, E. D. & Mason, B. S., *The Theory of Play* (New York: A. S. Barnes and Company, 1948): 105–106.
5. Roger Caillois, *Man, Play, and Games* (London: Thames and Hudson, 1961): 21.
6. Johan Huizinga, *Homo Ludens: A Study of the Play Element in Culture* (Boston: Beacon Press, 1944; 1960): 5.
7. Ginsburg, K. R. (2007). The importance of play in promoting healthy child development and maintaining strong parent-child bonds. *Pediatrics, 119*(1), 182-191. http://pediatrics.aappublications.org/content/119/1/182.short
8. Sigmund Freud, quoted in M. J. Ellis, *Why People Play* (Englewood Cliffs, NJ: Prentice Hall, 1973): 60.
9. M. Csikszentmihalyi, *Flow: The Psychology of Optimal Experience* (P.S.) (New York: HarperCollins Publishers, 2007).
10. Hayden Ramsey, *Reclaiming Leisure: Art, Sport and Philosophy* (New York: Palgrave Macmillan, 2005).
11. John Neulinger, *The Psychology of Leisure* (Springfield, IL: Charles C. Thomas, 1974): xi.
12. Geoffrey Godbey, *Leisure in Your Life: An Exploration* (Philadelphia: W. B. Saunders, 1981): 10.
13. James Murphy et al., *Leisure Service Delivery Systems: A Modern Perspective* (Philadelphia: Lea and Febiger, 1973): 73–76.
14. David Gray and Seymour Greben, "Future Perspectives," *Parks and Recreation* (July 1974): 49.

Leisure Motivation

Natalie Duran, Climber . . . What Climbing Means to Me

The first time was like, "This is really fun. It is awesome. Why didn't I think about this before?" The first day I did horrible but it was really fun. My muscles were really sore. . . . Climbing is a way that I can compete with myself and have fun with my peers. It's weird, because when you're climbing you get into this numb zone. There is a different state for everyone. Really it's like you are one with yourself and you're one with your surroundings.

It's a fun sport because even if it is competitive you are honestly only competitive with yourself. It is an individual sport. You climb to your most successful moments and you are at one with yourself and you are in a zen state and not when adrenaline is pumping. Adrenaline is what creates mistakes and mistakes aren't good.

I take fear as an opportunity to grow myself and gain experience. Every time I'm afraid that means I am experiencing something new or something is going wrong and I need to fix that in the future.

Climbing keeps me grounded from college. For some reason I love it. It has become my passion, my love, my lifestyle.

Source: Duran, N. [ndtitanlady]. (April 9, 2012). What Rock Climbing Is, to Me – Natalie Duran [Video file]. Retrieved from www.youtube.com/watch?v=76yyNVmXpA4.

Learning Objectives

1. Define and provide examples of physical, social, and psychological motivators to leisure.

2. Discuss the utilization of motivators in recreation programming.

3. Explain serious leisure as a unique form of leisure.

4. Define taboo recreation and identify examples of activities that would be classified as taboo recreation.

INTRODUCTION

Having reviewed the foundations of leisure and recreation, we now examine them from personal and social perspectives. This chapter outlines the varied motivations that impel individuals to take part in a wide range of recreational activities. These motivations are examined from the perspective of positive leisure experience, recreation activities that involve extreme risks, and those activities that are considered to be taboo, such as illegal drug use and gambling.

MOTIVATION: WHAT IS IT?

Why do people choose to watch television for hours on end, play competitive sports, or conquer Mount Everest? The reasons are as varied as people are. Recreation enthusiasts derive different qualities from their activities, and these qualities are what drive them to participate. These driving factors are called *motivators*. Motivation can be defined as an internal or external element that moves people toward a behavior. A recreation-related motivator could be the desire to develop soccer skills or to learn about the visual arts.

When discussing motivation at the theoretical level, the names Edward L. Deci and Richard M. Ryan always emerge. They have studied motivation for many years and developed Self-Determination Theory (SDT). SDT is a general psychological theory that assumes that "humans are inherently motivated to grow and achieve and will fully commit to and engage in even uninteresting tasks when their meaning and value is understood." SDT focuses on the intrinsic motivation of the activity and not the extrinsic (defined shortly).[1]

Ryan and Deci outline six different types of motivation on a self-determination continuum that spans from no control over a situation to complete autonomy:

1. *Amotivation:* Performance done without any intention of doing so. For example, amotivation is present when a parent takes a child to see a baseball game when the child has no desire or interest in seeing it. The child goes along because he has no choice and it is beyond his control.
2. *Extrinsic motivation:* Performance of an activity because of an external force or reward. For example, a professional athlete receives compensation for playing for his or her team. This compensation is an external reward and is most likely one of the driving factors behind the athlete's participation. Another example of an extrinsic motivator is that of the golfer who plays with a regular foursome and bets $5 per hole with her friends. If she plays because of the money involved, this is an extrinsic motivator.
3. *Introjected motivation:* Performance of an activity to alleviate guilt and anxiety or to enhance ego. Participation occurs in an activity because others desire that participation and the individual would feel guilty or anxious about letting people down. In terms of enhancing the ego, some participate in activities simply because they can demonstrate their skills to others. A professional athlete may continue playing the sport because of the admiration from the fans when in reality the athlete does not really enjoy playing.
4. *Identified motivation:* Performance is done because the individual sees the value in the activity and gets something out of it. This could be building skills or increasing physical fitness. For example, if a person is running to enhance her fitness level and increase weight loss and not for the pure love of running, she is experiencing identified motivation.
5. *Integrated motivation:* Performance of an activity matches the individual's values and desires, yet there are external reasons too. For example, the individual who runs for fitness and weight loss understands the need for physical health and has chosen running as an activity to achieve it.
6. *Intrinsic motivation:* Performance of an activity for the behavior itself and the feelings that result from the activity. For example, completing a half-marathon for the first time could lead to a sense of accomplishment and pride in the fact that a goal was reached. These feelings are intrinsic motivators. The half-marathon was done because of the benefits of the activity and not because an external reward was dictating or influencing the person's behavior. The rewards are internal to the person, and the activity is done for its own sake.[2]

In leisure services, intrinsic motivation is most desired. Ryan and Deci summarize the importance of intrinsic motivation by saying, "Perhaps no single phenomenon reflects the positive potential of human nature as much as intrinsic motivation, the inherent tendency to seek out novelty and challenges, to extend and exercise one's capacities, to explore, and to learn."[3] Intrinsic motivation is enhanced and more likely to occur when there is a sense of autonomy, competence, and relatedness. Autonomy is the freedom to determine your own behavior, to guide your own actions, and to be in control of the situation. Competence occurs when an individual feels capable, skilled, and able to meet an acceptable level of challenge. Feelings of competence result from effective and positive feedback from performance. Last, relatedness is a sense of belonging, security, and connection with others. These three things enhance the likelihood of intrinsic motivation. The following sections look at motivation from a variety of perspectives.

Although there is a plethora of ways to look at motivation, including by activity type, age, and gender, it is important to look at broad motivating factors that relate to leisure preferences. In describing the major areas of human development, behavioral scientists use such terms as *cognitive* (referring to mental or intellectual development), *affective* (relating to emotional or feeling states), and *psychomotor* (meaning the broad area of motor learning and performance). Because these terms are somewhat narrow in their application, this chapter instead uses the following more familiar terms: (1) *physical*, (2) *social*, (3) *psychological*, and (4) *emotional*. Most, if not all, motivators of leisure participation can fit into one or more of these four categories.

PHYSICAL MOTIVATORS

Active recreational pursuits such as sport and games, dance, and even such moderate forms of exercise as walking or gardening have significant positive effects on physical development and health. The value of such activities obviously will vary according to the age and developmental needs of the participants. For children and youth, the major need is to promote healthy structural growth, fitness, endurance, and the acquisition of physical qualities and skills. It is essential that children learn the importance of fitness and develop habits of participation in physical recreation that will serve them in later life. This is particularly important in an era of electronic games, labor-saving devices, and readily available transportation, all of which save time and physical effort but encourage a sedentary way of life.

Physical motivators can best be summarized as control of obesity and preserving cardiovascular health. Although each is discussed separately, they are intertwined. Most of what drives people who are motivated by the physical aspects of leisure is achieving wellness. A means to wellness is cardiovascular health and reduced obesity. Society is changing and starting to realize how important an active lifestyle is, and parks and recreation play an active role in this.

Youth baseball serves as a physical motivator where health, wellness, and other physical qualities are gained.
© Creatas/Thinkstock/Getty.

Control of Obesity

The Centers for Disease Control and Prevention (CDC) defines overweight and obesity in terms of body mass index (BMI). BMI is a calculation of height and weight. **Table 2.1** demonstrates the level of BMI in an adult 5'9".

BMI for children is calculated a bit differently and takes into account age and sex-specific percentiles. Scientists agree that physical activity plays a major role in weight control. Obesity among American adults has grown steadily and is now a serious health problem in this country. Nearly 73% of the U.S. population is overweight, and of those 35% are considered obese. Children are not exempt from this weight problem because one in three children are considered overweight[4] and 17% of these children are obese.[5]

TABLE 2.1 Sample Adult BMI Chart

Height	Weight Range (lbs)	BMI	Considered
5'9"	124 or less	Less than 18.5	Underweight
	125–168	18.5–24.9	Healthy weight
	169–202	25.0–29.9	Overweight
	203 or more	30 or higher	Obese

Reproduced from "Overweight and Obesity" by Centers for Disease Control and Prevention, www.cdc.gov/obesity/adult/defining.html.

Not only is there a difference in obesity rates based on age, race and geography also show differences. Non-Hispanic blacks were 51% more likely to be obese, and Hispanics showed a 21% greater prevalence of obesity when compared with non-Hispanic whites.[6] The states with the highest percentage of population who are overweight or obese include Mississippi (35.1%), West Virginia (35.1%), Arkansas (34.6%), Tennessee (33.7%), and Kentucky (33.2%). The healthiest states are Colorado (21.3%), Hawaii (21.8%), Utah (24.1%), Massachusetts (23.6%), and the District of Columbia (22.9%). In general, the states in the south have a tendency to be fattest, while the states in the West and New England are the slimmest.[7]

The main reason for obesity is inactivity. In 2015, less than half (49%) of Americans aged 18 and older met the 2008 federal physical activity guidelines for aerobic activity, and only 20.9% of them met the guidelines for aerobic activity and muscle-strengthening activity. For both categories, the highest levels of inactivity for every age group were found among women, with 52.9% of men meeting aerobic activity guidelines compared to 46.7% of women. The numbers are similar when adding muscular strengthening exercise into the mix, with 25.1% of men meeting the guidelines, while only 17.9% of women did. Age is also a factor; while 59% of adults aged 18–24 meet aerobic guidelines, the number plummets to 27.1% for those aged 75 and older. The same is true for the combination of aerobic and muscle-strengthening activity, with a drop from 29.8% of those aged 18–24 to 8.7% of those aged 75 and older meeting guidelines. With respect to race, 43% of Hispanics met the guidelines for aerobic activity compared to 42.4% of non-Hispanic blacks and 52.9% of non-Hispanic whites. The trend is similar for a combination for aerobic and muscle-strengthening activity, with 16.4% of Hispanics meeting guidelines compared to 20.2% of non-Hispanic blacks and 23.3% of non-Hispanic whites who met the guidelines.[8]

Education is also an indicator of regular physical activity levels. As education increases, so does physical activity. People without a high school diploma (23.3%) are least likely to get regular physical activity and those with advanced degrees are the most likely to exercise (61.4%). The same is true for income levels.[9] The benefits of getting regular physical activity are proven for both children and adults, with decreased obesity rates and decreased incidences of coronary disease, diabetes, high blood pressure, and stroke. Although many of these diseases do not occur in children, obese children are more likely to become obese adults.

Because of these statistics, public, nonprofit, and commercial agencies have come together to offer programs and education to help people become more active. For example, Healthy People 2020 is dedicated to helping people live longer and have a better quality of life. It includes 10 indicators as to what makes a person healthy, and physical activity is at the top of the list.[10]

Preserving Cardiovascular Health

Of all the fitness-related aspects of active recreation, maintaining cardiovascular health may represent the highest priority. Cardiovascular diseases include such things as high blood pressure, heart failure, stroke, and coronary

Case Study

. . . .

Calculating Your BMI

BMI is an indicator of healthy body weight. Go to the National Heart, Lung, and Blood Institute website (http://www.nhlbi .nih.gov/guidelines/obesity/BMI/bmicalc.htm) to calculate your BMI.

Questions to Consider

1. Were you surprised by your BMI? Do you have any risk factors as described by the National Heart, Lung, and Blood Institute?
2. What changes, if any, need to be made for you to maintain a healthy BMI?
3. If you are at a healthy weight, what do you do on a regular basis to maintain that healthy weight?
4. Think about your family, including grandparents, parents, aunts, and uncles. Is there a weight issue within the family as a whole? Explain.
5. What do you first think when you see an obese younger child?

Source

National Institutes of Health, National Heart, Lung, and Blood Institute, "Calculating Your Body Mass Index," http://www.nhlbi.nih.gov /guidelines/obesity/BMI/bmicalc.htm.

heart disease. Johns Hopkins Medicine reported that approximately 84 million people in the United States have cardiovascular disease, causing about 2200 deaths per day or one every 40 seconds. Furthermore, about approximately one third of cardiovascular disease deaths occur before age 75.

Even with these known statistics, physical inactivity is the main culprit, with a sedentary lifestyle being every bit as bad for one's heart as smoking, high cholesterol, or high blood pressure. The American Heart Association suggests that adults need 150 minutes of moderate-intensity aerobic activity per week or 75 minutes per week of vigorous-intensity aerobic physical activity. Moderate-intensity aerobic activity increases a person's heart rate and can be accomplished by participating in activities that increase the heart rate in episodes of at least 10 minutes. As such, a person could walk briskly or ride a bike three times a day for 10 minutes each time to achieve the standard. Vigorous-intensity activity, such as running or riding a bicycle at an accelerated speed, causes rapid breathing and a substantial increase in heart rate. It is also recommended that adults select activities that will increase muscle strength and endurance at least twice per week.

Case Study

A Park Hop Case Study

Americans are not moving—physical activity levels continue to fall or remain stagnant, and obesity rates continue to be high. As part of a countywide initiative to improve health and wellness in Greenville County, South Carolina, LiveWell Greenville was founded in 2011. LiveWell Greenville is a network of organizations partnering to ensure access to healthy eating and active living for every Greenville County resident. Coalition partners include parks and recreation agencies, faith-based organizations, schools, and other entities committed to facilitating a healthier population in Greenville County. The coalition focuses on the four values of sustainable impact, collaboration, engagement, and empowerment.

As part of LiveWell Greenville's programming, a Park Hop program was developed. The Park Hop program is an incentivized passport-style program to increase awareness, visitation, and active use of parks among youth in Greenville County. Developed within a family recreation program planning framework that focuses on facilitating enjoyable family experiences, increasing awareness of recreational activities, and reducing common leisure constraints, this free, summer-long scavenger hunt was designed to encourage children and their families to visit 17 selected parks and recreation facilities. While at each park or facility, participants were asked to a find the answer to a clue related to the park or facility. Examples of clues included asking participants to follow interpretive signs to gather information or to complete a fitness trail and ask which station challenged them the most.

There were four goals for the Park Hop program:

1. Increase parks usage and discovery.
2. Foster awareness and appreciation for the wealth of parks in Greenville County.
3. Increase the time spent in physical activity during park visits.
4. Establish an annual tradition for all to enjoy.

Passports were available as a downloadable file, as a hard copy at local facilities, or via the Park Hop mobile app. Participants who turned in partial or complete passports were eligible for prize drawings, with the more parks visited and clues answered, the larger the prizes they were eligible for. Evaluation found that parents and children enjoyed the program and that the program successfully influenced park awareness, discovery, and use of new parks.

Questions to Consider

1. Who can parks and recreation agencies work with to help increase physical activity among local citizens? What might that look like?
2. What are some other examples from your hometown of ways that local nonprofits or other groups are working to provide unique programs to encourage higher levels of physical activity for all ages?

Besenyi, G. M., Fair, M., Hughey, S. M., Kaczynski, A. T., Powers, A., Dunlap, E. (2015). Park Hop: Pilot evaluation of an inter-agency collaboration to promote park awareness, visitation, and physical activity in Greenville County, SC. *Journal of Parks and Recreation Administration*, 33(4), 69–89.

http://www.livewellgreenville.org

HEALTHY PEOPLE 2020

Healthy People is a governmental organization under the auspices of the U.S. Department of Health and Human Services that is dedicated to providing science-based national objectives to improve the health of Americans. This group has published three reports, or 10-year agendas, that give guidelines and strategies for building healthy people and communities—Healthy People 2000, Healthy People 2010, and Healthy People 2020. Healthy People 2020 strives to:

◆ Identify nationwide health improvement priorities.
◆ Increase public awareness and understanding of the determinants of health, disease, and disability, and the opportunities for progress.
◆ Provide measurable objectives and goals that are applicable at the national, state, and local levels.
◆ Engage multiple sectors to take actions to strengthen policies and improve practices that are driven by the best available evidence and knowledge.
◆ Identify critical research, evaluation, and data collection needs.

Reproduced from "About Healthy People," HealthyPeople.gov, U.S. Department of Health and Human Services. http://www.healthypeople.gov/2020/about /default.aspx.

However, in 2014, less than half (49.2%) of Americans aged 18 and older met the guidelines for aerobic activity and 20.8% for both aerobic and muscle-strengthening activities.[12]

The Department of Health and Human Services recommends children aged 6 years and older should get at least 1 hour a day of moderate-intensity physical activity. The American Heart Association lowers this age to 2 years and older.[13] Three days per week a child should do activities that are muscle strengthening, and another 3 days should include activities that are bone strengthening. Muscle-strengthening activities work the major muscle groups such as the legs, arms, and chest. These can include rope climbing, tree climbing, swinging, climbing walls, or cross-country skiing. Bone-strengthening activities put a force on the bones and help them grow and strengthen through impact with the ground. Bone-strengthening activities include such things as hopping, skipping, jumping, running, volleyball, and gymnastics.[14]

However, recent research involving thousands of men and women indicates that even moderate forms of exercise, including such activities as walking, stair climbing, gardening, and housework, have a beneficial long-term effect on one's health. Although high-intensity, pulse-pounding workouts yield the most dramatic benefits, more modest forms of exercise do yield significant benefits. Beyond these findings, other research demonstrates that regular exercise reduces the incidence of other diseases such as diabetes, colon cancer among men and breast and uterine cancer among women, stress, osteoporosis, and other serious illnesses.

Although there is a plethora of reasons why people should be physically active and the implications of not being active are widely known, the obesity rate is still quite high. A line of research on the constraints to physical activities demonstrates some of the reasons why. Constraints are things that keep people from participating in leisure activities or participating as much as they would like, or that compromise the quality of participation. A few findings that researchers uncovered about physical activity suggest the following:

◆ The healthier a person is, the less likely that person will find reasons not to participate in physical activity.[15]
◆ The more people see the benefits of being physically active, the more likely they are to choose these types of activities.[16]
◆ Time, family obligations, and lack of energy are main reasons people give for not participating in physical activity.[17]
◆ Enjoyment of an activity is a major predictor of selecting an activity, including sedentary activities.[18]
◆ Cost, work obligations, time, and other priorities diminish the likelihood of participating in physical activity.[19]
◆ An increased preference for sedentary activities has been found among children who are overweight or obese.[20]

Given all of this, the most effective forms of physical activity are those that are most enjoyable to different people. The challenge comes with those who prefer sedentary over physical activities.

NATIONAL PHYSICAL ACTIVITY RECOMMENDATIONS

The American College of Sports Medicine recommends 30 minutes of moderate physical activity five times per week as well as training each major muscle group 2 or 3 days each week through resistance training. However, it likely takes more than the minimum activity levels to facilitate weight loss or weight maintenance.

If people are motivated to participate in parks and recreation activities based on physical motivators, then there are plenty of opportunities to be found. More and more employers have fitness facilities, offer discounted memberships at local clubs, or give paid time off for employees to participate in fitness activities. Organizations such as the YMCA, YWCA, local parks and recreation agencies, and hospitals all provide activities to get people moving. Even the travel industry is trying to help. Seeing the value of health and fitness, the travel industry is taking action by making health easier for guests. Many hotels offer more healthy options on room service menus, but more importantly, they are catering to the health conscious and expanding beyond the typical fitness facility with a half dozen pieces of equipment. For example, Omni Hotels brings a workout kit to the guest's hotel room. The Get Fit Kit arrives in a canvas bag and includes a floor mat, dumbbells, exercise bands, and a workout booklet. The Hilton McLean Tysons Corner and the Hilton San Francisco Union Square have yoga and cardio rooms where guests can stay. These rooms have a king-sized bed and the equipment needed to work out. Other hotels are offering boot camp classes daily.[21]

SOCIAL MOTIVATORS

The need to be part of a social group and to have friends who provide companionship, support, and intimacy is at the heart of much recreational involvement. It helps to explain why people join sororities, fraternities, or other social clubs, sports leagues, tour groups, or other settings where new acquaintances and potential friends may be met. It is an underlying element in sport in terms of the friendships and bonds that are formed among team members. There are a number of specific social motivators that must be mentioned, including being with others, reducing loneliness, and developing social norms among people.

Being with Others and Reducing Loneliness

Many adults today find their primary social contacts and interpersonal relationships not in their work lives, but in voluntary group associations during leisure hours. Even in the relatively free environment of outdoor recreation, where people hike, camp, or explore the wilderness in ways of their own choosing, interaction among participants is a key element in the experience. Only 2% of all leisure activities are done alone. This indicates that people like to participate in activities with others.

Social contact, friendship, or intimacy with others is key to avoiding loneliness. Loneliness is a widespread phenomenon among all ages. Typically, as many as three-quarters of all college students report being lonely during their first term away from home. As adults age, they begin to experience increased loneliness as significant others and friends begin to pass away and children leave home. Loneliness can have unpleasant and even life-threatening consequences, and often is directly linked to depression, obesity, high blood pressure, and heart problems.[22]

Involvement in recreation activities with others can alleviate feelings of loneliness. People can join the YMCA, YWCA, their local recreation center, or take classes at their local parks and recreation department where they can learn new skills or exercise while

Building social relationships through leisure helps reduce loneliness.
© Rubberball Productions.

also meeting others who enjoy these same activities. Keep in mind, there is a difference between loneliness and solitude. Russell suggests that time spent alone is an important part of our lives and can be a much desired state. People participate in certain activities to reduce loneliness, but they also do things to escape or focus totally on themselves such as the case with solitude.[23]

THE RELATIONSHIP BETWEEN HAPPINESS AND SOCIALIZING

In a survey of 140,000 Americans, it was found that people are happiest when they spend 6–7 hours per day socializing. People who are alone all day are least happy and experience higher levels of stress than those who are more social. Furthermore, there is a weekend effect where people experience more happiness and less stress than during the week.[24]

Social Norms

Clearly, different types of recreation groups and programs impose different sets of social norms, roles, and relationships that participants must learn to accept and that contribute to their own social development. For children, play groups offer a realistic training ground for developing cooperative, competitive, and social skills. Through group participation, children learn to interact with others, to accept group rules and wishes, and, when necessary, to subordinate their own views or desires to those of the group. They learn to give and take, to assume leadership or follow the leadership of others, and to work effectively as part of a team.

As children age, their social groups increase in importance in their lives. Social peer groups for teens are a major sense of support and help them form their social identity. Into adulthood, social groups reflect our social status and position in society, whether it is playing golf at the country club or camping with family and friends. As people reach senior adulthood (65+), social connections increase in importance as the social group starts to decrease, and loneliness and isolation become more prevalent as our social networks diminish. Although social connections change throughout our lives, they always remain a significant part of our leisure lives.[25]

Introverts and extroverts view social interaction differently. It was found that people were happier when they were interacting with others.[26] However, this does not mean that introverts are unhappy or should force themselves to go to parties, hang out with large groups of people, or engage in other social activities. The difference in the two types of personalities is our tolerance for social stimulation. Extroverts need more social interaction, and introverts need less. Each need to get their own desired level to achieve happiness through social interactions.[27]

The social aspect of leisure is a significant motivator for many people. It may be a terrific opportunity to participate in activities with a friend or significant other or to participate in a setting to increase the possibility of meeting people for friendship or more.

PSYCHOLOGICAL MOTIVATORS

Often, recreational activities are seen as a means of providing excitement and challenge, as a means of relaxation and escape, as a way to relieve stress, or as a way to balance work and play. These are psychological motivators that contribute to our mental health.

People often seek adventure and challenge in their leisure activities.
© Dudarev Mikhail/Shutterstock.

Sense of Adventure, Excitement, and Challenge

A great deal of recreational involvement today is based on the need for excitement and challenge, particularly in such outdoor recreation activities as skiing, mountain climbing, or hang gliding, or in active, highly competitive individual or team sports. These activities are a part of adventure recreation, also called risk recreation. Adventure recreation is activity in the natural environment that has challenge, personal risk, uncertainty, and a reasonable chance for success.[28] People choose some of these leisure activities because they have an inherent risk associated with them. Participants thrive on the adrenalin rush, the challenges they are taking, and the thrill they get from completing the activity. As people participate in these types of activities, their perception of risk decreases and perception of skill increases.[29] In other words, people become less afraid while doing such things as backcountry backpacking or rock climbing, while they also feel their skills are increasing. Adventure recreation activities have also shown to enhance psychological well-being for people.

In addition to outdoor recreation, there has been tremendous growth in adventure sports because of the need for adventure, excitement, and challenge. For example, the 2015 X Games in Austin featured 21 sports such as motocross speed and style, rally cross (car racing), skateboarding, and BMX. The 2013 Winter X Games held in Aspen, Colorado featured 18 sports in three categories including skiing, snowboarding, and snowmobiling.[30] For those who are less skilled but who still crave that rush from adventure recreation, tourism companies are capitalizing on this motivational aspect. Some companies specialize in white-water rafting, sea kayaking, off-road vehicle trips, snowmobiling, and mountain trekking.

For many people, the urge for adventure, excitement, and challenge is met through spectatorship—by watching action-oriented movies or television shows—or in the form of video games based on high-speed chase or conflict. For others, ballooning, skydiving, parasailing, amateur stock car racing, or scuba diving satisfy risk-related motivations. Although varied forms of deviant social behavior, such as gang fighting, vandalism, or other types of juvenile crime, are not commonly considered as leisure pursuits, the reality is that they often are prompted by the same need for thrills, excitement, and challenge that other, more respectable recreation pursuits satisfy. This is discussed later in the chapter.

Stress Management

A closely related value of recreation is its usefulness in stress reduction. A leading authority on stress, Dr. Hans Selye, defines stress as the overall response of the body to any extreme demand made upon it, which might include threats, physical illness, job pressures, and environmental extremes—or even such life changes as marriage, divorce, vacations, or taking a new job. Increasing amounts of stress in modern life have resulted in many individuals suffering from pain, heart disease, sleep deprivation, excessive tiredness, and depression.

Once it was thought that the best approach to stress was rest and avoidance of all pressures, but today, there is an awareness that some degree of stress is desirable and healthy. Today, researchers point out that physical activity can play a significant role in stress reduction. Typically, people work off anger, frustration, and indignation by taking long walks or engaging in some kind of physical activity such as exercise. All of the body's systems—the working muscles, heart, hormones, metabolic reactions, and the responsiveness of the central nervous system— are strengthened through stimulation. Following periods of extended exertion, the body systems slow, bringing on a feeling of deep relaxation. Attaining this relaxed state is essential to lessening the stress reaction.

Relaxation and Escape

When you consider the positive side of leisure and why people choose the activities they do, often relaxation and escape are mentioned as key benefits to leisure. Escaping from work, home, or the everyday pressures of life can be done by taking a bike ride, going for a hike, or becoming absorbed in a creative activity through art or drama.

Relaxation allows people to forget the stresses they face. They can temporarily forget about upcoming deadlines, the need to find a job, or pressure to select a good graduate school. Choosing relaxing activities allows individuals to forget about these issues and become absorbed in the activity itself. Relaxation and escape can come from activities or doing nothing at all. Sitting in the backyard, lying on the beach, and taking a nap in the middle of the day are means for relaxation and escape resulting from use of leisure time. Relaxation experts often suggest deep breathing, meditation, exercise, sex, music, and yoga as ways to relax from stress.[31]

Healthy Balance of Work and Play

The role of work and leisure in our lives has changed dramatically from the thinking of the Greeks and Romans to whom leisure was the root of happiness and something enjoyed by those who did not have to work. Today, society sees leisure as something for all, and for most people, emotional well-being is greatly strengthened if they are able to maintain a healthy balance of work and recreation in their lives. Today, we recognize that there can be too much commitment to work, resulting in the exclusion of other interests and personal involvements that help to maintain mental health.

The emphasis on work and leisure is shifting in the United States. Much has been said in the news about the different generations and how the baby boomers (born in 1940–1964) are affecting our lives. The baby boomers are today's upper management. They live to work and view themselves as having a strong work ethic. A strong work ethic is characterized by this group as working long hours and weekends to meet customer demands. This group likes recognition for a job well done and sees working long hours as a way of getting this reward. It was with the baby boomers group that the divorce rates and stress levels skyrocketed and the number of latchkey kids increased.[32]

The tendency to place excessive emphasis on work, at the expense of other avenues of expression, has been popularly termed workaholism. For some people, work is an obsession, and they are unable to find other kinds of pleasurable release. For those who find their work a deep source of personal satisfaction and commitment, this may not be an altogether undesirable phenomenon.

The idea of workaholism will always be prevalent in society, but Generation X (born in 1965–1980) and the Millennial generation (born in 1981–1997) will most likely decrease this phenomenon. Generation Xers prefer

Case Study

Take Back Your Time

Take Back Your Time is a non-profit that seeks to challenge the epidemic of overwork, over-scheduling and time famine in the United States and Canada that threatens individuals' health, relationships, communities, and the environment. The organization's goal is to help others better appreciate the value of leisure time—particularly through vacation time—and the costs of time stress in our lives and workplaces.

While 9 out of 10 people report that their happiest memories are from vacation, 52% do not take all of their paid vacation time in a year. While 71% of vacationers are satisfied at work and 46% are not, 27% report taking less vacation time than 5 years ago, 54% do not take vacation time—saving it in case of an emergency that would require time off—and 34% never take vacation with family. In fact, 23% of people who get vacation time reported taking no vacation time in the past 12 months. Unfortunately, 25% of Americans get no paid vacation time at all.

Through events such as the annual "Take back your time day" and the "Vacation Commitment Summit," Take Back Your Time works to share the benefits of vacation time, as well as other types of paid leave (e.g., paid parental leave, limits on compulsory overtime work) that allow for more balance in people's lives. According to a broad array of researchers, among other benefits, vacations can:

◆ Relieve stress.
◆ Help prevent heart diseases.
◆ Help maintain focus.
◆ Help prevent illness.
◆ Make you happier.
◆ Strengthen relationships.
◆ Make you more productive at work.

http://www.takebackyourtime.org

Questions to Consider

1. Should all employers be mandated to provide at least 1 week of paid leave to their full-time employees? What are reasons why they might not want to?
2. Should employers actually make employees take all of their paid vacation time? Why or why not?

a balance of work and play. They are today's middle and upper managers who were the latchkey kids coming home to find their parents still at work. They feel work productivity is important but not at the cost of what is most important to them—their leisure, family, and friends. The Millennial generation works to live. They have a job so that they can make money to do the things they really want to do. They have been involved in a number of leisure activities their whole lives, from soccer to piano lessons, and they enjoy these things. This group sees the value of leisure and plans to take advantage of it rather than work excessive hours.[33]

Leading authorities on business management and personnel practices now stress the need for business executives to find outside pleasures that open up, diversify, and enrich their lives. The guilt that successful people too often have about play must be assuaged, and they must be helped to realize that, with a more balanced style of life, they are likely to be more productive in the long run—and much happier in the present. Generation X and the Millennial generation already know this and are probably better than their older supervisors and coworkers at taking advantage of the services offered by recreation professionals.[34]

EMOTIONAL MOTIVATORS

Emotional health is typified by positive self-esteem, a positive self-concept, ability to deal with stress, and a person's ability to control emotions and behaviors. Emotionally healthy people handle the daily stresses of life, build healthy relationships, and lead productive lives. Leisure is a major contributor to emotional well-being.

Leisure activity can provide strong feelings of pleasure and satisfaction, and can serve as an outlet for discharging certain emotional drives that, if repressed, might produce emotional distress or even mental illness. The role of pleasure is increasingly recognized as a vital factor in emotional well-being. Some researchers have

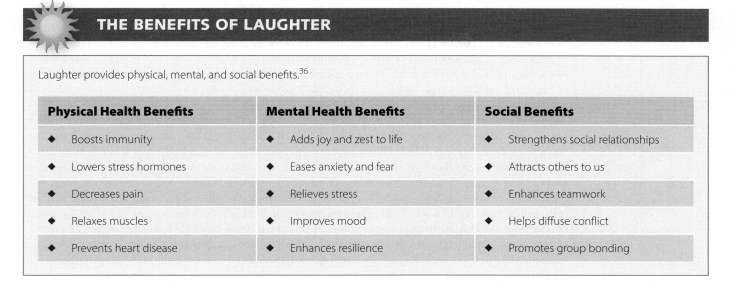

THE BENEFITS OF LAUGHTER

Laughter provides physical, mental, and social benefits.[36]

Physical Health Benefits	Mental Health Benefits	Social Benefits
◆ Boosts immunity	◆ Adds joy and zest to life	◆ Strengthens social relationships
◆ Lowers stress hormones	◆ Eases anxiety and fear	◆ Attracts others to us
◆ Decreases pain	◆ Relieves stress	◆ Enhances teamwork
◆ Relaxes muscles	◆ Improves mood	◆ Helps diffuse conflict
◆ Prevents heart disease	◆ Enhances resilience	◆ Promotes group bonding

begun to analyze the simple concept of fun, defined as intense pleasure and enjoyment and an important dimension of social interactional leisure.

In leisure, people predominantly seek fun in their free time. Why do a leisure activity if it is not fun? Fun is the reason we play, enjoy the outdoors, and socialize with others. Associated with fun is laughter. There are a number of benefits of laughter, including binding people together, enhancing intimacy, providing stress relief, and because it simply feels good. Fun and laughter can enhance emotional well-being and can be experienced through such activities as going to a comedy show, trying a brand-new activity with friends, or having a game night with family.[35]

In addition to fun and laughter, self-actualization has been linked to emotional well-being. Self-actualization is a term that became popular in the 1970s chiefly through the writings of Abraham Maslow, who stressed the need for individuals to achieve their fullest degree of creative potential. Maslow developed a convincing theory of human motivation in which he identified a number of important human needs, arranging them in a hierarchy. As each of the basic needs is met in turn, a person is able to move ahead to meet more advanced needs and drives. Maslow's theory includes the following ascending levels of need:

◆ *Physiological needs:* Needed for human survival, physiological needs include food, rest, shelter, sleep, and other basic survival needs.
◆ *Safety needs:* Safety needs encompass self-protection needs such as health and well-being and physical safety from danger and threats.
◆ *Social needs:* Sometimes labeled as love/belonging, these needs include association with others, friendship, intimacy, and connection with family.
◆ *Esteem needs:* People have a need for self-esteem, confidence, recognition, achievement, attention, and the respect of and for others.
◆ *Self-actualization:* The highest level of the hierarchy is the need for being creative and for realizing one's maximum potential in a variety of life spheres, and the need for spontaneity.

The lower-level needs—physiological, safety, social, and esteem needs—are considered deficiency needs and come from a lack of something in our lives. Unless something in these three areas is missing, these needs are considered met and are rarely acknowledged. When they do not exist, people experience unpleasant feelings. The higher-level need, self-actualization, is a growth need and results in a drive to grow and develop as individuals, to master something and to reach our full potential.

A group of backpackers seek to achieve social, ego, and self-actualization needs through a backpacking trip on the Appalachian Trail.
Courtesy of the Appalachian Trial Conservancy.

Obviously, play and recreation can be important elements in satisfying at least the last three levels of need in Maslow's hierarchy. Much discussion has already been attributed to social needs. Esteem needs can be met from participating in team sports, enhancing fitness levels, or building skills in an activity such as skiing, soccer, or diving. Self-actualization can be realized in both work and leisure. In leisure, creativity can come from art, theater, or drama. Continued participation can continually build self-esteem to the point of self-actualization, or continued participation and drive can help people become self-actualized by reaching a self-imposed goal of completing a marathon or climbing Mount McKinley.

A discussion of the emotional and psychological implications of leisure must also include the work of Mihaly Csikszentmihalyi, who developed flow theory. Csikszentmihalyi posited that people are most happy and content when they reach a state of flow. Flow is a state of mind that occurs when the challenge and skill in an activity are in synch with each other.[37] In other words, the person has the skill to meet the challenges presented in participating in the activity. When these two are out of balance, a range of emotions occurs. For example, when there is a low skill and low challenge required, a person will experience apathy and boredom, whereas low skill and high challenge can result in worry and anxiety because the individual is anxious about his or her ability to meet the challenge ahead. Activities that trigger flow in a person vary. It may be a night kayak, creating an oil painting, or playing the guitar that leads a person to experience flow. Notice that flow encompasses several motivational issues already discussed, including intrinsic motivation. However, one of the major benefits is escape because of the total absorption in the activity itself.

Happiness and Well-Being

In general, people want to be happy. Happiness is "frequent positive affect, high life satisfaction, and infrequent negative affect."[38] Lyubomirsky and colleagues analyzed many studies on the subject and learned that happiness generates many positive rewards including obtaining a positive state of mind, higher marriage success rates, having more friends and social connections, superior work outcomes, increased mental health, more activity and energy, and experiencing flow more often. They also found that happiness is determined from three sources. First, 50% of happiness is established by our genetics and is set with little chance of changing it. Another 10% is established by the circumstances we find ourselves in. This could be the part of the world we live in, our personal demographics, life events that we experience, and circumstantial factors such as marital status, job, and income levels. The last piece of happiness, which makes up 40%, is determined by intentional activity. Based on this model, 40% of happiness is determined by the actions we purposefully do. Recreation can play a major role in these intentional activities. The activities in which we participate in general are likely to contribute to happiness.

In addition to happiness, well-being is a major motivator in leisure. Well-being is "a state of successful, satisfying, and productive engagement with one's life and the realization of one's full physical, cognitive, and social-emotional potential."[39] In essence, happiness is central to well-being. When people experience well-being, they also experience happiness and are satisfied with most aspects of their lives.[40] Carruthers suggests that leisure plays several roles in well-being and happiness including the following:

◆ Positive emotion can result from leisure.
◆ Leisure serves as a mechanism for individuals to cultivate their personal strengths, and personal strengths enhance happiness.
◆ Leisure can help individuals attain their full potential by building their competence, sense of purpose, and ability to take risks.[41]

This insight into happiness and well-being demonstrates that leisure plays a major role in people's ability to be happy and feel good emotionally. Because intentional activities influence 40% of individuals' happiness and happiness enhances well-being, choosing leisure activities that fit well for individuals is an important motivator.

Intellectual Outcomes

Of all the personal benefits of play and recreation, probably the least widely recognized are those involving intellectual or cognitive development. Play is typically considered physical activity rather than mental, and has by definition been considered a nonserious form of involvement. How then could it contribute to intellectual growth? Researchers have come to realize that physical recreation tends to improve personal motivation and make mental and cognitive performance more effective. Numerous studies, for example, have documented the effects of specific types of physical exercise or play on the development of young children. Other research studies show a strong relationship between physical fitness and academic performance. Although a number of these studies focus on formal instructional programs, others use less structured experimental elements. Several studies show that playfulness as a personal quality is closely linked to creative and inventive thinking among children.

Children learn so much through play such as colors and shapes, how to build using blocks, and how to connect with other children and build social relationships. As they grow, they learn such things as how to follow rules, make up their own rules, build consensus, and solve problems.[42]

In the early age of games in North America, the sole purpose of playing was for intellectual stimulation. Although the focus has moved away from learning to that of a means of having fun, many games still have an intellectual aspect. For example, Monopoly was first developed so that people could begin to understand economic principles, and Snakes and Ladders (later renamed Chutes and Ladders) taught about morality and ethical behavior. Today, games also have been used to help children learn simple scientific, mathematical, and linguistic concepts. Games like Payday and Head Full of Numbers focus on math. Children and adults learn about geography from games such as Sequence—States & Capitals; logic and strategy from Clue, Sudoku, and Battleship; vocabulary from Scrabble and Boggle; and general knowledge from games such as Cranium or the vast array of Trivial Pursuit games on the market.

On another level, a reporter for Forbes magazine points out that business executives frequently enjoy high-level competitive play in games such as contract bridge, chess, or backgammon, and that they value competence in these pastimes in the people they employ. Investment advisors in particular recognize the risk-taking elements involved in such games and the need for strategic flair in taking calculated risks. Whether the game is poker, gin rummy, bridge, backgammon, or chess, the skills involved are all equally important in business.[43]

Spiritual Values and Outcomes

A final area in which recreation and leisure make a vital contribution to the healthy growth and well-being of human beings is within the spiritual realm. The term spiritual is commonly taken to be synonymous with religion, but here it means a capacity for exhibiting humanity's higher nature—a sense of moral values, compassion, and respect for other humans and for the earth itself. It is linked to the development of one's inner feelings, a sense of order and purpose in life, and a commitment to care for others and to behave responsibly in all aspects of one's existence.

How does recreation contribute in this respect? Josef Pieper, in his 1963 book Leisure: *The Basis of Culture*, and others suggest that in their leisure hours, humans are able to express their fullest and best selves. Leisure can be a time for contemplation, for consideration of ultimate values, for disinterested activity. This means that people can come together simply as people, sharing interests and exploring pleasure, commitment, personal growth, beauty, nature, and other such aspects of life.

Outdoor recreation is often linked to the spiritual side of leisure. The peace and serenity of the outdoors allows people to escape and experience a sense of freedom. Jensen and Guthrie suggest that nature-based recreation is a spiritual source, and "spiritual sources can help people navigate through life . . . spirituality often represents a person's higher nature—moral values and a respect for humanity, the environment, and the earth itself."[44]

So far, this chapter has examined the important personal values of recreation and leisure involvement from three different perspectives: physical, social, and psychological. It is essential to recognize that these are not distinctly separate components of motivation, but are instead closely interrelated from a holistic perspective. Furthermore, it must be understood that leisure means different things to different people. The motivators behind one person bicycling may be completely different from what another gets out of it. The same is true for the outcomes from participation. The first individual may feel great after biking because of the exercise element, whereas the second person may not think about the exercise portion but the feeling of joy he or she gets from contributing to a healthy environment by biking to work rather than driving. Leisure motivators are as unique as the participants themselves.

SERIOUS LEISURE

Much of the discussion so far on leisure motivation focuses on the average person who enjoys leisure time for a multitude of reasons, from physical and social to intellectual and spiritual. A different perspective on leisure is serious leisure. Serious leisure is "the systematic pursuit of an amateur, hobbyist, or volunteer activity sufficiently substantial and interesting for the participant to find a career there in the acquisition and expression of a combination of its special skills, knowledge, and experience."[45] People who undertake a leisure activity to the point it extensively extends into their everyday lives could consider that activity to be serious leisure. On the other hand, most people participate in what is labeled as casual leisure. Casual leisure is an "immediately, intrinsically rewarding, relatively short-lived pleasurable activity requiring little or no special training to enjoy it."[46] The difference for most between casual and serious leisure is time, money, and effort dedicated to the activity. For example, a musician who plays with friends a couple of times a month in someone's garage would be a casual participant. If that same person practiced every night, arranged for gigs every weekend, and invested many hours in music each week, that could be considered serious leisure.

Serious leisure has six defining qualities:

◆ *Perseverance:* Serious leisure is defined by the need to persistently persevere through adverse conditions over time. This may mean a runner must work through pain, fatigue, or poor weather conditions. A performer must deal with stage fright or embarrassment. People are willing to overcome what some would see as negative situations because of the positive feelings they ultimately get from the activity.
◆ *Leisure career:* Although the individual is most likely not paid for participation, serious leisure emulates a career in that it has stages of achievement. Individuals exhibit a career-like commitment to the leisure activity, where they work to improve and achieve set goals.
◆ *Significant effort:* Serious leisure is characterized by people developing special knowledge, skills, or abilities. This requires considerable effort that is beyond the ordinary skill development of casual leisure.
◆ *Durable outcomes:* Serious leisure pursuits are steeped in outcomes including enrichment, self-actualization, self-expression, enhanced self-image, self-gratification, recreation, and sometimes financial returns. Although these attributes can be found in casual leisure, it is the depth that distinguishes serious leisure. These activities may not be fun at times, but the skills people are developing are used and these durable outcomes emerge and make the activity more positive for the individual.
◆ *Unique ethos:* A unique ethos is a subculture among those who participate in serious leisure. These people share similar ideals, values, norms, and beliefs that pertain to the activity. Social relationships and networks emerge that focus on the leisure pursuit.
◆ *Identification with the pursuit:* The individual strongly identifies with the leisure activity. These people talk excitedly about their activity, are proud of the activity, and are quite committed to it.[47]

Given these six distinguishable characteristics, you can see that the commitment and motivation for serious leisure are far more intense than for casual leisure.

TABOO RECREATION

So far, this chapter has examined leisure motivation from the physical, social, psychological, and emotional perspectives. All of these motives have been positive, yet there is a negative side of leisure that requires some discussion. Russell suggests that leisure is not always done for the person's well-being, and these types of activities are considered taboo recreation.[48] Taboo recreation is leisure behavior that is restricted by law or society's norms. Because societal norms are subjective and change from group to group, it is difficult to decide what falls under taboo recreation and what are simply fringe activities. For example, some sects of the Catholic Church and some Scottish politicians have claimed that the Hokey Pokey was written to mock the actions and language of priests leading the Latin mass.[49] Other religious groups denounce dancing as evil. Because of the disagreement on a clear delineation of what constitutes taboo recreation, three common pursuits are discussed as examples.

Sexual Activity

Sexual activity by some can be classified as taboo recreation. Engaging in recreational sexual activity with a casual acquaintance, one night stands, having "friends with benefits," or engaging in sexual activity outside of a marriage may be deemed inappropriate by some in society. Taboo sex can also encompass such things as viewing pornography, visiting sex clubs, same-sex sexual activity, or engaging in swinging or partner swapping. While these recreational activities are not illegal, some sectors of society may view them as negative recreational activities. These judgments are often driven more by religious-based moral ideologies than legal ones. Like other taboo activities that will be discussed, sex is one that is classified as positive or negative based on the beliefs of the individual.

Motivation for these sexual activities is as varied as those engaging in them. Taboo sexual activity can be motivated by a sense of power, to learn more about oneself, to escape one's inhibitions, or to provide a sense of freedom.[50]

Gambling

Gambling is wagering money or something of value on a preselected outcome. Examples of gambling include betting on horse races, buying lottery tickets, and entering a National Collegiate Athletic Association (NCAA) Final Four Tournament pool. Gambling has a storied past and actually began during colonial times when lotteries were implemented to generate revenues. Lotteries were also used to fund some of the most prestigious universities in the United States, including Harvard, Yale, and Princeton.[51] It did not take long for gambling to become illegal and an underground activity. Gambling made a resurgence during the Great Depression because it was seen as a way to stimulate the economy.[51] Also at this time, Nevada legalized most forms of gambling. In these early years, gambling was infiltrated with organized crime. In the 1950s, the federal government cleaned up gambling and organized crime got out of the business. The variety of opportunities to gamble has increased across the United States. What started out as a few casinos has expanded to include parimutuel betting, Internet gambling, and riverboat casinos.

Because the focus of this chapter is not on gambling, per se, but motivation, the question arises as to why people gamble. Research shows a wide variety of reasons including fun, risk, excitement, challenge, adrenalin rush, and relaxation—all motivators that were previously discussed. If it stops at this, there would be no reason to discuss gambling separately from any other activity. However, gambling is taboo when it becomes a problem. Gamblers Anonymous defines someone with a gambling addiction as a compulsive gambler (**Table 2.2**).

GAMBLING STATISTICS

- The largest percentage of visitors to Las Vegas were in the age group of 65 and older (22%).
- 48 states have some form of legal gambling. Only Hawaii and Utah do not.
- Gambling generates more revenue than movies, spectator sports, theme parks, cruise ships, and recorded music combined.
- Gambling has become a $40 billion dollar a year industry in the United States.[52]
- 80 million Americans visit casinos annually.

TABLE 2.2 Problem Gambling Quiz

Gamblers Anonymous developed a 20-question quiz to ascertain if gambling is a problem for an individual.

1. Did you ever lose time from work or school due to gambling?
2. Has gambling ever made your home life unhappy?
3. Did gambling affect your reputation?
4. Have you ever felt remorse after gambling?
5. Did you ever gamble to get money with which to pay debts or otherwise solve financial difficulties?
6. Did gambling cause a decrease in your ambition or efficiency?
7. After losing did you feel you must return as soon as possible and win back your losses?
8. After a win did you have a strong urge to return and win more?
9. Did you often gamble until your last dollar was gone?
10. Did you ever borrow to finance your gambling?
11. Have you ever sold anything to finance gambling?
12. Were you reluctant to use "gambling money" for normal expenditures?
13. Did gambling make you careless of the welfare of yourself or your family?
14. Did you ever gamble longer than you had planned?
15. Have you ever gambled to escape worry, trouble, boredom, or loneliness?
16. Have you ever committed, or considered committing, an illegal act to finance gambling?
17. Did gambling cause you to have difficulty in sleeping?
18. Do arguments, disappointments, or frustrations create within you an urge to gamble?
19. Did you ever have an urge to celebrate any good fortune by a few hours of gambling?
20. Have you ever considered self-destruction or suicide as a result of your gambling?

Most compulsive gamblers will answer "yes" to at least seven of these questions.

Courtesy of Gamblers Anonymous. Available at: http://www.gamblersanonymous.org/ga/content/20-questions. Accessed March 8, 2013.

Case Study

Nude Recreation . . . Is It Taboo?

The American Association for Nude Recreation (AANR) has over 38,000 members who enjoy "living and experiencing nature in the most natural way possible." Nudists feel that they are comfortable in their own skin and see the human body as a vessel that carries it through life.

AANR focuses on protecting places for nude recreation to happen, including sanctioned nude beaches, public lands set aside for nude recreation, resorts, and campgrounds, among others. Nude recreation is legal in these designated areas.

The AANR stresses that nude recreation is about the family and is not considered an "adults only" activity. They promote body acceptance regardless of age or other factors and strongly oppose sexual exploitation of any kind.

Traditionally thought of as an activity for older generations, nude recreation organizations have recently emerged that target 18- to 35-year olds. The Florida Young Naturists and Young Naturists America have emerged to bring together a younger generation of adults interested in nude recreation. Both groups plan gatherings, trips, and other adventures to enjoy a clothes-free experience.

Questions to Consider

1. Is nude recreation considered taboo recreation? Why or why not?
2. Should children be allowed to participate in nude recreation with their parents and other adults?
3. A local nude recreation organization wants to rent out the indoor pool at the recreation center after hours. What are the pros and cons of allowing this?
4. Should public land be designated specifically as clothing optional? Why or why not?
5. A hotel several blocks from a popular Florida beach is declaring bankruptcy. The AANR wants to buy it and convert it to a clothing-optional resort. What are the pros and cons of doing this?
6. The Florida Young Naturists and Young Naturists America are coming to your campus to promote their upcoming spring break trip. How would this be received on campus by the students? Would students be more accepting because it is a group targeting 18- to 35-year-olds rather than the general population?

Sources

a. American Association for Nude Recreation: www.aanr.com/.
b. Florida Young Naturists: www.floridayoungnaturists.com/.
c. Young Naturists America: nudistnaturistamerica.org/.
d. R. Neale "Surviving the Economy, Clothing Optional," *USA Today*, (July 13, 2012): B1.

Compulsive gambling is an illness that progressively worsens, can never be cured, but that can be stopped.[53] The motivation to gamble at this point in a person's life is where it becomes taboo recreation.

Substance Abuse

Substance abuse is a pattern of using substances that alter mood and behavior beyond what they were originally intended. These substances include such things as legal and illegal drugs, inhalants, solvents, and alcohol.

For those using illegal drugs, binge drinking, or consuming alcohol underage, the taboo recreation label fits this behavior. Social drinking, on the other hand, is not considered taboo recreation until it becomes a problem. Just like sex and gambling, alcohol and drug use have signs that indicate when this activity becomes problematic. Also like sexual activity and gambling, there are motives for engaging in this activity. It could be for escape, relaxation, to fit in with a group, to socialize, to take risks, or to be more outgoing.

Social drinking is a major subculture in North America and not considered taboo recreation by most. A few examples are as follows:

- ◆ Young adults go to clubs and drink socially around their friends and to meet people.
- ◆ Wine tasting and beer making are leisure activities and social events.
- ◆ Tourism capitalizes on trips to wineries.
- ◆ Beermakers and restaurants are partnering to present beer and dinner events.
- ◆ Wine glass making is an art form.

There are far more examples of potentially taboo recreation pursuits that could be discussed here. For example, viewing pornography, adult entertainment and erotica, vandalism, dog fighting, or excessive Internet use can be deemed taboo by some portions of our society. To many people some sexual activities, gambling, the use of legal drugs and limited use of alcohol are no different than any other leisure activity. For those who see these activities as morally wrong or abuse any of them, the taboo recreation label emerges. Regardless of whether an individual sees these activities as acceptable and at what level they are acceptable, the motivation to participate varies for each person but focuses strongly on the social and psychological motivations for leisure.

Summary

Beyond the familiar motivations of seeking fun, pleasure, or relaxation, people engage in leisure pursuits for a host of different reasons. Recreational motivations include personal goals such as the need for companionship, escape from stress or the boredom of daily routines, and the search for challenge.

The outcomes of recreational involvement may be classified under four major headings: physical, social, psychological, and emotional.

Physical motivators have never been as important as they are in today's society. The obesity rates of both children and adults continue to grow. Recreational activities help people control weight, fight against obesity, and improve cardiovascular health. The social motivation for leisure results in reduced loneliness, strengthens relationships, and promotes social bonding. The psychological motivations for leisure are quite extensive. People seek adventure, relaxation, escape, stress reduction, and overall well-being and happiness. The emotional motivators involve fun, happiness, intellectual outcomes, and spiritual values. Leisure can bring all of these rewards to a person.

Serious leisure requires a person to be highly motivated to participate in their chosen activity. Those engaged in serious leisure have their leisure activities consume a major part of their lives and are quite committed to participation.

Although all of these motives are viewed as having positive outcomes, there is a part of leisure that not everyone sees as positive. Taboo recreation, or leisure that is seen as negative based on societal standards, can include such activities as some sexual activities, gambling, illegal drug use, and excessive use of alcohol. Society's views vary and some see any involvement in these activities as taboo while others base judgment on the frequency and extent to which participation occurs.

This chapter focused on why people choose the activities that they do and what outcomes they receive from participation. These motives are subjective and vary from person to person. No one activity provides the same outcomes for everyone. Because of this, people must assess their own needs and choose activities that meet these needs.

Questions for Class Discussion or Essay Examination

1. Define obesity. Give an overview of childhood and adult obesity. What is the role of parks and recreation in the fight against obesity? What things in society contribute to the obesity epidemic?

    _____

    _____

    _____

    _____

2. The chapter describes some of the specific contributions of recreation to emotional or mental health. What are they? On the basis of your own experience, can you describe some of the positive emotional outcomes resulting from recreational involvement?

    _____

    _____

    _____

    _____

3. Recreation centers are increasingly adding fitness equipment designed for children. This equipment includes such tools as smaller treadmills and stationary bicycles. Do you think this is a good use of money and will stimulate physical activity in children? Why or why not? What other activities could recreation centers implement to help fight childhood obesity? What role do parents play in this problem?

_____

_____

_____

4. Define taboo recreation. What motives do people have for participating in these types of activities? Give examples of other taboo activities that were not discussed in this text.

_____

_____

_____

5. A number of psychological motivators were discussed. What are they? How do they relate to your choices for leisure activities?

_____

_____

_____

6. Think of an activity that you could see yourself engaging in to the point of it being serious leisure. Describe your participation level and what would make that activity serious leisure.

_____

_____

_____

7. Select your five favorite recreational activities and then answer the following question: Why do you participate in these activities (motives)? Predict how this list will change in the next 10, 20, 30, and 50 years.

_____

_____

_____

Endnotes

1. D. Stone, E. L. Deci, and R. M. Ryan, "Beyond Talk: Creating Autonomous Motivation Through Self-Determination Theory," _Journal of General Management_ (Vol. 34, 2009): 75–91.

2. R. M. Ryan and E. L. Deci, "Self-Determination Theory and the Facilitation of Intrinsic Motivation, Social Development, and Well-Being," _American Psychologist_ (Vol. 55, No. 1, 2000): 68–78.

3. Ibid., 70.

4. American Heart Association, "Overweight in Children." www.heart.org/HEARTORG/GettingHealthy /Overweight-in-Children_UCM_304054_Article.jsp. Accessed March 8, 2013.

5. Centers for Disease Control and Prevention, "Prevalence of Obesity in the United States 2011–2014" (December 2016): www.cdc.gov/obesity/data/childhood.html.

6. Centers for Disease Control and Prevention, "Adult Obesity Facts" (September 2016): www.cdc.gov /obesity/data/adult.html.

7. Centers for Disease Control and Prevention, "Prevalence of Self-Reported Obesity Among U.S. Adults by State and Territory" (BRFSS 2013): www.cdc.gov/obesity/data/table-adults.html.

8.   Centers for Disease Control and Prevention, "Early Release of Selected Estimates Based Data from the 2014 Data National Health Interview Study. National Center for Health Statistics.": https://www.cdc .gov/nchs/data/nhis/earlyrelease/earlyrelease201605.pdf - Retrieved May 30, 2017.

9.   Nutrition, physical activity, and obesity: Data, trends and maps. https://www.cdc.gov/nccdphp/dnpao /data-trends-maps/index.html.

10. Center for Disease Control and Prevention, "Facts about physical activity" (May 2014): cdc.gov /physicalactivity/data/facts.htm.

11. Johns Hopkins Medicine, "Cardiovascular Disease Statistics." www.hopkinsmedicine.org /healthlibrary/conditions/cardiovascular_diseases/cardiovascular_disease_statistics_85,P00243/.

12. Centers for Disease Control and Prevention, "Early Release of Selected Estimates Based Data from the 2014 Data National Health Interview Study. National Center for Health Statistics." https://www.cdc .gov/nchs/data/nhis/earlyrelease/earlyrelease201506.pdf.

13. The AHA's Recommendations for Physical Activity in Children (2013): www.heart.org/HEARTORG /GettingHealthy/PhysicalActivity/Physical-Activity-and-Children_UCM_304053_Article.jsp.

14. Centers for Disease Control and Prevention, 2008 Physical Activity Guidelines for Americans: Fact Sheet for Health Professionals on Physical Activity Guidelines for Children and Adolescents. Department of Health and Human Services, Center for Disease Control and Prevention, www.cdc.gov /nccdphp/dnpa/physical/pdf/PA_Fact_Sheet_Children.pdf.

15. J. S. Son, D. L. Kerstetter, and A. J. Mowen, "Illuminating Identity and Health in the Constraint Negotiation of Leisure-Time Physical Activity in Mid to Late Life," *Journal of Parks and Recreation Administration* (Vol. 27, No. 3, 2009): 96–115.

16. Ibid.

17. S. A. Wilhelm Stanis, I. E. Schneider, D. J. Chavez, and K. J. Shinew, "Visitor Constraints to Physical Activity in Parks and Recreation Areas: Differences by Race and Ethnicity," Journal of Parks and Recreation Administration (Vol. 27, No. 3, 2009): 78–95.

18. J. Salmon, N. Owen, D. Crawford, A. Bauman, and J. F. Sallis, "Physical Activity and Sedentary Behavior: A Population-Based Study of Barriers, Enjoyment, and Preference," *Health Psychology* (Vol. 22, No. 2, 2003): 178–188.

19. Ibid.

20. J. Wardle, C. Guthrie, S. Sanderson, L. Birch, and R. Plomin, "Food and Activity Preferences in Children of Lean and Obese Parents," *International Journal of Obesity and Related Metabolic Disorders* (Vol. 25, 2001): 971–977.

21. N. Trejos, "Hotels make it easier to stay fit on the road," USA Today (October 10, 2012): https://www .usatoday.com/story/travel/hotels/2012/10/10/hotel-gyms-workouts/1622289/

22. E. Scott, "Top 10 Stress Relievers: The Best Ways to Feel Better." http://stress.about.com/od/ generaltechniques/tp/toptensionacts.htm.

23. R. Russell, *Pastimes: The Context of Contemporary Leisure*, 4th ed. (Champaign, IL: Sagamore Publishing, 2009).

24. J. Harter and R. Arora, "Social Time Crucial to Daily Emotional Well-Being in U.S." www.gallup.com /poll/107692/social-time-crucial-daily-emotional-wellbeing.aspx.

25. D. J. Jordan, *Leadership in Leisure Services: Making a Difference*, 3rd ed. (State College, PA: Venture Publishing, 2007).

26. W. Fleeson, A. B. Malanos, N. M. Achille, "An Intra-Individual Process Approach to the Relationship Between Extraversion and Positive Affect: Is Acting Extraverted as 'Good' as Being Extraverted?" *Journal of Personality and Social Psychology* (Vol. 83, No. 6, December 2002): 1409–1422.

27. S. Cain, "When Does Socializing Make You Happier," The Power of Introverts to Quiet Revolution: http://www.quietrev.com/when-does-socializing-make-you-happier/

28. C. R. Jensen and S. P. Guthrie, *Outdoor Recreation in America* (Champaign, IL: Human Kinetics, 2006).

29. S. Priest and G. Carpenter, "Changes in Perceived Risk and Competence During Adventurous Leisure Experiences," *Journal of Applied Recreation Research* (Vol. 18, No. 1, 1993): 51–71.

30. ESPN X Games (May 24, 2017): http://xgames.espn.com/xgames/events/2015/austin/results/

31. WebMD, "Stress Management: Ways to Relieve Stress." (May 24, 2017). www.webmd.com/balance /stress-management/stress-management-relieving-stress.

32. C. Raines, *Connecting Generations* (Menlo, CA: Crisp Publications, 2003).

33. Ibid.

34. Ibid.

35. Helpguide.org, "Laughter Is the Best Medicine: The Health Benefits of Humor and Laughter." (May 24, 2017). https://www.helpguide.org/articles/mental-health/laughter-is-the-best-medicine.htm

36. Ibid.

37. M. Csikszentmihalyi, *Finding Flow: The Psychology of Engagement With Everyday Life* (New York: Basic Books, 1997).

38. S. Lyubomirsky, K. M. Sheldon, and D. Schkade, "Pursuing Happiness: The Architecture of Sustainable Change," *Review of General Psychology* (Vol. 9, 2005): 111–131.

39. C. Carruthers and C. D. Hood, "Building a Life of Meaning Through Therapeutic Recreation: The Leisure and Well-Being Model, Part I," *Therapeutic Recreation Journal* (Vol. 41, No. 4, 2007): 276–298.

40. C. Carruthers and C. Hood, Beyond Coping: Adversity as a Catalyst for Personal Transformation. Educational session presented at the American Therapeutic Recreation Association Annual Conference, Kansas City, MO, 2004.

41. C. Carruthers, The Power of the Positive: Leisure and the Good Life. Educational session presented at the Nevada Recreation and Park Society Annual Conference, 2009.

42. D. Elkind, "Cognitive and Emotional Development Through Play," *Greater Good Magazine* (June 9, 2008): www.sharpbrains.com/blog/2008/06/09/cognitive-and-emotional-development-through-play/.

43. A. Hurd, "Board Games," in G. Cross, ed., *Encyclopedia of Recreation and Leisure in America* (New York: Charles Scribner's Sons, 2004).

44. C. R. Jensen and S. P. Gutherie, *Outdoor Recreation in America*, 6th ed. (Champaign, IL: Human Kinetics, 2006): 41.

45. R. A. Stebbins, *Amateurs, Professionals, and Serious Leisure* (Montreal: McGill-Queen's University Press, 1992).

46. R. A. Stebbins, "Casual Leisure: A Conceptual Statement," *Leisure Studies* (Vol. 16, 1997): 17–25.

47. J. Gould, D. Moore, F. McGuire, and R. Stebbins, "Development of the Serious Leisure Inventory and Measure," *Journal of Leisure Research* (Vol. 40, No. 1, 2008): 47–69.

48. R. V. Russell, *Pastimes: The Context of Contemporary Leisure*, 5th ed. (Champaign, IL: Sagamore Publishing, 2013): 165.

49. A. Cramb, "Doing the Hokey Cokey 'Could Be Hate Crime'." www.telegraph.co.uk/news/newstopics /howaboutthat/3883838/Doing-the-Hokey-Cokey-could-be-hate-crime.html.

50. M. Shores, "6 Reasons to Have Casual Sex" (August 20, 2010). AlterNet. Accessed March 8, 2013: www.alternet.org/story/147884/6_reasons_to_have_casual_sex.

51. History of Gambling in the United States, http://www.worldcasinodirectory.com/united-states/history

52. WGBH Educational Foundation (n. d.), "Gambling Facts & Stats." www.pbs.org/wgbh/pages /frontline/shows/gamble/etc/facts.html.

53. Gamblers Anonymous, "Questions & Answers about Gamblers Anonymous." (May 24, 2017): www .gamblersanonymous.org/ga/content/questions-answers-about-gamblers-anonymous.

Sociocultural Factors Affecting Leisure

Jen Welter reflects on what it means to be the first female coach (Arizona Cardinals) in the history of the NFL.

Why do I put myself out there like this? Well, football has often been referred to as the final frontier for women in sports, so for an NFL team to have brought a woman into the coaching ranks, that speaks volumes. It's an important step for girls and women to see. Being a woman is part of who I am. It's not all of who I am, and I'm not here just because I'm a woman. I'm here as a football coach.

If my opportunity in the NFL is a chance to show other women what's possible in this world, and to show guys that there is another dimension to a lot of women—that this game that they love can be loved and respected by a woman—why wouldn't I highlight that? At the same time, my most important obligation right now is helping Coach Arians and this team.[1]

Learning Objectives

1. Examine the influence of the following on leisure: age, gender, sexual orientation, racial and ethnic identity, and socioeconomic status.

2. Explain gender differences in leisure.

3. Identify how agencies can better serve the LGBT community.

4. Explain race and ethnicity factors influencing leisure.

5. Describe differences in leisure participation among social classes.

INTRODUCTION

Many sociocultural factors affect personal leisure values and involvement today including: age, gender, sexual orientation, racial and ethnic identity, and socioeconomic status.

It is easy to see the major changes that children experience as they grow. The same thing holds true for adults. Albeit, we change at a much slower pace, but differences exist based on age. Our leisure preferences evolve. We try new activities. Some of them remain activities for a lifetime and others stay with us until we reach a certain point in our lives. Interests may influence these changes as well as physical abilities, family status, education, or work, among others. Progress in this field has been striking with respect to expanded recreational opportunities for girls and women in sport and outdoor recreation. Although the chief concern has been about females and leisure, the role of boys and men in contemporary leisure has also been an issue.

Sexual orientation affects leisure pursuits in a number of ways. Focus is changing from ignoring those who identify as other than heterosexual to seeing them as a viable market as the numbers of identified lesbian, gay, bisexual, and transgendered people become more visible.

Racial and ethnic identity also has limited many individuals from full participation in organized recreation in the past, and continues to influence the leisure involvement not only of African Americans, but also of the growing number of Hispanics and those of Asian background. With continuing waves of immigration from other parts of the world, religion linked to ethnic identity will pose new policy questions as Muslims, as well as other people who are neither Christian nor Jewish, become part of the national landscape.

Socioeconomic status limits leisure participation as well as where people participate in leisure activities. Those who are in poor or working classes have fewer opportunities and get most of their services from the non-profit and public sector, whereas the upper class has relatively unlimited access to services and utilizes commercial services almost exclusively. This is only the beginning of the vast differences among classes.

AGE FACTORS INFLUENCING LEISURE

The influence of one's age on recreational values, motivators, and patterns of participation have been analyzed for many years. There are key periods of the life span as well as growth processes and development tasks to be accomplished at each stage. Apart from differences in individual personalities within each age group, there is also the reality that developments in modern technology, economic and social trends, and shifts in family relationships have been responsible for major changes in age-related norms of human behavior. People develop physically, socially, and cognitively throughout their lives, and recreation activities must reflect these changes and be age appropriate.[2]

We have seen dramatic shifts in life experiences. Today, children are exposed to the realities of life and mature physically at a much earlier point than in the past. At the same time, paradoxically, they have a longer period of adolescence and schooling before entering the adult workforce. Adults now tend to marry later and have fewer children, and many adults are choosing not to marry at all. Older people have a much longer period of retirement, and a significantly greater number of older persons live more active and adventurous leisure lives today than in the past.

To fully understand the impact of societal trends on public involvement in recreation, park, and leisure-service programs, it is helpful to examine each major age group in turn. Rather than discuss the development stages of each age group, an overview of some important issues is presented, from the perspective of children, adolescents, and adults including young adults, middle adults, and older adults.

Children develop physically, emotionally, and socially through play and recreation.
© Fuse/Thinkstock/Getty.

Recreation in the Lives of Children

Childhood is the age group that includes children from early infancy through the preteen years. Throughout this period, play satisfies important developmental needs in children—often helping to establish values and behavior patterns that will continue throughout a lifetime. Psychologists have examined the role of play at each stage of life, beginning with infancy and moving through the preschool period, middle and late childhood, and adolescence.

Children typically move through several stages: (1) solitary play, carried on without others nearby; (2) parallel play, in which children play side by side without meaningful interplay; (3) associative play, in which children share a common game or group enterprise but concentrate on their own individual efforts rather than group activity; and (4) cooperative play, beginning at about age 3, in which children actually join together in games, informal dramatics, or constructive projects. By the age of 6 or 7, children tend to be involved in loosely organized play groups, leading to much more tightly structured and organized groups in the so-called gang age between 8 and 12.[3]

Play contributes to children's physical, social, and cognitive development.

- ◆ Physical growth through play contributes to fine and gross motor development; body awareness; and physical growth, such as building or maintaining energy and increasing joint flexibility and muscular strength.
- ◆ Social skills are developed through interacting with other children and adults, including language, personal awareness, emotional well-being, and negotiation skills.

◆ Cognitive development in children improves creativity, problem solving and decision making, the ability to engage successfully in new situations, and learning ability. When young children use their imaginations in play, they are more creative, perform better at school tasks, and develop a problem-solving approach to learning.[4,5]

Change of the Family Structure   No longer is there a typical family structure with two parents raising their children together. The number of children in single-parent households (35% or 24,689,000) has remained steady over the last 10 years.[6] Of these, there are 16.2 million single mothers and 2.7 million single fathers raising their children.[7] Another 5.6 million children are living with an adult who is not their parent (e.g., grandparent, aunt, nonrelative). For many decades, there was a decline in the number of stay-at-home moms. However, over the last 12 years, in the U.S. a slight increase in stay-at-home moms can be seen. In 2012, 29% of all mothers were stay-at-home moms.[8] Dads represent the biggest increase among those caring for families as the total number has doubled since 1989.[9]

This change in family structure means an increased need for recreation services for working families. This includes such things as after-school and before-school programming, child and grandchild activities, and mentoring programs for children with single parents.

Overscheduled Children   The overscheduling of children is becoming a problem in today's culture. For example, there are increasing opportunities for youth to participate in sport clinics, camps, and leagues for children as young as 4. Many go on to be a part of traveling sport teams that go to different communities on the weekends to play in tournaments. Parents feel if they do not start their children in sports this young, they will be left behind. Couple this with the demands of household responsibilities, school assignments, and any number of other recreation activities, classes, and clubs and the result is dwindling free time for today's youth.

Although art and music lessons as well as sport and other educational activities may be beneficial to the child, there comes a point when the child has too many things going on in her life. This can result in damage to a child's self-esteem because she sees that her parents are always trying to improve her and she is not good enough the way she is. This overscheduling can add unnecessary stress to a child's life and quite possibly lead to escalated incidences of depression, anxiety, and a lack of creativity and problem solving skills. Experts on overscheduled children suggest a need for a balance between athletics, academics, and character-building activities. Athletics and academic achievement cannot be thrust upon children to the point they worry about not measuring up to adult expectations. These activities should be fun and meaningful. Free time with family and time to just do nothing builds character, reduces stress, and shows children they are loved.[10]

Overparenting   Each generation seems to increase its role of parenting and obsession with protecting its children. The recently coined terms "helicopter parenting" and "snowplow parenting" are becoming more common in our language. Helicopter parents are very involved in their child's education, experiences, and issues. They have a tendency to hover and are never far away from their children. Helicopter parents try to solve problems for their children, and, as a result, the children become reliant on their parents to do this for them. The snowplow parents are ones who plow right through any obstacles that stand in their child's way. Both helicopter and snowplow parents are raising children to believe they have few faults and will always be successful. These same parents are the first to confront a teacher or coach about unfair treatment of their child.

Helicopter parenting inhibits children's ability to make decisions for themselves—and not just young children but also young adults.[11] These children sometimes are also unable to accept responsibility for their actions because their parents bail them out of problems and issues they have gotten into.[11] Although helicopter parenting is often portrayed as a negative thing, and most parents deny they are helicopter parents, there are positives to this. A close relationship with a child and one where the parent helps a child make good decisions is beneficial to the child becoming a self-sufficient adult.

Influence of Commercial Media: Violence and Sex   Another important influence on the lives of children today stems from the overwhelming barrage of violence and sexual content contained in the movies, television shows, video games, and music that saturate their environment.

Because children spend more time watching television than any other activity, discussions about media portrayal of violence and sex have prevailed. Seventy-five percent of all children have televisions in their bedrooms and are exposed to 14,000 sexual messages each year. By age 18, children and teens will have seen 16,000 simulated murders and 200,000 acts of violence.[12]

Case Study

Helicopter Parents

Take the following quiz from your parent's perspective to see how closely your parent hovers over you as a college student.

- ◆ Do you call or email your student frequently (more than once a day)?
- ◆ Have you ever spoken to a professor about your student's grades?
- ◆ Do you frequently wake up your student in the morning to ensure they attend their classes?
- ◆ Have you played a heavy hand helping select the courses in your student's class schedule?
- ◆ Have you talked with university staff to resolve your student's problems (e.g., roommate conflict)?
- ◆ Have you completed your student's assignments or gone above and beyond assisting your student with their academic work?
- ◆ Do you remind your student of college-related deadlines (e.g., assignment or test, paying a fee)?
- ◆ Have you pressured your student to pursue a particular major or profession?

If you answered "yes" to three or more of the questions above (especially one in which your parent has contacted the university on your behalf), you may have helicopter parents.

Questions for Discussion

1. How did you score your parents on this quiz?
2. Before the quiz, did you think your parents were helicopter parents?
3. How do you view helicopter parents and their relationship with their child?
4. At what age do you consider yourself an adult and not need/want this level of help from parents?
5. How many questions can a parent answer yes to without being a helicopter parent? Why?

Source: University of Oregon.
http://counseling.uoregon.edu/Topics-Resources/Parents-Family/Helpful-Articles/Helicopter-Parents.

For the past 30 years, the American Psychological Association has posited that media increases aggressive behavior in children. Additionally, limiting violence seen on television can reduce aggressive behaviors in children toward their peers.[13]

Learning a new skill, expressing creativity through art, or experiencing nature all lead to enhanced personal well-being.
© sonya etchison/Shutterstock.

Lack of Outdoor Play Children are staying inside and spending more and more time with their computers, video games, and televisions rather than being outside experiencing all that nature has to offer. Richard Louv authored a book in which he explains how children do not have the same outdoor experiences previous generations had.[14] Parents keep a closer watch over children and limit where they can play and explore. They prefer the structured, supervised activities to free play in the outdoors. The radius that children are allowed to roam outside of their home is one-ninth of what it was 20 years ago. Much of this is because of safety concerns when in actuality child safety has steadily improved during the past decade, and they are far safer than they were 30 years ago.[15]

Louv reviewed research on the positive effects of children being close to nature. It was determined that nature can improve a child's emotional health. Furthermore, nature helps relieve everyday stress that leads to depression, and children with nature near their home had fewer problems with behavior disorders, anxiety, and depression.[16] Nature also is seen as an intellectual enhancer. Moore and Hong suggest that natural settings will stimulate a child's senses and bring together informal play with formal learning, and that these sensory experiences help a child grow intellectually.[17]

Attention Deficit Hyperactivity Disorder (ADHD) is a growing phenomenon among today's youth. More and more children are taking prescription drugs to curb the symptoms of ADHD that include a difficulty in paying attention, focusing, listening, and following directions. Researchers have claimed that being in nature can boost a child's attention span and relieve symptoms of ADHD.[18] Something as simple as taking a walk in the woods, playing in an open space such as a park, or spending time in the backyard can have tremendous rewards, yet these types of activities are on the decline.

Recreation in the Lives of Adolescents

The teenage population, which began to climb in the early 1990s following years of decline, is expected to keep growing until at least 2045, according to U.S. Census Bureau projections. By then, it is projected there will be more than 51 million Americans between the ages of 10 and 19.

This group of young people matures faster, is quite technologically savvy, and knows what they want from their leisure. The group is proving to be quite challenging for parks and recreation professionals for many different reasons, some of which are discussed here.

Teen Employment   The teen labor force has remained fairly steady since 2010 with teens working mostly in the summer months. Twenty-seven percent of employed youth work in the recreation and hospitality industry (including food service), 20% work in retail, and 11% work in education and health services.[19] Obviously this is a prime population to fill recreation jobs such as lifeguards or camp counselors. While many teens are employed, there are still many who do not have jobs until after they graduate from high school. This may be due to parents wanting teens to focus on a sport or academics. It could be a lack of viable jobs within the community or several other reasons. What this employment outlook means for parks and recreation departments is the continuing need to offer programs and services for this age group.

Trends in Negative Adolescent Leisure Pursuits   Negative leisure pursuits by teens include such things as drug and alcohol use, gambling, and sexuality, among others. Participation rates are changing with each one. For example, the National Institute on Drug Abuse saw a decline in alcohol, cigarette and illegal drug consumption in teens over the last 5 years. Marijuana use rates are steady with marked decrease in synthetic and prescription drug use. However, there has been a dramatic increase in the use of e-cigarettes.[20]

Alcohol is also a major problem with adolescents. The problem is not so much social drinking as it is binge drinking. Binge drinking is consuming a large amount of alcohol over a short period of time. This means that at least twice within the past 2 weeks males have consumed five drinks in a row and females four.[21] Binge drinking continues to decline from 41.2% of the population in 1980 to 23.7% in 2012.[22] The results or consequences of binge drinking are fighting, aggressiveness, blackouts, increased sexual activity, and memory loss.

Teen gambling is also on the rise. It is estimated that 60–80% of all teens have gambled at least once in the last year.[23] That may include buying lottery tickets, small bets with friends, online gambling, or participating in an NCAA basketball tournament pool. If gambling becomes a problem among adolescents, they may experience irritability, exhaustion from lack of sleep, declining grades in school, and an increase in petty crimes and delinquent activities to fund these bets.[24] Online gambling may be a major player in teen gambling behaviors because tens of thousands of websites are available to them as well as advertisements running on television. There is never a lack of exposure to gambling opportunities for this age group.

In 2013, the Planned Parenthood Federation reported that the United States had the highest rate of teen pregnancies among Western developed nations. However, teen pregnancy rates are at their lowest level in the United States in 40 years due to increased contraception use.[25] In 2013, 47% of all high school students reported ever having sex, which is a decline from 54% in 1991. Thirteen percent of females and 17% of males report having more than four sexual partners in high school, and 34% report being currently sexually active. Of these students, 22% reported using alcohol or drugs during their most recent sexual encounter.[26]

"Sexting," where explicit messages and/or photos are exchanged with others through their cell phones, has been in the news over the last several years. There is a lot of discrepancy about its prevalence, which has been reported as low as 7% of teens who have sexted up to 54%. Sexting gains media attention when it is used as a bullying tactic or results in negative consequences such as teen suicide.

Technology   Teens are avid users of cell phones and other technology. Seventy-three percent of all teens have a smart phone. Teens use their cell phones to access the Internet more than any other device. With this shift in cell phone use, teens are constantly connected. Teens text friends more than any other form of non-face-to-face communication and reserve phone calls for their closest friends.[27] Because of the amount of time teens spend with their phones, parents are concerned about relationships established through social media, cyber bullying, the impact their online activity will have on their future academic or employment opportunities, and inappropriate sharing of personal information.

Boredom and the Need for Excitement   Since the last decades of the nineteenth century, the perceived need to provide positive recreation programs and facilities for children and youth has been based on the belief that constructive free-time alternatives not only keep youngsters off the street but also help prevent the kinds of delinquent play that otherwise might result from boredom. Again and again, adolescents apprehended for criminal

Case Study
. . . .
The Challenge of Recreation Programming for Teens

Many of the teen issues discussed here influence their recreational needs. For many parks and recreation agencies, teens are one of the most difficult groups to develop programs, activities, and events for. Due to the changing teen experiences already discussed, agencies have tried many different approaches, including establishing teen centers and teen advisory boards. For example, the City of Palo Alto (CA) Recreation Department established the Teen Advisory Board and the Youth Council. The Teen Advisory Board is a group of high school students who plan and lead activities for their peers. They also have a teen center specifically for these activities. The Youth Council was established to give teens a voice in the community. They work closely with the Recreation Department and the City Council and study problems, activities, and concerns of youth in the community.

Questions for Discussion/Tasks to Complete

1. What were your recreation experiences as a teenager in your community? Were they focused on school, family, friends, or the neighborhood? Were these activities part of an agency such as the local parks and recreation department or the YMCA?
2. What challenges would parks and recreation agencies face in providing recreation opportunities for teens? How could they overcome some of these challenges?
3. Search and find three teen advisory boards across the country. Compare and contrast them.
4. Select a community without a teen advisory board. Outline how you would establish a board and how it would operate.

Source: http://www.cityofpaloalto.org/gov/depts/csd/teen_services.asp

activity use the excuse that they were bored, that there was nothing else to do, or that their delinquent actions were a form of fun. Often, however, such forms of thrill-seeking play end in tragic episodes of violence, drug- and alcohol-fueled accidents, or other self-destructive experiences.

Changing Teen Experiences   Adolescence is a challenging time for the teens, their friends, and their families. They are struggling with self-identity issues, moodiness, puberty, greater reliance on friends, and a greater need for privacy and independence.[28] They are overly concerned with being popular; they challenge the status quo; they are concerned with their appearance; and they are strongly influenced by their peers.[29] Although parents feel this is a difficult time for them, it also is difficult for the adolescent.

Recreation in the Lives of Adults

The adult population in modern society, defined as those in their late teens and older, may logically be subdivided into several age brackets, lifestyle patterns, or generations. Although many life experiences occur in this broad age range, it is important to look at an overall picture of how people progress through these years.

Young Adults   The population of young adults, extending from late teens through late 30s, includes Gen Y and a few of the older generations. For them, the single population has exploded. People are marrying later, if at all. In the past, the word *single* usually meant a lonely person, or someone whose solitary status was a temporary sidetrack on the way to happy matrimony. However, in the decade of the "Me Generation," with its emphasis on narcissistic pleasure and self-fulfillment, singlehood came to be regarded as a happy ending in itself—or at least an enjoyable prolonged phase of postadolescence. When this trend became obvious, a vast number of singles-only institutions sprang up to meet the needs of this newly recognized population that had an estimated $40 billion of annual spending power. Singles apartment complexes, bars, weekends at resort hotels, social groups at local churches, cruises, and a variety of other leisure programs or services emerged—including computer dating services.

As a subgroup of the young adult population, college students are usually strongly influenced in their choice of leisure activities by their status as students. Students living at home are likely to have relatively little free time, often holding jobs and traveling back and forth to school, and they frequently find much of their recreation with friends in their neighborhoods. Students living on college campuses generally take part in social or religious clubs, athletic events, fraternity or sorority functions, and college union programs, entertainment, or cultural activities. Many young college students regard their first experience in living away from home for a sustained period of time as an opportunity to engage in hedonistic forms of play without parental supervision. In part, this appears to be a response to the stress that challenges many first-year college students. Both male and female freshmen suffer from higher levels of anxiety and stress than in past generations. Many worry about the debt

![sun icon] **GENERATIONS**

> Generations are groups of people who share similar formative years by experiencing history, fads, and events. One way to divide the generations is as follows:
>
> *Silent generation:* Born between 1937 and 1945, they experienced the Depression, World War II, Amelia Earhart's solo flight across the Atlantic, and the passage of the Social Security Act.
>
> *Baby boomer generation:* Born between 1946 and 1964, this group saw Woodstock, the Korean War, Jackie Robinson break into Major League Baseball, and the assassinations of Bobby and President John Kennedy and Martin Luther King.
>
> *Generation X, or Gen X:* Born between 1965 and 1976, they experienced Watergate, the peak of Michael Jackson, break dancing, and Madonna.
>
> *Generation Y, or Millennial generation:* Born between 1977 and 1990, this group experienced the technology boom with MP3 players, cell phones, and handheld computers.
>
> *Generation Z:* Born between 1991 and 2012, this group is exposed to highly diverse environments in their community, school, and play; they have never known a world without the Internet, cell phones, or terrorism.[30]

they are incurring for their college education, job prospects upon graduation, having to work part time, and the pressure for success. This has resulted in today's college students having the lowest level of mental health in several decades.[31]

The majority of young single adults are able to use their leisure time in positive and constructive ways. Particularly for those who have finished school and are financially independent, travel, participation in sport or fitness clubs, social clubs, or forms of popular entertainment and involvement in hobbies and creative activities enrich their lives, both in college and in community settings.

Although millions of men and women have joined the trend toward a continuing single lifestyle, a majority of young adults today choose marriage and family life. Leisure behavior is markedly affected when people marry and have children. Social activities tend to center around the neighborhood in which the couple lives, and the home itself becomes a recreation center for parent and child activities. The family takes part in social programs sponsored by religious agencies, civic and neighborhood associations, or parent–teacher organizations (PTOs). As children move into organized community programs, parents begin to use their leisure time for volunteer service as adult leaders for Scout groups, coaches and managers of sport teams, or in similar positions.

The group in this age bracket that is most deprived of leisure consists of single parents who often must work, raise a family under difficult economic and emotional circumstances, and try at the same time to find needed social outlets and recreational opportunities for themselves.

Leisure for young adults often encompasses both family and friends.
© Monkey Business/Fotolia.com.

Middle Adults   The current middle adult age group is considered Gen X and baby boomers. They are approximately 40–65 years old and make up the largest section of the population.

Baby boomers have immense diversity in their lifestyles as well. Some are devoted to their families; others remain unattached. Some boomers are sport minded or wilderness oriented, whereas others are committed to the arts, hobbies, or literary pursuits. Growing numbers of this age group have begun to place a high value on the creative satisfaction found in work or to devote a fuller portion of their time to family and personal involvements.

For parents in the middle adult years, patterns of leisure involvement begin to change as children become more independent and even establish their own families. Many nonworking parents, who have devoted much time and energy to the family's needs, begin to find these demands less pressing. They have more available time, as well as a need to find a different meaning and fulfillment in life through new interests and challenges.

Many leisure-service providers are realizing the impact of the baby boomers and what it means for their agencies. As more of this age group moves into retirement, they are going to be looking for activities to keep themselves busy. This group is going to retire with money to spend, and they are healthier than retirees of the past. Furthermore, baby boomers are not afraid to try new things and go to new places. They refuse to retire and

BOOMER BITS

Boomers:

◆ are healthier, more active, and trendier than previous generations.
◆ are interested in travel and technology.
◆ see that time is of the essence. They have places to go and people to see.
◆ heavily rely on word of mouth for advertising.
◆ do not consider themselves old; they feel 10 years younger than their actual age.
◆ understand the importance of pampering themselves and are the largest purchasers of luxury cars, jewelry and gourmet foods.

St. Clair, S. (2008). A Booming Market: Recreation and Fitness for Baby Boomers. Recreation Management. http://www.recmanagement.com/feature_print.php?fid=200802fe03

Case Study

Programming for Baby Boomers

Baby boomers are currently the largest segment of our population. They have financial resources to spend, are retiring at rapid rates, are not afraid of technology, and want to travel and have new experiences. This makes them a prime target market for parks and recreation. Because of this, the local parks and recreation agency has recognized a significant need for increased programs for this group. You have been hired as the new director of adult activities in your community. Your charge is to develop programs targeted at the 65+ age group.

Tasks to complete:

1. Without doing any research, make a list of activities and events that you would like to offer for baby boomers. Compare your list to others in the class. How many of the activities are sedentary vs. active? How many are stereotypically for "old people"?
2. Find five agencies online that offer programs specifically for the baby boomer population. Gather the following information:
   a. What are these programs called (e.g. Senior Adults)?
   b. Are there active and sedentary programs?
   c. What type of fees are assessed?
   d. What programs do you consider to be stereotypical for older adults?
   e. What programs surprised you?
3. Select the best and most creative programs you found in your research. Develop a schedule of activities you would like to initially offer.

go quietly to a senior citizens center to play passive games, because they do not see themselves as seniors. They plan to stay active to show that they are not old, and will need recreation and tourism services to do it.

Recreation in the Lives of Older Adults

Older adults are defined here as people in their mid-60s and older, or the older baby boomers and silent generation. Given the increase in life expectancy, this group is quite large and diverse. They pass through several stages, much like those in the adult category do.

Active Older Adults Recreation and leisure assume a high priority in the lives of most older adults, particularly for those in their late 60s and beyond who have retired from full-time jobs. Without work to fill their time and often with the loss of partners or friends, such persons find it necessary to develop new interests and often to establish new relationships.

HOUSE-SWAPPING BECOMES A POPULAR VACATION OPTION

Older adults are increasingly engaging in house swapping, or home exchange. *House swapping* is when people offer their home to someone in another geographic location, often another country, in exchange for use of that person's home. So, a couple in Florida allows a couple in Spain to use their home for a 2-week vacation in exchange for the Florida couple using the home in Spain at the same time.[32]

It is now popular to assert that older adults are far more active, vigorous, economically secure, and happier than had been assumed in the past. With improved financial support and pension plans, a much higher percentage of older persons are relatively well-to-do and able to enjoy a far longer period of retirement. Research has shown that many older adults continue to enjoy sexual relations and to maintain active and creative lives well into their 70s and 80s.

The lives of older adults have changed dramatically over the past three or four decades. Not only can they expect to live much longer, but their living circumstances are likely to be radically different from those of past generations in terms of familial roles, social activities, economic factors, and other important conditions.

Changes in Family Structure   In the past, it was common for several generations of family members to live together. Older persons continued not only to receive the affection and support of their children and grandchildren, but also to play meaningful roles in family life. An increasing number of older adults continue to live by themselves for longer periods of time. Although many do not want to live in a nursing home, there is still need for some additional care as people age. The number of senior living communities, retirement communities, and assisted-living environments is growing. Depending on the level of care needed (from no care at all to full-time nursing care), these types of living situations can meet the needs of people as they age. These communities provide nursing care, daily living assistance, socialization, and recreation opportunities for the residents. Many see this as a better alternative than living with grown children and their families. Some retirement facilities have graduated living quarters where the level of care increases based on what the individual needs. An older adult may enter the facility being totally self-sufficient and, as health declines, can be moved to other areas within the same facility. This living arrangement lends itself to continuity and familiarity to the individual.

Older adults are breaking away from stereotypical leisure pursuits and engaging in a variety of activities.
© M.G. Mooij/Shutterstock.

Positive Changes   Even though these negative trends must be acknowledged, the reality still is that most older people are living longer, happier, and healthier lives than in the past. Indeed, there is striking new evidence that the very old are enjoying remarkably good health in comparison with other age groups. The average annual Medicare bill for people who live to their late 80s and 90s is significantly lower than that for those who die sooner. Part of the reason is that older adults tend to be relatively robust. Cancer and heart disease, the two chief killers of retired persons in the younger age brackets, tend not to affect the very old, and Alzheimer's disease also attacks slightly younger men and women. Today, there are more and more centenarians—people who have made it to their 100th birthday—80,000 with 85% of these being women.[33]

With improved medical care, people are not just living longer, healthier lives—they are living them differently. Particularly in the so-called retirement states of New Mexico, Arizona, Nevada, and Florida, which have fast-growing populations of older men and women, they are engaging in active sports, volunteering, going back to school, and developing new networks of friends and relationships.

Specific Contributions of Recreation and Leisure   Recreational involvement meets a number of important physical, emotional, and social needs of older adults. Regular physical exercise has immense health-related value for older persons, with a range of specific benefits that include preventing heart disease, stroke, cancer, osteoporosis, and diabetes; assisting in weight reduction; improving immunity against common infections; reducing arthritic symptoms; countering depression; and even helping to improve memory and the quality of sleep.

In terms of social benefits, one of the key problems affecting older adults is that they tend to become isolated and lose a sense of playing a significant role in family life or in the community at large. Therefore, community service and volunteerism are useful leisure activities for older adults. In fact, volunteerism is frequently conceptualized as a satisfactory substitute for paid work for older persons. Older adults gain an important sense of recognition and self-worth through volunteerism. It provides structure in their lives in terms of regular time commitments and offers social contacts that often lead to friendship and other group involvement.

Another important leisure pursuit for older adults consists of continuing education—either on a fairly casual basis with classes or workshops and community center programs or on a more formal basis in noncredit courses taken through Road Scholar (previously known as Elderhostel) or other college-sponsored programs.

Older adults are increasingly technologically savvy and use the Internet to gather information about travel and leisure. This further emphasizes the importance of leisure-service providers using electronic means to communicate with this group.

Other older adults break new ground by entering a new period of creative development in the arts, writing, social service, or other unknown kinds of personal involvement. Much of today's increased life expectancy has been added, it seems, not to the end but to the middle of our lives—extending the opportunity for "late bloomers" to realize their dreams.

GENDER FACTORS INFLUENCING LEISURE

Beyond the issue of one's age group, a second factor that plays an important role in leisure has to do with sexual or gender identity and values.

A distinction should be made between the two terms *sex* and *gender*. Although they are often used interchangeably, social scientists generally accept the principle that the term *sex* should be used to identify biological or physical classification in terms of the structure and functions that are possessed by one sex or the other. In contrast, the word *gender* is used to describe a broad range of characteristics, roles, or behaviors that society usually attaches to males and females. Stated simply, the words *male* and *female* apply to one's sex, whereas the words *masculine* and *feminine* are descriptive adjectives applying to gender traits.

Throughout history, distinctions between males and females have been made that extend beyond the procreative functions. These distinctions encompass family or marital roles, educational status, career opportunities, political influences, and all other aspects of daily life.

Among younger children, play has served to reinforce gender-related stereotypes. Little boys were given toy guns or cowboy outfits and encouraged to playact in stereotypically masculine roles such as doctors, fire fighters, or airline pilots. Girls were given dolls or play equipment designed to encourage stereotypically feminine roles such as caring for babies, cooking and sewing, or playing as nurses or flight attendants. Only after the resurgence of the feminist movement following World War II did society begin to question these roles and assumptions and challenge such sexist uses of play in childhood.

Leisure for girls and women has changed and improved from the impact of the feminist movement.
Courtesy of Deb Garrahy.

Women and Leisure

During the early decades of the twentieth century, leadership roles and activities assigned to girls and women, as well as the expectations regarding their ability to work well in groups, reflected past perceptions of women as weak and inferior in skills and lacking drive, confidence, and the ability to compete. Victorian prudery and misconceptions about physical capability and health needs also limited programming for girls and women.[34] Physical activity was seen as detracting from womanliness, having a negative effect on motherhood, and being detrimental to women's mental health.[35]

Impact of the Feminist Movement   Although times have changed since the Victorian age, there are still differences in experiences, attitudes, and expectations of women's participation in sport and recreation versus that of men. A major influential factor in the changes toward equality was the feminist movement.

Feminism is defined as political, social, and economic equality among men and women. This equality first came to light politically with women

TITLE IX

Title IX of the Education Amendments of 1972 states that "No person in the United States shall, on the basis of sex, be excluded from participation in, be denied the benefits of or be subjected to discrimination under any education program or activity receiving Federal financial assistance." Although many associate Title IX with athletics, it also covers education (including career and vocational programs), admissions and employment policies, standardized testing, and treatment of pregnant and parenting teens.

Title IX has been instrumental in improving opportunities for female athletes at both the high school and collegiate levels. Those opposed to Title IX often argue that it decreases athletic opportunities for men. However, this is not an accurate assessment. Here are the numbers of athletes from 1972–2015:[36]

	1972	1981	2011	2015
Men	170,384	225,800	235,800	273,114
Women	31,852	98,700	177,800	209,419

wanting the right to vote just as men could. With the passage of the Nineteenth Amendment in 1920 giving women this right, feminism virtually disappeared until women entered the workforce in large numbers starting in the 1950s. As women entered the workforce, they wanted equal pay as well as access to jobs that were stereotypically a "man's job." Political and economic aspects of feminism still exist today, but it is the social aspect of feminism that is most affected by leisure.

What did this mean for leisure? Feminism gave women an understanding that they had freedom in their choices of activities and participation. Limits and stereotypes could be removed. Furthermore, it gave women the same opportunities as men in terms of leisure.

Implications for Women's Leisure   Women's leisure has been a prominent topic in research for more than 20 years. By examining what scholars have learned, there are several implications regarding women's leisure.

◆ Women's participation in physical activity continues to grow. Women are moving beyond traditional physical fitness classes and staying active through activities such as outdoor recreation pursuits, cycling, running, and intense fitness programs such as CrossFit.
◆ Leisure has changed for women from being centered around family and household responsibilities, to women also taking time for their own recreational activities. They still enjoy attending their child's soccer game, but want their own activities as well.
◆ The difference between men's and women's leisure is diminishing. Once stereotypical activities have more blurred gender lines. Men can enjoy yoga as much as women can have a poker night with friends.
◆ Women value the social aspects of leisure. While time is a constraint to leisure for many, the resulting social opportunities with others and physical benefits drive women to pursue leisure activities.

AUGUSTA NATIONAL FINALLY ADDS FEMALE MEMBERS IN 2013

Many golf clubs have been resistant to having female members with full rights as allocated to men. One glaring example is Augusta National Golf Club, which admitted its first two women members—Condoleezza Rice and Darla Moore—in 2012.[37] Rice was the U.S. Secretary of State under President George W. Bush. Moore is vice president of Rainwater, Inc., a private investment company and the founder and chair of The Charleston Parks Conservancy, a foundation focused on enhancing the parks and public spaces of Charleston, SC. Augusta National is one of the most exclusive clubs in the world and host to the Masters Golf Tournament.

These issues make women's leisure quite complex. Their lives mean assuming several different roles over time that affect leisure choices.

Men and Leisure

Although most of the professional literature and research studies dealing with gender in recreation and leisure focuses on past discrimination against girls and women and the efforts made to strengthen their opportunities today, it is essential to examine the changing role of males in this area as well. Generally, men have been portrayed as the dominant sex within most areas of community life and have been seen as responsible for denying women access to a full range of leisure pursuits and professional advancement. However, it would be misleading to assume that men's lives are invariably richer and more satisfying than those of women.

Moreover, men and women are becoming more balanced. Men are spending more time in the home sharing day to day tasks, while more and more women are spending time outside the home with work and other demands.

Shifting Masculine Identities   Parents, family, friends, and teachers all play a major role in helping a child define what it means to be masculine. The media portrays males as being in control of themselves and situations around them, aggressive, physically desirable, and heroic. Male-oriented magazines show men with muscular bodies, well dressed, and successful. Although these images encourage men to behave in certain ways, not all men buy into this image. Increasingly, men are breaking free of these rigid stereotypes and behaving as they want, regardless of the associated stereotypes.

The Role of Fatherhood   A man's role as father has changed drastically over the past two decades. With more women entering the workforce, fathers are taking more responsibility for raising children and contributing to the household responsibilities. Some studies show that more men are beginning to take on childcare responsibilities, for reasons ranging from rising daycare costs to the growth in the number of working women. In addition, the stay-at-home dad is not quite so rare as he once was. As women's salaries are rivaling men's, many families are finding it just as beneficial if the father stays home to raise the children.

In addition to fathers who are living in the same household as their children, there are fathers who are living elsewhere or who started another family. There is an increased expectation that fathers will be more involved in their children's lives,[38] more emotionally connected to their children, and more egalitarian in terms of gender role expectations.[39] No longer is it a given that in a divorce the mother is automatically granted custody. The quality of parenting is a bigger dictator than gender is in most states.

Men, and fathers in particular, are using leisure as a means to build social relationships. For men in general, similar interests such as poker, hunting, fishing, or watching football on Sunday afternoons are used as social outlets. Fathers are participating in leisure activities to share experiences with their children. They may coach their child's soccer team, go to their piano lesson, or take their little girl to the Daddy–Daughter Dance at the local recreation center. Like mothers, these fathers are sometimes constrained in the fact that they choose leisure activities not because they particularly want to participate, but because their child wants to participate or the father understands the value of participating with the child.

Constraints to Leisure   It is evident that both men and women have issues that affect their leisure participation. These issues have been labeled as constraints to leisure. An entire body of research examines these constraints and their impact. Constraints to leisure occur when an individual is unable to participate in a leisure activity, unable to participate as much as the individual would like, or when the quality of the experience is diminished for some reason. Constraints are categorized as interpersonal, intrapersonal, and structural.

Interpersonal constraints are associated with the individual's relationship with others. The constraint occurs because of this relationship with friends, family, or even co-workers. An example of an interpersonal constraint would be lacking another person to participate with or participating in an activity because of the desires of others rather than an actual desire to do so. If a person goes along with friends to see a baseball game but really has no interest in the game, this is considered an interpersonal constraint.

Intrapersonal constraints are factors that affect an individual's preference for, or interest in, an activity. For example, a person may not feel he or she is skilled at an activity and as a result will choose not to participate. Another example is having feelings of self-consciousness. Women in particular sometimes feel self-conscious about their bodies. If this self-consciousness leads to a woman not joining a gym, she is experiencing an intrapersonal constraint. Likewise, if a man has interest in improving his cardiovascular fitness, he will most likely avoid an aerobics class because it is seen as an activity for women, even though he is interested in taking an aerobics class.

Finally, *structural constraints* are factors that intervene between the desire to participate and actual participation in an activity. The most common structural constraint is a lack of time. Other examples include lack of transportation, money, or opportunity.

While women face constraints to leisure, so do their male counterparts. A major constraint that men face more than women is the lack of companions with whom to participate. Women are much more likely to find a friend for such things as taking a class or attending a cultural event than men are. Furthermore, men are more likely to feel the constraints of gendered activities than women. Traditionally female activities such as ballet or aerobics are often seen as prohibitive for male participants because of the fear of being perceived as less than masculine.

Implications for Men's Leisure   What are the implications of these trends in masculine identity and lifestyle values for recreation and leisure? First, many boys and men who formerly felt pressured to be involved heavily in sports, both as participants and as spectators, may now feel free not to conform to this traditional masculine image. Further, growing numbers of males are increasingly likely to take part in domestic functions or hobbies, the creative arts, or other leisure pursuits that in the past might have raised questions about their degree of "maleness." This new freedom to engage in leisure pursuits once considered inappropriate for men also extends to attitudes toward women. Increasingly, many parents are becoming sensitive to the way they permit their sons to behave toward girls.

With respect to both sexes, it is important to note that many of the barriers that separated males and females in the past have been broken down in recent years. For example, a number of leading youth organizations that formerly were separate in terms of membership have now joined forces, as in the case of Boys and Girls Clubs of America. In other cases, national organizations such as the Young Men's Christian Association (YMCA) not only have substantial numbers of members who are girls and women, but also in some communities are directed by women executives and division heads.

SEXUAL ORIENTATION FACTORS INFLUENCING LEISURE

Leisure is affected by sexual orientation as well as by gender. Although everyone has a sexual orientation, whether it is heterosexual, homosexual, bisexual, or transgendered, the focus here is on those who identify themselves as lesbian, gay, bisexual, or transgendered (LGBT). This group of people faces additional situations, challenges, and obstacles in their leisure and their life as a whole.

Members of this group have had a difficult past in terms of acceptance by the mainstream population. In the 1930s and 1940s, a backlash developed against gay forms of entertainment, with state assemblies barring the performance of plays dealing with sexual "degeneracy" and Hollywood agreeing not to depict homosexuality in movies. State liquor authorities closed many bars that catered to gay and lesbian clientele, and in the 1950s, homosexual government employees lost their jobs because it was assumed that they could be easily blackmailed into spying for other countries on the basis of their hidden identities.

In the 1960s and 1970s, the effect of the Stonewall Riot in New York City (a mass protest against police persecution of gays and lesbians), the impact of the counterculture movement with its emphasis on sexual freedom, and the activism of leaders such as Harvey Milk, a San Francisco city supervisor who was assassinated in 1978, all converged to help homosexuals gain a greater measure of public acceptance.

A major change in attitudes toward the LGBT community resulted in the U.S. Supreme Court ruling 5–4 in favor of legalizing same-sex marriage on Thursday, June 25, 2015, making it the 21st country to legalize marriage for all LGBT couples. Although today there are more identified LGBT people than ever before—an estimated 29 million—there are still many who do not openly identify as LGBT for a variety of different reasons. It could be fear of not being accepted by friends and family, fear of losing their family support system, concerns about harassment and discrimination, or worry about losing a job. As a nation, we have seen tremendous improvements in acceptance of LGBT people. Much of this can be attributed to the millennial generation who are more open to different sexual orientations than their older counterparts. There are several reasons for this. For example, there are more people who are open about their sexuality, so millennials may be raised around someone who identifies as LGBT; there are LGBT characters regularly seen on television; millennials have access to technology to answer questions and keep them more informed; and more people talk about LGBT issues than ever before.[40]

While great strides have been made, those in the LGBT community sometimes experience discrimination and violence. One of the most recent examples occurred when an Orlando gunman attacked a gay nightclub, leaving 49 people dead. What started as a night of dancing to salsa and merengue music ended in tragedy. Many of those who survived said the club was a place for fun, where they could be themselves and enjoy an evening of entertainment.

Implications for Leisure

There are several issues to consider with this group in terms of recreation. First, LGBT people have been labeled a gold mine for recreation companies and agencies. This group is more highly educated and has a higher income level than the national average. It is estimated that they have $884 billion per year in buying power [41] and spend $70.1 billion per year on travel.[42] Second, on a more negative note, teens who identify as LGBT have a higher than average suicide rate among their peers. They often feel isolated and rejected by family or friends and have very few outlets for social and recreational opportunities where they feel comfortable. Third, LGBT people are increasingly becoming parents through past marriages, adoptions, or other means. All of these factors affect their leisure in a number of ways.

The following are a few examples of how these issues have sparked leisure-service providers to welcome and support LGBT people:

◆ In Boulder, Colorado, a play group has been established for young children of gay and lesbian couples.
◆ Olivia Cruise Lines focuses solely on cruises for gays and lesbians. R Family Vacations offers family cruises for gays and lesbians with children.[43]
◆ Key West, Florida, Portland, Oregon, New York City, and Palm Springs, California, specifically target gay and lesbian tourists by promoting the city as a tourism destination and providing information on gay/lesbian-friendly hotels, resorts, restaurants, and recreational opportunities.
◆ The Lavender Youth Recreation and Information Center (LYRIC) is a recreation center for youth aged 24 and younger. It was opened in 1988 and offers social and recreational programs and services for LGBT, queer, and questioning youth. The center provides community, education, and recreation programs and events.[44]
◆ In New York City, there is a nonprofit group called Services and Advocacy for LGBT Elders (SAGE). SAGE started in 1977 for adults, serving as a drop-in center and offering discussion groups and various recreational activities such as arts, exercise, dances, and trips.[45]
◆ FountainGrove Lodge is an LGBT retirement community that focuses on wellness and active lifestyles to maintain health for older adults. The community features such recreation amenities as a fitness center and classes, walking trails, pet park, golf course, and movie theater.[46]

Given the growing numbers of LGBT people, the economic impact of this group, and the special issues faced by them, it is important that recreation and leisure-service agencies understand the need to offer programs, activities, and events for LGBT youths to adults.

Case Study

. . . .

LGBT Sports League to Form?

A group of 10 LGBT people in the community come into the local parks and recreation department to discuss sport opportunities for those who identify as LGBT. They are requesting that a volleyball league and a co-ed softball league be formed. They also guarantee that they can put together at least six teams in each league, and that they will not limit players to just people who are LGBT. Your agency already has adult sports leagues, but this group wants their own league.

Questions to Consider

1. Assume you are part of the LGBT group seeking a league. What arguments would you use to convince the agency to start a league for you?
2. Take the other side of the argument. List potential reasons why forming the league would not be a good idea.
3. Because this is an adult sports league, it will generate revenue from the players and not rely on tax support. Does this make a difference in whether or not you would start this league? Why or why not?
4. You have decided to go ahead and run the softball league as a trial. You have two choices in location. One open field is in a complex of three other diamonds and is one of the best fields in the city. The other location is a decent field, but it is a standalone diamond on the edge of town. Which diamond would you choose for the league and why?

CLASSIFYING RACE IN THE CENSUS

The U.S. Census Bureau is confounded by the difficulty of classifying race for people in the United States. In 1990, people could choose from the following categories: white, black, Asian and Pacific Islanders, and American Indian or Alaska Native. In 2000, the census expanded to include 18 races including a category for "other" and the ability to select more than one race. In 2010, there were 15 racial categories with space to insert any specific races omitted.[47] Because of the difficulty in classifications, discussions are currently underway to eliminate the long list of options and to list a limited number of categories with examples within each category.[48]

RACE AND ETHNICITY FACTORS INFLUENCING LEISURE

A fourth major sociocultural factor is of key importance in determining leisure values and behaviors. A succession of past research studies shows that recreational involvement is heavily influenced by one's racial or ethnic identity. The provision of public, nonprofit, and other forms of recreation facilities and programs is also affected by these demographic factors, and the broader fields of popular culture—including the sport and entertainment worlds—continue to reflect their impact.

Meaning of Race and Ethnicity

Before examining the actual influence of race and ethnicity on recreation and leisure, it is helpful to clarify the meaning of the two terms. Although they are often used interchangeably, social scientists distinguish between them. *Race* refers to the genetic makeup of a person. The genetic makeup often results in biological characteristics that are exhibited among various groups. These characteristics include such things as the shape of one's eyes, texture of one's hair, and the color of one's skin.

In contrast, *ethnicity* involves having a unique social and cultural heritage that is passed on from one generation to another. Ethnic groups are often identified by patterns of language, family life, religion, recreation, and other customs or traits that distinguish them from other groups.

Despite the limitations of racial or ethnicity-based identification and its meaning in scientific terms, the reality is that the public continues to accept the concept of race and to apply it in terms of popular stereotypes about one group or the other. This is particularly significant for recreation and leisure because our traditional patterns of facility development and program planning were essentially based on the assumption that the public being served was predominantly a white, middle-class population familiar with the literature, traditions, and customs that came to North America from the British Isles.

Now, we are seeing the rapid growth of non-European populations in the United States as a consequence of recent immigration and birthrate trends. In a number of major cities throughout the country, nonwhites now outnumber those of European background, with the percentage of African American, Hispanic American, and Asian American children in the schools representing sizable majorities in some cases. States such as California are seeing nonwhite Hispanics become a majority group, and major cities across the country are not showing any majority groups.

This population trend has seen Hispanics become the largest minority group in the United States; it is estimated that by 2050 they will represent 30.2% of the U.S. population. Similarly, the number of Asian Americans has grown from 3.5 million in 1980 to more than 14.7 million in 2010 and is expected to climb steadily in the decades ahead.[49]

In addition to race, ethnicity can have a major impact on leisure preferences. One guiding force in ethnicity is religion. The United States continues to be dominated by Protestants (46.57%) and Catholics (20.87%). However, overall Christian religions are on a 7.8% decline from 2007 and 2014. During this same time period, non-Christian faiths (e.g. Jewish, Muslim) and non-affiliated (e.g., Atheist, agnostic, no religion) have both increased. Non-Christian religions grew by 1.2% and non-affiliated grew by 6.7%.[50] Another striking trend is the growing number of Muslims and Buddhists in the United States. The 2008 American

Dance in Hawaii is a tradition that tourists expect to see when visiting.
© Jose Gil/Shutterstock.

The Holi Festival of Colors in Malaysia is one of the largest traditional Indian cultural celebrations.
© Dimitry Berkut/Shutterstock.

DEFINING WHO IS HISPANIC

Hispanic or Latino are defined as Cuban, Mexican, Puerto Rican, South or Central American, or other Spanish cultures or origins regardless of race. Other Spanish culture can include such categories as Argentinean, Columbian, Dominican, Nicaraguan, Salvadoran, and others.

Source: United States Census Bureau. "Who's Hispanic in America?" www.census.gov/newsroom/cspan/hispanic/2012.06.22_cspan_hispanics.pdf.

Religious Identification Survey (ARIS) claims that there are 1,349,000 Muslims in the United States, which is a 156% growth since 1990. The number of Buddhists has grown 194% in that same time period, and that religion has 1,189,000 followers in the United States. Interestingly, 15% of the population claims no religion. This is an increase of 138% since 1990.[51]

The racial and ethnic composition of the United States is rapidly changing. Beyond the sheer numbers, it is evident that growing minority populations are also exerting powerful influences on the nation's cultural scene and recreational life. No longer is it acceptable to offer programs from a predominantly white, middle-class perspective and interest level. Leisure services need to be more inclusive than that. Programs can be offered from a "melting pot" perspective or a "mosaic" perspective. The melting pot perspective gives leisure-service providers the opportunity to merge groups to allow people to learn about different races, cultures, and ethnicities together, whereas the mosaic perspective allows programmers to offer activities, programs, and events tailored to the unique wants, values, attitudes, and beliefs of a particular group.

Implications for Recreation and Leisure

The approach to delivering services to people from different racial and ethnic backgrounds has changed and improved over time, but still has incredible room for growth. Scott[52] suggested that recreation services needed to be accessible, affordable, safe, culturally relevant, and welcoming in order to meet the needs of all racial and ethnic groups.

Accessible The importance of access to parks and recreation is immeasurable. People who live near a park are more physically active, healthy, and have higher levels of psychological well-being.[53] Accessibility can refer to financial resources, transportation, and physical access; accessibility to parks is not equal in most communities. The research on accessibility is limited, but people of color are less likely to live near a park, or the parks they do live near are smaller with fewer amenities than are found in predominantly white neighborhoods. Accessibility via transportation could be problematic both in terms of getting to local recreation opportunities as well as the ability to travel to rural locations for outdoor recreational activities. If there are no parks within walking distance, public transportation is limited, or there is little family discretionary income, people living in these areas face significantly more obstacles to using parks than anyone else.

Affordable and Safe Many research studies have shown that racial and ethnic minorities are limited in their recreation participation due to affordability and safety issues. Those who have lower levels of discretionary income do not have the financial resources to travel to a national park, go skiing in Jackson Hole, Wyoming, go to the Texas Rangers game, or pay the fee to take a cooking class. The link between income and safety is significant. For example, lower income neighborhoods often have elevated crime rates and residents who are concerned about their safety. This fear can diminish use of public spaces for many. Low income neighborhoods often have high traffic roads, railroads, or other barriers making access to parks difficult and unsafe, especially for those with limited transportation options.[54]

Culturally Relevant and Welcoming Many cultural factors prohibit the use of recreation facilities and programs. Some may not feel welcome because they view activities as being planned by and for whites, or that their own religious or personal values do not match those of others. For example, agencies that are not mindful of significant non-Christian religious holidays, or lack understanding of requirements regarding modesty and mixing of males and females in activities for such religions as Muslim will not draw these groups into their facilities. Essentially, some people do not feel there is anything for them, and see no need to participate. However, working with different groups to learn what activities they want and involving them in the planning can help them feel they have a voice and are welcome. Skokie, Illinois does this well through the Skokie Festival of Cultures. This citywide event has a planning committee with representatives from 24 different racial and ethnic groups residing in the community. Each group is represented and plans its facet of the event including food, art, entertainment, and activities.

Agencies must continually review their program offerings, marketing, administration, and staffing to best meet the needs of the community. Schneider, Shinew, and Fernandez[55] provide several suggestions for agencies to better serve the entire community:

◆ Show diversity in marketing materials through photos, content, and distribution to locations that reach diverse populations.
◆ Work with the city, public transportation agencies, schools, and nonprofit organizations to coordinate transportation options.
◆ Conduct an access assessment and include safety as a factor. Outline ways to increase access to parks, programs, and facilities.

Case Study
. . . .

Pokémon GO: Where Augmented Reality, Culture, and Race Intersect

Days before this text was sent to print, Pokémon GO was released and hit the public by storm. In less than a week, the number of users rivaled Twitter. Here is a brief description of the game:

Players or "trainers" use a GPS map to locate Pokémon or "pocket monsters." When a character is tapped, the smart phone camera is launched by the app for a mini-game where the Pokémon appear in the real world. Once Pokémon are captured, trainers use them to battle in specialized locations called Pokémon gyms. Pokémon can be found anywhere in the world including "Pokémon stops" that are cultural and historic landmarks. While this component adds to the educational benefits of the game, not everyone is pleased to be a stop. For example, the Holocaust Museum in Washington D.C. and the Auschwitz and Birkenau Concentration Camp sites in Poland have requested they be removed from the game because they feel the game dishonors Holocaust victims.

Pokémon GO has caused many millennials to be out in the community looking for the characters. The trainers can be seen with their heads down looking at a phone screen and wandering back and forth in an area chasing a character. Many communities have warned about the safety of the activity because of the disruption to traffic and trainers stumbling over fixtures on the sidewalk or bike racks in parks.

A USA TODAY article interviewed some African American men who felt recent racial tensions have become an issue for some who play the game. Pokémon GO was released at the same time that two African American men were shot and killed by police officers in Baton Rouge and a suburb of Minneapolis, followed by a fatal shooting of 5 police officers in Dallas who were working at a peaceful rally for the men. Those interviewed expressed their concerns that people could call the police on them because they look suspicious as they walk by a window three or four times trying to catch the character. One player said, "my brain started combining the complexity of being Black in America with the real world proposal of wandering and exploration that is designed into the game play of Pokémon GO, there was only one conclusion. I might die if I keep playing."

Questions to Consider
1. Should the Holocaust museum officials have asked that it be removed from the game as a location for a character? Why or why not?
2. Can games like Pokémon GO impact physical activity for the players? Why or why not?
3. Read the Guynn article in USA TODAY listed below. Discuss the points made in the article. Are the concerns legitimate?

Sources
Akhtar, A. (July 13, 2016). Holocaust Museum, Auschwitz want Pokémon Go hunts out. USA TODAY. http://www.usatoday.com/story/tech /news/2016/07/12/holocaust-museum-auschwitz-want-pokmon-go-hunts-stop-pokmon/86991810/
Guynn, J. (July 13, 2016). Playing Pokémon GO while black: Fear stifles the fun. USA TODAY. http://www.usatoday.com/story/tech /news/2016/07/12/playing-pokemon-go-while-black/86989554/
WRDW/WAGT Staff . (July 13, 2016). What exactly is Pokémon GO?. http://www.abc12.com/content/news/What-exactly-is-Pokemon -GO-386640661.html

MUSLIM RECREATION PARTICIPATION

Islam is a worldwide religion with more than 1 billion followers. Leisure is closely connected with religious activities for Muslims because free time is allotted to be spent with family and on religious activities and festivals.[56] Activity and sport are encouraged in Islamic countries for the purpose of a healthy body and mind. Livengood and Stoldolska found that Muslim Americans participate in the same mainstream leisure activities that the rest of Americans do, but their leisure style, location of leisure, and the individuals with whom they participate are different.[57] Lack of participation by Muslims in leisure has been attributed to such issues as disapproval from family, concern over contact with the opposite sex, which is discouraged, unacceptable facilities, immodest sport clothes, agency dress codes for participation that go against religious beliefs about what parts of the body should be covered, lack of experience in an activity, and obligations to family.

◆ Build culturally competent staff through ongoing diversity training. One-time training is insufficient, as employees must continue to learn about their community and the people within it.

◆ Develop social activities that can build relationships among community members, especially helpful to those new to the neighborhood such as recent immigrants.

◆ Hire a diverse staff. A customer seeing staff from their same racial or ethnic group can be an opening for groups to feel welcome.

A Muslim family plays cricket in London's Kensington Gardens.
Courtesy of Deb Garrahy.

Obviously, racial and ethnicity issues go beyond what recreation and park professionals are expected to deal with. However, within the total field of intergroup relations, it is essential that leisure-service managers plan programs that will contribute to intergroup understanding and favorable relations. This may be done through community celebrations, holidays, ethnic and folk festivals, friendly sport competition, and a host of other activities. It is also essential that leisure-service managers continue to strive to overcome the long-standing patterns of prejudice and racial discord that linger in many communities today.

SOCIOECONOMIC FACTORS INFLUENCING LEISURE

Socioeconomic status (SES), or *social class*, is a means of classifying people based on their income, education, occupation, and wealth. Although sociologists have developed several labels for the different social classes, there are five common ones: poor, working class, lower middle class, upper middle class, and upper class.

Social class affects leisure in a number of ways. The amount of education and/or the amount of money a person has dictates the amount of free time and discretionary income available for leisure. Traditionally, lower classes are underrepresented in recreation activity participation. It was seen previously that this was particularly true for health and fitness programs. On the other hand, those in higher classes usually have more education and money and look for more refined and prestigious leisure.[58]

In the United States, the poor, the working class, and the lower middle class have been the dominant users of public and nonprofit services. Depending on the agency, these sectors provide programs for all income levels but target the lower and middle classes in particular. Logically, as income increases, so does the ability to pay more for services; thus, the upper class will use commercial services almost exclusively. This could be for a number of reasons. For example, it may be an attitude of "you get what you pay for" where the commercial sector is seen as higher quality. Arguably, this is not an accurate assessment at all because many public and nonprofit agencies offer recreation services that rival commercial agencies. Another reason for using commercial services over the other two sectors may be a prestige or status issue. Status is assigned to such things as exclusive club memberships or exotic travel destinations booked through a travel agency.

Implications for Recreation and Leisure

Although there are several activities that transcend all social classes such as watching television, reading, or socializing, many others could be placed within each social class almost exclusively. For example, yachting, attending the symphony, or having a second home in the Hamptons would most likely be assigned to the upper class, whereas a trip to Disney World or playing golf at a public course, would more likely be activity choices of the middle classes.

Sometimes there are activities that are popular among all classes, but the way in which they are enjoyed differs. Travel is a common activity to all classes. However, the poor and lower class may take short day or overnight trips and stay with family and friends; the middle class may vacation in a popular tourism destination in the United States and stay at a Holiday Inn; whereas the upper class may take an extended cruise, travel abroad, or stay in a luxury hotel where a night's stay is equal to a month's rent for people in the lower classes.

In ancient Greece, leisure and upper classes were supported by the poor, slaves, and women. In some ways, this has not changed in modern society. The leisure of the middle and upper classes is often supported by the poor and working classes. Take tourism, for example: The economically stable classes travel to destinations and enjoy activities where the workers are making minimum wage. In today's economy, minimum wage is below the poverty level. In addition, when an area is tourism dependent, there is a tendency to drive up the cost of living, including housing and food. This makes it difficult for the workers to live in these communities that provide leisure for the middle and upper classes.

Age, gender, sexual orientation, race, and socioeconomic status all have some impact on leisure activity choices, and it is the responsibility of leisure professionals to understand these impacts and provide services that meet the needs of the community. Because it is not feasible for all agencies to provide services to all people, the different segments and agencies must find their niche and work to understand the needs, leisure patterns, and preferences of their intended population so that no group is underrepresented or denied leisure opportunities.

PROGRESS IN THE NEW MILLENNIUM

Although this chapter deals in detail with many of the past limitations that have affected the ages, genders, people of different sexual orientation, racial and ethnic minorities, and people with different socioeconomic status with respect to recreation and leisure, it must also be stressed that immense progress has been made over the past several decades.

While we have seen changes at all age levels, one age group has had a significant impact over the last 20 years. The aging baby boomers and their economic impact have driven leisure-service providers to rethink traditional services. The need for experiences; desire for physical activity, health, and wellness; and the ability to pay have created a whole new array of program opportunities as people age.

Women and people who identify as LGBT are treated today with far greater respect and have achieved impressive levels of public support—including the right to marry for LGBT—and have access to a wide range of recreational opportunities that were not available to them in the past. Furthermore, women and men alike have been more accepted in activities that are stereotypical for the opposite sex. Many disregard past stigmas and choose activities of interest rather than what they "should" choose.

In terms of race, similar gains have been achieved—particularly for African Americans—even though injustices and forms of discrimination continue. In many cities, particularly in such states as Florida, Texas, and California, large Hispanic American populations have begun to achieve economic success and a degree of political power. Agencies increasingly are recognizing this growth and the need to provide specialized services.

Ability to pay for leisure services by individuals and the ability of agencies to fund free programs for low-income people are issues. With the economy the way it is today, many agencies have to generate income to stay in business, even nonprofit and public entities. So, "pay to play" becomes the norm and, in turn, eliminates the poor and working classes. However, great strides have been made by nonprofit and public agencies to offer services to those who cannot afford them. Many agencies offer program scholarships, programs that are free to the public and supported by sponsors or tax dollars, or they seek local, state, and federal grants to pay for much needed programs. Although access to leisure is not equal, and probably never will be, continuous improvements are being made.

Summary

Major influences on recreation and leisure in contemporary society are the sociocultural factors of age, gender, sexual orientation, race and ethnicity, and socioeconomic status. This chapter defines these terms and shows how they have affected recreational participation in the past and continue to do so today.

As people age, their leisure preferences and patterns change. Children experience a tremendous amount of growth and try different leisure activities. As people enter and move through adulthood, family has a major influence on leisure participation. In an individual's latter years, physical abilities and social elements are key factors in leisure.

As the chapter notes, women and girls have historically been denied many of the leisure opportunities open to men and boys. However, the feminist movement has succeeded in urging colleges, school systems, and community recreation agencies to provide more support to female participants in a wide range of sports and physical activities. This helps women to develop positive self-images and feelings of empowerment. In addition, many women have overcome barriers to professional advancement in various types of agencies in the leisure-service field. Women are also being admitted to business and social groups that had excluded females in the past.

The status of males with respect to recreation and leisure is also discussed. In the past, many men were pressured to adopt stereotypical "macho" roles in leisure activities. Today, they are being encouraged to play a more open, sensitive, and creative role in their recreational pursuits, as well as in domestic life and their relationships.

The issue of sexual orientation is dealt with as well. LGBT people are increasingly gaining acceptance in the United States and are considered a key demographic for leisure-services providers. Not only are they forming their own social and recreational groups, but commercial recreation agencies and tourism bureaus in particular are targeting this group.

There is rapid change going on in the United States in relation to race and ethnicity. Given that not all forms of discrimination have been erased, it is essential that organized recreation services contribute to positive intergroup relations in community life. To better include all groups, parks and recreation services need to be accessible, affordable, safe, culturally relevant, and welcoming. Involving different groups in the planning of programs is a step in the right direction.

Socioeconomic status plays a powerful role in what leisure opportunities are available to people. There is a major difference in the leisure lives of the poor versus the leisure lives of the upper class; as with most other things in society, the upper class has more access than the poor. However, the public and nonprofit sectors understand their responsibility in providing services to a group of people who have a great need for quality recreation near their homes and at a price they can afford.

Questions for Class Discussion or Essay Examination

1.   Select one of the following age groups: children, teens, young adults, middle adults, or older adults. What are this group's special needs for recreation in modern society, and what barriers or problems does it face in the appropriate choice of satisfying leisure activity?

_____

_____

_____

_____

2.   Older adults make up a rapidly growing segment of the population. How has society traditionally considered the aging process and the role of older persons in community life? What new views have developed in recent years? What are the implications of these changes for recreation practitioners working with older persons?

_____

_____

_____

_____

3. How have women's roles with respect to recreation and leisure differed from those of men, in terms of societal attitudes and constraints, throughout history? How have they changed from the past? As a class, have male and female students analyze and compare their gender-related patterns of leisure interests and involvement.

_____

_____

_____

4. Although there is still some resistance to considering LGBT people as a minority population, there has been major progress in terms of their legal standing and status in community life. What issues do you perceive as critical in terms of involving gays and lesbians as identifiable groups in community recreation programs? How has this group been targeted by tourism agencies?

_____

_____

_____

5. In terms of the general cultural scene, members of different racial and ethnic minorities have gained prominence in recent years in film, television, and other artistic or literary areas. What images are generally presented in terms of gender, socioeconomic status, and age?

_____

_____

_____

6. How do you think race, ethnicity, and socioeconomic status interrelate? How is leisure affected by these sociocultural factors?

_____

_____

_____

7. Although LGBT people are increasingly gaining acceptance in the United States, there are still a large number of people who disagree with alternative sexual orientations. Should public agencies, which are supported with public tax dollars, provide programs for LGBT people? Should these same agencies provide programs specifically targeted at specific ethnic or religious groups such as Muslims?

_____

_____

_____

8. Define the three categories of leisure constraints. What constraints do LGBT people face? Men? Women?

_____

_____

_____

9. Differentiate between *race* and *ethnicity*.

_____

_____

_____

10. Define social class. Compare and contrast the leisure of the classes.

_____

_____

_____

_____

Endnotes

1. Welter, J. (June 20, 2016). I'm Here as a Football Coach. http://mmqb.si.com/mmqb/2015/08/04/jen-welter-first-woman-nfl-coach-arizona-cardinals.

2. D. A. Garrahy, Motor development and recreation. In A. R. Hurd and D. M. Anderson, _The Parks and Recreation Professional's Handbook_ (Champaign, IL: Human Kinetics, 2011).

3. G. V. Payne and L. D. Isaacs, _Human Motor Development: A Lifespan Approach_ 8th ed (Boston, MA: McGraw-Hill, 2012).

4. J.P. Isenberg & M. R. Jalongo. (Apr 30, 2014). Why is Play Important? Social and Emotional Development, Physical Development, Creative Development. Pearson Allyn Bacon Prentice Hall. http://www.education.com/reference/article/importance-play--social-emotional/.

5. Montessori, M. (n.d.) Play Is The Work of the Child. Child Development Institute. https://childdevelopmentinfo.com/child-development/play-work-of-children/

6. "Family Structure: Indicators on Children and Youth," Child Trends Databank. (December 2015): http://www.childtrends.org/wp-content/uploads/2015/03/59_Family_Structure.pdf.

7. G.C. Aramas, "Single-Father Homes on the Rise," ABC News (May 18, 2013) http://abcnews.go.com/US/story?id=93279&page=1.

8. D. Cohn, G. Livingston, and W. Wang, "After Decades of Decline, A Rise in Stay-at-Home Mothers," Pew Research Center (April 8, 2014): http://www.pewsocialtrends.org/2014/04/08/after-decades-of-decline-a-rise-in-stay-at-home-mothers/.

9. G. Livingston, "Growing Number of Dads Home with the Kids," Pew Research Center (June 5, 2015): http://www.pewsocialtrends.org/2014/06/05/growing-number-of-dads-home-with-the-kids/.

10. K. C. Mason, "The downside of no downtime for kids," PBS Newshour (July 2, 2015): http://www.pbs.org/newshour/updates/whats-conflicted-parent-scheduling-childs-summer/.

11. A. Michaud, "Michaud: Helicopter Parents Need Some Grounding," _Newsday_ (January 30, 2013): www.newsday.com/opinion/columnists/anne-michaud/michaud-helicopter-parents-need-some-grounding-1.4536491.

12. Parents Television Council, "Facts and TV Statistics," (June 20, 2016): http://w2.parentstv.org/main/Research/Facts.aspx.

13. T. N. Robinson et al., "Effects of Reducing Children's Television and Video Game Use on Aggressive Behavior," _Archives of Pediatrics and Adolescent Medicine_ (Vol. 155): 17–23.

14. R. Louv, _Last Child in the Woods: Saving Our Children from Nature-Deficit Disorder_ (Chapel Hill, NC: Algonquin Books of Chapel Hill, 2005).

15. K. C. Land, _The Foundation for Child Development and Youth Well-Being Index (CWI), 1974–2004, with Projections for 2005_ (Durham, NC: Duke University, 2006).

16. N. Wells and G. Evans, "Nearby Nature: Buffer of Life Stress Among Rural Children," _Environment and Behavior_ (Vol. 35, 2003): 311–330.

17. R. C. Moore and H. H. Hong, _Natural Learning: Creating Environments for Rediscovering Nature's Way of Teaching_ (Berkeley, CA: MIG Communications, 1997).

18. A. F. Taylor et al., "Coping with ADD: This Surprising Connection to Green Play Settings," *Environment Behavior* (Vol. 33, 2001): 54–77.

19. Bureau of Labor Statistics, "Employment and Unemployment Among Youth Summary" (August 18, 2015): http://www.bls.gov/news.release/youth.nr0.htm.

20. National Institute on Drug Abuse, "Monitoring the Future Survey: High School and Youth Trends" (June 2016): https://www.drugabuse.gov/publications/drugfacts/high-school-youth-trends.

21. TeensHealth, "Binge Drinking," (June 22, 2016): http://kidshealth.org/en/teens/binge-drink.html.

22. National Institute on Drug Abuse, "Monitoring the Future Survey: High School and Youth Trends" (December 2012): www.drugabuse.gov/publications/drugfacts/high-school-youth-trends.

23. National Council on Problem Gambling, High School Gambling Fact Sheet: (June 22, 2016): http://www.ncpgambling.org/files/HS_Fact_Sheet.pdf.

24. G. Le, M. Liao, S. Lee, and K. Woo, "Youth Gambling in the 21st Century: Prevalence, Impact, and Interventions," Problem Gambling Prevention Technical Assistance and Training Project (May 29, 2017): http://www.napafasa.org/resources/PGP.Youth%20Gambling%20in%20the%2021st%20Century.pdf

25. Planned Parenthood Federation of America, "Reducing Teenage Pregnancy," (2014): https://www.plannedparenthood.org/files/6813/9611/7632/Reducing_Teen_Pregnancy.pdf.

26. The Henry J. Kaiser Family Foundation, "Sexual Health of Adolescents and Young Adults in the United States" (August 20, 2014): http://kff.org/womens-health-policy/fact-sheet/sexual-health-of-adolescents-and-young-adults-in-the-united-states/.

27. Anderson, M., "How having smartphones (or not) shapes the way teens communicate," Pew Research Center (August 20, 2015): http://www.pewresearch.org/fact-tank/2015/08/20/how-having-smartphones-or-not-shapes-the-way-teens-communicate/.

28. Diana S. DelCampo, *Understanding Teens, Bringing Science to Your Life* (Guide F-122). This worked for me (June 22, 2016): http://aces.nmsu.edu/pubs/_f/F-122.pdf

29. Eileene Welker, "Understanding Teens: Opening the Door to a Better Relationship," News for Parents (June 22, 2016): www.newsforparents.org/expert_understanding_teens.html.

30. A. Renfro. Meeting Generation Z. Getting Smart. (September 21, 2013): http://gettingsmart.com/2012/12/meet-generation-z/.

31. Chew, K. "First-Year College Students Have Record-High Stress" (January 27, 2011): http://www.care2.com/causes/first-year-college-students-have-record-high-stress.html.

32. HomeExchange.com (June 22, 2016): www.homeexchange.com/.

33. The New England Centenarian Study, "Why Study Centenarians? An Overview," Boston University School of Medicine (June 22, 2016): www.bumc.bu.edu/centenarian/overview/.

34. F. R. Dulles, *A History of Recreation: America Learns to Play* (New York: Appleton-Century-Crofts, 1965): 96.

35. K. A. Henderson et al., *Both Gains and Gaps: Feminist Perspectives on Women's Leisure* (State College, PA: Venture Publishing, 1996).

36. National Collegiate Athletic Association (NCAA), "Student Athlete Participation 1981-82–2014-15," Indianapolis, IN: National Collegiate Athletic Association 2015. http://www.ncaa.org/sites/default/files/Participation%20Rates%20Final.pdf.

37. Boyette, J., "Augusta National admits 2 women members" (August 20, 2012): http://www.augusta.com/masters/story/news/latest-news/augusta-national-admits-2-women-members.

38. R. J. Palkovitz, *Involved Fathering and Men's Adult Development: Provisional Balances* (Hillsdale, NJ: Lawrence Erlbaum, 2001).

39. D. J. Eggebeen and C. Knoester, "Does Fatherhood Matter for Men?" *Journal of Marriage and the Family* (Vol. 62, No. 2, 2001): 381–393.

40. Samuels, A. (April 3, 2015). Study: Millennials more accepting of homosexuality than casual sex. USA Today College. (May 29, 2017): http://college.usatoday.com/2015/04/03/study-millennials-more-accepting-of-homosexuality-than-casual-sex/

41. Daily Grind Staff, "America's LGBT Buying Power In 2014 Estimated At $884 billion" (June 25, 2015): http://www.thegailygrind.com/2015/06/25/americas-lgbt-buying-power-in-2014-estimated-at-884-billion/.

42. Philadelphia Gay Tourism Caucus. (June 25, 2016): http://philadelphiagaytourism.com/.

43. R Family Vacations (June 25, 2016): http://www.rfamilyvacations.com/.

44. Lavender Youth Recreation and Information Center. (June 25, 2016): www.lyric.org.

45. *SAGE.* (June 25, 2016): www.sageusa.org.

46. FountainGrove Lodge LGBT Retirement Community: http://www.fountaingrovelodge.com/

47. Population Reference Bureau, "The 2010 Census Questionnaire: Seven Questions for Everyone. (June 25, 2016): www.prb.org/Articles/2009/questionnaire.aspx.

48. Cohn. D., "Census considers new approach to asking about race – by not using the term at all," Pew Research Center (June 18, 2015): http://www.pewresearch.org/fact-tank/2015/06/18/census-considers-new-approach-to-asking-about-race-by-not-using-the-term-at-all/.

49. United States Census Bureau, "2010 Census Shows America's Diversity" (March 24, 2011): www.census.gov/newsroom/releases/archives/2010_census/cb11-cn125.html.

50. Pew Research Center, "America's Changing Religious Landscape: Christians Decline Sharply as Share of Population; Unaffiliated and Other Faiths Continue to Grow" (May 12, 2015): http://www.pewforum.org/2015/05/12/americas-changing-religious-landscape/.

51. B. A. Kosmin and A. Keysar, "American Religious Identification Survey (ARIS 2008)," Trinity College (March, 2009): http://commons.trincoll.edu/aris/files/2011/08/ARIS_Report_2008.pdf.

52. Scott, D. (2014). Race, ethnicity, and leisure services: Can we hope to escape the past? In M. Stodolska, K.J. Shinew, M.F. Floyd & G.J. Walker (Eds.), *Race, ethnicity, and leisure: Perspectives on research, theory and practice* (Champaign, IL: Human Kinetics): 37–50.

53. Mowen, A.J. & Baker, B.L. (2009). Park, recreation, fitness and sport recommendations for a more physically active America: A white paper for the United States National Physical Activity Plan. *Journal of Physical Activity and Health*, 6(Suppl 2): S236–S244.

54. Noonan, D.S. (2005). Neighbours, barriers and urban environments: Are things "different on the other side of the tracks"? *Urban Studies*, 42, 1817–1835.

55. Schneider, I.E., Shinew, K.J., & Fernandez, M. (2014). Leisure constraints. In M. Stodolska, K.J. Shinew, M.F. Floyd & G.J. Walker (Eds.), *Race, ethnicity, and leisure: Perspectives on research, theory and practice* (Champaign, IL: Human Kinetics): 165–176.

56. W. Martin and S. Mason, "Leisure in Three Middle Eastern Countries," *World Leisure* (Vol. 1, 2003): 37–46.

57. J. Livengood and M. Stodolska, "The Effects of Discrimination and Constraints Negotiation on Leisure Behavior of American Muslims in the Post–September 11 America," *Journal of Leisure Research* (Vol. 36, 2004): 183–208.

58. K. van Eijck, "Leisure, Lifestyle, and the New Middle Class," *Leisure Sciences* (Vol. 26, 2004): 373–392.

CHAPTER

4

History of Recreation and Leisure

In the year AD 80, the Roman Colosseum opened with what must stand as quite the longest and most disgusting mass binge in history. Various sorts of large-scale slaughter, both of animals and men, were appreciatively watched by the Empire Titus and packed audient for 100 days.[1]

In the long run, industrialization brought the reduction of work-time. The hours per year committed to work have declined in the industrial West in a range from 3,000–3,600 to 1,800–2,000 from 1840 to present time. This redistribution of time has been accompanied by a drastic "repackaging" of leisure hours.[2]

Today, recreation and leisure services have come to be seen as an opportunity system to improve the quality of life, reduce social pathology, build constructive values in citizens, and generally make communities better places to live.[3]

Learning Objectives

1. Describe changing perceptions of leisure from ancient civilizations through modern day.

2. Describe the impact that religion had on recreation and leisure tolerance.

3. List forms of recreation activities popular during each major time period.

4. Describe current trends in recreation and leisure.

INTRODUCTION

To provide a meaningful background for the study of recreation and leisure in modern society, it is helpful to have a clear understanding of its role in the past. We can trace the origins of many of our contemporary views of leisure and related cultural customs to the traditions and practices of ancient cultures. The history of recreation and leisure is a rich tapestry of people, places, events, and social forces, showing the role of religion, education, and government and the customs and values of different cultures, their arts, sport, and pastimes. By becoming familiar with the evolution of our recreation and leisure, we are better able to understand and deal effectively with the present.

TRIBAL VIEW OF WORK AND LEISURE

Tribal people do not make the same sharp distinction between work and leisure that more technologically advanced societies do. Whereas the latter set aside different periods of time for work and relaxation, a tribal, pretechnological society has no such precise separations. Instead, work is customarily done when it is available or necessary, and it is often infused with rites and customs that lend it variety and pleasure. In such tribal societies, work tends to be varied and creative, rather than being a narrow, specialized task demanding a sharply defined skill, as in modern industry. Work is often accompanied by ritual that is regarded as essential to the success of the planting or harvesting or to the building or hunting expedition. The ritual may involve prayer, sacrifice, dance, or feasting, which thus becomes part of the world of work.

THE PLAY OF EARLY SOCIETIES

Relatively little is known about the nature of leisure and play in the early periods of the Paleolithic and Neolithic epochs. However, between archaeologists' discovery of artifacts providing evidence of leisure activities and societal accounts by missionaries and anthropologists, we have some understanding of early play.

ORIGINS OF GAMES AND SPORT

In primitive societies, play may have had many sources. Popular games were often vestiges of warfare, practiced as a form of sport. Musical instruments were likely created for use in religious rituals. Pottery, painting, drawings, and other early art provided a record of both daily life and cultural mythology. Beads and other types of jewelry were created as external symbols of individual status and group affiliations. When an activity was no longer useful in its original form (such as archery for hunting or warfare), it became a form of sport.

Native American tribes offer an example of how play was used to equip the young for adult life. Boys practiced warriors' skills and were taught to survive unarmed and unclothed in the wilderness. Girls were taught the household crafts expected of mature women. Through dancing, singing, and storytelling, both sexes learned the history and religion of their cultures.

RECREATION AND LEISURE IN ANCIENT CIVILIZATIONS

As prehistoric societies advanced, they developed specialization of functions. Humans learned to domesticate plants and animals, which permitted them to shift from a nomadic existence based on hunting and food gathering to a largely stationary way of life. Ultimately, ruling classes developed, along with soldiers, craftsmen, peasants, and slaves. As villages and cities evolved and large estates were farmed by lower-class workers, the upper classes gained power, wealth, and leisure. Thus, in the aristocracy of the first civilizations that developed in the Middle East during the five millennia before the Christian era, we find for the first time in history a leisure class.

Ancient Egypt, Assyria, and Babylonia

The Egyptian culture, lasting from about 5000 BC into the Roman era, was a rich and diversified one; it achieved an advanced knowledge of astronomy, architecture, engineering, agriculture, and construction. The culture was richly recorded in paintings, statuary, and hieroglyphic records. The ancient Egyptians engaged in many sports as part of education and recreation, including wrestling, gymnastic exercises, lifting and swinging weights, and ball games. Music, drama, and dance were forms of religious worship as well as social entertainment with complex orchestras that included various stringed and percussive instruments.

Early Chinese societies developed highly organized cultural events.
©IMAGEMORE Co, Ltd./Getty.

ARCHEOLOGISTS UNCOVER ANCIENT FLUTES USED IN CULTURAL CELEBRATION

In a period ranging from May 1986 to June 1987, archaeologists at the early Neolithic site of Jiahu in Henan Province, China, uncovered 25 flutes between 7,000 and 9,000 years old, most at grave sites. Six of the instruments were intact and are now believed to be the earliest, playable multinote instruments. The flutes, which were made of bone, contain seven holes that correspond to a scale similar to the Western eight-note scale. This tone scale indicates that musicians living in 7000 BC could compose and play music. Some believe that the flutes were part of religious rituals; others believe that music was simply a part of community life.[4]

Until the invasion by Alexander the Great in 330 BC, middle-eastern countries Assyria and Babylon were also powerful empires. Like the ancient Egyptians, the Assyrians and Babylonians had many popular recreation activities, such as boxing, wrestling, archery, and a variety of table games. In addition to watching dancing, listening to music, and giving banquets, Assyrians, particularly nobles, were also devoted to hunting, often in established parks.

Ancient Israel

Among the ancient Israelites, music and dancing were performed for ritual purposes as well as for social activities and celebrations as referenced in the Old Testament. Like other ancient societies, the ancient Hebrews also engaged in hunting, fishing, wrestling, and the use of such weapons as the sword and javelin for both recreational and defensive purposes. As for leisure itself, their major contribution was to set aside the Sabbath as a time for people to rest from work and to worship.

The highest form of leisure usually occurred among the elite in ancient societies.
© Pavel Mitrofanov/Dreamstime.com.

Ancient Greece

In the city-states of ancient Greece, particularly in Athens during the so-called Golden Age of Pericles from about 500 to 400 BC, humankind reached a new peak of philosophical and cultural development. The Athenians took great interest in the arts, in learning, and in athletics. These pursuits were generally restricted to wellborn, aristocratic noblemen. Craftsmen, farmers, and tradespeople were also citizens but had limited rights and less prestige, and labor was performed by slaves and foreigners.

The amenities of life were generally restricted to the most wealthy and powerful citizens, who represented the Athenian ideal of the balanced man—a combined soldier, athlete, artist, statesman, and philosopher. In fact, Athenian philosophers believed strongly in the unity of mind and body and that play activity was essential to the healthy physical and social growth of children. This ideal was furthered through education and the various religious festivals, which occupied about 70 days of the year. The arts of music, poetry, theater, gymnastics, and athletic competition were combined in these sacred competitions.

The ancient Greeks developed the art of town planning and customarily made extensive provisions for parks and gardens, open-air theaters and gymnasiums, baths, exercise grounds, and stadiums. Early Athens had many public baths and some public parks, which later gave way to privately owned estates.

A gradual transition occurred in the Greek approach to leisure and play. At first, all citizens were expected to participate in sports and games, and the Olympic Games were restricted to free-born Greeks only. Gradually,

WOMEN IN ANCIENT GREECE

Women did not enjoy the leisurely pursuits of men in ancient Greece, although there are some historical accounts of women receiving modest education and young girls participating in some athletic competitions. Citizens were, by definition, men.

however, the religious and cultural functions of the Olympic Games and other festivals were weakened by athletic specialization, corruption, and commercialism. In time, sport and other forms of activity such as drama, singing, and dance were performed only by highly skilled specialists drawn from the lower classes or even slaves.

Ancient Rome

Like the Greek city-states, the Roman republic during its early development was a vigorous and nationalistic state. The Roman citizen, although part of a privileged class, was required to defend his society and fight in its wars. Citizens participated in sport and gymnastics, intended to keep the body strong and the spirit courageous. Numerous games held in connection with the worship of various Roman gods later developed into annual festivals. The most important of the Roman games were those that celebrated military triumphs, usually held in honor of the god Jupiter, heads of the Roman pantheon.

Like the early Greeks, young Roman children had toy carts, houses, dolls, hobbyhorses, stilts, and tops and engaged in many sports and games. The Romans, however, had a different concept of leisure than the Greeks. Although the Latin words for "leisure" and "business" are *otium* and *negotium*, suggesting the same view of leisure as a positive value (with work defined negatively as a lack of leisure), the Romans supported play for utilitarian rather than aesthetic or spiritual reasons.

Even more than the Greeks, the Romans were systematic planners and builders. Their towns generally included provisions for baths, open-air theaters, amphitheaters, forums for public assemblies, stadiums, gymnasiums, and sometimes parks and gardens. Wealthier Romans often had private villas, many with large gardens and hunting preserves.

As the empire grew more powerful, the simple agricultural democracy of the early years, in which all male Romans were citizens and free men, shifted to an urban life with sharply divided classes. There were four social levels: the richest, land-holding *senators*; the *curiae*, who owned more than 25 acres of land and were officeholders or tax collectors; the *plebs*, or free common people, who owned small properties or were tradesmen or artisans; and the *coloni*, who were lower-class tenants of the land. In time, a huge urban population of plebs lived in semi-idleness because most of the work was done by *coloni* and slaves brought to Rome. Gradually, it became necessary for the Roman emperors and senate to amuse and entertain the *plebs*; they did so with doles of grain and with public games—in other words, "bread and circuses."

As early as the reign of the Emperor Claudius in the first century AD, there were 159 public holidays during the year, 93 of which were devoted to games at public expense. By AD 354, there were 200 public holidays each year, including 175 days of games. Even on working days, the labor began at daybreak and ended shortly after noon during much of the year.

As leisure increased with the necessity for military service and other forms of physical effort declining for the Roman citizen, the normal practice was for the citizen to be entertained or to follow a daily routine of exercise, bathing, and eating. No longer as active in sport as they once had been, the men now sought to be amused and to entertain their guests with paid acrobats, musicians, dancers, and other artists. Athletes performed as members of a specialized profession with unions, coaches, and training schools.

The Roman Colosseum is considered one of the greatest architectural achievements of antiquity. Built almost 2000 years ago, the Colosseum is a monument to the achievements and culture of ancient Rome.
© Tan, Kim Pin/Shutterstock.

Corruption of Entertainment Gradually, the focus on the traditional sports of running, throwing, and jumping gave way to an emphasis on human combat—first boxing and wrestling and then displays of cruelty in which gladiators fought to the death for the entertainment of mass audiences. Imported wild beasts, such as tigers and elephants, were pitted against each other or against human antagonists, often Christians.[5] Both animals and humans were maimed and butchered in cruel and horrible ways. By this time, competitive sport had become completely commercialized. To maintain political popularity and placate the bored masses, the emperors and the senate provided great parades, circuses, and feasts. Spectacles were often lewd and obscene, leading to mass debauchery, corruption, and perversion that profoundly weakened the Roman state.

EARLY CHRISTIAN ERA: DARK AND MIDDLE AGES

Under attack by successive waves of northern European tribes, the Roman Empire finally collapsed. For a period of several centuries, Europe was overrun

CHANGE COMES TO THE ROMAN LIFE IN THE DARK AND MIDDLE AGES

Many aspects of Roman life were forbidden during the Dark and Middle Ages. The stadiums, amphitheaters, and baths that had characterized Roman life were destroyed. The Council of Elvira ruled that the rite of baptism could not be extended to those connected with the stage, and in AD 398, the Council of Carthage excommunicated those who attended the theater on holy days. The Roman emphasis on leisure was replaced by a Christian emphasis on work. It would be a mistake, however, to assume that the Catholic Church eliminated all forms of play. Many early Catholic religious practices were based on the rituals of earlier faiths. Priests built churches on existing shrines or temple sites, set Christian holy days according to the dates of pagan festivals, and used such elements of pagan worship as bells, candles, incense, singing, and dancing.

with warring tribes and shifting alliances. The organized power of Rome, which had built roads, extended commerce, and provided civil order, was at an end. Gradually, the Catholic Church emerged to provide a form of universal citizenship within Europe. Having suffered under the brutal persecutions of the Romans, the early Christians condemned all that their pagan oppressors had stood for—especially their hedonistic way of life. Indeed, the early church fathers believed in a fanatical asceticism, which in the Byzantine, or Eastern, Empire was marked by the Anchorite movement, with its idea of salvation through masochistic self-deprivation.

Pastimes in the Middle Ages

Despite disapproval from the church, many forms of play continued during the Middle Ages. Medieval society was marked by rigid class stratification; below the nobility and clergy were the peasants, who were divided into such ranks as freemen, villeins, serfs, and slaves.

Life in the Middle Ages, even for the feudal nobility, was crude and harsh. Manors and castles were little more than stone fortresses. Knights were responsible for fighting in the service of their rulers; between wars, their favorite pastimes were hunting and hawking, with hunting serving as a useful preparation for war. Other pastimes during the Middle Ages were various types of games and gambling, music and dance, sport, and jousting. Gambling was popular, although forbidden by both ecclesiastical and royal authority.

As the chaos of the Dark Ages yielded to greater order and regularity, life became more stable. Travel in reasonable safety became possible, and by the eleventh century, commerce was widespread. The custom of jousting emerged within the medieval courts, stemming from the tradition that only the nobility fought on horseback.

Games of the Common People   Edward Hulme suggests that life was not all work for the lower classes. There were village feasts and sport, practical joking, throwing weights, cockfighting, bull baiting, and other lively games. As life in the Middle Ages became somewhat easier, a number of pastimes emerged. Many modern sports were developed at this time in rudimentary form. Peasants usually went to bed at dark, reading was a rare accomplishment, and there was much drinking and crude brawling.

The people of the Middle Ages had an insatiable love of sightseeing and would travel great distances to see entertainment. When the kings of France assembled their principal retainers once or twice a year, they distributed food and liquor among the common people and provided military displays, court ceremonies, and entertainment by jugglers, tumblers, and minstrels.

THE RENAISSANCE

Following the Dark Ages (AD 400–1000) and High Middle Ages, the Renaissance is said to have begun in Italy about AD 1350, in France about 1450, and in England about 1500. It marked a transition between the medieval world and the modern age. The term renaissance means rebirth and describes the revived interest in the scholarship, philosophy, and arts of ancient Greece and Rome. More broadly, it also represented a new freedom of thought and expression, a more rational and scientific view of life, and the expansion of commerce and travel in European life.

As the major European nations stabilized during this period under solidly established monarchies, power shifted from the church to the kings and their noblemen. Particularly in Italy and France, the nobility became patrons of great painters, sculptors, musicians, dancers, and dramatists.

Play as Education

Varied forms of play became part of the education of the youth of the nobility at this time. The Athenian philosophy that had supported play as an important form of education was given fuller emphasis during the Renaissance, with an emphasis on the need for physical exercises and games as well as singing, dancing, modeling and painting, nature study, and manual training.

INFLUENCE OF THE PROTESTANT REFORMATION

The Reformation was a religious movement of the 1500s that resulted in the establishment of a number of Protestant sects whose leaders broke away from Roman Catholicism. It was part of a broader stream that included economic, social, and political currents. In part, it represented the influence of the growing middle classes, who allied with the nobility in the emerging nations of Europe to challenge the power of the church.

The "Protestant work ethic" that emerged during the Reformation led to periods of strict limitations on leisure and recreation throughout the history of many Christian cultures, including societies in North America. This same ethic has heavily influenced our contemporary Western views of the relative value of work and leisure.

Puritanism in England

The English Puritans waged a constant battle to limit or condemn sport and other forms of entertainment during the period from the sixteenth to the eighteenth century. Maintaining strict observation of the Sabbath was a particular issue. Anglican clergy during the Elizabethan period bitterly attacked stage plays, church festival gatherings, dancing, gambling, bowling, and other "devilish pastimes" such as hawking and hunting, holding fairs and markets, and reading "lascivious and wanton books."

Types of Major Parks

During the Middle Ages, park planning was characterized in the city by a lack of space or open areas, and as residents moved out from the city, a lack of planning for satellite communities. However, as the Renaissance period began, European town planning was characterized by wide avenues, long approaches, handsome buildings, and similar monumental features, with nobility decorating their estates with elaborate gardens.

Three major types of large parks came into existence during the late Renaissance. In almost every instance, they were derived from private estates of nobles or the elite. The first were royal hunting preserves or parks, some of which have become famous public parks today, such as the 4,000-acre Prater in Vienna and the Tiergarten in Berlin. Second were the ornate and formal garden parks designed according to the so-called French style of landscape architecture. Third were the more naturalistic English garden parks.

In England, efforts at city planning began during the eighteenth century. Business and residential streets were paved and street names posted. Because it was believed that overcrowding led to disease (in the seventeenth century, London had suffered from recurrent attacks of the plague), an effort was made to convert open squares into gardens and to create more small parks. Deaths from contagious disease declined during each successive decade of the eighteenth century, and this improvement was believed to have been the result of increased cleanliness and ventilation within the city.

The English natural park school of thought emphasized using nature as the primary tool of creating a park rather than adding non-native species of plants to a park.
© Chris Lofty/Dreamstime.com.

THE PROTESTANT PURITANISM

The new Protestant sects tended to be more solemn and austere than the Catholic Church. Calvin established an autocratic system of government in Geneva in 1541 that was directed by a group of Presbyters, morally upright men who controlled the social and cultural life of the community to the smallest detail. They ruthlessly suppressed heretics and burned dissenters at the stake. Miller and Robinson describe the unbending Puritanism in Geneva:

"Purity of conduct" was insisted upon, which meant the forbidding of gambling, card playing, dancing, wearing of finery, singing of gay songs, feasting, drinking and the like. There were to be no more festivals, no more theaters, no more ribaldry, no more light and disrespectful poetry or display. Works of art and musical instruments were removed from the churches.[6]

Popular Diversions in England

Great outdoor gardens were established in England to provide entertainment and relaxation. Vauxhall, a pleasure resort founded during the reign of Charles II, was a densely wooded area with walks and bowers, lighting displays, water mills, fireworks, artificial caves and grottoes, entertainment, eating places, and tea gardens. The park was supported by the growing class of merchants and tradesmen, and its admission charge and distance from London helped to "exclude the rabble."

Among the lower classes, tastes in entertainment varied according to whether one lived in the country or city. Countrymen continued to engage vigorously in such sport as football, cricket, wrestling, or "cudgel playing" and to enjoy traditional country or Morris dancing and the singing of old folk songs.

Concerns About Leisure: Class Differences

Gradually, concerns about the growing number of holidays and the effect of leisure activities on the working classes began to be voiced. For example, in France during the eighteenth century, wealthy individuals had the opportunity for amusement all week long—paying social visits, dining, and passing evenings at gaming, at the theater, ballet, opera, or clubs. In contrast, the working classes had only Sundays and fête days, or holidays, for their amusements. La Croix points out, however, that these represented a third of the whole year. This excess in time off led many economists and men of affairs to argue that the ecclesiastic authorities should be called upon to reduce the number.

RECREATION IN AMERICA: THE COLONIAL PERIOD

We now cross the Atlantic to examine the development of recreation and leisure in the early American colonies. First, it needs to be recognized that when English and other European settlers came to the New World, they did not entirely divorce themselves from the customs and values of the countries they had left. Commerce was ongoing; governors and military personnel traveled back and forth; and newspapers, magazines, and books were exchanged regularly.

The first need of seventeenth-century colonists was for survival. They had to plant crops, clear forests, build shelters, and in some cases defend themselves against attack by hostile Native American tribes. In such a setting, work was all-important; there was little time, money, or energy to support amusements or public entertainment. Without nobility possessing the wealth, leisure, and inclination to patronize the arts, there was little opportunity for music, theater, or dance to flourish—but the most important hindrance to the development of recreation was the religious attitude.

Restrictions in New England

The Puritan settlers of New England came to the New World to establish a society based on a strict Calvinist interpretation of the Bible. Although the work ethic had not originated with the Puritans, they adopted it enthusiastically. Idleness was detested as the "devil's workshop," and a number of colonies passed laws binding "any rougs, vagabonds, sturdy beggards, masterless men or other notorious offenders" over to compulsory work or imprisonment.

Puritan magistrates attempted to maintain curbs on amusements long after the practical reasons for such prohibitions had disappeared. Early court records show many cases of young people being fined, confined to the stocks, or publicly whipped for such "violations" as drunkenness, idleness, gambling, dancing, or participating in other forms of "lascivious" behavior. However, despite these restrictions, many forms of play continued. Football was played by boys in Boston's streets and lanes, and although playing cards (the "devil's picture-books") were hated by the Puritans, they were freely imported from England and openly on sale.

Other ordinances banned gambling, drama, and nonreligious music, with dancing—particularly between men and women—also condemned. There was vigorous enforcement of the Sabbath laws: Sunday work, travel, and recreation—even "unnecessary and unseasonable walking in the streets and fields"—were prohibited.

The U.S. southern economy was built on the labor of slaves who had little time for recreation, which allowed slave owners to create a life of leisure and luxury.

Courtesy of Library of Congress, Prints & Photographs Division [reproduction number LC-USZ62-76385].

PLAY ATTACHED TO WORK GAINS ACCEPTANCE

Gradually, restrictions against play were relaxed in New England and elsewhere. Recreation became more acceptable when amusements could be attached to work, and thus country fairs and market days became occasions for merrymaking. Social gatherings with music, games, and dancing were held in conjunction with such work projects as house raisings, sheep shearing, logrolling, or cornhusking bees. Many social pastimes were linked to other civic occasions such as elections or training days for local militia.

Leisure in the Southern Colonies

A number of the southern colonies had similar restrictions during the early years of settlement. The laws of Virginia, for example, forbade Sunday amusements and made imprisonment the penalty for failure to attend church services. Sabbath-day dancing, fiddling, hunting, fishing, and card playing were strictly banned. Gradually, however, these stern restrictions declined in the southern colonies. There, the upper classes had both wealth and leisure from their large estates and plantations, on which the labor was performed by indentured servants and slaves. As southern settlers of this social class became established, plantation life for the upper class became marked by lavish entertainment and hospitality.

The lifestyles of slaves in the colonies were a stark contrast to the lavish lifestyles of their owners. The majority of slaves in the colonies were of West African ancestry. They were able to bring nothing with them to the colonies other than language and customs, both of which they were compelled to disregard upon arrival. The customs that thrived in the harsh life of the colonies included music, folktales and storytelling, and dance. In the colonies, and later in the southern states, slaves had very few opportunities for leisure. Slave masters used free time as a "reward" to improve morale and often enforced strict rules about what could happen during that free time.

Decline of Religious Controls

Despite the stern sermons of New England ministers and the severe penalties for infractions of the established moral code, it is clear that play became gradually tolerated in the colonies. The lottery was introduced during the early 1700s and quickly gained the sanction and participation of the most esteemed citizens. Towns and states used lotteries to increase their revenues and to build canals, turnpikes, and bridges. This "acceptable" form of gambling helped to endow leading colleges and academies, and even Congregational, Baptist, and Episcopal churches had lotteries "for promoting public worship and the advancement of religion."

The climate around drinking began to change despite the fact that under Puritan law, drunkards were subject to fines and imprisonment in the stocks, and sellers were forbidden to provide them with any liquor thereafter. By the early part of the eighteenth century, taverns were widely established throughout New England. By the mid-1700s, the stern necessity of hard work for survival had lessened, and religious antagonism toward amusements had also declined.

The Boston Common, often credited as the first community park in the United States because of its 1634 creation, continues to provide opportunities for recreation and park experiences.
© Marcos Carvalho/Shutterstock.

Parks and Conservation in the Colonial Era

Early American colonies showed little concern for developing parks in cities and towns with open space so plentiful around the isolated settlements. The earliest planned outdoor spaces were "commons" or "greens," found in many New England communities and used chiefly for pasturing cattle and sheep, but also for military drills, market days, and fairs. Similar open areas such as plazas were established in towns settled by the Spanish in the South and Southwest. As urban areas grew, cities such as Philadelphia, Savannah, and Washington, D.C. were among the first to give attention to the need for preserving or establishing parks and open spaces.

Early Conservation Efforts

From the early days of settlement, there was concern for the conservation of forests and open land in the New England countryside. As early as 1626 in the Plymouth Colony, the cutting of trees without official consent was prohibited by law. The Massachusetts Bay Colony passed the

Great Ponds Act in 1641, which set aside 2,000 bodies of water for such public uses as "fishing and fowling." Pennsylvania law in 1681 required that for every 5 acres of forest land that were cleared, 1 was to be left untouched.

As early as the late seventeenth century, Massachusetts and Connecticut defined hunting seasons and established rules for hunting certain types of game. As wildlife populations sharply fell, provinces such as New York started providing for closed seasons to protect different species. It is apparent that the colonists had shown a concern for the establishment of parks and urban open spaces and for the conservation of forests and wildlife in early days.

NINETEENTH-CENTURY CHANGES: IMPACT OF THE INDUSTRIAL REVOLUTION

During the late eighteenth through the twentieth century, great changes took place in both Europe and the United States. It was a time of growing democratization, advancement of scientific knowledge and technology, and huge waves of immigration from Europe to the New World. More than any other factor, the Industrial Revolution changed the way people lived. By the early twentieth century, leisure was more freely available to all, and a widespread recreation movement had begun in the United States.

Science and capital combined to increase production, as businessmen invested in the industrial expansion made possible by newly invented machines. Industry moved from homes and workshops to new mills and factories with mechanical power. The invention of such devices as the spinning jenny, the weaving machine, and the steam engine (all during the 1760s) drastically altered production methods and increased output.

THE CHANGING WORKWEEK

Overall, the average workweek declined from 69.7 hours per week for all industries (including agriculture) in 1860 to 61.7 hours in 1890, and to 54.9 hours in 1910 (see **Figure 4.1**). As a consequence, during the last half of the nineteenth century, concerns about increases in free time began to appear—including fears about the dangers of certain forms of play and the broader question of what the potential role of leisure might be in the coming century.

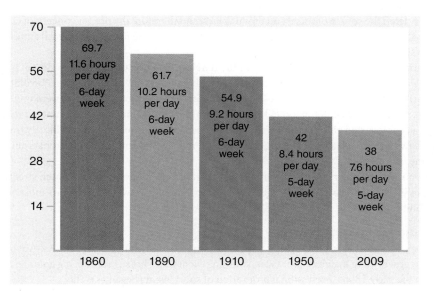

FIGURE 4.1 How the Average Workweek Has Changed (in hours)

Data from the Bureau of Labor Statistics. 2009. Available at: http://www.bls.gov. Accessed November 10, 2010.

Urbanization

Throughout the Western world, there was a steady shift of the population from rural areas to urban centers. Because factory wages were usually higher than those in domestic industry or agriculture, great numbers of people migrated to the cities. Millions of European peasant families emigrated because of crop failures, expulsion from their land, religious or social discrimination, or political unrest. During the latter part of the nineteenth century, tens of thousands of African Americans, disillusioned by the failed Reconstruction, immigrated to northern cities in search of a better quality of life.

The American population increased rapidly during this period. From 1829 to 1860, America's population had grown from 12.5 to 31 million. In the large cities, the proportion of foreign-born inhabitants was quite high: 45% of New York City's population in 1850 was foreign born, mostly Irish and German. While 85% of the population in 1850 was still rural, as more and more people moved into factory towns and large cities, the United States became an urban civilization.

Rural townspeople and foreign immigrants moved into the congested tenement areas of growing cities, living in quarters that were inadequate for decent family life with slums marked by congestion and disease. Their residents were oppressed by low wages and recurrent unemployment and by monotonous and prolonged labor, including the use of young children in mills, mines, and factories and at piecework tasks at home.

Reduction in Work Hours

Throughout this period, there was steady pressure to reduce the workweek, both through industry-labor negotiation and legislation. Benjamin Hunnicutt points out that the effort to obtain shorter work hours was a critical issue in reform politics in the United States throughout the nineteenth century and up until the period of the Great Depression.

The eight-hour day had been a union objective for many years in the United States, paralleling efforts to reduce the workweek in other countries. In 1868, Congress established the eight-hour day for mechanics and laborers employed by or under contracts with the federal government. Following the 1868 law, labor unions made a concerted effort to obtain the eight-hour day in other areas, and in 1890 began to achieve success.

Religious Revivalism and Recreation

Fueled by a religious revival before the Civil War, there was a strong emphasis on the importance of "honest toil" during the middle and latter parts of the nineteenth century. Many Americans believed, and continue to believe, that hard work alone is sufficient for an individual to improve his or her social and economic status. Clergy, policy makers, civic leaders, and scholars were particularly concerned that new immigrants and the urban poor develop appropriate social values through hard work and appropriate, disciplined use of leisure time.

Churches Attack Leisure

Work was considered the source of social and moral values, and therefore the proper concern of churches, which renewed their attack upon most forms of play. The churches condemned many commercial amusements as "the door to all the sins of iniquity."

Despite antiamusement efforts, the first half of the nineteenth century saw an expansion of popular amusements in the United States. The theater, which had been banned during the American Revolution, gradually gained popularity in cities along the eastern seaboard and in the South. Large theaters were built to accommodate audiences of as many as 4,000 people. Local stock companies throughout the country presented serious drama as well as lighthearted entertainment, which later became burlesque and vaudeville. By the 1830s, about 30 traveling shows were regularly touring the country with menageries and bands of acrobats and jugglers, ultimately evolving into circuses.

Drinking remained popular as the majority of American men were taverngoers. Printed street directories of American cities listed tavern keepers in staggering numbers, and taverns were the nation's most popular centers of male sociability.

Growing Interest in Sport

A number of sports gained their first strong impetus during the early nineteenth century. Americans enjoyed watching amateur wrestling matches, foot races, shooting events, and horse races during colonial days and along the frontier. In the early 1800s, professional promotion of sport events began as well.

Professionalism in Sport   Crowds as large as 50,000 from all ranks of society attended highly publicized boating regattas and 5- and 10-mile races of professional runners during the 1820s. The first sport promoters

☀ SOCIAL CLASS IMPACTS SPORT

Social class differences had a strong influence on sport involvement and attendance. George Will points out that professional baseball initially appealed to the brawling urban working classes:

> The sport was so tangled up with gambling and drinking that its first task was to attract a better class of fans. This it did by raising ticket prices, banning beer, not playing on Sundays, and giving free tickets to the clergy. Most important, baseball replaced wooden ball parks with permanent structures of concrete and steel [with impressive lobbies and other architectural features].[7]

were owners of resorts or of commercial transportation facilities such as stagecoach lines, ferries, and later, trolleys and railroads. These new sport impresarios initially made their profits from transportation fares and accommodations for spectators; later, they erected grandstands and charged admission. Horse racing, boxing, and basketball were among the first sports to gain large followings.

CHANGING ATTITUDES TOWARD PLAY

During the last half of the nineteenth century, the Industrial Revolution was flourishing, with factories, expansion of urban areas, and railroads crisscrossing the country. Free public education had become a reality in most areas, and health care and life expectancy were improving. As the industrial labor force began to organize into craft unions, working conditions improved, levels of pay increased, and the hours of work were cut back. Children who had worked long, hard hours in factories, mines, and big-city sweatshops were freed of this burden through child labor legislation while the strong disapproval of play that had characterized the colonial period began to disappear.

Sailing regattas were a popular form of recreation and a popular spectator sport in the early 1800s.
Courtesy of Library of Congress, Prints & Photographs Division [reproduction number LC-DIG-pga-00437].

By the 1880s and 1890s, church leaders recognized that religion could no longer arbitrarily condemn all play and offered "sanctified amusement and recreation" as alternatives to undesirable play. Many churches made provisions for libraries, gymnasiums, and assembly rooms.

Popular hobbies such as photography caught on and were frequently linked to new outdoor recreation pursuits. Sport was probably the largest single area of expanded leisure participation, with increasing interest being shown in tennis, archery, bowling, skating, bicycling, and team games such as baseball, basketball, and football.

The Muscular Christianity movement—so named because of the support given to it by leading church figures and because sport and physical activity were thought to build morality and good character—had its greatest influence in schools and colleges, which began to initiate programs of physical education and athletic competition.

College Sport

In the United States, colleges initiated their first competitive sports programs. In colonial New England, students had engaged in many pastimes, with some tolerated by college authorities and others prohibited. The first

☀ RISE OF SPORT

As the country neared the end of the nineteenth century, a series of athletic crazes swept through the eastern states.

> Baseball developed from its humble beginnings in the days before the Civil War to its recognized status as America's national game. The rapid spread of croquet caused the startled editors of The Nation to describe it as "the swiftest and most infectious epidemic the country had ever experienced. Lawn tennis was introduced to polite society by enthusiasts," and "archery was revived as still another fashionable lawn game. Roller-skating attained a popularity which extended to all parts of the country."[8]

college clubs had been founded as early as 1717, and social clubs were in full swing by the 1780s and 1790s. By the early nineteenth century, most U.S. colleges had more or less recognized clubs and their social activities. The founding of social fraternities in the 1840s and the building of college gymnasiums in the 1860s added to the social life and physical recreation of students.

Intercollegiate sport competition in rowing, baseball, track, and football was organized. The first known intercollegiate football game was between Princeton and Rutgers in 1869; interest spread rapidly, and by the late 1880s, college football games were attracting as many as 40,000 spectators.

Amateur Sport

Track and field events were widely promoted by amateur athletic clubs, some of which, like the New York Athletic Club, had many influential members who formed the Amateur Athletic Union and developed rules to govern amateur sport competition. Gymnastic instruction and games were sponsored by the German turnvereins, the Czech sokols, and the YMCA, which had established some 260 large gymnasiums around the country by the 1880s and was a leader in sport activities.

Other Activities

Women began to participate in recreational pastimes, enjoying gymnastics, dance, and other athletics in school and college physical education programs. Bicycling was introduced in the 1870s, and within a few years, hundreds of thousands of people had become enthusiasts. Moving outdoors, Americans also began to enjoy hiking and mountain climbing, fishing and hunting, camping in national forests and state parks, and nature photography.

GROWTH OF COMMERCIAL AMUSEMENTS

Particularly in larger cities, new forms of commercial amusement sprang up or expanded during the nineteenth century. The theater was more popular than ever. Dime museums, dance halls, shooting galleries, bowling alleys, billiard parlors, beer gardens, and saloons provided a new world of entertainment for pay. In addition to these, many cities had "red light districts" where prostitution flourished. Drinking, gambling, and commercial vice gradually became serious social problems, particularly when protected by a tacit alliance between criminal figures and big-city political machines.

Amusement parks grew on the outskirts of cities and towns, often established by new rapid transit companies offering reduced-fare rides to the parks in decorated trolley cars. Amusement parks featured such attractions as parachute jumps, open-air theaters, band concerts, professional bicycle races, freak shows, games of chance, and shooting galleries. Roller coasters, fun houses, and midget-car tracks also became popular[9].

Concerns About Leisure

Intellectual and political leaders raised questions about the growing amusement industry and new forms of recreation impacted by the growing urban centers of population. The English author Lord Lytton commented, "The social civilization of a people is always and infallibly indicated by the intellectual character of its amusements." In 1876, American journalist Horace Greeley observed that although there were teachers for every art, science, and "elegy," there were no "professors of play." He asked, "Who will teach us incessant workers how to achieve leisure and enjoy it?" And, in 1880, President James Garfield declared in a speech at Lake Chautauqua, "We may divide the whole struggle of the human race into two chapters: first, the fight to get leisure; and then the second fight of civilization—what shall we do with our leisure when we get it."

The Beginning Recreation Movement

The period extending from the mid-nineteenth through the early twentieth century is referred to by recreation scholars as the public recreation movement. The period was characterized by the widespread development of organized recreation activities and facilities by government and voluntary agencies with the intent of achieving desirable social outcomes. There were four major streams of development during the public recreation movement: the adult education movement; the development of national, state, and municipal parks; the establishment of voluntary organizations; and the playground movement.

The Adult Education Movement

During the early nineteenth century, there was considerable civic concern for improving intellectual cultivation and providing continuing education for adults. Again, this was found in other nations as well; in France, workers' societies were determined to gain shorter workdays and more leisure time for adult study and cultural activities.

In the United States, there was a growing conviction that leisure, properly used, could contribute to the idealistic liberal values that were part of the American intellectual heritage. One of the means of achieving this took the form of the Lyceum movement, a national organization with more than 900 local chapters. Its program consisted chiefly of lectures, readings, and other educational events, reflecting the view that all citizens should be educated to participate knowledgeably in affairs of government.

A closely related development was the expansion of reading as a recreational experience, which was furthered by the widespread growth of free public libraries that supported the increasing need for better educated workers. As an example of the growing interest in cultural activity, the arts and crafts movement found its largest following in the United States in the beginning of the twentieth century.

The Development of National, State, and Municipal Parks

Concern for preservation of the natural heritage of the United States in an era of increasing industrialization and despoilment of natural resources began in the nineteenth century. The first conservation action was passed in 1864, when Congress set aside an extensive area of wilderness primarily for public recreational use, consisting of the Yosemite Valley and the Mariposa Grove of Big Trees in California. This later became a national park. The first designated national park was Yellowstone, founded in 1872. In 1892, the Sierra Club was founded by John Muir, a leading Scottish-born conservationist who, along with Theodore Roosevelt, encouraged national interest in the outdoors and ultimately the establishment of the National Park Service.

The primary purpose of the national parks at the outset was to preserve the nation's natural heritage and wildlife. This contrasted sharply with the Canadian approach to wilderness, which saw it as primitive and untamed. Parks, as in Great Britain and Europe, were seen as landscaped gardens, and intensive development for recreation and tourism guided early Canadian policy. Indeed, Banff National Park was initially a health spa, and early provincial parks were designed to be health resorts[10].

©Library of Congress, LC-USZ62-52000.

State Parks   As federal park development gained momentum in the United States, state governments also became concerned with the preservation of their forest areas and wildlife. As early as 1867, Michigan and Wisconsin established fact-finding committees to explore the problem of forest conservation; their example was followed shortly by Maine and other eastern states. Between 1864 and 1900, the first state parks were established, as were a number of state forest preserves and historic parks.

Municipal Parks   Until the nineteenth century, North America lagged far behind Europe in the development of municipal parks, partly because this continent had no aristocracy with large cultivated estates, hunting grounds, and elaborate gardens that could be turned over to the public. The first major park to be developed in an American city was Central Park in New York.

There long had been a need for open space in New York City. During the first 30 years of the nineteenth century, plans were made for several open squares to total about 450 acres, but these were not carried out completely. By the early 1850s, the entire amount of public open space in Manhattan totaled only 117 acres. Pressure mounted among the citizens of the city for a major park that would provide relief from stone and concrete.

When the public will could no longer be denied, legislation was passed in 1856 to establish a park in New York City. Construction of the 843-acre site began in 1857. Central Park, designed by landscape architects Frederick Law Olmsted and Calvert Vaux, was completely man-made and planned with purpose. The park was to be heavily wooded and to have the appearance of rural scenery, with roadways screened from the eyes of park users wherever possible. Recreational pursuits permitted in the park included walking, pleasure driving, ice skating, and boating—but not organized sport.

Old Faithful and the geysers of Yellowstone have made this first national park a popular destination since 1872.
Courtesy of the National Park Service. Photographed by Ed Austin and Herb Jones.

JOHN MUIR

In 1901, John Muir wrote a book titled *Our National Parks* to make the general public more aware of the beauty and diversity of the existing parks. Writing about the national parks as a whole, and Yellowstone National Park in particular, Muir said the following:

> The National Parks are not only withdrawn from sale and entry like the forest reservations but are efficiently managed and guarded by small troops of United States calvary, directed by the Secretary of the Interior. Under this care, the forests are flourishing, protected from both axe and fire; and so, of course, are the shaggy beds of underbrush and herbaceous vegetation. The so-called curiosities, also, are preserved, and the furred and feathered tribes, many of which, in danger of extinction a short time ago, are now increasing in numbers—a refreshing thing to see amid the blind, ruthless destruction that is going on in the adjacent regions. In pleasing contrast to the noisy, ever-changing management, or mismanagement, of blundering, plundering, money-making vote-sellers who receive their places from boss politicians as purchased goods, the soldiers do their duty so quietly that the traveler is scarce aware of their presence.[11]

Central Park was America's first large urban park and was the prototype for other large city parks across the nation for the next 50 years.

© Christopher Walker/Shutterstock.

County Park Systems   Planning for what was to become the nation's first county park system began in Essex County, New Jersey. Bordering the crowded industrial city of Newark, it was outlined in a comprehensive proposal in 1894 that promised that the entire cost of the park project would be realized through tax revenues from increased property values. The Essex County park system proved to be a great success and set a model to be followed by hundreds of other county and special district park agencies throughout the United States in the early 1900s.

Establishment of Voluntary Organizations

During the nineteenth century, a number of voluntary (privately sponsored, nonprofit) organizations were founded that played an important role in providing recreation services, chiefly for children and youths. In many cases, voluntary organizations were the outgrowth of their founders' desires to put religious principles into action through direct service to the underprivileged. One such body was the Young Men's Christian Association (YMCA), founded in Boston in 1851 and followed by the Young Women's Christian

Case Study

. . . .

Types and Uses of Urban Parks, 1850–1965

Early urban parks in the United States were places seen as an antidote to the problems of cities, which were perceived as dangerous, dirty, and unhealthy places. Parks formed an important component of the urban environment, and cities embraced them. Those same parks today provide a type of precursor to the emerging sustainable park of the twenty-first century. Cranz and Boland define three periods of park development beginning in 1850 and continuing through 1965. The three periods include the following:

◆   Pleasure ground (1850–1900)
◆   Reform park (1900–1930)
◆   Recreation facility (1930–1965)

Each of the park types is described in terms of social goal, activities, size, relation to city, elements, promoters, and beneficiaries.

The importance of understanding the different park movements from 1850 to the mid-1960s is to gain a greater appreciation of how citizens, politicians, and social and environmental movements affected park design and use. The first wave saw the large urban parks created all across the country, including such places as Central Park in New York City, Golden Gate Park in San Francisco, and Grant Park in Chicago. These large urban parks became major components of large urban areas, most becoming the core of larger and more diverse park and recreation systems.

The three park systems described in **Table 4.1** show how the movements shifted, as did the population. In most cases, the park movement followed, rather than led, public needs and desires. As social reform advanced, the pleasure ground gave way to a more active and focused reform park, many of which still boast the same services and benefits today, although they have been changed several times. The recreation facility, a continuing popular model, was an expression of efforts to move from the city core to the suburbs.

TABLE 4.1 Typology of Urban Parks, 1850–1965

	Pleasure Ground (1850–1900)	**Reform Park (1900–1930)**	**Recreation Facility (1930–1965)**
Social goal	Public health and social reform	Social reform, children's play, assimilation	Recreation service
Activities	Strolling, carriage racking, bike riding, picnics, rowing, classical music, nondidactic education	Supervised play, gymnastics, crafts, Americanization classes, dancing, plays and pageants	Active recreation, basketball, tennis, team sports, spectator sports, swimming
Size	Very large, 1,000+ acres	Small, city blocks	Small to medium, follow formula
Relation to city	Set in contrast	Accepts urban patterns	Suburban
Elements	Woodlands and meadow, curving paths, placid water bodies, rustic structures, limited floral displays	Sandlots, playgrounds, rectilinear paths, swimming pools, fieldhouses	Asphalt or grass play area, pools, rectilinear paths, standard play equipment
Promoters	Health reformers, transcendentalists, real estate interests	Social reformers, social workers, recreation workers	Politicians, bureaucrats, planners
Beneficiaries	All citydwellers (intended), upper-middle class (reality)	Children, immigrants, working class	Suburban families

Data from Galen Cranz and Michael Boland. "Defining the Sustainable Park: A Fifth Model for Urban Parks." Landscape Journal, (Vol. 23, No. 2, 2004): 102–140.

Questions to Consider
1. Discuss how the three park movements mirrored society in the United States.
2. What were the actual benefits to the beneficiaries of the different types of parks?
3. How many of these types of parks have you visited? How have they changed?

Association (YWCA) 15 years later. At first, the Y's provided fellowship between youths and adults for religious purposes. They gradually enlarged their programs, however, to include gymnastics, sport, and other recreational and social activities.

Another type of voluntary agency that offered significant leisure programs was the settlement house—neighborhood centers established in the slum sections of the East and Midwest. Among the first were University Settlement, founded in New York City in 1886, and Hull House, founded in Chicago in 1889. Their staffs sought to help poor people, particularly immigrants, adjust to modern urban life by providing services concerned with education, family life, and community improvement.

The Playground Movement
To understand the need for playgrounds in cities and towns, it is necessary to know the living conditions of poor people during the latter decades of the nineteenth century.

The wave of urbanization that had begun earlier now reached its peak. The urban population more than doubled—from 14 to 30 million—between 1880 and 1900 alone. By the century's end, there were 28 cities

Case Study

The YMCA as the Prototype of the Social Movement of the Late 1800s

The Young Men's Christian Association was founded in London, England, in 1844 and migrated to the United States in 1851. George Williams was the founder of the YMCA, working with friends to find a way to get people off of London's streets. "The YMCA idea, which began among evangelicals, was unusual because it crossed the rigid lines that separated all the different churches and social classes in England in those days. This openness was a trait that would lead eventually to including in YMCAs all men, women and children, regardless of race, religion or nationality. Also, its target of meeting social needs in the community was dear from the start."[a]

> The movement grew rapidly. Within several years, YMCAs were started in Boston and other American cities. Initially, only those converted to evangelical churches could become members. Soon, however, young men were allowed to join even if not converted, although the management of the association was reserved to members of evangelical churches....

> Although the causes of the association's expansion are not clear, certain factors stand out. First, the definite Christian orientation of the movement tied it into the religious revivals of the time. The YMCA participated in organizing tent revivals as well as sponsoring prayer meetings, Bible readings, and lecture series. Thus the YMCA movement had definite goals and programs that focused its members' energies. Second, the movement spread by a diffusion process based on local enthusiasm rather than by a process of centralized direction and allocation of personnel. Visitors to the London YMCA or to the early YMCA in Boston became enthusiastic about the idea and took it back to their own communities. This method of expansion depended on strong local support, ensuring a continuing base in each community. Finally, each local YMCA usually had a reading room, a list of job openings, a coffee shop, and a list of wholesome boarding homes. These gave the association a material base in the community and also allowed it to minister to some of the basic needs of the young, single male."[b]

It became obvious to the leaders that if the YMCA was going to grow and serve a broader population it needed to adapt, so "the basic goal of the organization changed from evangelism to the broader and more secularized one of developing the 'whole man'; membership criteria were successively broadened to include all religions, ages, and both sexes; and control was extended to followers of any religion." Also, "program emphasis shifted away from the overtly religious to the development of the mental, physical, and social capacities of members. The inclusion of activities for physical training created more conflict than did programs for mental or intellectual development, because it challenged conservative religious views of the proper forms of recreation."[c]

One of the other factors that has made the YMCA successful was the effort to avoid politics. YMCA services have focused on prevention rather than rehabilitation. The YMCA "has generally implemented its goals by serving clientele rather than by attempting to change the environment."[d]

Questions to Consider

1. Explain the importance of the YMCA changing from an evangelical type of organization to a social organization.
2. It is suggested that the YMCAs grew "by a diffusion process based on local enthusiasm." Discuss how this is similar to movements created via social networks today. How do you think this diffusion process occurred in the late nineteenth century?
3. Discuss the differences between a preventive and rehabilitative organization.

Sources

a. YMCA, "About Us." Available at: http://www.ymca.net/about-us/
b. M. N. Zald and P. Denton, "From Evangelism to General Service: The Transformation of the YMCA." *Administrative Science Quarterly* (Vol. 8, No. 2, 1963): 216.
c. Ibid., 217–218.
d. Ibid., 221.

with more than 100,000 residents because of the recent waves of migration. A leading example was New York, where nearly five of every six of the city's 1.5 million residents lived in crowded tenements in 1891, characterized by dark hallways, filthy cellars, and inadequate cooking and bathroom facilities. In neighborhoods populated by poor immigrants, there was a tremendous amount of crime, gambling, gang violence, and prostitution.

Boston Sand Garden: A Beginning   Within poor working-class neighborhoods, there were few safe places where children might play. The first such facility—and the one that is generally regarded as a landmark in the development of the recreation movement in the United States—was the Boston Sand Garden. The city of Boston has been the arena for many important developments in the park and recreation movement in the United States. The Boston Common, established in 1634, generally is regarded as the first municipal park; a 48-acre area of green, rolling hills and shade trees, it is located in the heart of the city.

The famous Boston Sand Garden was the first playground in the country designed specifically for children. A group of public-spirited citizens had a pile of sand placed behind the Parmenter Street Chapel in a working-class district. Supervision was voluntary at first, but by 1887 when 10 such centers were opened, women were employed to supervise the children. Two years later, the city of Boston began to contribute funds to support the sand gardens.

New York's First Playgrounds   In the nation's largest city, Walter Vrooman, founder of the New York Society for Parks and Playgrounds, directed the public's attention to the fact that in 1890 there were 350,000 children without a single public playground. Although the city had almost 6,000 acres of parkland, none was set aside for children. Civic leaders pointed out that children of working parents lacked supervision and were permitted to grow up subject to various temptations. Vrooman wrote that such children

> are driven from their crowded homes in the morning … are chased from the streets by the police when they attempt to play, and beaten with the broom handle of the janitor's wife when found in the hallway, or on the stairs. No wonder they learn to chew and smoke tobacco before they can read, and take a fiendish delight in breaking windows, in petty thievery, and in gambling their pennies.[12]

Gradually, the pressure mounted. Two small model playgrounds were established in poor areas of the city in 1889 and 1891 by the newly formed New York Society for Parks and Playgrounds, with support from private donors. Gradually, the city assumed financial and legal responsibility as many additional playgrounds were built in the years that followed, often attached to schools.

The period between 1880 and 1900 was of critical importance to the development of urban recreation and park programs. More than 80 cities initiated park systems; a lesser number established sand gardens, and, shortly after, playgrounds. Illinois passed a law permitting the establishment of local park districts in which two or more municipalities might join together to operate park systems.

EFFECTS OF RACIAL AND ETHNIC DISCRIMINATION

Throughout this period, public and nonprofit youth-serving organizations often discriminated against members of racial or ethnic minorities.

Prejudice Against Minorities

Generally, the most severe discrimination was leveled against African Americans, who, though no longer slaves, were kept in a position of economic servitude through the practice of sharecropping, and were without civil, political, or judicial rights in the southern and border states. African Americans were increasingly barred from social contact, economic opportunity, or recreational involvement with whites by a wave of state legislation and local ordinances in the late nineteenth and early twentieth centuries.

There was also an extreme degree of prejudice against Mexican Americans and other Hispanics of mixed racial origins. For example, Anglo settlers in Texas regarded Mexicans as savage "heathens" who historically practiced human sacrifice and saw them as a decadent and inferior people.

There was also widespread prejudice expressed against Asian Americans, mostly Chinese nationals who began to arrive in California in the mid-1800s and who worked on the transcontinental railroad. As the number of Asians grew, so did xenophobia. Americans viewed them as heathens who could not readily be assimilated within the nation's essentially Anglo-Saxon framework and condemned them as unsanitary, immoral, and criminal. In fact, Chinese were barred from entry into the United States by the Oriental Exclusion Acts of 1882 and 1902.

RECREATION AND PARKS: EARLY TWENTIETH CENTURY

For the majority of Americans, however, the beginning of the twentieth century was an exciting period marked by growing economic and recreational opportunity. By 1900, 14 cities had made provisions for supervised play facilities. Among the leading cities were Boston, Providence, Philadelphia, Pittsburgh, Baltimore, Chicago, Milwaukee, Cleveland, Denver, and Minneapolis.

Playgrounds became more popular in the early decades of the twentieth century in large urban areas.

At the same time, municipal parks became well established throughout the United States. In addition to the parks mentioned earlier, the first metropolitan park system was established by Boston in 1892. In the West, San Francisco and Sacramento in California as well as Salt Lake City, Utah, were among the first to incorporate large open spaces in town planning before 1900. The New England Association of Park Superintendents, the predecessor of the American Institute of Park Executives, was established in 1898 to bring together park superintendents and promote their professional concerns.

Growth of Public Recreation and Park Agencies

Gradually, the concept that city governments should provide recreation facilities, programs, and services became widely accepted. By 1906, 41 cities were sponsoring public recreation programs, and by 1920, the number was 465. More and more states passed laws authorizing local governments to operate recreation programs, and between 1925 and 1935 the number of municipal recreation buildings quadrupled. Municipalities were also discovering new ways to add parks, including through mandated land dedications and gifts.

Federal Park Expansion

As president, Theodore Roosevelt, a dedicated outdoorsman, encouraged the acquisition of numerous new areas for the federal park system. Thanks in part to his assistance and support, the Reclamation Act of 1902, which authorized reservoir-building irrigation systems in the West, was passed, along with the Antiquities Act of 1906, which designated the first national monuments. Establishment of the U.S. Forest Service in 1905 and of the National Park Service 11 years later helped place many of the scattered forests, parks, and other sites under more clearly defined policies for acquisition, development, and use (see **Figure 4.2**).

EMERGENCE OF THE RECREATION MOVEMENT: THREE PIONEERS

As the recreation field developed during the first three decades of the twentieth century, several men and women emerged as influential advocates of play and recreation. Three of the most effective were Joseph Lee, Luther Halsey Gulick, and Jane Addams.

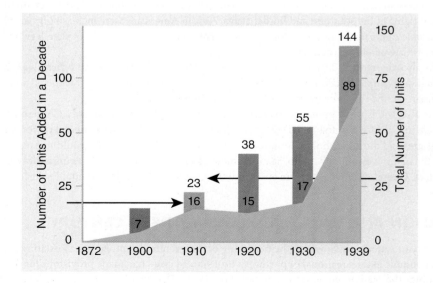

FIGURE 4.2   Growth of the National Park System 1900–1939

Joseph Lee

Regarded as the "father" of the playground movement, Joseph Lee was a lawyer and philanthropist who came from a wealthy New England family. Born in 1862, he took part in a survey of play opportunities conducted by the Family Welfare Society of Boston in 1882. Shocked to see boys arrested for playing in the streets, he organized a playground for them in an open lot. In 1898, Lee helped create a model playground on Columbus Avenue in Boston that included a play area for small children, a boys' section, a sport field, and individual gardens. With Lee's influence expanding, he served as vice president of public recreation for the American Civic Association. President of the Playground Association of America for 27 years, he was also the president and leading lecturer of the National Recreation School, a one-year program for carefully selected college graduates, as well as author of *Play in Education*.

Known as the Father of the Playground Movement, Joseph Lee was an advocate for the importance of play.
©Library of Congress, LC-DIG-ggbain-50026.

Luther Halsey Gulick

Another leading figure in the early recreation movement was Luther Halsey Gulick. A physician by training, he developed a special interest in physical education and recreation. Beginning in 1887, Dr. Gulick headed the first summer school of "special training for gymnasium instructors" at the School for Christian Workers (now Springfield College) in Massachusetts. He was active in the YMCAs in Canada and the United States, was the first president of the Camp Fire Girls, and was instrumental in the establishment of the Playground Association of America in 1906. He also vigorously promoted expanded recreation programs for girls and women.

Gulick distinguished play from recreation. He defines play as "doing that which we want to do, without reference primarily to any ulterior end, but simply for the joy of the process." But, he goes on to say, play is not less serious than work:

> The boy who is playing football with intensity needs recreation as much as does the inventor who is working intensely at his invention. Play can be more exhausting than work, because one can play much harder than one can work. No one would dream of pushing a boy in school as hard as he pushes himself in a football game. If there is any difference of intensity between play and work, the difference is in favor of play. Play is the result of desire; for that reason it is often carried on with more vigor than work.[13]

Luther Halsey Gulick, M.D., was a staunch supporter of girls' and women's right to access recreation.
©Library of Congress, LC-DIG-hec-25912.

Jane Addams

Jane Addams was a social work pioneer who established Hull House in Chicago. Her interest in the needs of children and youths, and in the lives of immigrant families and the poor in America's great cities, led her to develop programs of educational, social, and recreational activities. Beyond this, she was a leading feminist pioneer and so active a reformer that she was known as "the most dangerous woman in America."

Mary Duncan points out that Jane Addams was part of a wider radical reform movement in America's cities. Joining with muckraking editors, writers, ministers, and other social activists, they continually fought city hall, organized labor strikes, marched in the street, gave public speeches, and wrote award-winning articles deploring the living conditions of the poor. The issues and problems they faced were well defined: slavery, the aftermath of the Civil War, thousands of new immigrants, slums, child labor, disease, the suffrage movement, World War I, and a rapidly industrializing nation.[24]

EMERGING NEW LIFESTYLES

Such views of recreation, play, and leisure were not shared by the entire population. The early twentieth century was a time when the traditional Victorian mentality that had been taught and enforced by the home, school, and church was being challenged. For the first time, many young women took jobs in business and industry in cities throughout the country. With relative freedom from disapproving, stern parental authority, and with

Jane Addams worked tirelessly to support immigrants and the poor.
©Library of Congress, LC-USZ62-13484.

money to spend, they frequented commercial dance halls, boat rides, drinking saloons, social clubs, and other sources of popular entertainment. Kathy Peiss describes the new freedom for working-class youth in general:

Part of what appealed to young people were the playgrounds, parks, public beaches, and picnic grounds. However, often these were considered too tame and unexciting, and more and more young people became attracted to commercial forms of entertainment involving liquor, dancing, and sex that were viewed by the establishment as immoral and dangerous. Increasingly, organized recreation programs were promoted by churches, law enforcement agencies, and civic associations in an attempt to resist the new, hedonistic forms of play.

PUBLIC CONCERNS ABOUT THE USE OF LEISURE

To some degree, the support for public recreation was based on the fear that without public programs and facilities, adult leisure would be used unwisely. When the eight-hour workday laws first came under discussion, temperance societies prepared for increased drunkenness, and social reformers held international conferences on the worker's spare time and ways to use it constructively.

The major concern, however, was for children and youths in the large cities and their need for healthful and safe places to play. Indeed, much "juvenile delinquency" arose from children being arrested for playing on city streets. Authorities during this period reported reduced rates of juvenile delinquency in slum areas where playgrounds had been established.

Concern About Commercial Amusements

At this time, there was also fear that unregulated and unsupervised places of commercial amusement posed a serious threat to children and youths. Commercially sponsored forms of entertainment and recreation had grown rapidly during the early twentieth century, with many new pool and billiard parlors, dance halls, vaudeville shows and burlesque, and other amusement attractions. There was much concern about movies and stage performances, with frequent charges that they were immoral and led to the sexual corruption of youth.

A high percentage of privately operated dance halls that were freely patronized by young girls were attached to saloons and rooming houses. Dancing seemed to be only a secondary consideration. Pickups occurred regularly, often of young girls who had come to cities from the nation's farms and small towns with a presumed degree of innocence; so-called white slavers, who trapped or recruited girls and women into prostitution, appeared to ply their trade with little interference.

An examination of socially approved forms of recreation found that in many cities the schools were closed in the evening and throughout the summer, that libraries closed at night and on weekends, that churches closed for the summer, and that publicly provided forms of recreation were at a minimum. Jane Addams concluded that the city had "turned over the provision for public recreation to the most evil-minded and the most unscrupulous members of the community." Gradually, pressure mounted for more effective control of places of public amusement. In city after city, permits were required for operating dance halls, pool parlors, and bowling alleys, and for the sale of liquor.

There was also a fear that Americans were moving away from the traditional active ways of using their leisure to pursuits in which they were passive spectators. Some critics commented that instead of believing in the wholesome love of play, Americans now had a love of being "played upon."

Emerging Mass Culture

Such complaints and fears were the inevitable reactions of civic leaders to what they perceived to be a threat to traditional morality and values. The reality is that the United States in the early decades of the twentieth century was undergoing massive changes in response to changing economic and social conditions. These included the emergence of new middle-class and working-class people who had the time and money to spend on leisure, as well as a steady infusion of varied ethnic peoples who contributed new ideas and values to American society. Part of the change involved a growing rejection of authoritarian family structures and church-dominated social values, as well as a readiness to accept new kinds of roles for young people and women. All of these influences resulted in a new mass culture that emerged during the new century.

Defining Popular/Mass Culture

Popular culture (or pop culture) is the totality of ideas, perspectives, attitudes, memes, images, and other phenomena that are deemed preferred by an informal consensus within the mainstream of a given culture. Popular culture is heavily influenced by mass media and becomes ingrained in everyday life.[14]

Defining *popular* and *culture* is complicated with multiple competing definitions. The preceding definition represents mainstream perceptions of popular culture. Yet the definition of popular culture is often muddied with varying opinions on "high culture" versus "popular culture" as well as equating pop culture with mass culture or commercial culture which is focused on items produced for mass consumption. Regardless, what is known for sure is that popular culture changes constantly and occurs uniquely in place and time. Items of popular culture typically appeal to a broad spectrum of the public.

MAJOR FORCES PROMOTING ORGANIZED RECREATION SERVICES

At the same time that mass culture was providing new pastimes that challenged traditional community values and standards, the forces that sought to guide the American public in what they regarded as constructive uses of leisure were becoming active.

Billiard parlors, also known as pool halls, were often frequented by youths and adults alike as a form of entertainment.

Courtesy of Library of Congress, Prints & Photographs Division, National Child Labor Collection [reproduction number LC-DIG-nclc-04662].

Growth of Voluntary Organizations

In the opening decades of the twentieth century, a number of important youth-serving, nonprofit organizations were formed, either on a local basis or through nationally organized movements or federations. The National Association of Boys' Clubs was founded in 1906, the Boy Scouts and the Camp Fire Girls in 1910, and the Girl Scouts in 1912. Major civic clubs and community service groups such as the Rotary Club, Kiwanis Club, and the Lions Club were also founded between 1910 and 1917.

By the end of the 1920s, these organizations had become widely established in American life and were serving substantial numbers of young people. One of every seven boys in the appropriate age group in the United States was a Scout. The YMCA and YWCA had more than 1.5 million members in 1926.

Playground Association of America

In the early 1900s, leading recreation directors called for a conference to promote public awareness of and effective practices in the field of leisure services. Under the leadership of Luther Halsey Gulick, representatives of park, recreation, and school boards met in Washington, D.C., in April 1906. Unanimously agreeing upon the need for a national organization, the conference members drew up a constitution and selected Gulick as the first president of the Playground Association of America.

A basic purpose of the Playground Association was to develop informational and promotional services to assist people of all ages in using leisure time constructively. Field workers traveled from city to city, meeting with public officials and citizens' groups and helping in the development of playgrounds and recreation programs. To promote professional training, the association developed The Normal Course in Play, a curriculum plan of courses on play leadership on several levels.

In keeping with its broadening emphasis, the organization changed its name in 1911 to the Playground and Recreation Association of America, and in 1926 to the National Recreation Association. It sought to provide the public with a broader concept of recreation and leisure and to promote recreation as an area of government responsibility.

 DEVELOPMENT OF THE AMUSEMENT PARK

As a single example of the new craze for excitement and freedom in leisure, a host of amusement parks were developed close to various cities around the country. Typically, they put together a mélange of popular attractions, including bathing facilities, band pavilions, dance halls, vaudeville theaters, sideshows, circus attractions, freak displays, food and drink counters, and daredevil rides of every description.

The Boy Scouts have provided outdoor recreation experiences for youths since 1910.

Courtesy of the Library of Congress, Prints & Photographs Division, LC-USZ62-109741.

Recreation Programs in World War I

The nation's rapid mobilization during World War I revealed that communities adjacent to army and navy stations and training camps needed better programs of recreation. The Council of National Defense and the War Department Commission on Training Camp Activities asked the Playground and Recreation Association to assist in the creation of a national organization to provide wartime community recreation programs. The association established the War Camp Community Service (WCCS), which utilized the recreation resources of several hundred communities near military camps to provide recreation activities for both military personnel and civilians.

Role of the Schools

As indicated earlier, a number of urban school boards initiated after-school and vacation play programs as early as the 1890s. This trend continued in the twentieth century. Playground programs were begun in Rochester, New York, in 1907; in Milwaukee, Wisconsin, in 1911; and in Los Angeles, California, in 1914. These pioneering efforts were strongly supported by the National Education Association, which recommended that public school buildings and their resources such as playgrounds, gymnasiums, pools, and art rooms be used for community recreation and social activities.

With such support, public opinion encouraged the expansion of organized playground and public recreation programs. Between 1910 and 1930, thousands of school systems established extensive programs of extracurricular activities, particularly in sport, publications, hobbies, and social and academic-related fields. In 1919, the first college curriculum in recreation was established at Virginia Commonwealth University.

Case Study
. . . .

The Creation of the National Park Service

The creation of new federal agencies is a complicated and highly political process. Even though the need is apparent to those most concerned, there is always the task of convincing key leaders in the executive and legislative branches of government. Typically, a proposal for a new agency moves forward from the executive branch to the legislative branch. Although not always the case, the presence of a growing number of national parks administered by the Department of the Interior—but without a direct governing body—resulted in inconsistent administration of the national parks. "There military engineers and cavalrymen developed park roads and buildings, enforced regulations against hunting, grazing, timber cutting, and vandalism, and did their best to serve the visiting public. Civilian appointees superintended the other parks, while the monuments received minimal custody. In the absence of an effective central administration, those in charge operated without coordinated supervision or policy guidance."[a]

The National Park Service was created by act of Congress in 1916, 44 years after the establishment of the world's first national park—Yellowstone National Park. A number of national parks were created between 1872 and the early 1900s. By 1916, the Department of the Interior was responsible for a number of national parks and national monuments, and yet had no organizational structure to manage the growing number of areas dedicated to preservation and recreation. In the absence of a formal structure and, in many cases, guidelines, the areas set aside by Congress were vulnerable to competing interests. Matters seemed to have come to a head when in 1913, Congress authorized the creation of a dam in Hetch Hetchy Valley of Yosemite National Park.

"When San Francisco sought to dam Yosemite's Hetch Hetchy Valley for a reservoir after the turn of the century, the utilitarian and preservationist wings of the conservation movement came to blows. Over the passionate opposition of John Muir and other park supporters, Congress in 1913 permitted the dam."[a] In 1915, Stephen T. Mather, a well-connected and wealthy Chicago businessman, complained to Secretary of the Interior Franklin K. Lane about the mismanagement of the parks. Lane responded by inviting Mather to serve as his assistant for park matters, and Mather accepted. Serving as Mather's aide and guiding the legislation through Congress, Horace M. Albright, working hand in hand with his superior, crusaded "for a National Parks Bureau" and the two of them "effectively blurred the distinction between utilitarian conservation and preservation by emphasizing the economic value of parks as tourist meccas."[a]

Not relying wholly on their contacts within Congress, the two men initiated a public relations campaign that resulted in articles in the *Saturday Evening Post, National Geographic*, and other popular magazines. Mather "hired his own publicist and obtained funds from 17 western railroads to produce the National Parks Portfolio, a lavishly illustrated publication sent to Congressmen and other influential citizens." On August 25, 1916, Congress approved the creation of the National Park Service (NPS), and President Woodrow Wilson signed the legislation. The legislation specifically required the NPS "to conserve the scenery and the natural and historic objects in the wild life therein and to provide for the enjoyment of the same in such manner and by such means as leave them unimpaired for the enjoyment of future generations."[a]

Questions to Consider

1. Prepare a series of arguments in favor of creating a National Park Bureau/Service.
2. Prepare a series of arguments opposing the creation of a National Park Bureau/Service.
3. How do you think the National Park system would be different today if it did not have an agency to manage it?

Source

a. Barry Mackintosh, "The National Park Service: A Brief History," (May 26, 2017): http://npshistory.com/publications/brief_history/index.htm

Outdoor Recreation Developments

The role of the federal and state governments in promoting outdoor recreation was enlarged by the establishment of the National Park Service in 1916 and an accelerated pattern of acquisition and development of outdoor areas by the U.S. Forest Service. In 1921, Stephen Mather, director of the National Park Service, called for a national conference on state parks. This meeting made it clear that the Park Service was primarily to acquire and administer areas of national significance; it led to the recommendation that state governments take more responsibility for acquiring sites of lesser interest or value.

Park administrators began to give active recreation a higher priority in park design and operation.

The End of Shorter Hours

As the recreation movement continued to gain impetus, a reverse trend took place as the movement to shorten the workweek and provide workers with more free time gradually slackened. Benjamin Hunnicutt points out that the most dramatic increase in free time occurred in the period between 1901 and 1921, when the average workweek dropped from 58.4 to 48.4 hours, a decline never before or since equaled.[15]

Since the mid-nineteenth century, shorter hours and higher wages had been a campaign issue for progressive politicians. Union pressure, legislation, and court decisions achieved the eight-hour day in jobs under federal contracts, sections of the railroad industry, and certain hazardous occupations. The policy was supported by the findings of scientific management experts such as Frederick Taylor, who argued that workers' efficiency declined significantly after eight hours.

IMPACT OF THE GREAT DEPRESSION

Following the flourishing 1920s, the Great Depression of the 1930s mired the United States—and much of the industrial world—in a period of almost total despair. By the end of 1932, an estimated 15 million people, nearly one-third of the labor force, were unemployed. Individuals who were employed also experienced greater free time as the average workweek declined. During this period, scholars and public officials became concerned that leisure had become too commercial and passive and would contribute to the decline of American culture. Furthermore, there was widespread concern that excessive free time was linked to crime.

Civilian Conservation Corps camps were located throughout the United States during the Depression.
Courtesy of the Franklin D. Roosevelt Library and Museum.

In response to these concerns and in conjunction with a broad plan to combat the effects of the Depression, the federal government soon instituted a number of emergency work programs related to recreation. The Federal Emergency Relief Administration, established early in 1933, financed construction of recreation facilities such as parks and swimming pools and hired recreation leaders from the relief rolls. A second agency, the Civil Works Administration, was given the task of finding jobs for four million people in 30 days! Among other tasks, this agency built or improved 3,500 playgrounds and athletic fields in a few months.[12]

Both the National Youth Administration and the Civilian Conservation Corps (CCC) carried out numerous work projects involving the construction of recreational facilities. During the five years from 1932 to 1937, the federal government spent an estimated $1.5 billion developing camps, buildings, picnic grounds, trails, swimming pools, and other facilities. The CCC helped to establish state park systems in a number of states that had no organized park programs before 1933. The Works Progress Administration allocated $11 billion or 30% of their budget to recreation-related projects that spanned the nation and included 12,700 playgrounds, 8,500 gymnasiums or recreation buildings, 750 swimming pools, 1,000 ice skating rinks, and 64 ski jumps.[16]

Case Study

President Franklin D. Roosevelt's Legacy for Parks and Recreation

During the Great Depression of the 1930s, President Franklin D. Roosevelt created a legacy that has had enduring and significant influence on parks and recreation. It can be argued that Roosevelt's New Deal was a tool that initiated a growth of public parks and recreation areas, state parks, national parks, conservations, and wildlife areas.

The New Deal was a product of one of the most difficult periods in American history. Roosevelt was elected after the 1929 stock market crash and came to office in 1933. He saw the need to put Americans to work. The term "New Deal" was introduced during Franklin Roosevelt's 1932 Democratic presidential nomination acceptance speech, when he said, "I pledge you, I pledge myself, to a new deal for the American people."[a] Roosevelt summarized the New Deal as a "use of the authority of government as an organized form of self-help for all classes and groups and sections of our country."[a]

The New Deal represented a major shift in government involvement in everyone's lives. Its main purpose was to put people back to work and improve the economy. It is important to remember that during this period unemployment hovered at 30% nationwide. Among the important initiatives created, two significantly influenced parks and recreation. They were the Civilian Conservation Corps (CCC) and the Works Progress Administration (WPA).

The CCC initially targeted putting three million young men, between the ages of 18 and 25 years, to work. The CCC was involved in road building, forest maintenance and restoration, and flood control. The West saw the heavy use of CCC and the WPA's workers in national forests, national parks, on Indian reservations, and in municipal and state parks for work on natural resource–related projects.[b] During the existence of the CCC, members planted nearly three billion trees to help reforest America and constructed more than 800 parks nationwide that would become the start of many state parks.[c]

At the height of the program, 47 of 48 states participated in CCC programs, and in 1935 there were 475 CCC camps on state park lands. By the end of the CCC program, 405 state parks directly benefited from the program. In some cases, whole state parks were turned over to appreciative states. Georgia, as an example of a benefiting state, in 2010 identified 11 state parks that still had CCC-constructed facilities. The structures include a bathhouse, casino, dam, pumphouse, residences, comfort stations and picnic shelters, springhouse, bridge and walkways, museum building, blacksmith shop, and group shelters, to name a few. Georgia's legacy of the CCC is similar to many states that point to the WPA and CCC as an unexpected boon.[d]

The WPA, established in 1935 and renamed in 1939 as the Work Projects Administration, similarly focused on creating jobs for the unemployed. It became the largest of the New Deal programs carrying out public works projects that involved the construction of public buildings and roads, and it operated large arts, drama, media, and literacy projects. It fed children and redistributed food, clothing, and housing. Almost every community in the United States had a park, bridge, or school constructed by the agency. The WPA spent billions of dollars on reforestation, flood control, construction of facilities and parks and recreation areas, and many other conservation and community projects. From a municipal and state perspective, the WPA had a significant impact on communities and their ability to provide park and recreation resources and services. For example, the WPA hired artists, actors, and musicians to provide programming, create art, and hold concerts for local communities. In some cases, the construction of park shelters, restrooms, picnic shelters, swimming pools, and other facilities remain today.

An example WPA project from New York City is McCarren Pool, located in Brooklyn. McCarren Pool was the eighth of 11 giant pools built by the WPA, opening during the summer of 1936. With a capacity of 6,800 swimmers, the pool served as the summertime social hub. The pool was closed in 1984, but in 2006, the abandoned pool was the site of a series of Sunday afternoon concerts. The mayor of New York announced in 2007 that major renovations would be undertaken to reopen the pool.[e]

The National Park Service (NPS) has done the most effective job of chronicling the CCC and WPA involvement with their areas. The NPS budget was $10.8 million in 1933, and yet NPS took advantage of the New Deal, receiving $218 million for emergency conservation projects between 1933 and 1939. The NPS said, "Almost all federal conservation activities after 1933, including those in the national parks and monuments, were designed in part as pump-priming operations that would not only protect our national resources but also indirectly stimulate the economy."[f]

The work of New Deal organizations from 1933 to 1942 provided a foundation that would be expanded upon throughout the remainder of the twentieth century.

Questions to Consider

1. How do you think recreation areas, national parks, and wildlife areas would be different today without the New Deal?
2. Prepare a series of justifications for implementation of a New Deal program today.
3. Go on the Internet and find a state or community that is still using CCC- or WPA-constructed facilities and report on how they are used, how they were changed, and the legacy it has left upon the community or state. (Hint: do a search for "New Deal" facilities.)

Sources

a. Works of F. D. Roosevelt, Roosevelt's Nomination Address, Chicago, IL. March 31, 2017. http://newdeal.feri.org/speeches/1932b.htm
b. The National Archives, "The Great Depression and the New Deal," March 31, 2017. https://www.archives.gov/seattle/exhibit/picturing-the-century/great-depression.html
c. H. Unraw and G. F. Williss, *Expansion of the National Park Service in the 1930s: Administrative History* (Washington, DC: National Park Service, 1982), March 31, 2017. https://www.nps.gov/parkhistory/online_books/unrau-williss/adhi.htm
d. Georgia Department of Natural Resources, http://www.georgiastateparks.org.
e. New York City Department of Parks and Recreation, "McCarren Park," http://www.nycgovparks.org/parks/mccarrenpark.
f. Ibid., c.

Sharpened Awareness of Leisure Needs

The Depression helped to stimulate national concern about problems of leisure and recreational opportunity. For example, a number of studies in the 1930s revealed a serious lack of structured recreation programs for young people, especially African Americans, girls, and rural youths. In the early 1930s, the National Education Association carried out a major study of leisure education in the nation's school systems and issued a report, *The New Leisure Challenges the Schools*, that urged the educational establishment to take more responsibility for this function and advocated enlarging the school's role in community recreation.

Shortly thereafter, the National Recreation Association examined the public recreation and park programs in a number of major European nations with nationalized recreation programs and published a detailed report that included implications for American policy makers. The American Association for the Study of Group Work examined the overall problem and in 1939 published an important report, *Leisure: A National Issue*. In the report, Eduard Lindeman, a leading social work administrator who had played a key role in government during the Depression, stated that the "leisure of the American people constitutes a central and crucial problem of social policy."[17]

Lindeman argued that in the American democracy, recreation should meet the true needs of the people. Pointing out that American workers were gaining a vast national reservoir of leisure estimated at 390 billion hours per year, he suggested that the new leisure should be characterized by free choice and a minimum of

Recreation during the Depression came in many forms and frequently was family oriented.

restraint. He urged, however, that if leisure were not to become "idleness, waste, or opportunity for sheer mischief," a national plan for leisure had to be developed, including the widespread preparation of professionally trained recreation leaders.

A NATION AT WAR

World War II, in which the United States became fully involved on December 7, 1941, compelled the immediate mobilization of every aspect of national life. The Special Services Division of the U.S. Army provided recreation facilities and programs on military bases throughout the world, making use of approximately 12,000 officers, even more enlisted personnel, and many volunteers. About 1,500 officers were involved in the Welfare and Recreation Section of the Bureau of Naval Personnel, and expanded programs were offered by the Recreation Service of the Marine Corps. These departments were assisted by the United Service Organizations (USO), which was formed in 1941 and consisted of the joint effort of six agencies: the Jewish Welfare Board, the Salvation Army, Catholic Community Services, the YMCA, the YWCA, and the National Travelers Aid. The American National Red Cross established approximately 750 clubs in wartime theaters of operations throughout the world and about 250 mobile entertainment units, staffed by more than 4,000 leaders. Its military hospitals overseas and in the United States involved more than 1,500 recreation workers as well.

Many municipal directors extended their facilities and services to local war plants and changed their schedules to provide programs around the clock. Because of the rapid increase in industrial recreation programs, the National Industrial Recreation Association (later known as the National Employee Services and Recreation Association) was formed in 1941 to assist in such efforts. Also, the Federal Security Agency's Office of Community War Services established a recreation division to assist community programs. The Women's Bureau of the U.S. Department of Labor developed guidelines for recreation and housing for women war workers, based on their needs in moving from their home environments into suddenly expanded or greatly congested areas.

By the end of World War II, great numbers of servicemen and servicewomen had participated in varied recreation programs and services and thus had gained a new appreciation for this field. Many people had been trained in recreation leadership (more than 40,000 people were in the Special Services Division of the U.S. Army alone) and were ready to return to civilian life as professionals in this field.

POST–WORLD WAR II EXPECTATIONS

Immediately after World War II, expectations for the growth of leisure in the United States were high. In the 1950s and 1960s, it was predicted that leisure—usually defined as nonwork or discretionary time—would expand dramatically and have an increasing influence on the lives of Americans in the years ahead.

Think tanks such as the Rand Corporation and the Hudson Institute and special planning bodies such as the National Commission on Technology envisioned futurist scenarios with such alternatives as lowering the retirement age to 38, reducing the workweek to 22 hours a week, or extending paid vacations to as many as 25 weeks a year. Other authorities predicted that the 3-day or 4-day workweek, which some companies had been experimenting with, would soon be widespread.

In the early and mid-1990s and again on a much broader scale in 2008 and beyond, widespread company downsizing and other business trends led to the firing of millions of employees and an atmosphere of economic pessimism. There was a strong business recovery in the late 1990s, unemployment declined sharply, prosperity was widespread, and government budgets began to show surpluses on every level. By early 2009, however, there was a new decline with more far-reaching impact on personal income and government budgets, layoffs and unemployment at levels not seen since the Great Depression, loss of homes, and closing of businesses nationwide and a general sense of hopelessness among many.

EXPANSION OF RECREATION AND LEISURE

Over the last 60 years, recreation and leisure witnessed an immense growth in participation. There was a steady increase in sport, the arts, hobbies, outdoor recreation, and fitness programs, along with a parallel expansion of home-based entertainment through the use of computer, television, media players, handheld devices, and other electronic equipment.

Influence of National Affluence

An important factor in the growth of recreational participation was the national affluence of the postwar years. The gross national product rose from $211 billion in 1945 to more than a trillion dollars annually in 1971. In the late 1950s, it was reported that Americans were spending $30 billion a year on leisure—a sum that seemed huge then but that is dwarfed by the $841 billion spent in 2007.[18]

Involvement in varied forms of recreation exploded during this period. Visits to national forests increased by 474% between 1947 and 1963, and to national parks by 302% during the same period. Overseas pleasure travel increased by 440%, and attendance at sports and cultural events also grew rapidly. Sales of golf equipment increased by 188% and tennis equipment by 148%, and use of bowling lanes by 258%. Hunting and fishing, horse-racing attendance, and copies of paperback books sold all gained dramatically, and—most strikingly—the number of families with television sets grew by 3,500% over this 16-year period.[19]

Government recreation and park agencies dramatically expanded their budgets, personnel, facilities, and programs until the mid-1970s. Then, many federal, state, and local agencies were forced by funding cuts to cut back or freeze budgets. At the same time, the recreation and park profession continued to grow in numbers and public visibility. Preprofessional curricula were established in many colleges and universities during the 1960s and 1970s, and several national organizations, including the National Recreation Association, the American Recreation Society, and the American Institute of Park Executives, merged to form the National Recreation and Park Association.

Effect of Demographic Changes: Suburbanization and Urban Crises

In the years immediately after World War II—which had disrupted the lives of millions of servicemen and women—great numbers of young couples married. Within a few years, many of these new families with young children moved from the central cities to new homes in surrounding suburban areas. Most suburbs were quick to establish new recreation and park departments, hire personnel, and develop programs and facilities to serve all age groups—often in concert with local school districts.

At the same time, the population within the inner cities changed dramatically. With the rapid mechanization of agriculture in the South and the abandonment of the share-cropper system, millions of African Americans moved from the South to the cities and industrialized areas of the Northeast, the Midwest, and the West in search of jobs and better opportunities. Growing numbers of Hispanic immigrants surged into the cities from the Caribbean islands and Central America. Generally, these new residents faced economic hardships, including limited employment opportunities, resulting in health, housing, and welfare concerns for cities.

TRENDS IN PROGRAM SPONSORSHIP

As a result of such population shifts and changes in lifestyle, a number of trends in recreation program functions and in the role to be played by government emerged. These included (1) programs aimed at improving physical fitness, (2) emphasis on environmental concerns, (3) activities and services designed to meet specific age group needs, (4) recreation for persons with disabilities, (5) increasing programming in the arts, (6) services for people living in poverty, and (7) programs concerned with the needs of racial and ethnic minorities.

Emphasis on Physical Fitness

Beginning in the 1950s, there was a strong emphasis on the need to develop and maintain the physical fitness of youth. In both world wars, a disappointingly high percentage of male draftees and enlistees had been rejected by the armed forces for physical reasons. Then, after World War II, comparative studies such as the Kraus-Weber tests

Affluence is evidenced by the increase in attendance at resorts.
© Digital Vision/Photodisc/Thinkstock/Getty.

THE IMPACT OF ECONOMIC DECLINES ON SPENDING FOR LEISURE AND RECREATION

Over the course of the last quarter of the twentieth century and the first decade of the twenty-first century, the U.S. economy has experienced periodic economic declines. The declines are called recessions and take place when the economy contracts, or gets smaller. Recessions are characterized by high unemployment, stagnant wages, and falls in retail sales. Most recent recessions have been short-lived and their impact on public parks and recreation is documented elsewhere in this chapter. The impact on personal and public spending for recreation has broader implications. Not only does it affect public parks and recreation, but nonprofits providing recreation programs, the arts, and commercial recreation enterprises. The major recessions of the last 30 years occurred in 1981 (14 months), 1990 (8 months), 2001 (8 months), and 2007 (19 months). It was generally assumed that personal spending declines during a recession. However, spending data do not support that assumption. Between 1981 and 2009, there was only one quarter showing a decline in personal spending, and that occurred in 2001, during the dot-com bust. Through the early part of the twenty-first century, personal spending continued to increase in every quarter. That ended with the 2009 recession. This was the most broad-based recession since 1929, with a majority of Americans impacted. Some economists suggested that as a result of the 2009 recession, personal spending declined in excess of 3%, which translates into $300–$400 billion annually. Spread over the three plus years of the recession, spending declines had a major impact on public and nonprofit organizations. In 2010, evidence suggested people had continued to cut expenses and reduce personal spending. The Internet, which was a nonfactor in previous recessions, was a source individuals turned to for ways to reduce costs. Consumers bargain shopped, looked for coupons and special offers, did research on products, and so forth, all in an effort to reduce their spending.

Prior to the recession of 2009, conventional wisdom suggested that some spending reluctance would occur but would be short term. The widespread impact of the 2009 recession, although the recession was declared officially over in 2010, continued to affect states well into 2016. For leisure and recreation, the impact was felt in a variety of ways. From a positive perspective, public agencies experienced high levels of program demand from families and individuals replacing more costly commercial enterprises they used to patronize. Commercial enterprises also focused on cost effectiveness and efficiency, engaged in more effective marketing, and ensured that their products and experiences were perceived as a value.

Simultaneous with the increase in demand, public and nonprofit-based parks and recreation agencies faced the most significant funding crisis since the tax revolt of the early 1970s. Agencies laid off staff, closed recreation centers, raised fees for programs, and looked for partnerships, all focused on meeting the needs of citizens who were demanding more services.

The President's Council on Physical Fitness and Sport was created by President Eisenhower in 1956 and continues into the twenty-first century.
© Photodisc/Getty.

showed that American youths were less fit than the youths of several other nations. Vice President Richard Nixon convened the President's Conference on the Fitness of American Youth at the United States Naval Academy in Annapolis, Maryland, in 1956. The recommendations from the conference included increasing public awareness, increasing public funding of community recreation, supporting nonprofit youth-serving agencies through private and public funds, increasing and improving community recreation facilities, improving fitness opportunities for girls, and improving leadership for physical activity. In 1956, President Dwight Eisenhower also established the President's Council on Youth Fitness to serve as a catalyst for motivating communities and individuals to adopt active lifestyles. In response to the conference, schools strengthened their programs of physical fitness, and many public recreation departments expanded their leisure activities to include fitness classes, conditioning, jogging, and sports for all ages. Yet, despite these measures, today we are continuing to fight an obesity epidemic, with 38% of adults older than 20 years obese and 71% overweight. The picture is frightening for children as well, as one-third are categorically overweight or obese.[20]

Environmental Concerns

A key concern of the recreation field has been the environment. In the postwar period, it became evident that there was a critical need to preserve and rehabilitate the nation's land, water, and wildlife resources. U.S. citizens permitted the country's great rivers and lakes to be polluted by waste, forests to be razed by lumbering interests, and wildlife to be ravaged by overhunting, lack of adequate breeding areas, chemical poisons, and invasion of their environments. Greater and greater demands had been placed on the natural resource bank, with open space shrinking at an unprecedented rate.

A SHORT HISTORY OF THE LAND AND WATER CONSERVATION FUND

The legislation creating the Land and Water Conservation Fund (LWCF) was passed by Congress in 1964 and became law in 1965. The LWCF became the primary source of revenue for park and recreation agencies at the federal, state, and local levels and continues to play an important role. The LWCF initially had three sources of revenue: proceeds from sales of federal properties, motorboat fuel taxes, and user fees for recreational use of federal lands. This raised $100 million annually, but it quickly became evident the level of funding was inadequate to meet the goals of the program. In 1968, the funding level was raised to $200 million per year for five years, and an additional funding source, revenues from leasing of the Outer Continental Shelf oil and gas resources, was added. Congress gradually raised the funding level to $900 million annually.

Currently, approximately $900 million is annually accumulated into the fund. Through 2006, the fund accumulated $29 billion with 62% of the allocation going to federal land acquisition, 28% to state grant programs, and 10% to other programs. The major roadblock preventing greater success of the fund is that the allocation is not automatic but must be authorized annually by Congress. The president recommends a level of spending for the LWCF and in some years has recommended low levels of spending. Congress can override this recommendation and sometimes has. However, allocated funds (actual dollars spent) have often been below levels authorized by Congress (dollars appropriated by Congress). In 2015, facing the possibility of nonrenewal, the LWCF was granted a three-year reprieve and funded at a level of $450 million.

Appropriations from the fund have been made for three general purposes: (1) federal acquisition of land and waters and interests therein; (2) grants to states for recreational planning; acquiring recreational lands, waters, or related interests; and developing outdoor recreation facilities; and (3) other federal purposes.

One of the key provisions of the fund is a requirement that every state create a "state comprehensive outdoor recreation plan" to be eligible to receive monies from the fund. Another important aspect of the program requires that all grants made to states be matched by state or local dollars. At the state level, funding is administered through a state organization, with some money going to state parks, wildlife, and other outdoor recreation managers. The remainder of the funding is provided to cities and counties on a competitive basis. Between 1965 and 2008, 41,000 grants were made to states. "This figure includes 10,600 grants for acquisition; 26,420 grants for developing recreation facilities; 2,760 grants for redeveloping older recreational facilities; and 641 state planning grants for studies of recreation potential, need, opportunity, and policy."[21] From these funds the National Park Service reported, "2.6 million acres of state and local parkland through direct acquisition, and many times that number of acres is statutorily protected through development projects which protect lands acquired and developed from non-outdoor recreations uses in perpetuity."[22]

Results at the federal level have been equally impressive as the four recipient federal agencies (National Park Service, Forest Service, Fish and Wildlife Service, and Bureau of Land Management) have protected more than 4.5 million acres.

In the late 1950s, President Dwight Eisenhower and the Congress formed the Outdoor Recreation Resources Review Commission to investigate this problem. The result was a landmark, heavily documented report in 1962 that helped to promote a wave of environmental efforts by federal, state, and municipal governments. The Federal Water Pollution Control Administration divided the nation into 20 major river basins and promoted regional sewage treatment programs in those areas. The Water Quality Act of 1965, the Clean Water Restoration Act of 1966, the Solid Waste Disposal Act of 1965, the Highway Beautification Act of 1965, and the Mining Reclamation Act of 1968 all committed the United States to a sustained program of conservation and protection of its natural resources. Another major piece of legislation was the Wilderness Act of 1964, which gave Congress the authority to declare certain unspoiled lands permanently off-limits to human occupation and development.

Many states and cities embarked on new programs of land acquisition and beautification and developed environmental plans designed to reduce air and water pollution. Nonprofit organizations such as the American Land Trust, the Nature Conservancy, and the Trust for Public Lands took over properties encompassing hundreds of thousands of acres—many of them donated by large corporations—for preservation or transfer to public agencies for recreational use. Such programs were accompanied by efforts within federal agencies such as the National Park Service, the Forest Service, the Fish and Wildlife Service, and the Bureau of Land Management.

In the early 1980s, federal expenditures for parks and environmental programs were sharply reduced, the rate of land acquisition was cut back, and government policies regulating the use of wild lands for mining, timber cutting, grazing, oil drilling, and similar commercial activities were dramatically relaxed.

MEETING AGE-GROUP NEEDS

In addition to the demographic trends cited earlier, three important changes in the nation's population that gathered force in the postwar decades were (1) the dramatic rise in the birth rate, with millions of children

Outdoor recreation and nature areas have benefited from the environmental efforts that began with Yellowstone National Park and continue today.
© djgis/Shutterstock.

Persons with disabilities engage in a variety of sport and recreation activities today, including Special Olympics, tennis, basketball, and snow skiing.
© Bikeworldtravel/Shutterstock.

and youths flooding the schools and community recreation centers; (2) the lengthening of the population's life span, resulting in a growing proportion of older adults in society, at times resulting in increased demands of adult children to provide elder care; and (3) the increasing pressures on families with children due to growing numbers of single-parent households and the entrance of millions of women into the workforce.

In response to these trends, thousands of governmental and non-profit organizations expanded their programs for children and youths, and numerous youth sport leagues such as Little League, Biddy Basketball, and American Legion Football recruited millions of participants. At the other end of the age range, public and nonprofit organizations, including many municipal park and recreation agencies, developed golden age clubs or senior centers, often with funding from the federal government through the Administration on Aging.

Changing family households confirmed the need for recreation programs to provide day care services for children of working parents and to meet other leisure-related needs. Religious organizations in particular are stressing family-oriented programming in an effort to strengthen marital bonds and parent–child relationships.

Special Recreation for Persons with Disabilities

An area of increased emphasis in the postwar era was the provision of supportive services for persons with physical and mental disabilities. Various government agencies concerned with rehabilitation were expanded to meet the needs of individuals with physical disabilities, especially the large numbers of returning veterans who sought to be integrated into community life.

To better serve people with developmental disabilities, the federal government sharply increased its aid to special education. In recreation, assistance was given to programs serving children, youths, and adults with developmental disabilities. Beginning in the mid-1960s, there was an increased emphasis on developing social and recreational programs for aging persons in both institutional and community settings. Overall, the specialized field of what came to be known as therapeutic recreation service expanded steadily in this period. With the establishment of the National Therapeutic Recreation Society in the mid-1960s and the American Therapeutic Recreation Association in the 1980s, professionalization in therapeutic recreation service developed rapidly. The establishment of curriculum guidelines for professional preparation, the setting of program standards, and the development of registration and certification plans all served to make this field a significant specialized area within the broad leisure-service field.

Increased Interest in the Arts

Following World War II, the United States embarked on an expansion of cultural centers, museums, and art centers. In part, this represented a natural follow-up to the stimulus that had been given to art, theater, music, and dance by emergency federal programs during the Great Depression. Another element, however, was that Americans had come to enjoy the arts as both spectators and participants. Through the 1970s and early 1980s, community arts activities continued to flourish, with the assistance of federal funding through the National Endowment for the Arts, which helped to support state arts units, choreographers and composers, and individual performers and companies.

In the mid- and late 1980s, seeing declines in attendance at music, drama, and dance events, as well as a need to increase funding for many museums, libraries, and similar institutions, new methods of fundraising led to diversification of offerings and marketing them to a broader community audience. As an example, art, natural history, and science museums today offer lectures, tours, films, innovative displays, special fundraising dinners, and other events designed to attract a wide spectrum of patrons.

☀ THE SPECIAL OLYMPICS

In 1968, Eunice Kennedy Shriver (1921–2009) organized the first International Special Olympic Games in Chicago, Illinois. The Special Olympics were an outgrowth of a day-camp program started in 1962 by Shriver for people with developmental disabilities. During the first international games, 1,000 athletes from the United States and Canada competed. In 1977, the first winter games were held in Steamboat Springs, Colorado, and included 500 athletes. Today, over 3 million athletes from 220 countries compete in local, state, national, and international Special Olympics events. The Special Olympics movement and the tireless work of Shriver have had an extraordinary impact on the public's understanding of people with developmental disabilities and creation of supportive public policy. Her comments at the 1987 Special Olympics have become a rallying cry for the rights of individuals with disabilities:

"The right to play on any playing field?

You have earned it.

The right to study in any school?

You have earned it.

The right to hold a job?

You have earned it.

The right to be anyone's neighbor?

You have earned it."[23]

Recreation's Antipoverty Role

During the 1930s and 1940s, a number of federal housing programs provided funding to support small parks, playgrounds, or centers in public housing projects. In the 1960s, as part of President Lyndon Johnson's "war on poverty," a new wave of legislation, such as the Economic Opportunity Act of 1964, the Housing and Urban Development Act of 1964, and the Model Cities program approved in 1967, provided assistance for locally directed recreation programs to be conducted by disadvantaged citizens themselves in depressed urban neighborhoods. Other federal programs, such as the Job Corps, VISTA (Volunteers in Service to America), and the Neighborhood Youth Corps, also included recreation-related components.

Segregation and Integration in Recreation

The public recreation movement of the late nineteenth and early twentieth centuries did not equally benefit all Americans. Throughout most of the United States, separate recreation facilities had been built for African and Caucasian Americans. As with public education, the result of this segregation was highly disparate opportunities. The first widespread attempts at racial integration were in the late 1950s and early 1960s following the Supreme Court's landmark Brown v. the Board of Education decision.

Unfortunately, it was not until the late 1960s, following escalated racial tensions in many cities, that the federal government dedicated serious financial resources to serving African Americans, particularly those living in impoverished urban centers, and often for youth programs. These included sports and social activities, cultural pursuits, job training and tutorial programs, and trips and similar recreation activities. On a national scale, the Job Corps, VISTA, Neighborhood Youth Corps, and an aggregate of special projects known as Community Action Programs continued into the 1970s but were gradually terminated in the years that followed.

Red Rock Conservation Area is an example of an outdoor recreation resource located just minutes from the Las Vegas strip. It is a popular visitors site for tourists and residents and provides numerous free days each year so all residents can visit.
Courtesy of U.S. Bureau of Land Management.

COUNTERCULTURE: YOUTHS IN REBELLION

During the late 1960s, what came to be known as the counterculture made its appearance in America. The term counterculture, as John Kelly points out, is generally applied to a movement that develops in opposition to an

PROTESTANT WORK ETHIC REJECTED

The rejection of the Protestant work ethic was widely expressed in the music, art, and literature of the 1960s. The historical record of the baby boomers of the 1960s, however, indicates that the demise of Americans' obsession with work is more myth than reality. A study published by the Families and Work Institute in 2006 indicates that baby boomers are more likely to live work-centric lifestyles than the generations that preceded and follow them. A 2004 study by the same institute indicates that baby boomers work longer hours and are more likely to feel overworked than employees of other generations.

established and dominant culture—often in political, religious, or lifestyle terms—and that manifests itself in language, symbols, and behavior.

Rejection of the Work Ethic

A significant aspect of the counterculture movement was its rejection of work as the be-all and end-all of one's life, and of the widely accepted goal of "making it" in the business or professional world. A deep-rooted belief in the value of hard work, which was linked to an essentially conservative, industrious, and moralistic view of life, had long been a fundamental tenet of American society.

However, since World War II, there had been a retreat from the stern precepts of the Protestant work ethic. As establishment values and monetary success were undermined in the thinking of young people during the counterculture period, leisure satisfactions assumed new importance.

The counterculture movement in the United States during the 1960s was part of a larger youth movement that challenged the political, economic, and educational establishments in a number of other nations around the world. Here, it symbolized the rebellion of young people against parental authority and the curricular and social controls of schools and colleges. Much of it stemmed from mass protests against the Vietnam War. Rock music and lyrics that challenged traditional values became popular, and some young people joined "hippie" communes or fled to neighborhoods like Haight-Ashbury in San Francisco or the East Village in New York City, where they experimented with drugs and a variety of alternative lifestyles.

DRIVES FOR EQUALITY BY DISADVANTAGED GROUPS

Another important aspect of the counterculture movement was that it provided a climate within which various populations in American society that had historically been disadvantaged were encouraged to press vigorously for fuller social and economic rights.

Rock concerts began in earnest in the 1960s and continue today.
© Guitarsimo/Dreamstime.com.

Racial and Ethnic Minorities

For racial and ethnic minorities, there was a strong thrust during the 1960s and 1970s toward demanding fuller recreational service in terms of facilities and organized programs. In response, many public recreation and park departments not only upgraded these traditional elements, but also began to provide mobile recreation units that would enter affected neighborhoods to offer cultural, social, and other special services. Building on projects that had been initiated during the war on poverty and in response to escalating racial tensions in cities, many departments initiated classes, workshops, festivals, and holiday celebrations designed to promote ethnic pride and intercultural appreciation.

Through legislation, Supreme Court decisions, other judicial orders, and voluntary compliance, public, nonprofit, and commercial facilities were gradually desegregated through the 1970s and 1980s. Major youth and adult social membership organizations such as the Girl Scouts and the YMCA, which had tended either to maintain segregated units for racial minorities or not to serve them at all, opened up their memberships and in some cases identified racial justice as a high-priority mission for the years ahead. In terms of the broader culture, greater numbers of racial and ethnic minorities began to achieve great success in such leisure-related areas as college and professional sports and popular entertainment such as music, television, and motion pictures.

Progress for Women

In the 1960s and 1970s, feminist groups mobilized to attack two major areas of gender-based discrimination in recreation and leisure: employment practices and program involvement. In response to equal opportunity laws and other pressures, governmental recreation and park departments and other agencies began to hire more women.

A fundamental principle in community recreation has been that all persons should be given an equal opportunity, regardless of sex, religion, race, or other personal factors. However, in the postwar decades, it became evident that this principle had not been applied to participation of girls and women in public recreation programs in the United States. In 1972, growing pressure from women's groups led to the approval of groundbreaking legislation, Title IX of the Education Amendments Act. Title IX was the first legislation to prohibit sex discrimination in educational institutions. Although Title IX prevents discrimination in all aspects of public education, including recruitment, admission, and employment, the primary focus of public discourse over the past 40 years has been equality in athletics.

Case Study

Designing for Ethnic Minorities

One of the key concerns of outdoor recreation resource managers is the low number of racial and ethnic minorities visiting and participating in programs at outdoor recreation areas. Although not a new issue, land management agencies continue to struggle to find ways to engage these groups, especially as their population increases as a percentage of the total U.S. population. In a report prepared by the National Park Service (NPS) in 2008, five research hypotheses were reported that attempt to explain the lack of involvement in outdoor recreation. The hypotheses are marginality, subculture/ethnicity, discrimination, opportunity, and acculturation.

The *marginality* hypothesis suggests the differences in racial/ethnic minority representation are a result of socioeconomic factors caused by historical discrimination and include barriers such as limited financial resources, lower levels of education, and limited employment opportunities. The subculture/ethnicity hypothesis recognizes the influence of marginality on leisure and recreation patterns but argues the differences in park visitation, at least partially, are a result of cultural norms, value systems, social organizations, and socialization practices. Examples of cultural values or norms can include size of recreational groups, preferred activities (e.g., hiking, biking, swimming, picnicking), and development level of sites (e.g., bathrooms, pavilions, visitor centers).

The discrimination hypothesis places importance on contemporary, post–civil rights discrimination that occurs from interpersonal contact with other visitors or park personnel or through institutional policies. The opportunity hypothesis examines the relationship between the residential location of minority populations, recreational sites, and recreation preferences. The acculturation hypothesis examines the relationship between cultural assimilation into the majority culture and recreational choices. According to this hypothesis, as a minority culture assimilates into the majority culture, they begin to take on the recreational patterns of the majority culture.[a]

Understanding the hypotheses is important, and moving from hypotheses to action is much more challenging. It frequently requires agencies to rethink how they do business, change organizational culture, recognize the organization is not representative of the population it is designated to serve, and finally, strive to overcome bureaucratic inertia that promotes preservation of the norm over change. Each outdoor management agency deals with the challenge in its own way, and often in multiple ways. Federal agencies initiate plans and actions at the director, regional, and local levels. Much of the actual work falls to the local level because, at this level, the situation is direct and immediate. For example, in the mid-1990s, the Pacific regional director for the NPS determined that the public relations programs were focusing only on traditional media resources such as major newspapers, television, and radio stations. He organized a task force charged with identifying alternative media outlets in the San Francisco Bay area. In a short period of time, they identified more than 300 media outlets focusing on specific racial and ethnic minority groups, as well as women, gays and lesbians, and persons with disabilities.

The U.S. Army Corps of Engineers approached the development and renovation of recreation sites with a focus on providing facilities, amenities, and programs designed to meet the expressed needs of racial and ethnic minorities. In 2002, the Army Corps of Engineers published a report titled *Managing for Ethnic Diversity: Recreation Facility and Service Modifications for Ethnic Minorities* in which the premise was that ethnically universal designs can meet the needs of a progressively more diverse population. Ethnically universal design focuses on creation of programs and facilities that are more inclusive of ethnic cultural diversity. Specifically, the report suggests moving away from the traditional design model, called an ethnically neutral design, which focuses wholly on white middle-class nuclear families with the assumption that other ethnic groups would adapt to the design model. The new approach moves toward a model of embracing cultural pluralism. Further, the report argues that the development of day-use facilities are essential to the success of this model.[b]

The report suggests a variety of facilities and services that appeal to Hispanics, Asians, and African Americans. These services include the following:

- Group shelters to provide shade and protection from inclement weather
- Larger tables, or modular movable tables, to accommodate large family groups
- Larger and easier-to-maintain grills and cookers for recreational cooking for large groups
- Shade trees in picnic sites
- Playgrounds (kid zones) near picnic areas
- Open grassy play areas for sports that can accommodate a wide variety of activities
- Facilities for community events (e.g., large group shelter, gazebo, amphitheaters)
- Use of universal symbols on signs
- Interpretive signs on walking trails in Spanish and other dominant languages of the region
- Mass transportation facilities (bus loading areas) at the most popular areas
- Improved security through increased ranger patrols, bilingual rangers, and improved gatehouses at park entrances[b]

Questions to Consider

1. How has the move away from ethnically neutral design intended to improve attendance at outdoor areas?
2. Why is it important to understand the reasons why ethnic populations may not see the outdoors as a special place?
3. Put yourself in the role of a resource manager and determine how you would increase participation by racial and ethnic minorities.

Sources

a. R. S. McCowan and D. N. Laven, Evaluation Research to Support National Park Service 21st Century Relevance Initiatives (Washington, DC: National Park Service, 2008): 3.
b. R. A. Dunn, Managing for Ethnic Diversity: Recreation Facility and Service Modifications for Ethnic Minorities, ERDC/EL TR-02-14 (Vicksburg, MS: U.S. Army Research and Development Center, 2002).

During the 1970s and 1980s, community recreation organizations joined the nationwide effort to offer equal opportunities for girls and women. A significant development at this time was the merger of formerly sex-separated organizations into organizations serving both sexes, such as the Boys and Girls Club of America. As a result of these changes, girls and women today have a far greater range of sport and physical recreation opportunities than they did in the past.

WOMEN'S WORLD CUP SOCCER

From an international perspective, the Olympic Games were among the first true competitive events for women. Yet, it was Women's World Cup Soccer that captured the imagination of the world and firmly placed women as equals on the international sport stage. The International Federation of Association Football (FIFA) is the governing body for international football (soccer) and has been responsible for the men's World Cup since 1930. FIFA initiated the first Women's World Cup in 1991, and the event was held in China with 12 teams participating. Although it had an inauspicious start, the FIFA Women's World Cup has become an icon for women's equality in sport. The 1995 World Cup, held in Sweden, had a total attendance of 112,213 with one match only drawing 250 spectators. The 1999 World Cup, held in the United States, was the breakout World Cup with more than 1.1 million spectators and more than 1 billion television viewers. The Women's World Cup provided the American team's first international success, with championships in 1991 and 1999 and players such as Mia Hamm and Brandi Chastain becoming overnight household names. The success of the United States women's national soccer team, which resulted in three World Cups and four Olympic gold medals from 1990 to 2015, has helped earn soccer a place in the hearts of American society. Beyond that, it has opened women's sport on an international basis in areas where it might not otherwise have flourished as attendance at the 2015 World Cup in Canada reached 1,353,506 spectators, up from 997,433 in 2011 when hosted by China, and the highest number ever recorded.

Lesbians, Gays, Bisexual and Transgender

Lesbians, gays, bisexual, and transgender (GLBT) individuals compose a third group who traditionally have been disadvantaged in American society. During the counterculture era, gay activists began to mobilize as an economic and political force. In the 1960s and 1970s, many gay and lesbian groups began to organize and promote their recreational and social activities openly on college campuses and in community life.

In other cases, when homosexual groups sought to participate in big-city St. Patrick's Day parades, or when they held a huge gay festival at Florida's Walt Disney World, a number of conservative Christian organizations protested vigorously. In retaliation, when rural Cobb County, Georgia, passed a resolution condemning the gay lifestyle as incompatible with its values, gay groups and their allies pressured the International Olympic Committee to withdraw some of its featured events from the county after they had already been scheduled to take place there as part of the 1996 Olympics. Fights related to transgender individuals' right to compete based on their gender rather than biological sexual identity are ongoing.

Older Adults in Community Life

Although the counterculture was primarily a youth movement in the United States and abroad, it also prompted many middle-aged and older persons to examine their value systems and their status in community life.

Older adults at this time represented a fourth group of disadvantaged persons in the sense that they were generally regarded and treated as powerless individuals who were both physically and economically vulnerable. However, under the leadership of such growing organizations as the American Association of Retired Persons and the much smaller Gray Panthers, older adults began to mobilize and exert political clout to obtain improved benefits. With support from various federal programs, including the Administration on Aging, senior citizens' groups and golden age clubs around the United States began to offer diversified programs of health care, social services, nutrition, housing and transportation assistance, and recreation.

Programming for Persons with Disabilities

Although significant progress had been made following World War II, both treatment-centered and community-based programming for persons with disabilities received a major impetus during the counterculture period. Like other disadvantaged groups that had essentially been powerless, persons with disabilities began to act as their own advocates, demanding their rights and opportunities. Persons with disabilities began to mobilize politically to promote positive legislation and increased community services for those with physical, mental, or social disabilities.

At the same time that therapeutic recreation specialists began to include a broader range of disabilities within their scope of service, numerous organizations went one step further and promoted such innovative programming as theater arts for people with physical disabilities, skiing for individuals with visual impairments, and a full range of sports and track-and-field events for people with mobility impairments.

AUSTERITY AND FISCAL CUTBACKS: 1970s AND 1980s

Despite this general picture of positive progress, the recreation, parks, and leisure-service field faced a serious threat in the 1970s and 1980s as mounting costs of government led to tax protests and funding cutbacks in states and cities across the United States. As early as the mid-1970s, a number of older industrial cities in the nation's Rust Belt, an area of the Midwest where iron and steel are produced and manufactured, began to suffer from increased energy costs, welfare and crime problems, and expenses linked to rising infrastructure maintenance problems. Along with some suburban school districts confronted by skyrocketing enrollments and limited tax bases, such communities experienced budget deficits and the need to freeze expenditures.

In 1976, a tax limitation law was passed in New Jersey, and in 1978 California's much more radical Proposition 13 sharply reduced local property tax rates and assessment increases. A "tax revolt" soon spread rapidly across the United States. By the end of 1979, statutory provisions had been approved in 36 states that either reduced property, income, or sales taxes or put other types of spending limits in place. Austerity budgets had to be adopted in many communities, counties, and other governmental units. Typically, Proposition 13 resulted in major funding cutbacks for parks, libraries,

In periods of austerity and fiscal cut backs, states sometimes close state parks as a cost-saving measure.
Courtesy of Alan Levine.

recreation, social services, and street sweeping and maintenance, while police and fire departments tended to be protected against cuts.[24]

Expanding Use of Revenue Sources

Many local recreation and park agencies adopted the policy of instituting or raising fees and charges for participation in programs, for use of the facilities, for rental of equipment, and for other types of uses. In the past, it generally had been the practice to provide all basic play opportunities, particularly for children and youths, without charge and to impose fees only for classes with special expenses or for admission to facilities such as skating rinks, swimming pools, golf courses, or tennis courts—often with arrangements made for annual permits at modest cost.

Acceptance of Marketing Orientation   Directly linked to this trend was the widespread acceptance of an entrepreneurial, marketing-oriented approach to recreation and park programming and administration. It was argued by both educators and practitioners that it was necessary to be aggressive in seeking out new program opportunities and creative in responding to fiscal challenges.

It was argued that managers of recreation and park programs, directors of nonprofit youth organizations, and operators of commercial play facilities were all essentially in the same "business"—that of meeting the public's leisure needs and interests. Therefore, recreation was increasingly referred to as an "industry."

It was often argued that to compete, public recreation agencies had to adopt the philosophy and businesslike methods of successful companies. At every stage of agency operations—from assessing potential target populations and planning programs to pricing, publicizing, and distributing services—sophisticated methods of analysis and businesslike approaches to attracting and satisfying "customers" were to be used.

Privatization of Recreation and Park Operations

As a second type of response to the era of austerity that began in the 1980s, many recreation, park, and leisure-service agencies resorted to privatization—subcontracting or developing concession arrangements with private organizations—to carry out functions that they could not themselves fulfill as economically or efficiently.

Numerous parks and recreation departments have contracted with private businesses to operate golf courses, tennis complexes, marinas, and other facilities under agreements that govern the standards they must meet and the rates they may impose. Particularly in the construction of massive new facilities such as sports stadiums and arenas, similar arrangements have been made with commercial developers or businesses for private funding of all or part of construction expenses, with long-term leases being granted to owners of major sports teams.[25]

Impact of Funding Cuts

In 1978, the National Urban Recreation Study reported that hiring freezes and staff cutbacks had taken place in a majority of urban park and recreation departments during the preceding five years. Two years later, a study of U.S. cities with populations greater than 150,000 found that a majority of the responding recreation and park departments experienced cutbacks that necessitated personnel freezes, staff discharges, program elimination, rejection of bond issues, and reduced facility maintenance.

Some reports suggested that many municipal and county recreation and park agencies weathered the financial crisis that followed the tax revolt and reached a point of relative stability. A study of small-town public recreation departments in several Western and Midwestern states by Ellen Weissinger and William Murphy found that although these departments experienced somewhat similar cutbacks to those reported in larger cities, they generally avoided drastic reductions in staff and programs.[26]

PROMINENCE OF FEES AND CHARGES FOR ACTIVITIES

Even when recreation programs are provided by public local or nonprofit agencies, price tags are placed today on almost every kind of sponsored recreational opportunity. Typically, the annual or seasonal program brochures of public recreation and park agencies list various classes, aquatic or sport facilities, camps, tournaments, or special events—invariably with attached fees and charges that may run into several hundreds of dollars.

However, the reality is that in many larger cities, which have the greatest number of poor families and are marked by high welfare statistics, school dropouts, drug and alcohol abuse, youth gangs, and random violence, recreation and park programs today offer only the most minimal opportunities.

Beyond this, Jack Foley and Veda Ward point out that in the early 1990s the most severely disadvantaged communities, such as South Los Angeles, nonprofit sports groups like Little League, Pony League, AAU swimming, and gymnastic and track clubs (which use public facilities but rely on volunteer leaders and membership fees) do not exist. There is also no commercial recreation in the form of movie theaters, malls, skating rinks, or bowling alleys. They continue:

> Boys and Girls Clubs, YMCAs and YWCAs, Scouts, and so forth, which rely on business and community support, are under-represented and financed in poor communities. A market equity policy (one gets all the recreation one can buy) [has] created a separate, unequal, and regressive City of Los Angeles recreation system. City parks [in wealthier neighborhoods] raise from $50,000 to $250,000 annually from user fees and donations, while recreation centers in South Los Angeles exist on small city subsidies and money they can squeeze out of the parents of poor children.[27]

EXPANSION OF OTHER RECREATION PROGRAMS

In sharp contrast with this negative picture, other forms of recreation services have flourished over the past three decades. Today, the largest single component of leisure services is the diversified field of commercial recreation businesses. Travel and tourism; fitness spas; professional sport and sport equipment; the manufacture and sale of hobbies, toys, and games; and varied forms of popular entertainment represent only part of this major sector of leisure involvement.

THE IMPORTANCE OF INDIVIDUAL DONORS TO NONPROFITS

Nonprofit organizations are dependent upon the goodwill of individuals and organizations to provide financial donations. This is especially true when the nonprofit desires to renovate existing buildings or to construct new buildings. The annual operating budget of a nonprofit is highly dependent upon individual donations. Many organizations gain a share of their operating budget from the United Way, but this is rarely sufficient to maintain day-to-day operations, and for an organization to improve its physical facilities it is wholly dependent upon contributions and grants. Physical facilities can be as simple as furniture for a meeting room and a softball complex for girls and women or can be major structures, such as multisport facilities, community centers, hospitals, and the like. The Salvation Army was recipient to such a goodwill gift in 1998 and the gift has allowed it to change the way it delivers community services in some communities.

In 1998, Mrs. Joan Kroc, widow of McDonald's founder Ray Kroc, donated $90 million to the Salvation Army to build a comprehensive community center in San Diego, California. Her goal was to create a center, supported in part by the community, where children and families would be exposed to different people, activities and arts that would otherwise be beyond their reach. Completed in 2001, the center sits on 12 acres and offers an ice arena, gymnasium, three pools, rock climbing walls, a performing arts theatre, an Internet-based library, computer lab, and a school of visual and performing arts.

When Mrs. Kroc passed away in October 2003, she left $1.5 billion—much of her estate—to the Salvation Army, by far the largest charitable gift ever given to the Army, and the largest single gift given to any single charity at one time. The initial disbursements of this bequest began in January 2005. The gift had by then grown to $1.8 billion and was split evenly among the four Army Territories—Central, East, South, and West. The money was designated to build a series of state-of-the-art Salvation Army Ray and Joan Kroc Corps Community Centers nationwide patterned after the San Diego center. From the very beginning, the Salvation Army envisioned this as a long-term project, which could take up to 10 or 15 years to have all of the centers open and operational. No other U.S. charity—faith-based or otherwise—has ever undertaken such a sweeping fundraising or construction effort with the potential to impact millions of people.

By 2014, 26 centers had been opened. They are located throughout the United States in cities such as San Francisco, California; Atlanta, Georgia; Ashland, Ohio; Coeur d'Alene, Idaho; Omaha, Nebraska; Salem, Oregon; Dayton, Ohio; Grand Rapids, Michigan; Kerrville, Texas; Guayama, Puerto Rico; and Phoenix, Arizona.[28]

An example of the success of the Kroc Centers comes from Coeur d'Alene, Idaho, which saw its own center completed in 2009.

The Kroc turns 1 today—and what a year it has been. Before it opened, it shot for around 2,000 members, keeping its fingers crossed for 5,000 at the one-year mark. Today, it has 20,500 members, and has entertained around 630,000 visitors since May 11, 2009—while staff has increased to 272 employees compared to around 70 when it opened. And, a dozen cities, including Philadelphia, Chicago, Honolulu, and now Quincy, have toured the most populated Kroc Center in the West as a guide for their future hometown facilities.[29]

The Kroc Centers, operated by the Salvation Army, are major community centers that provide multiple services, including recreation.
Courtesy of Bryan E. Smith.

Similarly, most of the other areas of specialized recreation programming, such as therapeutic recreation, employee services, campus recreation, and private-membership and residential leisure services, have expanded steadily. These fields have sharpened their own identities by developing professional societies or business associations, sponsoring national and regional conferences, publishing newsletters and magazines, and in some cases establishing continuing education and certification programs.

TRENDS IN THE 1990s AND EARLY TWENTY-FIRST CENTURY

This section describes several important demographic, social, economic, and technological trends beginning in the 1990s that influenced the provision of recreation and leisure services in the years immediately before and after the turn of the century. We deal with these and more trends in greater detail elsewhere in the text.

Economic Stratification: Income Gaps and "Luxury Fever"

Historically, the United States was viewed as a land of opportunity, in which every individual might climb the socioeconomic ladder and in which the middle class represented the backbone of society. During the 1990s and into the twenty-first century, these assumptions were sharply reversed. Several new studies on the growing concentration of U.S. wealth and income challenged the nation's cherished self-image. Bradsher writes:

> They show that rather than being an egalitarian society, the United States has become the most economically stratified of industrial nations.... Indeed the drive [under the so-called Contract with America] to reduce federal welfare programs and cut taxes is expected to widen disparities between rich and poor.[30]

In part, this development stemmed from the emergence of a winner-take-all mentality in American business and public life, as more and more Americans compete for ever fewer and bigger prizes. In fact, a tiny fraction of the population controls much of the financial resources in America as just 1% of Americans control 40% of the wealth.[31]

The growth of the number of wealthy families in the United States in the 1990s was not accompanied by reduction of families living in poverty. In 1993, the nation's poverty rate rose to a 10-year high of 15.1%. In 2008, 13.2% of U.S. citizens, or 39.1 million people, lived in poverty. Although the poverty rate fluctuates a few percentage points across each decade, there has been very little change since the mid-1960s when a number of antipoverty social programs were implemented (see **Figure 4.3**).

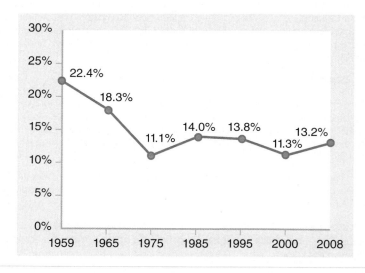

FIGURE 4.3   Poverty Level in the United States, 1959–2008.

Data from U.S. Census Bureau. Alternative Poverty Estimates in the United States: 2003 (Washington, DC: U.S. Census Bureau, 2005); and U.S. Census Bureau. Poverty: 2007 and 2008 American Community Surveys (Washington, DC: U.S. Census Bureau, 2009).

STRATIFICATION OF SALARIES AND THE MIDDLE CLASS

Much has been written about the stratification of salaries, including in this chapter. Less has been written about the impact on the middle class. Robert Frank's book *Falling Behind* is among several books addressing the effects of salary stratification on middle-class Americans.[33] A key premise of the book looks at the income gains at the highest level. Frank suggests that although the rich have gotten richer, the middle class has not kept up with income increases. There is no accepted definition of the middle class, so when annual income is considered as a measure, and individuals are asked if they are part of the middle class, people with annual incomes ranging from $40,000 to $250,000 say yes, they are middle class. These respondents typically say that they are stretched to make ends meet. They have not seen their salaries grow at a pace with the rich, yet they are purchasing more expensive homes, engaging in more expensive activities, and appear to be enjoying it less. Frank addresses the "rising cost of adequate" and uses homes as an example. When the rich build new homes or mansions, those at the top of the middle class begin to build larger homes, sometimes stretching what they can afford. There is a trickle-down effect to other levels of middle class as families see the community expectation for middle class rise. It is what Frank calls a cascading effect, where what top income earners spend their money on influences the spending patterns of the group directly below them, and on down until the effect reaches individuals at the bottom of the middle-class spectrum.

Starting in the 1990s, there were growing concerns about the ability of the middle class to make ends meet. Meanwhile, the middle class was declining, both in terms of numbers, income, and morale. In 1995, Labor Secretary Robert Reich concluded:

> Today's middle class is split into three groups. An underclass largely trapped in center cities, increasingly isolated from the core economy; an overclass of those who are positioned to profitably ride the waves of change; and in between, the largest group, an anxious class, most of whom hold jobs but who are justifiably... uneasy about their own standing and fearful for their children's futures.[32]

Implications for Leisure   What does this growing separation of U.S. society into rich and poor mean for recreation and leisure? First, a growing number of individuals have become immensely wealthy. In 1999, it was reported that 4.1 million of the nation's 102 million households had a net worth of $1 million or more and today that number is up to 10.1 million households.

In what seemed to be a vivid replay of Thorstein Veblen's view of "conspicuous consumption," these individuals were caught up in what Cornell economist Robert Frank described as luxury fever—a rage to spend wildly on vehicles, clothing, toys and hobbies, and a host of other possessions.[34]

Meanwhile, children in less affluent neighborhoods or school districts often attended schools that lacked even the most minimal resources for play, as well as spaces and equipment for classes. Throughout the nation at the century's end, the growing gap between rich and poor evidenced itself in jarring contrasts in terms of recreation, parks, and leisure opportunities.

Growing Conservatism in Social Policy

Accompanying the nation's division into rich and poor social classes, there was a pronounced shift in the late 1980s and the twenty-first century toward more conservative social and economic policies. This trend took many forms, including a sharp withdrawal of assistance for welfare and for inner-city programs serving the economically disadvantaged. Particularly in the mid-1990s (and again in the early twenty-first century), there were renewed efforts to open the nation's parks and forests to economic exploitation and to reduce support for environmental education programs.

The election of President Barack Obama and the initiation of the 2009 great recession for a short time loosened the growing social conservatism. However, once the initial crisis was over, Congress and the public became gridlocked in ideological discussions. There were continuing assaults on federal support for the National Endowment for the Arts and other cultural programs. Funding for the National Endowment for the Arts was cut from $162 million in 1995 to $99 million in 1996. The arts turned more and more to private funding.

Participation in recreation activities does not need to occur in large recreation centers; it can occur in almost any setting.

© Gennadiy Titkov/Shutterstock.

Throughout the past three decades, newspaper headlines illustrated the impact of conservative political thrusts on American life in such areas as mandates for child welfare, nursing home beds for the elderly, health care, environmental protection enforcement, legal help for the urban poor, and youth programs. The widespread decline in support for needed public services and the harsh resistance to government policies benefiting minorities and the poor inevitably posed a severe challenge to many public and nonprofit leisure-service organizations.

Commodification and Privatization of Leisure Services

There is a continued blurring of functions among different types of organizations in American society: governmental, nonprofit, private, and commercial. Instead of having clearly marked areas of responsibility and program operations in the leisure-service field, these separate kinds of organizations overlap each other through partnerships or cosponsorship arrangements; privatization by expanding their missions and undertaking new, innovative ventures; by adopting new fiscal policies; and by turning their operations over to the private sector. This overall trend had two related components: commodification and privatization.

Commodification Simply defined, commodification describes the process of taking any product or service and commercializing it by designing and marketing it to yield the greatest degree of financial return or profit. On the national scene, as part of the effort to gain fuller financial support in an increasingly consumer-oriented society, art museums, libraries, and theater, orchestra, and ballet companies all have become centers of popular entertainment, offering chartered trips abroad, film series and lecture programs, social events, and jazz concerts.

Privatization As described earlier, privatization refers to the growing practice of having private corporations take on responsibility for providing services, maintaining facilities, or performing other functions formerly carried out by government agencies.

During the 1990s, privatization grew increasingly widespread. In terms of public recreation and park privatization, the most striking event was the 1998 contract for a private group, the Central Park Conservancy, to operate New York City's Central Park, with joint public and private funding. A more common approach to privatization is to contract with a nonprofit to provide recreation services. This has been a frequent model in smaller communities where a nonprofit exists and no public recreation agency exists. The same model is present in large cities where existing recreation and park agencies cannot provide the level of service requested. A major recreation center is built, at public expense, and then leased to a nonprofit for operation. In many cases, the nonprofit continues to require a membership fee and may exclude some lower-income users.

THE NEW REALITIES: NEW, REVISITED, OR JUST PESSIMISM?

A consistent theme appearing in the literature of public and nonprofit recreation and leisure publications is that the recession of 2009–2010 has changed funding models forever. It is true that the recession diminished funding for public and nonprofit organizations. These organizations are almost always negatively affected by a recession, even when for-profit enterprises appear to be less affected.

One of the dilemmas faced by public and nonprofit organizations when the economy is in recession is an increasingly greater need for public services. People turn to public agencies for basic and recreational needs. Unfortunately, as demand increases, public agencies are facing similar financial challenges, frequently resulting in budget cuts and reduction of services. What was particularly challenging in the 2009 recession was the loss of revenue from multiple funding sources. Cities count on property, income, and sales taxes for the bulk of their operating revenues. Each source is somewhat volatile, but for the last 30 years property taxes have steadily increased until 2010, when property values dropped across major portions of the country. The new reality for recreation agencies may be that funding has changed forever. It did in the early 1970s when the tax revolt affected many states and communities. However, it is easy to assume things will not get better. That is a wrong-thinking attitude. Government funding sources, although traditionally stable, have not always been so, and to approach change from a negative perspective guarantees that opportunities such as those that can be provided through stimulus packages and other unique mechanisms will be missed.

It is important that public organizations and nonprofits maintain quality and focus on the future. In Las Vegas, Nevada, where more than 150 park and recreation employees were laid off and five community centers were closed, the director stated, "We will be a smaller, more efficient, and more responsive organization in the future." The new realities are that in the short term, public and nonprofit organizations will rethink, reorganize, and reprioritize their services and programs. Simultaneously, however, they need to plan for and aggressively act on the future.

The City of Rock Hill, South Carolina, offers a great example of utilizing a unique funding opportunity to develop recreation facilities. In 2000, Congress established the New Markets Tax Credits (NMTC) Program to incentivize new development in low-income communities by permitting investors to receive a tax credit against their federal income tax return in exchange for making equity investments in specialized financial institutions called Community Development Entities. With the opportunity to be part of a larger effort to develop the abandoned site of a former cellulose acetate manufacturing facility with housing, commercial and recreation facilities, the City identified NMTC as the most cost-effective avenue to fund a velodrome, BMX/supercross, cyclocross, and mountain biking trails as their part of the project. In essence, in taking advantage of the NMTC, the City of Rock Hill was able to ultimately reduce the cost of what was a $7,500,000 project (including interest) to $5,125,000 as they financed the deal as a NMTC with a Recovery Zone Designation.

Maturation of Organized Leisure-Services Field

The nature of municipal, state, and federal governments has changed dramatically in the almost 140 years of organized recreation in the United States. Government is more dependent on alternative income sources and less reliant on taxes. Where few fees once existed, now public agencies depend on fees and charges to make up as much as 90% of their operating budget. Parks and recreation agencies cannot serve all who either desire or have a need for services. Nonprofit and commercial agencies often fill the gap. In today's environment of rapidly changing demand for different types of leisure activities, public, commercial, and nonprofit organizations strive to respond, but often public agencies and nonprofits do not have the resources, financial capital, or ability to respond effectively. Commercial enterprises typically respond more quickly to what initially may appear to be fringe activities such as paintball, skateboarding, laser tag, and the like.

Commercial recreation is present in or near national parks as evidenced by the new glass walkway over the Grand Canyon—it exists on Native American land.
Courtesy of Grand Canyon Skywalk Development, LLC

Maturation does not suggest the organized leisure-services field is not changing, but rather that growth in the public and nonprofit sector is constrained by available funds, politics, public interest, and the perceived opportunity for growth. Public and nonprofit agencies have developed an infrastructure of parks, recreation centers, sports fields, cultural centers, and others that become a burden to agencies' ability to rapidly respond to change. The traditional programming of public and nonprofit agencies remains in place, although there is less of it and more of the emerging programs, but change is coming slowly. Where communities once built a 50-meter swimming pool, today they build a small to medium waterpark—except when politicians or other influential groups intervene and demand a traditional or old-fashioned approach. The leadership is changing and new, younger leaders are emerging. Values are being reassessed, commitments rethought, demands evaluated, and expectations challenged.

New Environmental Initiatives

As this chapter has shown, the nation's support for environmental protection and the recovery of polluted lakes and streams, as well as the continuing acquisition and preservation of wilderness areas, faced a sharp challenge through the end of the twentieth century.

Several decades of neglect and overcrowding left the nation's park system and forests in a precarious state. With national concern mounting, park authorities have instituted new fees to gather additional revenue and restricted automobile traffic into interior sections. Increasingly, corporate sponsors were recruited to assist in park maintenance, and major environmental organizations such as the National Park Trust provided support for the acquisition of new parks and wildlands.

Although public concerns focused chiefly on the ecological recovery of parks and wilderness areas, they also were directed to problems of clean air and water that affected major metropolitan areas. At the same time, major efforts were made in such older cities as Baltimore and Boston to revive waterfront and disused industrial areas. In such settings, cities developed new harbor facilities such as aquariums, museums, sport stadiums, marinas, theme parks, and other attractions—both to improve their image and attract tourists and to serve their own residents with appealing leisure programs.

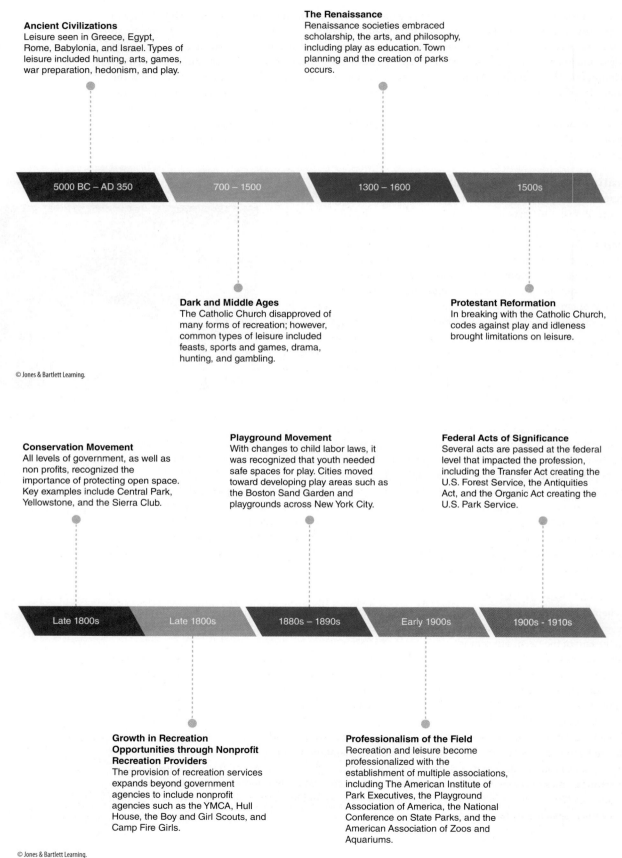

Ancient Civilizations
Leisure seen in Greece, Egypt, Rome, Babylonia, and Israel. Types of leisure included hunting, arts, games, war preparation, hedonism, and play.

The Renaissance
Renaissance societies embraced scholarship, the arts, and philosophy, including play as education. Town planning and the creation of parks occurs.

5000 BC – AD 350 | 700 – 1500 | 1300 – 1600 | 1500s

Dark and Middle Ages
The Catholic Church disapproved of many forms of recreation; however, common types of leisure included feasts, sports and games, drama, hunting, and gambling.

Protestant Reformation
In breaking with the Catholic Church, codes against play and idleness brought limitations on leisure.

© Jones & Bartlett Learning.

Conservation Movement
All levels of government, as well as non profits, recognized the importance of protecting open space. Key examples include Central Park, Yellowstone, and the Sierra Club.

Playground Movement
With changes to child labor laws, it was recognized that youth needed safe spaces for play. Cities moved toward developing play areas such as the Boston Sand Garden and playgrounds across New York City.

Federal Acts of Significance
Several acts are passed at the federal level that impacted the profession, including the Transfer Act creating the U.S. Forest Service, the Antiquities Act, and the Organic Act creating the U.S. Park Service.

Late 1800s | Late 1800s | 1880s – 1890s | Early 1900s | 1900s - 1910s

Growth in Recreation Opportunities through Nonprofit Recreation Providers
The provision of recreation services expands beyond government agencies to include nonprofit agencies such as the YMCA, Hull House, the Boy and Girl Scouts, and Camp Fire Girls.

Professionalism of the Field
Recreation and leisure become professionalized with the establishment of multiple associations, including The American Institute of Park Executives, the Playground Association of America, the National Conference on State Parks, and the American Association of Zoos and Aquariums.

© Jones & Bartlett Learning.

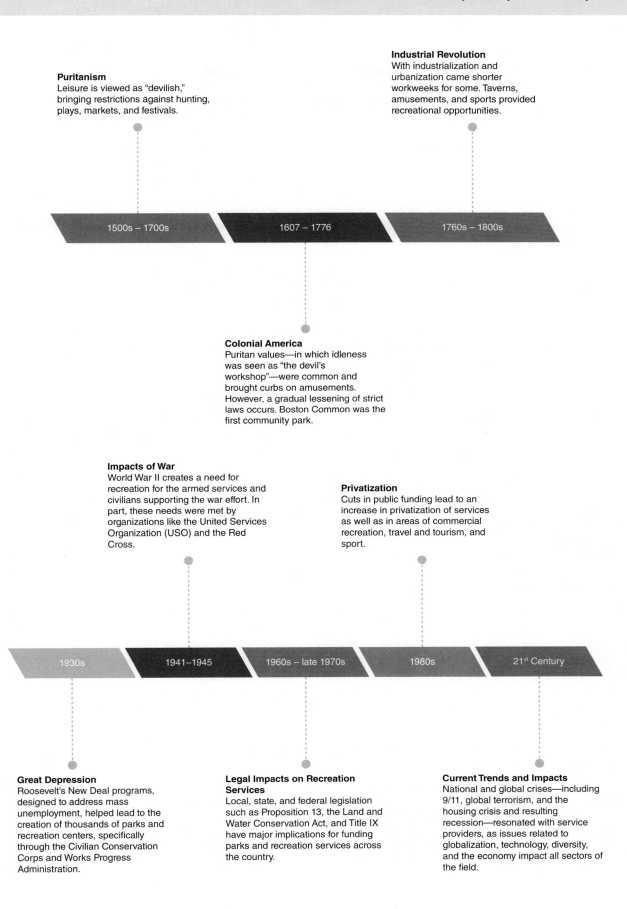

Puritanism
Leisure is viewed as "devilish," bringing restrictions against hunting, plays, markets, and festivals.

Industrial Revolution
With industrialization and urbanization came shorter workweeks for some. Taverns, amusements, and sports provided recreational opportunities.

1500s – 1700s

1607 – 1776

1760s – 1800s

Colonial America
Puritan values—in which idleness was seen as "the devil's workshop"—were common and brought curbs on amusements. However, a gradual lessening of strict laws occurs. Boston Common was the first community park.

Impacts of War
World War II creates a need for recreation for the armed services and civilians supporting the war effort. In part, these needs were met by organizations like the United Services Organization (USO) and the Red Cross.

Privatization
Cuts in public funding lead to an increase in privatization of services as well as in areas of commercial recreation, travel and tourism, and sport.

1930s

1941–1945

1960s – late 1970s

1980s

21st Century

Great Depression
Roosevelt's New Deal programs, designed to address mass unemployment, helped lead to the creation of thousands of parks and recreation centers, specifically through the Civilian Conservation Corps and Works Progress Administration.

Legal Impacts on Recreation Services
Local, state, and federal legislation such as Proposition 13, the Land and Water Conservation Act, and Title IX have major implications for funding parks and recreation services across the country.

Current Trends and Impacts
National and global crises—including 9/11, global terrorism, and the housing crisis and resulting recession—resonated with service providers, as issues related to globalization, technology, diversity, and the economy impact all sectors of the field.

Technological Impacts on Leisure

Beyond the effects of technological innovation described, a number of other scientifically based advances had a major impact on American leisure in the final decades of the twentieth century. Many of these had to do with forms of travel. Apart from the use of computers in tourism planning and reservations, global positioning system (GPS) services became able to direct an automobile trip through every turn until reaching the desired destination. Electronic navigation simulators created by companies such as Maptech, Inc., provided piloting assistance for boating enthusiasts. For the vacationing family, movies and video games replaced license-plate Bingo, as cars became entertainment centers with the latest audio and video technology.

Home environments became increasingly "smart." Home theater systems can control lighting; digital, CD, and MP3 systems; window shades; satellite service; and Blu-Ray players, while other lines wirelessly accommodate the family's telephones and computers—all at a distance.

Television, video games, and children's toys represent impressive examples of technology's impact on family leisure. As of the late 1990s, almost 80% of homes had cable or satellite television, and many studies reported that about 40% of Americans' free time was spent watching the home screen.

Into the twenty-first century, television watching has continued to be the most popular form of viewing media; however, it is receiving stiff competition from Internet-based sources used with computers and handheld devices. The Internet has had a huge impact on viewing. In the past, almost all viewing was on the television. Now television viewing is shared with watching television or videos on the Internet with a surge in on-demand services such as Netflix, Hulu, and Amazon Prime. The availability of handheld video devices means that individuals no longer need to be at home to watch videos. The most current figures suggest people watch 3.5 hours of video each month on their mobile phone.[35]

RECREATION AND WELLNESS REVISITED

Public health officials have recognized that the sedentary lifestyles led by a large percentage of adults and children in the United States are directly contributing to a prevalence of obesity in the population that approaches epidemic levels.[36,37] Unfortunately, the rise in childhood obesity has coincided with a decline in student time spent in physical education classes, recess, and outdoors.

Today, recreation and leisure-service providers and the federal government recognize the role of community recreation in encouraging physical activity. Federally funded initiatives include the establishment of community

Case Study

Smoking Policies in Public Parks

While physical activity is a hot button item with regard to parks and recreation programming, there are other health-related concerns at the forefront of professionals' minds. As more and more communities pass no smoking laws for indoor venues such as restaurants and bars, parks managers are frequently examining the issue of smoking regulations for their outdoor facilities. In 2015 the Office of Recreation and Park Resources, housed in the Department of Recreation, Sport, and Tourism at the University of Illinois, Urbana-Champaign, worked with the Illinois Department of Natural Resources to gain a greater understanding of how parks and recreation agencies in the state were regulating smoking in their outdoor parks and facilities. A total of 208 park districts, 119 municipalities, and 16 forest preserves completed a written survey asking about park policies and implementation of policies, with 42% indicating they had formal outdoor smoke-free policy areas, but few had complete bans. For most agencies the policies were specific to areas that saw frequent usage by children including playgrounds, pools, and youth athletic fields. Most agencies enforced behaviors in one of three ways: signage, citizen enforcement, and staff monitoring.

Questions to Consider

1. With an upswing in the use of e-cigarettes do you think agencies will move to limit their use on park property as well?
2. As states such as Colorado move to legalize marijuana, do you think its use should be allowed in outdoor park areas? Why or why not?

Owens, M. "Outdoor smoke-free policy development and enforcement in parks." *Parks & Recreation*, March 2016: 24–26. *Academic OneFile*. Web. 21 June 2016.

trail systems and support of after-school programs. The Surgeon General's Office recommended the development of public policy that addresses community access to safe physical activity. A growing number of nonprofits focusing on childhood obesity, lack of fitness orientations and programs, and the decline in children's contact with the outdoors and nature have emerged and are providing leadership.

Changing Demographics

The face of the United States began to change in the 1990s and will continue to change over the next several decades. In fact, it is predicted that by 2043 the "majority" will become the minority in America. As a result, the population served by recreation and leisure organizations in the twenty-first century will differ substantially from that served in the twentieth century. Some of the primary changes include the following:

◆ The number of adults 65 years and older grew from 25 million in 1980 to more than 41 million in 2011. By 2050, the 65-and-over population is projected to grow to more than 70 million.
◆ The composition of households in the United States will become increasingly diverse, as the number of households without children and single-parent households continue to grow.
◆ The growth of the Hispanic population in the United States will continue throughout the next few decades as Hispanic Americans become the largest ethnic minority group in the United States.

A changing population requires new approaches to delivery of leisure services. Agencies are challenged to serve an older population that will include several cohorts with different values and views of aging. Traditional recreation programs for older adults may not appeal to baby boomers, who highly value independence and resist aging stereotypes. Examples of the impact of a changing population might include decisions in facility development that reflect changing family structures that might demand alternative changing areas or areas that allow for more modesty for certain cultures where religion dictates its necessity. Programming examples might include health and safety programs targeted toward ethnic groups in light of risk factors such as diabetes prevention for Native American communities and Learn to Swim programs for African American children.

The changing ethnic composition of U.S. society will require leisure-service providers to examine the cultural framework that underlies programs and services. Agencies in certain geographic areas and some urban areas currently are responding to the need for truly multicultural programming.

Summary

This chapter shows the long history of recreation, play, and leisure by discussing their roles in the ancient civilizations of Assyria, Babylonia, and Egypt; then in the Greek and Roman eras; during the Middle Ages and the Renaissance in Europe; and from the pre-Revolutionary period in the North American colonies to the twenty-first century.

Religion and social class were major factors that influenced recreational involvement in terms of either prohibiting certain forms of activity or assigning them to one class or another throughout history. From the Catholic Church placing a strong value on work and worship to the Puritans that identified idleness as "the devil's workshop" to the impact of the Protestant Reformation and the related emphasis on work, religion continues today to have an impact on how we define appropriate leisure.

The chapter traces the influence of the Industrial Revolution, which brought millions of immigrants from Europe to America, where they lived in crowded tenements in large cities or in factory towns.

By the middle of the nineteenth century, however, religious opposition to varied types of play and entertainment began to decline. Sport became more popular and accepted and, after reaching a high point at mid-century, work hours began to decline. Four major roots of what was ultimately to become the recreation and park movement appeared: (1) the establishment of city parks, beginning with New York City's Central Park, and the later growth of county, state, and national parks; (2) the growing interest in adult education and cultural development; (3) the appearance of playgrounds for children, sponsored first as charitable efforts and shortly after by city governments and the public schools; and (4) the development of a number of nonprofit, youth-serving organizations that spread throughout the country.

Popular culture gained momentum during the Jazz Age of the 1920s, with college and professional sport, motion pictures and radio, new forms of dance and music, and a host of other crazes capturing the public's interest. Although the Great Depression of the 1930s had a tragic impact on many families, the efforts of the federal government to build recreation facilities and leisure services to provide jobs and a morale boost for the public at large meant that the Depression was a powerful positive force for the recreation movement in general.

By the early 1940s, organized recreation service was firmly established in American life, and both government officials and social critics began to raise searching questions about its future role in postwar society.

The years following World War II represented a period of immense change in the lives of Americans. From 1945 to the early 1970s, it was a time of prosperity and optimism for most families. As great numbers of young people—generally white and working- or middle-class—moved into suburban areas, recreation and park programs flourished, and leisure was seen as part of the good life.

Recognizing that a substantial part of the population continued to live in urban slums, with limited economic and social opportunities, the federal government launched a "war on poverty," in which recreation played a significant role. Under pressure from the civil rights movement, many recreation and park agencies began to give a higher level of priority to serving minorities. With the inner-city riots of the mid- and late-1960s, this effort was expanded throughout the country. At the same time, the counterculture movement, which saw young people rebelling against traditional authority and establishment values, transformed society with its resistance to the work ethic and its acceptance of drugs.

The late 1960s and 1970s were also a time when minority groups—including women, older adults, persons with disabilities, and those who are lesbian, gay, bisexual, or transgender—began to demand greater social, economic, political, and leisure opportunities. For them, recreation represented a means of gaining independence and achieving their fullest potential.

Beginning in the 1970s and intensifying during the decade that followed, recessions, inflation, rising costs of welfare and crime, and declining tax bases created an era of austerity that affected many government agencies. With sharp cutbacks in their budgets, many recreation and park agencies imposed severe staffing and maintenance cuts and relied more markedly on fees and privatization to maintain their programs. The entrepreneurial marketing strategy that prevailed widely at this time meant that many public departments were forced to give less emphasis to socially oriented programming.

At the same time, political conservatism in areas related to race relations, the criminal justice system, services for the poor, and environmental programs gained support. Studies in the 1980s and 1990s indicate that many Americans were working longer hours because of changes in family patterns and technological influences on business. At the end of the 1990s, with economic prosperity and more positive social and environmental concerns gaining acceptance, the place of recreation and leisure in contemporary life appeared to be more secure than ever.

Parks and recreation agencies face new challenges and opportunities in the twenty-first century. The population has started to change dramatically, requiring parks and recreation professionals to develop appropriate programs and services. Growing health concerns have provided an opportunity for agencies to play a greater role as public health advocates. The rapidly growing older population has time and resources for leisure but may reject traditional senior programs for more youthful and diverse opportunities. Changing household composition, including an increase in the number of singles, has challenged agencies that have historically focused on providing programs for families with children. Increasing ethnic diversity provides an opportunity for agencies to increase multicultural programming. In addition to changing demographics, parks and recreation agencies have experienced growing pressure to provide evidence of financial accountability through outcomes assessment. In the early twenty-first century, the place of recreation and leisure as a cultural and social institution seems secure.

Questions for Class Discussion

1.   Contrast the attitudes toward sport and other uses of leisure that were found in ancient Greece with those found in the Roman Empire. How did their philosophies differ, and how did the Roman philosophy lead to a weakening of that powerful nation? Could you draw a parallel between the approach to leisure and entertainment in ancient Rome and that in the present-day United States?

_____

_____

_____

_____

_____

2. Trace the development of religious attitudes and policies regarding leisure and play from the Dark and Middle Ages, through the Renaissance and Reformation periods, to the colonial era in seventeenth- and eighteenth-century North America. What differences were there in the approach to recreation between the northern and southern colonies at this time?

_____

_____

_____

_____

_____

3. Do you feel that it was appropriate that religion had such an impact on how individuals spent their free time in Colonial America? Why or why not?

_____

_____

_____

_____

_____

4. In the second half of the nineteenth century, the roots of what was to become the modern recreation and park movement appeared. What were these roots (e.g., the adult education or Lyceum movement), and how did they relate to the broad social needs of Americans?

_____

_____

_____

_____

_____

5. Three important pioneers of the early recreation movement in the United States were Lee, Gulick, and Addams. Summarize some of the key points of their philosophies and their contributions to the playground and recreation developments of the pre–World War I era. Describe the conflict between the traditional Victorian values and code of morality and the emerging popular culture, especially during the 1920s.

_____

_____

_____

_____

6. What do you feel are the three most influential events in history that have had a lasting impact on the provision of recreation services today? Explain.

_____

_____

_____

_____

7. Trace the expanding role of government in terms of sponsoring recreation and park programs during the first half of the twentieth century, with emphasis on federal policies in wartime and during the Depression of the 1930s. What were some of the growing concerns about leisure during this period?

    _____

    _____

    _____

    _____

8. The federal government has progressively pushed for stronger regulation of the environment since the mid-1950s. Explain how these efforts have affected, in positive and negative ways, the nation's perceptions and commitment to the environment and parks and recreation.

    _____

    _____

    _____

    _____

9. Explain the role that recreation and leisure had in helping to bridge the challenges of racial unrest and the counterculture movement of the 1960s and 1970s, and describe the influence recreation and leisure have on today's issues.

    _____

    _____

    _____

    _____

10. What are the current events occurring in society (e.g., elections, international political unrest, growth in conservatism, economic challenges) that you feel have a direct impact on the provision of recreation as we continue to move further into the twenty-first century?

    _____

    _____

    _____

    _____

11. Explain why free time has not met expectations. Take a position in favor of or against increased free time and defend your position.

    _____

    _____

    _____

    _____

12. Discuss the impact of the fluctuating economy on parks and recreation over the past 20 years.

    _____

    _____

    _____

    _____

13. Explain counterculture. How has the counterculture impacted parks and recreation?

_____

_____

_____

_____

Endnotes

1. John Pearson, *Arena: The Story of the Colosseum* (New York: McGraw-Hill, 1973): 7.

2. Gary Cross, *A Social History of Leisure Since 1600* (State College, PA: Venture Publishing, 1990): 73.

3. James F. Murphy, E. William Niepoth, Lynn M. Jamieson, and John G. Williams, *Leisure Systems: Critical Concepts and Applications* (Champaign, IL: Sagamore Publishers, 1991): 94.

4. Zhang Juzhong and Lee Yun Kuen, "The Magic Flutes," *Natural History* (Vol. 114, No. 7, 2005): 43.

5. Lincoln Kirstein, *Dance: A Short History of Classical Theatrical Dancing* (New York: G. P. Putnam, 1935): 57.

6. Norman P. Miller and Duane M. Robinson, *The Leisure Age* (Belmont, CA: Wadsworth, 1963): 66.

7. George Will, Review of G. Edward White, "Creating the National Pastime," *New York Times Book Review* (7 April 1996): 11.

8. Foster Rhea Dulles, *A History of Recreation: America Learns to Play* (New York: Appleton-Century-Crofts, 1965): 182.

9. David Nasaw, *Going Out: The Rise and Fall of Public Amusements* (New York: Basic Books, 1993): 2.

10. John Muir, (original 1901), *Our National Parks* (Madison: University of Wisconsin Press, 1981): 40.

11. Paul Heintzman, "Wilderness and the Canadian Mind: Impact upon Recreation Development in Canadian Parks" (NRPA Research Symposium, 1997): 75.

12. Walter Vrooman, "Playgrounds for Children," *The Arena* (July 1894): 286.

13. Richard Knapp, "Play for America: The New Deal and the NRA," *Parks and Recreation* (July 1973): 23.

14. Susan Currell, *The March of Spare Time: The Problem and Promise of Leisure in the Great Depression* (Philadelphia: University of Pennsylvania Press, 2005): 51.

15. Eduard Lindeman, *Leisure: A National Issue* (New York: American Association for the Study of Group Work, 1939): 32.

16. Art and Popular Culture, "Popular Culture," (May 26, 2017): http://www.artandpopularculture.com /Popular_culture.

17. Benjamin Hunnicutt, "Historical Attitudes Toward the Increase of Free Time in the Twentieth Century: Time for Leisure, for Work, for Unemployment," *Loisir et Societe* (Vol. 3, 1980): 196.

18. U.S. Census Bureau, "2010 Statistical Abstract," (May 26, 2017): https://www.census.gov/library /publications/2011/compendia/statab/131ed.html

19. Richard Kraus, *Leisure in a Changing America: Multicultural Perspectives* (New York: Macmillan College Publishing, 1994): 61.

20. Overweight and Obesity Statistics, National Institute of Health, (May 24, 2017): https://www.niddk .nih.gov/health-information/health-statistics/overweight-obesity

21. Carol Hardy Vincent, *Land and Water Conservation Fund: Overview, Funding History, and Current Issues* (Washington, DC: Congressional Research Service, 2006): 3, (May 26, 2017): https://fas.org/sgp/crs/ misc/RL33531.pdf

22. M. Walls, *Federal Funding for Conservation and Recreation: The Land and Water Conservation Fund* (Washington, DC: Resources for the Future, 2009): 5.

23. Eunice Kennedy Shriver, home page, (May 26, 2017): http://www.eunicekennedyshriver.org.

24. Kevin O'Leary, "The Legacy of Proposition 13," *Time* (June 27, 2009).

25. Richard Kraus, *New Directions in Urban Parks and Recreation: A Trends Analysis Report* (Philadelphia, PA: Temple University and Heritage Conservation and Recreation Service, 1980): 6.

26. Ellen Weissinger and William Murphy, "A Survey of Fiscal Conditions in Small-Town Public Recreation Departments from 1987 to 1991," *Journal of Park and Recreation Administration* (Vol. 11, No. 3, 1993): 61–71.

27. Jack Foley and Veda Ward, "Recreation, the Riots and a Healthy L.A.," *Parks and Recreation* (March 1993): 68.

28. Salvation Army, "Salvation Army Ray and Joan Kroc Corps Community Centers," (May 26, 2017): http://www.salvationarmyusa.org/usn/www_usn_2.nsf/vw-dynamic-arrays/E9D8660ADDBB36C7 802573F500587F26?openDocument&charset5utf-8.

29. Ray and Joan Kroc Center, "Kroc Center Celebrates One Year," (May 26, 2017): http://www.cdapress .com/archive/article-ba2d9c3c-1292-5d95-b886-c0f52c084c56.html

30. Keith Bradsher, "Gap in Wealth in U.S. Called Widest in West," *New York Times* (April 17, 1995): 1.

31. Robert Frank and Philip Cook, *The Winner Take All Society* (New York: Free Press, 1995).

32. Robert Reich, "A New Profile of Middle Class," *Employee Services Management* (May/June 1995): 4.

33. Cynthia L. Ogden, Margaret D. Carroll, Lester R. Curtin, Margaret A. McDowell, Carolyn J. Tabak, and Katherine M. Flegal, "Prevalence of Overweight and Obesity in the United States, 1999–2004," *Journal of the American Medical Association* (Vol. 295, No. 13, 2006): 1549–1555.

34. U.S. Department of Health and Human Services, *The Surgeon General's Call to Action to Prevent and Decrease Overweight and Obesity* (Rockville, MD: U.S. Department of Health and Human Services, Public Health Service, Office of the Surgeon General, 2001).

35. NielsenWire, "Americans Watching More TV than Ever; Web and Mobile Video Up Too," 20 May 2009, http://blog.nielsen.com/nielsenwire/online_mobile/americans-watching-more-tv-than-ever/.

36. Robert H. Frank, *Falling Behind: How Rising Inequality Harms the Middle Class* (Berkeley: University of California Press, 2007).

37. Robert Frank, *Luxury Fever: Why Money Fails to Satisfy in an Era of Excess* (New York: Free Press, 1999).

38. Luther H. Gulick, *A Philosophy of Play* (New York: Scribner, 1920): 125.

Social Functions of Community Recreation

Our nation's local parks and recreation are the gateways to healthy, prosperous, and connected communities. On any given day, someone is being positively affected through parks and recreation—whether they are taking a walk on a trail or fitness class at the community center, getting a nutritious meal, or just reaping the benefits of clean air and water because of preserved open space. The work of local parks and recreation takes on some of our nation's toughest challenges like obesity, the economy and environmental sustainability and offers solutions.[1]

Learning Objectives

1. Define community.

2. Discuss the factors that contribute to community well-being.

3. Identify and discuss each of the 10 functions of community recreation.

INTRODUCTION

Early definitions of recreation suggested that it served to restore participants' energy for renewed work but did not seek to achieve other, extrinsic purposes. Today, it is quite clear that this is no longer the case. Contemporary recreation programs and services—whether sponsored by public, nonprofit, or commercial agencies—are goal oriented and intended to achieve constructive outcomes for both participants and the community at large. These outcomes range from improving the quality of life for all community residents and reducing antisocial and destructive uses of leisure to promoting the arts, serving special populations, and protecting the environment. This chapter outlines the societal benefits of organized recreation service and provides a strong rationale for supporting recreation as an essential community function.

EMPHASIS ON COMMUNITY BENEFITS

Thus far in this text, recreation and leisure have been described conceptually as important aspects of human experience. We now examine their contribution to community well-being on a broader scale. The term *community* is used here to mean a significant clustering of people who have a common

Agencies like the YMCA of Greater Des Moines offer summer camps for youths that focus on setting values, building character, and enhancing creativity.
© Felix Mizioznikov/Shutterstock.

bond, such as the residents of a city, town, or neighborhood. It may also refer to other aggregations of people, such as the employees of a company or those who live and work on an armed forces base.

As community recreation has evolved and changed over the years, we have seen different philosophies emerge regarding the value of parks and recreation. What began as a social entity in the 1800s that provided services free of charge for the betterment of society has changed and grown. While agencies still provide these services, they must also justify their value as well as the economic efficiency of services. Our country has seen periods of economic austerity, such as after the September 11, 2001 attacks that forced many public and nonprofit agencies to cut programs and services. At that time, it became necessary to document the positive benefits derived from organized recreation programs and services to secure support for them. While communities called for more police and fire protection, park and recreation agencies had to show how they contribute to communities and how they can make their community a better place to live, work, and play.

Many agencies have placed an emphasis on showing economic and social value for their services. For example, Virginia Beach Parks and Recreation Department (VBPRD) understood their value to the community and tourism but needed a means to communicate it to the public with facts. To do this they did a study on this value and included seven major factors: clean air, clean water, tourism, direct use, health, property value, and community cohesion. They learned that VBPRD adds $701,814,399 in direct and indirect value to their community each year.[2] The City of New York Parks and Recreation Department analyzed property values within a 5 minute walk to the park, 5–10 minute walk and more than a 10 minute walk. They found that land values of residential properties increase the closer they are to a park. Properties that were within 5 minutes walking distance to the park were valued 11% higher than those 5–10 minutes away.

Given this understanding, we now examine 10 major areas of recreation's contribution to community life. In several cases, the benefits cited are similar to those presented in other chapters dealing with the personal values of recreation. However, here they apply to broader community needs and benefits.

FUNCTION 1: ENRICHING THE QUALITY OF LIFE

Purpose: To enrich the quality of life in the community setting by providing enjoyable and constructive leisure opportunities for all residents.

Quality of life encompasses elements that make a community good. Assessing quality of life looks at very quantifiable items as well as a personal perspective of the community. In terms of the quantifiable aspects of quality of life, Mercer's Quality of Living Survey is released annually and rates cities across the world on their perceived livability based on such factors as safety, education, health care, and political and economic environments. It also looks at factors such as recreation, the natural environment, and sociocultural environment.[3] In addition, International Living rates the livability of countries. They use categories of cost of living, culture and leisure, economy, environment, freedom, health and safety, infrastructure, and climate. In this index, recreation and tourism fall under the culture category.

As mentioned, some things contribute to quality of life that are not so quantifiable and are personal to the individual. In terms of recreation, these measure such things as available social opportunities, cultural activities, special events, parks, trails, lakes, restaurants, streetscaping, and facilities to enjoy ample recreation programs. Recreation's most obvious value is the opportunity that it provides for fun, relaxation, and pleasure through active participation in leisure involvements.

Parks provide a vivid illustration of the social value of leisure. During the warmer months of the year, they provide outdoor living spaces that are used by people of all ages and backgrounds. In swimming pools, zoos, playgrounds,

Parks, activities, and special events enhance the quality of life for community members of all ages and abilities.
© iStockphoto/Thinkstock/Getty.

Case Study

. . . .

Finding a New Community

You have recently graduated with your degree in recreation. You have decided to be adventurous, pack up all of your belongings and move to a new community in another state. You are leaving behind family and friends and want a new place to start your career. Your degree has made you marketable, and you are not worried about finding a job in your field. Let the search begin.

Tasks to complete:

1. List 10 factors you will look for when evaluating your community options.
2. Rank your factors from most to least important. Why did you rank the factors in this order?
3. What role does recreation play in your choice of factors?
4. Select 3 potential communities. Using your factors, rate these cities. Did your factors change as you started doing your research? Why or why not?
5. Which city did you choose?

nature centers, and sports facilities, community residents enjoy vigorous and sociable forms of group recreation. In community centers, children and adults can join clubs and special interest groups, take courses in a variety of enriching hobbies or self-development skills, and find both relaxation and challenge. The personal perspective of quality of life can be affected by family and friends, neighborhood, culture of the community, sense of well-being, love of a job, and overall life satisfaction. People place different values on these items and the indicators listed previously. Different people would view a 50-mile biking path, 5-minute access to a beach, and a premier theatrical venue quite differently, thus influencing their quality of life. In many ways, organized leisure service contributes significantly to the overall quality and enjoyment of community life.

FUNCTION 2: CONTRIBUTING TO PERSONAL DEVELOPMENT

Purpose: To contribute to a person's healthy physical, social, emotional, intellectual, and spiritual development, and well-being.

As other chapters in this text illustrate, recreation does far more than simply provide fun or pleasure for participants. It also makes an important contribution to their growth and development at each stage of life. Although we often tend to focus on such obvious goals as improving physical fitness or social adjustment, recreation participation also can help people reach their full potential as integrated human beings. For example, psychologists point out that many individuals have vivid memories of sports experiences in their childhood. Such experiences often play a key role in developing positive self-concepts and, beyond this, help to strengthen the bonds between parents and their children. In addition to providing benefits for children, these experiences may also contribute to the parent's own sense of well-being and mental health.

Varied types of community-sponsored recreation programs provide a rich setting in which children and youth are able to explore and confirm their personal values, experience positive peer relationships, discover their talents, and achieve other important personal benefits. For

Learning a new skill, expressing creativity through art, or experiencing nature all lead to enhanced personal well-being.
© Layland Masuda/Shutterstock.

example, Camp Fire, originally called the Campfire Girls of America, has expanded its services, mission, and goals from its inception in 1910. Today Camp Fire is committed to providing activities and services to all boys and girls and their families in the United States and has as its core purpose to help youth prepare for life through environmental and camp programs, out-of-school-time programs, and teen service and leadership programs.[4] Furthermore, the Children's Museum of Indianapolis has as its mission "To create extraordinary learning experiences across the arts, sciences, and humanities that have the power to transform the lives of children and families."[5]

While it is easy to focus on personal development for children, adults benefit from community-based recreation as well. For example, the City of Portland, Oregon Parks and Recreation Department has programs and facilities specifically designed with adult recreation in mind, including such things as 3 art centers, 6 golf courses, a motorsports raceway, 50 community gardens, 156 miles of trails, and 33 dog parks.[6] This is not a unique agency with a special emphasis on adults. They have a special interest in the community as a whole and provide services for everyone.

How effective are programs such as Campfire programs and children's museums? There is much research that demonstrates the effectiveness of these programs. Arguably, one of the better organizations at measuring their outcomes is the Girl Scouts of America. They outline end results for their programs, establish measurements, and compile data to show what they do works. For example, the Girl Scout Leadership Experience has 15 outcomes, including such things as developing a strong sense of self, gaining practical life skills, and advancing diversity in a multicultural world.[7]

There are several studies that have looked at outcomes of different types of programs. For example, when youths participate in out-of-school-time programs, juvenile delinquency reduces in the community, youths are exposed to less violence, and their education performance improves, which ultimately increases their economic contributions as adults.[8]

The National Endowment for the Arts showed that involvement in the arts increases academic achievement, high school graduation rates, college enrollment, and college graduation rates.[9] Research on community gardening programs has demonstrated that gardens bring neighbors of various ages, races, and ethnic backgrounds together; they offer educational opportunities and vocational skills for youth; increase physical activity; and provide open space for community gatherings and family events.[10] All of these programs within a community contribute to personal development throughout the lifespan.

Case Study
. . . .

A Planned Recreation Community

Green Valley Recreation, Inc. (GVR) is a nonprofit organization serving the leisure and social needs of the adult retirement community of Green Valley, Arizona, which is located 25 miles south of Tucson. Green Valley has a population of approximately 27,000 people in 13,200 households.

GVR owns and operated seven major facilities and six satellite centers that house things such as fitness equipment; pools; art studios such as ceramics, lapidary, woodworking, and clay; spas; and pickleball courts. They offer passive and active recreation opportunities for adults year-round. Given the makeup of the community, there are essentially no activities specifically for children. GVR is membershipdriven. Most homes in the community are GVR deed restricted where homeowners pay an initial capital fee when they buy their home and pay annual dues. This planned recreation community is an exemplary example of enhancing the quality of life and contributing to the personal development of its residents.

Questions for Discussion

1. Review the information on GVR at: http://www.gvrec.org/. Summarize what you learned.
2. Did any program offerings surprise you? Why or why not?
3. Look at the membership structure. Is this a good structure? If someone does not want to use the facilities, should they have to pay the fees? Why or why not?
4. As a retiree, would you want to live in a community such as this one? Why or why not?

FUNCTION 3: MAKING THE COMMUNITY A MORE ATTRACTIVE PLACE TO LIVE AND VISIT

Purpose: To improve the physical environment and make the community a more attractive place to live and visit by providing a network of parks and open spaces, incorporating leisure attractions in the redesign and rehabilitation of run-down urban areas, and fostering positive environmental attitudes and policies.

In local governments, the recreation function is closely linked to the management of parks and other open spaces, historical sites, and cultural facilities. Together, they help to make cities and towns more appealing as places to live. Inner cities and other communities have areas that have deteriorated over time. Gradually, we have come to realize that we no longer can permit our urban centers to be congested by cars, poisoned by smog, cut off from natural vistas, and scarred by the random disposal of industrial debris, ugly signs, auto junkyards, decaying railroad yards, and burned-out slum tenements. It is essential to protect and grace rivers with trees, shaded walkways, boating facilities, and cafés; to eliminate auto traffic in selected areas by creating pedestrian shopping centers; and to provide increased numbers of malls, playgrounds, and sitting areas that furnish opportunities for both passive and active uses of leisure.

The gardens at Temple Square in Salt Lake City, Utah, serve as an attraction for both residents and visitors.
Courtesy of Deb Garrahy.

Over the past few decades, numerous cities throughout the world have adopted ambitious projects of promoting recreation and tourism through the revitalization of their waterfronts—both in the redevelopment of decayed harbor areas and in the recreational uses of formerly polluted rivers. In a number of American cities, once abandoned freight yards, wharves, waterfront ports, or junk-filled streams winding through inner-city slums have been dramatically transformed into new, attractive open plazas and parklike settings. Frequently with the help of the business community, these eyesores have been rebuilt into condominium housing, offices, upscale shopping centers, marinas for boating or waterfront play, and outdoor amphitheaters for various forms of entertainment throughout the year. Run-down architectural masterpieces have been restored, and older ethnic neighborhoods preserved while adding restaurants, art galleries, and other cultural activities that appeal to tourists and residents.

Beyond recreation's role in helping to maintain and improve the environment in the central cities themselves, it also is a key player in helping to reclaim or protect natural areas within the larger framework of surrounding county or metropolitan regions. Environmental planners and park authorities are collaborating in many communities on remodeling abandoned railway corridors and establishing greenways to permit outdoor play or environmental education, provide hiking trails, or protect historic sites.

There are numerous examples of redeveloping land into usable space across North America. The Tampa Bay, Florida waterfront, once an industrial port, has been transformed into a major destination for community members and tourists. It has been labeled as an "active, pedestrian friendly environment for commerce, transportation, entertainment and fitness—all to enhance the city center."[11] Tampa Bay neighborhood parks were developed and later connected by a linear park for pedestrians, runners, and cyclists. Restaurants, cultural institutions, hotels, a convention center, and a dog park have been added to make the waterfront a focal point of the community.[12] In Manhattan, New York the High Line was opened in 1934 as a railway for transporting goods within the city. Use of the High Line discontinued in 1980, leaving an unused railway bed in the midst of a bustling urban area. After 10 years of planning, fundraising, and construction, the first section of the High Line opened to the public in 2009, followed by the second section in 2012, and the third section in 2014.[13] The High Line sees an average of 5 million visitors per year; it has increased property values near the park by 10%. The city recouped construction costs within a year through increased property values. In addition, the park led to more than $2 billion in private investments: restaurants, luxury apartment buildings, hotels, clubs, and a Whitney Museum branch all opened near the High Line.[14]

To foster environmental attitudes, the University of Colorado at Colorado Springs new Campus Recreation Center has earned Leadership in Energy and Environmental Design (LEED) Gold Certification. LEED

PEDESTRIAN MALLS SPARK TOURISM AND LIVABILITY

The Charlottesville (VA) Pedestrian Mall is a park within the Charlottesville Parks and Recreation Department system. This pedestrian mall is closed to automobile traffic and is a space where people walk from store to store without the hassle of traffic. The Charlottesville Pedestrian Mall is home to a vibrant collection of more than 120 shops and 30 restaurants, half-a-dozen art galleries, two historic theaters, multiple venues for live music, a movie theater, and an ice skating rink located in the historic buildings on and around old Main Street. The area has been called the "Community Living Room" and is a primary destination for locals and tourists.[15]

The University of Virginia has also implemented sustainability practices in its programming. They have done such things as purchase iPads for paperless administration of intramural and club sports, provided a bike share program, and purchased self-powered treadmills for the fitness center.[16]

certification requires buildings to be constructed and operated according to standards that are environmentally sustainable. The facility achieved the following to receive the certification:

◆ Low-flow toilet and sink fixtures cut down on facility water use, and the rec center uses 38% less water than comparable buildings.
◆ Where possible, unused construction materials were recycled instead of being added to a landfill.
◆ Highly efficient heating and cooling systems reduce energy expenditures, making the recreation center 30% more energy efficient than comparable buildings.
◆ Efficient landscaping reduces need for watering.

FUNCTION 4: PROVIDING POSITIVE OPPORTUNITIES FOR YOUTH DEVELOPMENT

Purpose: To provide positive recreation opportunities and experiences for youth to help them overcome or avoid negative use of free time.

One of the major objectives of the early recreation movement in the United States was to help prevent or reduce juvenile delinquency. Indeed, during the last decades of the nineteenth century and for much of the first half of the twentieth century, it was widely accepted that vigorous group activities were helpful in burning up the excess energy of youth, diverting their aggressive or antisocial drives, and "keeping them off the streets" and sheltered from exposure to criminal influences.

In the United States, there was widespread support for playgrounds, community centers, and other recreation programs for city youth by the police, juvenile court judges, and other youth authorities. A number of sociologists pointed out that much delinquent behavior on the part of younger children stemmed from the search for excitement, risk taking, and the need to impress their peers. It was argued that if other, more challenging, forms of constructive play could be offered to youngsters at this stage, it would be possible to divert them from more serious involvement in criminal activities.

This diversion concept has grown and changed over the past couple of decades. It was not until the mid-1980s that a strong focus on youth development and recreation emerged in the recreation research. Many terms have been used for the concept, such as *youth at risk*. This term in particular had a tendency to be viewed as only minority, inner-city, and low-income youth. In actuality, all children can benefit from recreation programs and focus should not be limited to those traditionally labeled as "at risk." Needing a broader and better perspective, the term *positive youth development* emerged and has been accepted in the profession. Peter Witt, a leading researcher in youth development, suggests that *youth development* is efforts made to "create organizations and communities that enable youth to move along the pathways to adulthood by supplying the support and opportunities necessary to develop beyond simple problem prevention."[17] The definition of youth development pushes recreation professionals

Keeping youths engaged in recreation activities can reduce incidences of delinquent behavior.
© Photodisc/Getty.

beyond simply getting kids off the streets, as was the idea in the early recreation movement. Youth development challenges recreation professionals to provide programs with a purpose and goal in mind.

Youth sports have been seen as a means to provide positive experiences for youth, despite some of the negatives seen in sport such as overly critical parents, adults fighting with officials, and crowds getting out of control. Extensive research in youth sports has shown that sport involvement often leads to improved academic performance, greater personal confidence and self-esteem, stronger peer relationships, development of an appreciation for diversity, and more restraint in participating in risky behavior.[18] Sports should be designed so that specific outcomes occur. Developing sport programs with specific benefits in mind can lead to sport programs that have moral, physical, mental, and cognitive development outcomes;[19] that reduce obesity and increase health;[20] and that build character.[21]

One model that has been used nationwide to develop youth is the Search Institute's 40 Development Assets for Adolescents. These assets are said to contribute to healthy, caring, and responsible young adults. The 40 assets are broken down into four age groups covering children 3–18 years of age.[22] Here are a few examples for 12- to 18-year-olds regarding what they should do as it relates to recreation:

> *Creative Activities.* Young person spends 3 or more hours per week in lessons or practice in music, theater, or other arts.
> *Youth Programs.* Young person spends 3 or more hours per week in sports, clubs, or organizations at school and/or in community organizations.
> *Time at Home.* Young person is out with friends "with nothing special to do" two or fewer nights per week.[22]

Here are a few examples of programs specifically designed to provide positive experiences for youth:

◆ Outward Bound's mission is to change lives through challenge and discovery. This nonprofit organization offers outdoor expeditions and programs such as canyoneering, backcountry skiing and snowshoeing, and sailing. Expeditions are designed to be challenging and character developing. The high impact skills learned will teach leadership, communication, and teamwork.[23]

◆ The Alex Fiore Thousand Oaks Teen Center is for seventh through twelfth graders and features a gymnasium, sound-proof music room, computer lab, classrooms, and a 1700-square-foot game room complete with three pool tables, two Ping-Pong tables, air hockey, foosball, assorted video games, and a 50-inch high-def plasma TV. Programs include sports leagues, surfing lessons, dance, fitness, music lessons, snowboarding, L.A. Lakers excursions, and a wide variety of special events.[24]

◆ Seattle (Washington) Parks and Recreation Department offers Late Night Recreation Programs for teens. The goal of the program is to provide a safe place for teens to hang out between 7 P.M. and midnight on Friday and Saturday. The city has 10 recreation centers with late evening programs such as tutoring, cultural and ethnic dance, and sports.[25]

Case Study
. . . .

Role of Recreation and America's Promise Alliance

America's Promise Alliance is a nonprofit organization founded by former Secretary of State Colin Powell and his wife Alma, which was created to ensure that youth received five promises. These promises contribute to youth growing into successful adults. The Alliance asserts that when at least four of these promises are at work in young people's lives, they are more likely to succeed academically, socially, and civically.

The Five Promises include the following:

1. Caring Adults: They are the centerpieces of children's development. They serve as guides, caretakers, and advisers, and give positive and productive guidance throughout their development.

2. Safe Places: To develop intellectually and emotionally, young people need physical and psychological safety at home, at school, and in the community. Without such "safe places"—environments that support and encourage inquiry, exploration, and play without fear of harm—children are not able to get support, form positive relationships, and concentrate on school.

3. A Healthy Start: Children grow and learn better when they are born healthy and practise healthy habits throughout childhood, including proper nutrition and exercise, and have access to high-quality learning opportunities. Healthy and well-nourished children are more able to develop their minds and bodies as they should, and they are far more capable of concentrating, learning, and thriving throughout their school years.
4. Effective Education: Our increasingly knowledge-driven world demands people who have the education and skills to thrive in a competitive marketplace and to understand the increasingly complex world in which they live. That means in order to compete and succeed, all young people will need an effective education that prepares them for work and life.
5. Opportunities to Help Others: Through service to others and their communities, young Americans develop the character and competence they need to be helpful, hopeful, and civically engaged all their lives, regardless of their own life circumstances. The chance to give back teaches young people the value of service to others, the meaning of community, and the self-respect that comes from knowing that one has a contribution to make in the world.

Questions for Discussion

1. What role can recreation play in each of these promises?
2. Look at programs offered in the following cities. Compare and contrast the communities and the demographic information provided. What programs have they implemented that are recreation related?
   Charleston, SC (http://www.americaspromise.org/charleston-south-carolina-0)
   Missoula, MT (http://www.americaspromise.org/missoula-montana)
   Bedford, MA (http://www.americaspromise.org/bedford-massachusetts-0).

Source: http://www.americaspromise.org/promises

FUNCTION 5: EDUCATING AND UNITING COMMUNITY MEMBERS

Purpose: To improve and develop positive relationships within the community by educating residents about similarities and differences on such things as culture, race, ethnicity, age, sexual orientation, religion, income, and more.

Recreation activities are an important means to developing intergenerational connections among families and community members.
© Blend Images/Shutterstock.

Our personal identity is formed by a variety of things including race, ethnicity, culture, sexual orientation, education, and income, among others. Community parks and recreation serve as a conduit to bring a variety of groups together in order to experience someone else's perspective. Special events, museums, programs, and sports leagues are used across the country to teach people about other cultures and shape our own leisure-related values and behaviors. Clearly, this presents a challenge to recreation and park professionals in terms of the need to provide program opportunities suited to the tastes and traditions of the various groups within the community.

Part of our role of a community parks and recreation agency is to provide people with different opportunities to try new activities, play a new sport, or learn a new game. Agencies should provide opportunities that encourage people to go beyond their socially constructed boundaries, which might allow them to see themselves and the world a bit differently.[26] In order to do this, Chavez suggests that if agencies want to make all groups feel welcome and want to participate in recreation activities, agencies need to (1) invite, (2) include, and (3) involve these groups.[27] Parks and recreation agencies cannot assume people feel welcome and that professionals know what people want without asking them and involving them in planning and providing programs.

Special events in particular represent a major area of opportunity for sharing cultural traditions and increasing the self-knowledge and pride of different racial and ethnic populations. These events are designed to celebrate culture because they are planned by people within the specific culture, but they are designed for everyone regardless of race or ethnicity. As an example, Milwaukee, Wisconsin is well-known for its ethnic festivals on the lakefront at Henry Maier Festival Park. Each year they hold such festivals as German Fest, Polish Fest, Irish Fest, Mexican Fiesta, and Festa Italiana.[28] The Skokie, Illinois Park District sponsors the Skokie Festival of Cultures, which features food, music, merchandise, and activities representing many of the 80 languages spoken in Skokie. Cultures represented at the festival include Armenian, Assyrian, Bangladeshi, Chinese, Cuban, Danish, Filipino, Finnish, Hellenic, Indian, Israeli, Japanese, Korean, Lebanese, Mexican, Pakistani, Scottish, Swedish, Thai, Turkish, West Indian, and more.[29]

ATLANTA ARAB FESTIVAL

The Atlanta, Georgia–based Alif (first letter of the Arabic alphabet) Institute is a nonprofit organization whose mission is to foster understanding and appreciation of Arab culture. They do this through education, culture, arts, and enrichment programs. The Atlanta Arab Festival is held by the Alif Institute each year and features cultural and educational exhibits related to the Arab culture and Arab Americans, music and dance performances, a fashion show, games, food, and shopping at the souk (market).[33]

In some cases, leisure-service agencies and programs may focus on problems of intergroup hostility and prejudice through meetings, staff training programs, workshops, and similar efforts. Organizations such as the YWCA have focused on the elimination of prejudice and discrimination as a key program goal, and in some cases youth camping programs have been established to promote intercultural friendship and understanding. In one such camp, the Seeds of Peace, teens from Egypt, Israel, Jordan, Palestine, and others are selected each year from their respective governments to participate in the camp, which is based on academic achievement and leadership abilities. The youth come together to share cultural traditions and to begin to build respect, friendship, and leadership skills and to confront their prejudices and deep-seated fears and tackle the issues that fuel violence, hatred, and oppression at home.[30]

Many larger communities host gay pride events, with one of the largest being in New York City. The festivities commemorate the Stonewall riots, which launched the gay rights movement in 1969. Events include such things as LGBT Pride March, family movie night, and a fundraiser for Broadway Cares/Equity Fights AIDS. All of these events are open to the general public to learn about the history and progress of the LGBT community.[31]

The City of Chicago has developed itineraries for visitors and community members to follow to learn about different cultures. For example, they have itineraries posted to learn about African-American heritage, and Asian culture, as well as budget-friendly attractions and family-orientated activities. The African-American heritage tour includes stops at public art displays, restaurants and jazz clubs, the DuSable Museum, the Black Ensemble Theater, and historic places such as the homes of heavyweight boxer Muhammad Ali and President Barack Obama.[32]

Community recreation is a place where people come together. They get to experience new things, see people who may be different from themselves, learn about the history of a group, acquire skills in a new sport such as cricket, develop salsa dancing skills, and simply build understanding through education. Given all of this, recreation is a pretty powerful component in a community seeking a high quality of life for all of its residents.

Case Study

. . . .

Religion and Recreation

You have had various religious groups in your community complain about the name and content of some of your events because they focus on Christian religious affiliation to the exclusion of other religions. For example, the community offers an Easter Egg Hunt, a Festival of Christmas Lights, and a Christmas Tree Lighting Ceremony. The local Jewish community has expressed concern about youth sports games being played on major Jewish holidays but cancelled on major Christian holidays.

Questions to Discuss

1. Should the community schedule around major holidays for all religions? If yes, why and how will this impact a local agency? If no, where do you draw the line on deciding what holidays warrant a change to program/league schedules?
2. Would you change the name of the events? Why or why not?
3. How could these events be made more inclusive of others outside the Christian faith?
4. Should a community recreation service provider respect the predominant religion in the community and exclude others? Why or why not?

FUNCTION 6: STRENGTHENING NEIGHBORHOOD AND COMMUNITY TIES

Purpose: To strengthen neighborhood and community life by involving residents in volunteer projects, service programs, and special events to enhance civic pride and morale.

An important tenet of the early recreation movement was that shared recreational experiences helped to strengthen neighborhood and community ties by giving residents of all backgrounds a sense of belonging and common purpose, helping them to maintain social traditions and cultural ties, and enabling them to join together in volunteer service roles. Recreation's role in strengthening neighborhood and community ties lies in the concepts of human and social capital. Human capital is the tools and training that can enhance individual or collective productivity. When people give their time and talent to the workforce or the community, they are using human capital. Although human capital is important, using it with social capital enriches the lives of those in the community. Social capital is defined as "connections among individuals—social networks and the norms of reciprocity and trustworthiness that arise from them."[34] Communities are made up of networks of people through schools, employment, the neighborhoods we live in, and of course recreation. These networks of people form valuable relationships that bond them together. Recreation and parks provide a plethora of opportunities for the human and social capital to merge and strengthen the community. Here are a few examples of how recreation and parks strengthen and improve communities:

Street rod owners form their own social community through a common hobby.
© Jamie Roach/Shutterstock.

In 2003, a group of residents in southwest Florida banded together to protect the bays, beaches, barrier islands, and watersheds in the area. They formed the Conservation Foundation of the Gulf Coast. One example of the group's impact since its inception over a decade ago was saving 150 acres of land from residential development and adding to the existing Robinson Preserve.

The New York Restoration Project (NYRP), founded by actress Bette Midler, strives to reclaim, restore, and redevelop parks, open space, and community gardens in New York City primarily in economically disadvantaged neighborhoods.[35] For example, Fort Tryon Park fell victim to neglect by the city in the 1980s and 90s. The NYRP stepped in and removed debris, downed trees, and uncovered and repaired paths that had been obscured under mounds of trash for many years. Within this park is the Cloisters Museum and Gardens and the New Leaf Restaurant and Bar. The New Leaf is a popular fine dining establishment, and net proceeds support the maintenance and beautification of NYRP's 55 community gardens and six New York City parks.[36]

COMMUNITY BUILT PLAYGROUNDS

Joshua's Park, a project of the Amherst Land Trust and Amherst Community Foundation, has brought together citizens of Amherst, New Hampshire to build a 3-acre park that was described as a chance to give kids a new place to play, to give adults a new place to garden, and to keep old farmland open. Community volunteers with expertise in real estate law, finance, banking, landscape design, and environmental science laid the groundwork, and hundreds of community volunteers contributed funds and labor to build the park that serves as a memorial to 9-year-old Joshua Savyon, an Amherst resident who was tragically killed in 2013.[37]

In times when disaster strikes, the communities impacted and those who simply want to help come together to provide immediate emergency relief and assist in long-term rebuilding efforts. When Hurricane Sandy hit the eastern seaboard in late October 2012, major damage and flooding impacted 24 states from Florida to Maine, in particular New York and New Jersey. Many communities opened their recreation centers to serve as emergency shelters for displaced residents. Rutgers University held fundraisers for the Hurricane Sandy NJ Relief Fund by selling t-shirts, having a food drive, and promoting the Red Cross text donation number.[38] After the immediate danger of the hurricane lessened, staff and volunteers worked to rebuild parks and recreation areas such as the Gateway National Recreation Area. A 1000-person staff from the National Park Service worked to stabilize the area and over the next 6 months 1700 volunteers dedicated 6250 hours in the effort to restore numerous parts of the park.[39]

Unselfish involvement in civic betterment activities is particularly important today, when many Americans see the signs of a spreading social and moral breakdown around them. At such a time, it is critical that every means be explored to develop a true sense of community, of sharing and mutual support in neighborhood life. Clearly, volunteerism and the kinds of projects just described help to promote such values and positive interactions among community residents.

More and more leisure-service providers are realizing the value of volunteers to the agency, the individual, and the community. For example, Champaign Park District in Illinois, which was one of the first public parks and recreation agencies to hire a volunteer coordinator, uses volunteers in all aspects of its operations, from recreation to maintenance. Each year, volunteers spend more than 20,000 hours working in day camps, at special events, planting flowerbeds, and coaching youth sports. In addition, the Champaign Park District has an adopt-a-park program in which neighborhoods take ownership of their area parks through such things as building flowerbeds, planting flowers, holding their own special events, raising money for playground equipment, and working with staff on park decisions. The adopt-a-park program allows the parks to be maintained at a higher level than ordinarily possible.

In many communities, recreational projects related to sports, the environment, the arts, people with disabilities, and similar concerns serve to promote civic pride and neighborhood cooperation.

FUNCTION 7: MEETING THE NEEDS OF SPECIAL POPULATIONS

Purpose: To serve special populations such as those with physical disabilities or cognitive impairments, both through therapeutic recreation service in treatment settings and through community-based programs serving individuals with a broad range of disabilities.

All people need diversified recreational opportunity; those with disabilities are no different. It is estimated that one in five people in the United States has a disability, and as adults age, this number is likely to increase.[40] Add to these the number of men and women who are returning from serving in Iraq and Afghanistan with disabilities ranging from amputations and visual impairments to traumatic head injuries and post-traumatic stress disorder. As such, it is important to focus special attention on providing leisure services in the community to this group.

Recreation for people with disabilities is provided from three different standpoints. First, recreation can be used as a form of physical or cognitive improvement and delivered in a hospital, a residential facility, or outpatient programs that focus on purposeful intervention to achieve a healthy leisure lifestyle. This form of recreation is often referred to as *therapeutic recreation*. Therapeutic recreation programs have been used to assist clients to become more independent, increase self-esteem, improve functional status, learn social skills, or learn to use leisure wisely. A second form of recreation for people with disabilities focuses on participation for the activity itself rather than as a means of therapy. This form of recreation is called *inclusive recreation*. Inclusive programs provide opportunities for people with and people without disabilities to interact together. The third form focuses on recreation programs designed for people with disabilities and is called *special recreation*. Opportunities for people with disabilities are as varied as the agencies that provide these services: Easter Seals, Special Olympics, and Disabled Sports USA.

Both inclusive recreation and special recreation can be found in community settings. For example, the South Suburban Special Recreation Association (SSSRA) is a public agency that provides programs for people with disabilities from eight park districts and three recreation and parks departments in Illinois. It is organized to provide individuals with disabilities or special needs the opportunity to be involved in year-round recreation. SSSRA programs are for individuals from birth through adult who are in special education classes, sheltered workshops, or who have recreational needs not met by traditional park district programs. This could include individuals who have varying degrees of physical disabilities, cognitive impairments, learning disabilities, emotional difficulties, hearing or visual impairments, and developmental delays. SSSRA offers Special Olympics programs, programs for veterans, adapted sports, trips, and special events each season.[41]

Many of the opportunities for people with disabilities arose because of federal legislation. The Americans with Disabilities Act (ADA), passed in 1990 and amended in 2010, mandated that people not be denied opportunities, segregated, or discriminated against because of their disability. Recreation-service providers had to ensure that equal opportunities were available for all constituents, and that if some specialized services were available that people with disabilities had a choice of participating in the general or the special program. The ADA also stipulates that facilities should be accessible and that programs be offered for all residents regardless of abilities. Furthermore, if a person has a disability, reasonable accommodations for participation must be made for that individual.

Conflicts have contributed to an increased need for programs for people with disabilities. Many servicemen and women return home injured in the line of duty, the most prevalent injury being traumatic brain injuries. Often referred to as "wounded warriors," these people initially receive services through the military medical centers and hospitals. Once released, some servicemen and servicewomen participate in recreation programs through parks and recreation departments in their communities. In addition to these opportunities, special programs are being designed to accommodate wounded warriors. Here are two examples:

◆ U.S. Paralympics has expanded to include programs for the United States Army Warriors Transition Units (WTU). The sports and fitness programs were created to help these servicepeople by providing postrehabilitation support. These programs are also done in partnership with local parks and recreation, as is the case with the Fort Bragg WTU and Fayetteville-Cumberland Parks and Recreation Department.[42]

Founded in London in 2014, The Invictus Games used the power of sport to inspire recovery; support rehabilitation; and generate a wider understanding and respect for wounded, injured, and sick servicemen and women. Established by Prince Harry, the Invictus Foundation manages the games, including the 2016 competition held in Orlando, Florida, which featured 10 competitive events including archery, indoor rowing, powerlifting, road cycling, sitting volleyball, swimming, track and field, wheelchair basketball, wheelchair rugby, and wheelchair tennis.[43]

◆ The Wounded Warrior Project Physical Health & Wellness program provides inclusive sports such as water skiing, snowboarding, and golf; fitness programs for weight management, strength, and overall health; nutrition education; and wellness.[44]

As our culture continues to be more inclusive, recreation provides both a means of therapy and a source of diversion for varied populations, both in clinical and community settings. Trends include not only serving the needs of veterans but also baby boomers, individuals with Autism Spectrum Disorder, our aging population, and many others.

FUNCTION 8: MAINTAINING ECONOMIC HEALTH AND COMMUNITY STABILITY

Purpose: To maintain the economic health and stability of communities by acting as a catalyst for business development and a source of community or regional income and employment, and by keeping neighborhoods desirable places to live.

Recreation has become a major focus of business investment and an essential element in the total national economy. It is estimated that leisure is a $400 billion industry annually; it is the nation's third largest retail industry, and the second largest employer behind the health industry. Communities with commercial, public, and nonprofit agencies have benefited economically from recreation. Such economic benefits may arise through taxes, such as bed taxes at hotels, or taxes from the lottery that go to support local parks and recreation. Furthermore, recreation increases property values, such as for homes on lakes, by parks, or on golf courses. For example, living on a golf course can increase property value from 5–19% although only 30–40% of the residents even play golf. This increase in property value may be attributed to the desire to live near green space and/or the natural beauty associated with many golf courses.[45]

Some cities have set out deliberately to transform themselves into centers of entertainment, culture, and sports. Indianapolis, Indiana, built nine major sports arenas between 1974 and 2008 to revitalize the city. These included a 10,000-square-foot tennis facility, a 12,111-seat track and field facility, a natatorium, a minor league ballpark, Bankers LIFE Fieldhouse (home of the Indiana Pacers and Fever), and Lucas Oil Stadium (home of the Indianapolis Colts). In addition, the cultural and entertainment opportunities were expanded. For example, White River State Park was built to connect city parks and cultural attractions—including the Indianapolis Zoo, White River Gardens, the Eiteljorg Museum of American Indians and Western Art, the NCAA Hall of Champions, the IMAX Theater, the Indiana State Museum, Victory Field and a premier outdoor concert venue, and Farm Bureau Insurance Lawn at White River State Park.[46]

To expand the convention opportunities in Indianapolis, once the Colts moved from the RCA Dome to Lucas Oil Stadium, the Indiana Convention Center was renovated and expanded into the RCA Dome.[47] In other cases, cities depend on special events and attractions to stimulate economic activity.

The Ice Rink at Rockefeller Center is an economic stimulant for New York City because of the large number of visitors throughout the winter holiday season.
Courtesy of Deb Garrahy.

Economic activity is better known as economic impact, or the measure of the amount of new dollars infused into the community by the agency. Economic impact is usually examined from the standpoints of direct and indirect. Direct economic impact is the amount of money that is directly generated by the event such as staff salaries, concessions, program fees, construction costs, and operating expenditures. Indirect impact is the money spent that results from the program or event. Examples are the money spent by a staff person or money spent at a hotel or in restaurants when a team is playing at a local softball tournament.

Here are some examples of economic impact from leisure services:

◆ The St. Louis Zoo, which has free admission, generates over $230 million for the local economy. This includes revenues from food, lodging, programs, and souvenir sales from its 3 million annual visitors and its 330 full-time employees and 950 seasonal part-time employees.[48]

◆ The Portland, Oregon, Rose Festival attracts over 1 million people and generates an estimated $75 million annually for the local and state economies.[49]

◆ Americans for the Arts conducted a study on the economic impact of nonprofit arts and cultural organizations (for example, museums) and found they had a $135.2 billion economic impact on communities across the country: $61.1 billion was from spending by the organizations, and the remaining $74.1 billion by the audience for event-related purchases. This industry also supports 4.1 million full-time jobs.[50]

◆ The 2015 Super Bowl and related events generated $719.4 million in direct and indirect spending for the state of Arizona.[51]

◆ Broadway shows and musicals generated nearly $12 billion in spending for the New York City economy during the 2012–13 season.[52]

In summary, evidence shows that public, private, and commercial leisure attractions and resources of cities are key elements in their economic health and stability, not only in bringing tourism revenues but also in the positive picture they present to potential residents and companies that are seeking to relocate.

FUNCTION 9: ENRICHING COMMUNITY CULTURAL LIFE

Purpose: To enrich cultural life by promoting fine and performing arts, special events, and cultural programs and by supporting historic sites, folk heritage customs, and community arts institutions.

It is generally recognized that the arts provide a vital ingredient in the culture of nations. Through the continued performance and appreciation of the great works of the past, in the areas of symphonic and choral music, opera, ballet, theater, painting, and sculpture, or through contemporary ventures in newer forms of expression, such as modern dance or experimental art forms, people of every age and background gain a sense of beauty and human creativity. Arts and culture manifest themselves in many different ways in communities. Art and culture can be found in the architecture of buildings, the design of parks, in museums, through educational programs, or by attending concerts. Enriching a community through art and culture does not require that one be an artist or have talent in the areas of drawing, painting, or music. A community benefits when art and cultural opportunities are available to be appreciated or to educate the community. In addition, art and culture are not just for the rich; opportunities should be available for all ages and income levels.

As such, it is imperative that community agencies, both public and nonprofit, play a strong role in presenting programs in the arts that improve the level of popular taste and provide an opportunity for direct personal expression through music, dance, theater, and arts and crafts. One such program is found in Prince George's County Department of Parks and Recreation (Maryland), which has six community recreation centers dedicated to the visual, performing, and literary arts. They offer such programs and facility space for art galleries, a store for local artisans to sell their work, learning studios for classes, a concert hall with several music series, and a public playhouse.[53]

In 2013 the City of Indianapolis debuted the Indianapolis Cultural Trail. The 8-mile trail is a curbed, buffered, beautifully paved, richly landscaped, and artfully lighted bike and pedestrian pathway that connects to every arts, cultural heritage, sports, and entertainment venue in the urban core. The inspiration for the idea was that it was going to connect to six designated cultural districts downtown in order to make those districts more vibrant and viable by connecting them and giving people a way to get to them that was walkable and bikeable.[54]

Dance is a popular means to experiencing and understanding other cultures.
© Boykov/Shutterstock.

PHILADELPHIA MURAL ARTS PROGRAM

The City of Philadelphia Mural Arts Program was established in 1984 as part of the city's anti-graffiti initiative. Those who were creating the unwanted graffiti were contacted and given an opportunity to put their artistic talents to work by creating murals throughout the city. The murals they created instantly added color, beauty, and life to an old, industrial city struggling with decades of economic distress and population loss. Since it began, the Mural Arts Program has produced over 3600 murals, which have become a cherished part of the civic landscape and a great source of inspiration to the millions of residents and visitors who encounter them each year.

Source: City of Philadelphia Mural Arts Program. http://muralarts.org/about/history.

Many public parks and recreation agencies sponsor summer concerts in the park featuring music that appeals to many different populations within the community.

© pcruciatti/Shutterstock.

Seattle, Washington, has the Olympic Sculpture Park that was opened in 2006. What once was an industrial site has been transformed into an 8.5-acre park on the waterfront that contains classic, modern, and contemporary permanent sculptures, temporary art installations, art-related musical and theatrical performances, and year-round educational programming in the arts.[55] Without parks such as these, many people would never be exposed to art at this level.

Art is not just for the rich and cultured. It benefits the entire community. As shown in these examples, art does not have to be in a museum. Art can be found in the parks, as murals on buildings, in flower gardens, and even in the architecture of buildings. Art enhances the livability and beauty of the community as a whole.

FUNCTION 10: PROMOTING HEALTH AND WELLNESS

Purpose: To promote community health and wellness by offering needed services, programs, and facilities to encourage active lifestyles for community members.

Public parks and recreation departments can be leaders in promoting health and wellness in their communities. They can combat some of the community's most pressing problems—poor nutrition, hunger, obesity, and physical inactivity.[56]

Many communities have developed programs such as fitness classes, dance programs, and sports leagues for all ages and abilities to promote health and fitness. Although these programs most likely have a fee attached to them, these same communities also are promoting free opportunities for health through their parks and trails so that all residents can become physically active and healthier. Parks and trails allow for close to home, low-cost activities for people. With any community, the key is to get people to use the parks. A National Recreation Foundation study found that people living near a park were twice as likely to use the park than those who do not live near one.[57]

In addition to parks, trails are also an important part of many cities. Walking and biking trails have been built through and around cities all over the United States. Trails have been built along rivers and streams, where railroads once stood, and on utility right of ways. These trails are used for fitness purposes as well as for transportation on foot, bike, or inline skates. People who live near trails are 50 percent more likely to get enough physical activity to help them stay healthy, and people who live in walkable neighborhoods are twice as likely to get enough physical activity as people who do not. Installing bike lanes within communities has increased cyclists by 69% in Portland, Oregon and by 225% in New Orleans, Louisiana.[58]

Parks offer unlimited opportunities for both children and adults to be physically active to improve their health.

© Seiya Kawamoto/Lifesize/Thinkstock/Getty.

Whether it is playing tennis with a friend, participating in a sand volleyball league, playing with a child on the playground, or biking on a trail, people who are in parks are physically active. There are thousands of examples of what local parks and recreation agencies are able to do in their communities to make their residents healthier. Here are a few examples:

◆ Many cities boast of their extended bike/walking trails built for residents as well as visitors to communities. For example, what once was a railroad bed connecting Chicago and Milwaukee has now become a continuous 100-mile bike trail that is promoted as a healthy tourism destination.

◆ The Minneapolis, Minnesota Park and Recreation Board contributes to the health of its residents by providing 200+ miles of bike trails and 180 parks. Ninety-four percent of Minneapolis residents live within 10-minute walking distance of a park. The residents benefit because the parks offer plenty of things to do, they are safe, and they are accessible. In addition to parks, there are many other aspects of the agency to improve physical activity in a community, including such things as dog parks, playgrounds, and golf courses, to name a few. Because of these things and many others, the Minneapolis (Minnesota) Park and Recreation Board was named the Best Park System in the United States by the Trust for Public Lands.[59]

In addition to physical and mental health and wellness, parks and recreation can contribute to the safety of its residents. Many community programs are focused on teaching safety skills through programs and events. These programs include such things as swim lessons, basic water safety programs, and boater and hunter safety programs. For example, Chehalem, Oregon Park and Recreation District and Newberg-Dundee Police offer a week-long summer camp for K–1 focused on safety, including personal safety, water, fire, electric, animal, pedestrian, bicycle, poison, and school bus safety.[62] Kokomo, Indiana Parks and Recreation Department offers hunter education courses, and many different local agencies offer programs such as wilderness first aid, lifeguard training, and swim lessons.

Health and wellness is increasingly being seen as a major player in the quality of life in a community. Cities and towns are making a concerted effort to provide programs and activities as well as facilities and open spaces to increase physical activity and mental health. When cities are planning for the future, they are more likely than ever to build biking/walking trails, add bike lanes to the streets, add parks to neighborhoods that do not have them, and promote the abundance of opportunities that keep people moving.

Park and recreational professions are instrumental in keeping children safe on playgrounds by adhering to national safety standards.
© iStockphoto/Thinkstock/Getty.

Leisure-service providers often offer programs to help people learn proper techniques of activities such as kayaking so that they can safely participate on their own.
© Bochkarev Photography/Shutterstock.

FITTEST AND FATTEST U.S. CITIES

Each year *Men's Fitness Magazine* ranks the 50 largest cities in the United States from the fittest to the fattest. Rankings are determined by such indicators as the number of gyms and sporting goods stores, participation in exercise and sports, the number of parks, the amount of open space, and the number and types of recreation facilities available. In 2014, Portland (Oregon), San Francisco, Seattle, and Denver were at the top of the fittest list and El Paso, Detroit, Louisville, and Memphis topped the fattest cities list.[60] The magazine tried a new approach and looked at the data from 10 million Fitbit users and found the fittest cities to be as follows: Madison (WI), Minneapolis, Spokane, Portland, and Boston.[61]

Case Study

. . . .

Make Your Community a More Fit City

You have been placed on a committee within your city to improve its overall fitness with the goal of becoming the fittest city in the state. As the committee develops, it plans to achieve this goal, and you have been given the following tasks to complete:

1. Look at the fitness opportunities that currently exist in your community. Make a list of those that have fees associated with them and those that are free.
2. Develop a list of criteria that you feel measure a fit city. Look at what other polls (e.g., *Men's Fitness Magazine*) measure.
3. Select four of the variables listed above and gather data about your city.
4. Review two cities that are considered to be fit cities such as Portland, Oregon and Minneapolis, Minnesota. What do these cities have that you could realistically suggest to make your city more fit?
5. Make a priority list of changes you would suggest be made to your community to increase its overall fitness level.

Summary

Far from simply providing casual or superficial amusement, organized recreation services help to satisfy a number of significant community needs, including the following:

1. *Quality of life.* Constructive and enjoyable leisure for people of all ages and backgrounds contributes significantly to their quality of life and satisfaction with their communities.
2. *Personal development.* Organized recreation promotes healthy personal development in physical, emotional, social, intellectual, and spiritual terms, thus contributing to overall community well-being.
3. *Attractive community.* Recreation and park agencies maintain parks, nature reserves, riverfronts, and other natural areas and may assist in rehabilitating or sponsoring historic and cultural settings.
4. *Positive opportunities for youth development.* As an important element in the community's educational, social, and other services for youth, organized recreation assists in preventing or reducing delinquency and other deviant forms of play, and giving youth positive alternatives to develop into health adults.
5. *Educating and uniting community members.* Recreation serves as a useful tool in promoting understanding and cooperation of cultural, ethnic, racial, and other sociodemographic characteristics.
6. *Strengthening community ties.* Volunteerism and taking part in neighborhood efforts to improve the community environment and similar involvement help to build civic togetherness.
7. *Needs of special populations.* In both treatment settings and in the community at large, therapeutic recreation service promotes inclusion and independence for persons with physical and cognitive disabilities.
8. *Maintaining economic health.* As a growing form of business enterprise, recreation employs millions of people today. By helping to attract tourists, industries that are relocating, or new residents, it also provides income and promotes community stability.
9. *Enriching cultural life.* Many public and nonprofit leisure-service agencies today assist or sponsor programming in the various artistic and cultural fields, strengthening this important dimension of community life.
10. *Promoting health and wellness.* Increasingly, recreation is recognized as a health-related discipline by helping individuals to maintain sound lifestyles and by helping to promote physical activity and safe access to leisure.

Questions for Class Discussion or Essay Examination

1. This chapter presents 10 different areas in which recreation, parks, and leisure services contribute to community life. If you had to present a positive argument for establishing or expanding a community recreation and park department, which of these areas would you emphasize, and why?

_____

_____

_____

_____

2. Explain and discuss the importance of community recreation within one of the following areas: (1) economic contribution; (2) health-related benefits; (3) promoting the cultural arts; or (4) educating and uniting residents of different socioeconomic, racial, or cultural backgrounds.

_____

_____

_____

_____

3. Think about the community in which you live. Give examples of how the 10 functions of community recreation are demonstrated in that community. Which ones are missing?

_____

_____

_____

_____

4. Think about the 10 functions of community recreation as they apply to your college campus. What are strengths and weaknesses of the campus in providing these 10 functions? Provide examples of each function that is demonstrated on campus.

_____

_____

_____

_____

Endnotes

1. Local park and recreation agencies provide crucial health and wellness opportunities for all populations in communities across the country. As America continues to face serious health issues including rising rates of chronic disease, an increased prevalence of sedentary lifestyles and poor nutrition habits, parks and recreation offer an affordable and accessible solution. http://www.nrpa.org/our-work/Three-Pillars/health-wellness/

2. Trust for Public Land, "The Economic Benefits of the Park and Recreation System of Virginia Beach, Virginia" (2011): http://cloud.tpl.org/pubs/ccpe-va-beach-park-analysis-report.pdf.

3. Mercer, "Quality of Living Reports" (May 15, 2016): www.imercer.com/products/2014/quality-of-living.aspx.

4. Campfire, http://campfire.org/

5. Children's Museum of Indianapolis, "Mission": www.childrensmuseum.org/about.

6. Portland Parks & Recreation Department, "PP&R by the Numbers" (May 15, 2016): www.portlandoregon.gov/parks/article/422533.

7. Girl Scouts of the United States of America, "Transforming Leadership: Focusing on Outcomes of the New Girl Scout Leadership Experience" (2008): www.girlscouts.org/research/pdf/transforming_leadership.pdf.

8. Witt, P.A. & Caldwell, L.L., "The Rationale for Recreation Services for Youth: An Evidenced Based Approach," NRPA (2010): http://www.nrpa.org/uploadedFiles/nrpa.org/Publications_and_Research/Research/Papers/Witt-Caldwell-Full-Research-Paper.pdf.

9. J. S. Catterall with Susan A. Dumais and Gillian Hampden-Thompson, "The Arts and Achievement in At-Risk Youth: Findings from Four Longitudinal Studies," Research Report #55 (2012), Washington, DC: National Endowment for the Arts. Retrieved from https://www.arts.gov/sites/default/files/Arts-At-Risk-Youth.pdf

10. Local Government Commission, "Cultivating Community Gardens: The Role of Local Government in Creating Healthy, Livable Neighborhoods" (May 29, 2017): http://lgc.org/wordpress/docs/freepub/community_design/fact_sheets/community_gardens_cs.pdf

11. *Friends of the Riverwalk* (May 16, 2016). http://www.thetampariverwalk.com/.

12. *Project for Public Spaces* (May 16, 2016). http://www.pps.org/places/squares-parks/tampa-riverwalk/.

13. *Friends of the High Line*, http://www.thehighline.org/about.

14. Staff (October 7, 2014), "Creating opportunity New York's High Line Fuels Wave of Urban Renewal Projects." *Free Enterprise* (October 7, 2014): http://www.freeenterprise.com/new-yorks-high-line-inspires-wave-of-urban-renewal-projects/.

15. Charlottesville VA Official Travel Website" *Visit Charlottesville, VA* (May 16, 2016): http://www.visitcharlottesville.org.

16. "Gallogly Recreation and Wellness Center: Sustainability" *University of Colorado, Colorado Springs* (May 16, 2016): http://www.uccs.edu/recwellness/campus-rec/facilities/sustainability.html.

17. P. A. Witt, "Youth Development: Going to the Next Level," *Parks & Recreation* (Vol. 37, No. 3, 2002): 52–59.

18. USADA, "True Sport: What We Stand to Lose in Our Obsession to Win": 2012 http://www.truesport.org/library/documents/about/true_sport_report/True-Sport-Report.pdf.

19. P. David, "Children's Rights and Sports," *International Journal of Children's Rights* (Vol. 7, 1999): 53–81.

20. R. Hedstrom and D. Gould, *Research in Youth Sports: Critical Issues Status* (East Lansing, MI: Institute for the Study of Youth Sports, 2004).

21. J. Coakley, *Sports in Society: Issues and Controversies*, 8th ed. (New York: McGraw-Hill, 2004).

22. Search Institute, "40 Developmental Assets for Adolescents." (May 18, 2016): www.search-institute.org/content/40-developmental-assets-adolescents-ages-12-18.

23. "Experiential Wilderness Education," *Outward Bound* (May 18, 2016): http://www.outwardbound.org/about-Outward-bound/outward-bound-today/.

24. Thousand Oaks Teen Center (May 18, 2016): www.thousandoaksteencenter.com/.

25. Seattle Parks and Recreation Department, "Seattle Parks Late Nite" (May 18, 2016): www.seattle.gov/parks/teens/programs/latenightprogram.htm#.

26. Kivel, P. & Kivel, B.D., (2016). Beyond cultural competence: Building allies and sharing power in leisure, recreation, and tourism settings. In I. Schneider & B. Kivel (Eds.), *Diversity and Inclusion in the Recreation Profession: Organizational,* 3rd ed. (Champaign, IL: Sagamore Publishing, 2016).

27.   D. J. Chavez, "Invite, Include, and Involve! Racial Groups, Ethnic Groups, and Leisure," in M. T. Allison and I. E. Schneider, eds., *Diversity and the Recreation Profession: Organizational Perspectives* (State College, PA: Venture Publishing, 2000).

28.   Henry Maier Festival Park Calendar of Events 2017 (May 29, 2017). http://www .milwaukeeworldfestival.com/calendar-of-events.

29.   Skokie Park District Festival of Cultures (May 19, 2016): www.skokieculturefest.org.

30.   Seeds of Peace (May 19, 2016): www.seedsofpeace.org.

31.   Alif Institute (May 19, 2016): www.alifinstitute.org.

32.   "Guide to Gay Pride 2017," *Time Out New York* (May 19, 2016): http://www.timeout.com/newyork/ lgbt/gay-pride-nyc.

33.   African American Heritage from (May 19, 2016): http://www.choosechicago.com/articles/view/ african-american-heritage/944/.

34.   R. D. Putnam, *Bowling Alone: The Collapse and Revival of American Community* (New York: Simon & Schuster, 2000): 19.

35.   New York Restoration Project (May 29, 2017): https://www.nyrp.org/about

36.   New York Restoration Project (NYRP), "Fort Tryon Park" (May 19, 2016): https://www.nyrp.org/ green-spaces/park-details/fort-tryon-park/.

37.   Amherst Land Trust and Amherst Community Foundation, "Joshua Park: A Project of the Amherst Land Trust and Amherst Community Foundation" (May 19, 2016): http://www.joshuaspark.org/ JoshuasPark/Welcome_files/Case%20statement-Joshuas%20Park%202016.pdf.

38.   Rutgers University Football, "Updated Details on Hurricane Sandy Relief Efforts at Rutgers Athletics Events" (May 27, 2017): http://www.scarletknights.com/sports/m-footbl/spec-rel/110812aaa.html

39.   National Park Service, "Hurricane Sandy—Six Months Later" (May 19, 2016): www.nps.gov/gate/ parknews/sandy-6.htm.

40.   U.S. Census Bureau (May 19, 2016), Americans with Disabilities: 2010: http://www.census.gov /prod/2012pubs/p70-131.pdf.

41.   South Suburban Special Recreation Association (May 19, 2016): http://www.sssra.org/index.html.

42.   D. Vaira, "A Soldier's Story," *Parks & Recreation* (Vol. 44, No. 12, 2009): 32–36.

43.   Invictus Games (May 19, 2016): http://invictusgames2016.org.

44.   Wounded Warrior Project, "Physical Health and Wellness" (May 19, 2016): https://www. woundedwarriorproject.org/programs/physical-health-wellness.

45.   Sarah Nichols, "Measuring the Impact of Parks on Property Values," *Parks and Recreation* (Vol. 39, 2004): 24–32.

46.   White River State Park (May 19, 2016): http://www.visitindy.com/indianapolis-white-river-state-park.

47.   M. M. S. Rosentraub, *Major League Winners: Using Sports and Cultural Centers as Tools for Economic Development* (Boca Raton, FL: CRC Press, 2010).

48.   St. Louis Zoo, "About Economic Impact" (2014): www.stlzoo.org/about/economicimpact/.

49.   Portland Rose Festival, 2016 Portland Rose Festival Advertising Kit. (May 19, 2016): http://www.rosefestival.org/wp-content/uploads/2016_Advertising-Kit.pdf.

50.   Americans for the Arts, *Arts and Economic Prosperity IV*, Washington, DC: Americans for the Arts (May 19, 2016): www.artsusa.org/information_services/research/services/economic_impact/ default.asp.

51.   Arizona Super Bowl Host Committee (May 19, 2016). https://azsuperbowl.com/wp-content/ uploads/2015/06/Economic-Study-2.pdf.

52. Cox, G. (May 30, 2014). Broadway's $12 Billion Impact on New York Economy Matches Film and TV Biz. Variety. http://variety.com/2014/legit/news/broadway-economic-impact-on-new -york-2012-13-1201199054/.

53. Prince George's County Department of Parks and Recreation (May 19, 2016): http://arts.pgparks. com/Home.htm

54. Indianapolis Cultural Trail: http://indyculturaltrail.org/alongthetrail/facts-and-figures/.

55. Seattle Art Museum, "Olympic Sculpture Park": http://www.seattleartmuseum.org/visit /olympic-sculpture-park.

56. (May 29, 2017) http://www.nrpa.org/our-work/Three-Pillars/health-wellness/

57. R. C. Brownson et al., "Environmental and Policy Determinants of Physical Activity in the United States," *American Journal of Public Health* (Vol. 91, No. 12, 2003): 1995–2003.

58. "Active Transportation, Parks and Public Health." National Recreation & Park Association (nd). http://www.nrpa.org/uploadedFiles/nrpaorg/Tools_and_Resources/Parks_and_Health/Fact _Sheets/Active-Transportation-Parks-Public-Health.pdf.

59. Callaghan, P. (05/26/16). Minneapolis edges St. Paul for title of nation's best park system MinnPost: https://www.minnpost.com/politics-policy/2016/05/minneapolis-edges-st-paul-title-nations-best- park-system.

60. Men's Fitness Editors (2016): The 2014 Fittest and Fattest Cities in America (May 21, 2016): The List, *Men's Fitness*: http://www.mensfitness.com/life/outdoor/2014-fittest-and-fattest-cities-america-list.

61. "Where the Fittest People in America Live in 2016," *Men's Fitness* (May 21, 2016): http://www .mensfitness.com/life/entertainment/where-fittest-people-america-live-2016.

62. Chehalem Park & Recreation District, "RE 8 Safety Town Camp" (2016): http://www.cprdnewberg .org/general/page/safety-town-camp.

The Leisure-Service System

America is a land of majestic beauty, and we are blessed with immeasurable natural wealth. Americans are united in the belief that we must preserve this treasured heritage and conserve these natural resources for the benefit and enjoyment of the American people.

As a nation, we can be proud of our diverse parklands, ranging from the rugged wilderness of snow-capped mountains, thick forests, sweeping desert sands, and remote canyons to national symbols such as the Statue of Liberty and the Lincoln Memorial. Our National Park Service has a long and important history. In 1864, the federal government ensured a grand natural landscape for generations to come when it designated Yosemite Valley and the Mariposa Grove of giant sequoias to be "held for public use, resort, and recreation . . . inalienable for all time." National parks, state parks, public parks, and recreation agencies grew out of the recognition of dedicated leaders of the need to provide opportunities, services, and places where people could renew, reflect, be active, enjoy social engagements, and bask in the beauty of the great outdoors. America's park and recreation system is comprised of public, private, and nonprofit organizations providing services and opportunities for individuals and groups.[1]

Learning Objectives

1. Identify the key elements in the leisure-service delivery system.

2. Explain the role of each of the elements in the leisure-service delivery system.

3. Selecting a leisure-service agency and program from that agency, assess how the program influences the steps in the leisure-service delivery system.

4. Understand the uniqueness and commonality of the leisure-service delivery system in the different types of agencies: public, nonprofit, and commercial.

5. Recognize the multiple agencies delivering leisure services and explain their unique and common goals.

INTRODUCTION

We now turn to a detailed examination of the overall leisure-service system in the United States at the turn of the twenty-first century. This chapter deals with three major types of recreation providers that share a broad responsibility for sponsoring recreation, park, and related leisure facilities and programs for the public at large: governmental agencies, nonprofit community organizations, and commercial recreation enterprises. In each case, the background, mission, and chief program elements of sponsoring agencies are described, with numerous examples drawn from the field that illustrate recreation and leisure services today.

KEY ELEMENTS IN THE LEISURE-SERVICE SYSTEM

There are 10 different types of leisure-service organizations in modern society, as shown in **Table 6.1**. Of these, three of the major types that meet a broad range of public needs are described in this chapter, with the other seven elsewhere in the text.

Understanding the 10 Major Elements in the Modern Leisure-Service Delivery System

Understanding the modern leisure-service delivery system is the essence of this chapter. Table 6.1 provides a matrix of how leisure services are structured and delivered. The table is a simple representation of a complex process of relationships, interchanges, and decisions leading to outcomes in the form of benefits.

Across the top of the table are the five categories representing the major processes (A through D) and outcomes of the delivery (E) of a leisure program by an organization. Below, each of the major processes is separated into more specific descriptors. These in turn allow processes to be classified as the examples will show.

Each major process is described as follows:

◆ The *types of recreation sponsoring organizations* (A) are categories reflecting types of groups or organizations that offer recreation programs. The 10 areas are the major providers in a modern leisure-service delivery system. Most delivery types can be grouped within this list of 10 types of sponsors.
◆ The *partnered with support groups and services* (B) is present when a program sponsor is working with one or more additional program sponsors to deliver a program.
◆ The *process to provide leisure programs* (C) category consists of types of delivery approaches. The delivery approaches represent traditional delivery models.
◆ To *satisfy public needs for* (D) represents (1) types of program areas and (2) variables that influence demand for leisure services and public needs and desires.
◆ The *yielding major benefits* (E) category addresses the importance of leisure activities in providing measurable benefits to individuals, groups, organizations, and communities.

Using Table 6.1

Step 1: Beginning with column A, Types of Recreation-Sponsoring Organizations, select an agency that provides a program. For example, the Boys and Girls Club provides an after school basketball clinic. In column A, nonprofit (2) is selected as the type of sponsoring organization.

Step 2: Are there any sponsoring organizations (column B)? In this case a local sporting goods store has offered to provide basketballs. The sporting goods company is a small business (8) and a sponsor of the Boys and Girls Club.

Step 3: The Boys and Girls Club are providing the basketball clinic (column C), taking on the role of direct program leadership (1).

Step 4: The basketball clinic satisfies a public need (column D) for games and sport as well as personal enjoyment (1). In this case, more than one spectrum of involvement is considered. The decision to offer the program was influenced by a number of factors such as age, gender, physical and emotional health, socioeconomic status, and ability (2). Other benefits unique to the situation could also have been considered.

Step 5: Participation in the basketball clinic should result in tangible and intangible benefits to the participant, and potentially to others (column E). This can include personal values (1) and social outcomes (2).

Table 6.2 shows how the basketball clinic moved through Table 6.1. The table allows the reader to look at the variables influencing leisure-service delivery and track the relationships of those variables. It is not a neat and clean process, but rather often is messy. What the table does is provide an improved understanding of the complexity of the delivery of leisure-service programs and offerings.

TABLE 6.1 The 10 Major Elements in the Modern Leisure-Service Delivery System

(A) Types of Recreation-Sponsoring Organizations	(B) Partnered with Groups and Services	(C) Provide Leisure Programs Consisting of	(D) To Satisfy Individual and Public Needs for	(E) Yielding Major Benefits
① Public agencies	① Trade associations	① Direct program leadership	① Full spectrum of involvement in:	① Personal values (health, emotional wellness, mental development, well-being)
② Nonprofit organizations	② Professional associations	② Provision of facilities and open spaces for undirected public use	Games and sport	② Social and community-based outcomes
③ Commercial recreation enterprises	③ Special-interest groups	③ Education for leisure	Outdoor recreation	③ Economic benefits, employment, taxes, and other fiscal returns
④ Employee service and recreation programs	④ Sponsors of special programs and events	④ Information referral services	Cultural activities	④ Environmental values, both natural and urban settings
⑤ Armed Forces morale, welfare, and recreation	⑤ Professional preparation institutions	⑤ Enabling facilitation	The arts	
⑥ Private membership organizations	⑥ Private groups that subcontract leisure functions	⑥ Advocacy and leadership in special areas	Hobbies	
⑦ Campus recreation programs	⑦ Other civic agencies and citizen groups	⑦ Jointly sponsored campaigns and events	Special events	
⑧ Therapeutic recreation services	⑧ Corporations	⑧ Authentic leisure experiences	Club and other social groups	
⑨ Sport management organizations	⑨ Small business enterprises	⑨ Opportunities for well-being	Personal enjoyment	
⑩ Tourism and hospitality industry	⑩ Individuals		Travel	
			Electronic media	
			Other social services	
			② With needs influenced by:	
			Age group	
			Gender	
			Socioeconomic status	
			Educational background	
			Racial/ethnic factors	
			Residential and regional factors	
			Physical and emotional health	
			Ability/disability	
			Family status	

TABLE 6.2 Simple Version

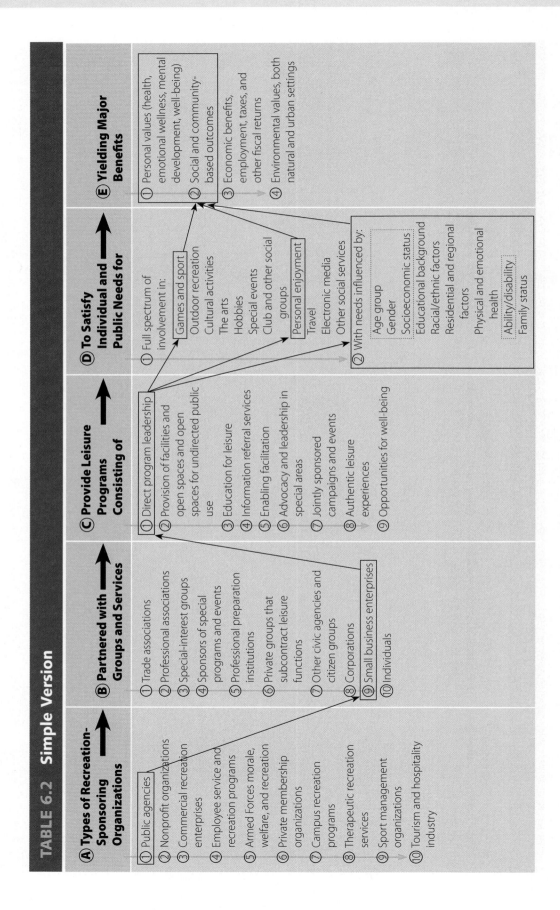

(A) Types of Recreation-Sponsoring Organizations →	(B) Partnered with Groups and Services →	(C) Provide Leisure Programs Consisting of →	(D) To Satisfy Individual and Public Needs for →	(E) Yielding Major Benefits
① Public agencies	① Trade associations	① Direct program leadership	① Full spectrum of involvement in:	① Personal values (health, emotional wellness, mental development, well-being)
② Nonprofit organizations	② Professional associations	② Provision of facilities and open spaces and open spaces for undirected public use	Games and sport	② Social and community-based outcomes
③ Commercial recreation enterprises	③ Special-interest groups	③ Education for leisure	Outdoor recreation	③ Economic benefits, employment, taxes, and other fiscal returns
④ Employee service and recreation programs	④ Sponsors of special programs and events	④ Information referral services	Cultural activities	④ Environmental values, both natural and urban settings
⑤ Armed Forces morale, welfare, and recreation	⑤ Professional preparation institutions	⑤ Enabling facilitation	The arts	
⑥ Private membership organizations	⑥ Private groups that subcontract leisure functions	⑥ Advocacy and leadership in special areas	Hobbies	
⑦ Campus recreation programs	⑦ Other civic agencies and citizen groups	⑦ Jointly sponsored campaigns and events	Special events	
⑧ Therapeutic recreation services	⑧ Corporations	⑧ Authentic leisure experiences	Club and other social groups	
⑨ Sport management organizations	⑨ Small business enterprises	⑨ Opportunities for well-being	Personal enjoyment	
⑩ Tourism and hospitality industry	⑩ Individuals		Travel	
			Electronic media	
			Other social services	
			② With needs influenced by:	
			Age group	
			Gender	
			Socioeconomic status	
			Educational background	
			Racial/ethnic factors	
			Residential and regional factors	
			Physical and emotional health	
			Ability/disability	
			Family status	

PUBLIC RECREATION, PARK, AND LEISURE SERVICES

Public, or government, leisure-service agencies have the following characteristics: (1) They were the first type of agency to be formally recognized as responsible for serving the public's recreation needs and, as such, have constituted the core of the recreation movement; (2) the primary means of support for most government recreation and park agencies traditionally has been tax funding, although in recent years other revenue sources have begun to be used more extensively; (3) government agencies have a major responsibility for the management of natural resources; and (4) they are obligated to serve the public at large with socially useful or constructive programs because of their tax-supported status.

ROLE OF THE FEDERAL GOVERNMENT

The federal government's responsibility for managing parks and recreation areas and providing or assisting other leisure services evolved gradually. The growth of the parks and recreation movement began with the early immigrants to New England, with Boston Common being an archetype of future park development across the United States. National and state parks grew differently from urban parks, and recreation evolved still differently—yet people talk of parks and recreation as if they were one. This is a U.S. institution ranging from Central Park in the late 1850s to the formation of the first national park in 1872. The growth of government and nonprofit involvement, beginning with experiences such as the Boston Sand Gardens and expanding dramatically under Franklin Roosevelt's New Deal policies, solidified government's role in parks and recreation.

The federal government in the United States developed a great variety of programs related to recreation in dozens of different departments, bureaus, or other administrative units. Typically, recreation functions evolved in federal agencies as secondary responsibilities. For example, the initial purposes of the Tennessee Valley Authority lakes and reservoirs were to provide flood control and rural electrification; only over time did recreation uses become important. The following list examines the responsibilities and role of the federal government.

- *Direct management of outdoor recreation resources:* The federal government, through such agencies as the National Park Service, the National Forest Service, and the Bureau of Land Management, owns and operates a vast network of parks, forests, lakes, reservoirs, seashores, and other facilities used extensively for outdoor recreation.

- *Conservation and resource reclamation:* Closely related to the preceding function is the government's role in reclaiming natural resources that have been destroyed, damaged, or threatened, and in promoting programs related to conservation, wildlife, and anti-pollution control.

- *Assistance to open space and park development programs:* Chiefly with funding authorized under the 1965 Land and Water Fund Conservation Act, the federal government has provided billions of dollars in matching grants to states and localities to promote open-space development. Also, through direct aid to municipalities carrying out housing and urban development projects, the federal government subsidized the development of local parks, playgrounds, and centers.

- *Direct programs of recreation participation:* The federal government operates a number of direct programs of recreation service in Veterans Administration hospitals and other federal institutions and in the armed forces on permanent and temporary bases throughout the world.

- *Advisory and financial assistance:* The federal government provides varied forms of assistance to states, localities, and other public or voluntary community agencies. For example, many community programs serving economically and socially disadvantaged populations have been assisted by the Departments of Health and Human Services, Housing and Urban Development, Labor, and others.

- *Aid to professional education:* Federal agencies concerned with education and the needs of special populations have provided training grants for professional education in colleges and universities throughout the United States.

- *Promotion of recreation as an economic function:* The federal government has been active in promoting tourism, providing aid to rural residents in developing recreation enterprises, and assisting Native American tribes in establishing recreational and

Providing interpretive services to visitors is essential to individuals understanding parks and natural settings.

Courtesy of John and Karen Hollingsworth/U.S. Fish and Wildlife Service.

tourist facilities on their reservations. Such agencies as the Bureau of the Census and the Coast Guard also provide needed information for those interested in travel, boating, and similar pastimes.

◆ *Research and technical assistance:* The federal government has supported a broad spectrum of research on topics ranging from outdoor recreation trends and needs and the current status of urban recreation and parks to specific studies of wildlife conservation, forest recreation, or the needs of special populations.

◆ *Regulation and standards:* The federal government has developed regulatory policies with respect to pollution control, watershed production, and environmental quality. It has also established standards with respect to rehabilitative service for those who are ill or those with disabilities and architectural standards to guarantee access to facilities for persons with disabilities.

The first two areas of responsibility (one, direct management and conservation, and two, resource reclamation) are carried out by seven major federal agencies that are either service units or bureaus in cabinet departments or separate authorities. They are the National Park Service, the U.S. Forest Service, the Bureau of Land Management, the Bureau of Reclamation, the U.S. Fish and Wildlife Service, the Tennessee Valley Authority, and the U.S. Army Corps of Engineers.

The National Park Service

The leading federal agency with respect to outdoor recreation is the National Park Service (NPS) (www.nps .gov), housed in the Department of the Interior. Its mission has been stated as follows:

The Appalachian Trail is an example of a national trail used by tens of thousands of people annually for one-day to multi-day trips.
Courtesy of the Appalachian Trial Conservancy.

The National Park Service preserves unimpaired the natural and cultural resources and values of the national park system for the enjoyment, education, and inspiration of this and future generations. The Park Service cooperates with partners to extend the benefits of natural and cultural resource conservation and outdoor recreation throughout this country and the world.

Most of the property administered by the NPS in its early years was west of the Mississippi, and it has since added major seashore parks and other areas throughout the country and closer to urban centers. For example, East Coast sites now include the Fire Island National Seashore on Long Island, Acadia National Park in Maine, Assateague National Seashore on the Maryland coast, Cape Hatteras National Seashore in North Carolina, and Gateway East in the New York and New Jersey harbor area.

The national park system consists of 84 million acres (33.9 million hectares) of land, about 5% of which remains in private ownership. The system generates a huge volume of tourism, with appeal for both domestic travelers and foreign visitors that yields major

 WHO REALLY OWNS THE WESTERN LANDS

The Federal Government is the largest land owner in the United States, and this is especially true in the western states. The federal government owns 62% of Alaska and 47% of the 11 coterminous western states, including 81% of Nevada, 66.5% of Utah, 61.7 percent of Idaho, and 53% of Oregon. By contrast, in the remaining states the federal government only owns an average of 4% of each state. For years, the western states have argued that the vast tracts of lands in their states should be state controlled rather than federally controlled. What's called the "sagebrush rebellion" see these vast tracts of land as revenue sources for mining, oil drilling, expanding ranches, and the like. Most of the states have smaller populations and need additional revenue sources to provide basic services such as schools, roads, and jobs. Western Congressmen have pushed this agenda for many years, but more recently activist ranchers have had standoffs with the Bureau of Land Management and other federal agencies. Simultaneously, western state legislatures, especially in the intermountain west, have become more aggressive in challenging federal control over so much of their land. The question of who really would provide the best stewardship is open for debate. Should the lands be used for revenue generation by the states and federal government, or preserved for wildlife and public enjoyment? This contentious debate is likely to continue for decades into the future.

Source: https://www.nps.gov/aboutus/upload/NPS-Overview-04-12-16.pdf

benefits for the nation's economy and the balance of trade with other countries. In 2014, the national park system experienced 307.2 million visitors, spread across the 412-unit system. The level of usage in the national parks has created overcrowding at what are frequently called the "crown jewels."[2]

The Forest Service

A second federal agency that administers extensive wilderness preserves for public recreation use is the U.S. Forest Service (USFS) (www.fs.fed.gov) within the Department of Agriculture. The resource management responsibilities of the NPS and USFS have blurred in recent years, even though their management mandates have not. Both agencies had responsibilities for managing national monuments, recreation areas, trails, and wild and scenic rivers. The USFS is best known for its management of huge areas of forests and grasslands. The USFS was a predecessor to the NPS and had a very different role. It adopted the multiple-use concept of federally owned land under its control; mining, grazing, lumbering, recreation, and hunting are all permitted in the national forests.

The recreation function of the USFS has continued to grow steadily. In 2016, it oversaw a total forest system of 192.9 million acres (78 million hectares), which included 36.6 million acres (14.8 million hectares) of wilderness as well as major elements of the National Scenic Byways and National Wild and Scenic Rivers Systems, national volcanic areas, 3.8 million acres (1.5 million hectares) of National Grasslands, wildlife and fish habitats, and numerous other special-use areas. In the same year, the USFS recorded 167.5 million visits on 14,077 recreation sites. Its major recreational uses in 2011 were for relaxation and viewing scenery; camping, picnicking, and swimming; hiking, horseback riding, and water travel; winter sports; and hunting and fishing.

Many threats are on forest service-administered lands. The USFS identified four main threats: fires and fuels, invasive species, loss of open space, and unmanaged recreation. Data suggest the loss of more than 3000 acres a day over a 6-year period, mostly to development, in lands near or adjacent to USFS areas. The loss of open space will place greater stress on forest service lands. Unmanaged recreation comes mostly in the form of off-highway vehicles (OHV). There were a reported 36 million OHV owners in 2000, a number that climbed until gas prices and the recession devastated the market. The use of OHVs in USFS lands has resulted in increased erosion, creation of new unplanned roads, and watershed and habitat degradation. The USFS has established action plans for each of the threats.

Other Federal Agencies

The Bureau of Land Management (BLM) (www.blm.gov) administers more than 245 million acres (99.1 million hectares), chiefly in the western states and Alaska. Its properties are used for a variety of resource-based outdoor recreation activities (including camping, biking, hunting and fishing, mountain climbing, and cycle racing), as well as mining, grazing, and lumbering activities that yield more than $800 million a year in revenues, much of it returned to state and local governments.

The U.S. Fish and Wildlife Service (USFWS) (www.fws.gov) originally consisted of two federal bureaus, one dealing with commercial fisheries (which was transferred to the Department of Commerce) and the other dealing with sports fisheries and wildlife (which remained in the Department of the Interior). Its functions include restoring the nation's fisheries, enforcing laws, managing wildlife populations, conducting research, and operating the National Wildlife Refuge System (www.fws.gov/refuges). This system includes 560 units comprising 150 million acres (60.7 million hectares) with at least one site in every state and vast acreages in the Caribbean

2016: 100TH ANNIVERSARY OF THE NATIONAL PARK SERVICE

On August 25, 2016, the National Park Service (NPS) celebrated its 100th anniversary. The first national organization of its kind, the NPS has been the champion of preservation of unique natural, historical, and cultural sites in the United States. The NPA was created by an act of Congress in 1916, signed into law by President Woodrow Wilson, and championed by John Muir, a naturalist often called "The Father of our National Parks." The NPS has been the world leader in conservation and preservation. In the beginning, the NPS was hampered by small budgets and a small core of dedicated people. In 2016, it had over 20,000 employees and 412 administered areas ranging from national parks to local historical and cultural sites. The original "Organic Act" states, "the service thus established shall promote and regulate the use of the Federal areas known as national parks, monuments, and reservations … which purpose is to conserve the scenery and the natural and historic objects and the wild life therein and to provide for the enjoyment of future generations." Throughout the NPS system, special events are planned. Hawai'i Volcanoes National Park also celebrated its 100th anniversary in 2016, created just weeks before the National Park Service. From an international perspective, the National Park System has been touted as "America's best idea" and if not that, it does represent American's best ideals.[3]

Participation in outdoor recreation continues to increase. The variety of outdoor activities increases demand on existing natural resource areas.

© Ammit Jack/Shutterstock.

and Pacific Ocean. In addition to meeting the ongoing needs of hunters and fishers, the USFWS particularly has been active in helping to ensure the survival of endangered species, conserving migratory birds, and administering federal aid programs that assist state wildlife programs and tribal lands programs. Its 2014 visitation exceeded 47 million.

The federal Bureau of Reclamation (BOR) (www.usbr.gov) is responsible for water resource development, primarily in the western states. Although its original function was to promote irrigation and electric power, it has accepted recreation as a responsibility since 1936. The policy of the BOR is to transfer reservoir areas wherever possible to other federal agencies; often these become classified as National Recreation Areas and are assigned to the NPS for operation. The emphasis is on active recreational use such as boating, camping, hiking, hunting, and fishing rather than sightseeing. The NPS, USFS, USFWS, and BOR have provided employment opportunities for thousands of young men and women through the Youth Conservation Corps (YCC), which has habilitated or built campgrounds and boating facilities at recreation areas throughout the West.

BLM'S CONTRIBUTION TO AMERICA'S NATURAL HERITAGE

The BLM manages 245 million acres (99.1 hectares), almost all of it in the western United States. The BLM's management program is called the National Landscape Conservation System (See **Table 6.3**), and includes more than 850 units dedicated to preserving natural resources.[5] The BLM-managed lands are home to approximately 30,000 free-roaming wild horses and burros; approximately 31,000 additional animals are cared for in short-term and long-term holding facilities. Managed areas include Wilderness and Wilderness Study Areas, Wild and Scenic Rivers, National Scenic and Historic Trails, National Monuments, and National Conservation Areas.

Additionally, the BLM manages 16,000 miles of multiple-use trails, including approximately 5300 miles of trails classified within the National Trails System; a vast array of geologic, historic, and archaeological sites, including 800 caves and 271,000 archaeological and historic recorded sites such as lighthouses, ghost towns, petroglyphs, pictographs, and cliff dwellings; and more than 117,000 miles of fisheries habitat and 4 million acres (1.6 billion hectares) of reservoirs and lakes.[6]

TABLE 6.3   BLM's National Landscape Conservation System

Category	Areas	Number	BLM Acres	BLM Miles
National Monuments and national conservation areas	National monuments National conservation areas Similar designations	16 16 4	9,709,615	
Wilderness	Wilderness areas Wilderness study areas	221 545	8,736,691 12,835,035	
Wild and scenic rivers		69	1,164,014	2419
Trails	National historic trails National scenic trails	11 5		5343 668
Totals		**890**	**Approximately 27 million**	**8425**

Reproduced from U.S. Department of the Interior, Bureau of Land Management, "National Landscape Conservation System Summary Tables." Available at: http://www.blm.gov/wo/st/en/prog/blm_special_areas/NLCS/summary_tables.html. Accessed Feb 20, 2013. https://www.blm.gov/wo/st/en/info/About_BLM.html; http://www.usace.army.mil/Missions/Civil-Works/Recreation/

The Tennessee Valley Authority (TVA) (www.tva.gov) operates extensive reservoirs in Kentucky, North Carolina, Tennessee, and other southern or border states. The TVA does not manage recreation facilities itself, but it makes land available to other public agencies or private groups for development.

The U.S. Army Corps of Engineers civilian side (www.usace.army.wil) is responsible for the improvement and maintenance of rivers and other waterways to facilitate navigation and flood control. It constructs reservoirs, protects and improves beaches and harbors, and administers more than 12 million acres (4.9 million hectares) of federally owned land and water impoundments. This includes 460 reservoirs and lakes; the majority of these are managed by the corps, and the remainder are managed by state and local agencies under lease. These sites totaled 370 million annual visits. Army Corps of Engineers recreation sites are heavily used by the public for boating, camping, hunting, and fishing.[4]

Several other agencies in the Department of Agriculture have important recreation functions. The Farm Service Agency's (www.fsa.usda.gov) conservation programs focus on several areas, three of which are relevant to parks and recreation. The Conservation Reserve Program is a state and federal partnership with farmers who, "In exchange for a yearly rental payment, farmers enrolled in the program agree to remove environmentally sensitive land from agricultural production and plant species that will improve environmental health and quality."[5] The Farmable Wetlands Program "reduces downstream flood damage, improves surface and groundwater quality, and recharges groundwater supplies by restoring wetlands." Finally, the Grassland Reserve Program "helps landowners restore and protect grassland, and provides assistance for rehabilitating grasslands."[7] The Farmers Home Administration (www.rd.usda.gov) gives credit and management advice to rural organizations and farmers in developing recreation facilities. The Extension Service aids community recreation planning in rural areas and advises states on outdoor recreation development, working in many states through extension agents at land grant agricultural colleges.

The Bureau of Indian Affairs (www.bia.gov) exists primarily to provide service to Native American tribes in such areas as health, education, economic development, and land management. However, it also operates (under civilian control in the Department of the Interior) Native American-owned properties of about 56 million acres, with more than 5500 lakes that are used heavily for recreational purposes, including camping, museum visits, hunting, and fishing.

Programs in Health and Human Services, Education, and Housing

A number of federal agencies related to health and human services, education, and housing and urban development have provided funding, technical assistance, and other forms of aid to recreation programs designed to meet various social needs in U.S. communities. Within the federal Department of Health and Human Services (www.hhs.gov), such units as the Administration for Children and Families (www.acf.hhs.gov), and the Public Health Service (www.usphs.gov) have been active in this area. For example, the Administration on Aging, authorized by the Older Americans Act of 1965 and reauthorized in 2016, promotes comprehensive programs for older persons and supports training programs and demonstration projects intended to prepare professional personnel to work with older people. It also gathers information on new or expanded programs and services for the aging and supports research projects in this field.

The Rehabilitation Services Administration (rsa.ed.gov) administers the federal law authorizing vocational rehabilitation programs designed to help persons with physical or mental disabilities gain employment and lead fuller lives. It has oversight of formula and discretionary grant programs. Other federal legislation, such as Section 504 of the Rehabilitation Act of 1975 (often called the "nondiscrimination clause") and the Americans with Disabilities Act of 1990, have been instrumental in pressuring school systems, units of local government, and other agencies to provide equal opportunity for persons with disabilities in a wide range of community opportunity fields.

The federal Department of Housing and Urban Development (HUD) (www.hud.gov) was established in 1965, with responsibility for a range of federally assisted programs, including urban renewal and planning, public housing, and open space. HUD's primary responsibility lies with urban development. Its mission is to increase home ownership, support community development, and increase access to affordable housing free from discrimination. Through its $49.3 billion budget, it administers a wide variety of programs focusing on community development. The Community Development Block Grant (CDBG) Entitlement Program, first authorized in 1974, is HUD's most valuable and effective community development program. Examples of use of CDBG funds include roads, sewers, and other infrastructure investments, or for community centers and parks. HUD also funds housing development and rehabilitation through CDBG, HOME, Youthbuild, and Lead Hazard Control grants.

Arts and Humanities Support

Another area of federal involvement in leisure pursuits in the United States has reflected public interest in the arts and a wide range of cultural activities. The National Foundation on the Arts and the Humanities Act of 1965 resulted in the creation of the National Endowment for the Arts (NEA) (www.arts.gov), and it celebrated 50 years of service in 2015. It functions as an independent federal agency supporting and encouraging programs in the arts (including dance, music, drama, folk art, creative writing, and the visual media) and humanities (including literature, history, philosophy, and the study of language).

Attendance at cultural events is an important component of public services provided by leisure-service and cultural arts agencies.
© Susan Montgomery/Shutterstock.

Although there was strong conservative resistance to some controversial programs in the 1990s, the NEA administered a $146 million budget in 2015.[8] Over its 40-year history, NEA has awarded more than 120,000 grants to communities, arts groups, and artists. In 2002, the NEA initiated the National Initiative Program and by 2013, 11 initiatives were available. They included both short- and long-term initiatives lasting from a single year to many years. The initiatives include NEA arts journalism institutes, Operation Homecoming: Writing the Wartime Experience, American Masterpieces, Shakespeare in American Communities, NEA Jazz initiative, Great American Voices, Poetry Out Loud, Big Read, Our Town, Mayors' Institute on City Design 25th Anniversary Initiative, and Blue Star Museums.[9] Creativity Connects, an initiative honoring and moving the arts forward, was initiated during NEA's 50th anniversary celebration in 2015 "to show how the arts contribute to the nation's creative ecosystem and how the arts can connect with other sectors that want and utilize creativity."[10] The initiative plans to address key resources that artists need in order to produce their best work, and includes a grant program supporting partnerships between arts organizations and the nonarts sectors.

Physical Fitness and Sports Promotion

Another recreation-related federal program has been the President's Council on Physical Fitness and Sports (www.fitness.gov). Created in 1956 to help upgrade the fitness of the nation's youth, and broadened in 1968 to include the promotion of sport participation, the Council has operated to encourage public awareness of fitness needs and to stimulate school and community-based sport and fitness programs. It has conducted nationwide promotional campaigns through the media and sponsored many regional physical fitness clinics. This effort continued through the 2000s, with a Presidential Youth Fitness Program providing for state and federal goals and guidelines, school championships, and participant fitness awards. Along with community school systems, many local recreation and park agencies and professional groups have assisted in such fitness programs.

RECREATION-RELATED FUNCTIONS OF STATE GOVERNMENTS

The role of state governments in recreation and parks generally has rested on the Tenth Amendment to the Constitution, which states, "The powers not delegated to the United States by the Constitution, nor prohibited by it to the States, are reserved to the States respectively, or to the people." This amendment, commonly referred to as the "states' rights amendment," is regarded as the source of state powers in such areas as public education, welfare, and health services.

Outdoor Recreation Resources and Programs

Each state government today operates a network of parks and other outdoor recreation resources. The National Association of State Park Directors (NASPD) (www.naspd.org) developed categories of facilities and areas:[11]

◆ *State parks areas:* Containing a number of coordinated programs for the preservation of natural and/or cultural resources and provisions of a variety of outdoor recreation activities supported by those resources.

◆ *State recreation areas:* Where a clear emphasis is placed on the provision of opportunities for primarily active recreation activities; this category includes recreational beaches, water theme parks, and so forth.

◆ *State natural areas:* Where a clear emphasis is placed on protection, management, and interpretation of natural resources or features; this category includes wilderness areas, nature preserves, natural landmarks, and sanctuaries.

◆ *State historic areas:* Where a clear emphasis is placed on protection, management, and interpretation of historical and/or archaeological resources or features; this category includes monuments, memorials, shrines, museums, and so forth dealing with historical and/or archaeological subjects, as well as areas that actually contain substantive remains (e.g., forts, burial mounds) and areas where historic events took place (e.g., battles, discoveries, meetings).

◆ *State environmental education sites:* Used exclusively or primarily for conducting educational programs on environmental subjects, natural resources, and conservation; this category includes nature centers, environmental education centers, "outdoor classrooms," and so forth.

◆ *State scientific areas:* Set aside exclusively or primarily for scientific study, observation, and experimentation involving natural objects, processes, and interrelationships; any other allowable uses are secondary and incidental.

◆ *State trails:* Linear areas outside any other unit of the state park system that provide primarily for trail-type recreational activities (hiking, cycling, horseback riding, etc.); they normally do not contain any land areas large enough to support nontrail activities.

During the 1960s and early 1970s, most state governments expanded their recreation and park holdings, primarily with funding assistance from the Land and Water Conservation Fund, but also through major bond issues totaling hundreds of millions of dollars in many cases. In the 1990s, many states again secured major bond issues for park renovation, new construction, and land acquisition. Open space and natural beauty were widely supported concepts, and the public enthusiastically supported programs of land acquisition and water cleanup. State parks are perceived as a close-to-home outdoor recreation experience available to most residents. Attendance at state parks exceeds all national agencies except the USFS. Attendance at state parks in 2014 was 409 million on 21 million acres (8.5 million hectares). State park acreage is only 18% of the size of the National Park system and yet state parks have more visitors. State parks are essential to outdoor recreation activities of many citizens. (See **Table 6.4.**)

Other State Functions

An important function of state government is to assist a nd work with local governments in environmental efforts. Just as no single municipality can clean up a polluted stream that flows through a state, so in the broad field of urban planning, recreation resource development, and conservation, problems must be approached on a

TABLE 6.4   Areas, Acreage, and Visitation for Selected Outdoor Recreation Agencies

Agency	Areas	Acreage[a]	Visitation[a]
National Park Service	412	84	307
U.S. Forest Service	1,477[b]	193	205
U.S. Fish and Wildlife Service[c]	560	150	47
Bureau of Land Management	238[d]	245	57
Army Corps of Engineers	460[e]	12	25
State Parks (all 50 states)	10,235	18	409

[a] number in millions—45 means 45 million
[b] recreation sites (may be more than one per area)
[c] National Wildlife Refuge System
[d] wilderness areas and national monuments
[e] reservoirs and lakes

Data from: https://www.nps.gov/aboutus/news/release.htm?id=1784; https://www.nps.gov/aboutus/faqs.htm; https://www.fs.fed.us/about-agency; https://www.fws.gov/refuges/about/pdfs/NWRSOverviewFactSheetApr2013revNov032013.pdf; http://www.usace.army.mil/Missions/Civil-Works/Recreation/; http://www.stateparks.org/about-us/state-park-facts/; https://www.blm.gov/wo/st/en/info/About_BLM.html; http://www.usace.army.mil/Missions/Civil-Works/Recreation/

statewide or even a regional basis. In such planning, as in many other aspects of federal relationships with local communities, the state acts as a catalyst for action and as a vital link between the national and local governments.

Many state governments have offices or sponsor arts councils that distribute funds to nonprofit organizations and performing groups or institutions in various areas of creative and cultural activity. A unique aspect of state-sponsored or state-assisted recreation is the state fair. This term covers a wide variety of fairs and expositions held each year throughout the United States and includes carnivals and midways, displays and competitions of livestock and produce, farm equipment shows, and a host of special presentations by corporations of every type. The majority of such fairs are run by nonprofit organizations that are publicly owned and operated, including a number of bona fide state agencies. Attended by about 160 million persons each year, they promote civic and state boosterism, offer a showcase for agricultural and other regional industries or attractions, and provide varied forms of entertainment.

Case Study

Alabama State Parks "Dirt Pass"

Every public park and recreation agency struggles to meet the demands and expectations of their constituents. State park systems as well as the National Park System are historically underfunded. With pressing infrastructure and social needs and demands, states often let their natural resources take a back seat during the funding process. As a result, state parks frequently have a medium to large unfunded maintenance and repair backlog. It is sometimes easier to convince state legislatures to fund new projects, rather than provide funds to maintain and renovate older facilities and parks. In 2016, Alabama's state park system faced an unusual challenge—even for a state park system—with 5 parks scheduled to be closed because of anticipated budget cuts.

Alabama's budget crisis was very real. Over a 5-year period, almost $30 million had been transferred from the state parks budget to cover what the state legislature deemed as essential services. Some communities and counties have negotiated with the state to keep parks in their area open. Fees have also been raised to aid in keeping the park system open. By 2016, the state park system was generating most of its meager operating budget from self-generated funds (such as entrance fees) and from federal earmarked funds, which have decreased significantly in recent years.

Even those parks that have remained open have reduced staffing significantly and have an almost nonexistent operations and repair budget. In 2016, an amendment to the Alabama state constitution was approved by a ballot initiative with a majority vote of 79.7% of those voting. The amendment prohibits the state legislature from reallocating state park funds for other uses and allows the parent state government organization, the Department of Conservation and Natural Resources, to contract with non-state entities for the operation and maintenance of land and facilities that are part of the state park system.

The state park system has looked for creative ways to increase park revenue. One approach has been the "Dirt Pass," a voluntary contribution to the state park system's trails program that individuals can purchase for $35. It is a rubber wristband and serves as a contribution to support maintenance and upkeep of the trails system in selected state parks. Walking outdoors is one of the most popular outdoor recreation activities nationally. The money generated from the Dirt Pass will focus on improvement and management of the state's trail system.

Questions to Consider

1. Do you know how your state park system is funded?
2. Do you think states should use their tax dollars toward maintaining a state park system?
3. Is it appropriate to ask people who use the state parks to pay an additional fee, above their taxes, to enter and use parks? Explain the rationale for your answer.
4. Would you be willing to pay a voluntary fee to show your support of your state parks if the fee was going back into the state park for operations and maintenance?
5. What ideas might be considered to increase alternative funding for state parks?

Sources

http://www.alapark.com/alabama-state-parks-funding; accessed 02/8/17;
https://ballotpedia.org/Alabama_Rules_Governing_Allocation_of_State_Park_Funds,_Amendment_2_(2016); accessed 02/8/17;

An important function of state governments is to promote all aspects of leisure involvement that support economic development. Many states assist or coordinate outdoor recreation ventures, tourism campaigns, regional recovery projects, and other efforts to attract visitors and revive local economies. Travel and tourism to urban and rural areas have become increasingly important to economies. States are providing leadership, assistance, and funding to local levels.

Therapeutic Recreation Service   Each state government provides direct recreation services within the institutions or agencies it sponsors, such as mental hospitals or mental health centers, special schools for people who are mentally retarded, and penal or correctional facilities. Many of the largest networks of facilities that employ therapeutic recreation specialists are tax-supported state mental health systems or similar organizations, although their overall numbers have been reduced because of deinstitutionalization policies.

Individuals with disabilities actively engage in sports, sometimes with individuals without disabilities.
© Shariff Che'Lah/Dreamstime.com.

Promotion of Professional Advancement   Although states promote effective leadership and administrative practices in recreation and parks by developing personnel standards and providing conferences and research support, their major contribution lies in the professional preparation of recreation practitioners in state colleges and universities. Of the colleges and universities in the United States with professional recreation and park curricula, a substantial majority are part of state university systems.

Many state agencies also assist professional development by conducting annual surveys of municipal and county recreation and parks departments and publishing their findings on facilities, fiscal practices, and personnel.

Development and Enforcement of Standards   States also have the function of screening personnel by establishing standards and hiring procedures, or by requiring Civil Service examinations, certification, or personnel registration programs in recreation and parks.

Some also have developed standards relating to health and safety practices in camping and similar settings. State departments enforce safety codes, promote facilities standards, ensure that recreation resources can accommodate persons with disabilities, regulate or prohibit certain types of commercial attractions, and in some cases carry out regular inspections of camps, pools, or other facilities.

THE ROLE OF COUNTY AND LOCAL GOVERNMENTS

Although federal and state governments provide major forms of recreation service in the United States, the responsibility for meeting year-round day-to-day leisure needs belongs to agencies of local government. These range from counties, special park districts, and townships (which embrace larger geographical areas) to cities, villages, and other political subdivisions.

THE ILLINOIS PARK DISTRICT SYSTEM

The Illinois Park District system is not unique in its organization, but is among the largest collection of park districts in the United States. A *park district* is a geographically and politically bounded separate taxing district, serving a distinct population with recreation, park and leisure services, and programs. The districts are created by state enabling legislation and voted into creation at the local level. Each district has an elected board that is responsible for the operations of the park district. Typically, they are policy-setting boards that hire an executive director and staff to run day-to-day operations. They are unique because most municipal park and recreation systems operate under a city government organization in which they compete for resources with other city agencies. A park district's independent status allows it to make investments and provide services with less conflict and competition than agencies that are part of city and county government. This does not remove the park districts from needing to create relationships with cities, counties, planning agencies, and the like. Park districts do not necessarily conform to traditional political boundaries such as cities and school districts. The Illinois Association of Park Districts (www.ilparks.org) has membership from 291 park districts, 9 forest preserve districts, 5 conservation districts, 25 special recreation associations, 27 city park and recreation agencies, 1 state agency, and 103 corporate members.[12]

For recreation and parks in the United States, all powers that are not vested in the federal government belong to the states. In turn, local governments must get their authority through enabling laws passed by state legislatures or through other special charter or home rule arrangements. Of all branches of government, the local government is closest to the people and therefore most able to meet the widest range of recreation needs.

County and Special Park District Programs

As an intermediate stage between state and incorporated local government agencies, county or special district park and recreation units provide large parks and other outdoor recreation resources as a primary function. They may also sponsor services for special populations; that is, programs for those aging or who have a disability, as well as services for all residents of the county, such as programs in the fine and performing arts.

During the early decades of the century, county governments had relatively limited functions. However, since World War II, the rapid growth of suburban populations around large cities has given many county governments new influence and power. Counties have become a base for coordinating and funneling numerous federal grants-in-aid programs. As a result, county park and recreation departments expanded rapidly.

Regional and Special Park Districts

Several states, including California, Illinois, Oregon, and North Dakota, have enabling legislation that permits the establishment of special park and recreation districts. Illinois has more than 300 such districts, including forest preserve and conservation districts. Other states with park and recreation districts include California, Ohio, Oregon, and North Dakota.

Many special recreation and park districts are in heavily populated areas; in some cases, they may encompass a number of independent, separate counties and municipalities in a single structure. Frequently, special park districts and counties are able to carry out vigorous programs of land acquisition in a combined effort, or to impose other means of protecting open space. Many counties enacted laws requiring home developers to set aside community recreation areas. Pennsylvania, for example, authorizes municipalities and counties to receive land from developers as "mandatory dedication" or other alternatives as outlined in the state code. Examples of alternatives include allowing the developer to pay a fee, making close-by park and recreation facilities accessible to development, construction of recreational facilities, or to privately reserve land within a subdivision for park and recreation purposes.[13]

Another common approach used by cities and counties to secure funds and lands is to require owners of new homes to pay an impact fee. The impact fee is based on the concept that current taxpayers should not have to pay for new development; it should be the responsibility of the new owner to pay for community improvements to the neighborhood. Park and recreation departments have been recipients of these funds. Some county governments are establishing permanently protected green belts to halt or lessen the tide of construction. Strengthened zoning policies and more flexible building codes that permit cluster zoning of homes with larger and more concentrated open spaces are also helpful.

MUNICIPAL RECREATION AND PARK DEPARTMENTS

Municipal government is the term generally used to describe the local political unit of government, such as the village, town, or city, that is responsible for providing the bulk of direct community service such as street

COUNTY PARK AGENCIES

County park systems across the United States are very common. King County, Washington, which includes Seattle, is representative of many county park agencies, with the majority of its efforts focused on natural resource management. Its mission is "to enhance the quality of life for communities by providing environmentally sound stewardship of regional and rural parks, trails, natural areas, forest lands, and recreational facilities, supported by partnerships and entrepreneurial initiatives." King County Parks has evolved from a relatively small 150 acres in 1938 to over 28,000 acres in 2011, and includes 200 parks, 175 miles of regional trails, and 180 miles of mountain trails. In addition to managing major natural resources, the system has had to change its approach to financing by becoming more entrepreneurial, increasing accountability for its operating budget, and establishing performance measures for the system and its employees.[14] County park systems across the United States are being challenged to develop new funding sources, become more efficient, and increase the use and effectiveness of partnerships.

maintenance, police and fire protection, and education. Most areas depend on municipal government to provide many important recreation and park facilities and program opportunities, in addition to those provided by voluntary, private, and commercial agencies.

With the widespread recognition of this responsibility, municipal recreation and park agencies expanded rapidly in the United States during the period following World War II, with a steady increase in the number of departments, amount of acreage in park and recreation areas, number of full- and part-time or seasonal personnel, and total expenditures.

Functions and Structure of Municipal Agencies

The most common structure for delivery of services is a combined parks and recreation department. In a few cases, parks and recreation may include other social service organizations such as libraries, assistance agencies, and the like. Some remain separate departments.

Other municipal agencies may also sponsor special leisure services that are linked to their own missions. They may include (1) police departments, which often operate youth service centers or leagues; (2) welfare departments or social service agencies, which may operate daycare centers or senior centers; (3) youth boards, which tend to focus on out-of-school youth or teen gangs; (4) health and hospital agencies, which sometimes operate community mental health centers or similar services; (5) public housing departments, which sometimes have recreation centers in their projects; (6) cultural departments or boards, which frequently sponsor performing arts programs or civic celebrations; and (7) school systems and local community colleges.

Programs of Municipal Agencies

Municipal recreation and parks departments operate programs within several categories of activity: games and sports, aquatics, outdoor and nature-oriented programs, arts and crafts, performing arts, special services, social programs, hobby groups, and other playground and community center activities.

In addition, public recreation and parks departments often sponsor large-scale special events such as holiday celebrations, festival programs, art and hobby shows, and sport tournaments. These departments also assist other community agencies to organize, publicize, and schedule activities. Frequently, sport programs for children and youth, such as Little League or American Legion baseball, are cosponsored by public departments and associations of interested parents who undertake much of the actual management of the activity, including coaching, fundraising, and scheduling. Similarly, many cultural programs, such as civic opera or little theater associations, are affiliated with and receive assistance from public recreation departments.

Varied Program Emphases

Cities tend to have common and unique emphases in their recreation and park operations. Henderson, Nevada, a city of over 270,000 residents, is an example of an established community and parks and recreation department that includes 4 year-round indoor aquatic centers, 7 seasonal swimming pools, 8 multi-use recreation centers (including a senior center), 5 major outdoor sports parks, a bird preserve, over 65 parks ranging from small vest-pocket parks to large parks, an outdoor events center and pavilion with an amphitheater, and a stand-alone convention center.[15]

Louisville, Kentucky has a rich heritage of parks and recreation with major early developments in their park system designed by Frederick Law Olmsted and considered one of the four ultimate park systems of his career. Since that time Louisville has kept the Olmsted legacy alive with rich investment in park development and simultaneously developing a strong recreation system with community recreation centers, golf courses, athletic fields, historic properties, and recreation programs focusing on seniors, the arts, youth, athletics, programs for individuals with disabilities, summer camps, and the like.

Fitness Programming   Many cities have undertaken special programs to promote health, fitness, and sport. The Parks and Recreation Department in San Antonio, Texas sponsors a broad range of programs under the title, "Fitness in the Parks," all of which are free. The variety of programs available includes Boot Camp, Circuit Training, Pediatrics in the Park, Mommy and Me Fitness, Body Combat, Zumba, Kettle Bell Conditioning, Yoga, Pilates, and many more. Classes target people of all ages, fitness levels, and ability levels, including those with disabilities. Some classes target specific groups such as seniors, expectant mothers, and youth. Beginning in 2011 the city focused on the installation of fitness equipment in parks and fitness programs. The project was a joint initiative of the mayor's fitness council, the city parks and recreation department, and the metropolitan health district.

Case Study
. . . .

The Next Generation of Urban Parks

Urban parks have been part of the American fabric since the creation of the Boston Common in the mid-seventeenth century and New York's Central Park in the early nineteenth century. Each defined parks in different ways, but it was the ideal of Central Park that brought about the large urban park movement. A movement that has defined public parks for 175 years, it has been rethought, discussed, challenged, but remains the ideal for many communities.

With burgeoning populations, the resurgence of urban areas, the recognition that communities must rethink how they provide public parks, and the desire to ensure that green spaces are available to many, the concept of the urban park in the twenty-first century is receiving much attention.[a] Traditionally park and recreation professionals have led the discussion, but increasingly the push for change is coming from nonprofits, community organizations, and community members, all devoted to their communities.

Louisville, Kentucky has a rich park heritage. In 1891, they contracted with Frederick Law Olmsted, one of two designers of Central Park, to create a park system. The results were three major parks connected with tree-lined boulevards. The Olmsted parks are considered to be national and local treasures and examples of a premiere park system. In 2001, the community was challenged by the chairman of the Louisville Olmsted Parks Conservancy to "help us think of something that our generation can do that will have a 100-year impact on Louisville like the Olmsted Parks."[b]

In Minneapolis, Minnesota, the Parks Foundation created a series of initiatives to foster community engagement in the development of parks. The foundation has embraced the concept of "The Next Generation of Urban Parks." A series of lectures were sponsored focusing on transformative park designs around the world; a curriculum for school children was created that helps them to see the community, share responsibility for its environment, and learn to participate in public decision-making processes. In addition, the Foundation has created partnerships with the University of Minnesota College of Design to help initiate creative design. One of their first initiatives, titled "RiverFirst," focuses on 5.5 miles of the Upper Mississippi River.[c] Parks developed along both sides of the river were conceived as a linear park, establishing a riverfront park for future generations. A series of design competitions were conducted as part of the creative process. The results have encouraged the Minneapolis Parks and Recreation Board to establish a 20-year development plan, with specific target tasks that will anchor the project and encourage ongoing investment.

The Trust for Public Land's Center for City Park Excellence is committed to research on parks; what makes them successful; how parks contribute to the social, economic, and ecological values of their communities and users; and how parks contribute to neighborhood revitalization.[d] The City Parks Alliance, another nonprofit organization, focuses its efforts on a broad spectrum of individuals committed to urban parks and their contributions to urban areas and environments.[e]

As communities address a broad range of social and economic issues, challenges, and expectations from their residents, they are discovering that government cannot do it alone. Rethinking the concept and role of urban parks has been a major national discussion since the early 1990s and has become even more acute as economic challenges have diminished many local and state governments' abilities to maintain existing services and provide new parks and recreation areas. Nonprofits are having a significant influence on the future potential of the concept, design, and management of urban parks. Part of the concept of "The Next Generation of Urban Parks" is the greater involvement of partnerships among government, nonprofits, corporations, and community groups and organizations to define, embrace, and serve as a catalyst for community understanding and commitment.

Questions to Consider

1. Does your community have an urban park?
2. Would it benefit from an urban park? If so, how would it benefit?
3. How could you help your community begin to think about creating or renewing its urban parks?

Sources

a. The Parklands of Floyd's Fork (21st Century Parks, Inc.), "A Dream Realized Through 21st Century Parks": http://theparklands.org.
b. 21st Century Parks, "Bringing Nature Into Neighborhoods": http://21cparks.org.
c. Walker Art Center Magazine, "The Next Frontier for Minneapolis Parks": www.walkerart.org/magazine/2012/next-frontier-minneapolis.
d. Trust for Public Lands (TPL) Center for City Park Excellence: www.tpl.org/research/parks/ccpe.html.
e. City Parks Alliance: www.cityparksalliance.org.

Denver, CO is constructing the Central Denver Recreation Center at a proposed cost of $20–$25 million. It is planned as a regional recreation center, will have more than 60,000 square feet of user space on two floors. It includes an indoor leisure and lap pools for recreation and competitive purposes, a large fitness/training area, a multicourt gymnasium, multipurpose classrooms, a child care/toddler area, and a large group exercise room. From the opposite end of the spectrum, White Pine County, NV—the 17th largest county by area (8,897 square miles) and with a population of 10,000, opened a new aquatic facility in Ely, NV in 2013. It was the first new facility in decades, and focuses on serving the population with a variety of aquatic recreation and fitness activities. Rural counties frequently struggle to provide recreation and park services to their residents.

Human Service Functions   Many local recreation and park agencies have moved vigorously into the area of programming to meet human and social service needs. The Recreation and Human Services Department of the city of Gardena, California, for example, offers many services, including youth services; individual, family, and group counseling; tutoring workshops; alcohol and drug abuse programs; after-school activities; licensed family child care; youth and adult counseling; senior citizen outreach and meals programming; and care for those suffering from Alzheimer's or mental disease.

A trend of the last two decades has been to develop multiservice departments in which recreation and park programs play a leading role. Thus, a merged department of community services might have responsibility for beaches, parking meters, special housing units, libraries, and other special public facilities or programs. Larger urban recreation and park departments may include management responsibilities for stadiums, convention centers, piers and marinas, or even municipal airports.

Exercise classes are frequently offered at local recreation centers.
© iStockphoto/Thinkstock/Getty.

Fee-Based Programs

In response to government efforts to become more business oriented, including seeking expanded revenue sources, fee-based programs have gained popularity with recreation and park departments. The trend toward imposing substantial fees for many program elements or facilities membership in public recreation and parks is firmly established. Those who favor it argue that it provides a logical means of developing rich programs and services and strengthens the role of the recreation and agency in community life. As tax revenues available for recreation and parks continue to decline, many agencies find fee-based programs a survival tool. Other agencies have implemented fee-based programs to offer services that would otherwise not be available through government funding.

Some critics argue that placing heavy reliance on fee structures discriminates against children and youth, people who are elderly, persons with disabilities, and the poor, who cannot afford to pay significant fees for participation in public recreation programs. As such, it represents a retreat from the fundamental mission of public recreation and leisure programs. In some cases, cities or other public recreation and park agencies have provided fee discounts, "scholarships," or variable pricing policies to enable participation by poorer families. Although such policies are generally acceptable in well-to-do towns or suburban areas, they are obviously not workable in socially and economically disadvantaged inner-city neighborhoods or in less affluent communities. Some cities developed models in which they assess the social priority that should be attached to recreation facilities or programs and base fee-charging policies on this assessment.

Aquatic centers with a variety of amenities have become popular year-round activities incorporated into public park and recreation agencies, commercial enterprises, and resorts.
Courtesy of Amy Hurd.

Innovative Developments in Larger Cities

As other chapters in this text have shown, problems related to inadequate budgets, increasing crime, and declining infrastructure and maintenance services tend to be most severe in older cities with limited public, nonprofit, and commercial leisure resources—yet, even in these communities, recreation and park administrators are working to expand and improve leisure facilities, programs, and maintenance. In 2014, Seattle, Washington residents approved the creation of the Seattle Park District with funding coming from property taxes. The park district was a response, in part, to the need for a more stable funding source for parks. In 2016, the first full year of funding, a $47 million budget was proposed for operations and capital

City parks allow residents to enjoy leisure time relaxing in open spaces.
© Siri Stafford/Lifesize/Thinkstock/Getty.

improvements. Like many American cities, funding for maintenance of parks and recreation facilities has not kept up with maintenance demands and expectations. When maintenance is not performed because of lack of funding it is called "deferred maintenance." Deferred maintenance can become an overwhelming budget and operations issue for an organization with limited fiscal resources. The 2016 budget identified $31 million for deferred maintenance and focused on new play equipment on playgrounds, rehabilitation of seven community centers, major renovations of the zoo, and other key projects in the community. The long-term capital budget (funds dedicated to major projects over several years) has targeted $137 million for "Fix it First" deferred projects; $44 million for building future projects; $4.4 million for redevelopment; and $1.6 million for maintaining parks and facilities.[18]

In addition to maintenance operations, construction of new facilities, and renovation of facilities, the Seattle Park District has set targets to improve community member experiences in community centers; create partnerships to provide more recreation opportunities; place a focus on enhancing arts in the parks through public performances and events; focus on programming for older adults as well as young people; and to meet the needs of persons with disabilities.[19]

Along with such environmental and marketing-based efforts, many municipal recreation and park agencies also have moved vigorously in the direction of benefits-based programming as a means of documenting and providing direction to their overall services.

Case Study

How is Public Parks and Recreation Funded?

Funding public parks and recreation is very different from operating a private enterprise. Governments are run by elected decision makers and federal, state, and local elected legislators, county officials, and city councils that enact laws and ordinances within bounds set by state governments for funding parks and recreation. Funding for public parks and recreation can come from multiple sources, including the community, county, state, or federal levels. This creates a complicated approach to achieve an adequate level of funding for public agencies. Parks and recreation rarely has its own funding base and is more likely in competition with other city, county, or state agencies for the local revenue sources. For the purposes of this case study, the four primary sources of income for a public agency (e.g., a city or county) are compulsory income, earned income, contractual receipts, and partnerships and collaborations. Compulsory income includes funds governments secure from taxes, licensing, or other sorts of government instituted income sources. The most common compulsory income includes property taxes, sales tax, and state and/or local income taxes. Other frequently used sources of compulsory income include special assessment taxes such as for street or sewer construction, but can also include parks and recreation development, dedication ordinances where a specific geographic area of the community is taxed such as a new housing development, which is taxed for the creation of a neighborhood park. Earned income includes cash revenues generated from fees and charges instituted by the public organization. These can include admission fees, program fees, entrance fees, charges for use of area and facilities, income from sales of supplies, equipment, gift shop, rental fees, and special user fees. Contractual receipts are funds generated from legal agreements with private and nonprofit organizations. Agreements can include the management of public properties (such as a tennis center), rental of facilities, rental of equipment, management of special operations (such as golf course, an indoor facility, or a marina). Partnerships and collaborations are agreements between two or more organizations who chose to work for a mutual goal. The partnership can be for a fixed or indeterminate length of time. The success of a partnership is dependent upon each organization clearly understanding and identifying their needs. In contrast, a collaboration is where organizations work together to achieve the common goal, but may not have the same vision, resources, or risks.

A public agency uses all of the sources of income to varying degrees. **Figure 6.1** depicts an example of revenue sources, contribution to the revenue budget. For example, compulsory income is a primary source of income for all public agencies, but is rarely present in the nonprofit sector. Earned income is an essential source of income to public park and recreation agencies and includes fees for classes, golf course fees, admission fees to swimming pools or other facilities, membership fees, and much more. It has become a key source of income for public agencies as tax dollars are not sufficient to meet public demands. Contractual receipts are common for almost all agencies, but vary in the importance of operations. For example, some communities have negotiated contracts with for profit or nonprofit organizations to manage golf courses, recreation centers, aquatic centers, and programs and services. Partnerships and collaborations focus on working with other organizations in sharing costs and resources to achieve a common goal, such as a special event (a sporting event, cultural event, or community event). Partnerships allow public, commercial, and nonprofit organizations to work together to meet community needs.

Public agencies construct their annual budget based on anticipated sources of income. For example, compulsory income typically is the single largest source followed by earned income and contractual receipts. Partnerships may or may not involve income. A budget might include 40% compulsory income, 36% earned income, and 24% contractual. Within the broad classes of income there are many different sources and will vary from state to state.

Budgeting for public parks and recreation is a complex mix of different local sources of income with the occasional addition of state and federal funds. Increasingly, public parks and recreation has relied less on tax dollars (compulsory income) for operations and increasingly on non-compulsory income sources.

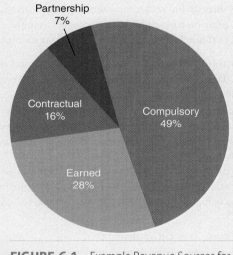

FIGURE 6.1   Example Revenue Sources for Municipal Park & Recreation Department
© Jones & Bartlett Learning.

Questions to Consider

1. Select a community or county park and recreation agency and explore its income sources. What are its balance of income sources? You should be able to find this on their web site.
2. Do the same process for a nonprofit organization, which will have no compulsory sources of income. This will be available on their web site; or possibly from the local United Way.
3. Find a partnership between a public agency and/or a private company, nonprofit, or another public agency. Identify the goals and outcomes for each agency, and if possible, the financial commitment each agency made to the partnership.
4. Explain how the four income sources complement each other.

Source: Brayley, R. E. & McLean, D. D. 2008. Managing Financial Resources in Sport, Tourism, and Leisure Services (Champaign, IL: Sagamore Publishing): 2008.

NONPROFIT ORGANIZATIONS: ORGANIZING THE VOLUNTARY SECTOR

Whereas government recreation and park agencies are responsible for providing a floor of basic leisure services for the public throughout the United States, a major segment of recreational opportunities is sponsored by nonprofit organizations, often called *voluntary agencies*. These consist of several different types of youth-serving, special-interest, and charitable organizations.

Organizations in this category may be completely independent or may be part of national or regional federations. Often they are described as "quasi-public" or "public/private." In some cases, they must meet government-imposed standards as charitable organizations to retain tax-exempt status. They tend to share the following characteristics:

♦ Usually established to meet significant social needs through organized citizen cooperation, community organizations represent the voluntary wishes and expressed needs of neighborhood residents. Thus, they are voluntary in origin.

♦ Governing boards of directors or trustees are usually public-spirited citizens who accept such responsibilities as a form of social obligation; thus, membership and administrative control are voluntary.

♦ For funding, voluntary agencies usually rely on public contributions, either directly to the agency itself or to Community Chest, United Way, or similar shared fundraising efforts. Contributed funds are usually supplemented by membership fees and charges for participation. In recent years, many voluntary organizations also have undertaken special projects for which they receive government funding.

♦ Leadership of voluntary agencies is partly professional and partly voluntary. Management is usually by directors and supervisors professionally trained in social work, recreation, education, or other related areas. At other levels, leadership is by nonprofessionals, part-time or seasonal personnel, and volunteers.

♦ In some cases, nonprofit organizations in the overall leisure-service system do not sponsor recreation activities directly, but rather represent organizations that do or that manufacture equipment or provide services, often on a for-profit basis. However, as in the case of educational institutions or professional societies in this field, they are nonprofit and tax exempt.

Nonprofit voluntary agencies regard recreation as part of their total spectrum of services, rather than their sole function. Typically, they recognize the importance of creative and constructive leisure and see recreation as a threshold activity that serves to attract participants to their agencies. In addition, they see it as a means of achieving significant social goals, such as building character among youth, reducing social pathology, enriching educational experience, strengthening community unity, and similar objectives. In general, even though voluntary agencies do not describe themselves as recreation agencies, this often tends to be the largest single component in their programs.

Nonprofits rely on volunteers for much of their work. Americans provide more volunteer service than any other society. In 2015, 64.5 million people, or 24.9% of all Americans, volunteered to serve organizations or other programs. Women represented 27.8% of all volunteers and those aged 35 to 44 provided 31.6% of all volunteers. Teens volunteered at a rate of 26.4%. Volunteers' median time spent was 50 hours annually.[20]

Nonprofit but Fee Charging

Many voluntary organizations, though they are nonprofit and interested in meeting important social goals, may charge substantial fees. For example, YMCAs or YWCAs in suburban areas are likely to have fees that are as high as several hundred dollars a year for full family memberships, and charge impressive sums for varied program activities. However, such fees are intended simply to help the organization maintain financial stability, without making a profit, and are frequently used to subsidize other services to marginalized populations who cannot afford to pay fees for membership or participation.

Because of the word *voluntary*, some assume incorrectly that such agencies are staffed solely by volunteer workers. The reality is that, although some nonprofit organizations such as the Boy Scouts and Girl Scouts rely heavily on volunteer leaders, most of them have full-time, paid professionals in their key management or supervisory posts.

It was estimated in 2012 that nonprofit organizations employed 10.3% of working Americans, involving 10.7 million paid workers.[21] Salaries for professional employees of nonprofits such as the Boy Scouts and Girl Scouts, the YMCA and YWCA, Junior Achievement, and Big Brothers/Big Sisters of America all have risen steadily in recent years.

TYPES OF NONPROFIT YOUTH-SERVING AGENCIES

Although voluntary nonprofit organizations fit under many headings—including the arts, education, health, and social service—the largest segment of such groups with strong recreational components is generally youth oriented. Included in this segment are the following:

♦ Nonsectarian youth-serving organizations
♦ Religiously affiliated youth-serving or social agencies
♦ Special interest organizations in such fields as sport, outdoor recreation, and travel
♦ Conservation and outdoor recreation

- Organizations promoting youth sports and games
- Arts councils and cultural organizations
- Service and federal clubs
- Promotional and coordinating bodies

Nonsectarian Youth-Serving Organizations

Nationally structured organizations that function directly through local branches, nonsectarian youth-serving groups have broad goals related to social development and good citizenship, and operate extensive programs of recreational activity. There are hundreds of such organizations: Many of them are junior affiliates of adult organizations, whereas others are independent. Sponsorship is by such varied bodies as civic and fraternal organizations, veterans' clubs, rural and farm organizations, and business clubs. Several examples follow.

Boy Scouts of America   Founded in the United States in 1910, the Boy Scouts of America is a powerful and widespread organization. In 2015, its youth membership consisted of 2.4 million youth, ranging from Tiger Cubs to Explorers. Together with adult leaders, a total of 3.5 million were involved in Boy Scouts of America.[22] In addition to its membership in the United States, Boy Scouts of America is part of a worldwide scouting movement involving more than 100 other countries. The program emphasizes mental and physical fitness, vocational and social development, and the enrichment of youth hobbies and prevocational interests, relying heavily on adventure and scouting skills and service activities.

The Boy Scouts of America has been regarded as a middle-class organization in U.S. society and as a small town or suburban rather than a big city phenomenon. As the urban environment has changed, so has Scouting's impact among youth living in large metropolitan areas and among diverse populations. For example, scouting has special focus programs for African American, Asian American, and American Indian groups. In addition, they have developed multicultural partnerships.

Girl Scouts of the U.S.A.   The largest voluntary organization serving girls in the world, the Girl Scouts of the U.S.A. is open to girls between the ages of 5 and 17 who subscribe to its ideals as stated in the Girl Scout Promise and Law. It is part of a worldwide association of girls and adults in more than 90 countries through its membership in the World Association of Girl Guides and Girl Scouts. Its membership in 2016 consisted of 2.7 million members and 800,000 adults, including volunteers, board members, and staff specialists.[23]

Founded in 1912, the Girl Scouts provides a sequential program of activities centered around the arts, the home, and the outdoors, with emphasis on character and citizenship development, community service, international understanding, and health and safety. Senior Girl Scouts in particular may take on responsibilities in hospitals, museums, child care, or environmental programs. Like the Boy Scouts of America, the Girl Scouts today conducts special programs for the poor; those with physical, emotional, or other disabilities; and similar populations.

Boys and Girls Clubs of America   The Boys and Girls Clubs movement is the fastest-growing youth-serving organization in the United States today. Originally composed of two separate organizations, the merged club movement holds a U.S. congressional charter and is endorsed by 21 leading service, fraternal, civic, veteran, labor, and business organizations. Today, the Boys and Girls Clubs movement serves almost 4 million youth members in more than 4,100 club locations with a staff of 56,000 full-time trained professionals and more than 239,000 adult volunteers. Its members are from underrepresented populations (70%), 6–9 years old (36%), 10–12 years old (30%), and 13 and older (29%), and are closely equal gender wise.[24] Programs include sport and games, arts and crafts, social activities, and camping, as well as remedial education, work training, and job placement and counseling. The national goals of the Boys and Girls Clubs of America include the following: citizenship education and leadership development; health, fitness, and preparation for leisure; educational vocational motivation; intergroup understanding and value development; and enrichment of both family and community life.

With the help of special funding from corporations, foundations, and government agencies, the organization has developed program curricula for several key projects in the social services area. Although each club is an independent organization with its own board and professional staff, the national headquarters and seven regional offices provide essential services to local clubs in such areas as personnel recruitment and management training, program research and development, fundraising and public relations, and building design and construction assistance.

The Girl Scouts are involved in their local communities through a variety of community service activities.

Used by permission of Girl Scouts of the USA.

Police Athletic Leagues In hundreds of communities today, law enforcement agencies sponsor Police Athletic Leagues (PALs). Operating in poverty areas, the league programs rely primarily on civilian staffing and voluntary contributions for support, although they sometimes receive technical assistance from officers on special assignment from cooperative municipal police departments. In a few cities, police officers provide the bulk of full-time professional leadership in PAL programs. PALs typically provide extensive recreation programming, indoor centers, and summer play streets, with strong emphasis on sport and games, creative arts, drum and bugle corps, and remedial education. Many leagues also maintain placement, counseling, and job training programs and assist youth who have dropped out of school.

The PAL is one of the few youth organizations that continues to have resisting juvenile delinquency as a primary thrust. One of its principal purposes has been to promote favorable relationships between young people and the police in urban settings, and it has been markedly successful in this effort. Like other voluntary agencies, PALs rely on varied funding sources, including the United Way, independent fundraising campaigns, contracts with government, and often partial police department sponsorship.

Best Buddies Established in 1989 by Anthony Kennedy Shriver, Best Buddies focuses on creating one-to-one friendships, integrated employment, and leadership development for people with intellectual and developmental disabilities.[25] The program currently has chapters on more than 1800 middle school, high school, and college campuses across the United States. There are six programs focusing on bringing one-to-one relationships to people with intellectual and developmental abilities with community members. The programs include Best Buddies Citizens, including the corporate and civic communities; Best Buddies Colleges; High Schools; Middle Schools; Best Buddies Jobs with supported employment; and *e*-Buddies focusing on an email pen pal program.

Best Buddies Massachusetts, an example state chapter, has an active program including participants and fundraising. In 2016, for example, its events included employment fairs, numerous friendship walks, and a Thanksgiving 5k Gobbler Run.[26] As with most nonprofits, there is a mix of activities for participants and fundraising to secure funding for operation of the program.

Religiously Affiliated Youth-Serving or Social Agencies

Many religious organizations sponsor youth programs with recreational components today, including activities sponsored by local churches or synagogues and activities sponsored by national federations that are affiliated with a particular denomination.

Recreation programs provided by local churches or synagogues tend to have two broad purposes: (1) to sponsor recreation for their own members or congregations to meet their leisure needs in ways that promote involvement with the institution and (2) to provide leisure opportunities for the community at large or for a selected population group in ways that are compatible with their own religious beliefs. Typical activities offered by individual churches and synagogues may include the following:

◆ Day camps, play schools, or summer Bible schools, which include recreation along with religious instruction
◆ Year-round recreation activities for families, including picnics, outings, bazaars, covered dish suppers, carnivals, single-adult clubs, dances, game nights, and similar events
◆ Programs in the fine and performing arts, including innovative worship programs involving dance and folk music
◆ Fellowship programs for various age levels, including discussion groups on religious and other themes
◆ Varied special interest or social service programs, including daycare centers for children, senior citizens clubs or golden age groups, and recreation programs for persons with disabilities
◆ Sport activities, including bowling and basketball leagues, or other forms of instructional or competitive participation

On a broader level, such organizations as the Young Men's Christian Association (YMCA), Young Women's Christian Association (YWCA), the Catholic Youth Organization (CYO), and the Young Men's and Young Women's Hebrew Association (YM-YWHA) provide a network of facilities and programs with diversified recreation, education, and youth service activities. Although their titles include the words *young* or *youth*, they tend to serve a broad range of children, youth, adult, and aging members.

YMCA and YWCA Voluntary organizations affiliated with Protestantism in general rather than with any single denomination, the Ys are devoted to the promotion of religious ideals of living, and view themselves as worldwide fellowships "dedicated to the enrichment of life through the development of Christian character and a Christian society." However, the actual membership of the Ys is multi-religious and multiracial. In 2015, there were 2700 YMCAs with 22 million members, making it one of the largest nonprofits providing recreation. There were an additional 500,000 volunteers and 19,000 full time staff.[27]

In many communities, the YMCA offers facilities and leadership for indoor aquatics, sport and games, physical fitness, social and cultural programs, and family-centered programs. These activities are usually aggressively marketed and bring in substantial revenues. Both the YMCA and YWCA derive funding from varied sources: membership fees, corporate and private contributions through the United Way, fundraising drives, and government and foundation grants.

Nonprofit organizations such as the YMCA provide important services for members, including fitness programs.
© muzsy/Shutterstock.

Muslim Youth Groups   There is no single national organization providing leadership for Muslim youth groups; rather, multiple groups are providing leadership, all with some or a total emphasis on youth. These include the Islamic Society of North America, Muslim American Society, and Young Muslims. The Islamic Society of North America (ISNA) provides information on aging, domestic violence, matrimony, leadership, and youth.

There are Muslim youth groups concentrated in local communities and regions. The Islamic Center of Southern California, for example, provides an educational, social, spiritual, and moral environment, and physical activities to motivate young American Muslims to live by and serve Islam and to identify themselves as Muslims, creating a nurturing learning environment in which a basic core knowledge of Islam is provided. In addition, they encourage education, self-expression, the creation of a social environment to build healthy interaction, and foster an American Muslim identity.

Catholic Youth Organization   The leading Catholic organization concerned with providing spiritual, social, and recreational services for young people in the United States is the Catholic Youth Organization (CYO). CYO originated in the early 1930s, when a number of dioceses under the leadership of Bishop Sheil of Chicago began experimenting with varied forms of youth organizations. It was established as a national organization in 1951 as a component of the National Council of Catholic Youth. Today, the National CYO Federation has an office in Washington, DC, as well as many citywide or diocesan offices. The parish, however, is the core of the Catholic Youth Organization, which depends heavily on the leadership of parish priests and the services of adult volunteers from the neighborhood for direction and assistance.

Young Men's and Young Women's Hebrew Association   Today, there are more than 275 YM-YWHAs, Jewish Community Centers, and camps serving more than 1 million members throughout the United States. Like the YMCAs and YWCAs, the Jewish Ys do not regard themselves primarily as recreation agencies, but rather as community organizations devoted to social service and having a strong Jewish cultural component. Specifically, the YM-YWHA has defined its mission in the following way:

◆ To meet the leisure-time social, cultural, and recreational needs of its membership, embracing both sexes and all age groups
◆ To stimulate individual growth and personality development by encouraging interest and capacity for group and community participation
◆ To teach leadership responsibility and democratic process through group participation
◆ To encourage citizenship education and responsibility among its members and, as a social welfare agency, to participate in community-wide programs of social betterment

Special Interest Organizations

Numerous other types of voluntary nonprofit organizations can best be classified as special interest groups, concerned with promoting a particular area of activity or social concern. Their functions may include leadership training, public relations, lobbying and legislation, establishing national standards or

Ethnic background affects the types of activities individuals participate in but does not diminish participation.
©Robert Kneschke/Shutterstock.

operational policies, or the direct sponsorship of program activities. Special interest organizations may be free of commercial involvement or may represent manufacturers of equipment, owners of facilities, schools, or other businesses that seek to stimulate public interest and support and, ultimately, to improve their own business success.

Conservation and Outdoor Recreation   Numerous nonprofit organizations seek to educate the public and influence governmental policies in the areas of conservation and outdoor recreation. In some cases, they lobby, conduct research, and sponsor conferences and publications. In others, their primary thrust is to mount projects and carry out direct action on state or local levels.

Sierra Club   Founded in 1892 and headed initially by the famous naturalist John Muir, the Sierra Club has sought to make Americans aware "of what we have lost and can lose during 200 years of continuing exploitation of our resources for commodity purposes and failure to realize their value for scenic, scientific, and aesthetic purposes." The Sierra Club has gained an international focus, emphasizing issues of global warming and the effects of recent disasters such as the tsunami in south Asia and Hurricane Katrina. Its activities are not restricted to conservation; it is also the nation's largest skiing and hiking club, operating a major network of ski lodges and "river runners," numerous wilderness outings, and ecological group projects.

Appalachian Mountain Club   This organization has a regional focus; its purpose when founded in 1876 was to "explore the mountains of New England and adjacent regions . . . for scientific and artistic purposes, and . . . to cultivate an interest in geographical studies." Since its inception, it has explored and mapped many of the wildest and most scenic areas in Massachusetts, New Hampshire, and Maine, in addition to promoting such sports as skiing, snowshoeing, mountain climbing, and canoeing.

Although practical conservation remains a primary concern of the club, it also has acquired various camp properties, published guides and maps, and maintained hundreds of miles of trails and a network of huts and shelters throughout the White Mountains for use by its members. It promotes programs of instruction and leadership training in such activities as snowshoeing, skiing, smooth and whitewater canoeing, and rock climbing.

Outdoor Leadership Programs   A number of other national nonprofit organizations teach outdoor leadership skills and promote sound environmental practices in the wilderness. The National Outdoor Leadership School sponsors a variety of courses in backpacking, mountaineering, rock climbing, sea kayaking, and other outdoor adventure activities in settings throughout the western states, Alaska, and such foreign countries as Australia, Mexico, Argentina, Chile, and Kenya. Outward Bound uses five core programs for character development and self-discovery through challenge and adventure. Initiated in the early 1960s, early programs trained the first Peace Corps volunteers. Since that time it has become a worldwide organization providing training and experiences to more than 500,000 people. The Association for Experiential Education is a professional membership association focusing on experiential education for students, educators, and practitioners. It provides program resources, a national conference, and accreditation for environmental education sites.

Nonprofits, art centers, and civic organizations offer art classes.
© Layland Masuda/Shutterstock.

Organizations Promoting Youth Sport and Games   There are thousands of national, regional, and local organizations promoting and regulating sport of every kind. Although many of these govern professional play or high-level intercollegiate competition, others are concerned with sports and games on a purely amateur basis. One example of such an organization is Little League.

Founded in Williamsport, Pennsylvania in 1939, Little League is the largest youth sports program in the world today. In its various leagues, including softball, it serves more than 2.6 million players in the United States and more than 2.4 million players in 80 countries. In 2015, there were about 6500 organized leagues; in the same year, 290 new programs were chartered, 135 of them outside the United States.[28] Vietnam was one of the new nations initiating a Little League program. Prior to the Little League Baseball World Series, up to 16,000 tournament games are played in a 6-week time frame. Little League operates an impressive headquarters complex and stadium in Williamsport, where camps, conferences, and the annual World Series are held. It has standardized rules of play, requirements for financial operation and fee structures, insurance coverage, approved equipment, and other arrangements for member leagues and teams. Little League also conducts research into youth sport and carries out a great variety of training programs for league officials, district administrators, umpires, managers, and coaches, as well as a series of publications.

Youth sports in general are assisted by national organizations that set standards and promote effective, values-oriented coaching approaches, such as the National Alliance for Youth Sports and the Positive Coaching Alliance. Examples of organizations that are particularly concerned with individual sport include Youth Basketball of America, the Young American Bowling Alliance, and the United States Tennis Association (USTA). The latter organization has mounted a vigorous campaign to promote tennis to children and youth through the schools and public recreation agencies. USTA has awarded more than $4 million to support community park and recreation tennis programs.

Arts Councils and Cultural Organizations   Another major area of activity for voluntary agencies is the arts. In addition to nonprofit schools and art centers that offer painting, drawing, sculpture, and similar programs, there are literally thousands of civic organizations that sponsor or present performing arts. These include symphony orchestras, bands of various types, choral societies, opera or operetta companies, little theater groups, ballet and modern dance companies, and similar bodies.

In many communities, special interest organizations in the arts are coordinated or assisted by umbrella agencies that help to promote their joint efforts. The Pasadena Arts Council was the first umbrella organization chartered in California. It provides a number of services to its members and the community, including a resource guide for artists, a business center for artists and new arts organizations, an information clearinghouse, networking events, financial sponsorship, an arts calendar, and a bimonthly publication. The Pasadena Arts Council efforts are similar to those in communities across the United States.

Service and Fraternal Clubs

Another category of nonprofit organizations that provide recreation for their own membership and sponsor programs for other population groups is community service clubs and fraternal organizations.

These include service clubs such as the Kiwanis, Lions, or Rotary clubs, which represent the business and professional groups in the community and which have as their purpose the improvement of the business environment and contributing to social well-being. A number of organizations established specifically for women, such as the Association of Junior Leagues, the General Federation of Women's Clubs, and the Business and Professional Women's Club, have similar goals.

The goals of such groups may include publicizing environmental concerns or issues, promoting the arts and other cultural activities, helping disadvantaged children and youth, and providing programs for persons with disabilities. For example, many Kiwanis organizations are involved in providing camping programs for special populations.

Promotional and Coordinating Bodies

A final type of nonprofit organization in the recreation, parks, and leisure-service field consists of associations that serve to promote, publicize, or coordinate activities within a given recreational field. In bowling, for example, the American Bowling Congress is composed of thousands of individuals whose careers or livelihoods depend on bowling and who therefore seek to promote and guide the sport as aggressively as possible, including setting standards and regulations and sponsoring a range of major tournaments each year.

There are hundreds of such nonprofit organizations in the fields of travel, tourism, entertainment, and hospitality, covering the range from associations of theme park or waterpark management to associations of tour directors or cruise ship operators. As an example, the Outdoor Amusement Business Association works to upgrade standards and services throughout the carnival and outdoor show industry. Its membership consists chiefly of manufacturers and distributors of trailers, tents and tarps, games supplies, and similar materials, as well as operators of many different kinds of traveling shows, concessions, and carnivals. Similarly, the International Association of Amusement Parks and Attractions conducts market studies, publishes standards and guidelines, and sponsors huge conventions and trade shows for thousands of companies worldwide in the tourism, entertainment, and amusement field. The World Waterpark Association assists waterparks with trend analysis, customer satisfaction, business skills, training, publications related to the waterpark industry, and an annual trade show.

Within local communities, there are often several types of coordinating groups that serve to exchange information, conduct studies, identify priorities, develop planning reports, provide technical assistance, train leadership, and organize events related to recreation and leisure. In some cases, these include councils of social agencies, including religious, healthcare, youth-serving, and social work groups.

COMMERCIAL RECREATION

We now turn to the type of recreation sponsor that provides the largest variety of leisure opportunities in the United States today—commercial, profit-oriented businesses. Such organizations have proliferated in recent years, running the gamut from small "mom-and-pop" operations to franchised programs and services; large-scale networks of health and fitness clubs, theme parks, hotels, and casino businesses; manufacturers of games, toys, and hobby equipment; and various other entertainment ventures.

The Nature of Commercial Recreation

Commercial recreation focuses on the retail provision of recreation opportunities for individuals. The retail orientation suggests that recreation enterprise has a goal of generating a profit for its owners.

The profit motive distinguishes a recreation business from any other type of leisure-service sponsor. Although public or voluntary agencies may charge for their services and may seek to clear a profit on individual program elements—or at least to run them on a self-sustaining basis where possible—their overall purpose is to meet important community or social needs. However, the commercial recreation organization has as a primary thrust the need to show a profit on the overall operation. Without commercial businesses that provide a host of important and high-quality leisure experiences, our recreational opportunities would be sharply diminished.

Commercial recreation sponsors today have the following characteristics: (1) They must constantly seek to identify and capitalize on recreational interests that are on the rise to ensure a constant or growing level of participation; (2) they are flexible and independent in their programmatic decisions and are not subject to the policy strictures of a city or town council or an agency board of trustees; (3) they constantly seek to promote and create experiences by packaging a product that will appeal to the public, by systematic marketing research, and by creative advertising and public relations; and (4) to be successful, they depend on effective entrepreneurship—a creative and aggressive approach to management that is willing to take risks to make gains.

Some of the most significant, creative, and cutting-edge facilities are provided by commercial recreation. Amusement parks, waterparks, mega-theaters, speedways, and sports stadiums may be the first to come to mind, but commercial recreation is present in almost every community. It may be the local dance studio, the combative-arts studio, or a crafts store that offers classes. Enterprises large and small continue to flourish in most communities. Quilt stores regularly have a room full of sewing machines, long-arm quilting machines, and the like, and classes are full. Stop by the Arthur Murray Dance Studio (arthurmurray.com) and see more full classes. Slot car tracks exist in many communities, as well as hobby shops, scuba shops, skydiving enterprises, tour buses, family recreation centers—the list could go on for pages. These commercial enterprises, regardless of their size, stay in business because they meet a need for recreation participation. It is not uncommon for commercial recreation enterprises to partner with public and nonprofit agencies.

Amusement parks are a growth industry serving millions of people annually.
© Edwin Verin/Shutterstock.

Categories of Service

Commercial recreation services may be classified under several major headings, including the following:

♦   Admission to facilities, either for self-directed participation (as in the use of a rented tennis court, an ice skating rink, or a billiard parlor) or for participation with some degree of supervision, instruction, or scheduling (as in admission to a ski center with use of a ski tow).
♦   Organized instruction in individual leisure activities or areas of personal enrichment, such as classes in arts and crafts, music, dance, or other hobbies.
♦   Membership in a commercially operated club, such as a for-profit tennis, golf, or boat club.
♦   Provision of hospitality or social contacts, ranging from hotels and resorts to bars, casinos, singles clubs, or dating services, which may use computers, videotaping, telephone contacts, or other means to help clients meet each other. At the socially less acceptable end of this spectrum of services are escort services, massage parlors, and sexually oriented telephone conversation operations.

◆ Arranged tours or cruises, domestic or foreign, which may consist solely of travel arrangements or which may also include a full package of travel, housing accommodations, meals, special events, side trips, and guide services.

◆ Commercial manufacture, sale, and service of recreation-related equipment, including sport supplies, electronic products, boats, off-road vehicles, toys, games, and hobby equipment.

◆ Entertainment and special events, such as theater, rock concerts, circuses, rodeos, and other such activities, when they are sponsored by a for-profit business, rather than a nonprofit, tax-exempt group.

Several of these types of commercial recreation businesses are described in the concluding section of this chapter. Others, such as sport and games and travel and tourism, are presented elsewhere in the text.

Family Entertainment Centers

Another recently evolved for-profit recreation enterprise includes family entertainment centers that combine children's play activities and equipment, video games, and other computerized activities with refreshments.

These businesses developed as an outgrowth of such "kiddie exercise" programs as Gymboree, which expanded as franchised chains that were usually situated in shopping malls. Family fun centers such as Malibu Grand Prix broadened their appeal, by adding more family-slanted activities, such as miniature golf, bumper cars, video games, and other indoor games, and packaged them with fast food options such as pizza, hot dogs, and soft drinks for birthday party and other group visits.

Theme Parks, Waterparks, and Marine and Wildlife Parks

Closely linked to the growth of tourism as a form of recreation has been the expansion of theme parks such as California's famous Disneyland. This major entertainment complex was built at a cost of more than $50 million in the 1950s and covers 65 acres in Anaheim, California. Its success led to the construction of a second major Disney complex, Walt Disney World, at Lake Buena Vista, Florida, and ultimately 11 Parks worldwide by 2016.

Growing with the amusement park industry is the International Association of Amusement Parks and Attractions (IAAPA). Started in 1918, it now boasts more than 4500 members from 93 countries and is the largest organization in the world that supports amusement parks. Its membership is associated with some areas of the amusement park industry. They include family entertainment centers, large parks and theme parks, museums, waterparks, zoos and aquariums, resorts, hotels, and casinos, small parks and attractions, and manufacturers and suppliers. IAAPA has an international perspective, hosting three international trade shows: one each in Europe, Asia, and the Americas. Each is called an *Attractions Expo* with content focusing on the industry, management, safety, education, marketing, operations, and products.

The list of top 10 performing amusement parks worldwide, in 2015, helps demonstrate how large this marketplace is and the dominance of the Disney brand:

1. Magic Kingdom (Florida)—20,492,000
2. Disneyland (California)—18,278,000
3. Tokyo Disneyland (Japan)—16,600,000
4. Universal Studios (Japan)—13,900,000
5. Tokyo Disney Sea (Japan)—13,600,000
6. EPCOT (Florida)—11,798,000
7. Disney's Animal Kingdom (Florida)—10,922,000
8. Disney's Hollywood Studios (Florida)—10,828,000
9. Disney's Park (Paris)—10,360,000
10. Universal Studios (Florida)—9,585,000[29]

Expansion of Disney Entertainment Empire   None of the other chains of theme parks or outdoor play centers could match the diversity and inventiveness of the Disney planners. In 1982, Disney opened EPCOT (an acronym for Experimental Prototype Community of Tomorrow), an $800 million, 260-acre (105.2 hectares) development that was conceived as being more than a theme park. Instead, EPCOT was intended to be a place that would offer an environment where people of many nations might meet and exchange ideas. It consists of two sections: Future World, which contains corporate pavilions primarily concerned with technology; and World Showcase, which has international pavilions designed to show the tourist attractions of various nations around the world.

WHAT'S NEXT FOR THEME PARKS?

Today, visitors to theme parks is expect more than just a decade ago. What was good enough for their parents is rarely acceptable to the current generations. They are accustomed to the presence of technology and set high expectations for their experiences. As a result, theme parks are becoming more tech savvy and integrating experiences for the millennial generation. This period has been characterized as the golden age of technology. Visitors and potential visitors are looking for the next big thing! Virtual reality, frequently talked about, has made its appearance in theme parks. Disney created the first virtual reality experience in 1955, operating on what today would be called dinosaur technology. Virtual reality is available in many attractions as a part of the total experience. This is expected to continue to expand. Another example of the use of technology and LED digital technology is Disney's Rivers of Light, based on traditional Asian lantern festivals, focusing on the use of technology to present a visual experience for guests. The technology controls the lighting, creating stunning visual effects, and provides guidance for various part of the event such as boats and barges, and sound. All of the technological components provide the visitor with a unique and engaging experience as a spectator. Other parks are experimenting and implementing virtual experiences that allow the participant to control the level and intensity of the experience, as opposed to just being a spectator.

Since then, Disney World has added a number of other spectacular and imaginative attractions, including Typhoon Lagoon, the Disney MGM Studios, and in 2012, Cars Land based on the popular Cars movie. In 1983, a Disneyland opened in Japan on 202 acres (81.7 hectares) of landfill in Tokyo Bay. It featured the traditional Disney characters and popular rides and attractions. Although the attraction was owned by a Japanese corporation, Disney provided technology and guidance during the construction and operation of Tokyo Disneyland for a share of the gross ticket take. Then, with the opening of Disneyland Paris, otherwise known as Euro Disney, the company created the largest theme park in Europe.

Throughout the 1990s, Disney continued to add new attractions and program features. In 1997, Disney's 200-acre (80.9-hectare) Wide World of Sports offered a 7500-seat stadium and other facilities as a venue for the Atlanta Braves, the Harlem Globetrotters, and the Indiana Pacers as well as thousands of other competitors on every age level in several different sports. Through a cooperative arrangement with the Amateur Athletic Union, national youth tournaments in baseball, basketball, softball, and tennis, among others, are held at this facility.

Disney continued its expansion into the 21st century with acquisition of Pixar, Marvel Comics, and Lucasfilm, all major participants in the movie industry. More recently, Disney opened a new Star Wars attraction and continued to expand its leadership in the movie, video, and amusement park arenas.

New Kinds of Theme Parks   Other entertainment entrepreneurs soon followed the Disney example, and by 1976 at least three dozen parks of similar scale had been built around the United States. Some parks concentrate on a single theme, such as Opryland, U.S.A. in Nashville, Tennessee, and Holiday World and Splashing Safari in Indiana. Others incorporate moving rides through settings based on literary, historical, or international themes; entertainment; and typical amusement park "thrill" rides such as roller coasters and parachute jumps. In 2015 there were over 400 theme parks reporting in excess of 375 million annual visits and $11.1 billion in revenues.

Another unusual facility, opened in the early 1980s by Busch Gardens, was Adventure Island in Tampa, Florida. This 30-acre waterpark provides vistas of white sand beaches, glistening waters, palm trees, and tropical plants. Built on varied levels with complex waterfalls, slides, pools, cliffs, and rocks, Adventure Island provides an all-inclusive water experience in which visitors slide down twisting water chutes.

Other Parks   There are literally hundreds of theme parks in the United States today. Orlando, Florida, can be considered the theme park capital of the United States. Universal's Orlando Islands of Adventure is typical of many of today's large theme parks. The park has five distinctive themes, similar to what Disneyland introduced. The themes are linked to Universal Studios films, cartoons, or specific activities. For example, Toon Lagoon, a waterpark, has rides named for different cartoon characters, such as Dudley Do-Right's Rip Saw Falls.

Cedar Point, located in Sandusky, Ohio, is an example of a regional theme park that provides multiple experiences on a single site. Typical of a growth industry in theme parks is the roller coaster. Cedar Point boasts 17 different roller coaster rides, ranging from the Wicked Twister, a 215-foot-tall (65.5 meters), 72-mph (115.9-kph) steel stunner, to the Millennium Force, a 310-feet-tall (94.5 meters) roller coaster with a top speed of 93 mph (149 kph) that is targeted toward young riders.

However, not all theme parks rely on such forms of entertainment. Dollywood, for example, a complex of shops, rides, shows, craft centers, restaurants, and other theatrical features based on folk themes, is an outstanding tourist attraction in the Great Smoky Mountain National Park Region. Linked to the image of Dolly Parton, the popular movie actress and country music star, Dollywood offers gospel music performances, harvest celebrations, a "showcase" series of well-known performers, and other programs attuned to its traditional Appalachian Mountain environment.

Waterparks   A specialized type of theme park today consists of waterparks—tourist destinations that feature wave pools, slides, chutes, shows, and other forms of water-based play and entertainment. There are almost 1000 waterparks today that provide such outdoor play in the United States. The largest concentration of waterparks is located in the Midwest, with the south a close second. They are not restricted to warmer areas, however. The Wisconsin Dells, for example, is famous for the number of indoor and outdoor waterparks in the region. One of the largest waterparks is located inside the West Edmonton Mall in Canada. Public agencies are the largest source of waterparks.

Often, water attractions are part of larger theme park operations. In Universal's Islands of Adventure, for example, the Jurassic Park River Adventure and Popeye and Bluto's Bilge Rat Barges offer either whirling and steep whitewater rides and sluice falls or swirling vortexes that spray riders thoroughly. Each year, dozens of new waterparks open, with the latest technology, marketing, and management skills taught to their operators at conventions held by the American Waterpark Association.

Amusement parks are present in almost every major community; the parks provide locally available thrill experiences for participants.
© Sergey Ivanov/Shutterstock.

Zoos, Marine Parks, and Wildlife Parks   The addition of rides and other entertainment features to animal attractions is making marine and wild animal parks increasingly popular among tourists. Annually, members of the American Zoo and Aquarium Association in the United States receive approximately 175 million visitors. Wild animal parks have seen steady growth in recent years where visitors of all ages are offered the opportunity to view big game and exotic animals in natural (or semi-wild) settings.

Other Fun Centers

In heavily populated metropolitan areas throughout the United States, other entrepreneurs have developed a variety of indoor fun centers, ranging from children's play, gymnastics, and exercise chains to family party centers, video game arcades, and huge restaurants with game areas. Fun centers are not just for children but adults as well. Dave and Buster's, an immensely successful chain of adult "fun and food" offerings in Dallas, Houston, Atlanta, Chicago, Philadelphia, and expanding into 20 states, Canada, and Mexico, offers a host of simulated fun experiences: golf, motorcycling, race car driving, space combat, and virtual reality, among others.

Similarly, the children's and family play centers that have been established in thousands of suburban neighborhoods and shopping malls around the United States offer a combination of computer and video games, billiards and other table games, miniature golf, entertainment by clowns and magicians, music, and popular fast-food refreshments. Offering packaged birthday parties and other family play services, they illustrate commercial recreation's success in providing attractive play activities that have supplanted more traditional home-based and "do it yourself" kinds of recreation.

Outdoor Recreation

The broad field of outdoor recreation—defined as leisure pursuits that depend on the outdoor environment for their special appeal or character—represents an important area of commercially sponsored services. Although a major portion of outdoor recreation is carried on in government-managed settings, many activities are provided by for-profit enterprises.

In 2011 the U.S. Fish and Wildlife Service reported that 90 million Americans aged 16 and older fished, hunted, or participated in wildlife-associated activities, including 34 million anglers and 12.5 million hunters. There was an increase in wildlife watchers from 61.4 million in 2001 to 71.1 million in 2011. Participants in these outdoor sports spent $43.2 billion on equipment, $32.2 billion on trips, and $14.6 billion on licenses and fees, membership dues and contributions, land leasing and ownership, and plantings for hunting. On average, each sportsperson spent $2407 in 2011.[30]

Commercial recreation in the outdoors takes many forms, including hunting preserves and guide services; charter fishing and other private fishing operations; marinas and other boating services; ski centers and schools; campgrounds, adventure recreation, vacation ranches, and farms; paintball centers; and numerous other pursuits.

In many cases, a single company, such as Pocono Whitewater Adventures in Jim Thorpe, Pennsylvania, may offer several different types of adventure activities, such as river rafting, whitewater kayaking, family biking excursions, or paintball, at different seasons of the year. Numerous hunting businesses throughout the United States offer the opportunity to shoot big game and in some cases exotic species imported from other continents. Both inland and ocean fishing represent another huge industry. Boating alone represents a major segment of the outdoor recreation market, with annual retail sales and service in 2010 estimated at almost $30.4 billion. It was estimated that 65.9 million adults (32.4% of the adult population) went boating in 2010. The Great Lakes has the largest concentration of boaters in the nation, while Florida led the nation in registered boats, followed by California, Minnesota, Michigan, Wisconsin, Texas, New York, South Carolina, Ohio, and North Carolina.

Health Spas and Fitness Clubs

Commercial fitness centers and health clubs constitute a major source of leisure spending in the United States. Although those who join such facilities may have varying kinds of motivations, ranging from actual health concerns to a cosmetic concern with appearance, the reality is that health spas often offer an attractive social setting, particularly for single men and women.

This overall field includes a variety of program emphases, such as aquatic and fitness centers with varied pool facilities, exercise equipment rooms, aerobics and Jazzercise classes, yoga, conditioning counseling or remedial services, and similar options with annual fees that may range up to thousands of dollars.

As a variation of such health-connected services, many nonprofit hospitals or long-term care facilities have established for-profit subsidiary companies that offer a wide range of exercise programs, physical therapy, aerobic classes, and innovative techniques that include hypnosis, pain management, acupuncture, and other alternative forms of treatment serving the public at large. They may also focus on holistic and homeopathic treatment, including meditation groups, clubs dealing with specific forms of illness such as arthritis, "overeaters anonymous," "living with loss," and massage and reflexology methods.

Other For-Profit Ventures

Beyond the examples just cited, commercial recreation today includes a host of other kinds of social and hobby activities and amusement or entertainment ventures. Private golf or tennis clubs, bowling alleys and billiard parlors, contract bridge or chess clubs, night clubs and dance halls, and even dating services and gambling casinos are all part of this picture. In a sense, movies, television, video games, book publishing, and electronic devices are all aspects of popular culture that represent forms of commercialized leisure. A growing marketplace is quilting. Long thought to be the domain of grandmothers, quilting stores are present in many communities. They sell material, quilting-related items, and specialized quilting machines, and sponsor classes, tours, cruises, exhibitions, and competitions.

In addition, both amateur sport participation and professional spectator sport and travel and tourism involve huge elements in the commercial recreation field and are discussed in detail elsewhere in this text.

DIFFERENCES AND SIMILARITIES AMONG AGENCIES

This chapter describes the provision of organized recreation services today by three types of organizations: public or governmental, nonprofit or voluntary, and commercial recreation businesses. Each of these types of leisure-service organization simultaneously provides unique and similar services.

Public recreation and park agencies, for example, have a major responsibility for maintaining and operating outdoor resources such as parks, forests, playgrounds, sport and aquatic facilities, and, in many cases, indoor centers, performing arts centers, conference or convention venues, stadiums, and similar facilities. Their obligation is to serve the public at large, including individuals and families at all socioeconomic levels and without regard to

Amateur sporting events in major urban centers are frequently integrated into existing parks where activities share spaces.

© Wendy Nero/Shutterstock.

ethnic, religious, or other demographic differences. However, given the intensified use of marketing-based fees and charges for many recreation programs, many government recreation and park agencies today are not reaching community groups with limited economic capability.

Nonprofit voluntary agencies are generally most concerned with social values and with achieving constructive outcomes either for the community or for specific population groups. They see recreation both as an end in itself and as a means to an end, are generally respectful of the social environment, and are sensitive to gender-, ethnicity-, and race-related issues. Particularly in terms of serving young people and special recreation interests, they are able to offer richer programs than many public agencies. Nonprofits fill voids that public and commercial agencies cannot or will not fill.

Of the three types of sponsors, commercial recreation sponsors provide the greatest range of recreational services and opportunities today, and they represent a steadily growing sphere of organized leisure programming. In some ways, profit-oriented businesses are similar to public and nonprofit recreation and park agencies in terms of their offerings and the leisure needs they satisfy. What distinguishes them is their ability to commit substantial sums to developing facilities and programs that will attract the public. Huge corporations that are able to design and build theme parks, aquatic complexes, stadiums, health and fitness clubs, and other types of specialized equipment or programs obviously have a tremendous advantage in appealing to those who are able to pay the necessary fees and charges. Commercial recreation sponsors have harnessed technology and industry in creating spectacular environments for play and have used the most subtle and sophisticated public relations and advertising techniques to market their products successfully.

Social Values in Recreation Planning

It would be wrong to assume that commercial recreation businesses are entirely free to provide any sort of leisure activity without considering its social impact.

Health clubs, camps, amusement parks, theaters, dance halls, gambling casinos, taverns, and a host of other facilities are subject to regulation under state, county, and municipal laws. These may include provisions regarding the sale of liquor, sanitary conditions, service to minors, safety practices, hours of operation, and similar restrictions. Many enterprises that require licenses may have these withdrawn if the operators do not conform to approved practices. Similarly, trade associations often influence practices, even though they may not have the legal power to enforce their rulings. Public attitudes—as expressed in the press, through the statements of leading citizens, civic officials, or religious organizations, or through consumer pressure—often are able to influence the operators in desired directions. For example, when Time Warner was sharply criticized in the press for its promotion of violent, racist, and sexist rap music products, it divested itself of the involved recording label.

The competition of other organizations and products is another key factor in the management of commercial recreation agencies. Often, better products and services within a branch of the industry will serve to drive out inferior competitors. The entire field of recreation service and participation may be viewed as a marketing system in which the economic forces of supply and demand work so that as a new product or service appears, existing products and services are threatened. Within this framework, there is a constant pruning and reshuffling of recreation enterprises as competing sponsors seek to maintain public interest and attendance.

PARTNERSHIPS AMONG MAJOR LEISURE-SERVICE AGENCIES

Although public, nonprofit, and commercial leisure-service agencies are dealt with separately in this chapter, it is important to emphasize that in actual practice they often join together in cooperative ventures. For example, a survey of more than 100 cities found that almost all municipal recreation and parks departments conducted programs with other agencies and organizations; more than half of the respondents had 10 or more synergetic programs during the year. They worked closely with voluntary agencies, schools and colleges, service clubs, and business and industry to promote sport, cultural, and other types of events and projects.

Partnering among public, nonprofit, and commercial recreation providers is commonplace. Where these agencies once jealously guarded their own areas, they have embraced the concept that partnering better serves the public and individual agencies. Public and nonprofit agencies are frequently judged on their effectiveness by the number and quality of the partnerships they establish.

Many forms of partnerships are created by park and recreation agencies working with nonprofits, commercial organizations, other government agencies, private individuals, special interest groups, and others. They can be as simple as the city parks and recreation department providing space for a model airplane club to construct

Sponsorship of recreation programs is increasing, as sponsors frequently have their organizations depicted at events.

© Joyce Vincent/Shutterstock.

a runway or as complex as multiple agencies working together to manage a unique natural resource. There is a long history of the National Park Service working with state park agencies and local parks and recreation departments. The Bureau of Land Management has transferred land to public agencies, such as the Grand Junction, Colorado, Parks and Recreation Department, to help maintain a buffer between urban development and natural areas. Special recreation associations, initially unique to Illinois, are the creation of multiple park districts joining together to develop a professional organization with the primary purpose of providing services to persons with disabilities. The special recreation associations operate as a separate service, yet integrate their services into existing park district programs using the resources of the association that exceed those of any individual park district.

There are numerous examples of partnerships in the areas of open space acquisition and environmental recovery. The Trust for Public Land (TPL) annually takes on numerous projects working with local public agencies, nonprofit, and neighborhood groups. TPL partnered with Cascade Bicycle Club in Puget Sound, Washington to start the remake of a defunct rail corridor which was 42 miles in length, completing it one section at a time. For example, Lakeview Elementary School allows students to ride their bicycles to school away from traffic corridor. Over 350,000 residents live within easy reach of the East Side Rail Corridor.[31] Two-thirds of the way across the country in Cleveland, Ohio, TPL is working with the Cuyahoga Metropolitan Housing Authority to bring together segments of urban trails into a greenway network that will ultimately bring users and residents to Cleveland's waterfront parks.[32] **Table 6.5** depicts TPL's impacts over a two year period.

Similarly, nonprofit organizations are frequently involved in collaborative program efforts. Typically, Boy and Girl Scout troops often work closely with churches and religious organizations or with school boards. The YMCA encourages numerous partnership arrangements with local parks and recreation departments, schools and colleges, public housing boards, hospitals, and even correctional institutions. In the mid-2000s the YMCA initiated in more than 160 communities collaborative projects working jointly with the Centers for Disease Control and Prevention and 20 other national organizations, nonprofits, and local community organizations, including parks and recreation departments, to expand community ability and to identify or create programs that establish positive health-related behavior change. The Healthier Communities Initiative has focused efforts on making healthy living available to community residents.

Different types of collaborations are beginning to emerge as agencies begin serving an older American population. Lewisburg, Pennsylvania, created the first multigenerational park as a destination designed to bring together different age groups to enjoy experiences while in close proximity. The emphasis was on the environment, families, and activity, recognizing that such an approach met the needs of many different age groups. Many communities are now recognizing that older Americans use parks more frequently than other age groups do and are beginning to cooperate within their communities to modify parks to fit the needs of older adults. The University of Illinois is working with a variety of groups, including parks and recreation agencies, to develop New Active Green Environments facilities that strive to improve the cardiovascular health, muscle strength, and flexibility of older Americans, understanding that the new older generation is different from all previous aging generations.[34]

TABLE 6.5 Trust for Public Land Impacts—Two Year Period[33]					
Year	Acres Protected	Ballots Help Pass	Projects Completed	Fitness Zones	Members, Friends, Volunteers
2015	92,978	19	140	70	192,744
2016	62,134	12	128	78	453,966

Data from The Trust for Public Land. 2015 and 2016 Annual Report. www.tpl.org. Accessed February 2, 2017.

Finally, the National Recreation and Park Association has successfully initiated a number of partnerships. These include joint ventures with NFL PLAY60 After-School Kickoff program; the United States Tennis Association; Soccer5 in the development of parks allowing more children to play soccer in a smaller space; and the National Basketball Association's "Jr. NBA" program for boys and girls 6–14, focusing on skills, sportsmanship, and values of the game. Collaborative arrangements of this type are growing in number and variety and are helping to build a climate of mutual assistance among the different elements that constitute the leisure-service system.

Revisiting the Major Elements in the Leisure-Service Delivery System

Early in this chapter, Tables 6.1 and 6.2 depicted how agencies, partnerships, programs, participants, and outcomes interact to create recreation and leisure opportunities. This chapter has demonstrated the diversity of recreation opportunities and the value of partnering to achieve greater opportunities for individuals to experience leisure. **Table 6.6** provides a more complex example of the interaction of these elements. The community orchestra is performing at the city's major outdoor park performance center. The city is cosponsoring the event with the orchestra. A local bank has agreed to pay for the labor to set up the sound, lights, and security for the performance. The city and orchestra have contracted with a local caterer who will provide food for purchase at the event. The parks and recreation department is advertising the event on its website and in its seasonal brochure and the local public television station is assisting the orchestra by webcasting the concert.

The view depicted in Table 6.6 is from that of the city parks and recreation department. The initiation organization was a community orchestra and the venue is managed by the parks and recreation department. These two organizations have a long-standing relationship. The bank is a sponsor of the community orchestra. The food caterer is approved by the parks and recreation department and contracted with by the community orchestra. The community orchestra has a partnership with the food vendor and receives a share of the profit of sales during the event. The webcasting of the performance is handled through the community orchestra, the parks and recreation department, and the local public television station, which determines what special needs the webcast may require.

By diagramming the program process in Table 6.6, it becomes easier to see the relationships and dependencies that are present. Seeing the type of agencies involved (A), the types of partnerships in place (B), the types of services provided (C), the reasons the programs or services are offered (D), and the influencers allows the agency to predict benefits (E).

Summary

Government's role with respect to organized leisure services is diversified. On the federal level, government is concerned with the management of outdoor recreation resources, either as a primary function or within a multiple-use concept, through such agencies as the National Park Service, U.S. Forest Service, Bureau of Land Management, and the Tennessee Valley Authority. The federal government also assists states and local political units through funding and technical assistance for programs serving children and youth, those with disabilities, older adults, and similar groups.

State governments operate major park systems and play an important role in promoting environmental conservation and outdoor recreation opportunities. They also set standards and pass enabling legislation defining the role of local governments in the area of recreation and parks. In addition, states have traditionally maintained networks of state hospitals and special schools for those with disabilities, although this function has been reduced in recent years as a result of deinstitutionalization trends that involve placing many such individuals in community settings.

The chief sponsors of government recreation and park programs are on the local level—city, town, county, and special district government agencies. They operate many different types of facilities and offer a wide range of classes, sport leagues, special events, the arts, social activities, and other leisure areas. They also provide or assist in many programs in the human services area. Although many municipal departments have expanded their revenue source operations, departments in other larger and older cities suffer from depleted staff resources and have limited program and maintenance potential.

Voluntary agencies place their greatest emphasis on using leisure to achieve positive social goals. Several types of youth-serving organizations are described, including both sectarian and nonsectarian groups. Such agencies rarely consider themselves to be primarily recreation organizations; instead, they generally prefer to be regarded as educational, character-building, or youth-serving organizations. However, recreation usually does constitute a sector of their program activities.

TABLE 6.6   Complex Version

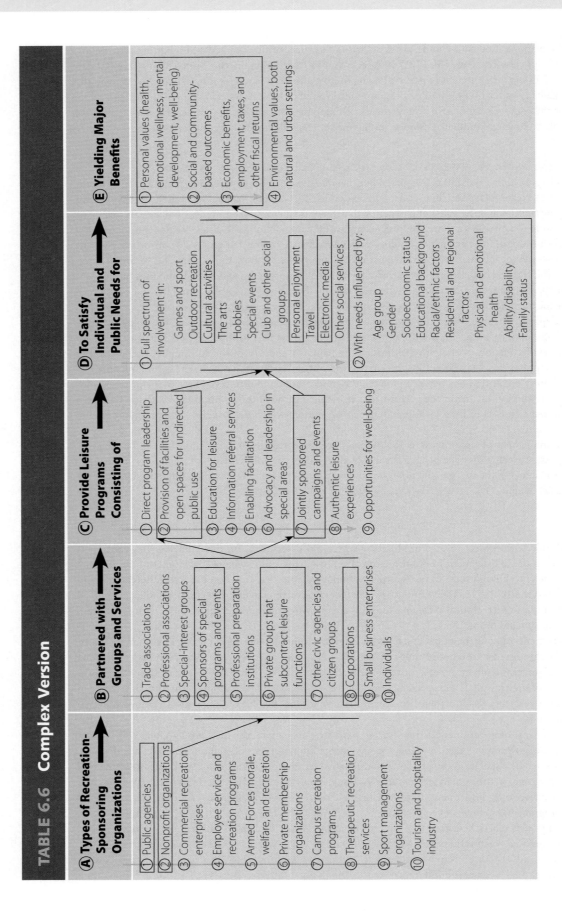

(A) Types of Recreation-Sponsoring Organizations	(B) Partnered with Groups and Services	(C) Provide Leisure Programs Consisting of	(D) To Satisfy Individual and Public Needs for	(E) Yielding Major Benefits
① Public agencies ② Nonprofit organizations ③ Commercial recreation enterprises ④ Employee service and recreation programs ⑤ Armed Forces morale, welfare, and recreation ⑥ Private membership organizations ⑦ Campus recreation programs ⑧ Therapeutic recreation services ⑨ Sport management organizations ⑩ Tourism and hospitality industry	① Trade associations ② Professional associations ③ Special-interest groups ④ Sponsors of special programs and events ⑤ Professional preparation institutions ⑥ Private groups that subcontract leisure functions ⑦ Other civic agencies and citizen groups ⑧ Corporations ⑨ Small business enterprises ⑩ Individuals	① Direct program leadership ② Provision of facilities and open spaces for undirected public use ③ Education for leisure ④ Information referral services ⑤ Enabling facilitation ⑥ Advocacy and leadership in special areas ⑦ Jointly sponsored campaigns and events ⑧ Authentic leisure experiences ⑨ Opportunities for well-being	① Full spectrum of involvement in: Games and sport Outdoor recreation Cultural activities The arts Hobbies Special events Club and other social groups Personal enjoyment Travel Electronic media Other social services ② With needs influenced by: Age group Gender Socioeconomic status Educational background Racial/ethnic factors Residential and regional factors Physical and emotional health Ability/disability Family status	① Personal values (health, emotional wellness, mental development, well-being) ② Social and community-based outcomes ③ Economic benefits, employment, taxes, and other fiscal returns ④ Environmental values, both natural and urban settings

A second type of nonprofit leisure-service agency consists of special interest groups, which usually promote a particular area of activity in outdoor recreation, sport, the arts, or hobbies. Such groups, although they may include many enthusiasts as members, are often formed to promote business interests within the particular leisure specialization.

Commercial recreation businesses offer an immense number of public recreation opportunities in such areas as travel and tourism, outdoor recreation, sport, popular entertainment, the mass media, hobbies, and crafts. Their primary goal is to make a consistent profit through the creation of experiences. In many cases, they are large and highly diversified operations, such as the Walt Disney organization, with its theme parks, resorts, and television, movies, Internet, and popular music components. From a social perspective, many for-profit businesses offer constructive, high-quality programs. However, in some cases—as in sectors of the entertainment industry—they are believed to contribute to youth violence, sexism, and racial hostility.

Questions for Class Discussion or Essay Examination

1. Identify the key recreation providers from the federal government as well as their core mission or purposes. Compare all the federal agencies and identify their commonalities and differences. Discuss with your classmates how these agencies collectively and individually influence the recreation landscape of the United States.

_____

_____

_____

_____

_____

_____

_____

_____

2. There appear to be different perspectives from providers of recreation opportunities from the federal level to the community level. Identify what you see as the major role at each level (federal, state, county, municipality). Second, identify what you see as common roles that cross three or more levels. Explain how you would justify to your community duplication of the roles of another agency (such as the National Park Service or your state park system).

_____

_____

_____

_____

_____

_____

_____

3. Select a park and recreation agency from your hometown or a larger community close to your hometown and look at their website. Identify the types of services and programs that they offer. Is this a small town, medium-sized town, or large city? Or is it a county system? Identify the core services provided and assess the quality and quantity of their level of service. Explain why you assessed their services in the way you did.

_____

_____

_____

_____

_____

_____

_____

4. Explain the importance of nonprofits in the leisure service industry. What do nonprofits bring to the leisure-service delivery system that make them unique and effective?

_____

_____

_____

_____

_____

_____

_____

_____

5. Select a commercial recreation enterprise in your community. Identify what its core business is and how it delivers that business. Describe how its delivery model is different from a public and a nonprofit organization.

_____

_____

_____

_____

_____

_____

_____

_____

Endnotes

1. President George W. Bush, excerpt from National Park Week Proclamation, 2003.

2. C. Bulson. 2012. PROQUEST Statistical Abstract of the United States 2013. Ann Arbor, MI: ProQuest. (Table 1270).

3. Mitchell, Brent A, "Projecting America's Best Ideals: International Engagements and the National Park Service," *George Wright Society*: www.georgewright.org/281mitchell.pdf. (Accessed October 26, 2013).

4. United States Forest Service (USFS), "Forest Service Global Change Research Strategy, 2009–2019" (2009): FS-917a.

5. USDA, "Conservation Reserve Program": https://www.fsa.usda.gov/programs-and-services /conservation-programs/index(https://www.fsa.usda.gov/programs-and-services/conservation-programs /index (Accessed May 29, 2017).

6. U.S. Department of the Interior. Bureau of Land Management. National Conservation Lands: Resources and Statistics: https://www.blm.gov/about/data/public-land-statistics (Accessed May 29, 2017).

7. U.S. Department of Agriculture, Farm Service Agency, "Conservation Programs": http://www.fsa.usda .gov/FSA/webapp?area=home&subject=copr&topic=landing.

8. National Endowment for the Arts, "2015 Annual Report" (April 15, 2016): https://www.arts.gov /sites/default/files/2015%20Annual%20Report.pdf, p. 3.

9. National Endowment for the Arts, 2013: "2012 Annual Report" (Washington, D.C.): https://docs .google.com/viewer?url=http%3A%2F%2Farts.gov%2Fsites%2Fdefault%2Ffiles% 2F2012-NEA -Annual-Report.pdf (Accessed May 30, 2013).

10. National Endowment for the Arts, "2015 Annual Report" (April 15, 2016): https://www.arts.gov /sites/default/files/2015%20Annual%20Report.pdf, p. 3.

11. Daniel D. McLean, *The 2006 Annual Information Exchange* (Raleigh, NC: National Association of State Park Directors, 2006).

12. Illinois Association of Park Districts, "2016 Annual Report": http://c.ymcdn.com/sites/www .ilparks.org/resource/resmgr/annual_reports/iapd_2016_final_for_web.pdf (Accessed February 10, 2017).

13. Pennsylvania Department of Conservation and Natural Resources, "A Guide to Using Section 503(11) of the Pennsylvania Municipalities Planning Code" (December 15, 2008): http://www.dcnr.state.pa.us /cs/groups/public/documents/document/dcnr_002299.pdf (Accessed February 18, 2017).

14. King County, Washington Natural Resources and Parks: www.kingcounty.gov/environment/dnrp.aspx (Accessed November 18, 2012).

15. CityofHenderson.com: http://www.cityofhenderson.com/henderson-happenings/home (Accessed February 8, 2017).

16. Denver: The Mile High City, "Central Denver Recreation Center Frequently Asked Questions" (June 3, 2014): https://www.denvergov.org/content/dam/denvergov/Portals/747/documents /planning/CentralDenverRecreationCenter/CDRC_FAQ.pdf (Accessed February 8, 2017).

17. White Pine County Nevada "White Pine County Aquatic Center": http://www.whitepinecounty.net /index.aspx?nid=471 (Accessed February 8, 2017).

18. Seattle.gov Office of the Mayor, "Mayor Unveils $47 million Seattle Park District Plan for 2016" (September 18, 2015): http://murray.seattle.gov/mayor-unveils-47-million-seattle-park-district-plan -for-2016/#sthash.bPbvLLaO.dpbs.

19. Seattle.gov Seattle Park District, "Programs for People": http://www.seattle.gov/seattle-park-district /projects/programs-for-people (Accessed June 12, 2016).

20. Bureau of Labor Statistics, "Volunteering in the United States—2012" (February 22, 2013): www.bls .gov/news.release/volun.nr0.htm.

21. LM Salamon, SW Sokolowski & SL Geller. 2012. Holding the Fort: Nonprofit employment during a decade of turmoil. *Nonprofit Employment Bulletin* 39, Johns Hopkins University: http://ccss.jhu.edu /publications-findings/?did=369 (Accessed December 28, 2013).

22. Boy Scouts of America, 2012 report to the Nation: http://www.scouting.org/About/AnnualReports /PreviousYears/2012/rtn.aspx (Accessed December 28, 2013).

23. Girl Scouts of America: http://www.girlscouts.org/who_we_are/facts/ (Accessed October 22, 2013).

24. Boys & Girls Clubs of America, "Our Facts and Figures": http://www.bgca.org/whoweare/Pages /FactsFigures.aspx.

25. Best Buddies: http://www.bestbuddies.org/best-buddies.

26. Best Buddies: "Our Impact": https://bestbuddies.org/our-impact/.

27. Young Men's Christian Association: http://www.ymca.net/organizational-profile (Accessed 10/22/13).

28. Little League Baseball: http://www.littleleague.org/Little_League_Online.htm (Accessed October 29, 2013).

29. MiceChat.com, 2011 "Theme Park Attendance Report": http//www.coastergrotto.com/theme-park-attendance.jsp (accessed 05/29/17).

30. U.S. Department of the Interior, U.S. Fish & Wildlife Service, 2012: 2011 "National Survey of Fishing, Hunting, and Wildlife-Associated Recreation: National Overview": 2011 "Theme Park Attendance Report":http://wsfrprograms.fws.gov/Subpages/NationalSurvey/National_Survey.htm (Accessed October 18, 2012).

31. The Trust for Public Land, "In the Seattle metro, a new bike path gets kids to school the old-fashioned way," (January 19, 2017): http://www.tpl.org/blog/eastside-rail-corridor#sm.01lwp1261b52dtu110i23341oygox (Accessed February 2, 2017).

32. The Trust for Public Land, "A Cleveland's neighborhood long-awaited link to the lakefront" (November 9, 2016): http://www.tpl.org/blog/cleveland-greenways-link-lakefront#sm.01lwp1261b52dtu110i23341oygox (Accessed February 12, 2017).

33. The Trust for Public Land, "2016 Annual Report": https://www.tpl.org/2016-annual-report#sm.01lwp1261b52dtu110i23341oygox (Accessed February 12, 2017).

34. Geoffrey Godbey, "Providing More for Older Adults," *Parks and Recreation* (October 2005): 76–81.

Specialized Leisure-Service Areas

Opportunities in recreation and leisure services are varied and numerous. The federal government provides career opportunities in national parks, forests, and other recreation areas. The military hires professionals to lead recreation activities for all of its personnel and families at bases around the world. All 50 states have parks, forests, and open space systems. Local community recreation and park departments hire recreation professionals with a variety of expertise including sports, aquatics, and the arts. Many nonprofit organizations such as the Ys, Scouts, and Boys and Girls Clubs offer leadership opportunities in recreation programs. There are a variety of private and semi-private clubs that hire managers to operate golf, tennis, or aquatic facilities.[1]

Learning Objectives

1. Demonstrate a basic understanding of the fields of therapeutic recreation, armed forces recreation, employee services recreation, campus recreation, and private-membership recreation clubs.

2. Explain the types of clientele that specialized leisure-service providers serve.

3. Name examples of organizations that provide specialized leisure services.

INTRODUCTION

Having examined three areas of organized leisure services that are designed for the public at large, we now turn to five categories of recreation services that meet more specialized needs and interests. These five areas are recreation for people with disabilities; armed forces morale, welfare, and recreation services; employee recreation services; campus recreation; and private-membership organizations. Each of these areas serves a specific type of population or organization, with goals and program elements geared to meet its specific needs.

Throughout the analysis of these five leisure-service areas, emphasis is placed on the dynamic changes that have occurred from the traditional models that evolved in the twentieth century to more innovative forms of service found today.

THERAPEUTIC RECREATION SERVICE

The roots of today's use of recreation to improve health conditions in treatment settings can be traced back to Benjamin Rush, an American physician, and Florence Nightingale, a British nurse. Both of these figures were advocates of the therapeutic value of recreation. Over the past 50 years, the expanded use of recreation and leisure in hospitals, physical rehabilitation, mental health, and long-term care settings has demonstrated its increased value as a treatment approach and the importance of having a recreation therapist on the treatment team. During this same period, there was tremendous growth in the provision of specialized or adapted recreation services in the community for people with disabilities.

This role in the recreation profession has a variety of names, including recreation therapist, therapeutic recreation specialist, inclusion specialist, and activity therapist, to name a few. The American Therapeutic Recreation Association (ATRA) defines recreation therapy as "a treatment service designed to restore, remediate and rehabilitate a person's level of functioning and independence in life activities, to promote health and wellness as well as reduce or eliminate the activity limitations and restrictions to participation in life situations caused by an illness or disabling condition."[2] Therapeutic recreation has been defined as "engaging people in planned recreation and related experiences in order to improve functioning, health and well-being, and quality of life, while focusing on the whole person and the needed changes in the optimal living environment."[3] These two definitions seem very similar and have sparked much discussion in the profession. One view is that *therapeutic recreation* can serve as the umbrella term where utilization and enhancement of leisure is the primary purpose, and recreation therapy has the primary purpose of intervention and improving functional abilities. For the purposes of this text, the term *therapeutic recreation* is used.

Early Development of Therapeutic Recreation

The history of past centuries provides a number of examples of the use of recreation in the treatment of psychiatric patients, in both Europe and America. The greatest impetus for therapeutic recreation, however, came in the twentieth century in three types of institutions: hospitals and rehabilitation centers for those with physical impairments, hospitals for people with mental illness, and special schools for those with developmental disabilities.

After both World War I and World War II, there were waves of concern about the need to rehabilitate veterans who had sustained major physical injuries or psychological trauma while in service. As a consequence, the Veterans Administration and military hospitals developed comprehensive programs of rehabilitative services, including physical and occupational therapy, psychotherapy, social services, vocational training, guidance, and recreation. In such settings, recreation was perceived as being one of several techniques that contributed to patient recovery.

At the same time, recreation gained recognition as a form of allied or adjunctive service within such civilian institutions as special homes or schools for individuals with cognitive or other disabilities, nursing homes and long-term care institutions, and state or private psychiatric hospitals or mental health centers. Gradually, *therapeutic recreation,* as it came to be known, gained acceptance in the healthcare field. Colleges and universities initiated major curricula or degree options in this field, and professional societies developed standards for practice and accreditation and certification procedures for practitioners.

Although all individuals need diverse recreation outlets, those with disabilities encounter barriers that those without disabilities do not, substantially narrowing their options for participation. In part this is because of significant and sometimes multiple disabling conditions that restrict physical, cognitive, and/or emotional functioning. Many times, however, the problems with access to recreation opportunities can be attributed to attitudinal, architectural, programmatic, and transportation barriers.

Smith et al.[4] explored the question of why persons with disabilities have been underserved by community recreation and leisure services. They suggest that in the first half of the twentieth century the way society generally treated people during this period who did not fit the norm was to separate and hide them away, and this produced a similar philosophy within the evolving field of recreation. Examples include the "old folks homes" for older people who were indigent, warehousing people with cognitive disabilities in large institutions away from populated areas, and placing people with mental health problems in similarly remote "insane asylums." While attitudes toward vulnerable populations were shifting during the 1960s, 1970s, and early 1980s, there were other barriers for public parks and recreation departments to contend with, both real and perceived. These included lack of funding, inaccessible facilities, untrained staff, lack of knowledge to develop such programs, lack of accessible community transportation, continuing attitudinal barriers, and lack of awareness of the great need for recreation participation by people with disabilities.

In some cases, recreation and park departments barred people with disabilities from their programs, arguing that serving such people would impose a higher risk of accident lawsuits and increased insurance costs. We now know this is not true. In other cases, parents, relatives, and schools have sheltered people with disabilities excessively, or the individual's perceived lack of ability or fear of rejection by others has caused him or her to limit recreation participation.

Therapeutic Recreation Job Settings

Therapeutic recreation (TR) professionals can find themselves working in the government sector, commercial sector, and nonprofit sector. TR specialists can predominantly work in one of two areas of practice—clinical settings or community settings.

TR specialists in a clinical setting often work in nursing homes and hospitals. Nursing home TR staff plan programs to help residents with their long-term, day-to-day function. There may be programs to enhance memory skills, social skills, and fitness levels. In hospital settings, TR specialists work with patients in four main areas: acute care, outpatient care, psychiatric care, and rehabilitation hospitals.[5] Acute care hospitals are for people with more serious illnesses and injuries on a short-term basis. TR specialists work with patients to prepare them for discharge or their next facility, such as a nursing home or rehabilitation center. Once discharged, a patient may move to outpatient care where they receive TR services while living at home. Psychiatric care is available for people with mental illnesses. Psychiatric care can be in a standalone facility or part of a general hospital and can be short or long term. Last, rehabilitation centers serve people with disabilities that have resulted from an illness such as a stroke or an accident. The TR specialist helps patients adjust to their disability and learn to use leisure to meet their needs. All of these clinical settings often have a treatment team that might include occupational therapists, physical therapists, social workers, physicians, and recreation therapists working together to help patients improve their health.

Not all people with disabilities need to experience leisure in a clinical setting. A far greater number of people with disabilities live in the community than live in hospital settings, and they have equally strong needs for recreation. Municipal parks and recreation agencies were given the charge to provide these much-needed services. Public parks and recreation agencies hire TR specialists to oversee programs specifically for people with disabilities or for inclusion purposes. People specializing in inclusion manage their own programs as well as assist staff in making programs and events accessible to people with disabilities. An inclusion specialist may help a program leader adapt a program so that someone who is deaf or who has a physical disability can participate with individuals who do not have a disability. The inclusion specialist most likely has extensive knowledge of the Americans with Disabilities Act,[6] which requires parks and recreation agencies to provide accessible services and access to all users. Community TR does not deliberately gear programs to achieve specific treatment or rehabilitative goals within a clinical framework, but those providing special or inclusive recreation do have important purposes. They value recreation as an important life experience for people with disabilities, and seek to achieve positive physical, social, and emotional outcomes, making adaptations in programming, facilities, equipment, or leadership methods as appropriate.

Therapeutic Recreation Models and Process

Two very distinct aspects of TR are the conceptual models and the TR process that drives practice. The TR profession uses conceptual models as a framework for delivery of service and to represent or guide practice. They help practitioners understand the comprehensive view of the profession and direct them in helping clients through intervention.[7] Although there are several different models used, two are discussed here so that the general perspectives held within TR are demonstrated. Those two models include the Leisure Ability Model and Health Protection–Health Promotion Model.

SPECIAL RECREATION ASSOCIATIONS

In Illinois, community parks and recreation agencies form special recreation associations (SRAs) to provide recreation services for people with disabilities. Rather than each Model and Health Protection–Health Promotion agency having its own staff trained in TR, they pool resources to provide a higher level of service for the communities involved. For example, the Fox Valley Special Recreation Association[8] is an extension of the Batavia, Fox Valley, Geneva, Oswego-land, St. Charles, Sugar Grove Park Districts, and South Elgin Parks and Recreation Department.

The Leisure Ability Model is based on the idea that everyone should experience leisure regardless of their abilities and disabilities. TR is a means to facilitate a quality leisure lifestyle, enhance quality of life, and improve health and happiness. The Leisure Ability Model has three components:[9]

Functional interventions: This therapy or rehabilitation component helps individuals improve related functional abilities needed for leisure participation. TR specialists help individuals participate by eliminating, improving, or adapting functional deficits that constrain leisure.

Leisure education: The purpose of leisure education is to help individuals learn leisure-related skills, attitudes, and knowledge.[10] TR specialists teach individuals new leisure-related skills to develop a healthy leisure lifestyle.

Recreation participation: The purpose of recreation participation is for structured leisure opportunities. The TR specialist provides the opportunity and acts as a facilitator or leader. This component of the Leisure Ability Model focuses on activity participation.

The Health Protection–Health Promotion Model of TR focuses on two areas: (1) treating and rehabilitating a client after an illness or disability; and (2) maintaining and enhancing good health. These two areas are considered a continuum because a client moves from less than ideal health to optimal health. TR specialists "contribute to health by helping persons fulfill their needs for stability and actualization until they are ready and able to assume responsibility for themselves."[11] Key to the Health Protection–Health Promotion Model are three elements:

Prescriptive activity: Prescriptive activity involves the TR specialist selecting activities that are specifically designed to achieve goals to enhance health. Prescriptive activity begins to move a client toward health and helps stabilize the client.

Recreation: Once stabilization occurs, the client moves into the recreation component of the model. The TR specialist provides an educational component by building skills and knowledge and helping clients value leisure so that they take more control over their lives. It is believed that the recreation experience is also for health protection.

Leisure: The leisure component focuses on health promotion rather than health protection as the other two components do. Individuals take control of their leisure lives and become self-determined and realize their full potential.[12]

In addition to working with a specialized clientele using a treatment model, TR is unique in the recreation field in that it follows a clinical process, called the TR process, to help clients. The TR process has four parts: assessment, planning, implementation, and evaluation. In the profession, this is known as APIE (pronounced *a-pie*).

The assessment piece of the TR process is information gathering. It is necessary to understand where the client currently is in functioning, strengths, and needs. Documents are gathered from physicians, other therapists, others involved in the care of the client, and from the client and/or the family. TR specialists also use TR-specific assessment tools designed to measure any number of factors needed to enhance care and reach a desired outcome. Once the initial assessment is complete, an individual program plan is developed outlining client goals, programs, and the overall treatment plan. Implementation of the individual program plan is facilitated by the TR specialist with the collaboration of the client. The TR specialist's level of involvement varies depending on the needs of the client. Last, evaluation is the systematic process where the TR specialist gathers information to assess whether the treatment plan and outcomes are appropriate. This information is used to modify the plan if needed.[13] This aspect of the TR process requires the evaluation of the client to assess the progress he or she is making on goals and outcomes. An evaluation is also done on the programs selected to ascertain their effectiveness for the individual.[14] This process is the crux of TR and requires the TR specialist and the participant to work together to establish what is in the best interest of the participant and how to achieve the goals created.

Certification

The practice of TR as a treatment discipline has become increasingly sophisticated. The body of research knowledge has expanded, protocols for treatment approaches have been developed, university curriculums have become broader in scope, and more populations are being served. There is also greater recognition of the discipline within healthcare systems and what it has to offer. Facilitating this is the reinforcement of standards by healthcare-accrediting bodies, such as the Commission of Accreditation of Rehabilitation Facilities and the Commission on Accreditation of Rehabilitation Facilities. These two major accrediting organizations have specific criteria for providing qualified therapeutic recreation services, which includes a requirement that said services be provided only by a certified therapeutic recreation specialist (CTRS).

TR TREATMENT MODALITIES

A treatment modality is the activity used to bring about a change or to reach a client's goals. TR specialists use a plethora of activities and approaches to help clients. The most common modalities used in TR include: (1) games, (2) exercise, (3) parties, (4) arts and crafts, (5) community integration activities, (6) music, (7) problem-solving activities, (8) sports, (9) self-esteem, and (10) activities of daily living. Some of these modalities are used more often with certain populations. For example, community integration, games, and exercise are often used for physical rehabilitation. Games, problem solving, and arts and crafts are more commonly used for people with mental health issues.[15]

In 1981, the National Council for Therapeutic Recreation Certification (NCTRC) was established as an autonomous credentialing body to oversee the development and administration of the CTRS professional certification. A research-based therapeutic recreation job analysis was performed and used to develop the certification exam, which was administered for the first time in November 1990. This exam and the requirements set by NCTRC to sit for the exam are the primary certification standards for both clinical and recreation applications of therapeutic recreation.

The most recent report by NCTRC in 2014 found the top-rated job tasks fall in the areas of professional relationships and responsibilities, document intervention services, implementation of interventions and/or programs, and assessment. The top-listed knowledge areas were foundational knowledge and the assessment process.[16]

Expansion of Sport and Outdoor Recreation Participation

At every level, people of all ages with physical or cognitive disabilities are taking part in varied forms of sport and outdoor recreation. Many of these activities are promoted by organizations such as Wheelchair and Ambulatory Sports, USA, a multisport organization for athletes who compete annually in regional, national, and international games. Included among the competitive events for both men and women are archery, athletics (track and field, pentathlon, road racing), basketball, swimming, table tennis, tennis, and weightlifting. Thousands of young athletes also participate in Special Olympics events, while many others compete in marathons, bowling leagues, and other individual or team sports.

In terms of outdoor recreation, programs have become increasingly geared for individuals with disabilities. Like sports, there are organizations specifically designed for outdoor recreation pursuits. For example, Outdoors Without Limits educates people about outdoor recreation opportunities for people with disabilities. The National Sports Center for the Disabled offers programs in sport and outdoor recreation. For example, they currently offer whitewater rafting, canoeing, mountain biking, rock climbing, alpine skiing, and more for all ages.[18]

Assistive technology has helped people with disabilities enjoy a wide variety of recreation activities.
© Eric Rodolfo Schroeder/iStockphoto/Thinkstock/Getty.

MORGAN'S WONDERLAND

Morgan's Wonderland, located in San Antonio, Texas, is a 25-acre amusement park designed specifically for people with disabilities. Gordon Hartman, whose daughter Morgan has a cognitive disability, raised $30 million to build this facility. Admission is free for people with disabilities. Everyone else is charged an admission fee. Amenities on the property include an event center and gymnasium, an interactive sensory village, butterfly-themed playground, Wonderland Express train, amphitheater, the first ever off-road adventure ride, a 36-foot-diameter carousel, music garden, water play area, and much more.[17]

Case Study

. . . .

Americans with Disabilities Act

The Americans with Disabilities Act of 1990 (ADA) is a civil rights law that prohibits discrimination based on disability.[a] There are five sections of the act:

Title 1: Employment: Qualified candidates cannot be discriminated against in the hiring process, employment, or discharge based on disability.

Title 2: State and Local Government: People with disabilities must have access to state and local government facilities and programs. This section also addresses accessibility of transportation such as on buses and trains.

Title 3: Public Accommodations (and Commercial Facilities): People with disabilities may not be discriminated against with regard to use of public accommodations including hotels, resorts, restaurants, and recreation opportunities, among others. In addition, buildings must be compliant with the ADA Accessibility Guidelines. Private clubs and religious organizations are exempt from the law. Public accommodations can include such things as sign language interpreters, assistive listening devices, Braille publications, taped publications, telephone typewriter (TTY)/Telecommunications Device for the Deaf (TDD), and facility accessibility.

Title 4: Telecommunications: Telecommunications companies must make their services available to people with disabilities. This is most focused on serving people who are deaf/hard of hearing and/or who have a speech impairment.

Title 5: Miscellaneous Provisions: This section covers the technical aspects of the law such as immunity under ADA, retaliation against claims, and responsibilities for technical assistance.

In 2008, the definition of the term "disability" was adjusted, effectively making it easier for an individual seeking protection under the ADA to establish that he or she has a disability within the meaning of the ADA.[b]

Questions to Consider

1. Walk through a building on campus such as the campus recreation facility. What examples did you find that the facility and/or programs were accessible to people with disabilities?
2. What aspects of the facility and/or programs were not accessible?

Sources

a. Council for Disability Rights, "The Americans with Disabilities Act: Frequently Asked Questions," www.disabilityrights.org/adatoc.htm.
b. Notice concerning the Americans with Disabilities Act (ADA) Amendments Act of 2008, www1.eeoc.gov//laws/statutes/adaaa_notice.cfm?renderforprint=1.

Use of Technology and Assistive Devices

Sophisticated technology is being brought into play to permit persons with disabilities to participate successfully in different leisure activities. For several decades, various modified instruments or pieces of equipment have been used to help people with disabilities take part in card and table games, arts and crafts, team and individual sport, and other pursuits. For example, for outdoor recreation there are adaptive gun and bow mounts for hunting, all-terrain tires for trails, and fishing pole holders. Adapted sports equipment includes ice hockey sledges, handcycles, mono- and bi-skis for alpine skiing, and Nordic cross-country skis.

Aerodynamic wheelchairs are now being used by racers with disabilities, and carbon-fiber prosthetic feet enable athletes with amputations to run almost as fast as athletes without disabilities. Research into the use of electrodes to stimulate the leg muscles of persons with spinal cord injuries is helping to maintain bone, joint, and muscle health, which has positive effects on cardiovascular functioning and recreation participation, while numerous other devices are being invented each year to facilitate independent functioning for people with disabilities. Electronic devices such as "aura interactor" strap-on vests enable deaf people to dance without straining to hear the music and help blind video game players to feel laser beams "bouncing" off the screen.

Cooperative Networks of Agencies

Because many community and nonprofit organizations lacked the staff resources or special facilities required to provide comprehensive leisure-service programs for persons with disabilities, the 1980s and 1990s saw a trend toward

Case Study
. . . .

Warfighters

The mission of Warfighter Sports is simple: to provide adaptive sports to severely wounded warriors free of cost. Since 2003, over 9,700 wounded warriors have been served through Warfighter Sports in 30 different activities including skiing, kayaking, and scuba diving. Warfighter Sports also provides grant opportunities through Disabled Sports USA to veterans and members of the armed forces with permanent physical disabilities (e.g., spinal cord injury, amputation, vision impairment, traumatic brain injury) who do not have nearby access to adaptive training in the sport of their choice. The goal of the program is to help veterans and members of the armed forces with permanent physical disabilities gain independence in their chosen sport, so that even if an adaptive club is not available nearby, they have the ability to participate in nonadaptive programs alongside family and friends. Expenses eligible for coverage include travel expenses to train in an adaptive sport if not offered locally, travel to attend classification opportunities or Paralympic competition, coaching fees for individualized instruction, and adaptive sports equipment not covered by the Veterans' Administration.

Question to Consider

1. What are the benefits of providing adaptive sports opportunities to wounded warriors?

Source

Disabled Sports USA: http://www.disabledsportsusa.org/programs/warfighter-sports/.

developing cooperative networks of such agencies. In such structures, two or more public or nonprofit human-service organizations—or a combination of both types—share their funding and facilities to provide needed recreation programs in a number of locations. For example, there are more than 20 independent special recreation associations (SRAs) in northern Illinois, based on revenue generated from special direct property taxes. All SRAs are coordinated by boards representing the cooperating communities. They interface with municipal recreation and park departments and offer programming for persons with all types of disabling conditions in both integrated and segregated groupings.

In another example of joint cooperation, Boston Children's Hospital, the University of Massachusetts–Boston, and the Institute for Community Inclusion have joined together to provide a variety of services for children with disabilities. One such service is Opening Doors: Project Adventure.[19] This program has three goals: (1) to provide inclusive activities that are physically active and fun, (2) to influence the career paths of the leaders who volunteer for the program, and (3) to serve as a respite and have a positive impact on families/caregivers. The volunteer leaders are matched one on one with a child with a disability. Another child in the household or a friend without a disability may also participate. The success of this program is dependent on the sponsoring agencies, the families, and the volunteer leaders who work with the children.

Throughout the country, numerous independent nonprofit organizations, such as HILLS (Healthy Independent Leisure Lifestyles)[20] have established facilities and programs that are designed to meet varied life needs—recreational, social, educational, and vocational—of people in different categories of disability.

New Emphasis on Inclusion

In the late 1990s, instead of the term *special recreation,* professional organizations began to use the term *inclusion,* meaning simply the involvement and full acceptance of people with disabilities in a wide range of community settings. In 2009, a research team of inclusion experts examined best practices employed by agencies deemed to be successful at implementing inclusive service delivery. Best practices are tied to participant assessment, accommodation plans, behavioral interventions, inclusion support staff, preparing nondisabled peers, and numerous other criteria. The study found that successful agencies use best practices but implement them in highly individualized manners.[21]

The efforts of researchers, ATRA, NCTRC, agencies that deliver services, and therapeutic recreation practitioners have combined to broaden the scope of services, improve the quality of services, and make therapeutic recreation services available to more people with illnesses and disabling conditions than ever before. Many factors are still unfolding in the areas of healthcare, community recreation services, efficacy-based research, university TR programs, and credentialing, which will affect the future of TR.

ARMED FORCES RECREATION

For many years, it has been the official policy of the military establishment to provide a well-rounded morale, welfare, and recreational program for the physical, social, and mental well-being of its personnel. During World War I, Special Services Divisions were established to provide social and recreational programs that would sustain favorable morale, curb homesickness and boredom, minimize fatigue, and reduce AWOL (absent without leave) and venereal disease rates.

Today, each branch of the armed forces has its own pattern of recreation sponsorship, although they are all under the same morale, welfare, and recreation (MWR) program, which is administratively responsible to the Office of the Assistant Secretary of Defense for Manpower, Reserve Affairs, and Logistics. They serve several million individuals, including active duty, reserve, and retired military personnel and their dependents; civilian employees; and surviving spouses of military personnel who died in active duty. In addition, MWR services are also provided to Coast Guard personnel, who are not part of the Department of Defense.

Goals and Scope of Armed Forces Recreation Today

The U.S. Army Morale, Welfare, and Recreation (MWR) exists because the U.S. Army states it ". . . is committed to the well-being of the community of people who serve and stand ready to defend the nation, to enhance the lives of soldiers, their families, civilian employees, and military retirees."[22] The mission is to serve the needs, interests, and responsibilities of each individual in the Army community for as long as he or she is associated with the Army, no matter where he or she is.

Total Army Strong, the newest revision to Army MWR that replaces the Army Family Covenant, seeks to provide a platform for programming that can be tailored to the unique needs of a unit's community—whether in the United States or abroad—and contribute to the Army's strength and readiness by offering services that reduce stress and build skills and self-confidence for soldiers and their families.[23]

Military recreation departments are structured and operate similarly to public parks and recreation agencies. They both offer a variety of programs for the community. The military community is far more defined and limited than a community such as a city or county. Potter and Ogilvie outline four major differences between MWR and community recreation.[24] First, the military community is quite transient and ever changing. Working in MWR requires staff to constantly focus on the changes in needs going on within the military community. Second, military communities are not always in the most stable parts of the world. They are in remote areas, combat zones, and less than desirable geographic locations. The staff, military personnel, and their families must be aware of these situations. Recreation can serve as a way to make life a little more stable for all involved. Third, MWR is exclusive in whom it serves. MWR provides services for active and retired military personnel and their families only. Last, MWR relies heavily on volunteers to carry out programs and events. Although municipal agencies also often rely on volunteers, MWR volunteers are transient, making it difficult to manage and recruit a consistent stream of volunteers.

Varying levels of health and wellness programs are major components of most MWR programs.

© Dmitriy Shironosov/iStockphoto/Thinkstock/Getty.

Program Elements

Sports   MWR programs include an extensive range of sport, fitness, social, creative, outdoor recreation, travel, entertainment, and hobby leisure pursuits. In the Air Force, for example, an extensive program of sports activities has typically included six major elements: (1) instruction in basic sport skills; (2) a self-directed phase of informal participation in sport under minimum supervision or direction; (3) an intramural program, in which personnel assigned to a particular base compete with others at the same base; (4) an extramural program, which includes competition with teams from different Air Force bases or with teams from neighboring communities; (5) a varsity program, which involves high-level competition with players selected for their advanced skills who compete on a broader national or international scale; and (6) a program for women in the Air Force.

In addition to such programs attached to individual services, the armed forces promote an extensive range of competitive sport programs. Through interservice competition in such sports as basketball, boxing,

FORT HUACHUCA FAMILY AND MWR PHILOSOPHY

Soldiers are entitled to the same quality of life as is afforded the society they are pledged to defend. Keeping an army ready to fight and win takes more than hard work and training. Soldiers need a balance of work and play.[26]

wrestling, track and field, and softball, all-service teams are selected; armed forces teams then are chosen to represent the United States in international competition.

Fitness Programs   Health and wellness have become a major focus of armed forces recreation. To improve fitness levels of personnel, the Air Force installed health and wellness centers (HAWC) on each base; these centers are well equipped and are staffed with leaders qualified to provide the following services: fitness and health risk assessments, exercise programming and weight counseling, stress management and smoking cessation assistance, and similar activities.[25]

On some military bases, fitness is promoted through well-publicized and challenging special events. At the Marine Corps Base at Camp Lejeune, North Carolina, the Lejeune Grand Prix Series is labeled the ultimate fitness challenge, and features a number of competitive events that involve hundreds of service personnel in a mud run, half marathon, sprint triathlon, duathlon, and other types of races.

Outdoor Recreation   Often, outdoor program activities are keyed to the location of a base. For example, Fort Carson, Colorado, offers such activities as ice climbing lessons, workshops, and trips; skiing and snowshoe trips; and rafting.[27] Responding to widespread interest in mountain climbing and rock climbing, this Army base constructed a 17,400-square-foot outdoor recreation center that features a 30-foot-high indoor climbing wall and a 60-foot outdoor wall with the look and feel of natural rock and climbing routes geared to different skill levels. Other bases offer instruction, equipment, and facilities for such water-based activities as fishing, wind-surfing, jet skiing, scuba diving, and similar pastimes.

Family Recreation   The Department of Defense has become increasingly aware of the need to provide varied family-focused programs to counter the special problems that may affect the spouses and children of military personnel.

All branches of the military have family programs. Marine Corps Community Services, through MCCS Forward, is committed to supporting both individual marines and family members with its fitness and wellness programs, as well as other services designed to enhance personal and family readiness such as the Family Team Building program that provides educational resources and services to foster personal growth and enhance the readiness of Marine Corps families.[28]

The Navy's program offerings are focused on "Serving the Fleet, Fighter and Family". The Navy has child and youth programs for children aged 4 weeks to 18 years. Programs are designed to foster emotional well-being, develop self-discipline, and cultivate respect and appreciation of differences and the uniqueness of diverse cultures and traditions.[29] The Air Force also offers a wide variety of programs for service members as well as their families as exemplified by the mission of the Little Rock Air Force Base's Airman and Family Readiness Center to "provide world class Airman and Family Readiness Center programs and services for members and families in an effort to build stronger communities, promote self-sufficiency, and foster resiliency; while enhancing mission readiness, retention and adaptation to the Air Force way of life."[30]

Community Relations   Many military bases in the United States and overseas place a high priority on establishing positive relationships between armed forces personnel and nearby communities. Civilian MWR personnel working around the globe in such settings as Europe, Korea, and Central America, and even Saudi Arabia, Turkey, and Africa, seek to provide a wealth of outdoor recreational experiences and positive intercultural experiences with local residents.

MWR programs are sometimes open to the general public. For example, MCAS Miramar Memorial Golf Course is open to the public. However, due to security and gate access at the course, player names must be submitted in advance to gain access. These players are also charged a higher fee than active duty soldiers, retirees, and their families.[31] There are also many services within MWR that help families acclimate to the communities in which they live. They do this by providing information about the community and participating in community events.[32]

Resorts   The Army maintains a full range of resorts for all military members. Armed Forces Recreation Centers (AFRC) are affordable Joint Service facilities operated by the U.S. Army Community and Family Support Center and located in different areas, including Germany, Florida, and Hawaii. They offer a full range of resort hotel opportunities for members of all branches of the military service, their families, and other members of the Total Defense Force. The resorts are self-supporting, funded by revenues generated internally from operations.

Fiscal Support of Armed Forces Recreation

Military recreation has traditionally depended on two types of funding: *appropriated funds,* which are tax funds approved by Congress, and *nonappropriated funds,* which are generated on the military base through a combination of post exchange profits and revenue from fees, rentals, and other recreation charges. As such, not all recreation activities are free to military personnel and their families. Just like other public agencies, some programs are free and supported by tax dollars (appropriated funds) and others are used to generate revenue.

With growing federal government budget cutbacks and the need to maximize revenues from clubs, messes, post exchanges, and varied forms of commercial sponsorship or partnerships, MWR planners have initiated a range of new fiscal strategies. The effort has been to reduce the costs of operations, standardize procedures, and eliminate redundant programs or personnel. The Navy, for example, established 10 major regions to simplify the planning and supervision of programs, increasingly encouraged public/private projects, and established new planning processes to "reinvent" facility development and other projects.

EMPLOYEE SERVICES AND RECREATION PROGRAMS

A third important area of specialized recreation programs involves the role of business and industry in providing recreation and related personnel services to employees and in some cases their families or other community residents.

Background of Company-Sponsored Programs

Employee recreation (formerly called "industrial recreation") began in the nineteenth century but did not expand rapidly until after World War II. At this time, the National Industrial Recreation Association was formed. This professional association provided resources for people working in corporate recreation, and at this point the emphasis was on fitness and wellness. Later, this organization became the Employee Services Management Association. Employee services management expands on recreation to provide other benefits to employees such as travel discounts and services.

Although the providers of employee services and recreation originally were manufacturing companies and other industrial businesses, today many different types of organizations also sponsor employee activities. They include such diverse groups as food market chains, airlines, insurance companies, hospitals, and government agencies.

Goals of Employee Recreation

The major goals of the institutions providing employee programs and services include the following.

Improvement of Employer-Employee Relations   Earlier in this country's industrial development, there was considerable friction between management and labor that often resulted in extended and violent strikes. A major purpose of industrial recreation programs at this time was to create favorable employer-employee

EMPLOYMENT IN MWR

MWR employs 100,000 people worldwide. Entry-level positions are often in specialty areas such as sports, youth, or special events. To find jobs in MWR, see these websites:

Coast Guard: www.uscg.mil/MWR/

Marines: www.usmc-mccs.org/careers/#

Navy: www.navymwr.org/jobs/

Army: https://www.armymwr.com/m/emplyee-portal/human-resources/employment/ (Retrieved June 3, 2017)

Air Force: www.indeed.com/q-Air-Force-Morale,-Welfare-&-Recreation-Center-jobs.html

relationships and instill a sense of loyalty among workers. It is believed that such programs tend to create a feeling of belonging and identification among employees, and that group participation by workers at various job levels contributes to improved worker morale, increased harmony, and an attitude of mutual cooperation.

For example, the Ford Employees Recreation Association was established "for the purpose of developing fellowship and understanding among the Michigan employees of Ford Motor Company through the promotion of social, physical, cultural and special programs."[33] In addition, Chevron Recreation provides health and work/life resources to Chevron employees to improve productivity, reduce safety risks, and enhance a healthy work environment.[34]

Directly Promoting Employee Fitness and Efficiency   Corporations large and small today have become concerned about maintaining the health of their employees. One reason may be the skyrocketing costs of health insurance for employers. A major factor in this increase is the nation's obesity epidemic. Obesity accounts for more annual healthcare costs than drinking and smoking. The American Public Health Association estimates that obesity costs the United States $152 billion annually in direct healthcare costs. Obesity also costs employers $6.4 billion per year in absenteeism, lost productivity, and insurance premiums.[35]

For example, HumanaVitality program incentivizes its members with rewards for making healthy choices and achieving individualized wellness goals based on measurable data in four categories: (1) fitness, (2) healthy living, (3) prevention, and (4) education. Members accumulate Vitality Points for their accomplishments within each category and then redeem their points from a selection of more than 600,000 reward choices, such as movie tickets, brand-name merchandise—like Oakley sunglasses—or hotel stays in the Caribbean.[36] Employers are also starting to recognize the health ramifications of employees not taking advantage of paid vacation time; in 2013, at least 75% of employees did not use all of their time. This behavior can lead to fatigue, burnout, health problems, and reduced productivity. A select number of companies are incentivizing employees to actually take vacation time through pay. Evernote provides unlimited paid vacation, but after not seeing a rise in requests for time off, they upped the ante by offering $1000 cash to employees once they return from a vacation. Software firm Full Contact offers employees $7500 per year for the same option, but again, employees only receive the money in return for "proof" of having taken a vacation.[37]

Recruitment and Retention Appeal

An attractive program of recreation and related personnel services that can meet the needs of both the employee and his or her family is a persuasive recruitment weapon. Agencies advertise employee recreation opportunities

HEALTH AND WELLNESS PROGRAM BENEFITS

The National Association for Health and Fitness suggests that a health and wellness program for employees benefits both the employee and the employer. Here's how:

Benefits for Employers
- Enhanced employee productivity
- Improved healthcare costs for management
- Decreased rates of illness and injuries
- Reduced employee absenteeism
- Development of employee leadership skills

Benefits for Employees
- Lower levels of stress
- Increased well-being, self-image, self-esteem, and improved physical fitness
- Increased stamina
- Potential weight reduction

More information can be found at www.physicalfitness.org/media_2013-01-29.php.

Many large companies offer recreation programs for current employees, retirees, and families. These programs are one means of increasing employee morale.

© Photodisc/Getty.

as a perk to employment. It demonstrates the company's commitment to its employees and makes the company appear to be a great place to work.

In terms of retention, many companies find that successful employee programs help reduce job turnover. Litton Laser Systems in Apopka, Florida, now owned by Northrop Grumman, for example, credits its low employee turnover and high morale to its social activities committee (SAC), a group of employees who manage social, recreational, and sports events and other services for all company members and their families.

Company Image and Community Role

An important part of the recreation and services function involves external relations—the company's external, community-based role. Eli Lilly and Company established the Eli Lilly and Company Foundation, which awards grants to initiatives that match the philosophy of the company such as healthcare, culture, and youth development. The company also matches gifts to charities by employees and financially supports organizations that staff volunteer with on a regular basis.[38]

In other settings, the employee services program provides a means through which company executives can move purposefully to transform the business's internal and external image. In 2011 Target employees donated $475,000 to projects in their community. Target supports these efforts because it makes for safer, healthier, and stronger communities.

Furthermore, in 2014, Target employees donated over 14.5 million dollars to the United Way, and more than one million volunteer hours, making this company a model business in its many communities.[39]

Program Activities and Services

Many companies established extensive and well-equipped recreation and fitness centers and staffed them with qualified personnel. The Texins Activity Center in Dallas, serving

Case Study

Employee Recreation Improves Morale

Business Insider published an article that featured the 18 best perks on the job provided by major corporations across the country.[a] Many of those were recreation related, including:

- Campbell Soup: On-site afterschool programs for children of employees
- Google: Access to company bowling alley, bocce courts, and gyms
- Smuckers: Holds bowling nights and softball games for employees
- Boeing: 12 paid holidays and a winter recess between Christmas and New Years
- Chesapeake Energy: On-site 72,000-square-foot fitness facility that includes an Olympic-sized pool, a sand volleyball court, rock climbing wall, and a quarter-mile walking track
- TIAA-CREF: Allows employees to play up to six sports on site through the corporate athletic program
- Yahoo: Offices have on-site fitness centers with yoga, cardio-kickboxing, pilates, and golf classes. Yahoo also provides its employees with discounts to ski resorts and California theme parks.

Questions to Consider

1. Which of these benefits would be important to you as an employee at a company?
2. List the pros and cons of having an employee recreation program within a company.
3. You have a company of 30 employees. Develop an employee recreation program.
4. You have a company of 300 employees. How does your employee recreation program change?

Source

a. M. Stanger, "18 Of The Best Perks At Top Employers," *Business Insider* (11 February 2013). http://www.businessinsider.com/companies-with-awesome-perks-payscale-2013-1.

employees of Texas Instruments, contains a multiuse gymnasium; strength and cardiovascular exercise areas; conference rooms; childcare rooms; club rooms; a natatorium with a six-lane, 25-lap pool; two aerobic studios; an indoor running track; and varied outdoor facilities. Other employers such as Double Encore and Airbnb offer alternative activities such as game rooms and company retreats.[40]

Administrative Arrangements

Various approaches to the management of employee service and recreation programs exist. In some, the company itself provides the facilities and leadership and maintains complete control of the operation. In other organizations, the company provides the facilities, but an employee recreation association takes actual responsibility for running the program. Other companies use combinations of these approaches. Frequently, profits from canteens or plant vending machines provide financial support for the program, as does revenue from moderate fees for participation or membership. Many activities—such as charter vacation flights—are completely self-supporting; others are fully or partly subsidized by the company.

Scheduling Flexibility: Off-Shift Programming

Employee service and recreation managers must adapt to the special circumstances of their organizations and the changing needs of the employees they serve. Often this may involve providing a wide range of special courses designed for vocational or career development, cultural interest, or personal enrichment.

Case Study

. . . .

Employer Wellness Programs

With the benefits of a healthy workforce ranging from lower absenteeism to higher productivity to lower healthcare costs, employers are looking for ways to incentivize wellness for their employees. Companies pay for wellness-related costs such as gym memberships, Weight Watchers memberships, and smoking cessation programs, and may also offer cash and other financial incentives for participation. However, there is disagreement with regard to the level of incentives that are allowable under ADA guidelines and the Health Insurance Portability and Accountability Act (HIPAA) and the Patient Protection and Affordable Care Act (PPACA). While the ADA allows employers to ask for medical information that is not job-specific in connection with *voluntary* wellness programs, the nature of voluntary is being called into question by the EEOC. There are instances where they feel that employees are being penalized unduly when they do not participate, thus negating the claim of "voluntary." However, HIPAA and PPACA allow rewards for both "health-contingent" and "participatory" wellness programs, albeit at different levels. Health-contingent programs require satisfaction of a standard related to a health factor to obtain a reward (e.g., not smoking), while participatory program requirements are satisfied simply by participating. To date, the PPACA permits rewards of up to 30% of the total cost (employer plus employee portions) of coverage under the plan and 50% for wellness programs designed to prevent or reduce tobacco use for health-contingent programs, while there is no limit on rewards for participatory programs. To date, there continues to be disagreement between the two bodies with regard to reward limits.

Question to Consider

Wellness program requirements are rarely, if ever, going to be "job-related and consistent with business necessity" as asserted as necessary by the EEOC to meet ADA guidelines. What does this mean for wellness programs?

Sources

S. Miller. (2013). Final Rule Provides Wellness Incentive Guidance. Society for Human Resource Management. http://www.hbsdealer.com/article/final-rule-provides-guidance-wellness-program-incentives (Retrieved June 3, 2017).

S. Miller. (2014) EEOC Sues Employers' Wellness Programs. Society for Human Resource Management. www.shrm.org/hrdisciplines/benefits/articles/pages/eeoc-sues-employers'-wellness-programs (Retrieved June 3, 2017).

Employer Wellness Programs Need Guidance to Avoid Discrimination. (2013). U. S. Equal Employment Opportunity Commission. http://www.eeoc.gov/eeoc/newsroom/release/5-8-13.cfm.

Employer Wellness Programs: What Financial Incentives are Permitted Under the Law? Jones Day (August 2013). www.jonesday.com/employer-wellness-programs-what-financial-incentives-are-permitted-under-the-law-08-01-2013/.

Some large corporations seek to meet the needs of their employees who work second and third shifts by scheduling facilities such as health clubs or weight rooms to be available at odd hours of the day and night. For example, Phillips Petroleum and Pratt and Whitney schedule morning and midnight softball and bowling leagues for off-shift workers and make gyms, tennis courts, and other facilities, as well as discount ticket operations, available to them at convenient times.

Innovation and Entrepreneurship

Just as in other sectors of the leisure-service field, employee service and recreation practitioners have experienced the need to become more fiscally independent by generating a fuller level of revenues through their offerings and by demonstrating their value in convincing terms.

The purposes of adopting businesslike values and strategies are (1) to enable employee programs to become less dependent on company financial support, and (2) to ensure that funds allocated to them by management yield significant, quantifiable benefits. A number of employee service and recreation directors in major corporations have been quite innovative in developing revenue sources based on businesslike ventures.

CAMPUS RECREATION

The nation's colleges and universities provide a major setting for organized programs of leisure services involving millions of participants each year in a wide range of recreational activities. Although their primary purpose is to serve students, faculty and staff members also may be involved in such programs on many campuses.

All institutions of higher education today sponsor some forms of leisure activity for their resident and commuter populations. Many of the larger colleges and universities have campus unions, departments of student affairs, or student centers that house a wide range of such activities. Frequently, a dean of student life is responsible for overseeing these programs, although intramural and recreational sports often may be administratively attached to a department or college of physical education and recreation or to a department of intercollegiate athletics.

The diversified leisure-service function may include operating performing arts centers (sometimes in cooperation with academic departments or schools in these fields), planning arts series, film programs, and forums with guest speakers, and similar cultural events. Student union buildings may include such specialized facilities as bowling alleys, coffee houses, game rooms, restaurants, bookstores, and other activity areas.

Rationale for Campus Programs

Several logical reasons for sponsoring college and university recreation programs may be cited. Discussion of some of these follows.

Leisure as Cocurricular Enrichment Not all of the learning that takes place in higher education is provided in the classroom or laboratory. Many special interests of students can be explored to the fullest only by *cocurricular* (nonclass) experiences, ranging from the journalism major who works on the staff of the campus newspaper or literary magazine to the botany major who becomes involved in wilderness backpacking or camping. Often such programs are carried on with the express cooperation of the campus department most directly involved with the leisure interest. Beyond enriching a student's formal academic experience, involvement in cocurricular experiences contributes significantly to his or her overall personal growth.

Maintaining Campus Control and Morale Historically, U.S. colleges acted *in loco parentis;* that is, they were obligated to maintain a degree of control over the private lives of their students in areas such as drinking, gambling, sexual behavior, or the general domain of health and safety. For centuries, they therefore maintained codes of behavior, rules for on-campus living, curfews, and numerous other restrictions that controlled various forms of leisure behavior. This strong control over students has lessened considerably. Rather than a university serving as a police force to control behaviors, they are using alternative activities as a means to guide the lives of students outside of the classroom.

Campus recreation seeks to promote positive student growth throughout the college experience. At a number of colleges and universities, students are drawn into outdoor recreation or community service projects, beginning with their freshman orientation period. At Lehigh University and Lafayette College, for example, new students are drawn into overnight canoe and backpacking trips and begin to make new friends immediately. Similarly, entering students at The University of Maine have the opportunity to participate in Maine Bound Outdoor adventure programs to introduce freshman to the programs offered at the university and to meet other people.[41]

Enhancing the University's Image   Particularly in an era in which colleges and universities must compete for the enrollment of high-quality students, maintaining an appealing and impressive institutional image is critical. Arguably the best-known vehicle for doing this is by fielding teams that play glamorous schedules in such popular sports as football and basketball. However, there are many other ways of building a positive image: through academic distinction, by winning prizes and awards, by having outstanding orchestras or theater companies, by having a distinguished university press, and through the accomplishments of alumni.

Certainly, having attractive recreational facilities and campus leisure programs also helps to build a positive image—particularly for potential students who visit a campus and are considering whether they want to live there for the next 4 years. Higher education appeals to a number of values and needs—not the least of these is the student's desire for an exciting and interesting social life.

Opportunities to Build Leadership Skills   Campus recreation offers undergraduate and graduate students an opportunity to develop leadership and other job skills. Universities hire student workers who staff the front desk, serve as personal trainers, work as officials, and lead trips, to name a few positions. Many campus recreation departments understand the value of student development and give students ample opportunities to broaden their skills in leadership, teamwork, decision making, problem solving, conflict resolution, and more.

Range of Campus Recreation Experiences

Campus recreation programs today are becoming more diversified, including a wide range of recreational sport, outdoor activities, entertainment and social events, cultural programs, activities for persons with disabilities, and various other services.

Recreational Sport   During the 1970s and 1980s, both intramural leagues and sport clubs expanded rapidly in many institutions, with a growing emphasis on lifetime sport and on coeducational participation. Due in part to changed sex-role expectations and the effect of Title IX, many more girls and women are involved in sport today than in the past. More and more colleges and universities are providing varied facilities for sport and games, including aquatic facilities, boxing/martial arts and exercise rooms, saunas and locker rooms, extensive outdoor areas with night lighting for evening play, and other special facilities for outdoor hobbies and instruction.

An outstanding example of college sport programming is found at Virginia Commonwealth University in Richmond, Virginia, which sponsors a host of recreational sport activities and events and fitness programs in six impressive campus facilities. Programs include a huge range of instructional, club, and intramural activities in such areas as individual, dual, and team sport; aerobics; dancing; yoga; martial arts; aquatics; and social programs. Participation in all programs and facilities is free for students through the general student fee. Spouses, staff, and faculty members pay modest annual fees. Similar sport programs are offered throughout the United States.

Outdoor Recreation   Outdoor recreation, which includes clinics, clubs, and outings, may involve hiking, backpacking, camping, mountain climbing, scuba diving, sailing, skiing, and numerous other nature-based programs. There are a number of outstanding campus recreation programs with outdoor recreation departments. The geography of the university obviously affects which programs are offered. It is not unusual for these universities to offer trips, rental gear, and do outdoor-related service projects. For example, Colorado State University offers snowshoeing trips, avalanche certification, and classes on ice and rock climbing.[42] University of Utah Campus Recreation rents outdoor equipment including camping equipment, mountain bikes, water craft, and winter sports equipment.[43] Southern Illinois University offers a diversified range of appealing trips and outings, clinics, and classes, including rock climbing and backpacking, spelunking (cave exploration), canoeing, and biking.

Campus recreation activities typically include intramural sports, special events, clubs, and fitness.
© Christian Bertrand/Shutterstock.

Special Events: Entertainment and Cultural Programs   Many campuses sponsor large-scale entertainment events and cultural series. Typically, singers, rock bands, and comedians are booked to entertain students in stadiums, fieldhouses, and campus centers. The college's or university's own departments of music, theater, and dance may provide performing companies that present concerts or other stage presentations, along with other kinds of specialized programs.

Large-scale special events that students plan and carry out themselves—such as sports carnivals or other major competitions—are highlights of campus social programs. They involve extensive interaction among leaders and participants and an intense outpouring of energy as people share fun in a crowded school or college setting.

Services for Special Populations   Students with disabilities are being encouraged and assisted to participate in general campus recreation programs whenever possible. However, for those students whose disabilities are too severe to permit this or who have not yet developed the needed degree of confidence and independence, special programs have been designed using modified equipment and adapted instructional techniques or rules.

Outstanding examples of such programs are those offered by the University of Illinois, which provides special teams in the areas of football, softball, basketball, swimming, and track and field for students with physical disabilities. Other activities, such as archery, judo, swimming, bowling, and softball, have been adapted for such special groups as people with visual impairment.

Community Service Projects   Many students also become involved in volunteer community projects such as repairing facilities, working with older adults, or helping with community special events. Such efforts are important for two reasons: (1) They illustrate how student-life activities may include a broad range of involvement beyond those that are clearly recognizable as recreational "fun" events; and (2) they serve to blend academic and extracurricular student experiences, increasing the individual's exposure to life and enhancing his or her leadership capability.

Overview of Campus Recreation

Campus recreation provides students with practical experience within a wide range of functions that supplement and enrich their academic programs. For example, many students may gain administrative or business skills, often on an advanced level. The Associated Students' Organization of San Diego State University in California provides a setting for such learning experiences. This multi-million-dollar corporation, funded by student fees, operates the Aztec Center, the college's student union building. Among its services are a successful travel agency, intramurals and sport clubs, special events, leisure classes, lectures, movies, concerts, an open-air theater, an aquatics center, campus radio station, childcare center, general store, campus information booth, and other programs. The bulk of its recreational activities is operated directly by the Recreation Activities Board, a unit within the overall Associated Students' Organization.[44]

Such experiences illustrate the important contributions made by campus recreation programs, along with other student cocurricular activities, to the college or university experience. They involve the whole student in meaningful and creative ways and thus provide a meaningful transition to adult life and potential career opportunities.

PRIVATE-MEMBERSHIP RECREATION ORGANIZATIONS

A significant portion of recreational opportunities today is provided by private-membership organizations. As distinguished from commercial recreation businesses—in which any individual may simply pay an admission fee to a theme park, for example—private-membership bodies usually restrict use of their facilities or programs to individual members and their families and guests.

Within the broad field of sport and outdoor recreation, many organizations offer facilities, instruction, or other services for activities such as skiing, tennis, golf, boating, and hunting or fishing. Whereas some private-membership organizations are commercially owned and operated, others exist as independent, incorporated clubs of members who own their own facilities. For these clubs, policy is set by elected officers and boards, and the actual administration and operation of the club are carried out by paid employees.

An important characteristic of many private-membership organizations has been their social exclusiveness. Membership policies historically have sometimes screened out certain prospective members for reasons of religion, ethnicity, gender, economics, or other demographic factors.

It is important to recognize that although the ostensible function of such private organizations is to provide sociability as well as specific forms of leisure activity, the clubs also provide a setting in which the most powerful members of communities meet regularly to discuss business or political matters and often reach informal decisions or plans for action. Those who are barred from membership in such clubs are thus also excluded from this behind-the-scenes, establishment-based process of influence and power.

Despite recent changes, many private-membership organizations continue to represent exclusive enclaves of the rich and powerful. Country clubs are generally of two types: (1) nonprofit "equity clubs," owned and operated by members; and (2) commercially owned, for-profit clubs. Equity clubs can be established as either nonprofit or for-profit organizations. A common equity club is a destination club where people buy in to vacation homes. They have the right to use the homes but have no real ownership in the individual home. Commercially owned for-profit clubs are quite common. For example, ClubCorp owns 200 golf courses, private business and sports clubs, and resorts and has over $2 billion in assets. ClubCorp owns such clubs as the Firestone Country Club in Akron, Ohio (site of the 2006–2014 World Golf Championships—Bridgestone Invitational) and Mission Hills Country Club in Rancho Mirage, California (home of the LPGA Kraft Nabisco Championship), and claims more than 430,000 members.[45]

Residence-Connected Clubs

Other types of private-membership recreation organizations continue to flourish—particularly in connection with new forms of home building and marketing. Many real estate developers have recognized that one of the key selling points in home development projects is the provision of attractive recreational facilities. Thus, tennis courts, golf courses, swimming pools, health spas, and similar recreation facilities are frequently provided for the residents of apartment buildings, condominiums, or one-family home developments, whether the residents are families, singles, or retired persons.

An important trend in society has been the rapid growth of housing developments in the suburbs, with community associations that carry out such functions as street cleaning, grounds maintenance, security, and the provision of leisure facilities such as tennis courts, golf courses, and swimming pools. Once found chiefly in the Southwest, such developments and community associations now have spread throughout the United States. In 1970, there were 10,000 such associations. By 2013, the number had grown to 333,600 associations with 66.7 million residents governed by associations.[46]

Although such real estate developments tend to be somewhat expensive and thus intended chiefly for more affluent homebuyers, there are exceptions. For example, a giant apartment development in Brooklyn, New York, known as Starrett City, was constructed in the mid-1970s to serve middle-income tenants drawn from varied ethnic populations—approximately half were African American, Hispanic, and Asian. Its thousands of residents enjoy a huge clubhouse with meeting rooms, hobby, craft, and dance classes, and an extensive pool program and tennis complex, as well as numerous classes, teams, and special events through the year.[47]

In some cases, large condominium-structured apartment buildings also have extensive leisure facilities and programs. For example, in Philadelphia, one such building with 776 residential units has a bank, restaurant, ten stores, doctors' and dentists' offices, garages, and two swimming pools, all under one roof. It also has a library, card room, fitness center, and numerous clubs and committees, including a welcoming committee, Weight Watchers, a writers' club, book club, and computer club.

Vacation Homes

A specialized form of residence-connected recreation is often found in vacation home developments. During the 1960s and 1970s, direct ownership and time-sharing arrangements for such homes became more popular, often in large-scale developments situated close to a lake or other major recreational attraction.

The baby boom, with millions of couples reaching the age and financial status at which they are able to afford vacation homes, has led to a rapid rise in the number of such developments. Nearly 6% of American households own a second home, typically within 150 miles of the primary residence. Most are located near recreation sites such as lakes or mountains.[48]

Typically, time-sharing apartments or condominiums in attractive vacation areas today cost as much as $15,000 to $20,000 for the right to use the facility one week each year. Although this may seem expensive, it is minimal compared with the cost in vacation areas where the "jet set"—the wealthy elite of U.S. society—enjoy their vacations. Illustrating the tendency to seek privacy in exclusive surroundings, a number of millionaires and billionaires who formerly enjoyed their vacations in Aspen, Colorado, left that area when it became too well known and popular. Today they fly their own jets to a stunningly beautiful mountain hamlet in Wyoming known as Saratoga. Members of the Old Baldy Club live in "cottages" that would be considered mansions anywhere else. When asked how much it cost to join the Old Baldy Club, a local resident received the reply, "If you have to ask, you can't afford it."

Case Study

. . . .

Do Private Clubs Discriminate?

A number of lawsuits have claimed discrimination in the membership practices of private clubs. Many of these clubs have been able to maintain their membership policies even though civil rights laws make it illegal to discriminate based on race, national origin, and other basis. However, these laws do not cover bona fide private clubs and religious organizations—these can discriminate on whatever basis they choose. Some states have extended the civil rights laws and prevent private clubs from discriminating, closing this loophole in the law. Because not all states have done this, discrimination still exists. Here are a few examples.

In 2009, 60 African American children were turned away from a northeast Philadelphia private swim club despite the fact that they had paid the $1900 fee. John Duesler, president of the Valley Swim Club, said they were turned away because "there was concern that a lot of kids would change the complexion . . . and the atmosphere of the club."[a]

Augusta National Golf Club just allowed women into the club in 2013. Prior to the first two women being admitted, Hootie Johnson, chairman of Augusta National, stated, "There may well come a day when women will be invited to join our membership, but that timetable will be ours and not at the point of a bayonet."

Birgit Koebke and Kendall French, a lesbian couple registered as domestic partners under the California Domestic Partner Rights and Responsibilities Act of 2003, sued Heights Country Club because of discrimination. Club membership pertains to member spouses but not domestic partners. The California Supreme Court ruled that domestic partners should receive the same benefits as legal spouses and mandated the club provide the same benefits to all couples.

Questions to Consider

1. If members own a private club, should they be able to establish policies that intentionally or unintentionally discriminate against a group?
2. Is a high membership fee a form of discrimination? Why or why not?

Source

a. A. Kilkenny, "Philadelphia Private Swim Club Forces Out Black Children," *Huffington Post* (July 8, 2009).

Retirement Communities

Similarly, large retirement villages offer recreation and social programs for their residents. A vivid example may be found in Sun City, Arizona. Established in 1960, this community has about 42,000 residents. Sun City is the country's first planned retirement community. The recreation opportunities are extensive because the community has 7 community centers with a pool in each one, 8 golf courses, 2 bowling alleys, 2 lakes, a wide variety of programs, and more than 120 social and civic clubs.[49]

Many retirement communities offer extensive recreation facilities and programs and encourage residents to attend cultural events in the surrounding area. Others, as in Sarasota, Florida's Pelican Cove, have uniquely beautiful natural surroundings, including a marina with easy access to open bay waters.

In numerous other retirement communities, such as Leisure World in Laguna Hills, California, such recreational facilities as pools, tennis courts, and riding stables often are found.

COMPARISONS AMONG SPECIAL-FOCUS AGENCIES

There are both differences and similarities among the five types of leisure-service organizations meeting special needs that are described in this chapter.

Therapeutic recreation is obviously concerned chiefly with meeting the needs of persons with disabilities as well as using recreation as a

Many retirement communities offer extensive recreation facilities and programs for their residents.

© Matthew Apps/Shutterstock.

purposeful tool to achieve goals of habilitation or rehabilitation. Although its major emphasis is on providing both clinical and community-based recreation programs, the strong thrust today is toward inclusion of individuals with disabilities within the larger population. As such, it shares many common program elements and facilities with the overall community recreation system.

Armed forces recreation involves a huge, sprawling, worldwide operation. It is essentially made up of hundreds of smaller individual programs on both domestic and foreign bases or on ships. Uniquely, it is governed by a bureaucratic structure and specific policies that originate within the U.S. Defense Department, while at the same time responding to the special needs and resources of different branches of the military services and to local capabilities and interests. Its services and programs range from businesslike and commercialized approaches to entertainment or hospitality to purposeful, social service activities meeting the needs of children and youth or dependent families.

Employee recreation service differs from other special branches of the leisure-service system in that it has become an important function designed to improve the quality of life in the work environment and to contribute to the effective operation of its sponsoring companies. Within this spectrum of service, recreation has the unique responsibility of upgrading company morale and human relationships, as well as promoting the positive image of the overall enterprise. As in both therapeutic and armed forces recreation, employee programs must be concerned with achieving important agency goals and with documenting their worth in concrete, measurable terms.

Campus recreation, whether primarily concerned with sport programming or with broader cultural and curriculum-connected activities, today is seen as an integral element in the overall higher education structure. Particularly in colleges and universities in which older adolescents and those just entering adulthood are faced with the challenge of their first real social independence, it is critical that campus recreation helps students develop positive lifestyle values and patterns of leisure choices. As part of this purpose, campus activities should serve as an attractive counterbalance to less desirable leisure involvements.

Finally, private-membership leisure-service organizations are heavily influenced by socioeconomic factors, in that they tend to be provided for individuals and families who are relatively elite in financial and demographic terms. Although they have been undergoing a gradual process of democratization, many such groups continue to be exclusive and focus on a narrow range of recreational interests. One exception is found in the growing number of retirement communities, which often sponsor a considerable variety of recreational programs, particularly for younger individuals and couples who are entering such communities.

Summary

Five specialized areas of leisure-service delivery described in this chapter illustrate the diversity of agencies that provide organized recreation opportunities today. In each case, they have their own goals and objectives, populations served, and program emphases—yet they are important elements within the overall leisure-service system and represent attractive fields of career opportunity for recreation, park, and leisure-service students today.

Therapeutic recreation service, in its two areas of professional emphasis—clinical and community-based special recreation—is probably the most highly professionalized of all the separate disciplines in the leisure-service field. It has a long history of professional development, with separate sections of state and national societies, early emphasis on certification, numerous specialized curricula, and a rich literature and background of research. With the possibility of lessened support being given to clinical therapeutic recreation in an era of cost cutting, hospital retrenchment, managed patient care, and deinstitutionalization, it is probable that community-based special recreation, with its emphasis on inclusion, will constitute an increasingly important element in therapeutic recreation.

Armed forces recreation professionals serve a distinct population composed both of large numbers of relatively young servicemen and women—and of families and dependants with special needs prompted by the military setting. MWR has many purposes including the physical, social, and mental welfare of its personnel and families. Military recreation has undergone major transformations in recent years, yet it continues to offer a wide range of attractive program opportunities and often has excellent facilities, both stateside and abroad.

Employee recreation and services today have gone far beyond their original emphasis on providing a narrow range of social and sports activities designed to promote company–worker relationships. They are carried on in many different kinds of organizations and include varied health- and fitness-related program elements, as well as such other personnel services as discount programs, company stores, community relationships, and other benefits-driven functions—all necessarily provided within a business-oriented framework that demands productivity and demonstrated outcomes.

Campus recreation is carried on within an educational setting and is designed to augment academic studies. At the same time, it has important responsibilities in terms of promoting the overall well-being of students, extending and enriching academic learning, developing leadership and other work skills, and contributing to other college and university goals.

The last type of organization described in this chapter, the private-membership association, includes a wide range of country clubs, golf clubs, yacht clubs, and other social or business membership groups that often tend to be socially exclusive. They represent a growing trend in the United States today, with millions of families now living in residential developments that have their own community associations to provide services, including recreation. This tends to limit their interest in or dependence on public, tax-supported recreation services.

Questions for Class Discussion or Essay Examination

1. Differentiate between clinical-based therapeutic recreation and community-based recreation.

   _____

   _____

   _____

   _____

2. Give specific examples of where recreation professionals could work within therapeutic recreation, MWR, campus recreation, employee recreation, and private-membership organizations.

   _____

   _____

   _____

   _____

3. Compare and contrast the two TR models of practice.

   _____

   _____

   _____

   _____

4. Describe the TR process.

   _____

   _____

   _____

   _____

5. Compare and contrast military recreation and public recreation agencies.

   _____

   _____

   _____

   _____

6. List the benefits of employee recreation for the employer and the employee.

   _____

   _____

7. What role does campus recreation play on a college campus?

8. Describe private-membership recreation and give some examples of clubs. Explain the issues with member discrimination.

9. Make a convincing case to an employer that the benefits of an employee recreation program outweigh the financial costs of such a program.

10. There has long been an ongoing discussion about the terms "therapeutic recreation" and "recreational therapy". Which of these do you think is a more accurate term for today's profession? Why?

11. Colleges and universities are spending millions of dollars on state-of-the-art facilities. Arguments for these this type of spending often center on the role campus recreation plays in the recruitment of new students. Explain your position regarding this type of spending—is it worth it? What about students who have no interest in campus recreation?

12. Discuss how Morale, Welfare, and Recreation contributes to combat readiness.

Endnotes

1. SHAPE American, "Fields of Study—Recreation and Leisure," Reston, VA: Society of Health and Physical Educators, http://www.shapeamerica.org/career/fields/recreation-leisure.cfm (Retrieved June 3, 2017).

2. ATRA, "What Is RT/TR?": https://www.atra-online.com/what/FAQ (Retrieved June 3, 2017).

3. F. Stavola Daly and R. Kunstler, "Therapeutic Recreation." In Human Kinetics (ed.), *Introduction to Recreation and Leisure* (Champaign, IL: Human Kinetics, 2006): 177–196.

4. R. Smith et al., *Inclusive and Special Recreation: Opportunities for Persons with Disabilities*, 6th ed. (Champaign, IL: Sagamore Publishing, 2011).

5. R. Williams, "Places, Models, and Modalities of Practice." In T. Robertson and T. Long (eds.), *Foundations of Therapeutic Recreation: Perceptions, Philosophies and Practices for the 21st Century* (Champaign, IL: Human Kinetics, 2008): 63–76.

6. Americans with Disabilities Act: www.ada.gov (Retrieved June 2, 2017).

7. D. R. Austin, M. E. Crawford, B. P. McCormick, & M. VanPuymbroeck, *Recreational Therapy: An Introduction*, 4th Ed. (Champaign, IL: Sagamore Publishing, 2015).

8. Fox Valley Special Recreation Association: www.fvsra.org/about/mission-vision.aspx (Retrieved June 2, 2017).

9. R. Williams, "Places, Models, and Modalities of Practice." In T. Robertson and T. Long (eds.), *Foundations of Therapeutic Recreation: Perceptions, Philosophies and Practices for the 21st Century* (Champaign, IL: Human Kinetics, 2008): 63–76.

10. N. J. Stumbo and C. A. Peterson, *Therapeutic Recreation Program Design: Principles and Procedures*, 5th ed. (San Francisco: Benjamin Cummings, 2009).

11. D. R. Austin, *Therapeutic Recreation: Processes and Techniques,* 7th Ed. (Champaign, IL: Sagamore Publishing, 2013).

12. R. Williams, "Places, Models, and Modalities of Practice." In T. Robertson and T. Long (eds.), *Foundations of Therapeutic Recreation: Perceptions, Philosophies and Practices for the 21st Century* (Champaign, IL: Human Kinetics, 2008): 63–76.

13. N. J. Stumbo and C. A. Peterson, *Therapeutic Recreation Program Design: Principles and Procedures*, 5th ed. (San Francisco: Benjamin Cummings, 2009): 63–76.

14. T. Long, "The Therapeutic Recreation Process." In T. Robertson and T. Long (eds.), *Foundations of Therapeutic Recreation: Perceptions, Philosophies and Practices for the 21st Century* (Champaign, IL: Human Kinetics, 2008): 79–97.

15. J. S. Kinney, T. Kinney, and J. Witman, "Therapeutic Recreation Modalities and Facilitation Techniques: A National Study," *Annual in Therapeutic Recreation* (Vol. 13, 2004): 59–79.

16. National Council for Therapeutic Recreation Certification, NCTRC Job Analysis: 2014 Job Analysis Study: http://nctrc.org/about-certification/national-job-analysis/ (Retrieved June 3, 2017).

17. Morgan's Wonderland, *Morgan's Wonderland*: www.morganswonderland.com/ (Retrieved June 3, 2017).

18. National Sports Center for the Disabled. http://nscd.org/ (Retrieved June 3, 2017).

19. Children's Hospital Boston, "Opening Doors for Youth: Project Adventure" (2010): www.openingdoorsforyouth.org/images/stories/let_the_fun_begin.pdf.

20. Healthy Independent Leisure & Lifestyles (HILLS): www.hills-inc.org (Retrieved June 3, 2017).

21. K. D. Miller, S. J. Schleien, J. Lausier, "Search for best practices in inclusive recreation: Programmatic findings," *Therapeutic Recreation Journal, 43*(1) (2009), 27–41.

22. U.S. Army MWR, "MWR History." www.armymwr.com/commander/history.aspx (Retrieved June 3, 2017).

23. Leipold, J. D. (2014). "Total Army Strong to succeed Army Family Covenant. https://www.army.mil/article/136184/_Total_Army_Strong__to_succeed_Army_Family_Covenant/ (Retrieved June 2, 2017).

24. C. Potter and L. Ogilvie, "Unique Groups." In Human Kinetics (ed.), *Introduction to Recreation and Leisure* (Champaign, IL: Human Kinetics, 2013): 217–250.

25. U.S. Air Force Health and Wellness: www.usafservices.com/Home/SpouseSupport/HealthandWellness.aspx (Retrieved June 2, 2017).

26. Fort Huachuca MWR: www.mwrhuachuca.com/ (Retrieved August 15, 2016).

27. Fort Carson MWR: https://carson.armymwr.com/programs/adventure-programs-and-education.

28. Marine Corps Community Services Camp Lejeune, "Marine Corps Family Team Building (MCFTB)": www.mccslejeune.com/mcftb/ (Retrieved July 15, 2016).

29. Navy MWR Programs: http://www.navymwr.org/programs/ (Retrieved June 2, 2017).

30. Little Rock Air Force Base: http://www.littlerock.af.mil/units/airman&familyreadiness/ (Retrieved June 2, 2017).

31. MCAS Miramar Memorial Golf Course: www.mccsmiramar.com/golfcourse.html (Retrieved June 2, 2017).

32. Army Community Service Outreach, Fort Campbell MWR: https://campbell.armymwr.com/programs/army-community-service-outreach (Retrieved June 3, 2017).

33. Ford Employees Recreation Association: https://web.vee.ford.com/FERA/index_files/FAQ.htm (Retrieved June 3, 2017).

34. Chevron Recreation: http://www.chevronretirees.org/sf-docs/default-source/benefits-messages/ChevRec_Navigational_Aid_04-09-14.pdf?sfvrsn=0 (Retrieved June 4, 2017).

35. The George Washington University School of Public Health and Health Services, "The Cost of Obesity" (April 2, 2013): http://publichealthonline.gwu.edu/cost-of-obesity-nphw-infographic-winner/.

36. http://healthcare.dmagazine.com/2013/01/11/employee-incentives-for-healthy-choices-reduce-health-care-costs/ (Retrieved June 3, 2017).

37. Fox News Travel, "Some Companies Pay Employees to Take Vacation": http://www.foxnews.com/travel/2014/08/14/companies-are-now-paying-employees-to-take-vacation/ (Retrieved June 30, 2016).

38. Eli Lilly Foundation, "Employee Giving": https://www.lilly.com/who-we-are/lilly-foundation/employee-giving (Retrieved June 3, 2017).

39. Target, "Volunteerism": https://corporate.target.com/corporate-responsibility/volunteerism (Retrieved June 15, 2016).

40. Forbes, "The Most Popular Employee Perks Of 2014": http://www.forbes.com/sites/kateharrison/2014/02/19/the-most-popular-employee-perks-of-2014/ (Retrieved August 1, 2016).

41. The University of Maine Campus Recreation: https://umaine.edu/campusrecreation/program/first-year/ (Retrieved April 15, 2017).

42. Colorado State University Campus Recreation: https://csurec.colostate.edu/programs/outdoor-program/ (Retrieved June 3, 2017).

43. University of Utah Campus Recreation, "Equipment Rental." http://campusrec.utah.edu/programs/outdoor-recreation-program/equipment-rental/ (Retrieved June 30, 2016).

44. San Diego State University, "Aztec Nights": http://go.sdsu.edu/aztecnights/Default.aspx (Retrieved July 26, 2016).

45. ClubCorp, "Company Profile": www.clubcorp.com/About-ClubCorp/Company-Profile (Retrieved July 13, 2016).

46. Community Associations Institute (CAI), "National and state Statistics Review for 2014": www.caionline.org/ (Retrieved June 23, 2016).

47. Starrett City Community: www.starrettcity.com/.

48. D. Lankarge and V. Nahorney, "The Evolution of Home Ownership," HomeInsight (2013): www.homeinsight.com/details.asp?url_id=7.

49. Sun City, AZ, Activities. www.suncityaz.org/ (Retrieved June 23, 2016).

CHAPTER

8

©Anton_Ivanov/Shutterstock.

Travel and Tourism

People always ask how travel has changed me. If I look back at who I was before I began traveling and compare that to who I am now, I would have to say that travel has made me a better and more well-rounded person. I'm way cooler now than I was at 25 when I first left to explore the world. Simply put, I'm a lot more awesome now than I used to be. In fact, I think travel makes everybody a more awesome person. We end our travels way better off than when we started.[1]

Learning Objectives

1.   Define travel and tourism.

2.   Understand the scope of tourism.

3.   Identify and explain tourism types.

4.   Describe technology advances in tourism.

INTRODUCTION

Tourism is the world's largest industry; spans across the public, nonprofit, and commercial sectors; is highly affected by changing technology; and encompasses culture, history, the environment, religion, the arts, agriculture, sport, education, and additional areas. Tourism is big business and is not confined to this country, as it is a global industry.

This chapter focuses on tourism and travel as well as the components that make up this massive industry. Before delving into the specifics of tourism, it is important to define what exactly travel and tourism are. On the surface, these may be easily defined, but think about the complexity. How far does one have to go to be considered a tourist? Do tourists have to stay overnight? Do tourists have to go outside of their home community? Does tourism have to be for pleasure or is business travel considered tourism?

Tourism is defined as "the activities of persons traveling to and staying in places outside their usual environments, for leisure, business, or other purposes."[2] In this instance, a person's usual environment means the community in which that person lives. The World Tourism Organization puts a time stipulation on the definition of tourism by saying that people must not remain in the location for more than a year.

The tourism industry can be divided into international and domestic tourism. International tourism is both inbound and outbound. Inbound tourism is when visitors from one country come to visit another country. Outbound tourism is when residents of one country leave and visit a different country. The other type of tourism is domestic tourism, when travelers stay within their own country.

Crossley, Jamieson, and Brayley do not separate commercial recreation and tourism because of the interconnectedness of these concepts.[3] They suggest that the tourism industry is made up of three parts. First, local commercial recreation is the entertainment, activities, and retail services within the community. It encompasses such venues and activities as theaters, festivals, water parks, golf courses, and shopping. The second piece of the industry is travel. *Travel* simply refers to the movement of people from one location to another. It may be carried out by plane, ship, railroad, bicycle, train, or other means. The last part of the commercial recreation and tourism industry is hospitality. *Hospitality* refers to the vast system of accommodations, food, and beverages that encompasses hotels, resorts, RV parks, bars, and restaurants. Tangential to the industry are the facilitators who make tourism happen. Travel agents, travel information services, convention and visitors bureaus, and meeting planners are facilitators of this industry and play an important role in making tourism happen.

SCOPE OF TOURISM

Overall, the travel and tourism industry has been described as one of the world's largest businesses. Approximately 2.67% of the gross domestic product in the United States is generated by travel and tourism, which is approximately $471.6 billion.[4] It is the nation's second-largest employer, second only to health services. In 2014 travel and tourism directly accounted for 5,302,000 jobs (3.6% of the U.S. total employment). These jobs include such things as accommodations, transportation, food and beverage, retail, and entertainment and attractions.[5]

According to the World Travel and Tourism Council, personal travel and tourism accounted for $660.3 billion (70.2%) and business travel accounted for another $280.2 billion (29.8.%) in 2014. Inbound international travel brings billions of dollars each year into the U.S. economy. These travelers accounted for 76 million people coming into the United States in 2015 and they spent $194.1 billion. Travelers coming into and out of the United States can be impacted by many events, including political and health issues. For example, the terrorist attack on the World Trade Center in New York City on September 11, 2001 had a significant impact on world travel, and particularly travel to the United States. Within the first 20 months after the attack, the U.S. economy was negatively affected by more than $74 billion. Political factors such as three months of protests in Thailand culminating in a week-long siege of the country's main airport (Suvarnabhumi), the political unrest in such places as Iraq, and the threats of terror attacks in Saudi Arabia and Indonesia can have a negative impact on tourism. In addition, health scares can negatively impact travel, including things such as the Zika virus, SARS, and cruise line–related illnesses. Despite these issues, tourism worldwide continues to grow.

International travelers come from a variety of locations, including Canada, Mexico, and the U.K. (**Table 8.1**). When these visitors come to the United States, they most often enter through New York, Miami, Los Angeles, and Honolulu.[6]

People living in the United States are also traveling abroad at high rates, with more than 68.2 million people traveling to other countries each year. The top five international destinations visited by travelers from the United States include Mexico (25.9 million), Canada (11.5 million), United Kingdom (2.8 million), Dominican Republic (2.7 million), and France (2.1 million).[7]

Many different kinds of organizations provide tourism opportunities. Thousands of commercial sponsors of tourist attractions and transportation services, theme parks and water parks, cruise ships, charter airline operators, group tour managers, hotel chains, sport arenas, entertainment venues, casinos, zoos, aquariums, wild animal parks, and numerous other businesses satisfy the tourism market. Many government agencies manage parks, historical sites, oceanfront areas, and other kinds of events that attract millions of recreational visitors.

Similarly, many nonprofit organizations sponsor sport events, cultural programs, educational tours, religious pilgrimages, and other special travel programs that serve millions of tourists each year. Armed forces morale, welfare, and recreation units offer travel services to men and women in uniform, and industrial and other business entities frequently schedule charter flights for their employees. Local convention and visitors bureaus facilitate vacation travel and promote regional tourist attractions.

Links Between Public and Commercial Sponsors
It is becoming apparent that both public and commercial agencies have an important stake in promoting successful tourism programs today. In the past, tourism has been regarded as a commercial economic phenomenon

TABLE 8.1 Visitors to the United States

	2014 Visitors to the United States	
Rank	**County**	**Arrivals**
1	Canada	23 million
2	Mexico	17.3 million
3	United Kingdom	3.97 million
4	Japan	3.58 million
5	Brazil	2.26 million
6	China	2.19 million
7	Germany	1.97 million
8	France	1.62 million
9	South Korea	1.45 million
10	Australia	1.28 million

Data from U.S. Department of Commerce International Trade Administration. International Visitation to the United States: A Statistical Summary of U.S. Visitation (2014). http://travel.trade.gov/outreachpages/download_data_table/2014_Visitation_Report.pdf

rooted in the private business sector. Today, with cities, states, and entire nations competing to attract large numbers of tourists because of their contribution to the overall economy, both government agencies and private entrepreneurs have joined forces in planning and promoting tourist attractions.

At another level, many states and local governments have moved vigorously into cooperative ventures to sponsor and promote varied forms of tourist attractions, both to heighten their positive image and to draw needed revenues and bolster local employment.

Case Study

Economic Impact: Where Does the Money Go?

Travel and tourism can have a tremendous economic impact on a community. There are direct, indirect, and induced expenditures that one must consider. Direct expenditures are those things purchased specifically for travel such as transportation, lodging, food, and activities. Indirect expenditures could be viewed as "respending" of the direct expenditures. They are the expenditures made for intermediate goods and services needed to do business with the tourist. For example, restaurants purchase food supplies from producers and souvenir shops purchase goods from suppliers. Part of the direct expenditure of food and souvenirs is used by the retailer to purchase the needed supplies, thus generating indirect expenditures. Lastly, there are induced expenditures. These expenditures account for the wages paid by companies to their employees in direct contact with tourists, and how the employees later spend these wages within the community. For example, induced expenditures include purchases made by the hotel manager for her own personal consumption such as a new car, bicycle, or gym membership. So, each dollar spent on tourism can be seen as having a ripple effect in the community as it purchases a hotel room, pays for hotel linens and cleaning supplies, and pays staff who buy goods to sustain their own lives.

Questions to Consider
1. Using a trip you have recently taken, list examples of direct, indirect, and induced expenditures.
2. If there is an economic crisis in the United States and tourism dropped by 75%, what industries would be hurt?
3. What are the advantages and disadvantages of being a major tourism community such as Las Vegas, Nevada or Daytona Beach, Florida?

Sources

Vellas, François. (October 25, 2011). The Indirect Impact of Tourism: An Economic Analysis. Third Meeting of T20 Tourism Ministers Paris, France. http://t20.unwto.org/sites/all/files/pdf/111020-rapport_vellas_en.pdf.

TOURISM TYPES

Tourists today seek to satisfy a remarkable range of personal interests and motivations.

Cruises

Over the past three decades, the growing prosperity of many Americans has made it possible for greater numbers of vacationers to indulge themselves with more varied forms of travel. Luxury cruise ships are no longer simply a vehicle for getting from one place to another or for extended, leisurely ocean voyages. Instead, they have evolved into floating amusement parks, health spas, classrooms, and nightclubs. The major cruise companies have developed huge new vessels and are catering to younger and less affluent individuals by offering relatively inexpensive short-term trips.

Today, more than 80 cruise ship lines offer a remarkable variety of vacation options afloat, ranging from small sail-propelled schooners to giant, luxurious ocean liners. In many cases, their attractions include gourmet meals, early morning workouts, nightlife and gambling, language classes, deck games, and visits to exotic ports. The cruise industry estimated 22.2 million passengers in 2015.

There are three major cruise line companies that dominate the industry: Carnival (48.1%), Royal Caribbean (23.1%), and Norwegian Cruise Lines (10.4%). These companies hold 81.6% of the industry market share, and the number of people taking cruises continues to increase each year. This is partially driven by larger capacity ships being built with a wider variety of amenities, more local ports, more destinations, and new on-board/on-shore activities that match demands of consumers.[8]

Case Study

International Travel: Is it Safe?

Adventurous travelers seek new and unknown destinations for their vacation destinations. They tend to stay away from the typical tourist spots and instead choose places that not many people place at the top of their vacation bucket list. Many countries have websites that help travelers determine the safety of such destinations. These websites assign a level of caution to the country, as well as things travelers should know before going. Use the following websites to answer the discussion questions.

Australia: http://smartraveller.gov.au/

Canada: http://travel.gc.ca/travelling/advisories

United Kingdom: https://www.gov.uk/foreign-travel-advice

United States: http://travel.state.gov/content/passports/en/alertswarnings/worldwide-caution.html

Questions to Consider
1. Look at each of these websites. What information is provided on each one? What is common among all of them?
2. Select a country that is on the list on one of the websites. Review the status of that country on each of the four websites. Do they agree in their assessment of travel to the country? Why or why not?

Tourism involves transportation in many forms, and international tourism frequently involves air travel.
© Mikael Damkier/Shutterstock.

Cruise ships continue to become more elaborate in the amenities offered to travelers.
© Bryan Busovicki/Shutterstock.

Cultural tourism involves experiencing the culture, whether it be indigenous or historical.
© WizData, Inc./Shutterstock.

Variety of Cruise Experiences   As in the overall tourism field, cruise passengers' motivations and interests take many different forms. While some travelers prefer luxurious, pampered, and relatively inactive trips, others enjoy excursions and activities that are demanding or that provide unusual leisure experiences. For example, a Cruise for the Cure benefiting Susan G. Komen for the Cure is a fundraising cruise where a portion of the cruise fee is donated to the charity.[9] The Ports of Apparitions Cruise stops in locations where passengers will search for ghosts and spirits, visit cemeteries, and hear paranormal presentations.[10]

Other specially designed cruises offer such themes as "clothing-optional" trips for "naturists," LGBT (lesbian, gay, bisexual, or transgender) cruises, golf cruises, trips combining shipboard lessons and stops at notable links, wine lovers cruises, and cruises specifically for people with disabilities, as well as many other unique travel tours with sea and land adventures.

Cultural and Historical Interests

The term *cultural* may have two possible meanings when applied to tourism motivation. It may suggest interest in attending major performing arts festivals, visiting famous art museums, or having other kinds of aesthetic experiences. Another meaning involves interest in being exposed to new and different cultures.

Cultural tourism is experiencing places and activities that promote the unique heritage, arts, traditions, and history of a location. This can include museums, art galleries, tours, events, and more. Cultural tourism allows travelers to learn about the diversity and character of the place.

The National Assembly of State Arts Agencies found 118.1 million people, representing 56% of all U.S. adult travelers, included a cultural, arts, heritage, or historic activity while on a one-way trip of 50 miles or more during the previous year. Of these travelers, visiting an historic site such as an historic community or building was the most popular cultural activity (31%), followed by visiting a museum (24%), visiting an art gallery (15%), and seeing live theater (14%).[11]

The purpose of cultural and historical tourism is to experience people and history in other places and countries because it helps us better understand and appreciate what currently exists and how that emerged. Cultural tourism may include exposure to such regional or ethnically different locations as the Amish countryside in Pennsylvania, smaller communities throughout French Canada where the culture is determinedly Gallic, or visits to Native American reservations throughout the West—destinations that have special appeal for many Europeans. It may also involve what Canadian authorities term "heritage tourism," with trips to see old mines, factories, or prisons that have been redesigned to provide today's visitors with a fuller understanding of the past.

Increasingly, festivals or holiday events commemorate famous battles of the past, scenes of the Civil War, or other historic events. Even rodeos, which illustrate the real-life work of cowboys in the American West, or lumberjack contests and similar competitions at state fairs, serve as experiences that make this kind of tourism meaningful.

Linked to this type of cultural and historic exploration, such organizations as American Youth Hostels or the Elderhostel movement, which serves older travelers, combine educational and cultural exposures with what are usually short-term stays in foreign lands or distant locations.

Sport Tourism

Sport tourism became a major force in the tourism marketplace beginning in the mid-1980s. There have always been major sporting events that draw tens of thousands and even millions of people (**Table 8.2**).

ANCESTRAL TOURISM

Americans are particularly interested in their family history and spend millions of dollars annually on ancestral tourism. Ancestral tourism involves such experiences as traveling to historical sites, visiting international destinations where ancestors were known or suspected to originate, attending conferences and workshops on genealogy, and so forth. The industry has continued to grow as Americans turn inward toward an understanding of their roots.

TABLE 8.2   Attendance Figures for Major Sporting Events

League	Games	Attendance	Year
Major League Baseball	2418	73,760,032	2015
National Football League	254	17,342,667	2015
National Basketball Association	1230	21,905,470	2015
NCAA bowl games	35	1,714,617	2013–2014
Indianapolis 500	1	Approx. 300,000	Annually

Data from ESPN Attendance reports 2015. Available at: espn.go.com/mlb/attendance/_/year/2015; http://espn.go.com/nfl/attendance/_/year/2015; Bowl Attendance figures: http://www.al.com/sports/index.ssf/2014/01/college_football_2013-14_bowl.html; The most-attended sporting events in the country? Races, baby http://sports.yahoo.com/nascar/blog/from_the_marbles/post/The-most-attended-sporting-events-in-the-country;_ylt=A0LEVv73oN1W2QUAC.snnIIQ;_ylu=X3oDMTEycXVsZXBqBGNvbG8DYmYxBHBvcwM4BHZ0aWQQDjE3NDdfMQRzZWMDc3l-?urn=nascar,243650.

Sport tourism has traditionally focused on two groups—participants and spectators. People travel to participate in such activities as softball tournaments, basketball tournaments, or to play golf. Arguably more common is travel to be a spectator at such events as the Super Bowl, NASCAR races, or the Kentucky Derby. Sport tourism has many different dimensions and means to experience sport. Here is an overview of the elements of sport tourism.

Sporting events and sport places both serve as attractions. The 1896 Olympic stadium sits in downtown Athens and receives more visitors than the now-closed Athens 2006 Olympic site. The College Football Hall of Fame, Professional Baseball Hall of Fame, and the NCAA Hall of Champions all draw many visitors. Visitations to sport facilities when teams are out of town or out of season are now commonplace. The Indianapolis Pacers and Bankers Life Fieldhouse charge an admission when visiting the fieldhouse, which goes to local charities. Yankee Stadium is probably the most visited baseball stadium in the United States because it holds a rich heritage of baseball greatness.

Sporting Events   Major sporting events draw large numbers of tourists and have significant impacts on the local, regional, and national economies. The Indianapolis Motor Speedway, home of the Indianapolis 500, is the site of the oldest auto race in the world. The Indianapolis Motor Speedway operated a single race from 1911 to 1993. In 1994, the Brickyard 400, a major new NASCAR race, was initiated and is now called the "Crown Royal 400 at the Brickyard." Six years later a Formula One race was added, making Indianapolis the race capital of the world. These events pale by comparison to mega sport events such as the Olympic Games. The 2012 London Summer Olympics drew 9.0 million people.[12]

Resorts   Resorts use sport as a means to attract tourists. For example, the Tourism Authority of Thailand uses resorts and their crystal-clear oceans to attract scuba divers. In addition, the country has more than 100 world-class golf courses with very reasonable greens fees. In the United States, golf and tennis resorts are abundant.

National and international sporting events, such as the Montreal Olympics, brand their events with logos promoting recognition among visitors, advertisers, and participants.

© meunierd/Shutterstock.

The Kiawah Island Golf Resort in South Carolina boasts five championship golf courses and was ranked the number one tennis resort in the world by tennisresortsonline.com.[13] Resorts also cater to winter sports such as skiing and snowboarding.

Cruises and Tours   Cruises were previously discussed in this chapter. However, sport cruises add a different dimension and have themes such as baseball greats, fans of specific teams, running, cycling, and golf. Companies such as Sports Travel and Tours set up sports-oriented tours for individuals and groups. They offer Pro Football Hall of Fame Enshrinement Festival tours, baseball road trips with stops at multiple baseball parks in a region, and Kentucky Derby Tours.[14]

Outdoor/Adventure Sports   The sale of outdoor equipment continually increases. This is an indicator of the popularity of outdoor adventure sports. Traditional outdoor vacations feature hiking, climbing, and fishing. People who are more adventurous can experience dog sledding, fly-in hiking, glacier tours, and heli-skiing, among other sports.

Fantasy Camps   Sport fantasy camps allow participants to train alongside current and previous professional sports players and often on the same fields and courts. These camps target diehard fans who want to be immersed in their favorite teams and play alongside players they have watched for years. Baseball offers many fantasy sport camps, usually during spring training. Participants wear the team jersey, get instruction from former players, and hear their name announced by legendary announcers. For $10,000 Duke fans over age 35 can participate in the K Academy with Coach Mike Krzyzewski and many former Duke players such as Mike Gminski, Christian Laettner, J. J. Redick, and Jason Williams.[15] Other sports stars such as Wayne Gretzky, Michael Jordan, Richard Petty, and Chris Evert offer their own fantasy camps as well.

Sport tourism has a major impact on the tourism industry whether the tourist is visiting a destination to participate or experience the attractions. Sport can be the reason to visit the community or a part of the overall vacation.

Religion-Based Tourism

Centuries ago, one of the motivations spurring international travel was pilgrimages. Today, religion-oriented travel is one of the industry's fastest-growing segments. Tours highlight Christian, Jewish, Muslim, and Buddhist places of importance.

Religious tourism, also called spiritual tourism, encompasses many aspects of religion. First, pilgrimages are quite common where individuals take long journeys to experience a location of religious significance. For example, Mecca in Saudi Arabia is the most sacred place for the Islamic religion. It is the place where all Muslims point themselves during their daily prayers, and they are encouraged to make the pilgrimage to Mecca at least once in their lifetime. Another popular pilgrimage destination is to the Western Wall in Jerusalem, which is a Jewish holy site.[16]

A second aspect of religious tourism is missionary travel where people travel to other locations as part of a religious group or church affiliation. On these trips, people help the local community with education, recreation, construction of needed facilities, health care, and economic development.

Third, conventions and crusades are held annually, bringing together people of specific religions for worship. For example, each summer 6000 members of Jehovah's Witness gather in Bloomington, Illinois, for their district convention.

Last, religious tourism has a focus on visiting attractions and locations that have religious significance. Attractions such as the Basilica de Guadalupe in Mexico, the Vatican in Italy, or the Reclining Buddha in Thailand are popular to those within these religions but also those outside of the religion.

Nauvoo, Illinois, has become an American religion-based tourism site. It was home to the Latter-Day Saints (Mormons) from 1839 to 1842 and has received increased tourism focus over the last 25 years as the Latter-Day

Religious-based tourism draws people to visit such places as St. Peter's Square in Vatican City, Italy.

© Sergii Figurnyi/Shutterstock.

Saint Church and nonprofit groups have restored much of the original area and in 2002 replaced the 1840 temple. Tourism exceeds 1.5 million annually.

Often, such trips are not narrowly denominational but bring members of various faiths together to explore their linked heritages and contrast their present beliefs and practices.

Health-Related Tourism

Recognizing that religious travel is for many people a means of obtaining spiritual well-being and emotional health, it should be stressed that for many other individuals health needs represent a primary motivation for travel. In Europe, particularly, visits to traditional health spas that are based on natural mineral springs are being gradually replaced by stays at more modern health and fitness centers. These destinations often combine varied forms of exercise, nutritional care, massage, yoga, and other holistic approaches to health care to provide a fuller range of services to visitors. Whereas weight reduction or recovery from alcohol or drug addiction is the primary focus of many such centers, others involve a much broader approach to achieving "wellness."

A recent trend related to health-motivated travel is medical tourism. In response to rising healthcare and insurance costs in their home countries, citizens from the United States and Great Britain are increasingly seeking cheaper medical and surgical care in developing countries such as India, Thailand, and Costa Rica. While some may think that medical tourism is of lesser quality and focuses only on elective surgeries, this is not accurate, as many healthcare facilities are accredited and have highly trained specialists. Different funding structures and the lower cost of living in many countries when compared to the United States often results in a 40%+ savings on such procedures as cosmetic, dental, and cardiovascular surgeries.[17] Medical tourism packages usually include luxury room accommodations in hospitals and are often combined with flights, transportation, resort hotel bookings, interpreters, and airport concierge services.

Ecotourism and Adventure Travel

With the growth of environmental concerns and programs over the past few decades, ecotourism has emerged and is deeply concerned with the preservation and protection of the natural environment. The International Ecotourism Society (IETS) defines ecotourism as "responsible travel to natural areas that conserves the environment and improves the well-being of local people."

Ecotourism may be carried on at various levels of personal challenge and comfort. For example, labeled as eco-luxurious, the Galapagos Culinary Adventure in Ecuador is designed for the active food enthusiast who wants to experience food sustainability, learn about natural history, enjoy activities such as deep sea fishing, and view wildlife such as the famous Galapagos tortoises in their natural habitat.[18]

A more rustic eco-vacation could have travelers camping in the Brazilian rainforest, learning about the indigenous people in the region.

The concept of ecotourism is entrenched in the principles of sustainable tourism. Sustainable tourism advocates tourism activities that are compatible with the ecological processes, sociocultural characteristics, and economic structure of the destination and that enhance the geographical character of a place.

As a variant of this approach, some tourist companies offer "action vacations" that provide the traveler the chance to visit foreign lands not simply to lie on a beach but to take part in an archaeological dig, study wildlife or the local environment systematically, teach English to children, or be involved in healthcare projects. As a result of heightened interest among tourists to make voluntary contributions to the communities they visit, a new form of tourism, *volunteer tourism*, is gaining popularity across the globe. Tours catering to "volun-tourists" provide cultural immersion along with opportunities for self-fulfillment through volunteer work. For example, Restoration Works International, a California-based nonprofit group, offers tours focusing on the renovation of Buddhist temples in Nepal. Another nonprofit, Project Abroad, plans trips for groups based on age and interest. There are trips for teens in high school, university students, gap year (18–19) young adults, professionals (30+), and those 50+. They will do such things as teaching English to children, preserving ecosystems, and building sustainable farms in places like Madagascar, Bolivia, and Fiji.[19]

With less of a social service orientation and more of an adventure recreation focus, some vacations may involve high-risk adventure pastimes such as trail rides through wild country, hang gliding, mountain climbing, or whitewater rafting on turbulent streams. Extreme versions of adventure tourism may involve the opportunity to track down tornadoes, offered as a package deal by a number of companies in the Midwest or Southwest regions of the United States during the tornado seasons of the year.[20]

Case Study

. . . .

Defining Ecotourism

The International Ecotourism Society is about *uniting conservation, communities, and sustainable travel*. Those who implement, participate in, and market ecotourism activities should adopt the following ecotourism principles:

◆ Minimize physical, social, behavioral, and psychological impacts.
◆ Build environmental and cultural awareness and respect.
◆ Provide positive experiences for both visitors and hosts.
◆ Provide direct financial benefits for conservation.
◆ Generate financial benefits for both local people and private industry.
◆ Deliver memorable interpretive experiences to visitors that help raise sensitivity to host countries' political, environmental, and social climates.
◆ Design, construct, and operate low-impact facilities.
◆ Recognize the rights and spiritual beliefs of the indigenous people in your community and work in partnership with them to create empowerment.

Ecotourism is touted as being a positive vacation option for those seeking a little more adventure, a different experience, and want to be environmentally conscious. However, there are some downsides to ecotourism that can cause harm to the very people ecotourism is designed to protect. The negatives include such things as follows:

◆ As the popularity of a destination grows, resources become overused. For example, too many people can disrupt the natural habitats of wildlife. This negatively impacts their mating and feeding habits.
◆ Ecotourism destinations are often in remote locations, requiring an increased carbon footprint to arrive by plane or motor vehicle.
◆ Developers see the potential revenue due to increased traffic and build resorts, stores, and other amenities to cater to the crowds without regard for the impact on the community and environment. These developments send money back to the corporations and take it away from the local economy.
◆ Increased tourism causes inflated prices for food and services, which is passed on to the local residents who must pay this same inflated cost.
◆ Increased tourism increases the number of jobs in a community, but the jobs are often low paying in the service industry.

Questions to Consider

1. What other positives and negatives can be associated with ecotourism?
2. Overall, is ecotourism a good or bad thing? Why?
3. Investigate the pros and cons of ecotourism further. Have a class debate to argue your points.

Sources

Woods, A. Problems with Ecotourism. USA Today. http://traveltips.usatoday.com/problems-ecotourism-108359.html.
International Ecotourism Society. Principles of Ecotourism. http://www.ecotourism.org/what-is-ecotourism.

Other well-heeled adventurers today embark on expeditions to climb the Matterhorn, fly to the North Pole, break the sound barrier in a Russian MIG-25 fighter jet, or pay deposits to take suborbital rides into space (defined as 62 miles up) scheduled to be offered by commercial rocket builders.

Hedonistic Forms of Tourism

Still other forms of tourism are designed to provide hedonistic forms of pleasure to participants. Gambling clearly represents the most popular such activity, with millions of individuals traveling each year to major casinos throughout the world or enjoying gaming as a convenient amenity on ocean cruises or major airline flights.

At another level, thousands of young people each year roam through the Far East, including unscheduled, free wheeling trips through Thailand, Cambodia, and Nepal, partly to experience their exotic environments, but also to take part in the drug culture that is readily available and inexpensive in these regions.

Finally, a form of pleasure-seeking tourism that has emerged throughout the world involves the search for sex. The sex industry has become extremely profitable, providing substantial revenues not only to individuals and the networks involved in human trafficking but to some nations that have come to depend on sex industry profits. Sex tourism thrives in countries such as Ukraine where the women are poor and unprotected by the government and law enforcement. Odessa is a Ukrainian port that has become a principal hub for international sex trade. This area is infused with police corruption and organized crime, making human trafficking and the sex industry thrive. In Costa Rica, prostitution is legal. However, prostitutes are supposed to register, be regularly examined by a doctor, and carry an ID card. Many do not, and so the sex industry is quite risky, but rampant.[21]

Hosteling and AirBnB

Many travelers are choosing cheaper and/or more social travel options by staying in hostels. Hostels are low-cost accommodations where people rent a bed in a dormitory-style facility. Guests share bathroom facilities and often have a common area for social interaction. Some hostels have private rooms for one to four people at an increased cost. En-suites are also becoming more popular. Prices for hostels vary depending on the location and amenities. For example, a hostel in Milan, Italy with rooms in a dorm with breakfast go for $25. A private room with two beds, breakfast, and sheets costs $68. A hostel two blocks from the beach in San Diego with the same amenities as Milan runs $32 per night.

Gambling is a growth industry in the United States, and it is a recognized form of personal recreation even if it is not perceived as psychologically and socially beneficial.
© Elena Ray/Shutterstock.

Case Study

. . . .

Park District to Consider Video Gaming

The Bensenville Park District in Illinois is considering adding video gaming machines to their White Pines Golf Course. To do this, they would need to ask to lift a ban on video gaming that was instituted in 2009 by the county when the state legalized video gambling. At the time of legalization, DuPage County opted out, making the video games illegal. However, since then, 10 cities within the county have opted back in so they could have video gaming machines. The Bensenville Park District board gathered data on the revenue from gaming and found that one business in Addison, IL, made $227,695 and three neighboring towns made at least $46,000 in profit in the previous year. In addition to the park district making money, the state of Illinois takes 25%, the county takes 5%, and the agency/business takes the rest.

Because tens of thousands of people visit White Pines each year to golf or attend weddings and other events, John Wassinger, President of the park board, said he believes video gambling machines could generate "a significant amount of money." He said, "The park district is always looking for new sources of revenue to offset rising expenses at the golf course."

Questions to Consider

1. Discuss the pros and cons of Bensenville Park District adding video gaming to the White Pines Golf Course.
2. Have a debate on this issue. Develop talking points and counterpoints for each side.
3. What steps should the park district take regarding this issue (e.g., public input)?

Source

Sanchez, R. (March 3, 2016). Bensenville Park District may ask DuPage County to lift video gambling ban. Daily Herald. http://www.dailyherald.com/article/20160303/news/160309625/.

Case Study

. . . .

The Growth of Marijuana Tourism

Licensed marijuana stores in Colorado and Washington can legally sell marijuana without a prescription to people 21 and over. Washington has begun to capitalize on marijuana tourism, seeing the revenue it can bring to the state. For example, the Original CannaBus Tour Company offers tours exploring Seattle's exploding cannabis culture, offering airport pick-up and hotel drop off with a stop at a legal recreational marijuana shop. Kush Tourism promotes cannabis-related lodging, tours, and activities such as Seattle airport layover specials, tours of cannabis growing facilities, and cannabis-friendly painting classes. Private clubs are opening catering to marijuana-using locals and tourists.

Questions to Consider

1. What are the pros and cons of advertising marijuana tourism as a regular part of tourism activities and attractions through the state tourism bureau (Go-Washington) or local convention and visitors bureaus?
2. If more states legalize marijuana, will advertisement of marijuana-related activities increase? Why or why not?
3. Look at how Washington and Colorado advertise marijuana-related activities. Compare and contrast their approaches.

Sources

Cogswell, D. (June 12, 2014). Marijuana Tourism Comes to Washington. http://www.travelpulse.com/news/destinations/marijuana-tourism-comes-to-washington.html.
The Original Cannabus. http://originalcannabus.com/2.
Kush Tourism. http://kushtourism.com/.

Hostels have traditionally been places in the countryside for young hikers to stop off for the night before continuing on their trek. Although this is a portion of the users of hostels, hostels are also starting to serve adults who want a simpler and less expensive place to stay. These people do not require the amenities of large-scale hotels such as room service and provided toiletries, and they can bring their own towels.

Hostels are most known for the social aspects. The common rooms entice conversations among guests. It is not unusual for people staying at hostels to get to know each other and go off for adventures together.

Part of the charm of hostels, in addition to the price, is that some can be quite unique. For example:

Carbisdale Castle Hostel (Scotland): The castle is a popular venue for groups, families, and weddings. Local attractions include distilleries, nature walks, and new mountain biking routes. This hostel is said to have great facilities, a statue gallery and art collection, a coffee shop, a restaurant, and a resident ghost.

Stockholm af Chapman & Skeppsholmen (Sweden): This hostel is an old sailing ship.

Stockholm 'Långholmen' (Sweden): Housed in a converted prison, this hostel was voted best hostel in Sweden in 2008. Inside this youth hostel visitors can see the prison museum, illustrating 250 years of prison history.

Point Montara Lighthouse (Montara, California): On the rugged California coast, 25 miles south of San Francisco, an historic 1875 fog signal station and lighthouse have been preserved and restored by HI-AYH and the California Department of Parks and Recreation, in cooperation with the Coast Guard.[22] AirBnB started in 2008 as a marketplace to connect hosts with unique spaces to rent with guests needing accommodations. Since its inception, AirBnB has expanded from an air mattress in the home of AirBnB's founders to the ability to rent shared spaces, private rooms, and entire apartments all around the world. This company has rentals in 190 countries and over 34,000 cities. Hosts set the pricing, rules for rentals, who can stay, and when they can stay. Both hosts and guests rate the other, and so the quality of the rental as well as the quality of the guest is known.

Some AirBnB options have become quite unique and include castles, boats, tree houses, tipis, and igloos. Travelers can stay in a glass tree house in Athens, Georgia, a 100-year-old houseboat docked under the Eiffel Tower, or in the St. Pancras Clock Tower guest suite in London.[23]

Food Travel

Food tourism is a relatively new phenomenon and a term that was first coined in 1998. The World Food Travel Association (WFTA) defines food tourism as "the pursuit and enjoyment of unique and memorable food and drink experiences, both far and near."[24]

Food tourism is quite vast and can include such things as attending cooking schools, visiting cooking supply stores, going on culinary tours, attending food festivals, visiting farmers' markets, stopping at street food carts or microbrews, or going to wineries and distilleries. The increase in food tourism is quite evident on television channels such as the Food Network and the Travel Channel. Andrew Zimmern consumes mainstream and exotic cuisine in all parts of the world, and Guy Fieri travels across the United States finding the best drive-ins, diners, and dives.

Some of the more extravagant food tourism happens with tours to well-known gastric regions. Here are a few examples:

◆ The Hess Collection Eastern Mediterranean Wine Cruise: Traveling from Athens to Venice, this 9-day cruise features the Hess Collection's Director of Winemaking, private parties, special tastings and winemaker's dinner, gourmet culinary program, and optional wine-focused shore excursions exclusive to the group.[25]

◆ *The Czech Republic: Independent Breweries and World Heritage Sites*: Starting in Prague, this 9-day trip features a tour through the small Czech breweries that are still adhering to the traditional methods of beer making.[26]

◆ *Chiang Mai Thai Cooking School:* This internationally renowned cooking school in Thailand teaches tourists how to cook Thai food. Classes run for 1 to 5 days and feature topics such as introduction to Thai ingredients, making curry pastes, and vegetable carving.[27]

TECHNOLOGY AND TOURISM

Technology has changed the way people plan their travel, move through the trip, and reflect on the experience. The Internet has now surpassed word of mouth as the primary source for location inspiration and travel information. When people are researching where to go, where to stay, and how to get there, they rely on many different websites and apps. For example, TripAdvisor.com website, which has 350 million unique monthly users,[28] allows tourists to post ratings of tourism businesses and discuss travel experiences with others. Websites and apps that monitor and alert you to flight price changes (e.g., FareCompare.com and webjet.com) and track flight performance (e.g., flight on time ratings, delay statistics, and cancellation history) are also becoming increasingly popular among travelers. Prior to arriving at a destination, the Internet allows travelers to research destinations and entertainment options, advance purchase tickets, hire a guide, book train tickets, rent a car, and many other things to make travel easier.

Technology also has a major impact during the trip. Social media has skyrocketed in the last several years where people post photos and commentary on Facebook, and Twitter, and Instagram immediately. Photos can also be uploaded to such sites as Flickr and Shutterfly to share. In addition, travelers are using travel blog sites such as bootsnall.com and travelblog.org to send notes or electronic postcards, photos, and sound recordings to others during the course of the trip. Smartphones are indispensable to many travelers. Smartphones are used in place of their cameras, and the GPS features help travelers find destinations in a city or a national park. These same phones will keep track of tickets, allow you to pay tabs, or search for needed information in the moment. If traveling internationally, there are many apps that can help navigate a new country, such as those that translate the language or help understand money conversion. After the vacation, technology is used for reflection on the journey via photos, updating social media posts, or reviewing the accommodations and destinations via the appropriate websites. Regardless of the trip taken or destination visited, technology plays a key role in how it is planned and experienced.

Case Study

. . . .

A Traveler's Best App

Many travel magazines and websites select their top travel-related apps. Here are a few examples on the list of favorites:

1. TripAdvisor: Checks hotel and restaurant reviews.
2. Hotel Tonight: Finds last-minute discounted hotels with bookings available until 2:00 AM.
3. TripIt: Keeps your travel itineraries and allows them to sync to your personal calendar.
4. Free Wi-Fi Finder: Locates free Internet hotspots in the area.
5. Google Translate: Translates 60+ languages, with 17 of those being voice activated.
6. Kayak: Allows you to rebook cancelled flights and find hotels nearby.
7. WhatsApp Messenger: Shares texts and pictures for free when traveling abroad, eliminating international charges.
8. Packing Pro: Creates packing lists based on number of children and adults and days traveled; takes into account temperature, destination, and laundry preferences; allows for custom lists.
9. OANDA Currency Converter: Translates any currency quickly, can factor in ATM charges and credit card rates.
10. GateGuru: Helps guide travelers through long delays, has maps of terminals, airport restaurant reviews, and average wait time going through security.

Questions to Consider

1. Develop your own app by creating an outline of the contents of the app. What would the app look like? Would it be a free app or have an associated charge? What makes your app different from what is already on the market?
2. Do some research to find other apps that could be beneficial to people traveling domestically and internationally.

Summary

Tourism involves huge sections of the leisure-service field, is provided by many different kinds of organizations, and has developed into a complex discipline in terms of job specialization and career opportunities. Tourism has a major economic impact on the United States and the rest of the world. Inbound and outbound travelers help stimulate economies domestically and abroad.

Travel and tourism represent diverse forms of leisure activity, with immense economic revenues. This chapter describes some of the most popular forms of tourism, such as cruises, cultural and historic interests, sport, religion, health, ecotourism, hedonism, hostels, and food tourism.

The Internet and smartphone apps have had a major impact on pre-trip planning, the trip itself, and the post-trip reflection. The Internet and apps play an important role in researching destinations, navigating through them, and is a means to share experiences through posting commentaries on the trip or sharing photos with friends and family. Technological advances will continue to affect travel and tourism in the years to come.

Questions for Class Discussion or Essay Examination

1. Tourism may be carried on for many purposes: exploration of different environments, cultural or educational purposes, adventure and risk, or hedonism. Give examples of such forms of tourism, based on class members' experiences.

   _____

   _____

   _____

   _____

2. Select either sport tourism or cruises and describe their role today in the tourism industry, including current trends and new formulas for appealing to the public.

   _____

   _____

_____

_____

3. Discuss the role of the Internet in tourism. How do you use the Internet for your travel plans?

_____

_____

_____

4. Consider the different generations within your family. Which type of tourism would most appeal to each group? Which would be least appealing? Why?

_____

_____

_____

5. Discuss the impact of the tourism industry on the world economy.

_____

_____

_____

_____

6. Define cultural and historic tourism. Give examples of these types of destinations.

_____

_____

_____

_____

7. Define ecotourism. Give examples of these types of destinations. Do you see this form of tourism increasing or declining in the future? Why?

_____

_____

_____

_____

Endnotes

1. Kepnes, Matt, "Why Travel Makes You An Awesome Person," _Huffington Post Travel_ (December 3, 2013): http://www.huffingtonpost.com/matt-kepnes/travel-is-awesome_b_4344632.html. (Accessed February 27, 2016).

2. J. C. Crossley, L. M. Jamieson, and R. E. Brayley, _Introduction to Commercial Recreation and Tourism: An Entrepreneurial Approach,_ 6th ed. (Champaign, IL: Sagamore Publishing, 2012): 11.

3. J. C. Crossley, L. M Jamieson., and R. E Brayley, _Introduction to Commercial Recreation and Tourism: The Entrepreneurial Approach,_ 6th ed. (Champaign, IL: Sagamore Publishing, 2012).

4. World Travel & Tourism Council, "Travel & Tourism, Economic Impact Report 2015, United States of America" (February 28, 2016): http://www.wttc.org/-/media/files/reports/economic%20impact%20 research/countries%202015/unitedstatesofamerica2015.pdf.

5. Ibid.

6. U.S. Department of Commerce International Trade Administration, "International Visitation to the United States: A Statistical Summary of U.S. Visitation (2014)": http://travel.trade.gov/outreachpages /download_data_table/2014_Visitation_Report.pdf.

7. U.S. Department of Commerce International Trade Administration, "U.S. Resident Travel to International Destinations Increased 10 Percent in 2014" (July 24, 2015): http://travel.trade.gov /outreachpages/download_data_table/2014_Outbound_Analysis.pdf.

8. Cruise Market Watch (March 1, 2016): http://www.cruisemarketwatch.com.

9. Cruise for the Cure (February 28, 2016): http://cruiseforthecure.com.

10. Theme Cruise Finder (February 28, 2016): http://themecruisefinder.com/CruiseAds/.

11. National Assembly of State Arts Agencies (NASAA), "Cultural Visitor Profile" (February 28, 2016): www.nasaa-arts.org/Research/Key-Topics/Creative-Economic-Development/Cultural-Visitor-Profile.php.

12. CNN World, "London Olympics by the Numbers" (July 27, 2012): www.cnn.com/2012/07/27 /world/olympics-numbers/.

13. Tennis Resorts Online, "Top 100 Tennis Resorts & Camps For 2015" (March 7, 2016): http://www.tennisresortsonline.com/trofiles/top-100-tennis-resorts-and-camps.cfm#Resorts.

14. Sports Travel and Tours (February 28, 2016): www.sportstravelandtours.com/index.php.

15. K Academy (February 28, 2016): http://kacademy.com.

16. Brie Cadman, "Top Ten Religious Pilgrimages," Divine Caroline (February 28, 2016): http://www.divinecaroline.com/entertainment/top-ten-religious-pilgrimages-0.

17. Patients Beyond Borders, "Medical Tourism Statistics and Facts" (February 28, 2016): www.patientsbeyondborders.com/medical-tourism-statistics-facts.

18. Greenloons, "Galapagos Culinary Adventure" (February 28, 2016): http://greenloons.com/ 322-galapagos-wildlife-culinary-adventure.

19. Projects Abroad, "Volunteer and Intern Abroad" (March 10, 2016): http://www.projects-abroad.org.

20. Storm Chasing Adventure Tours (February 28, 2016): www.stormchasing.com.

21. The Real Costa Rica (March 1, 2016): http://www.therealcostarica.com/travel_costa_rica/ adult_entertainment_costa_rica.html.

22. Hostel World (March 27, 2016): http://www.hostelworld.com.

23. Airbnb: https://www.airbnb.com

24. World Food Travel Association, "What is Food Tourism?" (June 2, 2017): http://www.worldfoodtravel .org/cpages/what-is-food-tourism.

25. Food & Wine Trails (March 1, 2016): http://foodandwinetrails.com/hess_2016.

26. Beertrips.com (March 1, 2016): www.beertrips.com/trips.html.

27. Chiang Mai Thai Cookery School (March 1, 2016): www.thaicookeryschool.com/index.html.

28. TripAdvisor (March 1, 2016): https://www.tripadvisor.com/.

Sport as Leisure

People desire spectator sport opportunities, and professional and amateur sports organizations have created substantial sporting events to fulfill that niche. [Many others] seek more active participation, and leisure professionals have attempted to create recreation sport opportunities for them, [in] public and private, nonprofit and for-profit, college and university, and employee service recreation settings.[1]

Learning Objectives

1. Explain how sport, from the perspective of a participation and a spectator, fits into leisure.

2. Understand the scope of sport.

3. Identify and explain sport participation and sport spectating.

4. Describe the influence of media on sport.

5. Discuss the impact of youth sport on the participants, looking at participation, injuries, and motivation.

INTRODUCTION

Sport, on its various levels, represents a major area of recreational programming today and constitutes a powerful economic force through the attraction for people of every age and background. Sport has a sociocultural heritage binding it to the Western ideal of leisure. This chapter presents an overview of sport, emphasizing its role within the leisure spectrum, the rapid expansion of sport over the past several decades, and the prospects for the years ahead as a physical pursuit, a leisure activity, and a maturing business.

SPORT AS POPULAR RECREATION

Sport in American society is viewed variously from a narrow to broad perspective, based on who is defining sport. A day of watching ESPN might convince an individual that football, basketball, soccer, baseball, poker, golf, or other traditional team and individual contests are major sports. Changing television channels might convince someone else that hunting and fishing are major sports. Watching

213

the Olympic games broadens the idea of sport to include winter and summer sports that may or may not be common in the United States. Our society tends to focus on sports that are portrayed in sporting magazines, in the broadcast media, on the Internet, and that are frequented in local communities. University and professional sport programs have strengthened the image of traditional sport programs. More than 100,000 people may attend a college football game while 1000 or less may attend a college cross-country event, and a women's volleyball match may draw fewer than 100 people.

Defining sport is grounded in personal perspectives. The literature of sport is inconclusive about what sport actually entails. *Sport* is defined as "an activity that is governed by a set of rules or customs and often engaged in competitively."[2] The open dictionary defines sports as "an activity involving physical exertion and skill in which an individual or team competes against another or others for entertainment."[3] The idea of sport and games as synonymous has fallen out of favor, except among some sport sociologists.

Sport management professionals generally define sports as physical activities demanding exertion and skill, involving competition, and carried on with both formal rules and general standards of etiquette and fair play. Some authorities describe them more concisely as activities with clear performance standards involving competition through physical exertion, governed by norms defining role relationships, typically performed by members of organized groups with the goal of achieving a reward through the defeat of other participants.

Clearly, sport activities, in terms of both participation and spectator involvement, represent key leisure interests for many youth and adults today. Apart from amateur, school, and college play, there are professional sports, which are a form of big business. They are moneymakers, sponsored by powerful commercial interests and promoted by advertising, public relations, television, radio, magazines, newspapers, and the Internet, and bolstered by the loyalty of millions of fans who identify closely with their favorite teams and star athletes.

In this chapter, the broadest possible view of sport is adopted. Traditional sport, as suggested in the preceding definitions, is given primary consideration, but from a leisure perspective the idea of sport extends beyond what occurs on the athletic field to outdoor recreation areas and to noncompetitive activities.

The Evolution of Sport and Leisure

The early history of sport was more closely related to military preparation than to leisure. The ancient Greek Olympic games were contests related to military prowess and included running with and without armor, wrestling, boxing, and discus as primary events. The earliest sporting events were frequently linked to festivals or religious celebrations.

As societies progressed, the evolution of sport as a social phenomenon seemed inevitable. At the beginning of the twentieth century, sport was seen as an amateur activity and those who participated in sport for financial reward were treated as outsiders. Sport, as a major component of society and as we know it today, is a relatively new phenomenon. For most of history, sport has been a leisure activity, engaged in after completing work. Even Roger Bannister, the first person to break the 4-minute mile, worked full time as a physician while training. Today many minor sport elite athletes follow the traditional model of work and sport as separate functions in their lives. This remains the norm for people engaged in sport as a leisure activity.

Sport participation is seen as an opportunity for members of society to engage in socially positive and healthy activity that contributes to society. Communities across the United States sponsor sport activities and have done so through most of the twentieth century and now into the twenty-first century. Sport as leisure has grown as the population and economy have grown. Sport participation and sport events vary from region to region. In the 1950s, soccer clubs were difficult to find for any age group. Today youth soccer represents one of the continuously fast-growing sports. In secondary schools, universities, and professional leagues, soccer has found a place in mainstream sport.

Sport, as a component of leisure experiences, is an integral part of many communities. It is expressed in youth sport programs, adult leagues, and senior leagues and programs, and has extended to include what were once called nontraditional sport activities. Government agencies no longer attempt to serve as the primary provider of leisure sport opportunities. Nonprofits and for-profit organizations are actively engaged in the provision of sport activities for people of all ages. As we shall later see, growth of opportunity does not always translate into greater participation. In some cases, traditional sport programs are losing participants to growing sports such as lacrosse, adventure sports, and the like.

Sports—in both participation and spectator involvement and regardless of age—are a major leisure activity in the United States.

© Rob Hainer/Shutterstock.

SPORT FOR INDIVIDUALS WITH DISABILITIES

Sport as a leisure and competitive activity has a strong following in the disabled community. Even before the wars in Iraq and Afghanistan, sport involvement by athletes with disabilities was strong, as was evidenced by the presence of a variety of competitions, at all skill levels, up through the Paralympics, which began in 1960 for the summer games and 1976 for the winter games.[4] A leader in the provision of disabled sports is Disabled Sports USA, founded in 1967 by disabled Vietnam veterans.[5] The organization focuses on three aspects: sport as rehabilitation, competition as rehabilitation, and a quest for excellence. The organization works directly with individuals with disabilities and rehabilitation organizations focusing on helping the individual to adjust to their disability. Some of the sports participants can participate in include snow skiing; water sports (such as water skiing, sailing, kayaking, and rafting); cycling; climbing; horseback riding; golf; and social activities.

The acceptance of what is called a sport is continuously changing. The concept of sport over the last 40 years has been challenged by the expansion of sport opportunities. The X Games did not exist 20 years ago. Snowboarding, as an Olympic sport, first appeared in 1998. The 1970s may ultimately become known as the era of the emergence of alternative sports, which were then known as nontraditional sports. Many of these sports have become traditional, in the sense that they are mainstream within groups in society. They will probably not replace baseball, basketball, football, and other traditional school-sponsored sports, but they have found their place and achieved societal acceptance. Skateboarding, for example, first appeared in the 1970s, but not until the mid-1990s did community-based skate parks begin to appear.

Sport participation is a large component of leisure involvement. Participation is defined in many ways. It does not necessarily involve active engagement in sport activities. In the 1930s and beyond, collecting sport cards (e.g., baseball cards, football cards) was and continues to be a form of sport involvement, albeit from the hobby perspective. Today's fantasy sport teams are similar to collecting baseball cards and fit into the concept of a hobby. Purists might argue the point, especially when professional teams and sport broadcasters and their websites devote considerable attention to fantasy teams, yet they do fit the description of a hobby. Watching sporting events is another major influence of sport and leisure. As we shall see later in the chapter, spectators make up a major segment of the sport and leisure involvement. Stebbins describes spectator involvement in sport as casual leisure.[6]

PATTERNS OF SPORT INVOLVEMENT

Participation in Sport Activities

Sport is an important form of leisure activity. It can range from casual to serious leisure, from passive to active involvement, and from leisure to lifestyle. In the same regard, it is difficult to clearly classify sport wholly or sometimes even partially as a leisure activity. One of the accepted ways of determining leisure involvement is to measure participation. Participation measures give a sense of involvement and commitment to a sport activity.

A selection of the most popular sport activities and participation levels are identified in **Table 9.1**. As indicated earlier, a number of the pastimes listed might better be described as outdoor recreation pursuits, such as exercise walking or camping. Others, such as skiing, swimming, or even fishing, are usually engaged in as noncompetitive recreation, although they may represent part of school or college competition or large-scale tournaments.

The measure of sport participation comes from multiple sources, including the National Sporting Goods Association (NSGA), the Sport and Fitness Industry Association, the Outdoor Foundation, and the Physical Activity Council. In this sense, we allow those who sell sports products to help define sport.

There are many ways to measure sport involvement and many groups collecting information about how people participate in sport. Measuring the number of participants in organized sport is much easier than identifying numbers participating in recreation leagues, pickup games, and the like. Any number of participants identified will be limited by the source of the information. For example, Little League only measures baseball players participating in their sanctioned programs. Their programs represent just a small part of the total youth participating in baseball in any given year. The measures that are available do provide indicators of how many people are involved in formalized sport activities on an annual basis.

TABLE 9.1	2014 Participation in Sport Activities (in millions)—Ranked by Total Participation*	
Activity	**Number (9.1 is 9,100,000)**	**Participation Change Since 2011**
Exercise Walking	104.3	Increase
Exercising with Equipment	55.1	Decrease
Swimming	45.9	Decrease
Aerobic Exercising	44.2	Increase
Running/Jogging	43.0	Increase
Hiking	41.1	Increase
Camping (vacation/overnight)	39.5	Decrease
Workout at Club	36.0	Increase
Bicycle Riding	35.6	Decrease
Bowling	34.4	Decrease
Weight Lifting	34.1	Increase
Fishing (freshwater)	29.4	Increase
Yoga	29.2	Increase
Basketball	23.7	Decrease
Billiards/Pool	20.7	Increase
Golf	18.4	Decrease
Hunting with Firearms	17.5	Increase
Boating, Motor/Power	14.1	Decrease
Soccer	13.4	Decrease
Tennis	12.4	Decrease
Backpacking	12.0	Increase
Baseball	11.3	Decrease
Dart Throwing	10.1	Increase
Volleyball	10.1	NO CHANGE
Table Tennis/Ping Pong	9.9	Decrease
Softball	9.5	Decrease
Fishing (saltwater)	9.4	Decrease

Kayaking	9.1	Increase
Archery (target)	8.3	Increase
Snowboarding	7.7	Increase
Football (tackle)	7.5	Decrease
Hunting with Bow & Arrow	5.9	Increase
Skiing (alpine)	5.6	Decrease
Gymnastics	5.4	Increase
Mountain Biking (off road)	5.4	Decrease
Skateboarding	5.4	Decrease
Target Shooting	5.1	Decrease
Target Shooting (airgun)	5.1	Decrease
Paintball Games	4.8	Decrease
In-Line Roller Skating	4.7	Decrease
Hockey (ice)	3.6	Increase
Water Skiing	3.4	Decrease
Lacrosse	2.8	Increase
Wrestling	2.8	Decrease
Muzzleloading	2.6	Decrease
Skiing (cross country)	2.4	Increase

Data from ProQuest Statistical Abstract of the U.S. 2016 Online Edition: Table 1258; Participants In Selected Sports Activities: 2014 [By Sex, Age, And Income] (Accessed: 06/15/2016)

Table 9.1 illustrates the breadth of participation in selected sport activities. The list, from NSGA, is indicative of the diversity existing in sport, how people view sport, and how those who are in the sport merchandising industry see sport. It is interesting to note that a participant in sport may view sport from a very narrow perspective, whereas those who represent sport merchandise sales see it from a much broader perspective.

Participation in sport is influenced by a variety of factors. Motivations for participation in leisure are discussed elsewhere in the text. These are similar for sport, but sometimes the nature of sport engages people for different reasons. It is instructive to understand who influences participants to engage in sport. In a study conducted by the Outdoor Foundation, respondents were asked, "Who influenced your decision to participate in outdoor activities?" For youth ages 6 through 17 years, parents were the major influencers, followed by friends. Friends became an increasingly important influencer until by ages 18 to 24, they had a primary influence. It is interesting to note that media icons, sports figures, and accomplished athletes had less than a 2% influence on participation.

Another question frequently posed asks if participants in one activity participate in other sport activities. The answer seems obvious and the data confirm this. Seventy-eight percent of freshwater, saltwater, and fly fishing participants participated in other outdoor activities. Hiking showed the greatest level of multiple activity involvement, with 87% of those who hike indicating they also participate in other activities. The numbers reported are indicative of other sport activities. However, participation is a function of accessibility, cost,

Parents and friends impact teens' decisions to participate in sports.
© wavebreakmedia/Shutterstock.

availability, socioeconomic status, skill, and self-perception. Considerable research is available that focuses on motivation for sport participation. As described earlier, parents may have a major influence on youth. As youth grow older, their parents have less influence, for the most part. One study reports the quality of the relationship with the athlete's mother and peer relationships were indicators of continuing involvement in sport.[7] Concerns about the transition into adulthood may influence youth sport participants to continue involvement.

Sport is sometimes seen as an activity that will prepare students for adulthood. In a similar vein, some continue to participate in sport because it demonstrates or extends their competence, and perceived competence is a primary motivation factor for teens. Between high school and college, participation in physical activity declines considerably, and following college it continues to decline. Sport participation must compete for an individual's time with work, family, and other social activities as individuals enter the workforce and see work as a primary motivator as opposed to recreation. Yet, recreational sport leagues flourish across the United States with millions of participants.

Reasons individuals continue to participate in leisure sport activities are varied but include the opportunity for affiliation with others, improving one's appearance, taking up a new or continuing challenge, competition, enjoyment, positive health, social recognition, stress management, and weight management, to name a few.[8] What we do know is that participation in strenuous and team sports, such as baseball, basketball, and football decline and are replaced with less physically stressful small-group or individual activities. As might be expected, there are exceptions to the decline in sport activities. Among older adults, for example, competitive sports continue to flourish, even if the numbers participating are a smaller percentage of their age group. Those participating in master sporting events are in better health, have experienced less physical decline than the older adult population as a whole, are motivated, and frequently were involved in sport throughout their life. Participation in traditional sport activities is highest during youth. The definition of traditional sport activities is expanding as opportunities to participate in sport are expanding. As people complete their secondary education and leave home, participation in sport declines throughout their lives. Despite repeated efforts to encourage greater participation in sport as a lifestyle choice, few people take advantage of sport. Typically, those who do actively participate in sport have done so throughout their lives.

TEAM SPORT PARTICIPATION

If any activity defines mainstream American sport, it is organized team sports, beginning with T-ball and soccer for 3-, 4-, and 5-years-olds and continuing throughout people's lives. Actual participation numbers in organized team sports are available only where governing organizations are present and data are collected. Participation is highest among high school students (see **Table 9.2**) and has grown steadily. Boys have the greatest opportunity for involvement in high school sports, with schools across the United States providing more than 148,000 sport teams, 10,000 more than provided to girls. The 7.8 million participants in high school sport represents over 40% of all high school students. However, many high school students participate in two or three or more sports, making the actual participation lower, but still involving a high number of high school students in sport.

College students are more likely to participate in recreational sports than intercollegiate sports.
© bikeriderlondon/Shutterstock.

Collegiate sport participation declines dramatically, but this is expected because the number of available opportunities to participate in sport teams declines dramatically. **Table 9.3** shows the participation levels in intercollegiate athletics. The number does not represent recreational sport involvement at the collegiate level, which is far higher. In addition to extensive intercollegiate sport facilities, today's college campuses have one or more recreational sport facilities that cater to the general student population. Over the last 30 years, universities have recognized the importance of participation in sport by students who are not engaged in intercollegiate athletics. The National Intramural-Recreational Sports Association is the professional association representing student-based sport opportunities.

TABLE 9.2 High School Participation in Interscholastic Sports[a]

Year	Boys	Girls	Combined
2015–2016	4,545	3,232	7,869
2014–2015	4,519	3,288	7,807
2011–2012	4,485	3,208	7,693
2008–2009	4,423	3,107	7,537
2005–2006	4,217	2,947	7,160

[a] Number is in thousands, i.e., 7800 = 7, 800,000 (number is rounded to nearest thousand)
Data from National Federation of State High School Associations, Indianapolis, IN, "Participation Statistics" (2016). Available at www.nfhs.org/ParticipationStatistics/PDF/2015-16_Sports_Participation_Survey.pdf. Accessed October 1, 2016..

Trends in Organized Team Sports Participation

The 2014 *U.S. Trends in Team Sports Report* and the *2016 Fitness and Leisure Activities Report* by the Sports and Fitness Industry Association reveal several key findings regarding team sports participation. These findings provide a realistic assessment of participation patterns in sport activities and are a useful tool for sport and recreation management professionals in developing successful strategies to serve the needs, desires, and interests of leisure product consumers, recreational organizations, sporting goods companies, and local, state, and federal governments.

Casual Team Sport Participation

An alarming situation is the millions of casual sport participants who have dropped out of team sport activities progressively for 25 years, every year since 1984. The overall number of children age 6 and older who participated in team sport at least once within each calendar year during the period since 1984 has declined. A similar trend is observed for participants who play team sport more frequently (that is 25 or more days per year). Since 1995, more than 4 million sport participants have quit participating and migrated to other leisure activities. Over the 2009 to 2014 period, there was a 9% decline (4.5 million youth) in 17 youth sports.[9]

Several factors contribute to this emerging problem. In inner-city environments, the availability of free space for recreational sport is extremely limited. Empty fields where children can gather after school and play a pickup

TABLE 9.3 Collegiate Participation in Organized Sport

Association	Participants	Number of Teams	
		Men	Women
National Collegiate Athletic Association	482,533	24	23
National Association of Intercollegiate Athletics	45,000	13	11
National Junior College Athletic Association	60,000	14	12
California Community College Athletic Association	27,000	12	12
Total	**614,533**	**63**	**58**

Data from National Collegiate Athletic Association. (http://www.ncaa.org/about/resources/media-center/news/number-ncaa-college-athletes-climbs-again - accessed October 1, 2016) National Association of Intercollegiate Athletics (http://www.naia.org/ViewArticle.dbml?DB_OEM_ID=27900&ATCLID=205679222 - accessed February 23, 2017) National Junior College Athletic Association (http://www.cccaasports.org/about/about - accessed February 23, 2017)

game are not the norm. At the same time, the lack of time for parental supervision and increased concerns for child safety have led a great number of parents to search for alternative ways (e.g., recreation centers, playgrounds, private or sectarian leagues) to introduce sport to their children. This is evident for single-parent families or families where both parents support full-time jobs.[10]

PHIT America reported in 2015 four key trends impacting sport participation that help explain why fewer people are participating in traditional sport activities and participating more frequently in nontraditional sport activities. For example, between 2012 and 2014, the fastest growing sport activity was High Impact Aerobics, followed by swimming for fitness and yoga.[10]

Trend 1 is, "It's all about the 'experience.'" As younger consumers move more toward experiences, they are seeking and finding nontraditional activities, and they that feel they are more likely to achieve the experience they desire. It's not just about getting fit. It's not only about having fun, but it also involves seeking enjoyable mental and emotional "takeaways" called experiences. These are rarely offered in traditional activities. Community park and recreation departments have discovered that low-pressure recreational leagues with modified rules, equipment, and field size draw individuals who are looking for fun and enjoyment at the expense of high competitiveness and skills.

Trend 2 proposes for sports event viewers, "That you watch is not what you do." Viewing sports does not show a direct correlation to participation in those sports. In other words, one may watch the World Series but not play baseball. As we shall see later, major sports have become entertainment, not pathways to participation. Entertainment is another form of experiencing.

Trend 3 asks, "Why keep score?" Participants have found great joy in participation and that the experience is more fun when not keeping score. It's just easier to focus on the experience when you are playing for enjoyment.

Trend 4 states, "Traditional sports are missing." Public park and recreation agencies continue to offer traditional sport opportunities for adults and youths, and they will always have a place. The concept of small and simple is becoming more popular. Examples include mini-soccer, Ultimate (Frisbee), body-weight training, shortened seasons, and adaptation of traditional sports to create more and/or better experience and less competition.[11]

Demographic changes also affect team sport participation rates. Today, research shows that team sport participation is as high as 70% for young children reaching age 11 and declines to 50% as youngsters reach age 18. It is evident that a combination of factors such as adolescence and school workload play a decisive role in this decline. Research suggests that early involvement in organized sport is not a factor influencing involvement during high school. Projections for the next 10 years are not encouraging for the same segment of the population. It is expected that participation for youth between 5–19 years old will grow only 3.6%, which translates to a greater decline in team sport participation.[12]

Sport as Big Business

Sport has become a large enterprise in the United States and across the world. Nations embrace major sporting events, cities and states embrace collegiate and professional sports teams, and communities mark their calendars by interscholastic sports contests. In higher education, sport management programs are appearing in business schools and the more traditional physical education and recreation programs. The *Statistical Abstract of the United States*, the National Sporting Goods Association, and the Sporting Goods Manufacturers' Association individually provide annual updates on select aspects of the sport industry. Their data are highlighted throughout this section and emphasize the financial size of the sport industry.

In 2015, Americans spent $63.6 billion on sporting goods. Stores selling sporting goods products accounted for 70.1% of all sales. There has been a drop-off in sales since 2007, when sales were $93.4 billion. **Table 9.4** provides an example of how age groups are represented in purchasing of sporting goods. The table depicts the percentage of sales for selected items by age groups and gender.

Individual purchasing habits and, in some cases, the purchasing habits of child care providers are notable. Age and gender are a predictor of sales and provide manufacturers and retailers target market information for manufacturing and purchasing decisions. It is not surprising that the 45- to 64-year-old age group has the most significant impact on the market. This age range has the highest disposable income. When you anticipate many of the sales of 17 and under age groups are also supported by the 45- to 64-year-old age groups, you can see the impact of children on sporting goods sales. Another interesting aspect is that women are primary purchasers of many items, with the exception of items often associated with men. Age is another predictor of sales. Look at golf, handguns, and walking shoes as examples. Also, note the significant drop in sales to the 65 years and older age group. It's projected that as current millennials and baby boomers have longer life expectancies and better health, spending patterns will also change.

TABLE 9.4	Consumer Spending by Age					
Age	Total %	Gym Shoes: Sneakers	Walking Shoes	Bicycles	Golf Club Sets	Handguns
13 and Under	18.0	17.2	3.5	20.6	7.2	5.9
14–17 years old	5.3	10.5	2.3	4.3	1.4	3.8
18–24 years old	10.0	10.8	5.0	5.9	0.2	6.8
25–34 years old	13.5	16.0	11.6	17.0	14.1	18.8
35–44 years old	12.8	13.2	11.7	15.8	6.9	14.9
45–64 years old	26.3	24.6	44.6	28.8	36.0	38.8
65 years or older	14.1	7.7	23.1	7.6	34.2	11.0
Total%	100.0	100.0	100.0	100.0	100.0	100.0

Data from http://www.nsga.org/research.

One of the challenges of measuring sporting goods sales centers around who is asking and who is reporting. Industry groups will ask different questions than market research companies about the same product, often using a different set of assumptions. For example, one research firm may only focus on the outdoor hunting, fishing, and hiking industry, while another looks at youth and adult competitive sports equipment. Depending on the lens one is using, the data can vary significantly. To understand what the reports actually portray, it is important to know the focus of the company that commissioned them.

Sporting good sales is organized around market segments. A market segment involves defining and subdividing a specific large market into smaller, clearly definable groups, called segments, for marketing purposes. Looking at one component of the sports industry provides additional insights. The Outdoor Industry Association published a report looking at the marketplace. They estimate that 60% of adults identify themselves as outdoor consumers. These individuals are classified into seven market segments: the achiever, the outdoor native, the urban athlete, the aspirational core, the athleisurist, the sideliner, and the complacent. The achiever is characterized as a traditional outdoor consumer who participates in a variety of outdoor activities, including team sports. They are highly focused on being outdoors and being active. The outdoor natives are seeking enjoyment and experience, are not competitive, and focus on family-related activities. The urban athlete's focus is on the activity; outdoors is the place where the activity—such

Surfing competitions in Hawaii are televised events.
© Epicstock/Dreamstime.com

as running, skateboarding, basketball—can be pursued. The aspirational core is "outdoorsy" and seeks adventure through running, mountain climbing, camping, mountain biking, and other similar activities. They often travel to get to their location. The athleisurists find their "center" in the outdoors and like working outdoors at home, such as in a garden, or relaxing on the hammock. The key emphasis is on being comfortable without seeking more adventurous or challenging activities. Getting outdoors with limitations due to age, weight, or physical ability characterizes the sideliner. They were once more active, but can no longer maintain that level of activity. The complacent is an indoors person, but their health, fitness, and mobility limitations are inhibitors to outdoor activity. They focus on low-intensity activities, such as sitting in the backyard or walking for a purpose. All sporting goods manufacturers and sales organizations, such as sporting goods stores, segment their population. Cabela's—an outdoor sporting goods store—would use these market segments to focus the organization of their store, establish sales, and determine what products to carry. Within its stores, Cabela could further segment sport shoes into the following categories: sporty, elite sports, everyday wears, fashion sports, and budget conscious.[13]

THE EXPLOSION OF WORLD CHAMPIONSHIPS

At the beginning of the twentieth century, there was one world game that was widely recognized—the Olympic Games. The Olympic Games represented the equivalent of world games for many sports. The Olympic Games still brings together athletes from many sports and from most of the countries of the world, remaining the premiere example of the purpose and focus of world game—or championship—events. During the twentieth century, and especially beginning in the 1950s, more sport governing bodies created their own global (or world) championship.

Many of these sporting events have big name recognition. Football (known as soccer in the United States) is a good example. The FIFA World Cup involves several years of competition between national teams to qualify. For example, the 2018 FIFA (Féderation Internationale de Football Association) World Cup involves five qualifying rounds for the North, Central America, and Caribbean region, with the first round beginning in March 2015. Qualifying participants compete in the playoff scheduled for November 2017, with the finals in Russia. A total of 209 teams (1 per country) will participate, and 561 games will be played before a champion is declared.

The diversity of world championships is almost staggering. FIFA World Cup may be the best known; the Tug of War (TWIF World Outdoor Championships) is an example of a lesser known competition. Although the availability of television- and sport-focused networks has encouraged the growth of world events, that is not the only reason. As world individual income has risen, individuals have more time for sport and recreation. As groups have come together, national and international bodies have formed and world championships were created.

In 1896, there were 5 world championships; by 1920, there were still fewer than 30 world championships. In 2016, there were over 500 different competitive sporting events, and there appears to be a championship for almost anything!

Examples include world championships in badminton, canoeing, darts, fistball, beach handball, air racing, pitch and putt, aeromodeling, touch football, and many more.

SPORT SPECTATORS

It has been said, "If there is sport, there are spectators." People enjoy watching sport activities, albeit the number of spectators varies from sport to sport and by individual and group interest. A bass fishing tournament draws far fewer spectators than does a collegiate or professional football game. Yet, both of these sports have strong print and electronic media followers.

Spectators have been described in a variety of ways. An overarching approach to understanding spectators focuses on motivation, or why people choose to watch sports and how they react to the sports they watch. Underwood and colleagues suggest, "Spectator sports are a unique group experience characterized by a sense of belonging that spectators feel and an inherent bias against out-group members. . . . For these individuals, sports are not merely a form of entertainment and recreation, but provide a sense of community and family."[14]

Giulianotti developed a taxonomy or classification for spectators.[15] He classified spectators as supporters, followers, fans, and flâneurs. His study, although focusing on English football (soccer) clubs with a corporate identity, has the potential to be related to American professional sports. The four categories are based on two continua, the first being attraction to the team (called hot and cool), with hot focused on an intense loyalty. Cool fans are at the other end of the continuum, exhibiting loyalty that is neither intense nor binding. The second continuum is a traditional consumer focus, or a cultural versus a market-centered approach.

A supporter is a traditional hot spectator with deep personal understanding and a strong commitment to the team. Giulianotti suggests supporters have a "relationship with the club that resembles those with close family and friends."[15] Followers are also traditionalists and can be described as knowledgeable spectators with a strong interest in the game, but not with a single team. As a result, single teams have minimal impact on their identity as a follower.

Fans are hot consumers. They are not traditionalists, but their focus is with a single team. "The individual fan experiences the . . . traditions, its star players, and fellow supporters through a market-centered set of relationships."[15] Consumption of market products and the display of those products is a driving force. Fans, because they are not traditionalists, are more transient in their loyalty to a team. If teams do not perform to their expectations, they may change their loyalty to another team. Finally, flâneurs have an almost aloof relationship with a team. Giulianotti suggests flâneurs may be more impressed with branding, such as logos, tattoos, and the like. They are transient, switching affiliations like surfing websites.

At a sporting event, or viewing a sporting event, all of these types of fans are present. The centerfield bleachers of the Chicago Cubs is composed of all four types but most probably supporters and fans.[16] The individual sporting Oakland Raiders tattoos, car stickers, T-shirts, and hats has a higher probability of being a flâneur, fan, or supporter. The typologies suggested can provide insights into how and why spectators are involved in sport. It can give clues to researchers, sport franchises, and commercial enterprises about how sport might be marketed and who to target.

Spectator Influence   The importance businesses attribute to major spectator sports is evident in associated business-related use of statistical data collected from fans who attend, watch, and follow teams and athletes. Attendance figures, average attendance, and percentages of stadium capacity filled are important indicators of fan support and influence the financial commitment that advertisers, partners, and governments are willing to invest in a team or individual. Similar to television shows, sports broadcasts are tracked for penetration into a given market, average ratings, peak ratings, and responses. This is discussed in greater detail in the next section.

Attendance at Sporting Events

For years the hallmark of a spectator's commitment to sport was attendance at sporting contests. To some degree, that remains true today for collegiate and professional sport franchises, although the cost of attendance has increased considerably and is discussed later in this chapter. Sport attendance is typically defined by sport teams and sport events by the number of people in attendance and viewing a contest.

Measuring attendance at sporting events can be challenging.
© Walter G Arce/Shutterstock.

Measuring attendance is, at best, problematic. Teams can count tickets sold, distributed, and given away. Estimated attendance is also a common approach, although less so than in the past. A surfing contest, for example, may not have formal tickets; people just show up and attendance must be estimated. This was common for many sporting events for a long time and continues to be the norm in smaller or less formally organized events. However, sport has become more formal and is following business models with more exact measurements expected. Regardless, it is difficult to get a handle on spectator attendance at park and recreation–sponsored programs, local youth leagues, and informal sport settings. Organized sports do a better, if not excellent, job of counting "in attendance" spectators. **Table 9.5** depicts attendance over the past decade at selected collegiate and professional sporting events. Professional baseball, including minor and major leagues, has the highest total attendance on a yearly basis. Professional baseball also has the largest number of teams and annual games.[17]

Media Use By and Influence on Spectators

Media long ago changed how people view their role as a spectator. An MLB baseball game was first broadcast via radio in 1921, and in 1935 the Chicago Cubs became the first team to broadcast their entire schedule on the radio. Radio broadcasts allowed people to be spectators during the contest when they were not present. No one could anticipate what the next 80 years would bring to professional, collegiate, and high school sports. The explosion of opportunities for spectators to watch sport over the last 10-plus years has been nothing short of spectacular. Professional teams have taken advantage of television and the Internet.

ESPN became the first "all-sports" television network, beginning in 1979 on a limited basis and becoming a 24-hour broadcast station in 1980. Beginning in the late 1990s, professional sports leagues began to establish their own television networks and financed them, in part, through viewer subscriptions through cable and satellite carriers. The actual number of subscribers varies, but MLB claims it has 55 million subscribers compared to NFL's 60 million and NBA's 12 million. The league networks, while in competition with major networks, did not sever their existing contracts, but instead expanded the availability for spectators to watch every game of their favorite team or teams. In 2009, the major networks (ABC, CBS, FOX, and NBC) reported to be in 114.5 million households, and TBS, TNT, ESPN, and Versus networks reported being in 75 to 99 million households each.[18] The ability for people to watch sports of any kind on television has expanded dramatically over the last 20 years. In 2015, the major sports reached almost 100 million households. ESPN reaches 94.5 million households, followed by the NFL Network, which reaches 73.6 million households. Other networks have emerged in the last 5 years, including SEC Network (69.1 million), Golf Channel (79.4 million), and the Big Ten Network (62 million). The newer collegiate networks reach more households than Major League Baseball, the National Basketball Association, and the National Hockey League.[19]

TABLE 9.5 Attendance at Selected Sporting Events*				
Sport	**2000**	**2007**	**2011**	**2016**
Baseball				
MLB	74,340	80,759	75,504	73,159
Minor League BB			41,279	37,345
Basketball				
NCAA Men	28,949	33,396	32,781	32,382
NCAA Women	8,825	11,121	11,211	11,367
NBA	12,134	20,272	21,841	13,351
National Hockey League	18,800	20,862	20,928	13,440
Football				
NCAA	39,059	48,752	46,699	49,058
NFL	20,954	22,256	20,959	17,509
Total	**203,061**	**237,418**	**271,202**	**247,611**

*millions of spectators (10,000 means 10,000,000)
Data from http://www.baseball-reference.com/leagues/current_attendance.shtml (Accessed February 23, 2017); http://www.baseballpilgrimages.com/attendance/minor-leagues-2016.html (Accessed February 23, 2017); http://fs.ncaa.org/Docs/stats/m_basketball_RB/Reports/attend/2016.pdf (Accessed February 23, 2017); https://www.espn.com/nba/attendance (Accessed February 23, 2017); http://www.espn.com/nhl/attendance (Accessed February 23, 2017); http://fs.ncaa.org/Docs/stats/football_records/Attendance/2015.pdf (Accessed February 23, 2017); http://www.pro-football-reference.com/years/2015/attendance.htm (Accessed February 23, 2017).

In 2014, the Super Bowl was the largest viewed sporting event, with more than 112 million U.S. viewers. This is the single largest American market sporting event. By contrast, the 2014 World Cup final was watched by over 700 million live viewers worldwide.[20]

The 2016 Rio Olympics, a multiweek event, was watched by 3.5 billion viewers worldwide down from 4.8 billion viewers for the 202 London Olympic Games. This does not represent separate viewers because many viewers tuned in more than one time and sometimes more than once a day. The opening ceremony for the Olympics had 342 million viewers. Estimates of actual viewers are always just that, an estimate based on historical statistical models. Actual numbers are impossible to identify because one or many people may watch a single television. Numbers of households subscribing, however, are a verifiable number, although they do not show actual numbers watching in a home. Americans are able to watch television in many different ways. Watching delayed broadcasts of television after recording a program, viewing from one of many sources on the internet, or purchasing a broadcast to watch later are all common. Nielsen reported that 66% of television shows were viewed live in 2015. However, sports has defied the trend to delay watching. In 2015, 95% of all sports were viewed live. People want to view their sporting events live. It is yet another example of the influence of seeking experiences.[21]

The most significant trend for spectators is the use of the Internet by viewers. Nielsen reports there are almost 134 million unique online viewers who video stream. More than 50% of men and just under 50% of women stream videos. That number is expected to increase as cell phones become a primary source of viewing the Internet. As an example, viewership of the 2016 NCAA Men's Basketball Tournament final game saw a 37% drop from the 2015 championship. It was the first time that a national championship was broadcast via cable, and not available on a traditional network. However, viewership on mobile devices was up. In today's video-rich environment, more individuals are watching television on mobile devices (at or above 50% for both men and women), and for sporting events, they more frequently check in for the scores and watch the highlights, rather than an entire game.

Spectators, as part of the sport marketplace, are key to its commercial success. At the same time, many spectators find leisure meaning in watching sporting events. Different types of fans achieve different emotional outcomes from viewing sporting events. During the 2008–2011 recession, attendance at sporting events declined initially and viewing via television and the Internet increased.

High television ratings lead to fierce negotiations between league officials and network executives when television contracts are about to expire or new media packages (Internet broadcasting, pay per view, and so forth) are available for bid.

All major professional sports teams and a large percentage of major college teams have medium to large revenue contracts with television and cable networks. For example, the 2016 NCAA basketball championship was broadcast on a cable-only network for the first time. Turner and CBS Sports and the NCAA agreed upon an $8.8 billion dollar contract over an 8-year period for the NCAA basketball championship. In 2014, the NFL agreed to a new Thursday night venue with NBC and CBS for a 2-year period. The networks agreed to pay $450 million per year to broadcast 10 games a year.[22] (Major League Baseball signed a 7-year agreement with Fox network for a reported $4 billion.[23] College conferences now bid for their own television rights. According to Forbes, the Southeast Conference has television deals worth $347 million, the Big 10 conference has televisions contracts valued at $279 million, and the Atlantic Coast Conference has television contracts valued at $98 million.[24]

Television allows sports fans to be spectators at home.
© Monkey Business/Fotolia.com.

Franchise Values and Player Salaries   The importance and magnitude of spectator sport are also evident in franchise financial worth and player salaries. Franchises in most major leagues have seen their values appreciating significantly in the last 5 to 10 years, with price tags reaching as high as $4 billion.

To help determine the fair market value of sport franchises, *Forbes* magazine conducts an annual survey evaluating factors such as the team's annual operating income, the size of the market the team operates in, stadium value, roster value, and so forth. By 2016, 20 teams were valued in excess of $1 billion, and 5 more were very close. The top three teams are the Dallas Cowboys ($4.2 billion), New England Patriots ($3.4 billion), and the New York Giants ($3.1 billion).[25] The New York Yankees are valued at $3.4 billion, the highest-valued MLB franchise and one of only three exceeding $1 billion in value.[25] *Forbes* determines team values by measuring four areas including (1) *sport* as a portion of a franchise's value attributable to revenue shared among all teams; (2) *market*, which includes the portion of a franchise's value attributable to its city and market size; (3) the *stadium* and that portion of a franchise's value attributable to its stadium; and (4) *brand management* as a portion of a franchise's value attributable to the management of its brand.[25]

The newest trend in sports broadcasting is streaming games over the Internet for use on individual computers.
© William Perugini/Shutterstock.

Players' values also have exceeded industry analysts' projections.

Tiger Woods, who has struggled with his golf game in recent years, earned $1.4 billion from prize money, endorsements, appearance fees, and golf course designs since turning pro in 1996. He has earned more than any professional athlete in history. The top paid athletes in the world are part of the new "international athletes" with international name recognition. The top among those in 2016 was Cristiano Ronaldo (soccer), followed by Lionel Messi (soccer), LeBron James (basketball), Roger Federer (tennis), and Kevin Durant (basketball), all with the potential—including bonuses—to earn over $70 million in the same year.[26]

Public Subsidy of Sport Facilities   Over the last 20 years, cities have invested billions of dollars into the construction and maintenance of sport facilities, primarily to retain or attract professional sport teams. The economic recession of 2008 to 2010 slowed that process, but did not halt it. Numerous teams today are housed in stadiums paid for wholly or in part by public taxes. In 2015, the Los Angeles Rams moved from St. Louis based on the promise of a new stadium estimated at $1.9 billion. When San Diego failed to pass a bond issue to build their NFL Chargers a new stadium, the team announced they were moving to Los Angeles in 2017, joining the Rams who moved from St. Louis the year before. Oakland is trying to move to Las Vegas, NV, on the promise of a $1.9 billion stadium with a significant amount paid for by an increased hotel and motel room tax.

Broadcasting sporting events has become a major source of income for sport teams and their sponsors.

© Pavel Losevsky/Dreamstime.com

Attendance Costs of Spectator Sports   The increasing cost of attending a sport event is one of the factors that creates discomfort for sport fans and their families. Attending a sporting event for any one of the major leagues today can be a personal account–draining proposition.

The Fan Cost Index (FCI), a survey conducted annually by Chicago-based Team Marketing Report, a sport marketing company, provides a comparable measure of how much a family of four likely will spend attending a professional sporting event. The survey assesses the costs of two average-price adult tickets, two average-price children's tickets, four of the cheapest soft drinks, two of the cheapest beers, four hot dogs, two programs, parking, one game program, and two of the cheapest-size caps.

The 2016 FCI reported that the most expensive place to attend an NFL game is the Chicago Bears stadium, with an average ticket price of $131.90. The total FCI for a Bears game is $685.10. By contrast, the average ticket price for the entire NFL was $92.98, with an average FCI of $502.84, showing an increase of 4.6% over the previous year. As a comparison, the FCI average for MLB was $219.53 and for the NBA was $339.02.[27]

EMERGENCE OF SPORT AS A REFLECTION OF SOCIETY

Sport as a Source of Moral Values

It was widely believed that sport had several important values: (1) contributing to health and physical fitness as a form of rigorous training, conditioning, and exercise; (2) building personal traits such as courage and perseverance, self-discipline, and sportsmanship; (3) encouraging social values linked to obeying rules and dedication to team goals, as well as providing a channel for social mobility, especially for individuals from disadvantaged backgrounds; and (4) serving as a force to build group loyalty, cohesiveness, and positive morale in schools and colleges and in communities throughout the nation.

Beyond these values, sport obviously has immense appeal, both for participants and for the vastly large audience of fans who often attach themselves to their favorite teams, wearing their colors or uniforms, cheering them enthusiastically, traveling to spring practice or "away" games, and contributing as loyal alumni to the recruitment or support of star athletes. This very fervor and degree of commitment to sport have led inevitably to a number of major abuses or problems affecting sport on all levels.

Case Study
· ·

How Old Is Too Old to Participate in Sport?

A growing body of research focuses on aging and fitness. Sport participation is part of the study of fitness. There are long-held traditions about aging and physical activity, and most of these support the notion that as one grows older, participation in sport and physical activity should be reduced. These perceptions can be described as barriers that are both real and perceived. Most older people agree that exercise is good, yet this same group often grew up without opportunities to participate extensively in sport and fitness activities, what is called socialization into organized fitness, and once leaving school, what few opportunities they had were diminished. The result of the lack of socialization and opportunity is that people are left with the real and perceived perception of vulnerability when participating in any level of fitness or sport.

Despite this understanding among researchers, most older adults describe their state of health in positive terms. Yet only a minority participate regularly in active physical leisure at a level sufficient to deter the onset of some level of incapacity. In fact, the research suggests that strenuous physical activity is more likely to be avoided when compared to other types of leisure opportunities. Another barrier to participation relates to how older adults perceive their own body and state of health. This includes the attitudes about what the older body should and should not be capable of doing. It includes biological process decline, but also attitudes, expectations, prejudices, cultural values, and ideals of society as well as those individuals' development as they grow old.[a]

Not all older people avoid activity. Many are engaged in physical activity, but, as opposed to younger participants who may be involved primarily for a better looking body as frequently suggested on infomercials, they engage in the activity to improve strength, mobility, and balance, all key elements to enhancing individual quality of life as one ages. One of the problems with the research literature, according to Grant, has been a singular focus on the "lived body" at the expense of a broader view encompassing the meanings of later life.[b]

Grant found that older individuals engaged in a variety of physical activities, and playing sport was important to them. Individuals found that the physical activity and sport had become an important part of their life. Even as they talked about the debilitating effects of aging, these individuals placed themselves in the discourse of good health, resisting the idea that aging was wholly a biomedical problem. However, existing stereotypes, especially for those older than 70 years, continue to exist and will into the foreseeable future. Even as more individuals enter the retirement years, there will be a core who maintain a level of fitness and others who will, for a variety of reasons, assume they cannot remain fit and will choose, either for themselves or have chosen for them, not to participate in physical activities.

Questions to Consider

1. Describe some of the potential arguments for not remaining engaged in physical activity and sport as one ages.
2. Think about someone you know who is physically inactive and older. Describe their physical and mental attitude toward exercise. If you don't know of someone, you may need to call a relative who is older.
3. Think about someone you know who is physically active and older. Describe that person's physical and mental attitude toward exercise.
4. How can this research help you adjust your lifestyle now?

Sources

a. B.C. Grant, 2001, 'You're never too old': beliefs about physical activity and playing sport in later life. *Ageing and Society,* 21(06), 777–798.
b. M. Featherstone and M. Hepworth, "The Mask of Aging and the Post-Modern Lifecourse." In *The Body: Social Processes and Cultural Theory* (London: Sage Publications, 1995).

Abuses and Problems of Sport Competition

Sports for children too often have been influenced by adult pressures to win at all costs. As a result, youngsters often feel excessive pressure to compete and to win, and the experience is no longer fun for them. Studies show that many children about to enter their teen years quit organized sport at this point or shift to a much more relaxed, recreational approach to games.

Linked to such pressures, adults frequently encourage overaggressive and violent play, as well as tactics that ignore sportsmanship and condone rule breaking. In extreme cases, parents may verbally or physically abuse players, parents, or coaches of rival teams, and even attack officials who have made decisions ruling against them.[28]

In the not too distant past, the influence of high-pressure sports occurred at the secondary school level as university coaches began to make contact with athletes and parents, inviting them to elite training camps that were financed by sport manufacturers. Now, in many cases parents and coaches are no longer the influencing factor in assisting young players to make decisions. High-pressure sport competition has moved down to the youngest ages, oftentimes with parents becoming the motivating force for involvement. **Table 9.6** shows just a few of the many national championships that are sponsored mostly by sports organizations. Some individuals call this movement in sport the "professional model" or more specifically the "professionalization of youth sports." Gould reflected, "the adoption of a 'professional model' within sport organizations is the single biggest problem we face in contemporary youth sports. It is adversely affecting the motivation of young people, exposing them to risks of injury, destroying an appreciation of sport, and often turning them away from sport and a recognition of the benefits of lifelong physical activity at the very time we need to turn them on to it."[29]

In 2012 the New York Giants had the highest Fan Cost Index in the NFL.
© gary718/Shutterstock.

TABLE 9.6 Youth Sport National Championships			
National Championship	**Age Group**	**Gender**	**Sponsor**
Callaway Junior World Golf Championship	6 years and under	boys/girls	Callaway Golf (a golf equipment company)
Amateur Athletic Union Basketball National Championships	8 years and under	boys/girls	Amateur Athletic Union (AAU)
U.S. Open Junior Tennis Championships	8 years and under	boys/girls	United States Tennis Association
Junior Pee Wee Pop Warner Super Bowl	8–11 years with weight limits	boys	Pop Warner Football
Junior Pee Wee Cheer and Dance Championships	8–11 years	girls	Pop Warner Cheer and Dance
Amateur Athletic Union Junior Olympic Swimming Meet	9 years and under	boys/girls	Amateur Athletic Union
Youth World Series	9 years and under	boys/girls	United States Club Soccer
Youth Basketball of America National Championships	9 years and under	boys/girls	Youth Basketball of America
Little League Baseball World Series	9–12 years	boys/girls	Little League Baseball
Little League Softball World Series	9–12 years	girls	Little League Softball
Amateur Athletic Union Girls Junior National Volleyball Championships	10 years and under	girls	Amateur Athletic Union
Cal Ripken Baseball 10-Year-Old World Series	10 years and under	boys/girls	Babe Ruth League

Data from A. Lumpkin, University of Kansas, "Sports as a Selection of Society," slide 13. Available at http://aahperd.confex.com/aahperd/2009/webprogram/ (Accessed: January 12, 2017).

Such abuses become more extreme in college competition, in which, especially in high-visibility sport such as basketball and football, there has been a long history of academic violations. Today, athletes are less often recruited with fraudulent course grades or altered school transcripts. At the extreme are athletes involved in fights in public places, sexual abuse, and other criminal activities. These abuses in sport are small in number but highly visible to the public. Again and again, there have been scandals and investigations involving gambling on college sport—sometimes with players betting their on games. In professional sport, conflicts between players and owners, the sudden departures of favorite athletes, or the transfer of sports franchises all have strengthened the public perception of sport as "just a business" and have eroded fan loyalty and attendance in some cities.

Other problems surrounding sport on all levels have involved physically dangerous and even life-threatening conditioning practices, concussions, playing with debilitating injuries and hazing in sport such as ice hockey or football, which has included physical, emotional, and even sexual abuse.[30]

Finally, the practices of building expensive new stadiums with costly skyboxes and adding charges for the right to buy season tickets have dramatically escalated the financial costs for fans. In many cases, the middle-class or blue-collar audience who has traditionally supported professional sport, particularly in large, older cities, is no longer able to do so. As a result, there is disturbing evidence that the fan base for professional sports is declining and that many members of the public are instead transferring their loyalties to local, minor league teams, in part because of nostalgic affection for sport "as it used to be."

On the international scene, sports corruption has been even worse. In late 2002, the British Broadcasting Corporation (BBC) reported a meeting of European sport ministers who were attempting to combat child exploitation in sport. In a number of documented cases, African youth were lured into contracts with professional soccer teams, but when they didn't make the team they were sometimes abandoned and became illegal immigrants without language skills or the ability to make a living. Belgium, France, and Holland have been cited as the countries most likely to bring in preteens and young teens on tourist visas and then abandon them.

Even the Olympic Games, traditionally viewed idealistically as amateur sport at its best, were revealed in 1999 as having involved widespread bribery in the awarding of the 2000 Summer Olympics to Sydney, Australia and the 2002 Winter Olympics to Salt Lake City.[31]

Beyond corruption at this level, the constant disclosure of prohibited performance-enhancing drugs and "blood doping" being used in international sport has helped to destroy public confidence in such events as the major bicycling event, the Tour de France, and other competitions.[32] Championship boxing matches have been shown to be under the control of criminal elements, and fixed soccer games have threatened the integrity of international competition at the highest level.[33]

One of the most relevant issue in youth sport is the prevalence of concussions. Concussions can lead to traumatic brain injury (TBI), hospitalization, partial or permanent disability.[34] The issue of concussions was brought to the forefront when a number of professional sport athletes lives were negatively impacted as a result of multiple concussions during their career. The awareness has resulted in changes in sport at all levels. A BlueCross/BlueShield 2016 reported concussion diagnosis increased 43 percent over a 5 year period beginning in 2010. For patients ages 10 through 19 diagnosis were up 71 percent. Some data on concussions reported 3.8 million youth sport concussions in 2012, double what was reported a decade earlier. The Centers for Disease Control (CDC) reports TBI as common in children, and sport as the leading cause.[35] Most children do not receive medical attention from a TBI, although this is changing as awareness is raised among coaches and parents. Youth football has been the focal point for concussion news reports, but data suggests concussions are spread across the whole spectrum of youth sport. For example, soccer is the most common risk for females (50 percent chance or a concussion). Some studies report that 50 percent of high school athletes and 70 percent of college athletes failed to report a concussion.

The impact on youth sport has been well documented. For example, the Aspen Institute reported an 8.8 percent drop in youth sport participation between 2008 and 2013 indicating that household income is a major determinant of sport participation. Some of this may be attributed to concussion awareness. High school football participation is down as students and parents become more aware of concussion potential. However, it is difficult to assign one cause to participation decline in youth sport.[36, 37]

FUTURE TRENDS IN SPORT

Whether such negative trends accelerate, sport managers and participants on all levels need to deal with the problems that have been presented in this chapter. Clearly, the continuing expansion of professional sport has reached a point of diminishing returns. If team owners and league policymakers are to retain or regain fan loyalty, it will be necessary to curb the growing costs of sport attendance, which are clearly tied to the astronomical salaries being paid to star players and the greediness of team owners.

Improving Youth Sport

In general, sport as a recreational pursuit appears to be on a healthier footing. Some critics complain that children and youth are excessively scheduled in athletics as well as other free-time activities and that organized play has driven out the kinds of spontaneous neighborhood games that children used to play. However, the reality is that the major national organizations in baseball, softball, basketball, football, and soccer, as well as many others in individual and team sports, have been successful in providing opportunities for play for many millions of young participants.

In terms of the need to control overemphasis on winning, excessive parental pressures, or the kinds of physical, emotional, and sexual abuse of participants by coaches that have received publicity in recent years, a number of leading national organizations have mobilized to improve youth sport. Such private, nonprofit organizations as the National Alliance for Youth Sport and Positive Coaching Alliance have developed ongoing campaigns, certification, and training programs to enlighten parents and promote positive coaching approaches.

Organizations representing individual sport, such as Little League Baseball, the American Youth Soccer Organization, or the United States Tennis Association, have not only developed guidelines and regulations for the same purposes but have also initiated campaigns to prevent drug use among youth and to encourage fuller participation by minority group children and in inner-city areas.

Changing Sport Interests

Sport participation is constantly changing and in today's fast-paced, mobile, and connected society, it is changing even more rapidly than ever before. With the growth of electronic media and analytics, trends that were traditionally tracked across decades are now measured in weeks, days, and sometimes hours. A search of the Internet using the term "sport trends 2017" revealed a variety of interesting sources, including "Youth Sports

ELECTRONIC SPORT IS GOING MAINSTREAM

It is always dangerous to project what the future will hold, but it appears that fantasy sport is growing dramatically. As recently as 2013, it was a term infrequently heard on ESPN, and now they have a corps of broadcasters almost wholly dedicated to the sport. Fantasy sport is changing American sporting culture; it has become big business almost overnight. Hundreds of millions of dollars have been invested as venture capital. Players build teams, project outcomes of sporting events, and trade players, all while betting on their knowledge of the sport. An ESPN study reported 118 million individuals participated in betting on sports, much of it illegally. Fantasy sport has grown as an alternative to local betting and allows participants to use their skills. Fantasy sports are organized around teams and leagues, with the player building his own team(s). There is the issue of gambling, and some fantasy sport groups have been banned because they violate state laws, such as in Nevada and New York. Professional teams have become engaged in the fantasy sports, seeing it as a way to expand their fan base, especially among younger people.[38, 39]

Participation in sport has increased among aging populations as they rediscover forgotten interests.

© Glenda M. Powers/Shutterstock.

Participation Statistics and Trends," "Trends in Membership & Sport Participation," "2016 Participation Report," "Sports Industry Trends that Will Disrupt and Dominate 2016." Trends focus on youth participation, professional sport development, athletes (professional, amateur, youth, seniors, etc.), technology, and commercial changes. During Olympic and soccer World Cup years, interest in a broader range of sports grows, especially if one's national team in a sport (such as gymnastics) does well. In the end, trend analysis can be helpful in suggesting growth in a particular area, but cannot guarantee it.

The Physical Activity Council's 2016 Participation Report suggests changing sport interests among U.S. residents. Between 2010 and 2015, individual sports showed a drop from 40% participation to 34.8%. The highest participation (all reported for 2015, and it is expected to continue, is in fitness sports (61.5%) and outdoor sports (48.5%). The lowest participation was in winter sports (7.4%) and racquet sports (13.5%). The latter require either a specialized facility or residence in a geographic region where winter occurs sufficiently long to engage in winter sports. Millennials participate more frequently in fitness sports, water sports, and racquet sports than other generations. As might be expected, Gen Z (those born since the year 2000) participate more frequently in team sports and outdoor sports. Overall, youth sport participation has shown a steady decline. Inactivity remains a concern with over 81 million individuals not participating in any type of physical activity.[40, 41]

The popularity of some extreme sports such as skateboarding and snowboarding for youth age 7 and older showed a decline after years of growth. Between 2006 and 2011 skateboarding experienced a decline in participation of 58% and snowboarding recorded a smaller decline at 16%.[42]

The X Games are an example of how the media have capitalized on and benefited from the move toward extreme sport. The list of events for the most recent Winter X Games included snowboarder X, skier X, moto X, snowboard superpipe, and other variations of skiing and snowboarding. The success of the X Games has breathed new life into a ski industry suffering from a lack of young participants. So successful has been the resurgence of snow sports that the 2002 Winter Olympics introduced several of the X Games events into their regular schedule and continued in the 2006 and 2010 Winter Olympics.

Summary

In this chapter, the discussion of sport has progressed beyond its primacy as a leisure activity. It has grounded sport in leisure and leisure in sport, reminding the reader that sport is only one component of leisure. This chapter demonstrates the growth of sport as a component of leisure, social engagement, culture, and big business. A discussion of participation levels in sport shows large youth involvement, gradually dropping off during and following high school, and then reemerging, at a lower level, during the mid- to late 20s and early 30s, and growing in diversity among seniors. Sport participation is a function of age, skill, commitment to sport, family commitments, social engagement, time, and money as well as lesser variables.

Spectator involvement in sport continues to grow. The availability of expanded television coverage through cable and satellite networks; creation of league networks for MLB and the NFL; the growth of Internet content through the use of computers, smart phones and tablets; and increased interest in international sporting events such as World Cup Soccer and the Summer and Winter Olympics, have resulted in the highest number of spectators in history. Yet it sometimes remains difficult to measure the actual number of spectators, especially when including electronic media.

The maturation of professional sport leagues on an international scale, and especially in the United States, has resulted in the integration of business models in sport. In short, sport has become big business, and like any business enterprise, it is expected to return a profit for the owners and shareholders. The individual worth of a growing number of professional sport teams exceeds $1 billion, including international teams such as the Manchester United Football Club. Sport as big business will drive the future of professional and collegiate sports for the near future. Although little was discussed regarding the value and business aspects of collegiate sports, they too have entered an era when they must be partially or fully self-supporting.

Finally, this chapter discusses trends and issues and includes the discussion of sport as a source of moral values, a topic that is frequently hotly debated; issues and concerns with youth sport participation and pressure; the influence of commercialism on young sport participants; efforts to rein in runaway youth sport programs and to bring fun back to the participants; the growth of extreme sports; and the influence of computer and video games.

Sport is a major influence in society. It is a topic of discussion at work, over the Internet, and among friends, and yet for all its engagement and involvement, only a moderate percentage of the population actually engages in sport participation or spectating.

Questions for Class Discussion or Essay Examination

1. Define what the word "sport" means to you. Include as part of the definition characteristics that you think a "sport" must have. List five different sports that meet your definition. Go online and search for "sports" that don't fit your definition. Be prepared to share and explain your definition of sport.

   _____

   _____

   _____

2. Do a survey of your friends and ask them if they know anyone who played a competitive sport and had a concussion—or if they had a concussion. Then, ask how knowing about the potential of concussions in sport changed their attitude toward a particular sport. If it did not change their attitude, why not? Share with them the statistics in this chapter and ask if that changes their mind about concussion and sport.

   _____

   _____

   _____

3. In a group, determine how many members of your group actually watch sporting events. Use the broadest possible definition of "watch" to include the news, ESPN, other sport channels, the newspaper, or mobile devices. Then ask how they most frequently watch sports—live attendance, on live television, live on a mobile device, record the event to watch later, or watch just the highlights on a television or mobile device. What is the most common way to watch a sporting event in your group? Is it consistent across other groups in the class?

   _____

   _____

   _____

4. Identify your motivations for participating in sport or exercise. Ask, "Why do I participate? What do I expect to get from my participation? Is it important to me? Why (yes or no)? What prevents me most from participating in sport or exercise? Do I do it for myself or as part of a group?"

   _____

   _____

   _____

5. Select a piece of sporting equipment (baseball glove, running shoes, badminton racquet, snowboard, gaming device, etc.). Track the evolution of that piece of sport equipment from inception until it gets to you. Does it require special manufacturing? Does it involve engineering to develop? Is it readily available or is it custom made? How does the manufacturer know what to make? Where did you purchase it (sporting goods store, other store, online, other)? How can this knowledge enhance your understanding of sport and recreation?

_____

_____

_____

Endnotes

1. J. B. Lewis, T. R. Jones, G. Lamke, and L. M. Dunn, "Recreational Sport: Making the Grade on College Campuses," *Parks and Recreation* (December 1998): 73.

2. The Free Dictionary, "Sport," www.thefreedictionary.com/sport (Accessed June 5, 2017).

3. Oxford Living Dictionaries: http://www.oxforddictionaries.com/us/definition/american_english/sport.

4. Official Website of the Paralympic Movement: www.paralympic.org.

5. Disabled Sports USA: http://dsusa.org/about-overview.html.

6. R. A. Stebbins, "Casual Leisure: A Conceptual Statement," *Leisure Studies* (Vol. 16, 1997): 17–25.

7. S. Ullrich-French and A. L. Smith, "Perceptions of Relationships with Parents and Peers in Youth Sport: Independent and Combined Prediction of Motivational Outcomes," *Psychology of Sport and Exercise* (Vol. 7, No. 2, 2008): 193–214.

8. All Star Activities, "Why Your Child Should Participate in Sports": www.allstaractivities.com/sports /sports-why-participate.htm (Accessed June 5, 2017).

9. "Team Sports: State of the Industry," *Sporting Goods Dealer* (January 1, 2006).

10. PHIT America, "America's 15 Fastest Growing Sports and Activities": http://www.phitamerica.org /News_Archive/America_s_Fast_Growing_Sports.htm (Accessed June 5, 2017).

11. Rainey, J. & Hamm, A. 2015, Trends in Sports and Fitness, *Leading Edge Newsletter*, GreenPlay LLC: http://www.phitamerica.org/News_Archive/America_s_Fast_Growing_Sports.htm.

12. R. R. Pate, M. G. Davis, T. N. Robinson, et al., "Promoting Physical Activity in Children and Youth," *Circulation* (Vol. 114, 2006): 1214–1224.

13. Outdoor Industry Association, "Consumer Segmentation Executive Summary": https://outdoorindustry.org/pdf/consumervue_executive_summary.pdf (Accessed January 23, 2017).

14. R. Underwood, E. Bond, and R. Baer, "Building Service Brands via Social Identity: Lessons from the Sports Marketplace," *Journal of Marketing: Theory and Practice* (Vol. 9, No. 1, 2001): 1–12.

15. R. Giulianotti, "Supporters, Followers, Fans, and Flaneurs: A Taxonomy of Spectator Identities in Football," *Journal of Sport and Social Issues* (Vol. 26, No. 1, 2002): 25–46.

16. Chicago Cubs, "Wrigley Field": http://mlb.mlb.com/chc/ballpark/index.jsp (Accessed June 14, 2014).

17. L. Igel, "Low Sports Attendance: Who Is Your Customer?" *Forbes*: http://blogs.forbes.com /sportsmoney/2010/09/28/low-sports-attendance-who-is-your-customer (Accessed June 14, 2014).

18. Sports Media Watch, "The 50 Most-Watched Sporting Events of 2012": www.sportsmediawatch. com/2013/01/2012-numbers-game-the-most-watched-sporting-events-of-the-year/ (Accessed November 18, 2012).

19. Outkick the Coverage, "The 15 Most Valuable Sports Networks": http://www.outkickthecoverage.com/ the-15-most-valuable-sports-networks-050715 (Accessed June 5, 2017).

20. S. Roxborough and B. Jones, "World Cup Finale Draws 700 Million Viewers," *Reuters* (July 13, 2010): www.reuters.com/article/2010/07/13/us-football-idUSTRE66C0ZV20100713.

21. Nielsen, "The Year in Sports Media Report: 2015": http://www.nielsen.com/us/en/insights/reports/2016/the-year-in-sports-media-report-2015.html (Accessed June 5, 2017).

22. Sports Cheatsheet, "5 College Conferences That Bring In Over $250 Million": http://www.cheatsheet.com/sports/the-5-most-valuable-conferences-in-college-sports.html/?a=viewall (Accessed January 23, 2017).

23. Forbes.com, "NFL Team Values": http://www.forbes.com/pictures/mlm45geihk/2-new-england-patriots/#1e42e0de1c39 (Accessed January 23, 2017).

24. Forbes.com, "The Business of Baseball: The New York Yankees": http://www.forbes.com/teams/new-york-yankees/ (Accessed January 23, 2017).

25. Kurt Badenhausen, Michael K. Ozanian, and Christina Settimi, "Recession Tackles NFL Team Values," Forbes.com (September 2, 2009): www.forbes.com/2009/09/02/nfl-pro-football-business-sportsmoney-football-values-09-values.html; and Michael K. Ozanian and Kurt Badenhausen, "Baseball's Most Valuable Teams," Forbes.com (April 22, 2009): www.forbes.com/2009/04/22/yankees-mets-baseball-values-09-business-sports-land.html.

26. Forbes.com: http://www.forbes.com (Accessed January 21, 2017).

27. "Team Marketing Report - NBA 2015–2016": https://www.statista.com (Accessed January 21, 2017).

28. James Kozlowski, "Sport League Held Liable for Brutal Attack on Coach," *Parks and Recreation* (November 1999): 45–52.

29. D. Gould, "The Professionalization of Youth Sports: It's Time to Act!" *Clinical Journal of Sport Medicine* (Vol. 19, No. 2, 2009): 81–82.

30. Joe La Points, "A Hard Winter in Vermont: Hockey Season Canceled Over Hazing," *The New York Times* (February 3, 2000): D1.

31. Robert Sullivan, "How the Olympics Were Bought," *Time* (January 25, 1999): 38.

32. Michael Lemonick, "Le Tour des Drugs," *Time* (August 10, 1998): 76.

33. Jere Longman, "Fixed Matches Are Darkening Soccer's Image," *New York Times* (June 7, 1998): 1.

34. Headcase, "Sports Concussion Statistics": http://www.headcasecompany.com/concussion_info/stats_on_concussions_sports (Accessed January 23, 2017).

35. Centers for Disease Control and Prevention, Nonfatal traumatic brain injuries related to sports and recreation activities among persons aged ≤19 years—United States, 2001–2009, MMWR Morb Mortal Wkly Rep. 2011:60.

36. https://www.bcbs.com/about-us/capabilities-initiatives/health-america/health-of-america-report/steep-rise-concussion.

37. https://www.aspeninstitute.org/blog-posts/7-charts-that-show-the-state-of-youth-sports-in-the-us-and-why-it-matters/.

38. Newzoo, "Esports Enthusiasts to Total 145 Million by 2017": https://newzoo.com/insights/articles/esports-enthusiasts-total-145-million-2017/ (Accessed January 23, 2017).

39. CNN.com, "Seven-Figure Salaries, Sold Out Stadiums: Is Pro Video Gaming a Sport?": http://edition.cnn.com/2016/05/31/sport/esports-is-professional-gaming-a-sport/ (Accessed January 13, 2017).

40. Physical Activity Council: http://www.physicalactivitycouncil.com (Accessed January 23, 2017).

41. http://www.forbes.com/sites/darrenheitner/2015/09/16/the-hyper-growth-of-daily-fantasy-sports-is-going-to-change-our-culture-and-our-laws/#521195d35f25 (Accessed January 12, 2017).

42. The Outdoor Foundation, "2012 Outdoor Recreation Participation Report," Boulder, CO: Outdoor Industry Association (2013): www.outdoorfoundation.org/research.participation.2012.html.

Leisure as a Profession

What does the park and recreation profession entail? *The park and recreation profession offers diverse job opportunities throughout the country. Whether you are working in an office or out in the field, a career in parks and recreation means enhancing the quality of life for all people through advancing environmental conservation efforts, social equity, and health and wellness. Going to a job you love every day is something everyone wants. If you have the passion for being outdoors, helping people, and bettering your community, you may want to consider a career in this field.*[1]

Learning Objectives

1. Discuss the career options in the leisure-service field.

2. Understand and discuss the seven criteria outlined for professional practice.

3. Identify appropriate professional certifications.

4. Describe operational philosophies of recreation and leisure.

INTRODUCTION

Recreation, parks, and leisure services have expanded greatly over the past several decades as a diversified area of employment. Today, several million people work in different sectors of this field, including amateur and professional sport, entertainment and amusement services, event planning, travel and tourism, recreation-related businesses, and government and nonprofit community organizations.

As a distinct part of this larger group, several hundred thousand people are directly involved as recreation leaders, supervisors, managers, therapists, planners, and consultants in public, nonprofit, and commercial agencies. These individuals with a primary concern for the provision of recreation services are generally regarded as professionals on the basis of their job responsibilities, specialized training, and affiliations with professional associations.

The prevailing image of leisure-service professionals has been that of public, governmental recreation and park employees. The leading professional associations, as well as most textbooks and college curricula, reinforced this narrowly defined identity. However, the reality is that vast sectors of employment in recreation and leisure services are not government related, but instead have to do with nonprofit community agencies; company-sponsored, commercial, and therapeutic recreation services; sport management; and travel and tourism programs. As such, they have their own professional associations, as well as goals, job functions, and strategies that differ from those of public recreation and park specialists.

RECREATION AS A CAREER

People have worked in recreation for many centuries in the sense that there have been professional athletes and entertainers throughout history. Musicians, tumblers, dancers, huntsmen, park designers, and gardeners were all recreation specialists meeting the leisure needs first of royalty and, ultimately, the public at large. However, the idea of recreation itself as a career field did not surface until the late 1800s, when public parks and playgrounds, along with voluntary social service and youth-serving organizations, were established.

After the beginning of the twentieth century, courses in play leadership were developed by the Playground Association of America and were taken by many teachers. In the middle 1920s, the National Recreation Association provided a graduate training program for professional recreation and park administrators, and leisure as a distinct area of public service came to be recognized. This recognition increased during the Great Depression of the 1930s as many thousands of individuals were assigned by the federal government to emergency posts providing community recreation programs and developing new parks and other facilities. However, it was not until the development of separate degree programs in a handful of colleges that higher education in recreation and parks as a distinct career field came into being.

By the second half of the twentieth century, careers in recreation and parks were seen as a growth area. A nationwide study of workforce requirements in the 1960s concluded that there would be a need for hundreds of thousands of new recreation and park professionals in the years ahead. The U.S. Department of Labor reported widespread shortages of leisure-service personnel in local government, hospitals, and youth-serving organizations. Several factors, such as the federal government's expanded activity in outdoor recreation and open space and the establishment of the National Recreation and Park Association, stimulated interest in this field. In the 1970s, as employment grew, curricula in recreation and leisure service gained increased acceptance in higher education.

Scope of Employment Today

People spend free time participating in sport, arts, and nature activities; visiting museums, zoos, and aquariums; and attending special events, shows, and performances; as well as traveling to tourism destinations. With all of this recreation going on, people are needed to work in these and many other jobs.

Employment opportunities in parks and recreation are highly diversified. Recreation workers are found in local parks and recreation agencies, on cruise ships, planning major festivals such as the Sundance Film Festival, planning promotional events for the Phoenix International Raceway, and working with people with disabilities in a therapeutic recreation setting. They can be found in all of our national parks from Acadia to Zion. They serve as park rangers, interpreters, guides, and activity planners. Throughout this chapter, you will find vignettes of people working in the field of parks and recreation. Some of them are brand new to the field, and others have several years of experience. Each shares his or her typical responsibilities for the job. It is easy to see how diverse this profession is.

The educational backgrounds of people working in recreation vary. A plethora of summer and part-time positions require a high school diploma—or less as is the case with many lifeguards and camp counselors. However, these positions are not considered professional positions, but rather a means to gather experience in order to obtain a professional position in the recreation field. As responsibilities increase in recreation-related jobs, so do degree requirements. Entry-level positions in the field such as after-school program supervisors, special-event planners, and facility supervisors may require a bachelor's degree, and middle- and upper-level management positions may require a master's degree.

Jobs in parks and recreation are quite varied—from working with the National Park Service to planning major special events to working with Special Olympics.

© spirit of america/Shutterstock.

Although data on the total number of jobs in recreation are limited, we do know that the tourism industry is one of the nation's largest employers, with 5.5 million people working in this industry.[2] The 2014 Bureau of Labor

As a Therapeutic Recreation Specialist, I implement programs for inpatient psychiatric and substance abuse patients of all ages. Within the facility, the inpatient unit can serve 88 patients, and I work with all of them on a daily basis. I assess and create goals for each new individual upon their admission to the facility. Some of the programming topics that I have implemented include pet therapy, mindfulness, relaxation, stress management, leisure education, communication, and more. The best part of my position is that I get to work alongside a variety of professionals to help individuals of all ages live a healthier and more holistic lifestyle.

Training for parks and recreation positions does not stop with a degree. Professionals take advantage of programs such as the Indiana University Executive Development program to enhance their skills.

Statistics estimates is that there are 18,600 people employed as recreation therapists,[3] 379,300 in recreation,[4] and another 100,000 employed as event planners.[5] Furthermore, the National Park Service employs 22,000 people to take care of its 84 million acres of land;[6] state parks employ 24,985 people full and part time.[7]

The Bureau of Labor Statistics expects the demand for most recreation jobs to grow faster than average through 2024, which means they expect a growth of about 10% through this time.[8] They also predict that therapeutic recreation will see a growth that is faster than average, with an increase of 12% over the next several years.[9] Part of what is driving this growth is the rate of retirement of baby boomers, previously discussed in other chapters. It is also the result of increased concern for health and wellness.

PROFESSIONAL IDENTIFICATION IN RECREATION

What does being a professional mean? At the simplest level, it indicates that one is paid for one's work—as opposed to an amateur, who is not paid for it. Thus, an athlete who receives pay for playing for a team is classified as a professional.

However, this obviously is not a sufficient definition of the term in that many forms of paid work are not considered to be professional. A more complete definition of the term would suggest that a professional is one who has a high degree of status and specialized training and provides a significant form of public or social service.

Within a number of specialized leisure-service areas today, such as company-sponsored employee programs, therapeutic recreation, or fitness and health clubs, professionalism might be narrowly defined as the possession of a required certification based on a combination of education, experience, and examination. In other situations, membership in a designated professional association or society may be recognized as a hallmark of professionalism. However, the following seven criteria have generally been accepted as key elements of professionalism.

My position requires me to fill many roles. Primarily I hire and continuously train staff, and manage our aquatics department, which makes up about 75% of our staff. I also oversee our park service department and the tasks related to that, including all maintenance, construction, and repairs for the pools and all other equipment in the park. Some days I'm a custodian. Others I'm a first responder to an emergency. Every day I get to be a teacher, a leader, and a manager who gets to do what I love without sitting behind a desk all day. It is an exciting environment to be in, and no single day is ever the same.

Criterion 1: Social Value and Purpose

The goals, value, and purpose of organized community leisure-service agencies are described in another chapter. In general, they deal with such elements as improving the quality of life, contributing to personal development and social cohesion, helping to prevent socially destructive leisure pursuits, and protecting the environment.

Public and nonprofit leisure services agencies have long been known for their social good. For example, the mission of the YWCA is to eliminate racism, empower women, and promote peace, justice, freedom, and dignity for all.[10]

Its member organizations provide safety, shelter, daycare, physical fitness and recreation programs, counseling, and other social, health, educational, and job-related services to millions of women and girls and their communities each year.

Although the public and nonprofit sectors are most often equated with social good, the commercial sector contributes to this as well and has its own social value and purpose. It may provide entertainment, support health and fitness, or expose people to other cultures, historic sites, or a multitude of other tourism-related destinations.

People are willing to pay for their own personal leisure and are more reluctant to pay taxes to support leisure for the public good such as parks and trails.
© Jim Noetzel/Shutterstock.

Criterion 2: Public Recognition

The rapid expansion of the leisure-service field over the past several decades does not necessarily mean that the public at large understands and respects it fully or that they regard it as a distinct area of professional service. To illustrate, most individuals today know what recreation is, and many regard it as an important part of their lives. Most are prepared to pay substantial portions of their income for recreational goods or services, such as memberships in health clubs, vacations, sport equipment, tickets to theater productions, and other leisure-related fees and charges. However, they are often less willing to pay taxes in support of public recreation and park facilities and programs than they are to spend privately for their own leisure needs.

A time-use study done by the Bureau of Labor Statistics found that 96% of people older than the age of 15 reported having some sort of leisure, whether it be socializing, sport, or exercising.[11] In 2014, there were more than 445.3 million visitors to state parks, and there were 4 million campers and another 6.7 million lodge and cabin guests.[12] The National Park Service reported another 11.7 billion visitors in 2009.[13] Nearly 74 million people attend major league baseball games each year.[14]

Although these are just a minute portion of the leisure-service opportunities available, it demonstrates that a large portion of the population uses recreation services.

Even though the value of organized recreation service may be acknowledged through participation and use, how aware is the public at large of the leisure-service field as a profession? The likelihood is that most individuals recognize the roles of recreation professionals within specific areas of service. For example, they are likely to be familiar with the function of a recreation therapist in a mental hospital or nursing home or the function of a community center director, a park ranger, or a sport specialist in an armed forces recreation program. What they tend not to understand is that recreation represents a field of practice that requires special expertise and educational preparation in a college or university. At issue is the image of the recreation professional.

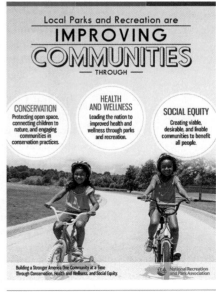

As a professional association, NRPA helps the public understand the value of parks and recreation in their communities.
Courtesy of National Recreation and Park Association.

Image of the Professional Unless one is an actual participant in organized leisure activities, people are most likely unaware that these jobs and careers even exist. Even with participation, the career acknowledgment may not happen. People attending a major special event may enjoy the special event and return year after year, but they are unlikely to understand all of the planning and preparation that goes into that event. People have the luxury of enjoying recreation services, whereas the people who provide them remain behind the scenes. The public often does not see the people who cut the grass in the park, plan and plant the flowerbeds, develop the tournament schedule, or schedule the concerts in the park. In many instances, a park and recreation professional is out of sight if the event or program is running smoothly. This can lead to the public not equating what is being done to a true profession or career.

JOHN TAYLOR, CITY OF ROCK HILL (SC), DIRECTOR OF PARKS, RECREATION & TOURISM

A typical day for me revolves around the needs of the community intertwined with the needs of staff and community leaders. On a community level, I communicate and mediate citizen requests regarding anything from recreation programs or leagues to facility needs. On a department or staff level, I communicate with staff on many pertinent topics, serve on citywide capital project teams, and lead coordination of major tourism or weather-impacted events. Daily life involves participation in Department Head and City Council planning sessions and meetings, and visiting construction projects and department facilities to assess needs for the benefit of the department. As a community leader, I confer with city management, department heads, commissioners, and major developers regarding community issues affecting the department. I also provide support to statewide and national legislative issues related to the parks, recreation, and tourism profession. There is no such thing as a typical day. One may only be assured that the day you plan is not the same one you finish.

Another misconception about this profession is that anyone can do it. People think anyone can plan a 64-team softball tournament, organize a special event that attracts 100,000 people, or manage a pool. On the surface, these activities may not seem very difficult. However, they require an extensive amount of academic preparation, experience, and organizational skills. In addition, if recreation and leisure-service employees are to sharpen their identity and support, they must enrich their own competence through specialized professional study and by joining organizations that strengthen their field.

Criterion 3: Specialized Professional Preparation

A measure of the professional authority of any given field is the degree of specialized preparation that people must have to function in it.

Parks and recreation is no exception. There are many jobs in the field that require no education, but many of these are part time and most are low paying. To obtain a full time, professional-level position, a post-high school education is often required. Two- and four-year degree programs, as well as master's degrees and doctoral degrees in parks and recreation related fields are available. These degrees provide the specialized training needed to hold entry-level and higher jobs.

Professional Preparation in Recreation and Parks The early period of the development of higher education in recreation, parks, and leisure services is described elsewhere in this text. Over the past five decades, college and university curricula in recreation and parks have been developed on three levels: 2-year, 4-year, and graduate (master's degree and doctorate) programs.

Two-Year Curricula During the late 1960s and early 1970s, many community colleges began to offer associate degree programs in recreation and parks. Typically, these sought to prepare individuals on para- or subprofessional levels, rather than for supervisory or administrative roles. Most community colleges offered recreation majors a choice of two types of programs: terminal and transfer. *Terminal programs* are intended to equip students immediately for employment and give heavy emphasis to developing basic, useful recreation leadership skills, often within a specific field of practice. *Transfer programs* are intended for students who hoped to transfer to 4-year degree programs.

Four-Year Programs The most widely found degree program in recreation and parks has been the 4-year bachelor's degree curriculum. Initially, most such programs consisted of specialized degree options in college departments of health, physical education, and recreation, although some were located in departments or schools of landscape architecture, agriculture, or forestry. Today, although many departments still are situated administratively in schools or colleges of health, physical education, and recreation, they have achieved a high level of curricular independence, with their own objectives, courses, degree requirements, and faculty.

Four-year programs typically have established degree options in areas such as recreation programming, resource management, outdoor recreation, therapeutic recreation, sport management, commercial recreation, and tourism. The normal pattern has been to require all department majors to take certain core courses representing the generic needs of all preprofessionals, including basic courses in recreation history and philosophy, programming, management, and evaluation and/or research, and then to have a separate cluster of specialized courses for each option.

BRYCEN TURNBULL, PARK GUIDE, LINCOLN HOME NATIONAL HISTORIC SITE, NATIONAL PARK SERVICE (SPRINGFIELD, IL)

The Lincoln Home National Historic Site is one of over 400 units of the National Park Service. As a Park Guide, I am responsible for interpretive programming and the logistics required for that programming. My duties include guided tours of Mr. Lincoln's home, neighborhood tours, visitor safety, outreach and partnership, group scheduling, programmatic accessibility coordination, and other duties. Examples of programs I have done include What's in Mr. Lincoln's Hat?, Journey to Greatness Afterschool Outreach Program, National Park Service Centennial talks, An Historic Christmas, various Every Kid in a Park Campaign outreach programs, and much more. As the programmatic accessibility coordinator, I am responsible for insuring that all programs offered are as accessible as possible. This includes updating and maintaining the iPads we use for our accessibility tours. These include not only the basic accessibility tour but also foreign language and American Sign Language tours. Working for the National Park Service is a very satisfying career as I enjoy working with the public, history, and being outside. When a visitor's eyes light up due to the connection they have made between their own life and the resource I am interpreting is one of the greatest parts of my job.

What once started as a training ground for public parks and recreation professionals has grown to meet the changing demands of the field. There was growing academic awareness of the job opportunities in other recreation areas. As a result, a number of college and university programs changed their titles and departmental affiliations to reflect the new interest in commercial recreation, travel and tourism, sport management, hotel and resort management, and similar specializations. Typically, a considerable number of departments added the term *tourism* to their titles and established enriched programs in this area—in some cases in collaboration with schools of business in their institutions. In other cases, therapeutic recreation majors were transferred administratively to departments or schools of public health or healthcare services. As the most striking example of proliferation in this field, as of 2015 there were more than 475 independent departments of sport management designed to meet personnel needs in this growing field.[15] This is up from 300 in 2010.

Master's Degree and Doctoral Programs   Although it is generally agreed that the 4-year curriculum should provide a broad base of general or liberal arts education along with the core of essential knowledge underlying recreation service, the specific function of graduate education in this field is not as clearly defined. Some authorities have suggested that graduate curricula should accept only those students who already have a degree in recreation and should focus on providing advanced professional education within a specialized area of service. However, there tends to be little support for this position, and many graduate programs accept students from other undergraduate disciplines as well as those holding undergraduate degrees in recreation.

In general, authorities agree that master's degree work should involve advanced study in recreation and park administration or in some other specialized area of service, such as therapeutic recreation or sport management. The assumption is that individuals on this level are preparing for supervisory or managerial positions or, in some cases, roles as researchers or chief executive officers.

Doctoral programs in leisure service-related fields prepare graduates to teach and conduct research at the university level. Degree programs are typically a minimum of three years of study culminating with a major research project in the form of a dissertation. Students specialize in an area of interest and build a research line in that area.

Specialized Body of Knowledge   At the outset, many recreation and park degree programs were established as "minor" specializations in other areas of study, such as physical education. As such, they tended to lack theoretically based courses within the field of study. Over the past four decades, this deficiency has been largely corrected.

The knowledge and skills components of higher education in recreation, parks, and leisure studies are formulated in terms that are specifically applicable to the recreation field, although they may involve content taken from other scholarly disciplines or fields of practice.

Given the recent impressive growth in both research studies and publication of findings, it seems clear that the field has a legitimate body of knowledge that must be possessed by professionals. Indeed, within some areas of practice, there has been systematic study of the competencies and knowledge that entry-level practitioners should possess. These skills, knowledge, and abilities guide curricula so that students are equipped with the skills needed to get their first job.[16]

Increasingly, undergraduate curricula have been redesigned to include specific areas of knowledge and job performance based on standards of practice or certification examinations that have been developed by professional societies.

For undergraduates, a major element of the degree program is a culminating internship, and so students are able to gain work experience and implement the knowledge gained in the classroom. Although these vary from institution to institution, in general they require at least a semester of full-time commitment to work in an agency of high quality within the student's expressed field of professional interest. Such placements should extend far beyond an agency's using field work or internship students in routine or mundane roles as a source of cheap labor. Instead, they are meant to involve a full range of realistic job assignments and exposures, supervision by professional staff members, and preparation for entry-level positions.

Accreditation in Higher Education   The most significant effort that has been made to upgrade curricular standards and practices in recreation, parks, and leisure studies has come in the accreditation process. *Accreditation* of a degree program involves meeting standards set by a larger governing body. These standards ensure that students are being exposed to standards of practices within the field.

The park and recreation accreditation program is administered by the Council on Accreditation of Parks, Recreation, Tourism and Related Professions. This group of academic faculty and practitioners in the field represent the National Recreation and Park Association (NRPA).

Academic programs become accredited for a number of reasons. First, and usually most important, is to ensure program quality and uncover areas in need of improvement. A secondary reason is that students graduating from an accredited university may take the Certified Park and Recreation Professional examination upon completion of their degree (certification is discussed later).

Undergraduate baccalaureate programs in parks and recreation are eligible for accreditation. At this time graduate programs cannot go through the accreditation process. In this process, there are set accreditation standards that programs must meet in the areas of administration, faculty, students, instructional resources, and learning outcomes. After completing a self-study of these areas, an outside review team visits the campus to judge how well standards are met. Suggestions for improving weaknesses are made with the understanding that these things are for the betterment of the degree program.

Accreditation began in the early 1980s with about 50 programs being accredited. There has been a steady increase in the number of programs being accredited, and this number has risen to 76 in 2016.[17]

In addition to accreditation from the NRPA's Council on Accreditation of Parks, Recreation, Tourism and Related Professions, sport management has a Commission on Sport Management Accreditation (COSMA). Accreditation in sport management is available for both undergraduate and graduate degree programs. COSMA accredited its first two programs in 2010, and by 2016 there were 45 accredited sport management programs across the country.[18] Accreditation requires review of many of the same aspects of general parks and recreation programs, but these standards are sports specific in terms of curriculum and faculty.

Criterion 4: Existence of Related Professional Associations

Another important characteristic of professions in modern society is that they have strong organizations, shared values, and traditions.

In North America, professional recreation associations have been in existence for a number of years. Like their counterparts in other professions, recreation and park associations have the following functions: They (1) regulate and set standards for professional development; (2) promote legislation for the advancement of the field; (3) develop public information programs to improve understanding and support of the field by the general public; (4) sponsor conferences, publications, and field services to improve practices; and (5) press for higher standards of training, accreditation, and certification. There are a number of professional associations available for park and recreation professionals that provide those and other services.

NATIONAL RECREATION AND PARK ASSOCIATION

Each year, thousands of recreation and park professionals, civic officials, board members, educators, and students attend the National Recreation and Park Congress. Varied workshops, general sessions, exhibitor displays, and continuing education events provide expertise and exposure to outstanding programs in different regions of the country.

National Recreation and Park Association   Because of the varied nature of professional service in recreation and parks and the strong role played by citizens' groups and nonprofessional organizations, many different associations were established through the years to serve the field. Five of these (the National Recreation Association, the American Institute of Park Executives, the National Conference on State Parks, the American Association of Zoological Parks and Aquariums, and the American Recreation Society) merged into a single body in 1965, with Laurance S. Rockefeller as president. Within a year or two, other groups, such as the National Association of Recreation Therapists and the Armed Forces Section of the American Recreation Society, merged their interests with the newly formed organization.

This national body, the National Recreation and Park Association (NRPA), is an independent, nonprofit organization intended to advance parks, recreation, and conservation efforts that enhance the quality of life for all people.[19] This organization is arguably the broadest in scope for the recreation profession by embracing most of the professional categories listed earlier in the chapter. NRPA is directed by a board of trustees, which meets several times each year to guide its major policies.

NRPA plays a vigorous role in helping to bring about a fuller national consciousness of the value of recreation and leisure through various public information campaigns, publications, research efforts, and legislative presentations. The organization responds to thousands of inquiries and requests for technical assistance from practitioners, establishes national partnerships for local departments, oversees conferences and training opportunities, and provides numerous publications for members. In addition, NRPA representatives regularly testify before congressional subcommittees in support of legislation and funding proposals dealing with the environment, social needs, and similar national problems.

Other Professional Organizations   While NRPA welcomes membership from all over the world, it is predominantly focused on the United States. The Canadian Parks and Recreation Association has much of the same charge for parks and recreation professionals in Canada. They serve as advocates, build partnerships, promote the value of parks and recreation, and offer educational opportunities to its members.[20] For organized camps, the American Camp Association (ACA) strives to be the leading authority in child development, provides resources to camp managers and staff, holds annual conferences, and administers the ACA camp accreditation program, among other services.[21]

Other organizations that have made important contributions to this field include those listed in **Table 10.1**.

It is clear that no one organization can possibly speak for or represent the entire leisure-service field today. As each specialized area of recreation has become more active and successful, it has tended to form its own professional society to deal with its unique needs and interests.

TABLE 10.1 Common Professional Associations in Recreation, Sport, and Tourism

Purpose/Focus	Agency	Website
General Recreation	Canadian Parks and Recreation Association	http://www.cpra.ca/
	National Correctional Recreation Association	http://www.strengthtech.com/correct/ncra/ncra.htm
	National Recreation & Park Association	http://www.nrpa.org
	World Leisure Organization	http://www.worldleisure.org/
	Shape America Society of Health and Physical Educators	http://www.shapeamerica.org/
Outdoor/Camping	American Camp Association	http://www.acacamps.org/
	Association for Experiential Education	http://www.aee.org/
	Association of Outdoor Recreation and Education	http://www.aore.org/
	Canadian Parks and Wilderness Society	http://www.cpaws.org/
	National Association for Interpretation	http://www.interpnet.com/

	Society of Outdoor Recreation Professionals	http://www.recpro.org/
	Outdoor Industry Association	http://www.outdoorindustry.org/
	Student Conservation Association	http://www.thesca.org/
	Wilderness Education Association	http://www.weainfo.org/
	North American Association for Environmental Education	http://www.naaee.org/
Resorts/Commercial Recreation	International Association of Amusement Parks and Attractions	http://www.iaapa.org/
	National Ski Areas Association	http://www.nsaa.org/
	Resort and Commercial Recreation Association	http://www.rcra.org/
	American Hotel and Lodging Association	http://www.ahla.com/
	Club Managers Association of America	http://www.cmaa.org/
Special Events & Meeting Planning	Convention Industry Council	http://www.conventionindustry.org/
	International Association of Venue Managers	http://www.iavm.org/
	International Festivals & Events Association	http://www.ifea.com/
	International Special Events Society	http://www.ises.com/
	Meeting Professionals International	http://www.mpiweb.org/
	Professional Convention Management Association	http://www.pcma.org
	Association of Collegiate Conference and Events Directors-International	https://www.acced-i.org/
Sport	NIRSA: Leaders in Collegiate Recreation	http://www.nirsa.org/
	North American Society for Sport Management	http://www.nassm.org/
	National Association of Sports Commissions	http://www.sportscommissions.org/
Therapeutic Recreation	American Therapeutic Recreation Association	http://www.atra-online.com
	National Recreation & Park Association	http://www.nrpa.org/
Tourism	The International Ecotourism Society	http://www.ecotourism.org
	Tourism Industry Association of Canada	http://www.tiac-aitc.ca/
	World Travel & Tourism Council	http://www.wttc.org/
	World Tourism Organization	http://www.unwto.org/index.php
	American Society of Travel Agents	http://www.asta.org/

Criterion 5: Credentialing, Certification, and Agency Accreditation

Credentials are qualifications that must be satisfied through a formal review process before an individual is permitted to engage in professional practice in a given field. Obviously, this is a very important criterion of professionalism. If anyone can call him- or herself a qualified practitioner in a given field—without appropriate training or experience—that field has very low standards and is not likely to gain or hold the public's respect.

Because the recreation and park field has been so diversified, no single standard or selection process has been devised for those who seek employment in it. However, within the field of recreation and parks, certification programs have been developed to increase the professionalism of the field as well as set some standards that all certified professionals should possess.

Certification in a profession indicates that a certain level of skill and knowledge has been attained. Certification in parks and recreation is no exception. Although there are several different certifications available for different specialties in the field, the most recognized are the Certified Park and Recreation Professional (CPRP) and the Certified Therapeutic Recreation Specialist (CTRS).

Certified Park and Recreation Professional   The Certified Park and Recreation Professional program as we know it today has existed since 1990. To qualify to receive the CPRP designation one of the following criteria must be met:

◆ Have received, or are set to receive, a bachelor's degree from a program accredited by the Council on Accreditation of Parks, Recreation, Tourism and Related Professions. (Students who have not yet graduated from a COAPRT-accredited program with a major in recreation, park resources, and leisure services but who are in their final semester on campus may qualify for exam status.)

◆ Have a bachelor's degree or higher from any institution in recreation, park resources, or leisure services; and also have no less than 1 year of full-time experience in the field.

◆ Have a bachelor's degree in a major other than recreation, park resources, or leisure services; and also have no less than 3 years of full-time experience in the field.

◆ Have an associate's degree and have 4 years of full-time experience in the field.

◆ Have a high school degree or equivalent and have 5 years of full-time experience in the field.[22]

Once the criteria are met, an exam must be passed. The exam covers four broad content areas including the following:

1. *Communication* (16% of the exam): Public input, mission, marketing, partnerships, and planning
2. *Finance* (18% of the exam): Purchasing, program budgets, alternative funding, cash handling procedures, collecting financial data
3. *Human resources* (22%): Recruiting, hiring, and supervising staff and volunteers
4. *Operations* (24%): Risk management, facility management, customer service, external relationships, needs assessments, emergency management, maintenance
5. *Programming* (20%): Program leadership, planning, implementing and evaluating programs and events[23]

Once an individual receives certification, he or she must recertify every 2 years. Recertification requires individuals to receive 2.0 continuing education units (CEUs). One CEU is equivalent to 10 contact hours in an educational program. CEUs can be obtained from state, regional, and national conference educational sessions, university courses, or professional service points. Professional service experience points come from service given to the profession in the form of speaking at a conference, writing articles for a professional magazine, or serving on committees within the professional association.

In scanning the latest job search announcements, it is clear that more and more public parks and recreation departments are requesting applicants be certified. These employers see the value in obtaining a certain level of education and a commitment to staying current by continually attending workshops and conferences.

Certified Therapeutic Recreation Specialist   Certification in therapeutic recreation (TR) is administered by the National Council for Therapeutic Recreation Certification (NCTRC). To obtain a CTRS certification, professionals may follow either an academic path or an equivalency path. The academic path is for people who have completed a bachelor's degree or higher with a concentration in therapeutic recreation. The equivalency option is for people without a degree specifically in therapeutic recreation, but a bachelor's degree in another area as well as full-time work experience in therapeutic recreation. Regardless of the path chosen, both require successfully passing the CTRS exam.[24]

CERTIFIED PARK AND RECREATION EXECUTIVE

In 2012 a new certification was unveiled—the Certified Park and Recreation Executive (CPRE). This exam establishes a national standard for managerial, administrative, and executive parks and recreation professionals and reflects mastery-level credentials. It is designed for upper-level administrators who seek to be directors or department heads.[26] There are currently 177 CPREs in the United States.

Based on the 2014 job analysis study, the NCTRC Certification exam has the following five content areas: foundational knowledge (20%), assessment process (19%), documentation (18%), implementation (26%), administration of TR/RT Service (10%), and advancement of the profession (7%).[25]

Both the CPRP and CTRS certification programs have resources available to help candidates prepare for the exams. Resources include practice exams, study guides, and in some cases study groups.

Standards in Nonpublic Leisure-Service Agencies   The NRPA and the NCTRC have been the prime movers in the attempt to strengthen professionalism in leisure-service agencies. In general, the employees in nonprofit and commercial agencies have not been identified as key players in the recreation certification movement. Hiring in such agencies therefore has not been influenced by the NRPA accreditation efforts or certification.

However, national organizations such as the Ys, Scouts, and Boys and Girls Clubs are obviously concerned with helping their local councils, branches, or other direct-service units maintain a high level of staff competence. They do that through specialized training. For example, the YMCA has its own professional organization dedicated to providing training to all levels of staff. The Association of YMCA Professionals provides chapter, regional, and national training opportunities for YMCA staff, career and human resources manuals, and financial support for training needs.[27]

Other Certifications   Because not all jobs in the leisure-service profession are best associated with the CPRP or CTRS certification, a number of others available may better reflect job responsibilities.

Certified meeting professional: For people who plan meetings, conventions, and exhibitions.[28]

Certified playground inspector: This certification is offered by the National Playground Safety Institute.

Aquatics facility operator and certified pool operator: These certifications focus on managing and operating aquatics facilities.

Certified special-events professional (CSEP): Awarded by the International Live Events Association, certification is earned through education, experience, and service to the industry. Professionals are required to earn 35 points through education attainment, professional association leadership, and special-event industry experience; then they must pass an examination that includes objective questions, solving a case study, and the review of a professional portfolio.[29]

National Association for Interpretation: Offers certifications in a number of outdoor-related areas including Certified Interpretive Guide, Certified Interpretive Host, Certified Interpretive Planner, Certified Interpretation Trainer, Certified Heritage Interpreter, and Certified Interpretive Manager.[30]

Certified Destination Management Executive: This certification is often obtained by people working with convention and visitors bureaus.

Agency Accreditation Process   Another example of the thrust toward fuller professionalism in the organized recreation, park, and leisure-service field is found in the accreditation process for local public departments initiated in the mid-1990s. For an agency to become accredited, it must examine all aspects of its operations, from maintenance to marketing, and adhere to carefully developed standards of excellence. An outside team of park and recreation practitioners visit the agency to see how well it is meeting the set standards and to offer suggestions for improvements to the agency. Currently, there are 142 accredited agencies.[31] Many of the directors of the accredited agencies have used accreditation as a benchmark for improving services offered to the community and to show the public their tax-supported agency is using its resources wisely.[32]

Case Study

. . . .

The Job Search

Using **Table 10.1**, select two professional associations that have job listings. Review the listings for four positions you would be interested in after graduation.

Questions to Consider

1. What skills or experiences are required for these positions? What are some commonalities among the jobs?
2. What education is needed for the positions?
3. Are there any certifications that are needed? If so, which one(s)?
4. What surprised you most about the jobs in the field?

MAYA STRONG, ACTIVE LIFE COORDINATOR, WATERS SENIOR LIVING COMMUNITY (MINNEAPOLIS, MN)

I mainly work with our residents with memory issues due to such things as dementia or Alzheimer's disease, or with enhanced care residents who need more medical assistance. My days are never the same. I do assessments on residents who haven't had them done yet or any new residents who come in. I get to plan, create, and implement programs based on the assessments. The job can be physically demanding since I am usually the one who sets up chairs and tables, and moves furniture and anything else to set up for a program or upcoming event. It can be emotionally demanding because I use Validation Therapy with my residents, but it is very beneficial long term. Although my job can take up a lot of my energy, I love it! Most importantly, I enjoy working with my residents and their families. I love being a recreational therapist, and my education is what has helped me fulfill my dreams of making a difference in peoples' lives.

Agency accreditation is also done in the camping industry. The American Camp Association accredits camps that meet specific safety, health, and program quality standards. An onsite visitation team examines such areas as facilities, transportation, human resources, programs, and health and wellness.[33]

Criterion 6: Code of Ethical Practice

An important measure of any profession is that it typically outlines the public responsibilities of practitioners and establishes a code of ethical behavior. In fields such as medicine and law, where the possibility of malpractice is great and the stakes are high, strict codes of ethics prevail.

In the field of leisure services, it might appear that any issues related to ethical practice are not as critical as in these other professions. However, in specialized areas such as therapeutic recreation, where patients or clients are likely to be physically, emotionally, or economically vulnerable, the opportunities for harmful, negligent, or unprofessional behavior are great. In other areas of leisure service as well, professionals should have a strong sense of obligation to those they serve, to their communities, and to the profession itself.

The American Therapeutic Recreation Association's Code of Ethics is outlined in 10 principles guiding practices such as justice, confidentiality, and competence.[34] The American Camp Association stresses integrity, truthfulness, fairness to all people, and an agreement to comply with relevant laws of the community. There is a Global Code of Ethics for Tourism that serves as guiding principles for tourism development. These 10 principles cover the economic, social, cultural, and environmental components of travel and tourism, including such things as sustainability, rights of workers and entrepreneurs in the tourism industry, and mutual understanding and respect between peoples and societies.[35]

International Live Events Association (ILEA) Principles of Professional Conduct and Ethics   Special events are important—the last thing someone wants to worry about is the integrity of the special-events professional. That's why all ILEA members subscribe to the ILEA Principles of Professional Conduct and Ethics, listed here.

Each member of ILEA shall agree to adhere to the following:

◆   Promote and encourage the highest level of ethics within the profession of the special events industry while maintaining the highest standards of professional conduct.

- ◆ Strive for excellence in all aspects of our profession by performing consistently at or above acceptable industry standards.
- ◆ Use only legal and ethical means in all industry negotiations and activities.
- ◆ Protect the public against fraud and unfair practices, and promote all practices which bring respect and credit to the profession.
- ◆ Provide truthful and accurate information with respect to the performance of duties. Use a written contract clearly stating all charges, services, products, performance expectations and other essential information.
- ◆ Maintain industry accepted standards of safety and sanitation.
- ◆ Maintain adequate and appropriate insurance coverage for all business activities.
- ◆ Commit to increase professional growth and knowledge, to attend educational programs, and to personally contribute expertise to meetings and journals.
- ◆ Strive to cooperate with colleagues, suppliers, employees, employers, and all persons supervised, in order to provide the highest quality service at every level.
- ◆ Subscribe to the ISES Principles of Professional Conduct and Ethics, and abide by the ISES bylaws and policies.[36]

[Used with permission from the International Live Events Association. © 2007. All rights reserved.]

Criterion 7: Existence of Extensive Professional Development Opportunities

A true profession has many avenues for professionals to develop their skills, knowledge, and abilities in their chosen career after their degrees are completed. Conferences, workshops, seminars, and institutes are held at the state, regional, and national levels, focusing on training opportunities in all areas of the profession. For example, the International Festival Event Association has an annual convention; an annual expo (trade show) featuring vendors for ticketing, crowd management, and equipment rental; and a webinar series covering such topics as sponsorship retention, dealing with severe weather, and maximizing revenue.[37] The National Intramural Recreational Sports Association offers workshops and institutes throughout the year such as National Women's Leadership Institute, Emerging Recreational Sports Leaders Conference, and the Marketing Institute.[38]

Recreation is a changing profession and it is necessary to continually educate its practitioners for them to continue to provide quality services.

In addition to workshops and trainings, most professional associations have monthly, quarterly, or annual publications with articles focusing on issues in the field. The Association for Experiential Education has the *Journal for Experiential Education*; the North American Society of Sport Management has the *Journal of Sport Management*; and the Resort and Commercial Recreation Association has *The Journal of Tourism Insights*.

Current Level of Professional Status

When the seven accepted criteria of professionalism reviewed here are used as the basis for judgment, it is apparent that the recreation, parks, and leisure-service field has made considerable progress toward becoming a recognized profession.

KAREN SUNSHINE SPECIAL EVENT MANAGER, DISNEYLAND RESORT, ANAHEIM, CA

As an Event Manager with the Walt Disney Company, I work on a team that designs the event concepts to ensure we are properly focusing on the marketing message. My event planning job is unique in that 90 percent of the events I work on take place in a theme park that is open to guests 365 days a year. So we do not negatively impact the operation of the theme park, it is critical that I am part of a team that communicates all the logistics that are taking. Part of the planning process involves creating a detailed working itinerary with a thorough summary of what is happening at detailed points in time, who is responsible for the action, and where the specific activity takes place. This process insures all partners are aware of what the others are doing and avoids any conflicts of timing, space allocation, etc. During the planning phase of an event, a majority of my time is spent in collaborative meetings and e-mail follow up. It is not uncommon for an event to generate hundreds of e-mails. In addition to managing logistics, I manage the overall project budget from estimation through reconciliation. Once in the execution phase of the event, I am on site ensuring all phases—from guest arrival through departure—are executed without a flaw and with lots of "Disney magic!"

Some elements are already securely in place, such as the development of a unique body of knowledge and the establishment of a network of college and university programs of professional preparation. As for the professional organization element, the National Recreation and Park Association and other national associations or societies represent a significant force for upgrading and monitoring performance in the recreation field, but their attempts to serve the interests of a wide variety of leisure-service agencies also illustrate the field's diversity of services. Realistically, many practitioners in such specialized disciplines as special-event planning, employee recreation, and varied aspects of commercial recreation tend to identify more closely with their separate fields than they do with the overall leisure-service field.

Professionalism in recreation, parks, and leisure services has increased greatly over the past several decades, along with the growing recognition of the field's value in modern society. Because of the immense scope of the diversified recreation field in terms of employment, it has the potential for becoming even more influential in contributing to community well-being in the years ahead.

NEED FOR A SOUND PHILOSOPHICAL BASIS

As discussed, several elements define a profession. Whereas these factors legitimize a profession, a profession has a philosophy that drives its values, ethics, ideas, and approach to service delivery. A sound philosophy of recreation and leisure also can serve the leisure-service field in ongoing policy formulation and program development.

Meaning of Philosophy

The term *philosophy* often conveys an image of ivory tower abstraction, divorced from practical or realistic concerns. Understandably, many practitioners are likely to be suspicious of any approach that appears to be overly theoretical, rather than pragmatic and action-based. The nature of practitioners is to be in the here and now. They look for answers that assist them today and tomorrow, not 6 months or 3 years in the future. Philosophy, more often than not, provides more questions than answers. In far too many instances, it is easier to deal with the present than to anticipate the future and one's appropriate role in shaping that future.

The term philosophy has many definitions. As it applies to a profession, a philosophy is the most basic beliefs, principles, perceptions, and approach to delivering services. A philosophy will guide why the profession or agency exists, guide decision making, and even influence what programs are offered.

Throughout the text many trends and purposes of recreation have been presented. All of these are guided by one of the philosophies presented here.

OPERATIONAL PHILOSOPHIES OF RECREATION AND LEISURE

It is possible to identify several approaches or orientations found in leisure-service agencies today that may be called *operational philosophies*. These include the following: (1) the quality-of-life approach, (2) the marketing or entrepreneurial approach, (3) the human services approach, (4) the prescriptive approach, (5) the resource manager/aesthetic/preservationist approach, (6) the hedonist/individualist approach, and (7) the benefits-based approach.

Quality-of-Life Approach

The *quality-of-life approach* has been the dominant one in the field of organized recreation service for several decades. It sees recreation as an experience that contributes to human development and to community well-being in various ways: improving physical and mental health, enriching cultural life, reducing antisocial uses of leisure, and strengthening community ties.

The quality-of-life orientation stresses the unique nature of recreation as a vital form of human experience—one that is engaged in for its own sake rather than for any extrinsic purpose or conscious social goal. Generally, proponents of this view have agreed that recreation satisfies a universal human need that has been made even more pressing by the tensions of modern urban society, the changed nature of work, and other social conditions.

Those holding this view argue that the pleasure, freedom, and self-choice inherent in recreation and leisure are their most vital contributions to the lives of participants. Quality-of-life advocates have tended to assume that public recreation should be supported for its own sake as an important area of civic responsibility, and that adequate tax funds should be provided for this purpose. In today's era of intense competition for limited tax dollars, the quality-of-life issue remains important, yet the concept of full tax support for parks and recreation is recognized as no longer viable.

HERE ARE TWO EXAMPLES OF AGENCY MISSION STATEMENTS THAT DEMONSTRATE THE QUALITY OF LIFE PHILOSOPHY

Park Ridge Park District's mission is to enhance Park Ridge's quality of life by providing park and recreation opportunities for all residents while being environmentally and fiscally responsible.[39]

The Johnston Senior Center's mission is to enrich the quality of life and support independence and vitality for seniors.[40]

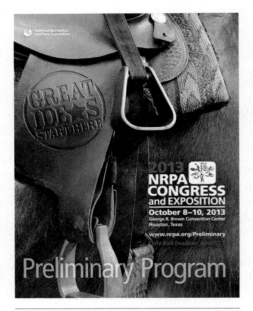

Linking commercial, public, and other special interest recreation organizations, the National Recreation and Park Association offers a variety of special conferences and management schools each year. Other associations in such areas as theme or water park management, conference operations, zoo and aquarium maintenance, and other specializations sponsor similar national programs.

Courtesy of National Recreation and Park Association.

Marketing or Entrepreneurial Approach

The *marketing* or *entrepreneurial approach,* a business-oriented approach to providing organized recreation and park programs and services, evolved rapidly during the latter part of the twentieth century as a direct response to the fiscal pressures placed on public and voluntary leisure-service agencies. As noted in other chapters, steadily mounting operational costs and a declining tax base during that time forced many recreation and park departments to adopt what has come to be known as the marketing approach to agency management. This approach is based on the idea that public, voluntary, or other leisure-service providers will flourish best if they adopt the methods used by commercial enterprises. It argues that they must become more aggressive and efficient in developing and promoting recreation facilities and programs that will reach the broadest possible audience and gain the maximum possible income.

Proponents of the marketing approach take the position that recreation and park professionals should not have to plead for tax-based support solely on the basis of the social value of their programs, but rather should seek to become more independent as a viable, self-sufficient form of community service.

This self-sufficiency can come from either increasing participation in programs, thus generating more revenue, or looking at cost recovery policies. Agencies with a cost recovery approach look at how much programs actually cost and the fees that are charged. They establish a cost recovery benchmark where some programs will be priced to have expenditures higher than revenues (a loss), break even (revenues=expenditures), or where revenues exceed expenditures (a profit). For public agencies, programs operating at a loss can be offset with tax revenue. Nonprofit agencies could use fundraising or profits from other programs to cover costs, and commercial agencies will most likely eliminate programs that are not profitable.

It should be recognized that the marketing trend has influenced far more than public recreation and park agencies alone. Many large nonprofit youth-serving organizations, such as the Y, YWCA and YM-YWHA, have been forced to increase their reliance on self-generated revenues and to move into more aggressive marketing of a wide range of leisure programs, including their fitness services.

Although the marketing approach has been enthusiastically received by many recreation and park managers, it raises a number of issues with respect to the essential purpose of public and voluntary leisure-service agencies. The argument has been made that increased fees and charges—whether imposed by the agencies themselves or by concessionaires or contractors working under privatization plans—tend to exclude the people in greatest need of inexpensive public recreation opportunities, such as children, people with disabilities, and people who are economically disadvantaged.

Human Services Approach

In direct contrast to the marketing approach is the *human services approach* to organized recreation service. This approach regards recreation as an important form of social service that must be provided in a way that contributes directly to a wide range of desired social values and goals. The human services approach received a strong impetus during the 1960s, when recreation programs were generously funded by the federal government as part of the war on poverty and recreation was used to offer job training and employment opportunities for economically disadvantaged youth and adults.

Case Study

. . . .

A Marketing Approach to Program Delivery

Select three similar leisure services agencies, one in each sector (e.g., fitness programs in a public agency, a YMCA, and a commercial gym). Gather a listing of programs they offer. Compare and contrast the services offered and the costs of these services.

Questions to Consider

1. Are the services offered comparable?
2. Which of the 3 agencies best uses the marketing approach to leisure? How do they differ?
3. Should a public agency use a marketing approach to leisure? Why or why not?
4. How can a marketing approach be used if an agency serves low income constituents?

The human services approach is similar to the quality-of-life approach in its recognition of the social value of recreation service. However, it does not subscribe to the latter's idealization of recreation as an inherently ennobling kind of experience, carried on for its own sake. Instead, within the human services framework, recreation must be designed to achieve significant community change and to use a variety of appropriate modalities.

This does not mean that recreation personnel should seek to be health educators, employment counselors, nutritionists, correctional officers, legal advisors, or housing experts. Rather, it implies that they must recognize the holistic nature of the human condition, provide such services when able to do so effectively, and cooperate fully with other practitioners in the various human services fields when appropriate.

Operating under this approach, many public recreation departments have sponsored youth or adult classes in a wide range of educational, vocational, or self-improvement areas and also have provided daycare programs, special services for people with disabilities, roving leader programs for juvenile gangs, environmental projects, and numerous other functions of this type.

In its forceful emphasis on the need to meet social problems head on and achieve beneficial human goals, the human services approach to recreation and park programming may at times be at odds with the marketing approach to service. In the marketing approach, efficient management and maximum revenue are often the primary aims. In the human services orientation, social values and human benefits are emphasized.

Prescriptive Approach

Of the orientations described here, the *prescriptive approach* is the most purposeful in the way it defines the goals and functions of the recreational experience. The idea that recreation should bring about constructive change in participants has been stressed in a number of textbooks on programming. Rossman and Schlatter suggest that leisure programs have goals that describe what change or experience will result from participation.[41]

The clearest cases of prescriptive recreation programs are found in therapeutic recreation. The prescriptive approach to leisure supports the idea that leisure is a part of health and that health and wellness do not totally involve the use of medical intervention. The prescriptive approach recognizes the needs of the participants such as improvement of social or motor skills. Therapeutic recreation professionals use a standard approach to developing programs that are prescriptive in nature. This approach is assessment, planning, implementation, and evaluation (APIE). The participant is assessed to determine his or her needs, a plan is developed to address these needs, the plan is then implemented and evaluated. The evaluation phase reverts back to the assessment and the goals that resulted from the assessment.

Although it is similar to the human services approach in its emphasis on deliberately achieving significant social goals, the prescriptive approach differs in its reliance on the practitioner's expertise and authority. In contrast, a recreation professional working within a human services framework would be much more likely to value the input of community residents and to involve them in decision making.

Regardless of sector, some agencies may have enterprise facilities that generate a profit.
© FloridaStock/Shutterstock.

Resource Manager/Aesthetic/Preservationist Approach

The unwieldy title *resource manager/aesthetic/preservationist approach* is used as a catch-all model to lump together three elements that are not synonymous but that exhibit a high degree of similarity. The *resource manager* obviously is concerned with managing, using, and protecting the outdoor environment. The balance between use, preservation, and protection is a difficult issue that is hotly contested by planners and stakeholders.

Many outdoor recreation agencies strive to balance managing, using, and preserving the natural environment.
© tusharkoley/Shutterstock.

The *aesthetic* position is one that values the appearance of the environment, both natural and artificial, and stresses the inclusion of cultural arts and other creative experiences within a recreation program. The *preservationist* seeks to maintain the physical environment not simply out of a respect for nature, but to preserve evidence of a historical past and a cultural tradition.

This approach to recreation planning is more likely to be evident in agencies that operate extensive parks, forests, waterfront areas, or other natural or scenic resources. Thus, one might assume that it would chiefly be found in such government agencies as federal and state park departments that administer major parks and outdoor recreation facilities. However, this is not the full picture. Many urban recreation and park planners are responsible for large parks. Recent years have seen a growth of new large urban parks in areas that are experiencing growing populations with economically advantaged residents. Often they may help to rehabilitate or redesign rundown waterfront areas, industrial sites, or gutted slum areas. In many cases, their purpose is to preserve or rebuild historic areas of cultural interest that will maintain or increase the appeal of cities for tourism and cultural programming. Preservation and restoration are the primary focuses for older parks while new development with revenue-producing facilities is becoming more common in newer or newly developed park and recreation agencies and communities.

Environmental Awareness   A key element in this approach is the deep reverence that many individuals have today for nature in its various forms. A common theme throughout this text is the need for nature and the lack of time children spend in nature. The value of the outdoor experience is extensive. It helps people understand a lost culture, face the challenge of adventure activities, find a spiritual connection, and experience the beauty and serenity of the outdoors.

However, environmental programming approaches cannot be carried out simply through a poetic evocation of the beauty and experience of nature. Political and economic realities also come into play when environmental decisions must be made.

Natural areas such as the Wakodahatchee Wetlands in Delray Beach, FL serve as a means to preserve wildlife and endangered species.
Courtesy of Deb Garrahy.

State and national parks have seen dramatic budget cuts that have negatively impacted park land and services. For example, the National Park Service has a $12 billion maintenance backlog in 2016, a $440 million increase from 2015 due to deferred maintenance. Examples of park maintenance problems include the Jefferson Memorial sinking into the Tidal Basin, Yosemite National Park road repairs, and crumbling walls in Alcatraz.[42]

If this trend continues, parks will stop some programming, open later in the season, reduce hours, turn to corporate sponsors, and continue to backlog maintenance.

Hedonist/Individualist Approach

The *hedonist/individualist approach* to recreational programming is concerned chiefly with providing fun and pleasure. It regards recreation as a highly individualistic activity that should be free of social constraints or moral purposes. The term *hedonist* is used to mean one who seeks personal pleasure, often with the implication that it is of a sensual, bodily nature. The term *individualist* is attached because this philosophical approach stresses the idea that each individual should be free to seek his or her own fulfillment and pleasure untrammeled by group pressures or social expectations.

Obviously, certain forms of leisure activity that have gained increased popularity in U.S. life fit this description. The accelerated use and generally freer acceptance of drugs, alcohol, gambling, and sex as a commercialized recreational pursuit, and other forms of sensation-seeking entertainment and play, illustrate the hedonist approach to leisure. These forms of play may best be described as morally marginal, in the sense that they are legal in some contexts or localities and illegal in others, regarded as acceptable leisure experiences by some population groups and condemned by others.

Case Study
....

How Do Values Drive an Organization?

The National Recreation and Park Association has built its mission and core values on three important functions that parallel some of the seven philosophies discussed here:

1. Conservation: Protecting open space, connecting children to nature, and engaging communities in conservation practices.
2. Health and Wellness: Leading the nation to improved health and wellness through parks and recreation.
3. Social Equity: Ensuring all people have access to the benefits of local parks and recreation.

Review a complete description of these values at: http://www.nrpa.org.

Questions to Consider

1. How is NRPA using these values?
2. How do the values compare to the philosophies discussed?
3. Review one of the position statements on these three values found online. Summarize the position.

Drug and alcohol use, gambling, legalized marijuana, and some forms of sexual activity are discussed in other chapters. Another form of morally marginal leisure that is a key component of the hedonist approach to recreation and leisure is the use of sex as a form of play or entertainment. Commercialized sex takes many forms, including prostitution and escort services; sex films, books, and magazines; the widespread rental of X-rated movies for home viewing; Internet pornography; and the increased showing of explicit sexual images and themes on network television programs.

Although public, nonprofit, and other types of community-based leisure-service organizations generally do not sponsor substance abuse, gambling, or sex-oriented types of entertainment, such activities are widely available through commercial sponsorship and, in many cases, have governmental approval or tacit acceptance.

Benefits-Based Management Approach

The final philosophical approach to the design and implementation of recreation, park, and leisure-service programs is the *benefits-based approach*. Essentially, this approach holds that it is not enough to verbalize a set of desirable goals or mission statements or to carry out head counts of participation and tally the number of events sponsored by a leisure-service agency. Instead, governmental, nonprofit, therapeutic, armed forces, and other types of managed recreation agencies should more clearly define their roles and purposes in terms of community and participant benefits. A benefit is defined as something that is good for an individual.

Within this process, it is essential that target goals be defined in terms of concrete and measurable benefits. A benefits-based approach focuses on *outcomes* that measure long-term change or effect, rather than *outputs* that simply describe a program.

Philosophical Approaches: No Pure Models

It should be stressed that although these seven approaches to the definition and management of organized leisure services are separate and distinct philosophical positions, it is unlikely that any single agency or government department follows one approach exclusively.

The changing nature of the political, economic, and social environment has forced parks and recreation agencies to reevaluate traditional approaches to delivering public parks and recreation. No single approach has been discarded, but some have fallen out of favor with politicians and professionals. Especially affected has been the human services approach. As mentioned elsewhere, the availability of funding for parks and recreation has not kept up with inflation and in many cases has been significantly reduced. The influence of the war on terror and the ongoing conflicts in Iraq and Afghanistan have had a negative influence on funding for public parks and recreation—yet agencies are expected to provide more programs and services and to maintain existing and new facilities, constituencies, and markets. The business marketing approach, the fastest growing approach to delivery, has been embraced at all levels of government. Services remain available, utilizing the human services approach, especially in major urban areas. In suburban areas, with higher family incomes, supersized recreation centers are replacing older neighborhood centers or are being created in the place of smaller centers. In growing urban fringe areas where recreation services or centers have never been present, or present as only a small operation, the supercenter is an attractive amenity for their growing population. Supercenters typically charge membership fees, charge higher prices for programs, cater to an upscale economic population, and are located in areas of the community where disadvantaged individuals may not have ready access. In addition, the supercenters have more of a club ambience than traditional recreation centers, representing a move away from the human services approach.

Summary

Recreation, parks, and leisure services have grown immensely as a career field, with several million people now employed in organized recreation. Of this overall group, it is estimated that several hundred thousand individuals should be regarded as professionals because of their academic training, job functions, and organizational affiliations.

This chapter describes several important criteria of professionalism, including the following:

1. Having a significant degree of social value, in terms of providing benefits to individual participants and/or to community life
2. Being recognized by the public as a meaningful area of social service or as a legitimate occupational field
3. Requiring specialized professional preparation at the college or university level, based on a distinct body of theoretical and practical knowledge
4. Having profession-related associations that involve national and regional organizations that sponsor conferences, research, publications, and other efforts to upgrade practice and that promote collegiality and a sense of commitment among the practitioners
5. Having a credentialing system to ensure that only qualified individuals—usually identified through a system of certification—are permitted to undertake professional-level tasks
6. Having a code of ethics to ensure that responsible and effective service is provided to the public
7. Having extensive professional development opportunities

The recreation, parks, and leisure-services field has made substantial progress in most of these areas. As recreation and leisure become increasingly important aspects of life in the years ahead, the challenge to the leisure-service field will be to become even more highly professionalized by building on the foundation that has already been laid.

In addition to the criteria for professionalism, a profession also has a philosophical foundation. This chapter identifies seven distinct operational philosophies that influence the provision of organized recreation services today. These range from the quality of life and marketing orientations to a more recent model of service, the benefits-based management approach. Most leisure-services agencies use a mix of these philosophies in their policy development and program delivery. Given the current state of the profession, many agencies blend the benefits-based and marketing or entrepreneurial approaches to leisure-services delivery.

Questions for Class Discussion or Essay Examination

1. Several criteria are generally accepted as hallmarks of professionalism, such as having a social mandate or set of important social values or having a body of specialized knowledge. Select any four of these and discuss the extent to which you believe the recreation, park, and leisure-service field meets these criteria of professionalism.

_____

_____

_____

_____

2. What are the two certifications that are most prominent in parks and recreation? What are the criteria and requirements to obtain these certifications?

_____

_____

_____

_____

3. Several professional associations are listed. What associations would best match your future career interests?

_____

_____

_____

_____

4. Seven different philosophies and approaches to leisure are presented (for example, quality of life). Which of the seven approaches do you find most compatible with your own view?

_____

_____

_____

_____

Endnotes

1. National Recreation and Park Association, "Choosing a Career in Parks and Recreation": http://www.nrpa.org/careers-education/careers/choosing-a-career-in-parks-and-recreation/ (Accessed February 5, 2016).

2. World Travel & Tourism Council, "Economic Impact of Travel & Tourism 2015": https://www.wttc.org/-/media/files/reports/economic%20impact%20research/regional%202015/world2015.pdf (Accessed June 2, 2017).

3. Bureau of Labor Statistics, "Occupational Outlook Handbook: Summary: Recreation Therapists": http://www.bls.gov/ooh/healthcare/recreational-therapists.htm (Accessed February 5, 2016).

4. Ibid.

5. Ibid.

6. National Park Service, "Frequently Asked Questions": http://www.nps.gov/aboutus/faqs.htm.

7. America's State Parks, "State Park Facts": http://www.naspd.org/about-us/state-park-facts/ (Accessed February 5, 2016).

8. Bureau of Labor Statistics, "Occupational Outlook Handbook. Job Outlook": http://www.bls.gov/ooh/personal-care-and-service/recreation-workers.htm#tab-6 (Accessed February 5, 2016).

9. Ibid.

10. YWCA, "Mission & Vision": http://www.ywca.org/site/c.cuIRJ7NTKrLaG/b.7515887/k.9633/Mission__Vision.htm (Accessed February 5, 2016).

11. Bureau of Labor Statistics, "American Time Use Survey-2014 Results": http://www.bls.gov/news.release/atus.nr0.htm (Accessed February 5, 2016).

12. America's State Parks, "State Park Facts": http://www.naspd.org/about-us/state-park-facts/ (Accessed February 5, 2016).

13. National Park Service, "Frequently Asked Questions": http://www.nps.gov/aboutus/faqs.htm (Accessed February 5, 2016).

14. ESPN, "Major League Attendance Report": http://espn.go.com/mlb/attendance (Accessed February 5, 2016).

15. North American Society for Sport Management, "Sports Management Programs: United States": http://www.nassm.org/Programs/AcademicPrograms/United_States (Accessed February 5, 2016).

16. A. R. Hurd and B. E. Schlatter, "Establishing Cooperative Competency Based Internships for Parks and Recreation Students," _Journal of Health, Physical Education, Recreation & Dance_ (Vol. 35, 2007): 32–37.

17. National Recreation and Park Association Professional Development, "COAPRT Accredited Academic Programs" (2016): http://www.nrpa.org/certification/accreditation/coaprt/coaprt-accredited-academic-programs/.

18. Commission on Sport Management Accreditation (COSMA), "Accredited Programs": http://www.cosmaweb.org/list-of-accredited-programs1.html (Accessed February 7, 2016).

19. National Recreation and Park Association, "Our Mission": www.nrpa.org/About-National-Recreation-and-Park-Association/.

20. Canadian Parks and Recreation Association: http://www.cpra.ca/ (Accessed February 7, 2016).

21. American Camp Association: http://www.acacamps.org/ (Accessed February 7, 2016).

22. National Recreation and Park Association, "CPRP Eligibility": http://www.nrpa.org/certification/CPRP/eligibility/.

23. M. A. Mulvaney and A. R. Hurd, *Official Study Guide for the Certified Park and Recreation Professional Examination*, 5th ed. (Ashburn, VA: National Recreation and Park Association, 2017).

24. National Council for Therapeutic Recreation Certification, "Certification Standards": http://nctrc.org/about-certification/certification-standards/ (Accessed February 5, 2016).

25. National Council for Therapeutic Recreation Certification, "NCTRC Exam Content Outline: 2014 Job Analysis Study": http://nctrc.org/wp-content/uploads/2015/02/MM8-HT3-exam-content-outline.pdf (Accessed February 7, 2016).

26. National Recreation and Park Association, "Certified Park and Recreation Executive (CPRE) Certification": www.nrpa.org/CPRE/ (Accessed February 5, 2016).

27. Association of YMCA Professionals: www.ayponline.org (Accessed February 5, 2016).

28. Event Industry Council, Certified Meeting Professional (CMP) Program: http://www.eventscouncil.org/CMP/Applications.aspx (Accessed February 6, 2017).

29. International Live Events Association, Certified Special Events Professional: www.ileahub.com/CSEP (Accessed February 5, 2016).

30. National Association for Interpretation Certification Program: www.interpnet.com/nai/Certification/Overview/nai/_certification/NAI_Certification.aspx?hkey=fa8b1be4-ee12-436d-ac61-7cdd7efd3926 (Accessed February 5, 2016).

31. National Recreation and Park Association, "Accredited Agencies": www.nrpa.org/accreditedagencies/ (Accessed February 5, 2016).

32. National Recreation and Park Association Professional Development, "CAPRA Accredited Agencies": http://www.nrpa.org/accreditedagencies/ (Accessed February 5, 2016).

33. American Camp Association, "About ACA Accreditation": http://www.acacamps.org/staff-professionals/accreditation-standards/accreditation/about-aca-accreditation (Accessed February 7, 2016).

34. American Therapeutic Recreation Association, "Code of Ethics": http://www.atra-online.com/welcome/about-atra/ethics (Accessed February 7, 2016).

35. World Tourism Association, "Global Code of Ethics for Tourism": http://ethics.unwto.org/en/content/global-code-ethics-tourism (Accessed February 8, 2016).

36. International Live Events Association, "ILEA Professional Conduct and Ethics": http://www.ileahub.com/about/ilea-professional-conduct-and-ethics (Accessed February 8, 2016).

37. International Festival Event Association, "Education": http://www.ifea.com/p/education (Accessed February 8, 2016).

38. National Intramural Recreational Sports Association, "Upcoming NIRSA Events": http://nirsa.net/nirsa/grow/ (Accessed February 8, 2016).

39. Park Ridge Park District, "About Us": http://parkridgeparkdistrict.com/general (Accessed February 14, 2016).

40. Johnston Senior Center, "Mission Statement": http://johnstonsc.net/2.html (Accessed February 14, 2016).

41. J. R. Rossman and B. E. Schlatter, *Recreation Programming: Designing Leisure Experiences*, 7th ed. (Champaign, IL: Sagamore Publishing, 2015).

42. Daly, M., "Parks $12 billion behind in maintenance work," *The Pantagraph, 170,* D1-2: Associated Press (February 14, 2016).

CHAPTER 11

Future Perspectives

Defining the Future: The future is a product of imagination based on experience and desire. It is a place where people like to anticipate, plan, fantasize, and hope. It is a product of the mind. It is perhaps possible to argue that the evolution of the human brain is in great part an evolution in cognitive abilities necessary to forecast the future, i.e., abstract imagination, logic, and induction. Imagination permits us to "see" (i.e., predict) a plausible model of a given situation without observing it, therefore mitigating risks. Logical reasoning allows one to predict inevitable consequences of actions and situations and therefore gives useful information about future events. Induction permits the association of a cause with consequences, a fundamental notion for every forecast of future time.[1]

Learning Objectives

1. Recognize the key agendas for the twenty-first century.

2. Understand the influence of key agendas of the twenty-first century on the leisure industry.

3. Investigate and propose how the leisure industry might respond to the key agendas.

4. Explain one or more of the key agendas, potential impact on the delivery of leisure services.

5. Assess and explain how one or more of the key agendas will personally impact you.

INTRODUCTION

The remarkable growth of organized recreation, parks, and leisure services is documented throughout this text. Despite the impressive history of this social movement and field of professional activity, a number of continuing and emerging issues and concerns affect the regard for the role of recreation, parks, and leisure in personal, community, and national life.

The new century, now almost 20 years old, is already experiencing new challenges, opportunities, and approaches to the leisure mosaic. Former traditional models of leisure are changing in many communities; traditional approaches to the provision of recreation services are changing; opportunities for leisure are more abundant than at any time in recorded history; governments and people are rethinking the role of parks, recreation, and leisure in the national fabric; and nonprofits are expanding services while commercial enterprises are engaging in new and creative leisure opportunities.

Decisions about parks and recreation facilities are frequently debated in public hearings.
© Yurico/Shutterstock.

As the United States and the world experienced its most serious economic decline in 70 years, following almost 30 years of sustained economic growth, decisions about what government can do, should do, and what citizens are willing to pay for remain under discussion over a decade later.

The notion of parks, recreation, and leisure as a social welfare model remains viable, especially in consideration of those who are underprivileged; but for many others, the social welfare model has become outdated and the public, politicians, and leisure practitioners are looking for new models. The relevant question of the twenty-first century is how do public parks, recreation, and leisure provide effective services and programs in an era of economic uncertainty? What is the appropriate role and responsibility of urban, suburban, and rural recreation agencies, as well as nonprofit and commercial organizations? This chapter discusses issues, challenges, and changes in the American fabric that influence parks, recreation, and leisure.

How should the major priorities of organized recreation service in the United States be determined? In what ways can or should government provide more effective and efficient services? What are the key responsibilities of organized recreation toward people with physical and mental disabilities, toward the new aging, or toward those who may have had inadequate opportunities in the past because of their gender, race, ethnic background? How is the millennial generation changing our perception, operation, and access to parks and recreation?

How has technology affected the planning, delivery, operation, and marketing of parks and recreation—in the public, nonprofit, and commercial sectors? Social media, smartphones, tablets, and a whole host of technology supported by rapidly emerging apps has changed the way people look at, use, and embrace their world. Long-held assumptions about how information is shared and exchanged are no longer valid. How will leisure-service professionals respond and anticipate such changes in the years ahead?

How will the changing social and economic conditions in the coming decades affect the public's leisure values and patterns of participation, and how can recreation, parks, and leisure-service professionals and organizations respond effectively to the challenges of the future?

KEY RATIONALE GUIDING LEISURE-SERVICE DELIVERY TODAY

For recreation, parks, and leisure-service practitioners, it is possible to identify a number of key principles that should be used to guide their professional operations today. First, it is assumed that such individuals—no matter what their fields of specialization—regard recreation and leisure as important to human growth and community development. A contemporary philosophy of organized recreation service therefore should deal with such important issues as the place of recreation and leisure in modern life, the role of government, the development of experience-based programming, and building relationships with partners to meet social needs.

Place of Recreation in the Modern Community

In U.S. society, our view of recreation as a social phenomenon and area of community involvement is influenced by our governmental systems. In our Constitution and in court decisions that have influenced government policy through the years, we have accepted the view that, on various levels, government has the responsibility for providing certain major services to citizens. These include functions related to safety and protection, education, health, and other services that contribute to maintaining the quality of life of all citizens.

Linked to this system of governmental responsibility is our general acceptance of the Judeo-Christian concepts of the worth and dignity of all human beings and the need to help each person become the most fully realized individual that he or she is capable of being. Through government and through many voluntary community associations, we have accepted the responsibility for providing needed services and opportunities for people at each stage of life and for those who because of disability have been deprived in significant ways.

Needs of Individual Citizens

Recreation and leisure are important aspects of personal experience in modern life for the physical, social, emotional, intellectual, and spiritual benefits they provide. Positive leisure experiences enhance the quality of a person's life and help each person develop to the fullest potential. To make this possible, government and other responsible social agencies should provide recreation resources, programs, and, where appropriate, leisure education to help people understand the value of free time when constructively and creatively used.

Government's Responsibility

In addition to providing personal benefits, recreation helps a community to meet health needs, gain economic benefits, and maintain community morale. On each level (local, state, and federal), appropriate government agencies should therefore be assigned the responsibility for maintaining a network of physical resources for leisure participation, including parks, playgrounds, centers, sport facilities, and other special recreation facilities. Government should be responsible for planning, organizing, and carrying out programs, under proper leadership, for all age levels.

Government cannot and should not seek to meet all of the leisure needs of the community. It must recognize that other types of community organizations—including voluntary, private, commercial, therapeutic, industrial, and educational groups—sponsor effective recreation programs, which are often designed to meet specialized needs or more advanced interests. Therefore, its unique role should be to provide a basic floor of recreational opportunity, to fill the gaps that are not covered by other organizations, and to provide coordination and overall direction to community leisure-service programs.

There has been a growing body of opinion that local government recreation and park agencies should take less responsibility for the direct provision of program activities, particularly when limited by fiscal constraints, and should move instead into the role of serving as an advocate for recreation and leisure in community life and providing coordinating or facilitating assistance to other agencies. There is an ongoing debate regarding how much service can be provided, who should be the director or primary provider, who should pay and who should not pay, and at what level services should be provided.

A major concern should be to ensure an equitable distribution of recreational opportunities for the public at large. This would not guarantee that all residents have totally equal programs and services, but rather would represent a pledge that, within the realities of community needs and economic capabilities, facilities and programs will be distributed so as to bring about a reasonable balance of such opportunities for different neighborhoods and community groups.

Influence of the Nonprofit Sector

The nonprofit sector has accepted an increasingly larger role in the provision of recreation and leisure-based social services. An important part of the effort has focused on youth-serving agencies in at-risk neighborhoods. There are several reasons why nonprofits have taken an increasing role. First, this is not a new model for nonprofits to assume, but rather a continuation and expansion of services when local members of the community realize that the government cannot provide needed services. Second, more individuals are willing to give to nonprofits, are able to give substantial sums of money, and are willing to give to their community. Nonprofits are frequently seen as a more desirable and effective organization to address social ills than is government. Finally, government has recognized its inability to meet all of the needs of a community and either encourages nonprofits and/or works jointly with them.

Influence of the Commercial Sector

The commercial sector serves a unique and increasing role in the provision of recreation and leisure opportunities. Its engagement is infrequently focused on a particular social group or those economically disadvantaged, but instead looks at the broad sector of recreation opportunities for the masses. The services can be broad, such as resorts, theme parks, cruise lines, and the like, or very narrow, such as river tours, backcountry excursions, flights over and into wilderness areas, and specialized recreation services such as bike shops, tours, and races; shooting ranges and hunting ranches; and mountain climbing manufacturers, schools, and expeditions. Online delivery of recreation experiences is expanding, as evidenced by the rapid growth of virtual technology. The breadth of involvement by the commercial sector is staggering. Commercial enterprises are often seen as innovative, able to react to trends, and appropriate providers for certain mass and specialized recreation services.

FACING THE CHALLENGE OF THE FUTURE

Those who read this text—primarily college and university students in recreation, park, tourism, sport, and leisure-studies curricula—are looking ahead to careers in the future. What will the twenty-first century bring in terms of demographic, social, and economic changes that can radically impact our perceptions, expectations, and demand for our leisure?

Traditional forms of leisure are growing, but at a slower rate than the population. The election of a Republican President and a Republican majority in Congress has already resulted in a new direction for the country. New diverse forms of leisure, often individual or Internet-based, are growing outside of traditional program areas. Academic programs and curricula based on a twentieth-century model no longer prepare students and professionals for the challenges of the twenty-first century. Recognition of a social responsibility ethic grounded in community engagement structured in the context of a "do-more-with-less" government reality is what students and professionals are already dealing with. Challenges to our social fabric, mores, and openness as a society must endure among park and recreation professionals. The awareness of environmental and social justice in society and how public parks and recreation will address these issues are paramount to the profession's future.

Many contemporary authorities in the leisure-service field emphasize that bringing about needed changes will require a new wave of entrepreneurship. Recreation and park professionals in all spheres of service need to think more imaginatively and innovatively, need to be content experts in leisure, politically astute in government, and able to build coalitions among support and disparate groups. They need to cultivate an organizational and professional climate that is interactive, community focused, and politically and socially responsible.

EFFORTS TO PREDICT THE FUTURE

Almost 20 years into the twenty-first century there remains much discussion about the role of parks and recreation. Whatever discussions were held in the early part of this decade, the recession in the latter part of the decade changed the ability and willingness of government to deliver parks, recreation, and leisure services, programs, and facilities. Nonprofits and commercial enterprises were equally challenged by the economic decline. The face of the profession has changed in the midst of these new challenges.

The "business as usual" model that dominated the latter part of the twentieth century and the early part of this century has been challenged in ways not anticipated. The impact on the public parks and recreation sector's ability to provide services and facilities is the most significant in 50 years. Local and state governments and park and recreation agencies have adapted to new organizational models and mandates. As a result, they are changing the vision of their role in their communities

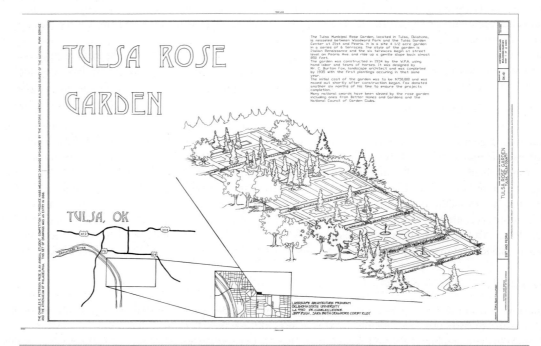

Designing park settings incorporates past experiences and anticipates future expectations.
Courtesy of the Library of Congress, Prints and Photographs Division.

Agendas in the Twenty-First Century

There has been no single national effort by parks and recreation organizations to address the twenty-first century's impact on parks and recreation; individual organizations have focused on trends that affect themselves. The broader societal impact has been left for others to deal with. The U.S. Forest Service operates an outdoor recreation trends center; states generate 5-year state comprehensive outdoor recreation plans that are of varying quality with some to significant trend analysis. Many municipalities have master plans for development and have strategic plans. In both instances, trend analysis may be a small or significant part of the plan. Some state parks and recreation associations, especially California, make efforts to keep their members abreast of trends. The problem facing trend analysis in parks and recreation is the diversity of the profession itself. Some trends cross boundaries between urban recreation, outdoor recreation, city parks and recreation departments, state park systems, national parks, and nonprofits, but there are many other trends that do not. National trends paint a broad picture, whereas regional and local trends may be significantly different. Making assumptions that trends will occur as predicted is equally dangerous. In 2004, the economy looked as if it would continue to be positive. In October, 2007 the economy collapsed around the housing market and had a worldwide ripple effect on global investment banks, and international, national, and local economies. Unemployment reached levels not seen since the depression of the 1930s. By 2016 the economy had recovered from the recession, but the damage inflicted on public and nonprofit agencies was still present and has altered how people see the roles of government and nonprofits.

How then do parks and recreation organizations focus on trends that have some basis of validity? There are those who are considered futurists and have a track record of success. Trends, at their best, are educated guesses about the future. They are influenced by those who are suggesting them—their knowledge, biases, and creative ability to anticipate change.

The trends have led to conclusions about the future of parks and recreation, and especially about public and nonprofit agencies that requires a response. Some of these trends emerged at conferences and workshops held in the mid- to late-1990s and remain current.

Agendas in the Twenty-First Century

- Parks and recreation professionals must embrace rapid societal change as the new norm and learn to anticipate needed service provision.
- Demographic complexity, as demonstrated by shifting social issues of gender, lifestyle, and life stage, provides indications of social sous chefs in society that require parks and recreation agencies to rethink for whom, what, and how they offer programs.
- The trend toward greater public participation in decision-making is a reality, and public agencies must be on the cutting edge of the movement.
- Obesity is increasingly a major societal health crisis. Partnering in community-based efforts is critical to overcoming the obesity crisis, as is focusing on the broader issue of individual and community wellness.
- Public agencies are receiving smaller shares of available public dollars for operations, maintenance, and repairs. The public continue to support and fund land acquisitions through bond referendum and other resources, and simultaneously expect services to continue at the same level.
- Public agency success depends on an organization's ability to build quality relationships and establish networks and coalitions with other community-based organizations.
- Federal leadership in the recreation and parks movement will become more narrowly focused, as the challenges of an aging society, globalization, international commitments, tax revolts, and other unforeseen mandates reduce the ability to support the broad range of traditional services.
- Park and recreation agencies need to enhance their technological competence to introduce new generations to the outdoors, fitness, community engagement, and expanded leisure opportunities.
- An understanding of current users, nonusers, potential users, and their motivation is the foundation for anticipating change and meeting the needs of the current and future generations.
- Public agencies must provide environmental leadership at the local level.
- Embracing the role of a community change agent through engagement on issues focusing on quality of life, community visioning, creation of public places and spaces, and building whole and healthy communities in partnership with community, regional, and national organizations.
- Public park and recreation agencies are increasingly moving beyond the quality of life role and becoming partners in community economic development, oftentimes providing impetus for regional and multistate sport, recreation, and cultural events.

◆ There is a mandate to embrace tourism, the world's largest economy, on a local, regional, and national level in new and creative ways. Public agencies can be the catalyst for community and regional tourism development.

Agencies must rethink the recreation experience in light of increased technology impacting leisure activities, segmentation and specialization of participation, individualized personal recreation, time-deepening, time-shifting, and activity-stacking.

CHALLENGES AND STRATEGIES FOR THE FUTURE

Demographic Shifts and Population Diversity

Demographic shifts and population diversity are two of the major issues today. Public agencies, accustomed to serving single or fixed cultural groups, have discovered that the demographic dynamic is rapidly changing. In California the total minority population is now larger than the traditional white population. This trend will continue. At the same time, immigration and migration (movement within the United States) is changing the makeup, population size, and diversity of communities. We are part of an aging society, the traditional family defies definition, and children and teens are increasingly at risk. Understanding these trends and their impact are part of the leisure profession's responsibilities.

However, these changes are more than just geographic. Examples of some key population shifts, both geographic and generational, include the following:

◆ More than 59% of all Americans live in the South and West, and that number is growing.
◆ Hispanics are projected to make up 24% of the population by 2065.[2]
◆ Asians have become the largest immigrant group, replacing Hispanics.[2]
◆ Millennials, young adults born after 1980, have become the largest generation, surpassing Boomers. They are the generation to watch.
◆ The United States has moved from a rural to a metropolitan nation, with four of five Americans now living in metropolitan areas (84%).
◆ Millennials are making key personal choices regarding resource and energy consumption and family size, taking into consideration ecological and environmental impacts and sustainability.[3]
◆ By 2050, blacks, Hispanics, and Asians will make up 46% of the working-age population and account for almost 90% of the growth in that age group during the same period.[4]

Shifts are cultural, geographic, demographic, and environmental. The shifts have important impacts on the delivery of parks, recreation, and leisure services. In the early stages of migration from the urban core to the suburbs, loss of free time was measured in commuting time. It was assumed most commuting was done from the suburbs to the urban core. More recently, the commute has stretched both ways, with increasing numbers of people choosing to live in the urban core and work in the suburbs. Beyond the urban core, the exurbs have become the new growth area, outpacing growth within cities. Land in this area has been developed twice as fast as in the urban and suburban cores. In addition, developed land occupies 20% more space than it did just 20 years ago. It is the twenty-first century version of sprawl.[5]

In 1915, the population reached 100 million people. Fifty-two years later in 1967, it reached 200 million, and 50 years later, it reached 324 million. Foreign-born residents represented 15% of the population in 1915, 8% in 1967, and 12.9% in 2010. In 1915 and 1967, the largest percentage of the foreign-born population came from Europe. In 2012, it was Latin America, followed by Asia.[6] The immigrant population held relatively steady at 8–12% of the total population from 1860 to 2000, but between 2000 and 2050 it is projected that the major growth in population will come from immigrants. The United States is the third most populous nation in the world behind China and India. The steady growth in population and diversity has increasing impacts on recreation demand, participation, and types of programs.

The Generations America is a land of generations. In recent years, the terms *baby boomer*, *Gen X*, *Millennials*, and *Net Generation* have garnered much public press. Only more recently has the term *generations* taken on a marketing connotation. Some authors have adjusted the names to fit marketing terminology. For example, the Pew Internet Project classifies six generations between 1937 and 1990 (**Table 11.1**).

What matters in understanding generations is defining how they are different from each other. Every generation has been different from the generations preceding it. Gen X and Millennials are the first generations to have

TABLE 11.1 Generations of Americans

Generation	Birth Years in 2016	Percentage of Total Adult Population		
		2015	2036	2050
Millennials	Born 1977–1995	30.9%	43.0%	57.7%
Gen X	Born 1965–1976	27.0%	31.8%	36.5%
Boomers	Born 1946–1964	30.7%	23.9%	5.8%
Silent Generation	Born 1937–1945	11.5%	1.3%	0.0%

Data from Fry, R. 2016. Millennials overtake Baby Boomers as America's largest generation. Pew Research Center. http://www.pewresearch.org/fact-tank/2016/04/25/millennials-overtake-baby-boomers/. (Accessed Feburary 15, 2017).

broad access to computer technology and to fully embrace it as a part of their lives. The influence of technology is discussed in more detail later in this chapter. A study of generations is a study of American history and how culture, war, poverty, technology, social movements, education, and other influences affect individuals within generations, their attitudes, expectations, and leisure participation.

A similar perspective of generations can be applied to the history, challenges, influences, and actions within parks, recreation, and leisure. Comparing the concept of generations to the discussion in the chapter "Recreation and Leisure in the Modern Era" can enhance one's understanding of how the profession has grown and matured.

Ethnic and Racial Diversity As previously shared, the United States is becoming more diverse. The immigration of Europeans has lessened dramatically, replaced by rapid integration of Hispanics, and lesser of Asian, Middle Eastern, and African populations. The 2010 U.S. Census showed a growing diversity. Hispanics are the largest minority in the United States. Between 2000 and 2010 the Hispanic population grew 43%, from 35.5 million to 50.5 million. The total estimated U.S. population is depicted in **Table 11.2**.

Research into the influence of race and ethnicity has received greater attention over the last decade. Most important, it has shown that ethnicity is a factor in levels of recreation participation, types of activities engaged in, and comfort levels with the natural environment. Some early research set the stage for a better

MEET THE MILLENNIAL GENERATION

The Pew Research Center (pewresearch.org) has actively tracked the generations for years. The Millennial generation has just supplanted the Boomer generation as the largest generation. Coming in a period of rapid technological and social change, this generation is facing opportunities, challenges, and is redefining America in their own image. Pew conducted a study of Millennials and arrived at six conclusions:

1. Millennials have fewer attachments to traditional political and religious institutions, but they connect to personalized networks of friends, colleagues, and affinity groups through social and digital media.
2. Millennials are more burdened by financial hardships than previous generations, but they're optimistic about the future. Millennials are the first in the modern era to have higher levels of student loan debt, poverty, and unemployment, and lower levels of wealth and personal income than their two immediate predecessor generations had at the same age. Yet, they are extremely confident about their financial future.
3. Singlehood sets Millennials apart from other generations. Just 26% of Millennials are married. When they were at the age that Millennials are now, 36% of Gen Xers, 48% of Baby Boomers, and 65% of the members of the Silent Generation were married.
4. Millennials are the most racially diverse generation in American history. Some 43% of Millennial adults are non-white.
5. Millennials are less trusting of others than older Americans are. In a survey, only 19% say that most people can be trusted.
6. Few Millennials believe that Social Security will provide them with full benefits when they are ready to retire, but most oppose cutting current benefits as a way to fix the system.[7]

understanding of why there are differences. A study by Virden and Walker reports that Caucasians found a forest environment more pleasing and safer than did African Americans and Hispanics.[8] Hibbler and Shinew identified four factors that explain the differences in leisure patterns. The four reasons are (1) the limited socioeconomic resources of many African Americans; (2) a historical pattern of oppression and racial discrimination towards African Americans; (3) distinct cultural differences between African Americans and European Americans; and (4) feelings of discomfort and constraint by African Americans in public leisure settings.[9]

There is a growing realization that assimilation of immigrants is a complex issue. They are more ethnically diverse, may have complex intergenerational changes, and are growing rapidly in number. For example, Mexican immigrant women have seen it as their responsibility to maintain their culture. Beyond immigrant and generational issues, different ethnic groups view leisure at once similarly and differently. African Americans prefer shopping, going to church, and open spaces that serve active recreation-related functions. Caucasians show a greater preference for open space for land; wildlife; passive-, individual-, or family-based recreation; and conservation. Hispanics and Asians tend to come to outdoor areas in larger family groups for social purposes. African Americans, Caucasians, and Hispanics all shared similar views toward social-setting attributes such as sharing experiences, being by oneself, and so forth. Research has made progress in explaining differences in race and ethnic decisions and preferences for leisure, but the field is still not well understood.[10,11]

Age Diversity Generations are represented by age diversity. The baby boomer generation, as a percentage of the total population, is staggering in its size and impact. In addition, the population distribution has changed dramatically over the last 50 years with its influence on society and government already significant. Births are declining while immigration and births among first- and second-generation Hispanics are higher than the national average for all other ethnic groups.

In 1967, the median age in the United States was 29.5 years. In 2015, the median age increased to 37.8 years. America is an aging society and it suggests that we are moving from an economy where there are more workers than retirees to a society where there are insufficient workers to maintain retirees. The senior or boomer population will continue to be a significant

New immigrants bring with them their own culture and customs. Integration into American society is often difficult.
Courtesy of Martha Reed.

TABLE 11.2   2016 Race and Ethnicity of the United States Population

Race/Ethnicity	2016 Population (199 in millions)	% Total Population
White	199.0	60.1%
Hispanic	56.9	17.2%
Black or African-American	43.0	13.0%
Asian	18.1	5.5%
American Indiana & Alaska Native	3.9	1.2%
Native Hawaiian	0.5	0.2%
Some other race	0.6	0.2%
More than one race	9.0	2.7%
Total	**331.0**	**100.0%**

Data from U.S. Census Bureau. 2016. QuickFacts. Available at https://www.census.gov/quickfacts/table/PST045216/00 (Accessed February 15, 2017).

but dwindling part of the total population. The first boomers were born in 1946 and are retiring. The later boomers were born in 1960 to 1964 and are past their child-bearing years, and have made their contributions to society's population growth. The 36- to 54-year-old age groups (49 to 67 in 2013) include the boomers and represent 28% of the total U.S. population.[12]

Aging Society   The United States has an aging society. For the first time in history, Americans are reaping the benefits of advances in science, technology, healthcare, nutrition, and affluence. The life expectancy of Americans has nearly doubled in the past century; in 1900, the life expectancy was 47 years, and by 2000, it had risen to 77. Individuals living into their late 80s and mid-90s is no longer uncommon. This population represents the most financially independent aging group in history. The 55-plus age group controls more than 75% of the country's wealth.

Between 2012 and 2050, the growth of an older population will expand dramatically. By 2050, the 65 and older population is expected to grow to 83.7 million, almost double the 2012 population.[13] By one estimate, the United States will need 31,000 geriatricians, compared to the 1000 in 2004.[14] It is suggested that 20% of the workforce could focus on providing services to and caring for aging boomers. In some states, particularly in the Midwest and Northeast, healthcare is already the largest industry.

Yet, can we expect the boomers, as they enter retirement, to do the same as earlier seniors? The answer is no. They will make their own mark on society and do it their way, which is a continuation of their lifelong contributions to change society. The early assumption was that boomers would go into full retirement as so many other generations have. Changes in the economy, retirement benefits, concerns about Social Security and Medicare, healthcare costs, longevity, and overall health have changed perceptions about retirement. In a 2015 census.gov report, 20% of the population over age 65 worked at least 1 to 14 hours a week, with 57.6% of the 65- to 69-year-old male population working an average of 35 or more hours a week, while 36% of women of the same age range worked. Overall, 36% of the 65- to 69-year-old population worked, while only 12.4% of the 70 or older population worked.[15]

More and more adults are celebrating the "new old," which is a new generation of seniors who are aging on their own terms.
© digitalskillet/Shutterstock.

In a report by Merrill Lynch, they found only 17% of boomers surveyed said they would never work again, and this 17% was the least financially prepared for retirement.[16] By contrast, 76% of those surveyed plan to work during stages of retirement. When asked why they will continue to work, 34% said it was important to earn money and 67% wanted the continuing mental stimulation and challenge to motivate them. The end of mandatory retirement in 1986 allowed many older adults to continue to work and contribute to the workforce. Simultaneous with the end of mandatory retirement, the Social Security system retirement ages were raised to 66 and 67. Between 1990 and 2010, there was a 20.8% increase in the number of men working between ages 62 and 64, a traditional retirement period. Overall, the workforce of men and women ages 60 to 64 grew from 52.8 million to 58 million. Boomers do not see retirement as a period of relaxation and reduced lifestyle, but rather a continuation of challenges and personal growth—but on their own terms. The decision to retire is based more on the ability to do what they want and having the resources to do it than it is on the need to retire in a more traditional sense.

POVERTY AND OLDER AMERICANS

Poverty in America has been a long hard struggle for those in poverty and for those working to help individuals and groups move out of poverty. Seniors are not only not exempt from poverty, but sometimes are more susceptible to poverty. Just as among the normal population, ethnic groups have higher levels of poverty, and so do older ethnic Americans. In a 2016 report from multiple federal agencies (Older Americans: Key Indicators of Well-Being), the prevalence of poverty among those 65 and over has lowered since a 1966 report showed that 29% of older Americans lived at or below the poverty level. This was the highest rate among any population in the United States. By 2014 that number had dropped to 10%, but ethnic populations continued to lag. Non-white ethnic groups were more likely to live at or below the poverty level. Among Asian men, 13% were at this level, and 16% of Asian women. Older Hispanic men and women were at 16%, while older Black men were at 17% and older Black women were at 21%.[17]

Case Study

. . . .

Serious Leisure Contributes to Successful Aging

Serious leisure is a concept first proposed by sociologist Robert Stebbens in 1982, who contended that "serious leisure is the systematic pursuit of an amateur, hobbyist, or volunteer core activity that people find so substantial, interesting and fulfilling that . . . they launch themselves on a (leisure) career centered on acquiring and expressing a combination of its special skills, knowledge, and experience."[a] In the context of Maslow's hierarchy of needs, serious leisure fulfills multiple need and growth roles for individuals, ranging from belonging to creativity. Stebbens sees serious leisure as a substitution for work for those who may have left the workforce, whether voluntarily or involuntarily, yet he says serious leisure is not a livelihood and one should not get caught up in seeing serious leisure as a substitute for work. Serious leisure carries with it "numerous pleasant expectations and memories, doing so to a degree only rarely found in work."[b]

As part of his description of serious leisure, Stebbens identified six qualities, or descriptors, that are present. In some ways, they are similar to life challenges and do not always represent positive emotions, but they do represent challenges individuals must face in the pursuit of serious leisure. There are linkages to Maslow's hierarchy of human needs at the creativity level as well as Csikszentmihalyi's flow theory. The six qualities are as follows:

Serious leisure activities help seniors maintain successful aging.

© Photodisc/Getty.

- ◆ The occasional need to persevere to overcome difficulties
- ◆ The presence of a career that involves achievement, occurring through stages of development and involvement
- ◆ A significant personal effort focusing on unique acquired knowledge, skill, or training
- ◆ Eight durable benefits including social interaction and belongingness, self-expression, self-enrichment, enhancement of self-image, feelings of accomplishment, lasting physical products, self actualization, and renewal
- ◆ A strong identity formed among participants in their chosen pursuits
- ◆ A unique ethos formed related to the activity resulting in a special social world[a]

Today's aging population, as reported elsewhere in this text, no longer conforms to the concept of a slow downward spiral or the notion that involvement, physical activity, and learning are not part of acceptable retirement activities. Rather, as the baby boomer population ages, this group is challenging all of the notions of what is appropriate for an aging population. Involvement, engagement, physical activity, and extended work or work-related activities are becoming the norm. As part of this change in the approach to and views of aging, serious leisure is receiving more attention from researchers. Linked with predictors of successful aging, serious leisure is showing promise as a way to enrich successful aging. Rowe and Kahn identify three factors crucial to successful aging: "the absence of disease and disability; maintaining mental and physical functioning; and continuing engagement with life."[d] Brown and colleagues studied older adults involved in a dance program and identified six themes related to the qualities of serious leisure.[c] They found *perseverance* among the participants as they learned how to dance. The perseverance was manifested among the participants in attitude and behaviors as they attempted to master basic and advanced dancing steps. Second, the notion of a *leisure career* included achievement or involvement among the participants. For those so engaged, "the concept of a leisure career reflects the successful aging components of learning, involvement, and keeping active."[d] The third quality and theme involved *considerable personal effort* to acquire specific knowledge of the leisure activity. The characteristic of a *unique ethos* reflects directly upon the development of a new and specialized social world, resulting in a strong social network, both of which are recognized components of successful aging. The *benefits of involvement* in serious leisure as they relate to this study involved self-actualization, self-enrichment, self-expression, feelings of accomplishment, enhancement of self-image, regeneration of self, self-gratification, lasting physical products, and social interaction and belongingness. The benefits of involvement may have the most long-lasting impact on the participants and successful aging.

Identity formulation, another quality, comes from the other five characteristics and the researchers found the participants formed a strong identity with their pursuits. More important, it suggests the power of serious leisure as a contributor to successful aging.

Questions to Consider

1. Explain how you participate in serious leisure.
2. Do you have a grandparent who is actively engaged in serious leisure?
3. Explain why serious leisure is important to successful aging.

Sources

a. R. Stebbens, *Serious Leisure*, (New Brunswick, NJ: Transaction Publishers, 2007): 5.
b. R. Stebbens, "Serious Leisure," *Society* (Vol. 38, No. 4, 2001): 55.
c. C. A. Brown, F. A. McGuire, and J. Voelkl, "The Link Between Successful Aging and Serious Leisure," *International Journal of Aging and Human Development* (Vol. 66, No. 1, 2008): 74.
d. Ibid, 82.

What does all of this mean? First, the 72-and-out rule is gone. It has been assumed for generations that most people would die by the age of 72. That has not been true for decades, but never more so than with boomers. There are 75 million over-50s in the United States and they hold approximately 90% of America's $44 trillion in liquid assets. The wealth is not evenly spread across this population. An amazing 42% of all boomers plan to move in retirement. Boomers are moving south and west to warmer climates. Boomer men are planning to retire late, transition from work to retirement, work less, spend more time with their spouses, and relax more. Women see retirement as an opportunity for career development, community involvement, and continued personal growth. Demands for recreation and leisure will increase, but not necessarily for traditional services. The boomers will be better able to pay for services and activities and will be more demanding of creative and nontraditional services.

The aging of Americans has significant implications for recreation participation and delivery. Parks and recreation professionals will be challenged to determine how to serve boomers. The new aging population cannot be considered older adults in the traditional sense. The days of senior centers, bingo, cards, Friday afternoon movies, and bus tours will not be over but will fail to attract the large number of older adults who see themselves as independent. They are already more active, have a more mobile lifestyle, are healthier, have a longer life expectancy, and use technology as a compensation for particular deficiencies, and will do so even more in the future. They are as diverse as any group in society and are changing the way recreation is considered for an aging population. Cities are establishing separate senior service departments or integrating them into existing government organizations. There will be a need to continue to provide traditional services to those older adults who desire them, but many will seek new experiences and greater challenges. This group utilizes their financial resources to remain involved; to engage in travel, sport, and active leisure; and to continue their involvement in family and society.

Recent research holds promise for improving recreation programming for boomers and other older adults. Some research suggests that older adults will focus on more meaningful relationships at the expense of less important relationships. Fitness programs are growing and being adapted to the needs of older adults' health, mobility, and strength levels. Healthy older adults may benefit from activities that focus on goal selection and optimization. Older adults with more limited health should benefit from adapted and facilitated activities.[18] Regardless of the approach taken, public parks and recreation agencies need to understand that older adults are more diverse and have higher expectations than any previous generation.

The Changing Family   Over the last 30 years, family structure and definition have changed more than in the previous 200 years. The era of the stay-at-home mother, the single-income source, three or more children, family dinners, church on Sunday, and marriage as a lifetime commitment has all but disappeared. World War II changed the United States as a society. Women experienced freedom; soldiers coming home from the war had the GI Bill and gained more education than any generation before them. The 1960s and 1970s saw a change in societal mores, traditional family values, and perceptions. The notion of a traditional family changed with society. Politicians and the conservative religious movements have focused on the decay of the nuclear family, yet the facts show that the nuclear family has been in decline for more than 40 years. As early as 1960, the traditional nuclear family comprised only 45% of American households. The 2000 U.S. Census reported for the first time that less than one-quarter (23.5%) of American households consisted of a married man and woman and one or more of their children.[19] The percentage remained unchanged in the 2010 census.

Today's families are characterized in a variety of ways. It may be as a traditional nuclear, an adoption with no marriage, a wedding after the baby, single mom, two dads, two moms, or single dad. David Elkind calls these *permeable families*: "The permeable family is more fluid, more flexible, and more obviously vulnerable to pressures from outside itself."[20]

A major concern of social service organizations is children growing up in single-parent homes. They frequently have fewer opportunities and financial resources than do children growing up in two-parent homes, even if both parents are in the workforce. The Annie E. Casey Foundation reported in 2014 that 24.7 million children are in single-parent homes, but the disparity of opportunities, based on ethnicity and race, is dramatic.[21] **Figure 11.1** depicts the differentiation of single-parent families by race and Hispanic origin. The presence of high levels of single-parent homes among ethnic groups, other than non-Hispanic whites, mirrors poverty rates and suggests the importance of providing recreation programs, after-school programs, and other social support services to these children.

Today, less than 25% of American households are composed of a single wage earner, meaning 75% of households are dependent on two or more wage earners. This places greater stresses on families, parents, and children. The notion of the mother as the primary caregiver has changed. Fathers are becoming more involved in the lives of their children—from changing diapers to taking time off for sick children. The roles of fathers are in transition as larger numbers of men are indicating a desire to be more nurturing with their children. Mothers traditionally assumed the extra burden of the home, work, and child rearing and now are more frequently sharing these duties with others.

The challenge for recreation and family service agencies is to determine how to serve the new permeable family. Traditional after-school programs may no longer work when mothers expect to pick children up later in the day. Many agencies have gone to extended after-school programs, frequently partnering with schools to mix education, tutoring, and leisure.

Children at Risk   Between 1950 and 2008, Americans experienced the most sustained economic growth of any time in history. For the most part, U.S. children are growing up in relative luxury compared to their grandparents, who grew up in relative luxury compared to their grandparents.

The youth population has been declining as a percentage of the total population for several decades: 26% in 2000 and 24% in 2010. In 1964, the end of the baby boomer generation, youth represented 36% of the population. Youth population since 2000 is not declining as a total number, but only as a percentage of the total U.S. population. The U.S. Census Bureau reported 74.2 million youth in 2010, 1.8 million more than in 2000.[22]

The shift to an urban society continued to increase, with more than 80% of children living in urban areas, including the suburbs and exurbs. Generations of contact and grounding with a rural environment have been replaced by city parks, community recreation centers,

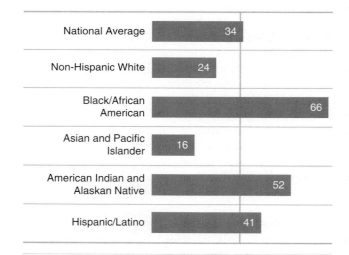

FIGURE 11.1   Percentage of Children in Single-Parent Families by Race and Origin.

Data from The 2016 Kids Count Data Book. 2016. © The Annie E. Casey Foundation. http://www.aecf.org/resources/the-2016-kids-count-data-book/. (Accessed February 18, 2017).

Note: Data for Blacks/African Americans, Asians and Pacific Islanders, and American Indians and Alaskan Natives include those who are also Hispanic/Latino. Data for Non-Hispanic Whites, Blacks/African Americans, Asians and Pacific Islanders, and American Indians and Alaskan Natives are for persons who selected only one race.

YMCAs, YWCAs, Boy Scouts, Girl Scouts, Camp Fire USA, and other organizations. In many cases, these organizations changed their orientation from a rural to an urban perspective. Today's camps are less likely to be overnights away from home than they are to be day camps in parks or on nonprofit-owned properties, usually in or near the neighborhood where the children live. State park organizations nationwide have reported decreases in the number of children participating in outdoor recreation–based activities and attending parks and recreation areas in rural areas.

Yet there are also greater challenges facing today's youth than at any time in modern history. Numerous groups are investigating children and the issues they face. Three such organizations at the forefront are:

Social service organizations offer support to homeless families.
© Vladislav Gajic/Shutterstock.

◆ Childstats.gov (www.childstats.gov), a federal interagency forum focusing on collecting, analyzing, and reporting data on issues related to children and families.

◆ Child Trends (www.childtrends.org), a nonprofit organization focusing on trends affecting children and providing research, a databank of trends and indicators, and best practices.

◆ Kids Count (www.kidscount.org), a major initiative of the Annie E. Casey Foundation that tracks the status of children on a state-by-state basis. It measures the educational, social, economic, and physical well-being of children and reports them in a variety of research publications. It also has funded projects in many states.

A major area of concern of public and private agencies is youth well-being. Child well-being has been variously described as those conditions affecting children in the United States. ChildStats.gov includes indicators from "three demographic background measures and 40 selected indicators [that] describe the population of children and depict child well-being in the areas of family and social environment, economic circumstances, healthcare, physical environment and safety, behavior, education, and health."[22] The Annie E. Casey Foundation sponsors the Kids Count report on the well-being of America's youth, which is updated every other year. It measures items such as children's access to healthcare, environmental conditions, economic growth of families, education, and the education of young children.

Table 11.3 depicts selected data focusing on youth well-being gathered in 1999, 2001, and 2011. The snapshot captures multiple areas of concern. A review of the table suggests areas of social concern, such as tobacco use, lack of child-care services, illicit drug use, violent crime, and the like. Poverty is the most pervasive and abusive condition affecting children in the United States. UNICEF, in a 2004 report, said,

"Children living in poverty experience deprivation of the material, spiritual, and emotional resources needed to survive, develop and thrive, leaving them unable to enjoy their rights, to achieve their full potential or to participate as full and equal members of society."[24]

NATIONAL CHILD AND YOUTH WELL-BEING INDEX

The National Child and Youth Well-Being Index (CWI) is an important resource and has provided information on the well-being of children and youth since 1975. The index is composed of 28 key indicators focusing on family economic well-being, safe/risky behavior, social relationships, emotional/spiritual well-being, community engagement, educational attainment, and health. The 2014 report looks at 2013 and compares it with previous years. Concerns remain about family income. It has not returned to the 2000 pre-recession level. Safe/risky behavior has improved, with a decline in teenage births per thousand; violent crime victimizations for ages 12 to 19 years went down; and children were found to be more connected to their communities. The number of children in single-parent homes has not decreased, but grown larger. Obesity has shown a slight decline in children since the mid-1980s. Overall, child and youth well-being is marginally up. It rose rapidly from 1993 to 2003 and then stabilized, fluctuating after 2003 through 2013.[23]

TABLE 11.3 America's Children at a Glance

Characteristic	1999/2001[a]	2016[b]
Children ages 0–17 in the United States	70.4 million	73.9 million
Children ages 0–17 as a proportion of the population		23.7%
Children ages 0–17 by race and ethnic group[c]		
White		
White, non-Hispanic	64.0%	52.0%
Black, non-Hispanic	15.0%	14.0%
Asian, non-Hispanic	4.0%	5.0%
All other races	1.0%	4.0%
Hispanic (of any race)	16.0%	25.0%
Children 0–17 living with two married parents	69.0%	65.0%
Children 0–17 in poverty	16.0%	21.0%
Children 0–17 in households classified by USDA as "food insecure"	4.0%	21.0%
Children 0–17 covered by health insurance	85.0%	90.0%
Children 6–17 who are obese		19.0%
12th graders reporting regular cigarette smoking	22.0%	6.0%
12th graders reporting having five or more alcoholic beverages	32.0%	18.0%
12th graders reported using illicit drugs over the past 30 days	26.0%	24.0%
Youth victimization rate for ages 12–17 by serious violent crimes		40 per 1000
Young adults aged 18–24 who have completed high school At least 1 foreign born parent	86.0% -	92.0% 25.0%

[a] Two reports are combined to secure data. Data collected and reported has changed since the inception of the report in 1997.
[b] Data from U.S. Census Bureau, 2010 Census of Population and Housing, "United States: Summary Population and Housing Characteristics," Washington, DC: U.S. Government Printing Office (2013). Available at www.census.gov/prod/cen2010/cph-1-1.pdf (Accessed February 25, 2013).
[c] Children percentages by race and ethnic group has changed due to refined definitions by the U.S. Census Bureau.
Data from Federal Interagency Forum on Children and Family Statistics. America's Children in Brief: Key National Indicators of Well-Being, 2010. Washington, DC: U.S. Government Printing Office Available at: Childstats.gov. https://www.childstats.gov (Accessed February 18, 2017).

The child poverty rate in 2015 was 20%[25] for children between 0 and 17 years of age. The economic recession had a significant impact on families as unemployment grew to more than 10% nationally and more than 13% in some regions, suggesting that the number of children living in extreme poverty (half the poverty level) would climb to between 4.5 and 6.3 million. This was up from 2.5 million in 2008. Children in poverty remain a significant national concern.

Globalization is contributing to major societal change, with particular impact on children. This era of globalization is evidenced by advances in investment, technology, manufacturing, and mobility coinciding with dramatically increased prosperity. Although corporate decision making may be influenced by globalization, it is the social frameworks that are frequently being negatively affected. It has created a scale of migration from Mexico and Central America previously unseen. As previously discussed, Hispanic populations represent the fastest growing immigrant group over the last 20 years. Youth from developing countries are less likely to be academically, socially, economically, physically, and emotionally prepared to enter the U.S. social fabric and lead full and productive lives. Already the Hispanic population has the highest high school dropout rate in the United States.

Leisure is a commodity in the lives of children that is essential and developmental. Leisure professionals have addressed concern for child well-being. Government and nonprofit agencies are working together to serve at-risk youth by providing intervention, services, and opportunities. The challenges are significant and public agencies are attempting to balance needs while simultaneously serve more affluent populations of taxpayers who demand services and are willing to pay for them. Urban parks and recreation agencies are expanding their partnerships with social service nonprofits and government organizations to meet the needs of disadvantaged youth and families. This includes joint programming, provision of facilities, redirecting individuals to social service agencies, expanding existing services, and developing innovative interventions targeting specific at-risk populations.

Social networking and cell phone use are up for teens.
© Syda Productions/Shutterstock.

Teens and Tweeners: Movers of Change   Any discussion of children is incomplete without a discussion of teens and tweeners. The Harris Poll regularly tracks trends among teens and has become an important source for information about this age group. Many other organizations watch trends in teens for various reasons, including market forces, college directions, family issues, social stresses, and so forth. The Partnership for a Drug-Free America identified five teen trends: (1) they are stressed; (2) they are hypersexualized; (3) friends are the new family; (4) the traditional family has been redefined; and (5) diversity isn't something they are taught—they live with it.[26]

Today's researchers have discovered that any study of teens must also include tweens, that age group from 8 to 12 years of age. Tweens are between being children and teens and the 5-year time frame represents a period of dramatic physical, emotional, and social growth. For example, 61% of tweens said their mother understands them best, but only 20% of teens said the same thing.[27] These groups are different and create sometimes challenging dynamics in family lifestyles. Activities families do most often together include eating dinner at home, watching television, going out to eat together, food and grocery shopping, watching rented movies, and visiting relatives.[28] In a recent study, youth ages 13 to 17 years are three times more likely to prefer spending time with their friends than with their family. Tweeners, by contrast, remain strongly linked to their family.[29]

Teens' interaction patterns change between 12 and 18 years. They begin to rely more heavily on their peers, are trend conscious, and react to peer pressure. The Harris Poll and Pew Internet Initiative found teens to be major users of the Internet; teens have become the innovators in social networking. Social networking is a growing source of finding new friends. Facebook, Google, and Twitter are contemporary examples of how teens connect on the Internet. Social networking sites have become increasingly important communication sources for teens. They are putting more and more of their lives online for others to see, comment on, and to expand their network of relationships. The Pew Internet and American Life Project tracks teen activities online. **Table 11.4** reports teen usage of different social media apps.

Twittering, a social networking use of a tool that did not exist 10 years ago, is a contemporary social networking mechanism that has individuals, organizations, and groups involved. The Pew Internet Project reports that 71% of teens use more than one social network site. Smart phones provide opportunities for talking, texting, emailing, and, more important, teens see them as a primary tool for staying connected to their friends. These devices give teens a freedom previous generations did not have and move parents out of a controlling communications mode.

Teens aged 16 to 19 years are more likely to volunteer than any age group under 35 years. Research further suggests a correlation between teen volunteering and positive academic well-being. Additional studies have linked teen volunteerism to an enhanced work ethic and improved psychological and occupational well-being. Teens are more likely to vote, show a great respect for others, and demonstrate leadership skills. Thirty-nine percent of those volunteering sought out the experience, reinforcing concepts of self-worth.[30]

Engaging youth in parks and recreation is challenging, at best, and daunting if they are not involved in the planning. Too many organizations continue to provide traditional activities for youth, and although beneficial, this fails to draw and provide the services needed. These youth now see the cell phone as an entertainment

Rank	Social Media Platform	Percent Using
1	Facebook	71%
2	Instagram	52%
3	Snapchat	41%
4	Twitter	33%
5	Google+	33%
6	Vine	24%
7	Tumblr	14%

TABLE 11.4   Teen (13–17) Reported Use of Social Media Applications

Data from 18. Teens, Social Media & Technology Overview 2015. Pew Research Center. http://www.pewinternet.org/files/2015/04/PI_TeensandTech_Update2015_0409151.pdf (Accessed February 18, 2017).

device, not just a communication device. They expect to be able to communicate with their current friends, make new friends, and engage in social groups, all online. Organizations that capture the desire for community engagement and strengthen opportunities for social inclusion will find greater involvement by youth and simultaneously meet some of their needs.

The Environment

Americans have and continue to struggle to think beyond their borders. As a group, they, for the most part, fail to see a global picture as it relates to the environment. Americans are not alone in this narrow view of the world, yet they seem to epitomize a lack of concern for the environment. Whether it be a loss of open space, the continued purchasing of gas-guzzling vehicles, or a supersized approach to living and buying, it seems our indifference amid our wealth is considered by some of the world community as selfish and inexcusable.

Outdoor recreation activities such as camping, biking, backpacking, boating, hunting, fishing, skiing, and mountain climbing depend heavily on parks, forests, and water areas operated chiefly by public recreation and park agencies. The concern of many people regarding the health of the nation's outdoor resources stems from more than the need for outdoor recreation spaces. LaPage and Ranney point out that one of the most powerful sources of America's essential cultural fiber and spirit is the land itself: "The roots of this new nation and its people became the forests and rivers, the deserts and mountains, and the challenges and inspirations they presented, not the ruins of ancient civilizations most other cultures look to for ancestral continuity. Thus, America developed a different attitude and identity."[31]

For such reasons, the environmental movement receives strong support from many recreation advocates and organizations. At the same time, it is recognized that such activities as fishing and hunting are part of a bigger scene requiring clean—and safe—air and water and wise use of the land.

Growing national concern about the need to protect the environment was buttressed by the 1962 report of the Outdoor Recreation Resources Review Commission. During the following two decades, there was a wave of federal and state legislative action and funding support in the United States that was designed to acquire open space; to protect imperiled forests, wetlands, and scenic areas; to help endangered species flourish; and to reclaim the nation's wild rivers and trails. This movement was threatened during the early 1980s, when a new administration sought to reduce park and open space funding, eliminate conservation programs and environmental regulations, and subject the outdoors to renewed economic exploitation. In the mid-1990s, and again under the second Bush administration in the early- and mid-2000s, the effort to open protected wilderness areas to increased oil drilling, cattle grazing, lumbering, and other commercial uses gained strong political support. The election of Donald Trump as President in 2016 may indicate a change in environmental commitment and action.

Organizations such as the nonpartisan League of Conservation Voters, National Audubon Society, National Wildlife Federation, Wilderness Society, Sierra Club, and Nature Conservancy have been in the forefront of the continuing battle to protect the nation's natural resources. Numerous outdoor recreation organizations have joined with such groups, and the struggle will clearly continue to be an important political issue in the years ahead.

As the world celebrated Earth Day 2010, 40 years after the first Earth Day in 1970, it was clear that North American air was cleaner and its water purer than it had been for many past decades. Earth Day has gained an international following as demonstrated by the fortieth anniversary efforts that included a goal of a "Billion Acts of Green": One million students abroad participated in community green activities, an effort to plant one million trees in 16 countries was initiated, 400 elected officials in 40 countries held dialogues with community members about the creation of sustainable green economies, 22,000 worldwide partners, and much more. In 2016, Earth Day was celebrated with 50,000 partners in 196 countries, engaging 1 billion people.

In the United States there was more protected open space in national parks and wildlife areas, yet there is still cause for concern. Americans continue to purchase large, inefficient vehicles, but smaller, more efficient vehicles are a growing segment of the auto industry. Government, at all levels, has embraced the presence of global climate change and has joined the international community in efforts to reduce impacts on the environment. Yet, Americans are growing away from their traditional environment ethic. Attendance, over a period of 5 years, is down at state and national parks, children are not exposed to the natural environment, and campers who stay in the parks in their motorhomes demand electricity, water, sewer, and cable and broadband hookups. Going outdoors is no longer fashionable. America's appreciation of the outdoors and the environment is clearly in jeopardy. In response, organizations, individuals, researchers, and governments are finding ways to make people aware of the importance of the outdoors in their lives. Governments and schools are creating campaigns and educational requirements introducing and encouraging families and youth to return to the natural environment.

Environment and Population The United States represents just 5% of the world's population and consumes almost 25% of every natural resource—more than any other nation in the world.[32] Americans have the largest "ecological footprint" of any country in the world.[33]

Population growth at current levels has the potential to negate efforts to reduce impact on the climate. Even as federal, state, and local governments move forward with plans to reduce greenhouse emissions, the continued rapid growth of population in high-density population centers and centers of ecological vulnerability may offset gains in addressing climate change. **Figure 11.2** illustrates the impact of population on energy consumption and greenhouse gases. Compared to the world and developing countries, our contributions to global warming, on a per-capita basis, are staggering. The United States accounts for almost half (46%) of the annual carbon dioxide emitted into the environment and represents the primary cause of global warming. Americans produce 5 pounds of garbage per day, five times the average amount in developing countries.[34]

The Center for Environment and Population suggests that the United States is now a metro nation, a "lifestyle [that] differs from urban-centered lifestyles in that it requires extensive use of motor vehicles and rapid, extensive land development."[35] The McDonalds influence on U.S. culture to supersize everything has moved from French fries to houses, shopping centers, recreation centers, and land and resource consumption. The Center goes on to report, "the 'supersized' lifestyles of so many people affect the quality of everyday life causing, among other things, more frequent, worse traffic jams, and expenditure of more money and effort to heat and keep-up more and/or larger homes."[36] The impact on recreation is not lost. Demand for recreation facilities, park areas, and access to these is growing in metropolitan and adjacent areas. Congestion in this country's premiere natural resources has been well documented by the National Park Service, and similar patterns are occurring at the state and community levels.

Where People Live: Urban, Suburb, Exurb History has recorded the decline of rural populations, the growth of cities, industrialization, postindustrialization, the growth of suburbs and exurbs, the decline of the inner city, and the simultaneous revitalization of cities and urban areas. In the 1950s, people began to commute into the city. In the twenty-first century, commuting has become a norm for millions of people, but urbanites are as likely to commute to the suburbs to work as suburbanites are to commute to cities' business centers. The average commuter spends over 100 hours a year commuting to and from work.

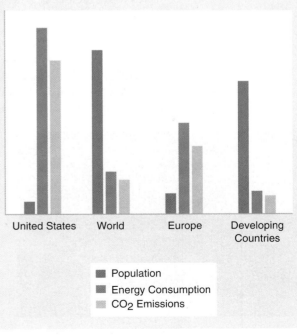

FIGURE 11.2 U.S.–World Population and Climate Change.
Data from U.S. Census Bureau, U.S. Energy Information Administration, World Resources Institute, 2008.

A METROPOLITAN REVOLUTION

Metropolitan areas are traditionally defined by size, as prescribed by the U.S. Census Bureau. This designation has served well, but hardly begins to address what a metropolitan area is. Nationally and internationally, metropolitan areas are growing at a steady pace. One source suggested that, internationally, one million people move to a metropolitan space every five days! The Brookings Institute suggests, "a city's true measure goes beyond human-made structures and lies deeper than daily routine." They are "defined by the quality of the ideas they generate, the innovations they spur, and the opportunities they create for people...."[37]. Urban recreation, park, cultural, and sport organizations have great opportunities to provide services in a metropolitan region. There is frequently a wealth of opportunities, but they are not always equally distributed among the population. Public and nonprofit organizations are the primary source of support for disadvantaged populations in metropolitan areas. In recent years, these organizations have partnered with corporations and other social service organizations to bring opportunities to underserved areas.

In 2014, the average commute was 52 minutes a day.[38] However, New York and Maryland each averaged 60 minutes or more commuting each day and three counties in metropolitan New York averaged more than 80 minutes daily in commutes.

Beyond the suburbs are the exurbs, difficult to define, but an easy area to describe. They exist beyond the suburbs in traditionally rural areas, which are now dotted with individual homes on acreage or subdivisions, and may include cities of 50,000 or more people. They are adjacent to large metropolitan areas and their distinctive feature is the residents' choice of place over people, where the primary commonality is the need to commute to work. The exurbs are growing population areas because individuals are more willing to increase travel time for a perceived improved quality of life.

Open Space Loss and the Environment   The environment is coming under increasingly difficult challenges, both as a part of national policy, and among Americans as a whole. In Iowa, the state government gives new homeowners a 5-year tax relief if they purchase a new home on previously open space or farmland. Between 1982 and 2012, the United States developed or took out of farm production 5 million acres (9.9 million hectares).[39] Americans experienced a daily loss of 3000 acres (1214 hectares) of farmland over the last decade. Land converted for development occurs at twice the rate of population growth. We have become a nation of sprawl represented by low-density development in the suburbs and exurbs. The exurbs are growing at a rate almost three times that of urban areas.

Youth prefer computers to the outdoors. Parents are afraid to send their children outdoors because they too have lost their outdoor ethic. As a society, Americans have almost fully transitioned from a generation raised on or near farms to a generation raised in an urban environment. Like a zoo or museum, the outdoors is a place to visit and see, but not to partake of. Scares such as polluted beaches, Lyme disease, wasting disease in elk, and others have encouraged parents already unfamiliar with the outdoors to keep their children home. Attendance at national parks, national forests, state parks, and other rural recreation and preservation areas has been on decline at a time when the population is increasing (see **Table 11.5**). The influx of immigrants without an outdoor ethic has affected the response to wilderness, outdoors, and preservation. This has been reflected in Congress as it has become more difficult to secure funds for parks and recreation lands. For example, the Arctic National Wildlife Refuge is continuously under attack by politicians and oil interests in an effort to open the area to increased oil production.

Many national associations focusing on the environment are encouraging individuals to express concern and demand action. Often this action is local and even bounded by the property owned. The National Wildlife Federation encourages individuals to certify their backyards for wildlife. The Audubon Society encourages individuals to take the healthy yard pledge by reducing pesticides, conserving water, planting native species, protecting water quality, and supporting birds and other wildlife.

Many of the same organizations that are promoting local environmental awareness and action are also active at the national and international levels.

Urban sprawl consumes 6000 acres of land daily.
© Losevsky Pavel/Shutterstock.

TABLE 11.5	Changes in Attendance at State & National Parks: Compared to Total Population Growth				

Year	State Parks[a]	National Parks	Population	% Change in Relation to Total Population	
				% State Park[a]	% National
2015	409,300,000	307,247,252	325,032,763	-47.51%	3.75%
2010	740,733,000	281,300,000	308,745,538	-2.26%	-1.56%
2005	725,361,000	273,500,000	295,507,000	-9.92%	-6.94%
2000	766,842,123	279,900,000	281,424,602	-3.45%	-1.66%
1995	752,266,297	269,600,000	266,557,000	-5.76%	-2.76%
1990	744,812,234	258,700,000	248,718,302	13.04%	-5.83%

Data from 1) https://irma.nps.gov/Stats/SSRSReports/National%20Reports/Annual%20Park%20Ranking%20Report%20(1979%20-%20Last%20Calendar%20Year); 2) http://naspd.wpengine.com/about-us/state-park-facts/; (Accessed February 20, 2017).

[a]National Association of State Park Directors changed criteria for calculating state park attendance for 2014 (2015 data not available)

Loss of Environmental Ethic   At the same time, Americans appear to be participating at a lower rate in traditional visits to state and national parks. Table 11.5 shows a mixed picture of attendance, with a decline between 2000 and 2005 for state and national parks. The right-hand columns compare park attendance to the reported U.S. population. The state park 2015 attendance is significantly different from previous years, suggesting they altered their reporting methods. The comparison shows that the percentage of Americans visiting state and national parks has become more variable based on economic factors, population growth, and competing outdoor recreation opportunities. It would appear that visiting these areas is becoming either less important to or out of the reach of Americans. The numbers remain large, but the vast majority of state and national parks are in remote areas, not close to urban populations. Some data suggest as much as 50% of visits to some national parks are international tourists. Repeat visits by individuals account for another large portion of the attendance.

Data from one study specifically linked a decline in park attendance to the economy. State parks have shown an increase even as state budgets have been reduced, state park areas closed, and park staff furloughed.

The issue is less clear than it might at first appear. Attendance may be down for state and slightly higher for national parks, yet the willingness of Americans to vote for funding for parks and open space remains high. From 2011 through 2016, Americans voted $64 billion in 599 local and state elections, 77% of which were successful,

FFA ADAPTS TO RURAL POPULATION DECLINE

The National FFA organization, originally the Future Farmers of America, traditionally represented rural farming America. As families moved to urban areas and farms became larger and corporate, membership began to decline and FFA recognized the need to rethink who their membership base was. For example, between 2007 and 2012, the United States lost 100,000 farms, mostly to larger farming operations. FFA realized that its future lay in attracting not only traditional rural youth but also urban youth. They looked at the larger agricultural market place and began to adapt. The traditional farm-related programs were expanded to include business, marketing, science, communications, education, horticulture, production, natural resources, and other related fields. Today, FFA has almost 650,000 members in all 50 states plus U.S. Puerto Rico and U.S. Virgin Islands. As it grew into urban areas, it also began attracting a more ethnically diverse membership base. FFA is an example of a youth-based organization who has adapted to meet new demographic realities.

The number of visitors to national parks is down.

Courtesy of the National Park Service. NPS Photo by Michael Quinn.

providing funding for parks and open space acquisition, maintenance, and operation. **Table 11.6** shows the number of referenda voted on between 2007 and 2016. The amount of funding approved in almost 50 states is staggering. In years when large amounts have been approved by voters, it frequently involved a statewide initiative and ballot supporting conservation funding. The difference between total funding and conservation funding, as described by the Trust for Public Lands, is important to understand. The total funds include support for "parks and playgrounds, farmland preservation, watershed protection, trails and greenways, forests, and wildlife habitat" as primary examples. Conservation funding is more narrowly focused, looking at "measures that preserve natural lands, create parks, and protect farmland."[40] These are state, county, and local endeavors where voters choose to tax themselves to provide open spaces and parks. The vast majority of the funds were for acquisition of lands. The money has not been equally distributed across the United States. The Mid-Atlantic, a major center of population in the United States, voted for considerably more measures than any other region. The West, another population center, voted for far fewer conservation and recreation measures, but for larger expenditures of money. As a whole, since 1988, Americans have voted to tax themselves for over $75 billion in conservation and outdoor recreation areas, not including federal park, conservation, and outdoor recreation areas. Does this mean local spaces are more important than national or state places? Probably not, but there are clearly shifts in preferences and only part of those shifts can be attributed to ethnic and cultural influences.[41]

In addition to federal, state, and local agencies providing recreation and park opportunities and places, there are many watchdogs of government agencies. The federal government's handling of environmental issues that affect national parks and wilderness areas has been a particular area of criticism. The National Environmental

TABLE 11.6   Summary of Conservation Measures by Year

Year	Number of Measures	Number of Measures Passed	Total Funds Approved	Conservation Funds Approved
2007	100	66	$2,245,755,926	$1,952,415,707
2008	128	91	$11,102,012,360	$8,046,960,160
2009	40	25	$1,059,164,056	$607,668,083
2010	49	41	$2,378,635,217	$2,186,464,866
2011	24	14	$539,231,467	$312,765,748
2012	68	53	$2,317,328,913	$797,680,495
2013	21	16	$1,401,972,735	$343,072,735
2014	37	52	$30,765,304,044	$13,203,357,243
2015	35	26	$698,990,736	$324,693,947
2016	97	77	$12,385,278,910	$3,395,519,633
Total	**599**	**461**	**$64,893,674,364**	**$31,170,598,617**

Data from the Trust for Public Lands, "Access TPL Land Vote Database."

Available at: 26. https://tpl.quickbase.com/db/bbqna2qct?a=dbpage&pageID=8 (Accessed February 18, 2017).

Trust has pointed to air quality significantly diminishing the quality of individual experiences of visitors. They point to a 27-year-old requirement administered by the Environmental Protection Agency that has not been enforced. The Natural Resources Defense Council points to the impact of climate change on western U.S. national parks stating,

> Many scientists think the American West will experience the effects of climate change sooner and more intensely than most other regions. The West is warming faster than the East, and that warming is already profoundly affecting the scarce snow and water of the West. In the arid and semi-arid West, the changes that have already occurred and the greater changes projected for the future would fundamentally disrupt ecosystems. The region's national parks, representing the best examples of the West's spectacular resources, are among the places where the changes in the natural environment will be most evident. As a result, a disrupted climate is the single greatest threat to ever face western national parks.[42]

Climate Change   Humans have affected the environment as never before. The 1997 Kyoto Protocol (named after an international conference convened in Kyoto, Japan) is often credited as the most significant environmentally based international agreement of the twentieth century. The essence of the agreement was for developed nations to reduce their greenhouse gases (CO_2 emissions) to 5% below their 1990 levels and for less developed countries to be allowed to make a lesser contribution to reductions. Of the 166 countries that signed the protocol, only the United States and Australia refused to ratify it. Other countries including India and China and other smaller developing countries were exempt from the protocols because most greenhouse gases are coming from developed countries.

International engagement in climate change is growing. In late 2011 in Durban, South Africa, the international community met and agreed to create a universal legal agreement on climate change. Agreeing to create a document is far from achieving consensus, but it is a major step forward. Individual countries, including the United States, have moved forward with developing and implementing initiatives. New Zealand, for example, now generates two-thirds of its energy from renewable resources. Korea is building a smart grid power system to assist regions in becoming self-sufficient with renewable energy. Saudi Arabia is home to the world's largest thermal power plant and Germany is the largest solar energy producer in the world. If large industrialized nations are moving slowly on addressing climate change, it is the emerging countries where achieving positive action on climate change is most challenging. In these countries there is a lack of awareness of climate change and many see a response to climate change as an effort to prevent their country from achieving higher standards of living for their citizens.

In the United States, the Obama administration has actively moved forward with action to mitigate climate change. It is unclear what the Trump administration will do, but early indications suggest a less friendly perspective toward climate change. There remain many individuals who do not believe that humans are the primary influencer of climate change, but the body of evidence and individual and nonprofit and commercial organizations are beginning to recognize the importance of responding to and providing leadership on climate change. Nonprofits have taken the lead on making Americans aware of the potential damage of climate change. In a recent effort to identify key nonprofits focusing on climate change, a panel of experts identified over 100 organizations actively engaged in promoting the dangers of climate change. In many cases they have gone beyond promotion and are funding research programs and encouraging grassroots efforts. Some nonprofits, such as the Environmental Defense Fund, Greenpeace, and the Nature Conservancy, have long histories in the environmental movement. Others, including the Center for Climate and Energy Solutions, Pew Center on Global Climate Change, and the Alliance for Climate Protection, U.S. Climate Action Network, The Climate Reality Project, 350.org, and the Coalition for Environmentally Responsible Economies (Ceres) are less well known, but all are playing key roles in changing attitudes about climate change.[43]

The federal government has created a Global Change Research Program (www.globalchange.gov) composed of 13 departments and agencies. The agency existed under another name from 2002 through 2008 and reports directly to the president. Its function is to coordinate and integrate federal research on changes in the global environment with potential implications for society. The United States, over the last 20 years, has not ignored global climate change but has quietly made the "world's largest scientific investment in the areas of climate change and global change research."[45]

The agency produces regular reports, including *2009 Global Climate Change Impacts in the United States*, identifying anticipated national and global impacts. In 2014 the *National Climate Assessment Report* was released

350.ORG - GRASSROOTS CLIMATE DEFENSE

"350.org" is a self-described grassroots organization with a short and vigorous commitment to targeting youth worldwide to organize for climate change action. Founded in 2008 in the United States, it went global in 2011. They named their organization 350 in terms of the level of CO_2 in the atmosphere (parts per million) must be reduced to achieve climate safety. The current level is 400 ppm. The organization operates under three principles: (1) We Believe in Climate Justice; (2) We're Stronger When We Collaborate; and (3) Mass Mobilizations Make Change. These core principles allow the organization to focus its energies on world decision makers. They self-report membership in 188 countries with some level of organization. As an example, at the 2015 Paris Climate Change Conference, 350.org was instrumental in organizing a major demonstration the weekend before the conference began that included thousands of youth from across the world. They self-reported 785,000 people taking to the streets in 175 countries and 2,300 events.[44]

Climate change impacts our daily lives, including rush hour traffic in crowded areas.
© Rorem/Dreamstime.com.

The report reaffirms the primary influence of human activity on global climate change and the already visible impacts, such as Hurricane Sandy in late 2012, a rising sea level, and melting of glaciers and arctic sea ice. The perceived impacts are not just hotter days, but more broadly on environmental patterns, agricultural capability, human health, water supplies, transportation, and energy, to identify some of the more significant issues.

Impact of Nature on People's Lives: Issues of Wellness, Well-Being, and Human Development
The environmental concerns discussed earlier go beyond issues associated only with the environment. It has become personal for many who have recognized that the absence of involvement with nature negatively affects human growth and development, especially among children. Numerous researchers have begun to link environmental and ecological issues to health and well-being outcomes for individuals and society as a whole.

Richard Louv, with the publication of *No Child Left in the Woods: Saving Our Children from Nature-Deficit Disorder*, became the spokesperson for a growing movement to reconnect children with nature. The term *nature-deficit disorder,* referred to as human environment interaction in the research literature, captured the imagination and has become a rallying cry to address the issues of children, and adults, who are becoming more separated from nature with every generation. Daily contact with nature has become the exception rather than the norm. There are a number of reasons for the decline in contact with nature, including the loss of natural areas in and near urban areas, the absence of parks close to where people live, the over-scheduling of children, safety concerns, more homework, and fear of stranger-danger.[46]

The correlation of the absence of nature in our lives with the developmental growth of children has raised a concern among public health officials, child development specialists, urban environmentalists, and parks and recreation practitioners. As stated in a report titled *Healthy Parks, Healthy People*, "An ecological theory of public health recognizes that not only is health itself holistic and multidisciplinary, but also that a holistic or multidisciplinary approach is needed to promote and manage health successfully."[50]

Nearby nature refers to the presence or absence of nature in close proximity to an individual. Parks and natural areas in urban environments are seen as important contributors to the opportunity of individuals, and especially youth, to experience nature. The backyard, neighborhood, and areas where individuals, work, play, and go to school are also important. Research is beginning to show that the presence of nearby nature has an impact on individual wellness and well-being.[51] The ideal situation is for individuals to have regular contact with natural areas, but, in the absence of those opportunities, nearby nature in urban environments can have positive mediating effects on individuals.

Childhood Experiences with Nature and Its Influence on Adult Behavior and Attitudes   There are indicators that adults who had positive childhood experiences with wild nature have a more positive attitude about the environment than those who had experiences with domesticated nature. Wild nature involves being in an outdoor setting where hiking, camping, hunting, and related activities can occur and these are usually away from urban areas. Domestic nature is more reflective of nearby nature in that it is at or close to home and may involve flowers, planting trees, shrubs, a garden, or caring for indoor plants. The

THE 2030 AGENDA FOR SUSTAINABLE DEVELOPMENT: SUSTAINABLE DEVELOPMENT GOALS

A key outcome of the 2015 Paris Climate Change Conference was 17 sustainable development goals that were agreed upon by the majority of the participants at the conference, including the United States. The sustainable development goals cover a wide range of economic, social, poverty, and people issues. The goals appear below:

1. End poverty in all its forms everywhere
2. End hunger, achieve food security and improved nutrition and promote sustainable agriculture
3. Ensure healthy lives and promote well-being for all at all ages
4. Ensure inclusive and quality education for all and promote lifelong learning
5. Achieve gender equality and empower all women and girls
6. Ensure access to water and sanitation for all
7. Ensure access to affordable, reliable, sustainable, and modern energy for all
8. Promote inclusive and sustainable economic growth, employment and decent work for all
9. Build resilient infrastructure, promote sustainable industrialization, and foster innovation
10. Reduce inequality within and among countries
11. Make cities inclusive, safe, resilient, and sustainable
12. Ensure sustainable consumption and production patterns
13. Take urgent action to combat climate change and its impacts
14. Conserve and sustainably use the oceans, seas and marine resources
15. Sustainably manage forests, combat desertification, halt and reverse land degradation, halt biodiversity loss
16. Promote just, peaceful, and inclusive societies
17. Revitalize the global partnership for sustainable development

Source: http://www.un.org/sustainabledevelopment/sustainable-development-goals/

Louv suggests several factors influencing the amount of time children spend in nature, including the following:

◆ The explosive growth of electronic media, later identified as videophilia[46]
◆ The increasingly litigious nature of American society creating risk-averse managers and citizens who prevent or limit various nature experiences (e.g., climbing trees, building tree forts)
◆ The prevalence of neighborhood covenants that place severe limitations on what, where, and when children can play outdoors
◆ The climate of fear generated by intense media attention of child abduction cases
◆ The longer work and commuting hours of parents and increased amount of scheduled activities for children that create time constraints
◆ The explosive rate of land development in the past two decades and the corresponding lack of nearby nature (i.e., vegetation and open space with natural features in close proximity to urban residents) in the developed areas

The loss of contact with nature results in additional health and wellness issues for children. Some of the results include increasing levels of obesity in children and adults; a decline in physical, social, and mental well-being; issues of psychological well-being; linkages to attention deficit disorder in children and adults; increasing levels of stress; and lowered immunity to illness. Some argue that this may be because of the pace of life throughout the world, but the literature on nature, wellness, and well-being increasingly confirms the need for contact with nature, even if it is just a small green space.[49]

frequency of involvement in such activities is also important. A single camping experience has little long-term impact, whereas repeat camping experiences influence future environmental attitudes and visits.[52] However, although it would be expected that frequent visits to wild nature as a child would carry over to adult behaviors, that is not necessarily the case. Visits to wild nature as a child are not a good predictor that such activities will continue into adulthood. However, lack of visits to wild nature as a child is a predictor that as adults they are less likely to visit wild nature. The research suggests that adults who continue to visit wild nature do so for opportunities for physical activity and emotional and spiritual renewal.[53]

The connotation from this research strongly suggests the importance of wild nature experiences among youth. Further, such experiences are strengthened when youth are with their parents. Sending children to a regimented camp has a lesser impact on youth and their future perspectives of the environment. In camp settings, natural experiences are lessened and group experiences are strengthened, which may or may not be related to the camp setting. Kellert's work regarding nature and childhood development is groundbreaking.

CLIMATE CHANGE AND RECREATION: CONSEQUENCES AND COSTS

Americans who like to play outdoors may soon find that climate change–induced warming trends around the nation will put some of their favorite recreational retreats in jeopardy—from trout streams to waterfowl preserves, from ski areas to mountain biking trails, and from beaches to forested parkland. "Climate impacts on natural resources are pervasive," write Daniel Morris and Margaret Walls in a background paper titled, "Climate Change and Outdoor Recreation Resources."[47] Their paper highlights the stresses climate change will put on water resources, which could result in reduced mountain snowpack levels; increased drought conditions across public lands; decreased waterflows into streams, reservoirs, and wetlands; and forests weakened against fire and insect infestations.

Walls, a senior fellow at Resources for the Future (RFF), and Morris, an RFF research assistant, included a number of possible scenarios, among them:

Snowpack: Extended warm seasons may result in more rainfall than snow, which would reduce skiing and snowboarding opportunities, particularly in comparatively warmer areas in California, Nevada, Arizona, and New Mexico.

Fresh waterways: Reduced snowpack and more rain in winter months would mean earlier spring runoff into streams and reservoirs. That could mean less fresh water flowing in the summer months, when sport fishing and boating are most popular. Fishing depends on water temperature, streamflow levels, and ecological quality, while boating is more sensitive to lake, reservoir, and stream levels.

Noncoastal wetlands: Stretching across 216 million acres of the northern plains and Canada, these wetlands are rich sources of many species of ducks and other waterfowl. By one estimate, lower water levels caused by climate change in the Upper Great Lakes could reduce regional duck populations by nearly 40% in the area.

Beaches: Rising sea levels over time could reduce the size of beachfront recreation areas, national seashores, and coastal waterways, the authors find. A full 85% of tourism-related revenues in the United States are generated by coastal states.

Forests and parks: Tree cover, particularly in the western United States, is already feeling the impact of climate change, particularly as a result of drought. Insects have decimated millions of acres of evergreens in the Rocky Mountain region, and dryness has fueled damaging wildfires. Tree dieoffs also resulted in closures of campgrounds, trails, and picnic areas in public parks.

What is clear, the authors conclude, is that impacts from climate change will vary among such leisure pursuits as skiing, camping, boating, fishing and hunting, outdoor sports such as golf, and wildlife viewing. That prospect may require more assertive efforts by public officials to adapt policies that will help preserve outdoor recreation areas.

"Longer and warmer summers are expected to increase the demand for outdoor recreation, from hiking, fishing, hunting, and camping to simple beach visits," the authors write. "This makes it all the more important that government policy at all levels develop climate adaptation programs and funding."[48]

Children need to experience the outdoors, not be protected from it.

© Van Truan/Fotolia.com.

His identification of direct, indirect, and vicarious experiences with nature frame much of the research currently conducted. Where the previous paragraphs discussed wild nature and domestic nature, Kellert frames the same descriptions as direct, indirect, and vicarious contact with nature. **Table 11.7** describes each of the types of contact with nature with examples. Similar to other research, he finds that direct contact as having the most significant impact on individuals, regardless of age; indirect contact has a lesser impact but is still positive; and vicarious contact has an influence but one considerably less than direct or indirect contact.[54]

The importance of childhood experiences with nature is more evident and cannot long be ignored. As others have suggested, the absence of experiences with nature, at any level, causes potential health, wellness, and well-being issues for children and adults, but especially for children. In 2008, politicians reacted to the need to provide children with nature experiences when the U.S. House of Representatives Education and Labor Committee voted in June to send the *No Child Left Inside Act* (HR 3036) to the House floor for a full vote. The legislation was unsuccessful, but the message was clear.

Benefits and Outcomes of Contact with Nature   Our understanding of the benefits and outcomes of contact with nature is growing as additional research is conducted. Forty years ago, few people outside of leisure scientists and landscape architects explored the importance of outdoor recreation. Today, the list of those researching this area includes experts in public health, early childhood education, child psychology, urban planning, medicine, psychology, and sociology, among others. A number of authors discuss the benefits and outcomes of

TABLE 11.7 Types of Contact with Nature

Type of Contact	Description	Examples
Direct	Interaction with large self-sustaining features and processes in the natural environment	Relatively unmanaged areas such as forests, creeks, sometimes a backyard or park
Indirect	Involves actual contact with nature occurring in highly controlled environments dependent on ongoing human management and intervention	Highly structured, organized and planned occurring in zoos, botanical gardens, nature centers, museums, parks
Vicarious	Symbolic experiences of nature not involving contact with actual living organisms or environments, but rather with the image, representation, or metaphorical expression of nature	A teddy bear, various cartoon and book characters, Mickey Mouse, *Lassie*, films focusing on nature, television programs such as on the Discovery Channel

Data from S. R. Kellert. Building for Life: Designing and Understanding the Human–Nature Connection. (Washington, DC: Island Press, 2007).

participation in natural settings. **Table 11.8** depicts what Maller calls contributions of parks to human health and well-being. The categories expressed in Table 11.7 are generally agreed upon by researchers, even if different terms are used.

Parks and recreation agencies have the opportunity to take the lead in providing direct and indirect contact with nature for individuals. The approach demands creativity and a willingness to challenge the norm. Godbey provides a list of policy recommendations for enhancing direct and indirect contact with nature, including planning for outdoor recreation in urban areas involving schools and recreation and park departments, public health, transportation, public utilities, hospitals, and nonprofit environmental organizations.[55] Maller states, "Parks, in fact, are an ideal catalyst for the integration of environment, society, and health (which have been demonstrated to be inextricably linked) by promoting an ecological approach to human health and well-being based on contact with nature."[56]

Public parks and recreation organizations, environmental- and outdoor-based nonprofits, and federal land management and protection agencies traditionally have been proponents of protection and rationality. The organizations sometimes have been at odds, especially at the national level when the executive branch of government has been perceived as unfriendly to the environment. Local government has a mixed response to environmental issues and city, county, and state agencies have not provided the level of leadership that once was common. Park and recreation agencies can provide leadership by example in their communities in the twenty-first century.

TECHNOLOGY AND TIME

Technology affects the way people live and the way they experience leisure. The California Park and Recreation Society issued a trends report in 2005. In 2017 it is appropriate to rethink those trends.

Technology has changed the way we communicate. As little as 30 years ago, mail was the most common communications method. There was only one long-distance telephone company. Long-distance telephone calls were expensive and usually reserved for special occasions or for business enterprises. Most families subscribed to a morning newspaper and watched the network news on one of three commercial channels. They listened to one or two local stations and only in larger markets was there a variety of music available on the radio.

Today Americans, on average, spend more waking time communicating and using media devices such as the television, radio, MP3 devices, and smartphones, than any other activity. The cell phone is an example of how technology has affected individuals, families, work, and communities. Even

A family camping trip allows family members to benefit from their connections to the wilderness.

© Oleg Kozlov/Dreamstime.com.

TABLE 11.8 A Summary of the Contributions of Parks to Human Health and Well-Being

Component of Health	Contribution of Parks
Physical	Provide a variety of settings and infrastructure for various levels of formal and informal sport and recreation, for all skill levels and abilities (e.g., picnicking, walking, dog training, running, cycling, ball games, sailing, surfing, photography, birdwatching, bushwalking, rock climbing, camping).
Mental	Make nature available for restoration from mental fatigue; solitude and quiet; artistic inspiration and expression; educational development (e.g., natural and cultural history).
Spiritual	Preserve the natural environment for contemplation, reflection, and inspiration; invoke a sense of place; facilitate feeling a connection to something beyond human concerns.
Social	Provide settings for people to enhance their social networks and personal relationships, from couples and families to social clubs and organizations of all sizes, from casual picnicking to events days and festivals.
Environmental	Preserve ecosystems and biodiversity, provide clean air and water, maintain ecosystem function, and foster human involvement in the natural environment (Friends of Parks groups, etc.).

Reproduced from C. Maller, C. Henderson-Wilson, A. Pryor, L. Prossor, and M. Moore. *Healthy Parks, Healthy People: The Health Benefits of Contact with Nature in a Park Context: A Review of Relevant Literature.* 2nd Edition. Burwood, Melbourne. Deakin University and Parks Victoria. Reprinted with permission.

older adults use their cell phones to make contact while traveling, even if most of the time the phone sits turned off while at home. As late as 2002 a cell phone was primarily a phone. People carried cell phones and digital handheld devices for scheduling, note taking, and the like. Today's smartphones have replaced these two devices and expanded their level of services. In 2016, 95% of Americans had cell phones and 77% had smartphones. Smartphones dominate the market. Many continue to use a cell phone primarily as a phone, but many more use it as an email client; note taker; camera (still and movie); calendar; a link to online services such as Twitter, Flicker, Facebook, the global positioning system (GPS); game console; newsreader; address finder with map; and much more. Apple iPhone users spend more time using their mobile devices as an Internet access tool than as a telephone.

We are becoming a mobile generation. "Cast a glance at any coffee shop, train station, or airport boarding gate, and it is easy to see that mobile access to the Internet has taken root in our society. Open laptops or furrowed brows staring at palm-sized screens are evidence of how routinely information is exchanged on wireless networks."[57] The Pew Internet and American Life project states that mobility changes the way people interact with each other and the ways they use their computer. We have reached a level where businesses and others expect to have broadband always on or be always connected. Questions remain unanswered about the impact of continual information exchange on individuals. For example, does it stress social norms, or cause continuous partial attention? In Pew's typology, the sophisticated user of technology has mobile access and becomes an elite, replacing home access as an elite status. Many of today's teens and young adults see being always connected as a necessity and a right.

Citizens can attend town meetings, business meetings, and the like without leaving their home or office. They can attend these meetings from anywhere with their mobile devices. Skype became the first free or low-cost Internet-based international telephone service. It has had a major impact on the developing world. The Internet has even had a significant influence on how people deal with illness. One study reported 54% of the adults responding saying the Internet played a major role as they helped another person cope with a major illness. The number who said the Internet played a role as they coped with a major illness increased 40% over a 2-year period.[58]

By 2016, 88% of Americans were on the Internet and the number of users varied by age, gender, ethnicity, income: Men and women used the internet almost equally; rural users lagged in use of the internet; college graduates were the highest users, while those with less than a high school education lagged behind. Race, which had been a factor for internet usage in 2000, has largely been eliminated as a determinant of internet use. However, age remains a factor influencing internet use; seniors—those over 65—have the lowest rate of use (65%), while the 18 to 29 and 30 to 49 age groups are almost equal in their use. Social media has defined use of mobile devices.

TABLE 11.9   A Comparison of 2005 and 2017 Trends and Reality

2005	2017
Americans love their toys, and baby boomers expect "amenity-rich" experiences.	Millennials, now the largest generation, are digital natives, and what was a desire in previous generations is now an expectation.
Technology will continue to affect how we work and how we plan.	The boundaries around IT are fading as technology becomes integral to almost every business function and social relationship.
Each generation is better educated, more adept with, and more dependent on technology than the previous generation.	Privacy and security linked to personal data concerns are growing as companies are mining more and more data of customers.
Technological advances affect the affordability, accessibility, and required skill level of many recreation activities.	Technology has created an "ambient user experience" allowing individuals to preserve their experiences across traditional boundaries of time and space.
Technology allows "mass customization."	Technology allows "built-to-order" personal customization.
New activities will be developed around innovative devices and procedures.	Americans have become cord cutters—in 2015 24% of Americans did not have cable TV—a trend that is growing.
Technology creates entirely new recreation uses.	Technology has allowed the development and growth of adventure recreation opportunities not even dreamed of by previous generations—this growth will continue to expand.
People tend to self-define and organize around their chosen form of recreation.	This continues to be true, but organization has become seamless for many activities through the use of technology.
Each group tends to want (demand) their own exclusive allocation of resources.	Technology has created an awareness for specialized activities and has less community involvement.

Data from:
1. Anderson, M. (2016, March 10). 8 conversations shaping technology. Retrieved from www.pewresearch.org/fact-tank/2016/03/10/8-conversations-shaping-technology/.
2. Briggs, B., & Hodgetts, C. (2017) Tech Trends 2017. Retrieved from www2.deloitte.com/global/en/pages/technology/articles/tech-trends.html.
3. Cearley, D. W. (2016, February 15). Gartner IDs Top 10 Strategic Technology Trends for 2016. Forbes. Retrieved from www.forbes.com/sites/gartnergroup/2016/01/15/top-10-technology-trends-for-2016/#61282cd22655
4. Poushter, J. (2016, February 22). Smartphone Ownership and Internet Usage Continues to Climb in Emerging Economies. Retrieved from www.pewglobal.org/2016/02/22/smartphone-ownership-and-internet-usage-continues-to-climb-in-emerging-economies/.
5. Romero, P., Hong, S., & Westrup, L. (2005, March). Trends Worth Talking About. California and Pacific Southwest Recreation and Park Training Conference, Sacramento, CA. Retrieved from www.parks.ca.gov/pages/795/files/cprs%202005%20trends%20final.pdf
6. Smith, E. (2014, October 23). Effects of Technology on Recreation and Leisure. Retrieved from www.prezi.com/9p2wdqdataqw/effects-of-technology-on-recreation-and-leisure/.

FINDING LEISURE AND FUN IN THE "GIG ECONOMY"

Characterized by individuals who operate as independent contractors, the "gig economy" is the digital platform economy, and it has been growing faster than traditional payroll employees. Examples of gig economy include Uber, TaskRabbit, Managed by Q, and WashClub. Increasing numbers of people are entering this marketplace for a variety of reasons. Reportedly, the gig economy has outperformed the traditional job market over the last few years.

Why engage in the gig economy? For many it is an economic reality. They need the additional funds to make ends meet or to stabilize their income. Others participate because they can't find a job anywhere else. But, surprisingly, a large group of participants, as measured by the Pew Research Center (42%), reported they did it because it was fun and something to do in their spare time.

What does this mean for leisure? Has "killing time" and "extra income" become a fun activity? Could it be classified as a leisure activity? It begs the question of the need to educate individuals about the value of leisure time vs work time. What starts as fun can quickly turn into a burden as the money generated from the gig economy ventures moves from fun to essential.

Source: http://www.pewresearch.org/fact-tank/2016/11/18/why-join-the-gig-economy-for-many-the-answer-is-for-fun/(Accessed February 22, 2017)

With a lack of leisure time, Americans feel the need to multitask.

© PeterMooij/Shutterstock.

About 7 of every 10 individuals use social media. Peak users of social media are 18- to 29-year-olds, closely followed by the 30 to 49 age group. Social media is widely used among individuals to keep up to date, to see what is going on, to pass along information and gossip, and to stay in touch with their friends. During the 2016 presidential race, it was highlighted as a key source of information, even when that information was proven to be false.[59, 60]

A number of implications result from technology that parks and recreation professionals need to consider. They include, but are not limited to, the following:

◆   Teens are less engaged in traditional recreation activities than their predecessors. They are more engaged in technology-based activities such as creating Web pages, posting photos and videos on social network sites, modifying music, sharing music, and being involved with their peers through texting, Facebook, and similar mobile platforms.

◆   There is greater competition for an individual's time. The notion of "free time" is almost a lost term. Technology has made this generation the most connected in history.

◆   Community members want active involvement, even if it is through the Internet. They do not want to be talked to, but talked with. The same is true for participating in programs offered by public and nonprofit agencies.

◆   Communicating images, program information, and building brands is far more difficult because of the plurality of communications alternatives. Sending home flyers through the public schools, sending brochures out in the mail, and advertising on traditional television stations will no longer reach the desired public. Knowledge about how different groups communicate, where they get their information, and how that information is determined to be important becomes essential for public agencies attempting to reach community members.

◆   Understanding that the old "word-of-mouth" model is magnified a hundred- or even thousandfold is essential. Administrators used to believe that one person could influence five to eight people he or she came in contact with. Today that one person can influence thousands and even hundreds of thousands without ever making physical contact with people. Images of organizations and their public goodwill can be positively or negatively influenced by minor as well as major events.

◆   Public parks and recreation agencies must learn to think and act in a digital age. Members must embrace technology as an important part of their operation, but more important, they must understand how their community members have embraced technology, whether they be 92 or 2. This suggests professionals need to be flexible and able to transition between digital natives, digital immigrants, and digital refusers.

Technology is influencing recreation and leisure in ways that were never imagined. As parks and recreation professionals embrace technology, they do so from multiple perspectives: Professionals need to ask: (1) "How can technology help me?"; (2) "How can I use technology to help our community, residents, and program participants?"; (3) "How do I reach those who we are not reaching or those who chose not to take advantage of our services?"; and (4) "How do we position ourselves to make the most of technology today and in the future?"

The Changing Nature of Time   The growth of individual discretionary time, sometimes referred to as free time or time without obligation, has long been considered a major influence on the increased participation in recreation activities. Between 1900 and 1995, the growth in leisure time was steady, if not spectacular. Freedom from an agrarian economy, increased holidays, paid vacations, and shorter workweeks combined to give people more opportunities for participation in recreation than at any other time in history. A debate about the actual availability of free time began in the early 1980s and continues. Today the 40-hour workweek is nonexistent for many. Manufacturing firms frequently mandate 20 or more hours of overtime for their employees. Corporate executives, midlevel managers, supervisors, and service employees experience a 24/7 (24 hours a day, 7 days a week) work life. The digital age has made everyone more accessible. The introduction of electronic communications exemplified by the iPhone has made the Internet available anywhere and any time. Smartphones now provide continuous connectivity. Business travelers use their smartphones until flight attendants ask everyone to turn off their electronic devices, and then they turn off the cell phone function and use the device to take notes, work offline, watch videos, read books, and listen to music. Vacations no longer provide time away from work, just time away from the office.

The availability of discretionary time is based on age, education, gender, and the presence or absence of a disability. Children, those who are unemployed, and retirees have considerably more discretionary time than do individuals who are in the workforce. Children have less discretion about what they might participate in and older adults' physical, mental, or economic condition may limit their ability to participate in some recreation activities. Professionals and those with a college education typically work fewer hours than those in nonprofessional jobs, such as in the service industry, manufacturing, construction, and the like. Many individuals with severe disabilities have limited opportunities to explore a range of recreation activities but have long enforced hours of free time.

The Bureau of Labor Statistics maintains annual data on how people use their time. The American Time Use Survey (ATUS) is released annually and measures the average amount of time per day that individuals worked, did household activities, cared for household children, participated in educational activities, and engaged in leisure and sports activities. Personal care, including sleep, is the largest consumer of individual time. During the weekdays, work is the largest waking time-consumer, with leisure and sports a close second. On weekends, leisure and sports are the largest activity time is spent on, although about half of this time is spent watching television. (See **Table 11.10**.)

Several issues related to the perception of time have become more apparent in recent years. *Time deepening, time shifting, time compression*, and *time famine* have entered the vocabulary of researchers, leisure providers, and the general public. Time deepening suggests more efficient use of the time available by engaging in several activities simultaneously, such as driving and talking on the cell phone, or watching a television show and knitting at the same time. Time shifting refers to the viewing of broadcast media, such as network television, at times and in ways other than the intended time and method, such as broadcast news at 6 pm. Almost 15% of all viewing is now done at times other than scheduled times. Time compression is a perspective that relates to acceleration of time and making experiences seem shorter. It is related to technology and by some, it is suggested as the driver of lifestyle changes. Going on a picnic with the family used to be an all-day activity where the focus was on the family. Today mom and dad bring their cell phones, talk to other people, make plans, respond to email, and so forth, while children play with their hand-held game devices. At the end of the day, the family feels they have had little time together. Time famine is present when an individual has insufficient time to accomplish all of the tasks required for work, leisure, and necessities. Time famine is particularly prevalent among people in jobs demanding large amounts of a person's available time.

TABLE 11.10   Distribution of How People Use Their Time, 2015 Annual Averages

Activity	Weekday Hours	Percentage	Weekend Hours	Percentage
Personal Care Activities	9.21	39.28%	9.94	44.02%
Eating and drinking	1.18	5.03%	1.37	6.07%
Household activities	1.23	5.25%	1.88	8.33%
Purchasing goods & services	0.54	2.30%	0.74	3.28%
Caring for and helping household members	0.31	1.32%	0.33	1.46%
Work and work-related activities	5.31	22.64%	0.52	2.30%
Educational activities	0.4	1.71%	0.12	0.53%
Organizational, civic, and religious activities	0.2	0.85%	0.52	2.30%
Leisure and sports	4.96	21.15%	7.02	31.09%
Telephone, calls, electronic communication	0.11	0.47%	0.14	0.62%
Total	**23.45**		**22.58**	

Data as of June 22, 2012, from Bureau of Labor Statistics, "American Time Use Survey." Available at: http://www.bls.gov/tus/home.htm. (Accessed March 6, 2013).

Layered on top of time compression, time famine, time shifting, and time deepening is technology and how it has changed people's lifestyles. Social networking tools such as Facebook, Twitter, Flickr, blogging, and the ability for smartphones to "push" email and other information to consumers means that people no longer have empty free time. In a sense, free time, or time with no obligation, has ceased to exist for some people. With the implementation of these mobile technologies, people attempt to maximize the content available in every minute, increasing the pace of their lives. The inability to keep up with all of the available information results in increased anxiety, stress, and feelings of time famine.

The feelings of time compression and time famine lead many to believe that they have less time available than preceding generations did. With the exception of a small percentage of people, most people have more discretionary time available today than at any time in history. The term *real time* is one reflection of today's perception of time. Real time "applies not to any device but to the technologically transformed context of everything we do. Real time is characterized by the shortest possible lapse between idea and action, between initiation and result."[61]

LEISURE ISSUES IN THE TWENTY-FIRST CENTURY

The beginnings of the twenty-first century held little indication of how the latter part of the first decade would bring changes that may have long-term influences on the profession. At the community level, public parks and recreation programs are being challenged to survive in many communities. As the economy shows signs of recovery, local and state governments have yet to feel the elusive benefits of economic growth. What defined economic growth at the start of this century did not define economic growth midway through the second decade of this century. Reduction of services, closing of facilities and parks, furloughs, and elimination of staff are becoming accepted tools to deal with the economic decline. The federal government operated in a crisis mode for almost half of that time. Nonprofits are finding ways to secure funding particularly challenging while simultaneously attempting to provide desperately needed services to a large number of unemployed and underemployed. Recreation providers have had to rethink the delivery of services and programs.

The first decade of the twenty-first century gradually saw a turnaround in state and local government as economies began to grow once again. However, the damage of the great recession has yet to be overcome. Governments, whose primary source of income comes from taxes, typically take longer to recover (up to 3 to 5 years) from a recession than commercial enterprises. There is always a lag in tax collections, making it difficult for city, county, and state governments to respond. Pensions of state and local government employees have changed forever. Investments in programs and services, organization of departments, and staffing of park and recreation programs continue to lag.

The unanswered question facing the leisure-services profession is what the future will look like. However, by looking at the past we can glean some ideas for the future. The recent recession may be the worst since the Depression of the 1930s, but there are parallels in the 1960s and 1970s that we can draw on. Organizations will recover, tax income will increase, staff will be expanded, new facilities and services will be designed, built, and operated. It has happened before and it will happen again. That is the one constant that economists agree on. However, how governments, nonprofits, and commercial enterprises structure and deliver their services most assuredly will change from what has been done in the past. New models are already emerging, partnerships are becoming more common, and new sources of revenue generation will be created. More difficult decisions regarding service levels, land acquisition, staffing, organizational focus, and future direction are receiving greater attention from policy makers.

In the 1930s, leisure and recreation were seen as critical to the success of the New Deal and to society. Whether that will be the same today is unknown, but early trends suggest it is unlikely. Public safety continues to receive the majority of available tax dollars. People want to feel safe. Recreation and leisure, essential elements of quality of life, fall much lower on individual taxpayers' perception of need. After almost 100 years, one might expect that the profession would have done a better job of positioning itself. The conclusion to that statement remains to be seen.

Growth of Special Interest Groups

Throughout this chapter are discussions on the influences of the Internet, media, and social networking on leisure and recreation. As these influences have affected how leisure and recreation services are delivered, they have also affected how people interact and react to the debate about services, needs, and future directions. Social networking has allowed individuals and small organizations to influence policy, decision making, and planning. Before the Internet, special interest groups were not always well organized and struggled to make their voices heard at local and national levels. That has changed considerably as small, local, and traditional groups, such as the Sierra Club, National Trust for Historic Preservation, and the Environmental Defense Fund, have embraced the use of the Internet as a social networking tool. At their websites one can join; sign up for a newsletter; download specialized information; discover what is going on in the community; find information for special events, trips, and activities; be alerted to proposed local, state, and federal changes in laws and rules; and provide financial support. Where an organization previously would send out letters or make phone calls, both time consuming, it can now send e-mail and tweets alerting interested parties about issues and request support for targeted funding.

The explosion of involvement by special interest groups is having a profound impact on how public agencies, at all levels, look at their delivery of services. For the most part, special interest groups have a positive impact on recreation and leisure. Organizations can more effectively coordinate with the groups, track involvement, and draw upon their interests. **Figure 11.3** is a graphic depicting types of social interest groups that might affect recreation, leisure, and parks. Each of the descending branches identifies a major type of special interest group. Twenty years ago, this same mind map might have had only two or, at most, three trunks. Special interest groups are challenging recreation and leisure organizations to rethink and expand their view of services and programs. In

Public parks and recreation agencies are embracing partnerships with fitness and health organizations.
© Paul McKinnon/Shutterstock.

the 1990s, when the benefits of the parks and recreation movement was emerging, the number of researchers was small. Today, expanding on the notion of benefits, there are literally hundreds of organizations involved in addressing, researching, and applying the benefits message. The term *benefits*, however, is less prominent as groups external to the recreation and leisure profession have addressed these topics from their own academic discipline. For example, positive psychology (in the process of being renamed positive science) draws heavily on leisure research literature. Yet discussions of the use of positive psychology are all but absent from the mainline recreation and park literature. At a recent conference involving hundreds of people from across the world, fewer than five leisure researchers were present.

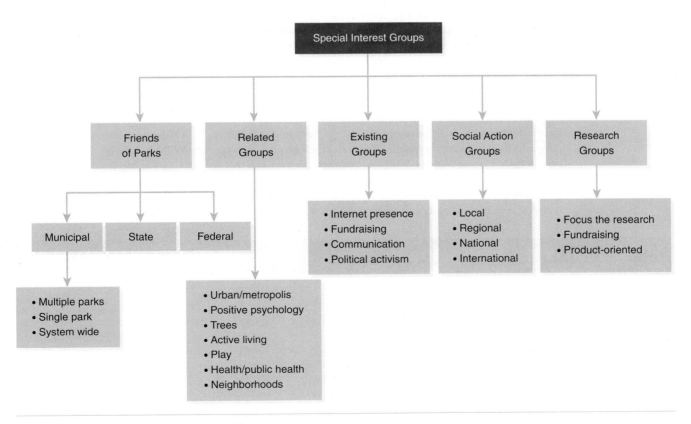

FIGURE 11.3 Typology of Special Interest Groups

Other groups are having an equivalent influence, or lack of, on the leisure and recreation profession. The Active Living Research initiative directs research toward the elimination of childhood obesity in low-income and high-risk racial/ethnic communities. The Robert Wood Johnson Foundation, sponsor of the program, has focused its funding efforts on directing research on these topics.

Commodification of Leisure

The contrast in leisure opportunity among the rich, the middle class, and the poor is heightened by what has been termed the "commodification" of leisure. Increasingly, varied forms of play today are developed in complex, expensive forms by profit-seeking businesses. More and more, giant conglomerates such as Time Warner, Disney, and Viacom have taken control of huge corporations that run music, television, and movie businesses. These conglomerates also own sports stadiums, professional sports teams, cruise ships, theme parks, and other leisure enterprises.

Ogden, UT, proposed a $38 million indoor recreation center with an Olympic-sized pool plus a large water park, an indoor velodrome, and six tennis courts. Such investments are a drain on local economies if they are not heavily marketed (which they often are not) and operated like a commercial enterprise and not like a city-owned facility. There are good and bad examples of such facilities across the country. Public agencies should be wary of facilities that are based on high revenue projections, realizing they are often out of reach of many of their citizens.

Lippke shares concerns about the effects of commercialization of leisure on individuals and society.[62] He suggests individuals "are subtly and not so subtly encouraged to indulge themselves in a consumption binge that, temporarily at least, distracts them from the cares and concerns of everyday life." The problem lies not with the distraction, but with the use of such leisure-time activities to replace what leisure theorists have called personal development, creativity, and flow. Lippke suggests that the commercialization of leisure promotes a lack of self-development, and an increase in the inability of persons to direct their own lives as they become dependent on external stimulators. Third, the effects on social life are that people focus on shallow relationships such as are promoted on today's reality-based television shows, including *American Idol*, *Fear Factor*, and *Survivor*. The Harris Interactive Poll reports that teens particularly find reality television a common ground for discussions with other teens. In 2006, 70% of surveyed teens watched *Fear Factor*, 67% watched *American Idol*, and other reality shows fared well.[63] Commercialization of recreation has created a competition for everyone to have the same things, or what one author calls, "sneer group pressure." The cell phone marketplace is an example. The ever-increasing "all-in-one" cell phone has captured the market as youth in particular desire the newest and coolest. Finally, there is confusion about values and what is important. Advertisers and sellers of commercialization create expectations among potential buyers that life should be "filled with glamorous, exciting, or dramatic moments."[62]

Recreation's Integration into the Health, Fitness, and Well-Being Movements

A key trend continuing in U.S. society is public interest in well-being, exercise, and physical fitness programs. Well-being, discussed previously, is being embraced by the leisure profession in recognition of the need for and importance of individuals improving their lives beyond just the physical. Well-being research focuses on the physical, emotional, and psychological domains through a holistic approach. Well-being embraces an ecosystem perspective: "Human well-being key components: the basic material needs for a good life, freedom and choice, health, good social relations, and personal security."[64] Research on well-being is increasing, and the leisure field is but one of many disciplines engaged in research and delivery of programs. Other fields including psychology, medicine, environmental studies, and sociology have linked well-being to leisure and recreation and park places.

 ## SITTING IS THE NEW SMOKING

Reports of the obesity crisis are increasing in the media. A recent report suggested that within a few years obesity will outpace smoking as the leading cause of death in the United States. "Sitting Is the New Smoking" is the rallying cry of researchers as they attempt to alert the public to the dangers of prolonged sitting, overeating, and lack of exercise. Americans sit an average of 9.3 hours per day. Some research has suggested that uninterrupted sitting may be an overlooked risk factor for cancer and other conditions associated with increased inflammation and insulin levels. What is more alarming is that research is beginning to suggest that going to the gym a few times a week, or even working out every day may not overcome the effects of sitting. In addition to workouts at home or the gym, researchers are suggesting 1- to 2-minute breaks every hour or two may be essential to long-term health. It appears that increasing numbers of researchers are encouraging people to change their daily routine to include more walking and climbing stairs and less sitting. Standing, while not sitting, does not replace walking. The evidence suggests all Americans need to engage in more activity, at all ages.

Realizing that modern life is frequently inactive, sedentary, beset by tensions, and subject to a host of unhealthy habits such as overeating, smoking, and drinking, popular concern developed about improving one's health, vitality, and appearance through diet and exercise. Participation in such activities as walking, aerobics, swimming, running and jogging, racket sports, and similar vigorous pursuits has more than physiological effects. It also has psychological value: Those who exercise regularly look and feel better physically and mentally. Experts conclude that fitness is not a passing trend; the public's desire to be healthy and physically attractive is supported by continuing publicity, social values, personal vanity, and solid business sense.

Research shows that the most successful fitness programs are likely to be those that provide an ingredient of recreational interest and satisfaction. The National Recreation and Park Association (NRPA) recognizes the value of fitness and health, and sponsors local involvement in Step Up to Health: Start in the Parks, a nationwide fitness program delivered by local park and recreation agencies. Each agency is to develop fitness programs that encourage employee and community participation. Sandy, Utah held a sprint triathlon that included a 400-yard swim, a 9-mile bike ride, and a 5-kilometer run. Columbus, Georgia sponsors two annual festivals, one in the spring and one in the fall, to encourage fitness in the parks. The Decatur, Illinois Park District hosted a teen fitness summit. The Robert Wood Johnson Foundation has focused much of its effort on a healthy communities initiative. They recognize that while many are served well in communities, there are those who are not served well. It may be poverty, transportation, lack of care facilities, housing, recreation, or public transportation that impedes an individual and neighborhood's ability to achieve a healthy community. They have championed the need to have parks that promote health by documenting that parks play a significant role in human health including spiritual, mental, and physical health. In addition, parks promote physical activity, they help children flourish, and combat chronic disease. It is all about being outdoors in a safe environment where children and adults can relax, play, and enjoy one another. The research is replete with the restorative power of nature, regardless of where that nature occurs.[65]

Recreation and leisure organizations have always been associated with social movement, but over the last 30 years they have expanded their understanding and role of recreation and leisure in the community. Increased focus on better trails, fitness, wellness, happiness, and community engagement have contributed to the broader perspective of how public parks and recreation crosses many community boundaries and can be an active and effective contributor to community growth and development.

Recreation and Leisure as an Economic Force

Many think of recreation as free time, something done when not working; for example, an activity, event, or trip that may or may not be planned. Even in the leisure research literature that perception is reinforced. Yet, for a large segment of the United States economy, recreation is a major factor in individual and family expenditures. **Table 11.11** illustrates the amount of individual spending on recreation products, attendance at different types of events, and other types of expenditures for recreation, not including travel and tourism, totaling in excess of $900 billion annually. Looking at outdoor recreation, a single segment of the recreation industry, the Bureau of Economic Analysis ranked spending for outdoor recreation behind financial services and insurance, and outpatient healthcare, but ahead of expenditures for motor vehicles and parts, gasoline and other fuels, household utilities, and pharmaceuticals. Put another way, Americans spent $81 billion on bicycling gear and trips. This is more than they spent on airplane travel ($51 billion).[66] The White House, in a 2011 report, stated "one in twenty U.S. jobs are in the recreation economy—more than there are doctors, lawyers or teachers."[67]

The recreation, sport, and tourism industries are essential components of local, state, and national communities. They rarely gain recognition in the media beyond the local region. Idaho, for example, reported in 2013 that recreation expenditures exceeded $6 billion and were responsible for over 76,000 jobs.[68] There were over 17,000 bed-and-breakfast inns, with 79% of the owners living on the premises. What makes recreation an economic force is, in part, the variety and type of commercial enterprises that provide equipment, supplies, travel, lodging, guides, instructors, lessons, and the like directly to the industry and are supported by other commercial enterprises.

Take, for example, the bed-and-breakfast industry that directly employs support staff to clean rooms; maintenance staff or specialists to deal with equipment upkeep and repairs; marketing firms or collaborations to sell their product; tour companies to provide special services to guests; food vendors for meals prepared on site; cleaning supplies from building maintenance services; and they pay local, state, and federal taxes. Expand the concept of the local bed-and-breakfast to that of the local bait shop, or the bicycle shop, the sporting goods store, local tour companies, sporting goods companies, specialized recreation services, both local and online, and suddenly the real impact of the recreation industry is significant.

Recreation is a major contributor to the economy. It plays significant roles, often built around small to midsized local vendors. Larger enterprises are expanding in the marketplace and in some instances, such as sporting

TABLE 11.11   Annual Personal Spending on Recreation, 2000–2014

Type of Product or Service	2000	2005	2010	2014
Video and audio equipment, computers, and related services	181.2	239.0	276.4	306.6
Sports and recreational goods and services	146.0	184.1	174.2	213.2
Membership in clubs, sports centers, parks, theaters, and museums	91.9	117.9	41.8	168.8
Amusement parks, campgrounds, and related recreation services	31.1	33.6	38.8	50.3
Admissions to motion picture theaters, live entertainment (including sports), and spectator sports	30.6	43.7	57.3	65.4
Museums and libraries	3.8	6.1	5.8	7.2
Magazines, newspapers, books, and stationary	81.0	85.6	92.5	107.6
Gambling	67.6	96.5	115.6	123.3
Pets, pet products, and related services	39.7	57.2	75.9	92.8
Photographic goods and services	19.7	17.7	15.4	16.9
Package tours	6.7	7.2	9.1	11.5
Total Recreation Expenditures	**699.3**	**888.6**	**902.8**	**1163.6**

All numbers are billions of dollars. Hence, 81.1 represents $81,100,000,000.
Data from Bureau of Economic Analysis. Last Updated: Dec. 2015 Edition: 2016, www.bea.gov/national/consumer_spending.htm (Accessed February 20, 2017).

goods stores and outdoor supply stores, may come to dominate the market, yet the small local and regional retail merchant remains a key player.[67] Recreation expenditures are subject to prevailing economic conditions, and like much of the economy, rise and fall based on individual perceptions of the economy. However, over the last 20 years the recreation, sport, and tourism industry has grown at a steady rate.

Recreation as an Experience

Researchers and recreation providers have often talked about the recreation experience and done so in generic terms. More recently, the discussion of experience has become broader, especially among economists and market specialists. The context of experience was from the provider and the focus was on giving a service to the individual or group. The focus was on delivery and process. The central point of the structure in recreation programs was the program itself and the process of moving it from concept to delivery to a potential end user. It worked for many years and is still the core of much of what recreation providers do, but society has changed, and so have the expectations of receivers of traditional recreation experiences. As far back as 1970, Toffler suggested the emergence of an experience industry. In 1999 Pine and Gilmore published "The Experience Economy," focusing on a new economic model, superseding the traditional service model. They propose that engaging the customer through experience is necessary to create value in an increasing competitive business environment. Moving beyond traditional recreation concept of experience, they saw experience as an economic offering.

Experience requires two key components. The first is the participation or involvement by an individual, and an understanding that experiences are internal in nature, making them individualized and each participant unique. This second is not far from how leisure researchers have discussed experiences, especially the Csikszentmihalyis and their discussion of optimal experiences.[69] The second component was a common component of developing recreation programs, but almost always from a group perspective. The new concept of experience argues that each consumer is unique. We each bring different backgrounds, values, attitudes, and beliefs to the situation; we experience it through our individualized "rose-colored glasses." The idea of individual experiences resulted from the convergence of three major forces: "(1) new technology to fuel innovative experiences; (2) a more sophisticated, affluent, and demanding consumer base; and (3) escalating competitive intensity."[70]

Redesigning the process of creating a recreation experience, moving it from a group to individual experience opportunity, is the foundation for change. Outcomes focus on participant perception of value. "Value may be reflected in many ways. Among these expressions of value are participants' decisions to commit time to the offering; their willingness to persist in participation; their decisions to accept social, psychological, and physical risks associated with participation; or their decision to spend money that, in many settings, is necessary to secure rights to engage in the offering."[71] Creating value for the participants is grounded in the development of program delivery models.

Application to the recreation and leisure industry is important and gaining momentum across the industry—from public agencies to large commercial recreation enterprises. In many instances the commercial sector has understood and applied the concept of individual experiences better than the public and nonprofit sectors. The provision of experiences will continue to grow. Its adherents are expanding and academic programs are embracing the concept.

Globalization of Leisure

Globalization has been equally called a blessing and a curse, sometimes by the same person. In the context of change, globalization is a relative newcomer. Economists first used the term in the early 1980s. Globalization was initially referred to as the Americanization of the world. However, more recently globalization represents a the integration of economic, political, cultural, and environmental systems and structures worldwide. From a leisure perspective, cultural and environmental influences have the greatest potential for current and future impacts.

Environmental globalization viewed from a protected-areas perspective provides a good example of globalization impacts. In the United States, we call protected areas parks, wilderness areas, national parks, state parks, national forests, and the like. Internationally, they are called protected areas. The International Union for the Conservation of Nature (IUCN; www.iucn.org) defines a *protected area* as "an area of land and/or sea especially dedicated to the protection and maintenance of biological diversity, and of natural and associated cultural resources, and managed through legal or other effective means."[72] The impetus for protected areas originated with the United States National Park Service, which early on was, and continues to be, a leading proponent of creating protected areas. Early models tended to follow a national parks approach. As described, the concept of protected areas on a global scale was strongly influenced by the American model, but as the movement matured, the American model became but one model that has been globally shared. Other models have evolved that fit the cultural, economic, and environmental issues of host countries. The IUCN developed a list of types of protected areas that applies to most areas internationally. The seven types of areas include: strict nature preserve, wilderness area, national park, national monument, habitat/species management area, protected landscape/seascape, and managed resource protected area. In some instances, protected areas have been created and indigenous populations continued to live on and utilize the lands as they have done for generations. In other instances, transnational boundaries have been crossed, where two or more countries joined together to create a larger protected area. Environmentalism is not independent of its social context and is linked with other social and economic issues, politics, and competitors. The globalization of environmentalism as related to protected areas has benefited from the ability to share models, lessons learned, adaptation to local settings, and the greater awareness a global perspective brings to resource managers.

Tourism provides the most easily identifiable impact of globalization. Some authors have suggested that globalization is replacing sustainability as an organizing concept for tourism. According to Reiser, tourism and globalization have numerous examples of connections (see **Table11.12**) and include "the movement of people, the movement of ideas and the movement of capital across borderlines."[73] Tourists, or visitors, come with a set of expectations and are frequently challenged by the experiences. Visitors to Guatemala's Mayan cultural sites are often surprised by the tourist maps overlaid with transnational corporation logos. It moves the perception of a colonial site to a transnational site, potentially affecting the visitor's experience. In heritage tourism, the plazas and barrios of Central America are the traditional gathering spots of local residents. Historic sites are residential areas, or as one described these areas, the communal urban "front porches" that globalization is changing.

The impact of globalization on culture is significant and challenges long-held traditions, mores, and customs. It has been suggested that globalization is a time–space compression, emphasizing the way modernity restructures time–space relations and uproots social meanings and identities.[74] Globalization is changing the way we view, interact with, and respond to the world. It has forced individuals and organizations to rethink their role in the homes, communities, and society. Williams argues that, "by recognizing modernity's fragmenting and disorienting qualities we can begin to focus on the strategies people have available and draw on to assemble a coherent narrative of self."[74]

TABLE 11.12 Tourism and Globalization: Examples of Connections

Tourism	Globalization
Movement of people (tourists, workers in tourism industry)	Movement of people (immigrants and their cultures)
Movement of ideas (new cultural values with tourists; ways of doing business in tourism industry)	Movement of ideas (new technologies across the globe)
Movement of capital (tourism industry investment; foreign exchange earnings through tourism)	Movement of capital (instant movement of capital across borderlines)
Needs new technology to expand (wide-bodied jets)	Spread of new technology around the globe
Started at the latest in ancient Greece (limited to particular groups in society)	Started with first movement of humans (from Africa to Indonesia in 17,000 years using some of their original tools, maybe domesticated animals, etc.)
Enormous growth in the last 100 years	Time–space compression, in particular in the last 30 years
Toward traveling as a right for everyone; development of a world tourism culture?	World tourism culture?
Tourism needs local culture, or at least the image of it (differentiation between destinations)	Toward a world culture

Data from D. R. Williams. "Leisure Identities, Globalization, and the Politics of Place," *Journal of Leisure Research* (Vol. 34, No. 4, 2002): 351–367.

WORLD HERITAGE PLACES

Heritage is the legacy of the past, what we live with today, and what we pass on to future generations. Cultural and natural heritage are both irreplaceable sources of life and inspiration. Places as unique and diverse as the wilds of East Africa's Serengeti, the Pyramids of Egypt, the Great Barrier Reef in Australia, and the Baroque cathedrals of Latin America make up the world's heritage. Eighty-one countries have designated World Heritage Sites.

What makes the concept of world heritage exceptional is its universal application. World Heritage Sites belong to all the peoples of the world, irrespective of the territory on which they are located. How can a World Heritage Site in Egypt "belong" equally to Egyptians and to the peoples of Indonesia and Argentina?

The answer is to be found in the 1972 convention concerning the protection of the world cultural and natural heritage, by which countries recognize that the sites located on their national territory, and which have been inscribed on the World Heritage List, without prejudice to national sovereignty or ownership, constitute a world heritage "for whose protection it is the duty of the international community as a whole to cooperate."

Without the support of other countries, some of the world's outstanding cultural and natural sites would deteriorate or, worse, disappear, often through lack of funding to preserve them. The convention is thus an agreement, ratified almost universally, that aims to secure the necessary financial and intellectual resources to protect World Heritage sites.

How does a World Heritage Site differ from a national heritage site? The key lies in the words *outstanding universal value*. All countries have sites of local or national interest, which are quite justifiably a source of national pride, and the convention encourages them to identify and protect their heritage whether or not it is placed on the World Heritage List. Sites selected for World Heritage listing are inscribed on the basis of their merits as the best possible examples of the cultural and natural heritage.

The list of United States World Heritage Sites is reflective of the country's national treasures and includes the Grand Canyon, Everglades, Hawaii Volcanoes, Mammoth Cave, Yellowstone, and Great Smokey Mountains National Parks. It also includes national monuments such as the Statue of Liberty, Monticello and the University of Virginia, and Independence Hall. The United States ranks fourth internationally in the number of acres designated as World Heritage Sites, behind Australia, the Russian Federation, and Canada.[75]

Maturation of the Organized Leisure-Services Field

The nature of municipal, state, and federal governments has changed dramatically in the nearly 140 years of organized recreation in the United States. Today's city government is markedly different from that of previous generations. Government is more dependent on alternative income sources and less reliant on taxes. Public parks and recreation agencies have, of necessity, become entrepreneurial. Where few fees once existed, now public agencies are dependent on fees and charges to make up as much as 90% of their operating budgets. Parks and recreation agencies are hard pressed to serve all of those who either desire or have a need for services. Nonprofit and commercial agencies fill the gap in many instances. In today's environment of rapidly changing demand for different types of leisure activities, public, commercial, and nonprofit organizations strive to respond, but often public and nonprofits do not have the resources, financial capital, or ability to respond. Commercial enterprises typically respond more quickly to what initially may appear as fringe activities such as paintball, skateboarding, laser tag, and the like.

Maturation does not suggest the organized leisure-services field is not changing, but rather that growth in the public and nonprofit sector is constrained by available funds, politics, public interest, and the perceived opportunity for growth. Public and nonprofit agencies have developed an infrastructure of parks, recreation centers, sports fields, cultural centers, and other types of facilities and areas that become a financial and maintenance burden. The traditional programming focus of public and nonprofit agencies remains in place, although it is frequently unable to grow with public demand. Where communities once built a 50-meter swimming pool, today they build a small to medium water park, except when politicians or other influential groups intervene and demand a traditional or old-fashioned approach. The leadership is changing and new, younger leaders are emerging. Values are being reassessed, commitments rethought, demands evaluated, and expectations challenged.

As the economic and political climate of public agencies has changed over the last half-decade, there is a recognition of all involved that government must change. What has been accepted for years as a government responsibility, especially in the parks and recreation profession, is now under debate. The change, as described earlier, began decades ago, but in a post-recession era where all government programs are held to a higher level of scrutiny and relevance, public agencies must rethink how they operate and redefine themselves within the context of the political, economic, and public perceptions of expectations, importance, and relevance.

Summary

This chapter moves from the past and the present to focus on contemporary issues, challenges, and the future of leisure and recreation. It began by focusing on agendas for recreation and leisure in the twenty-first century. Emerging issues related to population include gender, ethnic, racial, and age diversity; demographic shifts; the impact of an aging society; and the changing nature of the family, including children, tweeners, and teens. The discussion moves from demographic issues to other agendas such as where people live and the influence of location on the delivery of recreation and leisure services. Technology has become a major influence on how people use their free time and engage in leisure activities.

The environment, environmental concerns, global climate change, and nature-deficit disorder are all emerging and potentially society-changing challenges. The linking of these issues to nature and well-being is one of the fastest growing areas of concern, especially among urban dwellers and providers of natural areas and environmental experiences.

Other issues that were presented in the chapter focus on globalization of leisure, economic issues, how discretionary time has changed, the growth of special interest groups, and the changing nature of the leisure-service delivery system. All of these issues are cause for concern or opportunity for the leisure profession.

Questions for Class Discussion or Essay Examination

1. Select one agenda for the future, such as the recreation experience, and describe how that agenda impacts the delivery of recreation experiences and influences the user experience. Select two very different recreation experiences and explain how the experience is different and why.

_____

_____

_____

_____

2. Based on your reading of this chapter, what do you see as a major concern that you feel should be addressed by public park and recreation agencies? Explain and justify your response.

_____

_____

_____

_____

3. How does America's changing demographic impact the future delivery of recreation, park, tourism, and other related leisure systems? Think in terms of delivery of programs, diversity of Americans, social and political challenges, and desires for the future.

_____

_____

_____

4. Explain how you think the three sectors (government, nonprofit, and commercial) should address the future of provision and delivery of recreation and leisure. Highlight what you believe to be the key differences in the future of the three sectors and where you think they should work together and work independently. Use the information from the text and external readings to address your assessment.

_____

_____

_____

_____

5. Select a metropolitan area (population in excess of 100,000) and investigate the commercial recreation opportunities available in the community. Select a single category such as sports, fitness, swimming, libraries (reading), or some other activity and show the presence in the community. You might need to answer questions such as "How available is the recreation service geographically?" or

_____

_____

_____

_____

Endnotes

1. Opentopia, "Future," http://encycl.opentopia.com/term/Future.

2. Pew Research Center, "10 demographic trends that are shaping the U.S. and the World," http://www.pewresearch.org/fact-tank/2016/03/31/10-demographic-trends-that-are-shaping-the-u-s-and-the-world/ (Accessed February 15, 2017).

3. V. D. Markham, _U.S. Population, Energy and Climate Change_ (Washington, DC: Center for Environment and Population, 2008): 7.

4. United States Department of Labor: https://www.dol.gov/dol/aboutdol/history/herman/reports/futurework/report/chapter1/main.htm (Accessed February 21, 2017).

5. Markham, _U.S. Population_, 6.

6. The United States Census, "The Foreign Born Population in the United States - 2010," https://www.census.gov/prod/2012pubs/acs-19.pdf (Accessed February 21, 2017).

7.   Pew Research, "6 new findings about Millennials," http://www.pewresearch.org/fact-tank/2014/03/07/6-new-findings-about-millennials/ (Accessed February 21, 2017).

8.   C. Maller, M. Townsend, L. St Leger, et al, *Healthy Parks, Healthy People: The Health Benefits of Contact with Nature in a Park Context*, 2nd ed. (Burwood, Melbourne: Deakin University, 2008): 11.

9.   Dan K. Hibler and Kimberly J. Shinew, "Moving Beyond Our Comfort Zone: The Role of Leisure Service Providers in Enhancing Multiracial Families' Leisure Experiences," *Parks and Recreation* (Vol. 37, No. 2, 2002): 26.

10. Ching-hua Ho et al., "Gender and Ethnic Variations in Urban Park Preferences, Visitations, and Perceived Benefits," *Journal of Leisure Research* (Vol. 37, No. 3, 2005): 281–306.

11. Kimberly J. Shinew, Myron F. Floyd, and Diana Parry, "Understanding the Relationship Between Race and Leisure Activities and Constraints: Exploring an Alternative Framework," *Leisure Sciences* (Vol. 26, 2004): 188–191.

12. K. Zickhur. 2010, Generations 2010, Pew Internet & American Life Project, Pew Research Center: http://www.pewinternet.org/Reports/2010/Generations-2010.aspx (Accessed February 25, 2013).

13. Ortman, J. M., Velkoff, V. A., & Hogan, H. 2014, *An Aging Nation: The Older Population in the United States: Population Estimates and Projections*, U.S Census Bureau: https://www.census.gov/prod/2014pubs/p25-1140.pdf (Accessed February 18, 2017).

14. Douglas Knudson, *Outdoor Recreation* (New York: Macmillan, 1980): 31.

15. Working in America: New Tables Detail Demographics of Work Experience: https://www.census.gov/newsroom/blogs/random-samplings/2015/10/working-in-america-new-tables-detail-demographics-of-work-experience.html (Accessed February 18, 20–17).

16. Stephen Mitchell, "Retirement Evolution: Reexamining the Retirement Model," *LIMRA's Market Facts Quarterly* (Vol. 25, No. 1, 2006): 82–85.

17. Federal Interagency Forum on Aging-Related Statistics, "Older Americans: Key indicators of well-being. Federal Interagency Forum on Aging-Related Statistics," https://agingstats.gov/docs/LatestReport/Older-Americans-2016-Key-Indicators-of-WellBeing.pdf (Accessed February 18, 2017).

18. Sarah Burnett-Wolle and Geoffrey Godbey, "Active Aging 101," *Parks and Recreation* (2005): 30–40.

19. U.S. Census 2000, "Your Gateway to 2000 Census," www.census.gov/main/www/cen2000.html.

20. M. Scherer, "On Our Changing Family Values (Interview with Sociologist David Elkind)," *Educational Leadership* (April 1, 1996).

21. KIDS COUNT Data Book © Annie E. Casey Foundation (2012): www.aecf.org/~/media/Pubs/Initiatives/KIDS%20COUNT/123/2012KIDSCOUNTDataBook/KIDSCOUNT2012DataBookFullReport.pdf.

22. Childstats.gov, "America's Children: Key National Indicators of Well-Being, 2009," www.childstats.gov/americaschildren/index3.asp.

23. Duke Center for Child and Family Policy, "Child and Youth Well Being Index (CWI) Report," http://childandfamilypolicy.duke.edu/wp-content/uploads/2014/12/Child-Well-Being-Report.pdf (Accessed February 21, 2017).

24. UNICEF, "The State of the World's Children Report ," New York: United Nations (2004).

25. Child Trends, "Children In Poverty," http://www.childtrends.org/indicators/children-in-poverty/ (Accessed February 18, 2017).

26. Partnership for a Drug-Free America, www.drugfree.org (Accessed January 15, 2017).

27. Harris Interactive, "Parents, Changing Roles in Tweens' and Teens' Lives," *Trends & Tudes* (Vol. 2, No. 5, 2003).

28. Harris Interactive, "Kids and Online Privacy," *Trends & Tudes* (Vol. 2, No. 4, 2003).

29. Harris Interactive, "Youth and Mental Health Stigma," *Trends & Tudes* (Vol. 5, No. 9, 2006).

30. Child Trends, "Volunteering," http://www.childtrends.org/indicators/volunteering/ (Accessed February 18, 2017).

31. W. F. LaPage and S. R. Ranney, "America's Wilderness: The Heart and Soul of Culture," *Parks and Recreation* (July 1988): 24.

32. Center for Environment and Population, "U.S. National Report on Population and the Environment," New Canaan, CT: Center for Environment and Population (2006): 4.

33. J. Loh et al., eds., *WWF Living Planet Report* (Switzerland: WWF International, New Economics Foundation, World Conservation Monitoring Centre, 2004).

34. U.S. Environmental Protection Agency, "Basic Information," https://www.epa.gov /environmental-topics/land-waste-and-cleanup-topics (Accessed June 12, 2017).

35. Center for Environment and Population, "U.S. National Report on Population," 55.

36. Center for Environment and Population, www.cepnet.org (Accessed January 15, 2017).

37. Brookings, "The Metropolitan Revolution," https://www.brookings.edu/book/the-metropolitan-revolution-2/ (Accessed February 22, 2017).

38. https://factfinder.census.gov/faces/tableservices/jsf/pages/productview.xhtml?src=bkmk (Accessed February 18, 2017).

39. Farmland Information, "National Statistics," http://www.farmlandinfo.org/statistics (Accessed February 18, 2017).

40. Trust for Public Land, "LandVote," https://tpl.quickbase.com/db/bbqna2qct?a=dbpage&pageID=8 (Accessed June 12, 2017).

41. The Trust for Public Land, http://www.tpl.org. (Accessed February 12, 2017)

42. Stephen Saunders and Tom Easley, *Losing Ground: Western National Parks Endangered by Climate Change* (Louisville, CO: Rocky Mountain Climate Organization and the Natural Resources Defense Council, 2006).

43. Philanthropedia, "Ranked Nonprofits: National Climate Change 2012," www.myphilanthropedia.org/ top-nonprofits/national/climate-change/2012 (Accessed May 12, 2012).

44. 350.org: https://350.org (Accessed February 17, 2018).

45. U.S. Global Change Research Program, "Program Overview," www.globalchange.gov/about/overview.

46. Charles et al., *Children and Nature 2008: A Report on the Movement to Reconnect Children to the Natural World* (Santa Fe, NM: Children's Nature Network, 2008): 13.

47. O. R. W. Pergams and P. A. Zaradic, "Is Love of Nature in the U.S. Becoming Love of Electronic Media?" *Journal of Environmental Management* (Vol. 80, 2006): 387–393.

48. D. Morris and M. A. Wells, *Climate Change and Outdoor Recreation Resources* (Washington, DC: Resources for the Future, 2009).

49. Resources for the Future, "Climate Change and Recreation: Consequences and Costs" (April 24, 2009), http://www.rff.org/files/sharepoint/WorkImages/Download/RFF-BCK-ORRG_ClimateChange.pdf.

50. Maller et al., *Healthy Parks, Healthy People*, 11.

51. City of Long Beach, Office of Sustainability, "Urban Nature," www.longbeach.gov/citymanager/ sustainability/urban_nature.asp.

52. G. Godbey, *Outdoor Recreation, Health, and Wellness: Understanding and Enhancing the Relationship* (Washington, DC: Resources for the Future, 2009): 27.

53. C. W. Thompson, P. Aspinall, and A. Montarzino, "The Childhood Factor: Adult Visits to Green Places and the Significance of Childhood Experience," *Environment & Behavior* (Vol. 40, No. 1, 2008): 111–143.

54. S. R. Kellert. *Building for Life: Designing and Understanding the Human–Nature Connection* (Washington, DC: Island Press, 2007).

55. G. Godbey, *Outdoor Recreation, Health, and Wellness: Understanding and Enhancing the Relationship* (Washington, DC: Resources for the Future, 2009): 27.

56. Maller et al., *Healthy Parks, Healthy People*, 21.

57. J. Horrigan, "The Mobile Difference: Wireless Connectivity Has Drawn Many Users More Deeply into Digital Life," Washington, DC: Pew Internet and American Life Project (2009).

58. J. Horrigan and L. Rainie, "The Internet's Growing Role in Life's Major Decisions," Washington, DC: Pew Internet and American Life Project, (April 2006): 1.

59. Pew Research Center, "Internet/Broadband Factsheet," http://www.pewinternet.org/fact-sheet/internet-broadband/ (Accessed February 20, 2010).

60. Pew Research Center, "Social Media Fact Sheet," http://www.pewinternet.org/fact-sheet/social-media/ (Accessed February 20, 2017).

61. J. Wajcman, "Life in the Fast Lane? Toward a Sociology of Technology and Time," *British Journal of Sociology* (Vol. 59, No. 1, 2008): 59–76.

62. R. L. Lippke, "Five Concerns Regarding the Commercialization of Leisure," *Business and Society Review* (Vol. 106, No. 2, 2001): 107–126.

63. S. Martin and D. Markow (eds), "Youth and Reality TV," www.HarrisInteractive.com.

64. P. Morrow, "Outdoor Recreation Drives Idaho Economy," KLTV News (March 11, 2013). www.kivitv.com/news/local/197088951.html.

65. Robert Wood Johnson Foundation, "Healthy Communities," http://www.rwjf.org/en/our-focus-areas/focus-areas/healthy-communities.html (Accessed February 20, 2017).

66. Outdoor Industry Association, "The Outdoor Recreation Economy" (2012), www.outdoorindustry.org/pdf/OIA_OutdoorRecEconomyReport2012.pdf.

67. K. Salazar, "The Economic Power of Outdoor Recreation," Washington, DC: U.S. Department of the Interior (August 22, 2011), www.doi.gov/news/blog/The-economic-power-of-outdoor-recreation.cfm.

68. P. Morrow, "Outdoor Recreation Drives Idaho Economy," KLTV News (March 11, 2013). www.kivitv.com/news/local/197088951.html.

69. M. Csikszentmihalyi and I. S. Csikszentmihalyi (eds), *Optimal Experiences: Psychological Studies of Flow in Consciousness* (Cambridge, UK: Cambridge University Press, 1988).

70. B. J. Knutson, J. A. Beck, S. H. Kim, and J. Cha, "Identifying the Dimensions of the Experience Construct" [Electronic Version], *Journal of Hospitality & Leisure Marketing* (Vol. 15, No. 3, 2006): 31–47.

71. G. D. Ellis and J. R. Rossman, "Creating Value for Participants through Experience Staging: Parks, Recreation, and Tourism in the Experience Industry," *Journal of Park and Recreation Administration* (Vol. 26, No. 4, 2008): 1–20.

72. World Commission on Protected Areas, *National System Planning for Protected Areas* (Cambridge, England: World Commission on Protected Areas, 1998).

73. Dirk Reiser, "Globalisation: An Old Phenomenon That Needs to Be Rediscovered for Tourism," *Tourism and Hospitality Research* (Vol. 4, No. 4, 2003): 310.

74. Daniel L. Williams, "Leisure Identities, Globalization, and the Politics of Place," *Journal of Leisure Research* (Vol. 34, No. 4, 2002): 355.

75. UNESCO World Heritage Centre, *World Heritage Information Kit* (Paris, France: UNESCO World Heritage Centre, June 2008), whc.unesco.org/uploads/activities/documents/activity-567-1.pdf.

Index

Note: Page numbers followed by *n*, *f*, and *t* indicate material in footnotes, figures, and tables, respectively.